LISTENING WITH THE THIRD EAR

BOOKS BY THEODOR REIK

Listening with the Third Ear

THE INNER EXPERIENCE OF A PSYCHOANALYST

by

THEODOR REIK

The Noonday Press
Farrar, Straus and Giroux
New York

Tenth printing, 1991

First Farrar, Straus and Giroux paperback edition
Printed in the United States of America
Published in Canada by HarperCollins*CanadaLtd*
Designed by Stefan Salter

Library of Congress Cataloging in Publication Data
Reik, Theodor, 1888-1969.
    Listening with the third ear.
    Originally published: New York: Farrar, Straus, 1948.
    1. Psychoanalysis.   I. Title.
BF173.R42   1983   150.19'50924 [B]   83-11615
ISBN 0-374-51800-9 (pbk.)

FOR MARIJA

*Who Puts Up with Her Husband
and His Strange Profession*

Introduction

IN A psychoanalytic session the other day, I controlled the impulse to remark, "When I was five and twenty, I heard a wise man say . . ." A young man had come to consult me about two decisions that he had to make: should he follow a certain profession and ought he to marry a certain girl. Something in him or in his situation reminded me of myself at his age. He had just received his doctorate in psychology. I, too, had won my Ph.D. at this age and I was a student of Freud.

One evening I ran into the great man on his daily walk along the Ringstrasse in Vienna, and walked home with him. Friendly as always, he asked me about my plans and I told him of my problems, which resembled those of my present patient. Of course, I hoped Freud would give me advice or resolve my doubts.

"I can only tell you of my personal experience," he said. "When making a decision of minor importance, I have always found it advantageous to consider all the pros and cons. In vital matters, however, such as the choice of a mate or a profession, the decision should come from the unconscious, from somewhere within ourselves. In the important decisions of our personal life, we should be governed, I think, by the deep inner needs of our nature."

Without telling me what to do Freud had helped me make my own decision. Like marriage, the choice of a profession is a matter of destiny. We should welcome our destiny, readily accepting what comes with and out of it. On that evening thirty-five years ago when I decided to become a psychoanalyst, I married the profession for better or for worse.

Most middle-aged men, asked whether they have ever wished to

LISTENING WITH THE THIRD EAR

change their profession for another, would answer in the negative. If one expressed astonishment and perhaps a slight skepticism ("What, never?"), quite a few might reconsider and say, "Well, hardly ever."

Let me freely admit that in these thirty-five years of psychoanalytic practice, I have had this wish more than once. I have had moods in which being a psychoanalyst appeared to me less a profession than a calamity. Such temporary discouragement is unavoidable when demands are made that only God can fulfill. An analyst, I have often said to myself, is expected to be a sorcerer who, in the opinion of many people, could introduce himself like the Gilbert and Sullivan figure:

> Oh! my name is John Wellington Wells;
> I'm a dealer in magic and spells.

In my younger days, when my ambition was still uncurbed, I had moments of discouragement that did not concern the limitations of psychoanalytic practice, but the very nature of the profession itself. What I mean can best be illustrated by a little story about the magnificent Viennese actor, Josef Kainz, who lives in memory as the top tragedian of the German stage. Near the end of his brilliant career (he died in 1910), Kainz was asked by the director of the Vienna Burgtheater to play the role of Prospero in Shakespeare's *The Tempest*. Kainz considered the offer for some time but finally declined. "To act the part of Prospero," he said, "one has not only to be a great actor but also a great man. But would a great man become only an actor . . . ?" In the same sense that Kainz meant it, I am rather skeptical whether a great man would become just a psychoanalyst. I hope that nobody will argue that Freud, who *was* a great man, was merely a psychoanalyst. He created a new science; he discovered psychoanalysis. He was a great thinker and one of the greatest psychologists of all times.

There were moments in which the importance of my own practical activity became questionable and the social impact of my profession dubious. There are, however, no such doubts about the value of the insights that depth psychology has to give. Here is a method of research that offers singular opportunities for gaining incomparable insight into the dynamics of emotional and mental life. The torch that psychoanalysis puts into the hands of the investigator lights up the darkest corners and throws a beam down the deepest shafts. It reaches the remotest recesses and makes transparent what stirs and moves in the hiding-places of the netherworld. No other psychological method shows us how thousands of emotional varieties follow the same laws, laws as valid as those of physics and chemistry. To find the laws that govern the unconscious processes, to discover what is concealed behind the psychical façade—these are the satisfactions a psychoanalyst may experience.

The following pages tell the story of the strange adventure that is the most important work of a psychoanalyst: the story of an expedition into the last dark continent on earth. I want to show how new psychological insights are won either as a result of long and patient mining, or of sudden flashes emerging from unconscious depths.

The person who approaches psychoanalysis is not psychologically unprepared for it. Long before he enters the consultation room of the analyst he has become aware of some strange experiences, has felt anxieties or inhibitions, and has observed symptoms and behavior traits that have made life difficult and sometimes unbearable for him. He has tried to find out what it is that interferes with his work, disturbs his social behavior, or his capability of loving. Many times he has attempted to answer the question whether there are some unknown things in himself which are responsible for his troubles. He has himself tried to find the way out of the labyrinth of his emotions. It was a kind of abortive self-analysis, attempted with insufficient insight and knowledge, performed with inappropriate tools. Without elementary self-analysis he never would have gotten to the analyst's door. Long before he saw a psychoanalyst the patient became interested in psychological problems by inner necessity, because they were his own problems. The world around us is full of fascinating questions. Why should a man turn his attention inward, why should he be interested in what takes place in himself? The answer to this question that faces us at the beginning of our research goes beyond the realm of the individual patient. It will help us to find how psychoanalysis was discovered.

Inquiry into one's own emotional difficulties, an attempt to master inner unrest, marks the origin of the new science. It was self-observation and self-analysis which led to the fundamental convictions which Freud presented to an unbelieving world. He would also have become one of the world's greatest psychologists even if he had restricted his observations to himself, if he had published only the discoveries made about his own person, and if he had never treated a single neurotic patient. His psychological insights would have been incomplete, had he not compared the results of his self-observation and self-analysis with what analys˙ of others showed, but his decisive insights were gained in the vivisection of his own person.

This book retraces the steps by which Freud reached his goal. It is an introduction to psychoanalysis from a new angle: from the point of view of self-observation and self-analysis. It attempts thus to introduce the reader to a strange, new field by starting where other investigators stop.

In the first part of this book quite a few instances of such psychological self-observation and self-analysis are presented. They appear here, so to speak, as samples of what the emotional netherworld has to offer when the psychologist descends into this dark region, equipped with the tools of his science. The following part allows the reader a glance into the workshop of the analyst during his search and research. The inner process by which he reaches his results is presented in its decisive initial phases, with its peculiarities, its rewards in understanding, and its failures—in its possibilities and its limitations. Hundreds of case histories are presented here, not in dry scientific terms, which refuse to come to life, but as an inner experience of the analyst. I want to show how a psychological insight dawns upon him in his daily silent wrestling with an invisible antagonist. Such presentation has, of course, to be restricted to the essentials, but failures and mistakes are discussed as frankly as gratifying results are.

My book investigates the unconscious processes of the psychoanalyst himself; it shows the other side of the coin. It is an attempt—so far as I know, the first—to describe what an investigator into the unconscious mental processes of another person does and what he achieves.

People have had books about what a symptom of a neurosis means; the nature and the hidden content of a psychotic disease; the sense behind the manifest content of a dream. I am here interested in what takes place in the mind of the psychoanalyst—the same scene viewed from the other side, inside out.

Not everything in this book is new. What is new is that it is stated.

After five decades of development psychoanalysis has acquired a new aspect. In the beginning the analyst was a mental therapist of a new school. The methods of psychoanalysis at its inception were felt to be in direct conflict with the spirit of medical science, which it was easy in those days to interpret as rudely materialistic and mechanistic. And in truth, say what we will, the analyst was really nearer akin to the medicine man than to the medical man of that period. To me, today, the analyst is primarily a psychologist, and analysis a psychological method which can be used for psychotherapeutic purposes among others. The future will show that the use of analysis in the treatment of individual neuroses is not its most important application.

The way we come to conjecture unconscious processes, their nature, their hidden meaning, and their intent, is of the utmost educational importance from the point of view of the training of analysts. It appears to me dangerous to accord first rank to the therapeutic, clinical aspect of analysis in our methods of training. The psychological aspect must predominate. I know psychoanalysts who are nerve specialists with a wide knowledge of psychiatry, but nowise psychologists. Indeed, I believe, incredible as it may sound, that there are psychoanalysts whose main interest is not their psychological work. *But psychoanalysis will either be psychology, or it will not be.*

Americans are practical people and my colleagues are primarily interested in the practical aspects of psychoanalysis. But I take the liberty of reminding them of one of the greatest sons of our country, Benjamin Franklin. Perhaps not all of them know that Louis Pasteur invoked the spirit of Franklin in his opening speech as professor at Lille on December 7, 1854.

Without theory, practice is but routine born of habit. Theory alone can bring forth and develop the spirit of invention. It is you especially who are obliged not to share the opinion of those narrow minds who reject everything in science which has no immediate application. You know Franklin's charming saying? He was witnessing the first application of a purely scientific discovery and people around him asked, "But what is its use?" Franklin answered them, "What is the use of a newborn babe?" Yes, gentlemen, what is the use of a newborn child? And yet, perhaps, at that tender age, germs already existed in you of the talents which distinguish you. Among your baby boys, fragile things that they are, there are incipient magistrates, scientists, heroes as valiant as those who are now covering themselves with glory under the walls of Sebastopol. And thus, gentlemen, a theoretical discovery has but the merits of its existence; it awakens hope and that is all. But let it be cultivated, let it grow and you will see what it will become.

Thus spoke Louis Pasteur, who, if not a medical man, was one of the greatest scientists and benefactors of mankind.

Another reason for confining myself to the psychological aspect is a personal one: the little that I could contribute on the subject of therapy that would be new—or at least not hitherto stated—I have not yet tested enough to venture to bring it forward before a wide circle of educated readers.

Let me take this opportunity to add a second personal statement to this one: that I only now, after thirty-seven years of analytic practice and theory, venture to speak on the subject of technique, is due to two peculiar characteristics which necessarily prevented me from appearing earlier in print. The first is an inability to learn from other people's mistakes. All the wisdom of proverbs and all exhortations and warnings are useless to me. If I am to learn from the mistakes of others, I must make them my own, and so perhaps cast them off. And with this kind of mental stubbornness or intellectual contumacy, another is combined: I am almost incapable of learning from my own mistakes unless I have repeated them several times. Only in the case of one or two minor awkwardnesses have I been able to cure myself of them the second time that I recognized them as such.

Moreover, I would beg my readers to consider right at the outset one difficulty that is involved in the special nature of our subject. We are concerned with processes that are hard to grasp and, for the most part, peculiarly hard to describe. If I do not succeed—and it is impossible that I should succeed—in presenting them so as to satisfy strictly scientific demands, I shall not deplore that fact as much as might be expected. I am less concerned with providing my readers with scientifically unchallengeable theories than with giving them an insight into the very remarkable psychological process by which we conjecture and comprehend the unconscious processes in another mind. I shall endeavor to seize upon as many as possible of the representative elements in this singular process, hitherto unexplored by psychologists, and to give some idea of the stream of mental power, flowing freely and yet under control, that is at work.

New York, December, 1947.   THEODOR REIK

Contents

PART ONE

"I AM A STRANGER HERE MYSELF"

CHAPTER I

How Does a Man Become Interested

in Psychology?

PSYCHOLOGISTS—that is, psychologists who, in our sense, are curious about emotional problems—are born, not made. Psychological interest and the gift for psychological observation are as inborn as a musical sense or a mathematical talent. Where it is not present, nothing—not even courses, lectures, and seminars—will produce it. The comparison with musicianship is justified in more than one sense. Musicians, like psychologists, are born; but, in order to become what they are, they must be trained and they must work long and hard. Talent alone is not enough; but work and industry alone, without talent, are nothing. Lack of psychological endowment becomes especially conspicuous when a psychoanalyst is ready to turn to creative work, to present new psychological findings in a book or paper. Nowadays we read many books and articles in psychoanalytic periodicals, that are cleverly written and present interesting material of a medical, sociological, psychosomatic, or physiological nature. I do not doubt their value, but there is not the slightest trace of psychology in them.

Rossini went to hear the opera *The Huguenots* for the first time. "What do you think of this music, maestro?" he was asked. "Music—I did not hear any music," the composer answered. Similarly, the reader of certain psychoanalytic books and magazines may have read and learned many things, but no psychology. That music is essential to an opera might be a prejudice, but one we would like to keep.

The German scholar, O. Klemm, has stated that psychology has a long past but a short history. Psychology is, as a matter of fact, one of the youngest sciences. The naïve man, living under the command of his

instinctual needs, is not concerned with psychological matters. He turns
his interest to the external world and the knowledge he acquires is
directed toward mastering the world outside himself, and making it
serve his wishes. He tries to conquer a piece of material reality and does
not covet any other kind of mastery. The kingdom of the psychologist
is not of this world, not material reality. When conflicts arose in the
mind of primitive man, when his wishes remained unfulfilled, he tried
to master them by projecting their power into the external world, into
lightning and thunder, rain and fire. He used magic and spells; he
became a sorcerer, and finally, renouncing his omnipotence in favor of
his gods, he became a religious person, a worshipper of deities. He cast
his passions, needs, conflicts, and frustrations into the realm of the
powers of nature, as we cast a picture on a screen. He looked at these
pictures and was unaware that they only mirrored processes within
himself. For many hundreds of thousands of years, the unconscious projection of his own psychical processes into the outside world remained
the natural way of dealing with them, of understanding them. What
forced man finally to discover them in himself? The sincere answer is
that we do not know.

But something must have happened to bring this change about.
Paul Moebius, the German psychologist, says: "It is, so to speak, natural
to direct one's look to the external world; it is unnatural to turn it
inwards. We can compare ourselves with a man who looks from a dark
room through a small window at a world in sunshine; outside everything is easily discernible. When he turns around, he has difficulty finding himself at home in his dark room."[1] The comparison helps. Only
when there is no longer anything to be seen there, or when something
happens in the room itself which forces him to turn around, will this
man's attention be turned away from the world in sunshine.

Psychology does not begin as self-observation. It ends there. Yes,
self-observation, as possibility and fact, sets a psychological problem of
its own. Every scientific research demands an object and a subject—an
object to be studied and a subject that tries to recognize its nature. The
objects of the other sciences are facts and connections between facts in
the outside world. The subject is the observer, the research worker.
In introspective psychology, the object is the investigator's own psychical
processes; the subject is himself. Here, then, is an identity of object
and subject that is puzzling. This fact is so extraordinary that the best

[1] Paul Moebius, *Die Hoffnungslosigkeit aller Psychologie* (1907), p. 12.

way for psychologists to deal with it was to take it for granted, without wasting any thought on it. If Aristotle's assertion that research starts with wonder is true, then it must be admitted that most psychologists did not bother with this superfluous emotion.

Think of the famous inscription on the temple of Apollo at Delphi: "Know thyself." This statement was apparently simple enough. There was no mystery about one's self. What the son of Zeus meant seemed to be as clear as a textbook on psychology: Turn your attention to your own personality and know yourself.

Today, however, we seriously doubt whether such was the real meaning of the admonition of the Delphic god. Oracles were full of obscure and double meanings. Behind those two words, "Know thyself," hides another idea. They impose the most difficult task imaginable—a task which something in human nature resists. To fulfill it a man must fight against heavy odds. The Delphic words do not mark the point of departure but rather the end of psychological research. If to know oneself were so easy, it need not have been put as a demand.

William James has described the puzzling phenomenon of self-observation in the words, "The *I* observes the *Me*." It is obvious that the precondition for such a phenomenon—observation of one's own mental and emotional processes—must be a split within the ego. This split makes psychology possible. In fact, this split makes psychology necessary. If the ego were undivided, it could not observe itself. It would have no need to observe itself.

Self-observation is the result of a late phase of psychology. Nietzsche remarked, "The *Thou* is older than the *I*." Every child is selfish, but it is at first not interested in itself. There is not even a clear-cut self. Primitive observation is directed to the person or the persons in the environment. There is no direct path from observation of others to self-observation. The *Thou* remains for a long time the only object. The *I* is but newly an object of observation—so young that many psychologists had not discovered it as an object worthy of their attention until recently. Your own psychical processes are inappropriate material for statistics, curves, graphs, tables, tests, and schedules.

Where is the transition from observation of others, as we see it in children, to self-observation? There must be an intermediary phase which has been neglected. Here it is: The child realizes at a certain age that it is an object of observation on the part of its parents or nurses. Stated otherwise, the *I* can observe the *Me* because *They—She* or *He—*

once observed the *Me*. The attention the persons of his environment paid to the child will be continued by the attention that the child pays to itself. Self-observation thus originates in the awareness of being observed. The intermediary stage between the observation of others and self-observation is thus the realization that one is observed by others.

Where the personality is split, as in certain psychotic diseasès, self-observation is again transformed into hallucinations of being permanently observed by others. In another form the phenomenon of depersonalization, in which the person complains that he does not feel but only observes himself, reinforces this point. A man gives a speech and suddenly becomes aware of peculiarities in his voice, of certain gestures that he makes, of some personal ways of expressing himself. This awareness is not independent of the fact that he sees or senses the impression his speaking or the content of his speech makes upon his audience. We have a good expression for this kind of recognition. The speaker becomes self-conscious. One does not become self-conscious only in the presence of others, although that is usually the case. The occurrence of this reaction when one is alone is much more rare, and of a secondary character.

I repeat, self-observation is not a primary phenomenon. It must be traced back to being observed. One part of the self observes another part. I assume that differences in the kind and intensity of this observation may be significant for the future psychological interests of the individual.

A little girl I know asked her mother, "Why do you always smile when a lady in Central Park smiles at me?" The child had observed that her mother smiled at another woman who looked with pleasure at the pretty little girl. Such a case shows not so much self-observation as observation of others who react to one's self.

By primitive observation the child learns early in life to interpret the reactions of his parents or nurses as expressions of approval or disapproval, of pleasure or annoyance. Being observed and later on observing oneself will never lose its connection with this feeling of criticism. Psychology teaches us again and again that self-observation leads to self-criticism, and we have all had opportunity to re-examine this experience. Add that self-observation is from its inception a result of self-criticism. This self-criticism continues the critical attitude of mother, father, or nurse. They are incorporated into the self—become introjected. Introjection, or absorption of another person into oneself, is an indis-

pensable precondition for the possibility of self-ob...
a child cannot transform the feeling of being observ...
tion. The process describes a circle: attention directe...
and others; awareness of being observed, often criticiz...
of the observing or critical persons into oneself; self-ob...

We know that many psychologists have wondered—
even wonder—about the possibility that the *I* can observe...
see now who this observant and observing *I* is. It is the ... ...n
into oneself, the mother, the nurse who observed the child. ...ne split,
which enables one to observe oneself, comes about through the introjection of the supervising person into oneself. We make one part of the
self the supervisor of the other part. The observant *I* is a survival of
the observing mother or father. We are reminded at this point of the
genesis of religious belief in the omniscience of God, the belief that
God sees everything. A little girl was very indignant when she heard
this and said, "But that is very indecent of God."

Freud once remarked that the introspective perception of one's own
instinctual impulses finally results in inhibition of these tendencies. We
would like to add that such self-observation of one's tendencies is already the result of a previous inhibition. If there were no memory-
traces that persons in the child's environment reacted with disapproval
or annoyance, with withdrawal of affection, to certain instinctual expressions, no self-observation would develop. Let us return to our
speaker. When he becomes self-conscious, and if this feeling reaches
a certain intensity, he becomes embarrassed. He begins to stammer, to
hesitate, to make slips of the tongue, to grow uncertain. That would be
the result of the impression he gets that his speech is not being received with approval, but is being met with negative criticism. To become self-conscious means to become conscious of the negative attitude
of others, to realize or to anticipate that the others are critical of one.

Psychology makes the presence of two persons necessary—even if it is
introspection done by a researcher in a lonely study. There is always a
second person there who observes the *Me*. We know this person was
originally the father (or mother) who now continues his existence
within us. The seer of oneself has an overseer; he who has received a
vision of himself has taken on a supervisor.

Psychoanalysis has given a name to this invisible superintendent of
the self; it calls him the superego. We thought we were masters in our
own household until Freud discovered this inspecting and introspective

he superego—the image of the father incorporated, taken into elf as a part of it. The superego is also the second person present in self-observation.

I want to avoid the impression common among many analysts that the superego is a factor that only criticizes, punishes, forbids. If this part of ourselves, this concealed roomer in our psychical household, is a survival of the father and mother of our early childhood, he cannot have only these functions. We learn in psychoanalytic practice that the superego can have pity on the individual, and we call this experience self-pity. It is really nothing but the unconscious idea: If mother or father could see me in this misery she or he would feel sorry for me.

The superego can smile, console, and seem to say, "Take it easy; it isn't half as bad as you think it is." We call it humor. We even know situations in which the superego forgives the person who is aware of his misdeeds or sinfulness, and we call this self-forgiveness. Religion calls it grace that descends upon the worshipper. In many cases where we use words with "self" (like "self-confidence"), "self" refers to the part of the person which is the representative of the father within him. Without knowing it, we mean the superego.

The ego is primarily an organ of perception directed toward the outside world. It is unable to observe the self. The superego is the first representative of the inner world. It is the silent guide in the subterranean realm of our psychical life. Psychology started with the supervision of emotional processes by this superintendent, this proxy-parent within us. It was this factor which examined what took place in our thought and emotional life. Its attention and vigilance were directed to those tendencies and impulses that were socially disapproved. It would criticize, condemn, suppress, and finally repress them. The first discoveries in the field of psychology were made in the service of those suppressing powers. The origin of psychology can be easily recognized in our psychological descriptions and judgments. Language has immortalized this origin. How do we characterize or describe a person? We say, for instance, that he is stubborn or avaricious or pedantic or kind or friendly. Does not the voice of the superego sound in such psychological descriptions? We want to observe and describe without preconceived ideas, but our miserably poor language forces us to put an undertone of approval or disapproval into scientific statements. Psychology was for a long time in bondage to moralistic and religious conceptions, and the superego is a witness to this servitude to ideas foreign to the spirit of research. The superego knows more about what takes place in the human mind than the other parts of the ego, exactly as worldly-wise, clever priests often know more about people than people know about themselves.

Psychology, I asserted, was at first put into the service of those powers that supervise the thoughts and emotions of the individual and of the community in order to keep away forbidden impulses and ideas. The psychologist was once a censor of the human soul; sometimes a stupid one, sometimes a wise one; sometimes tolerant and sometimes severe. The best way to deal with especially rebellious and ferocious elements is to ban them, to eliminate them. Thus psychology became a servant in the service of the repressing powers. It ignored, disavowed, and disowned certain tendencies within the ego. When their existence could no longer be denied, psychology gave them other names, distorted their nature by classifying and describing them. Even when psychology apparently freed itself from the supervision of the suppressing power, its attitude of liberty was an official one only. Proud of its independence, it continued to hold on to preconceived ideas. It was—and to a great extent it still is—a situation that calls to mind the cartoon in which two men get into a furious argument with one shouting at the other: "You shut up! Don't you know that you are living in a free country?" That was the nature of psychology for many hundreds, perhaps for a couple of thousand years.

Then there slowly came a change. It was heralded not by psychologists, or at least not by professional psychologists. It took its point of departure from the discovery of the hidden, disavowed, disowned, and forbidden tendencies. They had appeared before only in the plays of Shakespeare, and other poets, in novels, and in poems. Their voices began to be heard in the writings of Montaigne, of La Rochefoucauld, of Chamfort, and other, especially French, searchers after truth. Free or freed spirits, they labored to unmask the hidden, to disenchant a world in bondage to self-deception and magic. Another part of the ego, the same that lent its power to the suppressed tendencies, helped now to remove the chains. The great turn in modern psychology began. Heralded by the French moralists, it was brought to its most significant expression by Friedrich Nietzsche (here considered only as one of the great psychologists) and reached its peak in Sigmund Freud.

Psychology started its research in the service of the censorship of the emotional life. The observing and controlling station within the ego called conscience (or social fear) examined the ideas and tendencies that should not trespass upon the land of conscious thoughts. Psychology in this phase of its development furnished a kind of alibi for these forbidden impulses. The admonition "Know thyself" was very necessary because psychology was then the best method by which to deceive oneself about oneself. Later, very late indeed, psychology realized that its task was the removal of repressing powers, the lifting of the ban of repression, the search for the forbidden forces. This was at first an underground movement. With Nietzsche and louder still with Freud, the voice of the suppressed instincts and disavowed impulses sounded from hidden recesses. The underground movement of psychology came at last into the open and made itself known.

The organ of psychological observation, and therefore of psychological research and discovery, is to be found within oneself. This book wants to search for this organ, which observes, recognizes, and discovers what happens in us. This organ is not yet found. It is unknown; more than that—it is unconscious.

CHAPTER II

How Freud Discovered Psychoanalysis

IT TAKES two to practice psychology, even psychological self-observation. When you want to recognize and understand what takes place in the minds of others, you have first to look into yourself. Such a searching is only possible when a division of yourself has preceded the observation. The premise for psychological interest is thus a disturbance within the person. Without it no possibility of psychological recognition exists. Moreover the emotional disturbance has to be overcome to a certain degree, the conflict almost resolved—otherwise psychological interest would not arise. When a man is very angry, he will not be inclined, nor will he be able, to observe his own psychical processes. We would thus presuppose that Freud, who was a genius at psychological observation, must have been subjected to emotional conflicts of such a nature that they made psychological interest not only possible, but also necessary.

We put aside here the problem of his special gifts and ask: What enabled Freud psychologically to make his great discoveries, to solve the riddle of the dream, to penetrate into the recesses of human motivation; what forced him to descend into the netherworld of the neuroses while so many others remained on the surface? He himself often enough described how he came to the new science: "Psychoanalysis was born of medical necessity. It originated in the need for helping the victims of nervous disease to whom rest, hydropathy, or electrical treatment could bring no relief." These are his words.[1] In order to help these patients he

[1] In the Preface to my book, *Ritual* (New York: Farrar, Straus & Co., 1946), p. 7.

had to understand their hitherto unfathomed symptoms. This is the route by which Freud arrived at psychoanalysis. But how did psychoanalysis come to Freud?

This question remains unanswered. Up to the present it has not even been asked. What were the personal motives which impelled him? What was the conflict-situation that made this psychological interest so strong, so governing, so consuming?

The explanation Freud himself gives is, so to speak, only the official one. Is there another one besides? One need not preclude the other; they can coexist like two rooms, in one of which a lustre sheds its light while the other is illuminated only by a small candle that leaves the corners dark.

Here we are interested only in this dark room. I once compared Freud with Rembrandt. There is no artist comparable to Rembrandt for exactitude of observation, but light came to him only as a contrast to the darkness in which great portions of his pictures are kept. Similarly, Freud left some of his motives in darkness, and it could be said of him what Eugène Fromentin wrote of Rembrandt: "It is with the night that he has made the day." Freud was a confessor, an autobiographer of admirable moral courage and frankness, but at the same time he kept certain personal secrets to himself. He was a self-revealer and a self-concealer. In a certain passage he writes of the "discretion which one owes also to oneself."

This discretion was rarely breached. It was as if he felt he had to keep personal things to himself, even from those of us who were his most loyal students. In his old age he sometimes spoke to one or another of us almost casually of a fragment of his own life he had never mentioned before, as if he had suddenly tired of his secrecy. In his *Interpretation of Dreams,* in the *Psychopathology of Everyday Life* and other writings, he had presented startling discoveries that he had made about himself, magnificent instances of self-analysis, forever belonging to the most precious self-revelations of great minds. All that psychoanalysts throughout the world have since written pales into insignificance beside those pages, distinguished by unheard-of sincerity, by an unequaled moral courage, and by a cool, pitiless observation that is always self-searching and never self-seeking. There were, however, limitations that he imposed on himself—not because he shied away from certain things, but because he knew this hypocritical world and realized it would misunderstand or fail to understand his fearlessness before the shadows that fall on everybody.

"The very best that thou dost know thou dar'st not to the striplings show," we often heard him quote from Goethe's *Faust*.

There were self-revealing reports about suppressed and repressed emotions, conflicts, doubts, fears unearthed by the analyst—by Freud himself—in many a book he published and in many a conversation with us, his students. There was always, however, a remarkable restraint and discretion about himself—a distance from himself, so to speak. In a conversation with me he once emphasized the difference between "privata" and "privatissima," between private things you talk about when there is a scientific need for it, and things so private that you do not talk about them even when it would be valuable to discuss them.

Is there no way that leads to this secret room now, after his death? Our wish to find it is not dictated by idle curiosity of a personal nature; no spying into Freud's secrets is intended. We want to discover what led him to the psychology of the neuroses. It is thus psychological interest of an important kind that makes us ask. He himself would not mind it; he often admitted that he felt indifferent to personal things after his death. He did not believe in survival and immortality, and thought with Heine that the resurrection would be a long time in coming.

What follows is, as far as I can see, the first attempt to discover what determined the intensive personal interest of Freud in the psychology of neuroses. The approach to the secret room is difficult, particularly because of his discretion. Where is it located?

Most psychoanalysts have not observed that psychoanalysis has, so to speak, two branches. One is the research into the symptomatology and etiology of the neuroses, of hysteria, phobia, compulsion neuroses, and so forth. The other is the psychology of dreams; of the little mistakes of everyday life such as forgetting, slips of the tongue, and so forth; of wit and of superstitions—including all that Freud called metapsychology.

The first branch led to the contributions to the theory of sex, to the concept of impulses, especially of the libido. It goes in the direction of biology or tries to build a bridge between psychology and biology. It is clear that these theories are the results of experiences and observations of others. Here are the most precious discoveries used for the understanding of neurotic and psychotic diseases.

The other branch concerns purely psychological phenomena, emotional processes—no connection with biology is sought—inner experiences of the individual, best observed by himself. Dreams, wit, slips of the tongue, old superstitions conflicting with our free, conscious thinking—all these and many other phenomena are analyzed by Freud mostly from instances taken from his own life.

These two branches, it is true, are not always clearly separated. They sometimes appear intertwined, and deep down their two roots must invisibly meet; but one is bent more in the direction of the pathological, and the other more in the direction of general psychology. Nevertheless, they are two clearly distinguishable branches. The future of psychoanalysis—perhaps the future of psychology—will depend upon the choice of the research worker as to which branch he considers the more important one, which of the two will bear better and richer fruits for future generations.

Freud told us many times—and he repeated it in his writings—that he had no great liking for the profession of physician. The therapeutic ambition, the need to help sick people, was not strongly developed in him and for a long time he could not make up his mind whether to study medicine or follow his other interests. He heard a lecture on an essay of Goethe's entitled "Nature," and this experience decided his choice. Was ever a profession wooed in this humor? In Freud's case it was not only wooed but won. He considered it, he said, a personal triumph that he returned on this "detour" (the study of medicine a detour!) to his first and primary wish—to discover something new in the field of psychology. He considered himself first and last a psychologist, not a physician, and here is the line of demarcation which separates many psychoanalysts from the founder of their science, to whom they pay lip service and little else.

Their concept of psychoanalysis is basically different from his. They consider it a branch of medicine and their memory makes them conveniently suppress Freud's explicit sentences. He emphasized that he takes it for granted that psychoanalysis is not a "special branch of medicine. I cannot understand how one can resist recognizing that psychoanalysis is part of psychology; not medical psychology in the old meaning and not psychology of the pathological process, but pure psychology; certainly not the whole of psychology but its underground, perhaps its foundation. One should not be deceived by the possibility of its application to medical purposes. Electricity and X-ray are also applied to medicine, but the science of both remains physics. Neither can historical arguments change the fact that psychoanalysis belongs to psychology. . . . The argument has been brought forward that psychoanalysis was discovered by a physician in his efforts to help patients. But this is immaterial in its evaluation."[2] These remarks are followed by the confession that he realizes after forty-one years of medical practice that he has not really been a physician and that he became a physician professionally only by a deviation from his original intentions. He had, he says, passed all his medical examinations without having felt any interest in medicine; external necessity forced him to renounce a theoretical career. He arrived at neuropathology and finally "on account of new motives" at the study of the neuroses.

Here is a purposeful rejection of the view that psychoanalysis is a medical science. It is, of course, possible that the majority of physicians in America know more and know better than the founder and the greatest representative of the new science what it is—but it is rather unlikely.[3]

There is a very clear warning to physicians not to consider Freud as one of themselves in his "Please count me out." There was more than the Atlantic between psychoanalysis in New York and psychoanalysis in Vienna. There was an ocean of difference in the conception of it.

What interests us at this moment is the question: What personal stimulus led Freud to the research into the psychology of neuroses? What were the "new motives" he mentions that made him turn his attention in this new direction? It is clear that his older interest was to discover something new. He says in the years of his youth the wish to understand something of the mysteries of the world and to contribute something to their solution had become especially strong. He had never played "doctor" as a child, and his curiosity turned in other directions.

What follows now is my attempt to build the bridge of motives between what we think were Freud's earlier interests and his later intellectual preoccupation with the problems of the neuroses. The bridge is narrow enough, but, it seems to me, capable of bearing the burden. As I have said, Freud did not often speak about himself and his intimate life. My impression is that he became more confidential after his seventieth birthday; at least he then told me some things about himself which I could never have guessed. One memory is the most important. I accidentally met him one evening in the Kaertnerstrasse in Vienna and accompanied him home. We talked mostly about analytic cases during the walk. When we crossed a street that had heavy traffic, Freud hesitated

---

[2] Freud, *Gesammelte Schriften,* XI, 387.

[3] In one of his last letters to me dated London, July 3, 1938, Freud sharply criticized this concept of our New York colleagues "for whom analysis is nothing else but one of the maidservants of psychiatry."

as if he did not want to cross. I attributed the hesitancy to the caution of the old man, but to my astonishment he took my arm and said, "You see, there is a survival of my old agoraphobia, which troubled me much in younger years." We crossed the street and picked up our conversation after this remark, which had been casually made.[4] His confession of a lingering fear of crossing open places, his mention of this remnant of an earlier neurosis, made, of course, a strong impression upon me. It took me by surprise and his casual way of telling it to me intensified, rather than weakened, my astonishment. If such a thing had been possible, the free admission that his neurosis had left this scar on his emotional life would have added to my admiration of his great personality.

The other day Siegfried Bernfeld published a paper, "An Unknown Autobiographical Fragment by Freud,"[5] in which he showed that an article of Freud's on screen-memories contains a piece of self-analysis, in this case disguised in the form of a report about a patient. This analysis concerns a man of thirty-eight years "who had maintained an interest in psychological problems in spite of his entirely different profession." Freud asserts that he "had been able to relieve him of a slight phobia through psychoanalysis." Bernfeld proves by means of a careful examination of details that this unknown patient is Freud himself disguised. Freud used the same method of speaking of himself as of another person when he wanted to disguise his identity in another paper later on.[6] Bernfeld, when he published his paper, did not know of Freud's remark made in that conversation with me.

What interests us here is not the biographical significance of Freud's phobia itself, but the fact that it reveals the hidden missing link between his primarily psychological interests and his later occupation with the neuroses. Here is the personal motive that made necessary for him the understanding of neurotic disturbances. In addition to the wish to help nervous patients, there was the demand: Physician, heal yourself. In this case the postulate took the form: Physician, understand your own symptoms and your own disease. But such an understanding was impossible without self-analysis, which could not remain restricted to the symptoms only. From here on we can apply the explanation given by Freud of his own case as a general one. He described how psychoanalysis led away

[4] The scene must have taken place before 1928 because I remember that I saw Freud in later years only at his home.

[5] *The American Imago* (August, 1946), IV, No. 1.

[6] Freud, "Der Moses des Michelangelo," *Gesammelte Schriften* (1914), X, 414.

from the study of the nervous conditions "in a degree surprising to the physician," how it had to concern itself with emotions and passions, how it learned to recognize the significance of memories and the strength of unconscious wishes.[7] "For a time it appeared to be the fate of psychoanalysis to be incorporated in the field of psychology without being able to indicate in what way the mind of the sick patient differed from that of the normal person." In the course of the development of psychoanalysis, Freud declares, it came upon the problem of the dream, which is "an abnormal mental product created by normal people." In solving the enigma of the dream, "it found in unconscious mentality the common ground in which the highest as well as the lowest mental impulses are rooted, and from which arise the most normal mental activities as well as the strange mechanisms of a diseased mind. The picture of the mental mechanisms of the individual now become clearer and more complete. . . ."

Freud himself clearly realized the connection between the interest necessitated in the first instance by his own neurosis and that arising from his concern with general pathology and psychology. The dream—and certainly also wit and the little mistakes belonging to the psychopathology of everyday life—secured the bridge from one shore to the other. The analysis of these phenomena presented the clue to the secret room of his own mental life. In helping himself he brought understanding, help, and recovery to thousands of others. When he learned to recognize the meaning, hidden to himself before, of what takes place behind the façade of his own conscious thinking, the meaning of unconscious processes of all people dawned upon him. He could not have discovered the most valuable secrets of the human mind had he not found them in himself first.

Everybody who has read Freud's most important works knows that these insights were reached by analysis of his own dreams, his own slips of the tongue, and so forth. They were arrived at by self-observation and self-recognition, directed by an extraordinarily fine ear for his inner voices. When, later on, observation of others and research into other minds were added, comparison with his own emotional processes helped him to understand others. Criticism of premature analogies, of conclusions too quickly reached, corrected such comparisons and led to deeper insights, made recognition richer and extended it beyond the frontiers of Freud's ego; but the first and most important source of psychological

[7] In Freud's preface to my *Ritual*, p. 7 ff.

understanding remained this self-observing factor in the psychoanalysis of himself.

Here are the results to which these introductory remarks inevitably lead, results that separate me from the majority of psychoanalysts in this country: psychoanalysis is psychology. Its application in the service of the therapy of neuroses and psychoses means making use of a method that is purely psychological in origin and nature. The most important and the most valuable insights of psychoanalysis are found by self-analysis. Wherever and whenever psychoanalysis makes really important scientific progress, it will be accomplished by an experience in which self-analysis plays the greatest role. No deep insight into human minds is possible without unconscious comparisons with our own experiences. The decisive factor in understanding the meaning and the motives of human emotions and thoughts is something in the person of the observer, of the psychologist himself.

The following pages will, I hope, show to what important scientific consequences our first conclusions will lead. Before that I must, however, point out what will forever separate Freud's way from that of other psychoanalysts, setting aside now the differences between a great man and mediocre minds. His discoveries were made by himself. They were therefore not only a personal experience of unique value but also a triumph comparable to that of the greatest inventors we know. They were the triumph of a mind in search of itself, which, in reaching its aims, discovered the laws governing the emotional processes of all minds. We learn these discoveries with the help of books and lectures; we make them again, rediscover them, when we are in the process of analysis— that is, when we are analyzed or when we analyze others. Our psychoanalytic institutes seem to be unaware of the fact that being analyzed cannot compete in experience-value with unearthing these insights oneself. The one experience cannot be likened to the other. It remains for us a poor substitute, a second or third best. It is ridiculous to consider one's own psychoanalysis as equivalent to the original experience. One's own psychoanalysis—however important, indeed indispensable, for the understanding of oneself and others—is, of course, not comparable to the process by which Freud arrived at his results by a heroic mental deed, by a victory over his own inner reluctances and resistances. When we are analyzed by others, it is an entirely different process, induced from outside even when we ask for it ourselves. It lacks the intimacy and the depth of experience felt in discovering one's secrets oneself.

Nothing said to us, nothing we can learn from others, reaches so deep as that which we find in ourselves. The most a psychoanalyst can do for the patient and for the student is to act the mental midwife or obstetrician. Everybody has to bring his own child into the world. The psychoanalyst can help only in the delivery; he can mitigate the labor pains. He cannot influence the organic process of birth—either in himself or in others.

Many psychoanalysts who train psychiatrists think that the analysis of the students is sufficient. They are so sadly mistaken that it is not even funny. As if being analyzed were enough of an emotional and mental experience to become a psychoanalyst! As if this other, more penetrating experience—to arrive oneself at psychological insight into oneself—were superfluous! Or do they really think that study, attending courses and seminars, can be a substitute for self-acquired knowledge? It is as if listening to a poem were psychologically equivalent to writing the same poem. If being analyzed is not continued and supplemented by a man's own creative experience in finding himself, without the guidance and supervision of a psychoanalyst, it remains an isolated experience, which has no deep roots in himself and bears no rich fruit. Of the psychoanalyst, too, it may be said: By their fruits ye shall know them.

I said before that I do not share the belief of many psychoanalysts that the most valuable things in psychoanalysis can be learned. They can only be experienced. I am certainly far from underestimating the requirement that everybody who studies psychoanalysis be analyzed. This demand appears to me as imperative as it does to them, my stepbrothers in Apollo. But I do not agree with them that one's personal experience of psychoanalysis is finished with this process. I would almost say it begins with it. If there is any possibility of coming even close to the neighborhood of Freud's original experience, it can only be by a self-analysis that follows the process of being analyzed, continues and completes it.

Let me explain what I mean with the help of a comparison. A young man decides to become an actor. Reading the classical authors he becomes convinced he will one day act Hamlet, Othello, Faust. He has to learn to act; he goes to the best dramatic academy and is trained by the best teachers. He is taught how to pronounce words, to achieve the right intonation, to time sentences, to speak verses, and to give them their actor's due. He learns how to move on the stage. Now when he speaks Hamlet's great monologue, when as Faust he discusses ethical and religious subjects with Mephistopheles, he knows how to apply what he has learned, how to give emphasis and theatrical effect to his acting. For all that, he may remain a bad or mediocre actor who fails to strike a chord in us, the people sitting in the theater. What must be added, if he wants to reach us emotionally, to make us believe him?

It seems to me that two more steps, one negative and one positive, must be taken. The actor should, when he walks out upon the stage, forget what he has studied at the academy. He must brush it aside as if it had never been there. If he cannot neglect it now, in the moment of real performance—if it has not gone deep enough that he can afford to neglect it—then his training wasn't good enough. If he has to consciously think and remember how he should speak, move, make gestures, he had better give up his career.

What he has been taught has by now reached tissues so deep—and I mean this literally: his nerve tissues in both brain and body—that he can afford to act as if he had never seen the inside of a dramatic academy.

The man in the audience takes the technical routine for granted and looks for something more: that the actor recover the essential part of the emotion that made him want to be an actor in the first place. On stage, in other words, he becomes Hamlet or Faust, feels what they feel. He must be transformed into Hamlet or Faust when he acts them. There is only one way for such a thing to happen. He has to feel again and anew what he felt and experienced when he met Hamlet and Faust the first time—in a book or at the theater as the case may be. Otherwise he will never touch us; he will leave his audience cold.

Psychoanalysts are like actors applying what they have learned in the academy. I know psychoanalysts who—to continue my comparison—have not learned enough at school. And I know a second group technically perfect but with no style of their own. They are unable to recapture the zeal of their first experiences. Finally, I know the rare psychoanalysts—the masters—who have studied their field thoroughly and behave in the manner of sovereigns, rulers of the stage whom nobody can think of as previous students of an academy.

This analogy is as valid for analytic self-recognition as for the analysis of others. No good psychoanalyst has to think back consciously to what he learned from his own analysis. Nobody can be a good analyst for whom analysis—of himself or others—has lost the value of a personal experience, of *a search* and research.

Apply this test to the field of psychoanalytic writing, and what do you get? There are papers published in psychoanalytic magazines nowadays that are as far from personal experience as Sirius is from our planet. Sterility in psychoanalytic research, its distance from men's lives, has gone so far that some of the papers look like mathematical operations— purely formalized thinking in its most abstract form. Reading such papers I sometimes wonder if many analysts haven't taken a common and solemn vow to stay awake while reading them. It would take a wilder fantasy than any Shakespeare dreamed to imagine that the investigator got his results by way of experience. Science practiced this way remains science for science' sake; it can have no practical outcome. Nothing that does not originate in an experience can become an experience for others.

The element of personal experience can, of course, remain hidden. It may not appear, but it will be felt in the quality of the psychoanalyst's work, whether in practice or in his research. I therefore repeat: By their fruits ye shall know them.

CHAPTER III

"Dere's No Hidin' Place Down Dere"

THE overvaluation of intelligence among cultured people in our country has reached a frightening degree. Not only our public schools and our colleges and universities but also our research institutes give the impression that the intelligence test is the only criterion of man's mental endowment. It is as if intelligence, nowadays called "smartness," were the one and only decisive factor in measuring or in evaluating a person's qualities. It is as if other gifts were not even to be considered; as if imagination, moral courage, creative faculties were of no importance. I am convinced that Beethoven had a lower I.Q. than a bank director, but I am willing to exchange all bank directors for the one Beethoven. One is inclined to believe that Mozart's I.Q. was not equal to that of many college graduates. It was, I am sure, even lower than that of most psychoanalysts.

This general, silly overvaluation of mere intelligence has led to a misconception about the origin of psychoanalysis or about Freud's way of discovering it. The first is that this new research method was discovered by hard and penetrating thinking, by a great intellectual effort. Freud in his incomparable sincerity denied it energetically. He emphasized again and again that he was led to his most important discoveries by a prejudice, a preconceived opinion. He used the German *"Vorurteil,"* which really means "pre-notion" or "pre-judgment." What he really meant can be better expressed by the English word "hunch." What is a hunch? It seems to me that it is an impression reached by intuition, a kind of foreknowledge—sensing something rather than knowing it or judging it by means of reason. The birth of psychoanalysis out of a hunch—that is perhaps not a comfortable idea for us scientific minds, for us psychoanalysts. But the birthplace of an idea is not the decisive factor. Jesus was born in a stable and his idea conquered the world.

As a matter of psychological fact, many of the greatest discoveries and inventions originated as hunches, as every textbook on the history of science reveals. Freud stated again and again that he gained his best insights by trusting to hunches. He did not agree with the accepted opinion of the scholars, that the dream is only a physiological process, but with the average man and woman on the street that it has a secret meaning and can be interpreted. He had another hunch: he did not accept the official view of the physicians who explained hysteria as a physically determined disease, but thought of it as resulting from emotional conflicts. He felt that the generally valid theory of psychiatry did not explain the genesis and the nature of the neuroses, but he preferred rather the concept of the uncultured masses who considered neurosis as an emotional disturbance. He generally preferred concepts in the field of psychology that nobody took seriously. He was not afraid to remain in the minority and his strong will as well as his moral courage enabled him not to give a tinker's damn about what the majority of his professional colleagues thought of him and his new views. For us psychoanalysts it is hopeless, of course, to try to emulate Freud's genius and mental endowments. We should, however, at least wish to emulate him with regard to his fearlessness, his moral courage, his readiness to suffer for his convictions and to remain lonely. Alas, I see very few signs of such a wish among psychoanalysts today.

The technique of psychoanalysis as we know it at present was born as a hunch about the essential nature of the dream and the neuroses. The simple and leading thought, which seems to be so near now and was so far from the minds of Freud's contemporaries, is that men reveal themselves—all their emotional secrets—when they talk freely about themselves; not just when they talk about their secrets, but about everything concerning themselves. They give away what bothers them, disturbs and torments them, all that occupies their thoughts and arouses their emotions—even when they would be most unwilling to talk directly about these things.

Freud has said that mortals are not made to keep a secret and that self-betrayal oozes from all their pores. The ego has built mighty defenses against the forbidden impulses that drive and push to gain some measure of expression. They are pressed into oblivion, into the dark abyss of rejected and condemned emotions and thoughts. They are disavowed, banned, and outlawed, and live in the netherworld, never to be mentioned. In panic fear of their power, man has rolled obstacles as strong as the rock of Gibraltar before the door to prevent their return. They betray themselves, nevertheless, and give notice of their subterranean existence and activity in little, unsuspected signs, words, and gestures. They give themselves away in spite of shame and fear. The old Negro spiritual knows it:

> . . . . I went to de rock
> To hide my face,
> De rock cried out, "No hidin' place,
> Dere's no hidin' place down dere."

Here are the roots of that basic rule of psychoanalytic technique, the only rule which the student or patient need promise to follow. At first hearing it sounds simple enough. Yes, one cannot easily imagine that there could be anything simpler than to say just what occurs to you. But how difficult it is! How much training, what a long will-training will be necessary, not to reach, but merely to approach this aim!

The basic rule is known by the name of free association. Modern writers like to speak of the "stream of consciousness." The comparison is not without merit, but it has its demerits too. The stream sometimes changes into a sea that threatens to drown the person. Sometimes it degenerates and declines into a trickle and it often seems to run dry. It is, it seems, a peculiar kind of stream.

What course this stream takes was, of course, recognized by psychology and formulated in the shape of laws of thought-association long ago. We are following certain laws when we think of an apple, a garden, blossomtime, or of an apple and apple-strudel in succession; when we look at a portrait and think of the person who posed for it; when we smell something and think of a certain dish. We are as obedient to these laws of association as when we think of cold-hot or low-high. Freud had a hunch that this stream had undercurrents to be investigated that determined its course to an even greater extent perhaps than the factors then known to psychology. These undercurrents are the unconscious impulses and interests, the repressed emotions of men. Free associations are only free on the surface. They are dictated by a power behind the throne of reason.

Freud followed his hunch. He asked his patients to say whatever occurred to them without any exception and without using the censorship
to which we submit our thoughts otherwise. In general we try to follow
a certain direction in speaking. We tend to speak logically and to the
point (the effort frequently fails, as the speeches of our senators show).
The patient in psychoanalysis should say what occurs to him without
such order and restriction. He should jump about in his thoughts.

We might contrast the different types of mental activity thus: thinking is like marching on the beaten path of custom to a certain aim;
saying what comes into one's mind is like walking about without any
destination. But are not the two ways of mental activity mutually exclusive? Certainly not; there is room enough for both in our psychical
life. They take place in different layers. It is possible that on the fourth
floor of a building a pianist is practicing a Clementi sonata, while another artist in a room in the basement is playing a Beethoven sonata.
They do not disturb each other as long as they do not hear each other.

It is obvious that the two ways of thinking have separate realms, with
a border between them that neither may cross without creating disturbances of one kind or another. A corporation lawyer would reach
no satisfactory result were he to follow every fancy in thinking about a
difficult legal problem. A poet, on the other hand, would write a very
poor poem if he were to examine each metaphor in his love poem to
see whether it met the tests of strict logic. One way of thinking is not
appropriate in the first case, the other would have no place in the second. The lawyer will do his work best when he thinks and concludes
logically and uses all the reason at his disposal. The poet cannot write
his verses after long reflection and mature consideration. If he should
meditate and ponder about the expression of his feelings, they would
lose all spontaneity. The French poet, Paul Valéry, said that thinking or
reflecting means to lose the thread, *"perdre le fil."* The lawyer thinks
he has lost the thread if he follows a capricious idea, a whim, while
working on his brief. One man's meat is another man's poison.

Is it not easy simply to tell what occurs to you? Should it not be very
easy to speak without order and logical connection, to say everything
that flashes through your mind without rhyme or reason? No, it is
rather difficult; it is more like a steeplechase than a flat course. Every
minute a new obstacle blocks your way. You will be surprised by the
kinds of thoughts that occur to you. You will not only be surprised; you
will be ashamed and sometimes even afraid of them. More than the

conventions of society have to be thrown overboard when you want to say everything that occurs to you. Fear and shame, which is perhaps a special kind of fear itself, have to be discarded before you can succeed. Thoughts and impulses concerning sexual and toilet activities and needs are not easy to utter. Mean, aggressive, and hostile tendencies—especially against persons near and dear to us—are difficult to admit.

It would, however, be erroneous to assume that those tendencies are the only ones that are hard to confess. An analyst often makes the surprising discovery that a man is more ready to talk about a perversion than about a tender feeling he has had. In one of Zola's novels a defendant is willing to speak in a matter-of-fact way about a lust-murder he has committed, but is hindered by shame from admitting that he once kissed the stocking of a woman. Often a petty or trivial thought is much harder to tell than a mean deed. The psychoanalyst finds men are often more ashamed to speak about ideas they consider stupid or superstitious than about impulses that they condemn as criminal or antisocial.

But why enumerate and evaluate all the hindrances and obstacles in the road, when a simple experiment can convince the reader how difficult the task is? The experiment, it is true, is not equivalent to the real psychoanalytic situation; but it has some of its elements and it has the advantage that it can be made here and now. The reader is invited to take paper and pencil and to write down whatever occurs to him during the next half-hour. He should eliminate all censorship of his thoughts while he writes, take no consideration of logic, esthetics, or morals, and concentrate only on jotting down what occurs to him, lost to the social world that at other times dictates his train of thought. If he is sincere with himself and overcomes all tendencies seeking to prevent him from writing down all his thoughts, whether they are clever or silly, conventional or indecent, important or trivial, without bothering about their order, aim, and connections, without selection or censorship—just as if they had been dictated to him by another person—he has done a good job. He should then put the written sheets into a drawer and leave the room. When he takes them out the next day and carefully reads them, he will meet a person there who reminds him of himself in many ways but is in other ways an unknown man. Was it he who thought all that? Here is a new *I* to whom he gets introduced.

Today the experiment can be considerably improved, thanks to an instrument that modern invention has provided. This instrument is called the dictaphone. When one speaks all that one thinks into a dictaphone for an hour under the conditions just mentioned and disconnects the instrument, one has the possibility of listening in comfort to one's thoughts the next day, as one might listen to a third person. The advantages compared with writing are clear. The road from thought to speech is shorter than from thinking to writing. It is really a return to the original, because what we think is only what we say within ourselves without pronouncing the words. Everybody has observed that many people make mouth movements as if they would speak when they read and even when they write. The spoken words have an emotional quality different from the words that have only been thought. The Catholic church does not recognize a confession which is only thought or written down. The confession must be *vocalis*, spoken; it must be articulated, vocalized. A comparison between written and thought words shows that the effect of articulate speech is different not only upon the hearer but also upon the speaker himself. I know a girl who said, "I never know what I think until I hear myself saying it." The advantage of the dictaphone is that one can "hear oneself think." Such experiments can, of course, never replace the psychoanalytic situation, but they can convince the skeptic that he has thoughts and impulses that are unknown to him. There are hidden roomers that live in his mental house without being registered.

There are certain other conditions necessary; certain requirements have to be fulfilled before such experiments can even approach an elementary self-analysis, but one thing is clear: a person has to become at least capable of making such an experiment before he can hope to "analyze himself."

Anybody who tries the experiment will soon realize that one quality is more important than any other in psychoanalysis: moral courage. This quality and this alone enabled Freud, as he once emphatically stated,[1] to make his most valuable discoveries. Many psychoanalysts think that their intellectual endowments qualify them especially for their profession. The truth is that every psychoanalyst with a long experience has had patients who were intellectually his superiors by far; and every psychoanalyst will be ready to admit that to himself. I have had the good luck to treat and to help men who were famous as writers and scientists, and I have often had the opportunity to admire their

[1] Freud, "Josef Popper-Lynkeus und die Theorie des Traumes," *Gesammelte Schriften*, XI, 297.

genius. Two factors render the analyst in the situation in the consulting room an authority. The first—his knowledge and experience in psychology—could be acquired easily by every one of his gifted patients. The other factor is the moral courage that enables the psychoanalyst to face in others as well as in himself unpleasant and repressed thoughts and tendencies, which the patient in his present situation avoids. To help the patient stand his ground before these impulses and ideas is the most important part of the analyst's task. The analyst plays the role of the midwife in helping to bring those unborn thoughts and impulses to the daylight of conscious processes and to convince the patient that they have a right to exist and to be considered.

The psychoanalyst himself is subject to the same dangers as his patient: to disavow and repress thoughts and impulses he does not want to realize in himself, to play hide-and-seek with himself. Every analyst should put himself to the test periodically to determine how sincere he can be with himself. Such self-analysis will teach him a lesson he will remember whenever he is inclined to become impatient with the patient's resistance against recognizing some unpleasant truths. Such self-managed experiments will remind him that he has much to learn and recognize about himself long—in many cases even a few decades—after he was analyzed by another. Only superficial and shallow thinking can make an analyst believe that he knows himself thoroughly and that he does not need any added analysis to become acquainted with himself. He will experience some surprises whenever he faces himself. Meeting oneself is rarely a pleasant experience even for the psychoanalyst.

Every experience of this kind will bring him new insights and added psychological knowledge brought up from the deep wells of his emotional life. At this point I hear a voice saying, "It is easy enough to give advice that one is unwilling to take oneself."

I accept the challenge and interrupt my writing to subject myself to the experiments.

What are my thoughts at this moment? I see the pussy willows on my bookcase . . . a prehistoric vase . . . spring, youth, old age . . . regrets . . . the books . . . the *Encyclopedia of Ethics and Religion* . . . the book I did not finish . . . My eyes wander to the door . . . A photograph of Arthur Schnitzler on the wall . . . my son Arthur . . . his future . . . the lamp on the table . . . What a patient had said about the lamp once when it was without a shade . . . the table . . . it was not there a few years ago . . . my wife bought it . . . I did not want to spend the money at first . . . she bought it nevertheless . . . These are my thoughts as I should tell them to a person in the room ⸱to whom I have to report them the moment they occur. It is clear that most of them are determined by the objects I see; the connections between them seem to be made only by the sight of the objects and by thoughts of the persons they remind me of. Some, as for instance the two sequences, *Encyclopedia of Ethics and Religion*—the book I did not finish and pussy willows—spring—old age—regrets, do not follow the same laws of association, it would seem.

But are they really my thoughts? Aren't they rather abbreviations, clues to my thoughts, not the thoughts themselves? As such, they give nothing but the most superficial information about what I was thinking. If I want to tell what I really thought, I shall have to fill the gaps between these clues, put flesh on this skeleton. Here is what I really thought (and not all, not by a long shot, but enough to make me realize what occupies me at this moment).

I see the pussy willows on my bookcase . . . they are in a prehistoric vase that I brought with me when I came from Austria . . . the flowers remind me of my youth in Vienna . . . I am getting old . . . next year I shall be sixty . . . I regret that I have not enjoyed my youth more . . . I remember a joke I heard from Dr. S. when I last saw him: "When one is six years old, one thinks the penis is there for urinating; when one is sixty, one knows it." . . . unpleasant thoughts about impotence, which threatens with old age . . . return of the regrets that I have not enjoyed my younger years sexually . . . a French proverb: "*Si jeunesse savait, si vieillesse pouvait*" ("If youth but knew, if old age but could") . . . I try to console myself . . . I worked, I achieved something . . . I wrote many books . . . how many? Twenty? Thirty? . . . only six are translated into English . . . the *Encyclopedia of Ethics and Religion* reminds me of the second volume of my *Psychological Problems of Religion* which is not finished . . . without saying it I promised Freud to continue the studies . . . the door . . . leaving . . . dying . . . the photograph of Arthur Schnitzler . . . I remember him and I see him as I took a walk with him in Vienna on the Sommerhaidenweg . . . we lived in the same street and my son was named after him . . . I once wished that Arthur would become a writer like Arthur Schnitzler, whom I loved . . . Schnitzler was once a physician but he left his practice because he preferred writing . . . I hoped my son would study medicine; that was in Holland, but he had to break off his studies and preferred to become a bookseller . . . perhaps he would not have finished his studies even if the Nazis had not come . . . a slight disappointment, because I wanted him to have a brilliant career . . . will he succeed in his profession? . . . the son of Arthur Schnitzler occurs to me . . . his name is Heinrich . . . Like my son he is now in this country. I have not heard anything about him for a long time. Perhaps he is in Hollywood. His father may have wished another career for his son, too. I am sure he did not like Hollywood. I remember his blue eyes, his gray beard . . . the story I heard in Vienna when Heinrich, Arthur Schnitzler's son, was in the first grade of public school. The teacher had asked the boys whether they knew who Goethe was. No one knew, but little Heinrich said, "I am not certain but I believe he is a colleague of my father." . . . clever saying of my son Arthur when he was a child. Once after listening to a concerto by Mozart, he asked his mother, "Is he not called Mozart because his music is so *zart?*" (German for "gentle, fine, delicate") . . . affection for Arthur . . . his passionate interest in music . . . It used to worry me, he seemed too interested. Grillparzer (the great Austrian poet) said about his sweetheart: "She gets drunk on music as another on wine." . . . I once hoped Arthur would become a composer . . . he showed a great musical gift but like myself was too lazy to study an instrument . . . I remember that as a small boy he sang tunes from the symphonies of Mahler . . . he loves this composer as I do . . . the lamp on the table . . . it is a big lamp with curves . . . once the shade was broken and the bulb was visible . . . a lady who was a patient of mine at the time said, "The lamp looks so nude." . . . the table on which the lamp stands was not there . . . my wife suggested that we buy a table for this place near the wall . . . I thought it unnecessary and did not want to spend the money . . . we have so little money . . . my wife did not argue, but a few weeks later the table was there and the lamp stood on it . . . she got around me . . . am I henpecked or indulgent? . . .

Here are my thoughts, and not all the thoughts at that. Many I have skipped because, as Freud once said, one owes discretion even to oneself. There are other associations that do not appear here because I owe discretion to my wife, my son, and other persons who would otherwise be mentioned in this report. It also does not put my train of thought to good account because it considers only what takes place in the center of my mental activity. It does not take the marginal thoughts into account and does not consider the fringes of my thoughts. I would have to write many more pages if I wanted to report them too. When I thought of Arthur, for instance, a memory flashed through my mind. In a moment the image of his mother, whom he resembles, occurred to me. I remembered a conversation we had when he was a small boy. I had even then expressed my ambitious hopes for his future, but my wife said she wished only for his happiness. Here my thoughts turned in the direction of the contrast of fame and achievement with happiness, Arthur Schnitzler was not happy although he was very famous at the time my son was born and named after him.

Such thoughts really belong to the essential psychical process and should not be excluded from this report, especially since they touch a problem that has occupied me in the last few years (see the regrets about my youth which is gone).

How does the name Mahler occur in this train of thought? Apparently only on account of the fact that my son, when only a small boy, was able to remember many tunes from Mahler's symphonies. Between the reported associations there were at least two other connections that I have neglected to give here; one superficial and the other reaching into deeper layers. First the other photograph, beside the one of Arthur Schnitzler, that hangs on the wall is that of Gustav Mahler. This association seems to correspond with the laws of association which W. Wundt and other psychologists follow. Not so the second association: both men lived many years in the Vienna of my youth without having met, until Schnitzler expressed what a deep impression Mahler's Sixth Symphony had made upon him. My son Arthur and I attended a performance of this symphony together in Vienna.

Here we meet the factor of over-determination of associations. This means that many threads connect one thought with the preceding and the following ones. As a matter of fact, no description can give a full account of this over-determination because it is not possible to describe the simultaneous interplay of thoughts moving on different levels. One must change simultaneousness into succession, and the dimensions of surface and depth in the psychical process can only be hinted at.

It is also difficult to give an adequate impression of the rich life on the margins and fringes of the thoughts. I shall give only one instance: at a certain point in my thoughts the name Goethe appeared (little Heinrich Schnitzler said in public school that he thought Goethe was a colleague of his father). But this was not the first time a memory of Goethe occurred in my train of thought. It was there before, although only on the fringes of the process: When I thought of my son's not continuing his studies, I thought also that his engagement to a Dutch girl and his early marriage had a share in his decision; and mysteriously a half-forgotten line from Goethe's *Hermann and Dorothea* occurred. There the mother of the son wishes that he would marry "so that the night will become a beautiful part of thy life." Here, connected with Goethe is an allusion to the sexual motive of marriage. The other obvious thread to Goethe is the name of Schnitzler's son. Heinrich is the name of Faust, the hero of Goethe's tragedy, whose verses accompanied my own youth. From this point thoughts branched off to my psychoanalytic study of Goethe, to my ambitions and hope that Farrar, Straus will publish the book in an English translation in 1949, when the nations of the world celebrate the two hundredth anniversary of Goethe's birth . . . doubts whether I will live so long . . . my heart ailment . . . Schnitzler died of a heart disease.

There are further precursors and lingering notes in the train of thought that are not considered in my report above. On the walk on the Sommerhaidenweg in Vienna, Schnitzler and I had talked about marriage. He had married a girl who was much younger than himself. Here thoughts went forth to my present wife, whom I married after my first wife, Arthur's mother, died. But this same road, the Sommerhaidenweg, plays a part in Schnitzler *Der Weg ins Freie* ("The Way into the Open") a novel which also discusses the Jewish problem. It was partly the influence of the Nazi danger that made my son decide to leave Europe—here is the Jewish problem again.

There are further thoughts—connections that I have not given their psychological due because the explanation would take too long, psychologically important and informative as they are. I can give only two instances. I remembered Arthur's bright remark about Mozart; then followed my thought that my son is too interested in music; and then Grillparzer's words about the passionate love of his girl friend Kathi, for music. The associative threads seem clear enough; the links are all there. But to appreciate the inner operations of the mind, one should follow the connections between the names Mozart and Grillparzer. Grillparzer appears here, in his characterization of Kathi Froehlich's enthusiasm, almost as an opponent of music, as I myself am opposed to my son's overfondness for this art. But Grillparzer was himself a music lover. He played the piano excellently, worshipped the great classical masters, often talked with Beethoven, for whom he prepared a libretto for an opera. He wrote the speech that was spoken at Beethoven's grave, over which he wept with many another Viennese.

It must be psychologically determined that Grillparzer appears here as a contrast to Mozart, whom he adored. The justified criticism of Kathi Froehlich's musical enthusiasm is not sufficient to make a bridge between Mozart and Grillparzer. The bridge was prepared in my thoughts long before this particular train of thought. It was not built on the spur of the moment; it has been there since my youth. Like all boys who attended college in Vienna, I read most of Grillparzer's plays and knew much about his life. To tell the truth, I never liked the man, although we were educated to see in him the great poet of our Austria. As an expression of this concealed dislike, I discovered in my college years an inclination to forget the year of his birth, and I once got a bad mark in an examination on account of it. But an accident helped me keep this date (1791) in memory with such certainty that I know it even now, almost forty years later. My dislike for Grillparzer was not greater than my love for another Austrian, Mozart, who died in the year Grillparzer was born. By a simple mnemonic device that coupled the disliked date, which one is inclined to forget, with another that reminded me of a loved personality, I succeeded in retaining 1791 as Grillparzer's birth year.

My second instance of a marginal association was a visual image. Remembering Schnitzler, I recalled suddenly a caricature of him that appeared in a Vienna newspaper on the occasion of his sixtieth birthday. The cartoon, teasing rather than malicious, shows the writer comfortably smoking his cigar. The rings that the smoke makes seem to transform themselves into seductive faces and bodies of beautiful women. The writer of *Hands Around* looks thoughtfully at these rings as if absorbed in enjoyable memories. The caption expresses his thoughts: "Oh, my, those were times!"

Clearly the memory of the cartoon, which I saw only once almost twenty-five years ago (Schnitzler was sixty years old in 1922), did not occur merely because my glance had fallen on his photograph. If the reader will again follow my previous thoughts, he will meet ideas about my own age—I shall become sixty myself next year—then regrets about my youth and some unpleasant thoughts about the threat of sexual impotency. Here are the highly personal associative threads. In the memory of the caricature with its delicate reminder of fading youth and sexual power, there is an echo that resounds and re-echoes subterraneous thoughts about myself, which have built a bridge of associations to the writer because I am now myself near the age he was when we were friends.[2]

I have given here the main thoughts that crossed my mind in those few minutes of the experiment, which was made on the spur of the moment. It was, of course, impossible to give the reader even a vague idea of the emotions that, distinct or vague, diluted or concentrated, accompanied this train of thought. Words like "regret over my youth, which is gone," "memory of my wife, who died," or "tenderness for Arthur when he was a small boy" are hints at those emotions rather than expressions of their nature.

If I had these thoughts during an analytic session, my psychoanalyst would certainly get an impression of what these emotions accompanying my thoughts were. Intonation, changes of my voice, the rise and fall of the sentences, as well as pauses and other signs would betray not only what I think but also what I feel. If he is a psychoanalyst worthy of the name, he would guess or sense what emotions came alive when I remembered Schnitzler or when I felt sorry that I did not finish the book that I wanted to write because I had promised Freud I would. The most personal factor of these emotions, the intimacy of the inner experience is, it is true, not sayable, but its reflex will communicate itself like a song without words and express emotions that the listener in his turn will sense.

Besides and beyond such impressions, this succession of thoughts, ostensibly so unconnected and meaningless, would give any analyst an excellent idea of what occupies me at this time. Following my train of association, he could not fail to know that I have some thoughts about getting old, worries about sexual potency, and that I try to console myself for my lost youth with satisfaction of another kind. He would realize that I must have been a very ambitious person in my younger days and that I tried to displace this ambition on to my son and was as disappointed with him as with myself, and so forth. All these and many other thoughts and feelings emerged from dark recesses to the surface of my associations, like moles crawling out of their hills between the lights. In such experiments hearing is believing.

[2]My book *Arthur Schnitzler als Psychologe* (which is not translated into English), was published in 1913, but I became his neighbor much later.

When we express what occurs to us, we do not always know what we are saying. But when we read or listen to our words later on, they are oddly enough, not odd any more. We did not know what we were saying, but even so we did better than many people who do not know what they are talking about.

I believe that exercises in thought-association in self-analysis have a value beyond their immediate, practical use for understanding what is one's own psychological situation at a given time. They renew and deepen the experience of the analytic process, make it a living experience again, one which is part of one's life. There is always a danger that the psychoanalyst, who every day sees nine or ten patients, will consider his work a "profession," that he will see himself as an "expert" on the heights and depths of psychical life, and that psychoanalysis may become for him a standard operation procedure. He is not forever "analyzed" after he has once been analyzed.

The psychoanalyst as well as his patient must renew the impression that it is impossible to speak absolute nonsense when one sincerely expresses what has crossed his mind. What emerges from *unconscious* depths has an order, a continuity, and a reason of its own. The analyst has plenty of opportunity to observe how little sense it makes when some people say what they *consciously* think.

CHAPTER IV

Eine Kleine Nachtmusik

THE great German writer, Gotthold Ephraim Lessing, asserted two hundred years ago that the man who does not lose his mind in certain situations has no mind to lose. It is doubtful whether we could go on thinking and acting like reasonable people if we did not from time to time think and act as if we were almost crazy. In our dreams we return to ways of thinking that we deserted long ago, to emotions we no longer feel while awake. Out of the night messages come to us of events taking place in us without our knowledge. Whereas life goes on as usual during the day, we experience exciting things while we sleep. "Great nature's second course," as the poet calls sleep, does more than comfort us and help us to forget what worries us. Perhaps the Viennese physician who tried to prove more than twenty years ago that the poet we know as Shakespeare suffered from insomnia, was right; no one has praised sleep, "Balm of hurt minds," as he has.

Freud repeated that the analysis of his own dreams gave him his deepest insights into his own emotional life. The analyst cannot but follow the master. He will discover secrets about himself, hitherto hidden from him, when he looks into his dreams. He will also refresh his impression of how thin the veneer is that separates him, the reasonable and law-abiding citizen of a modern cultural pattern, from the insane, the criminal, and the savage. He will see traits in his own face that he has never observed and that cannot be discovered in any other mirror. The person he sees in this magnifying looking glass is part of himself, and what he finds in the enlarging process of dream-interpretation are his clandestine thoughts and feelings. The story of his dreams belongs to his autobiography as much as—and sometimes more than—the events and experiences of his days.

Freud emphasized again and again[1] that dream-interpretation marks the turning-point where psychoanalysis changed from a psychotherapeutic method to depth psychology. He admitted, too, that the analytic study of the dream was the first help in understanding the mental processes of the neuroses. The dream is a pathological phenomenon produced by normal persons, the "first link of a chain that leads to the hysterical symptoms, to obsession ideas, and to the systems of the insane." It is a remarkable fact, and one upon which Freud laid stress, that "the analysts behave as if they had nothing to add about the dream and as if the theory of the dream were finished." Those words, written in 1932, are as valid today as they were then. Is nothing new to be discovered about the dream since Freud revealed its greatest secrets? I do not believe it. So much more about the dream remains unsolved: its relation to the real destiny of the dreamer;[2] the connections between the thoughts before falling asleep and the latent dream-content; the resemblance of the dream to artistic visions; the threads that run from the visions of the dreams to the systems of psychotic persons, and many other problems.

I really believe that the fact that research in dream psychology remained so unproductive in the last twenty-five years is due to the reluctance of psychoanalysts to interpret and to publish their own dreams. It is as if we ourselves were too—shall I say—cautious to talk about what we dream and what we discover about ourselves in interpreting our dreams. The instances in which analysts have published interpretations of their own dreams since Freud's lectures can be counted on the fingers of two hands. It is not easy to understand why we, who should know better, observe here the better part of valor. Demanding moral courage and sincerity from our patients, are we not obliged to set them a good example? No double standard should exist here. If our self-revelations were to discredit us in their eyes, then we have never deserved the credit they willingly give us. And if we were to disgrace ourselves by talking about our unconscious processes, then we have been in their good graces only through a mistake that must be rectified.

[1] The last line in his *New Introductory Lectures* (1933).
[2] A contribution to this theme was made by this writer in the chapter, "A Dream a Possible Life," in *Masochism in Modern Man* (New York: Farrar & Rinehart, 1942).

Things are bound to get worse before they get better, but the following interpretations of two of this writer's dreams are perhaps harbingers of this predicted change. Neither of the two brings startling or new discoveries about the dream and its interpretation. Some of their features, however, seem to me remarkable enough to justify their publication—not the least of them being that dreams of psychoanalysts have a curiosity value among psychoanalytic publications. Other features concern the emotional function of the dream, a special way of arriving at their interpretation, and the finer psychological conclusions to which this interpretation leads. Last but not least, it will be of some interest that the two dreams are separated by an interval of twenty years—as far as I know, the only instance of two dreams produced, interpreted, and published by the same person. Perhaps it makes a contribution to the minor problem of whether and how far character-change over a long period modifies the unconscious layers of the dreamer. Considerations of space do not permit me to present more than a part of the interpretation.

The first dream was dreamed in September, 1926.[3] Here is the content: *I see myself standing before judges and I deliver a great plea. I am accused of murder and I have committed this crime.*

The emotion in the dream was not all anxiety, repentance, or depression. After waking up, I remember that I got up from my chair in the dream and that I felt a great emotion of redemption or relief the moment I started my address. Awakening, I wondered about this mood, which was so inappropriate to the situation. I stayed in bed half asleep and half awake for a few minutes after the dream. (While I am writing these lines, the mysterious words "in after-enjoyment" obtrude themselves upon me.) It was as if I wanted to recapture the dream, but I did not consciously intend to do that. In this half-asleep state two isolated fragments of my speech delivered in the dream penetrated to the conscious surface. The first was the address: *"Your honor! Gentlemen of the Jury!"* The second fragment, obviously detached from an unknown text, was an entirely clear sentence, which I liked as I thought it over. *"In my life I have done many things of which I am ashamed—I presume as every one of you has, gentlemen—but nothing of which I have to be ashamed."* It seems to me in recollection that I emphasized the stylistically effective contrast between *of which I am ashamed* and *of*

[3] First published in my book, *Der Schrecken* (Vienna and Leipzig: 1929), p. 75 ff.

which I have to be ashamed theatrically, like an actor who brings out a line.

As I mentioned, the dream did not contain anything analytically remarkable. It was written down because the process of its interpretation is of interest. I never made any conscious attempt to interpret the dream; it interpreted itself, so to speak. This happened as follows: The memory of the dream occurred from time to time at certain moments during the following year. There were, it seemed, no reasons why I remembered the dream just then, but it was as if the recollection wanted to remind me of something. Superstitious people, or dream-interpreters inclined to a kind of scientifically disguised superstition, would perhaps acknowledge such insistent recollection as an expression of a prophetic quality or function of the dream. The analytic interpretation will show that such a conception of a function pointing to the future cannot be found in it.

The fragmentary analysis of the dream took place in sudden jerks or surprise thrusts. Whenever the memory of the dream emerged in subsequent months, together with it there came a thought or an idea, and this thought seemed always to say something about a part of the dream which brought its hidden meaning nearer to the surface. It was as if an object long submerged was being brought to the surface of a lake by the waves so that it could be seized. Let me add a few words about these recollections, which succeeded each other at irregular intervals. They occurred, it seemed, without any connection with preceding thoughts and were not related to the situations in which they surprised me. Why did they occur just then? They concerned something whose secret meaning became suddenly obvious, as if a curtain that covers something were pulled away. Sometimes the recollection came of the dream as a whole, as a unity. Then no insight into its meaning followed, but something else evolved: a feeling like that of meeting some well-known or familiar person. When the memory occurred in the last months of the following year, it had scarcely any visual character left. The accompanying feeling was like that of recognizing an old, dear acquaintance: "Ah, the dream of the compulsion to confess." (I had named the dream thus in my thoughts.) The emotion that saw the dream to the door of conscious thinking was always pleasant, similar to the feeling in chancing upon a daydream in which one had previously indulged. This emotion and the content of the dream were as ill-matched as the feeling of relief that I experienced in dreaming and the situation before the judges.

It would be incorrect to say that these recollections had an obsessive character. They did not pursue me; they only followed me. Sometimes many weeks passed by without any thought of the dream. When I remembered it, the thought never occupied me more than a few minutes. In these short minutes the thoughts occurred that later on fitted together like parts of a jigsaw puzzle to make the essence of the interpretation. This kind of recollection is very different from the other well-known kind in which the dream trespasses upon the waking state for hours and even days, as if it were a piece of the day, a part of the business of living. In this case the thought of the dream had rather the character of remembering something one had once thought. In those intervals my thoughts returned again and again to the dream, as if they wanted to remind me of something that was important or significant to me.

I had no intention of interpreting the dream and never turned my attention to it consciously. My interest in it was thus felt in spite of myself, *malgré moi*.

The remnants from the preceding days that were responsible for the production of the dream are the following: The evening before I had read a paper, "Psychoanalysis and Criminal Law," in which a lecturer of law at the university reviewed my book, *Compulsion to Confess and Need for Punishment,* which had been published the year before.[4] The reviewer had praised the book, but his appreciation had made little impression upon me because he had partly misunderstood and partly rejected precisely the essential elements in my book. He had not grasped the psychological import of the theory of an unconscious compulsion to confess and had denied that certain crimes are committed under the influence of an unconscious guilt-feeling that does not follow but precedes the deed. On the way back from the university library, where I had read the law journal, I had felt annoyed with the professor and had charged him in my thoughts with underestimating the importance of my book.

I do not believe in the value of polemics in science, but I have the bad habit of arguing in thought with my opponents. In these imaginary discussions I show—so I flatter myself—sagacity, quick repartee, and wit; in short, qualities I sadly lack in real life. Also a great eloquence, a rich vocabulary, sharp, logical gifts are at my disposal when I see my opponent before my mental eye only. I crush him with irresistible arguments; I overwhelm him with biting irony; I wound him in his

[4] *Gestaendniszwang und Strafbeduerfnis* (Vienna: 1925).

weakest and most vulnerable spots with refined cruelty—things I am quite unable to do in a real discussion. Especially when I am attacked and when my pride is hurt, I develop this kind of after-sagacity, those splendid ideas that occur to you only when you are leaving a party or discussion, and for which the French have the apt expression *esprit d'escalier*. Almost incapable of reacting immediately to an offense in an adequate way, I find it difficult to forget it. I develop this kind of delayed reaction and I enjoy the deep satisfaction of vengeance in imagination.

And sometimes not in imagination only. I never understood why the Lord declared that vengeance is His. He has got so much and it is almost superhuman to renounce entirely the satisfaction of revenge for a wrong purposefully and maliciously inflicted. Understanding the motives for harming others can sometimes make us feel more forgiving, but it is remarkable how much more ready we are to forgive the wrong inflicted upon others. The sentence of Madame de Stael, "To understand everything means to forgive everything," seems to me to be in a feminine way sentimental and false. When the German explorer, Karl von der Steinen, studied the natives of central Brazil in 1893, he found that they had no word for "pardon." He had great difficulty explaining to them what we meant by it. The oldest of the tribesmen decided after long reflection that the best translation of "I forgive" is "I strike back."[5]

I did not understand that the origins of my dreams were in the emotions and thoughts awakened by reading this critical review until a new occasion reawakened the recollection. A few months after reading Professor B.'s paper in the law journal, there was a discussion of my book in the Vienna Psychoanalytic Association. In the middle of the discussion the recollection of my dream emerged, seemingly without connection; and its hidden meaning representing its wish-fulfillment, suddenly became clear. Other elements of it had analyzed themselves on previous occasions.

B., the professor of criminal law and psychology of law, had expressed his doubts in the review as to whether an unconscious guilt-feeling could really be of such an impulsive and compulsive kind and whether its intensification could really make a man commit a murder, as I had asserted in my book. This point was also being debated in the current discussion—a few colleagues criticizing just this theory in what I considered an unjustified manner. The theory of the unconscious guilt-

[5] *Unter den Naturvoelkern Zentral Brasiliens* (Berlin: 1894).

feeling which precedes the deed and has a share in its motivation was then, in 1926, new.

I realized then the latent meaning of the situation which the dream shows. *I stand before the judges; I have committed a murder myself; I am pleading for myself.* That is to say, I must know very well what emotional processes take place since I have become a murderer myself and since I have myself as an object of psychological research. I can now give information about the psychology of the murderer to my critics, information the authenticity of which no longer can be doubted. I am a criminal myself and I can convince them now that all the emotional processes described in my book—the anxious suspense before the deed, the guilt-feeling that propels it, and the release in the deed—really are as I have described them. I know best because I am a murderer; the theory I had presented is correct and my opponents are wrong.

I was not as horrified by the potentialities for murder that I discovered in my soul as one might expect. Did not John Bradford, seeing a murderer led to execution, say: "There but for the grace of God goes Bradford"? Most psychologists, judges, and public prosecutors either consider such a psychical potentiality excluded as far as they are concerned, or they have an admirably strong faith in God's mercy.

Thus the wish that formed the dream was the desire to demonstrate to my critics that I was correct and they were mistaken. I did not consciously desire to murder anybody. The dream's center of psychical gravity was not the fact of murder itself, but rather the wish to prove that my psychological theories presented the real emotional situation of the criminal. That also explained why I was not afraid or repentant, why I was not worried about the verdict. It was as though I had been convinced that I could get away with murder. More than that, that the murder I committed would lead to a triumph for me. But was not something more hidden in this corner?

The emotion remembered from the dream was that of impatience to deliver my great address before the jury. I wanted to appear at last before the judges to defend and justify myself (my theories) and to give expression to my hatred of my critics. It was certainly this impatience to convince my opponents of the truth of my psychological theories, but there was something else, too, behind such scientific interest. When one pursued those impulses into the realm of unconscious drives, one discovered a wish to murder those critics, the benevolent Professor B. and my less benevolent colleagues of the Vienna Psychoanalytic Association. I neglected, so far as my unconscious went, the praise they had given my book and I reacted only to their critical attitude toward some theories with the wish to murder them. In my waking state I was only aware of a slight annoyance, and I was now astonished at the passionate hate that my dream showed.

Looking back at the dream now, twenty-two years later, I realize that intense reactions of this kind against people whose criticism is malicious or who wrong me are part of my character, however well they are controlled and concealed in life. It seems that I go out of my way in thought to retaliate with fantasies against a person who has tried to humiliate me. Such fantasies have, it seems to me, psychotherapeutic value as well. When not accompanied by guilt-feelings, fantasies of such a violent kind protect me, I suppose, from becoming neurotic. If it is permitted to joke in such serious matters, I would say they are to be recommended as useful counter-advice against a boy-scout mentality. A thought-murder a day keeps the doctor away.

On another occasion it dawned upon me that it made good sense that I knew in my dream that I had committed the deed, that I freely admitted it, and that I felt a strong emotion of release and satisfaction in making a clean breast of it. I confessed. I was demonstrating thereby the depth-effect of the unconscious compulsion to confess, the theory of which I had presented in my book, and I was feeling the release and instinctual satisfaction described there. In my book I tried to prove that the confession is the verbal repetition of a deed and that a part of the emotional satisfaction in confessing lies just in this repetition, as if the deed were being committed again. At the same time confession ex-presses unconsciously all the emotions leading to the crime and thereby enables the person to master the experience psychically, to overcome it. In my confession in the dream I also wanted to prove my theories about the psychology of confession. It seems thus that I wanted to convert my psychological theories into practice in order to prove their correctness; but it seems, on the other hand, that I drew them from my own experience: and I wanted to demonstrate that, too, by my confession. In the aforementioned irregular intervals some associations emerged that showed against what persons, near and dear to me, my murderous wishes were really directed. Moreover, the details of my speech became understandable to me later on. The address, *"Gentlemen of the Jury,"* and the contrast *"of which I am ashamed . . . of which I have to be ashamed"* can be traced to thoughts that were turned sarcastically and aggressively against my opponents among my psychoanalytic colleagues.[6]

The hidden, "latent" content of the dream was the fulfillment of the wish to convince my opponents of the correctness and significance of my psychological view. This wish appeared to be so imperative and urgent that it led to the extreme where I was ready to commit a murder to reach my goal. But such zeal for a psychological theory is unimaginable if it does not concern something very personal. My great speech of defense did not relate in reality to the presentation of my theories, but to the justification of those strong impulses of hate and bitterness that had awakened a murderous wish (the murder in the dream) in me. My own business is dealt with here, *mea res agitur,* no abstract psychological theories: I myself am a potential murderer. The continuation of my dream-thoughts about the correctness of my theories thus led to the confession of my murderous wishes. When one considers the dream as a whole, it appears as a confession not only in its content ("I have committed the deed") but also in its secondary function as confession of my murder-wishes. In other words, the dream presents itself sometimes as a confession. Thus another motive that was operating in the production of the dream: I wanted to demonstrate that the compulsion to confess was also one of the factors working in the creation of dreams, a secondary factor, it is true, but one that had not been discovered before the publication of my book. Thus, not only was it once again proved that I was right and the others wrong, but another secret wish was fulfilled: if my theory is correct, I, too, have made a contribution to the theory of dream psychology.

Here another hidden feature came to the conscious mind. I used to compare and measure my analytic achievements against those of two older colleagues Otto Rank and Hanns Sachs who had finished their psychoanalytic study a few years before me. The theory of dream-interpretation was enriched by contributions from both of these colleagues, who were figures representing my two older brothers; but I had contributed little and nothing significant to the dream-theory. The hypothesis dealing with the secondary function of the dream as a confession before the ego thus represented my small contribution to the dream-theory.

[6] The viciousness of my aggressions can only partly be excused when one recognizes that I felt hurt. *"Cet animal est très méchant; quand on l'attaque, il se défend."*

The emotions in the dream can be followed through its layers. The feelings of release and liberation correspond to the satisfaction about the deed, the realization of my murderous wish. At the same time they fulfill the desire to convince my critics; they confirm the liberating effects of confession. The connecting link between the personal and the theoretical factor is secured by the view that a part of the emotional effect of confession is that it is a repetition of the (real or imagined) deed by means of words. There is a single, uninterrupted emotional stream that goes from the deepest layer (satisfaction about the fulfilled murderous wish) to the highest (gratification that my theory appears confirmed).

The factor of the repeated and seemingly unmotivated recollection of the dream at irregular intervals in the following months is noteworthy. There was nothing common to these occasions on which the recollection appeared; but they were always followed by associations that made a part of the latent dream-content understandable. The interpretation of these parts was not searched for; it fell into my lap, so to speak. This particular psychical course interests us here only because it shows how one sometimes finds clues to one's own unconscious processes. Many psychoanalysts think that you race after those clues. However, they sometimes emerge, when you least expect them. We may also perceive here why recollections of a dream dreamed long ago present themselves at certain points in the patient's stream of associations and why they recur.

The recollection of the dream occurred on occasions which had nothing to do with its manifest content. Most of these occasions are still present in my mind. Here are a few.

While taking a walk, I thought of a problem in religious psychology, of the ideas of resurrection in different religions. With this thought the recollection of the last movement of Mahler's Second Symphony must have been awakened because I caught myself humming a tune from this symphony. It was the passage describing the great Recall that gathers all the resurrected from the four corners of the earth on doomsday. I imagined the crescendo scales, the stormy chords that express in their powerful aggravation the fear of the resurrected before the highest judge, the roll of the drums, and the answer of the four trumpets. Then with an increase in the volume of the instruments and with a greater panic scarcely possible, the great chorale of resurrection in low voices emerged. Contrasting with this increasing fear came the deeply comforting and consoling words: "Oh, believe my heart, Oh, believe nothing will be lost to you"; and, pressing from minor to major: "You were not born in vain, you have not lived and suffered in vain! That is what you desired; that which you fought for." While my imagination drove to the triumphant and roaring melody of the finale:

> You will rise again, my dust,
> After a short rest.

The recollection of the dream was suddenly with me. At the time I did not know why. Today the thought-connection is obvious. It is the contrast between the terror and the fear that grasp all creatures on Judgment Day and that glorious feeling of release and relief that overcomes all anxiety and finally becomes an intoxicating triumph. The recurring memory of the dream was determined by that contrast between the fear of the criminal before confession and the freeing of anxiety by confession. That here in the symphony the feeling of relief appears after the intensified fear before the judges is certainly worthy of consideration. It reflected my own emotions.

On another occasion, in a conversation with my wife, I was pointing out that she had once rejected an opinion often expressed by me as untenable and even nonsensical . . . and had referred to another person whom she considered an authority and who had a contrary opinion. Then recently she concluded that my opinion was justified after all. I now insisted that she had underestimated me and I enjoyed a long-expected, really not noble, satisfaction of the "I-told-you-so" character. It must have been this factor, beside others irrelevant here, that made the memory of the dream reappear: In the end I am right, after having withstood humiliation for a long time, and I enjoy my triumph.

On a third occasion, in a discussion with other psychoanalysts, a colleague sharply criticized an opinion which I had expressed. While I was listening to his criticism, which grew rather personal, the memory of the dream occurred suddenly. It was like a signal, like a flash pointing to a familiar situation; and the thought disappeared after a moment. But this time was quite different from the earlier meeting in which my book was discussed. I now know why the recollection of the dream occurred at this moment, it turned out to be one of the few occasions when I have been able to overcome my inhibitions against aggression. The signal indicated what took place in the next ten minutes: now I was witty, sarcastic, and cruel in my counterattack. Starting with some sly allusions understood by all the others, I passed over to an especially vicious attack and subjected my opponent to the ridicule that kills.

Then on the way home the memory of the dream reappeared, and the connection became immediately clear. Early in the evening, it had acted like a cue: Now is my opportunity; I can tear someone who has been very nasty to me to pieces (verbally, of course). Later the recollection of the dream recurred as a confirmation that it had become realized. A real situation seemed to be so favorable that it appeared as an appropriate substitute for the one of which I had dreamed. Since then no spontaneous memory of the dream has recurred.

It surprises me how deep the wish to be right in the end must work upon me unconsciously, while during my wakeful state it does not matter much to me whether I am right or wrong. (I understand quite well that even the writing and discussion of this dream is not accidental and expresses this wish.)

We almost forgot that our task is not the demonstration of the usefulness or necessity of self-analysis, but to show that self-analysis must precede analysis of others. The quality of the experience is different in its feeling-tones. In the one you look into a room in which you live. It is very likely that you do not observe many things in this room just because you spend your days in it. A visitor sees and realizes things that have escaped you, but his discoveries are not comparable with your own. There are things, corners, hiding places that are not recognizable to the person who looks into this room as a stranger. And what you hide from yourself has a familiar quality when you finally find it that it never has when another points it out to you. The other day I heard about a little boy who was spending the night at his aunt's and complained about the fact that she had turned out the light. "What is the matter with you, Tommy?" asked the aunt. "You sleep in the dark at home, don't you?" "Yes, Auntie," replied the boy, "but it is my own dark "

CHAPTER V

Twenty Years Later

W E HAVE just told a dream of our own. But it is not important whether the object of the search or research is ourselves or others. What matters is the experience itself, or better, that it should be an experience and not just routine analytic office work.

There is no rule by which one reaches these insights. Sometimes they come after long and hard work and sometimes they present themselves without being summoned. (Sometimes they are summoned and they do not come.) It is just as it is with babies. Their birth and growth is an organic process and cannot be hastened. (Analytic literature shows that there are premature births and miscarriages of ideas, too.) Psychoanalysts themselves know very little about how they reach their results and little about the evolution and growth of this kind of experience. In some cases insights emerge from thinking the problem over, in others they appear like flashes from nowhere, or rather from we know not where.

The interpretation of the dream reported in the last chapter was reached by way of installments. The understanding of the dream that follows was immediate, paid in cash, so to speak.

It was dreamed in August, 1946, during the vacation we spent on a farm in Canada. The day before had been very hot and I could not fall asleep for a long time. The way I reached an understanding of the secret meaning of this dream is at least as important as its content, so I shall describe the detailed circumstances surrounding the dream-interpretation before reporting the dream. This, as far as my knowledge of the literature goes, has never before been done. It is unusual, I know, but to do the unusual would be only appropriate in this case.

I awoke in the middle of the night after dreaming the dream; it was very dark in the room and I tried to fall asleep again. I could not fall asleep, I felt depressed, and I tossed around. It was very hot and I did not find any comfort in my bed. My thoughts were not directed to the dream, although I was aware I had dreamed of a small boy in Ottawa who spoke French, I remembered nothing else. I looked at my wife who was sound asleep and I listened to the sound of her quiet breathing. I took her hand and put it to my cheek and I felt myself gliding into sleep from which I awoke in a better mood about seven o'clock in the morning. At the moment of awakening the dream occurred to me with great clarity as a visual image, first the situation of the boy surrounded by a crowd, and then what he had said.

The interpretation of the dream took place during the next hour while I shaved, washed, and breakfasted. The ideas for it pressed forward while I visualized the dream-situation. It was as if thoughts were all ready to present themselves as soon as I turned my attention to each part of the dream. I knew the essence of what the dream wished to say within the first fifteen minutes; other features occurred to me in the remaining time. They followed the essential thoughts like a straggler following an army on the march. I was, in more than one sense, an on-looker in this process of interpretation because it took place while I shaved. I saw my face while I interpreted the dream, or rather while the dream interpreted itself. I have never thought of myself as hand-some, but I was almost frightened by the ugliness of the features that I saw in the mirror making grimaces, now grinning, now sad, reflecting the changing expressions of gaiety and tearfulness, depending on the emotions that the understood parts of the dream aroused in me. The whole impression was almost impersonal, as if I disliked the face of the old and bald ugly Jew who looked at me out of the mirror. Only later it occurred to me that such self-criticism fitted the content of the dream. I have not met any situation similar to this in analytic literature, that is, where a dream-interpretation was made in which a material and a mental mirror were held before the self at the same time; but I can assert that it is hardly a pleasant experience. At least it was not pleasant in my case, although I was amused by some of the things the dream re-vealed about me.

This is the dream: *I am in a street in Ottawa and I have just come out of a restaurant where I have had a meal. I am entering a park and I begin to talk with an urchin who is shabbily dressed. He is five to six years old, almost six. He complains that he must leave his home because his people treat him badly. He mumbles now that he has done something. I ask him why he has stayed so long with his people. He replies,* "Il faut vivre."[1] *He then says,* "Je veux aller aux montagnes."[2] *People come and gather around us. There is a girl with two children. Everyone looks with astonishment at the old boy. I say to them,* "Il ne veut pas dire ce qu'il a fait."[3] *I now realize that he has quite white hair under his cap, which has a slouch brim in front.*

In the moment of awakening in the morning (I do not know why and how) I knew that I was the "old boy." Just before falling asleep I had heard a man speaking to another below our windows. They were speaking French and I could not catch what they were saying; only the last words, *"Bonne nuit, vieux garçon!"* were clearly audible. Just before falling asleep I thought that *"vieux garçon"* had the same connotation as "old boy." There is no doubt, I was the old, white-haired boy. *He is five to six years old, almost six.* At the time of the dream I was between fifty and sixty years old, namely fifty-eight, almost sixty.

After this immediate identification of the old boy, I went over the dream sentence by sentence, and I listened to what the free associations that arose told me.

I am in a street in Ottawa and I have just come out of a restaurant where I have had a meal. Ottawa is the nearest city, a few hours distant from the farm where we are spending the summer. I am very dissatisfied with the food we get here and I often wish to have a good meal in a restaurant in Ottawa. We spent two hours there on our way from New York to the farm, and we had a good lunch at the station. The dream starts thus with a simple wish-fulfillment: I want to have a satisfying dinner. As a matter of fact, I mentioned this wish to my wife during dinner the previous evening as the meal was again not to my taste. In the dream I had already had a good meal. *I am entering a park.* Here, too, is a memory of our sojourn in Ottawa. After our lunch I took a short walk through the streets of the unknown city, looked at the Rideau River, and sat down on a shady bench in the park near-by. *I*

[1] You have to live.
[2] I want to go to the mountains.
[3] He does not want to tell what he has done.

begin to talk with an urchin who is shabbily dressed. Nothing of this kind happened in reality. We already know who this shabbily dressed urchin is and know what it means that he is five to six years old, almost six. But what does it mean that I talk to him, that I appear as two characters in the dream? It is not frequent that the same figure, who is the dreamer, too, ascends the dream-stage in different roles; but it sometimes occurs on the real stage as well that one actor plays two parts. The extraordinary, very unusual case here is that I *began to talk* with myself. This seems inexplicable and is almost as impossible as having an actor carry on a dialogue with himself as another figure on the stage. The text of the dream as well as the comparison just used help us to interpret this element. It was a dialogue with myself. I really began a conversation with myself before I fell asleep. The content of this *dialogue intérieure* (why a French expression?) will be mentioned immediately.

He complains that he must leave his home because his people treat him badly. The dream becomes at this point completely uninterpretable as long as the events of the day before are not reported. It had been intolerably hot the last few days and I, who am quite corpulent, suffered intensely from the heat. I had had a tiff with my wife that evening about our summers. Every summer I give up my great desire to spend my vacation in the high mountains and let myself be persuaded to go to a place that has a lake, which the children can enjoy. I am always told it will be cool there and I am always disappointed because it becomes very hot, so that I become bad-tempered and gloomy. This summer, too, people had told me that this farm in Quebec would be cool and again the heat had become so intolerable that I could not work. I had planned to finish a book this summer that had been a long time in preparation and now I felt unable to do this. I accused my wife of being more concerned about the welfare of the children than about me and my work. I said it was her fault that we had to spend our summers in hot places, where I could not find desirable recreation. She had answered that high mountain air such as I wish would not agree with the children, and that I should have gone alone to spend the summer on a mountain. In reality I am reluctant to spend these weeks away from my family and would feel lonely. When the dream says: *He complains that his people treat him badly,* it reflects this mood of self-pity and reproach. I feel unfairly treated by my wife and children, who expect me to sacrifice my well-being for their comfort. Of course, all this is very much exaggerated. Neither my wife nor my children would demand such a thing, but I feel neglected and am hurt that they do not consider me enough.

In the interval before falling asleep, which was difficult on account of the extreme heat as well as the remorse that I felt because I had hurt my wife's feelings, I had a few sad thoughts that ran in the following direction: "If one could live one's life again, if one only had a second chance!" Some distant memory of Sir James Barrie's *Dear Brutus,* which I had once read and which deals with such an imagined possibility, occurred to me. If one had such a second chance, how differently one would spend one's second life! But the chance alone would not be sufficient, I thought; one had also to change one's character. How would a second chance help if I were still the same—a man who cannot enjoy life naïvely, who knows only work and no play, who yields to the wishes of others and then begrudges them their enjoyment? No, a second chance alone would be insufficient; one should also start life as another person. And how would a second chance help a man who is old? It would be necessary to give him not only his youth in years but also a young mind, a soul fresh and receptive to new impressions—yes, he would have to be young in body and in mind. If one lived one's life again with the same character, life would be the same. I looked back at my own life and told myself that I had lived for others and, now that life waned, it was too late and there was too little left of it to change. With an old heart one cannot enjoy life. These were some of the thoughts that occupied me before falling asleep. They concerned, of course, my situation at the moment. The heat, which had not lessened much by night and did not let me sleep, my regrets about my sharp words to my wife, and my wish, nevertheless, to escape from this farm, made me restless. I was thus repentant and defiant at the same time. Finally I fell asleep.

The dream really starts here. I see myself again as a boy. At the same time I know I am old (white-haired). That odd creature, a small boy with white hair, reflects the result of these thoughts; I want to be a boy again, but I am old. Such bizarre situations or odd figures are the only means at the disposal of the mind during sleep to express the opinion: "That is nonsense. That is grotesque." The dream takes its point of departure from the wish to go to Ottawa and have a good dinner there, and glides into deeper waters. Prior to the train of thought in which I regretted the lost opportunities of my youth, I had toyed with the idea of leaving the farm secretly, taking the train to Ottawa, and going to a tourist or travel bureau to ask for information about a hotel high in the mountains where I could spend the remaining weeks of the summer. Before that I had asked my wife to break our stay at the damned farm and to go with me and the children to a mountain hotel, but she had rejected this suggestion. She had argued that we had promised to stay on the farm the whole summer, that the work of packing and unpacking would be too much for her since her health was not good, and so forth. In my dream I see myself in Ottawa. I have had dinner there in a good restaurant, and now is the time to consider the entire situation. I begin to talk with myself. Here follow parts of the inner dialogue, my reflections before falling asleep. The dream shows me as a boy, but as an "old boy," that is a boy and old. (The expression *vieux garçon* presents the remnant of the evening before.)

The element of the old boy is thus highly condensed and compressed. It says: I want to be a boy again, to have my freedom, to be a vagabond (urchin!); but it knows also that I am too old to be such a freely roaming and irresponsible adventurer. The compromise formation of the old boy contains even more: an acquaintance once called me a "white-haired boy" teasingly or mockingly. The dream also uses this familiar expression and transforms it from its metaphorical character back into its original, literal meaning: a small boy with white hair.

This boy has a cap with a slouch brim in front. At this point in my interpretation I stopped and did not know what this detail could mean. It was significantly enough the only passage of the dream-text that puzzled me. Nothing occurred to me that would elucidate the meaning of the cap on the white-haired head. I thought of cap, then of hat, and then of the French word for it, *chapeau*. Out of nowhere there suddenly came to me the well-known anecdote of the American whose wife died and who goes into a store in Paris to buy a black hat. He asks for a *capeau noir* (black contraceptive), instead of a *chapeau noir*. The salesman is astonished and the husband explains that he wants a *capeau noir* because his wife died the other day. The salesman says, *"Quelle delicatesse!"*

What an idiot I had been! Of course, I knew the sexual symbolical meaning of cap as well as the next psychoanalyst. It did not occur to me, and I would need the detour over the French word *chapeau* and the anecdote about *capeau* to know something I had always known. I made a grimace at my image in the mirror while I was shaving, and I remembered how often we analysts are astonished by the resistances we meet in our patients.

Of course, I know now what kind of resistance it was that did not let me recognize the secret meaning of the dream-detail of the cap. I need not assure myself that I did not consciously think of the possibility of an extramarital affair and of such equipment. Such a thought must nevertheless have been unconsciously connected with my plan to go alone to the mountains. Nothing of these wishes is known to me; I have not the slightest desire to be disloyal to my wife; but the cap, together with the anecdote, tells a tale no conscious alibi can invalidate. It cannot be accidental that the use of a contraceptive in the anecdote is connected with the death of the wife. I discontinue this train of thought here; it becomes unbearable.

The cap, the hat, the slouch brim have certainly an unconscious sexual significance, but besides and beyond that there is another meaning connected with the article. It occurs to me now. When I awoke, I had felt a slight pain in my back and the need to urinate. Both symptoms, which have awakened me at times during the last months, are due, as my physician has told me, to the enlargement of the prostate gland, a complaint to which most older men are subject. Such signs of approaching old age did not go well with the unconscious wishes that emerged during my sleep. It is likely that the awareness of the need to urinate was misinterpreted by the dream-manufactory powers as a sexual sensation. Everywhere in the dream there appears the wish to be young again!

He mumbles now that he has done something. This concerns self-reproaching thoughts about what I have done to hurt my wife's feelings. Before I fell asleep I had had the uncomfortable feeling of a man who has lost his temper unjustifiably and regrets it, as well as the impression that I was, to use a slang expression, "in the doghouse." The detail of mumbling belongs in this context too. I wanted to speak to my wife and apologize, but did not. I would have had to speak in a low voice or I might have awakened the children in the next room.

I ask him why he has stayed so long with his people. That is really a question I had asked myself: Why can't I go away alone to the mountains, why is it so difficult for me to spend my vacations alone? *He replies, "Il faut vivre."* This is the first sentence in French. Apparently an answer to the question, the connection is, so to speak, artificial, mock-logic. In reality it concerns a self-justification: I cannot go away on vacation during the year because I have to earn a living. I cannot afford to have vacations in addition to those in the summer. This point also had been raised in my conversation with my wife the previous evening. I had mentioned that I sometimes felt like interrupting my analytic practice for a few days because I had an urgent wish to breathe mountain air, but I could not do it. I had to earn money—and now, during the summer, I have such a miserable time! *"Il faut vivre"* would thus correspond to the thought: I have to earn money.

But why do I speak French? Well, most people in Ottawa speak French, but this explanation is too superficial. In my defiant thoughts before I fell asleep, I had considered the possibility of going to Ottawa to get information about mountain hotels. Such plans—or rather flirtations with a plan—had met some hindrances in my thoughts. Will my French be good enough in Ottawa? As a boy I spoke French quite well, and when I was in Paris as a student I could express myself satisfactorily. Later on I once gave a guest lecture in French at the Sorbonne, but I have not spoken French for many years. To my pleasant surprise, I found I could speak French fluently enough when I talked with the people on the farm. Yes, in my thoughts I even critically compared their "Canadian" French with mine, which I considered Parisian (sic!). I was, however, often annoyed with myself and ashamed of myself when I could not find the French word for everyday things like a vegetable, an instrument, a piece of furniture. My memory, of which I used to be proud, failed me often, while at other times the French words came fluently and easily. I have a suspicion that my linguistic capabilities depend upon my attitude toward the people with whom I am speaking— whether I feel welcome or anticipate unfriendliness. There must have been a slight fear in me that I would not be able to ask all my questions and get all the necessary information at the tourist office because my French is so poor. In the dream this fear is entirely overcome. The old boy speaks French as if it were his mother tongue, which it would be in reality if he were an Ottawa urchin, but which is, of course, not so since I was born in Vienna.

He then says: "Je veux aller aux montagnes." I would really say something like that in the tourist office in Ottawa, if I should go there. Here is the real core of the dream where my self-assertion expresses itself most strongly. I am saying: I want to go to the mountains; nobody and nothing will prevent me. If the dream as a whole anticipates the situation in Ottawa where I want to go for information, this sentence expresses vigorously my irrevocable decision and wish.

People come and gather around us. There is a girl with two children. Everyone looks with astonishment at the old boy. Here the dream describes the situation on the farm when I leave. People would come and gather around us, me and my family. The girl with the children is, of course, my wife, who is so many years younger than I am, with my two daughters. Everyone would look with astonishment at the old boy, me, who has found the will-power and the energy to leave his family alone in the middle of the summer. I am a kind of hero; I have done the deed. *I say to them, "Il ne veut pas dire ce qu'il a fait."* That relates, of course, to the fact that I do not want to confess that I have offended my wife by my remarks. At the same time I do not feel inclined to explain why I am leaving the place. I want to leave secretly. I say to them that I have nothing to say; that is, no comment. Of course, there is also a defiant note that runs through the whole dream: no one has a right to call me to account for what I do. It is as if this defiance would overcome a slight fear: what will people think? What should I say to them, how explain why I leave? The *il*, the "he" of the dream, is, of course, myself as I appear in my plans, observed by myself.

I would not be astonished if the reader who has patiently followed me to this point—granted that he accepts this interpretation—was to think: "What a villain and what a brute! A man near sixty, father of a family, who dreams that he wants to desert them in a foreign country and go to the mountains alone like a hobo!" I cannot disavow my responsibility for the dream and I would have to admit: *Voilà, comme je suis* (again French?); that's how I am, or at least a part of me, the part coming to the foreground in the dream. There is no blinking at the psychological fact the dream reveals; that I would have liked to have left my family alone and to have lived by myself for a few weeks high in the mountains, finishing my book. I have no apologies to offer. The dream was to be sure, not a considered action, but it shows that I considered an action, unconsciously, at least. Facing severe judges, I can only present a few extenuating circumstances. I really suffer from the heat. I had hoped so much to finish my book in mountain air, and it was the eighth year in which this wish to live on a high mountain had remained unfulfilled. Moreover, in reality I remained, of course, with my family, sat during the day in the somewhat cooler cellar of the farm, and did not finish my book.

It seems to me that the circumstances following the dream are worth psychological consideration. That I could not fall asleep again and that

I tossed about restlessly were, of course, conditioned by the emotions the dream aroused in me. I must have felt guilty—not on account of the dream, but on account of my bad behavior toward my wife the evening before. I felt affectionate when I thought how she bore with me and my temper. I took her hand as if I wanted to ask her forgiveness and I fell asleep almost immediately.

The dream released feelings that had not been fully expressed during the day. It not only showed the fulfillment of my wishes in the images it presented but also gave the emotions connected with them free rein. In realizing both tasks the dream had fulfilled its healing or psychotherapeutic function. When I awoke in the night I scarcely remembered the dream and the emotions in it. It was as if they only resounded like a distant echo. In the morning the dream reappeared in my memory, but the curtain had come down on the emotions of bitterness and annoyance. It is noteworthy that the dream, which used an expression heard a few minutes before in the sense of my wish ("old boy") to be young again and free of responsibility, maintained the knowledge that I was no longer young and that I was a husband and a father. It was defiant with bad conscience.

From this dream-analysis we return to our theme, which is research into the strange ways by which we arrive at our insights into unconscious processes. It is really unimportant whether they are one's own or those of others, when one approaches the problem in the spirit of a psychologist. The intellectual satisfaction in finding something that hides itself is almost impersonal when "out of the night" secrets of one's own self emerge. The deep gratification derived from looking into one's own concealed thoughts and drives even outweighs the intensity of the other emotions that are aroused in the psychologist. The satisfaction that originates in the recognition and understanding of the nature and motives of unconscious processes is equal to that of every other adventure of the mind. The psychoanalyst who loves his science will enjoy this intellectual pleasure, which has the controlled suspense of the chase and the gratification of reaching that which eludes all conscious effort. Freud gave us much more than a method of treating neurotic or psychotic patients. He let us understand a language every human being speaks, although he neither knows it nor understands it himself.

In speaking and in thinking we reveal ourselves without wanting to. In our dreams, in our everyday mistakes and slips of the tongue, in our associations of thoughts, we give away more than we think. When we speak we allude to and suggest more than we say, and we say more than we suggest. In trifles we are not even aware of, in *petits riens* of observation, is contained all that is vital in our lives. In our dreams we keep a blind date with an unknown self.

If we then try to analyze what comes to the surface, we are introduced to a new acquaintance. Most people lose out when you get to know them better, including ourselves. But when you penetrate deeper into the hidden parts of their personality—your own, too—you find that there is something of the worst in the best of us and something of the best in the worst of us.

CHAPTER VI

"Ask Your Heart What It Doth Know"

EVERY self-analysis that leads into a certain depth convinces the analyst that there is no basic psychological difference between him and the patients he is treating. An occasional blind date with oneself is here recommended to the analyst, not only as a way to enlarge the knowledge of his own personality but also as an excellent method of self-education. Many analysts are inclined to exaggerate in their thoughts the distance that separates them from their neurotic and psychotic patients. Nothing but luck has decided that we are on this side of the fence and not on the other or that we are sitting behind the couch and not on it. Where this sober insight threatens to lose its strength, self-analysis will restore it. It makes the analyst humble and prevents him from feeling that he is the master of his soul.

Students at the Vienna University thirty years ago told the following story: A rather stupid and conceited clinical assistant who knew how to use his social connections became a professor of psychiatry. All his colleagues were astonished and could not understand how such a pompous ass could get the position, which was the goal of many gifted and ambitious physicians. One of these colleagues shrugged his shoulders and said, "It was perhaps the mildest way of bringing him into the psychiatric clinic." Really, the distance between the psychiatrists and their patients is not as tremendous as it frequently appears to laymen and sometimes even to the psychoanalysts. We are all wrestling with the same emotional problems, and it is often only a matter of proportion that determines whether we are victorious or defeated.

A little more or a little less inner sincerity, a small plus or minus of moral courage, is what decides whether we understand ourselves and others. Reading the dream-interpretation of the preceding chapter, I suddenly realized that I must confess that I had been almost tempted into such a lack of inner sincerity myself. The following paragraphs will present not only my confession, but, what appears to me more important, my analysis of the omission of which I found myself guilty.

As I was writing the dream-interpretation, I had the vague impression that I was omittting something in my thoughts or in the description of the situation that led to the production of the dream. I had forgotten something or skipped over something, but what was it? I knew where I had to search for it, but I could not find it. It was somehow connected with the reproach I had made to my wife: that she was responsible for the fact that I had to suffer so much from the heat. I knew that this reproach was to some extent unjust, but to what extent? I had the uncomfortable feeling that I was myself more responsible than she, but how? I knew I ought to correct the mistake in the presentation here; I knew that I had made a mistake, but did not know what to add or what to replace. There remained, however, the vague feeling of having suppressed something that should have been said. I had the uncomfortable sensation of having forgotten something and being constantly reminded of this fact without being able to remember what the forgotten object was.

The reminder, which I could not brush aside, was itself irksome. A strange comparison came to mind: it was as if a man occupied with some serious work is annoyed because a little boy, his son for instance, pulls him by the sleeve to call his attention to some insignificant thing.

Let me dwell a moment on this analogy. I am aware—sometimes painfully so—that the comparisons I introduce into my thoughts are often not well chosen and sometimes not even appropriate, but such self-criticism does not improve matters. In spite of it, I am tempted to make psychological things clear to myself and to others by comparing them with phenomena from other fields of observation. But the analogy between an inner reminder and a little boy trying to arouse the attention of his father goes too far! It is really so remote that not only its content but also its form appear almost childish or silly. I tried in vain to get rid of this infantile comparison, but it was stubborn and stayed in my thoughts. Let me hasten to state that it was the understanding of just this "stupid" comparison which at last gave me the clue to what I had suppressed. This is a thread which we shall follow later on.

First here is what I had suppressed. It was true that my wife decided she wanted to stay with the children at the farm where it was so hot, but I was myself responsible for the fact that we had to spend our vacation on the farm, which had been recommended to me. I had given up the search for mountain hotels where we could have spent these summer weeks in a more pleasant manner. I had been discouraged because I had not found a hotel in the mountains, a hotel located high enough, not expensive—and not reserved for Christian clientele. In the weeks before we started our vacation, I had had an unpleasant experience or two with the managers of some mountain hotels, and it was the memory of these experiences that led to the suppression of a not unimportant fact and to an unconscious distortion in the presentation of the material. What I had skipped over was the Jewish question, which had been a determining factor in the choice of our vacation place. Inquiries at several mountain hotels in Vermont and New Hampshire had shown that they were "restricted" or "reserved for Gentiles." A lecturer at Harvard, a friend of mine, had at last recommended me to the manager of a hotel whose location and rates appeared satisfactory. We had reserved rooms there and I had already received the acknowledgment of my check. Friends of ours, who have a Jewish-sounding name, wished to reserve rooms in the same hotel. They received a polite letter from the manager of the hotel answering their questions. At the bottom of the letter was one typewritten, underlined word: "Restricted." Of course, I canceled our reservation at the hotel where the manager regarded Jewish guests as unwelcome. In my letter I expressed my disappointment and indignation. After some similar experiences I gave up hope of finding a satisfactory place that did not discriminate against Jews.

What are the reasons that led to the suppression of this thought? In the first place it was certainly the wish not to admit to myself as well as to my wife that I had not taken enough trouble to search further after having experienced some disappointment. Of course, the wish to avoid the unpleasant memory of these experiences was the element that did not let the thought of those other mountain hotels come to conscious mind. I have also to admit that I tried to avoid this subject in my thoughts later on. I did not like to think of the humiliating feeling I had at not being admitted as a guest, like anyone else, to a hotel in a country I now consider my home. After having lived in Europe for fifty years, I had hoped that we could avoid racial or religious discrimination in the United States. I had to admit to myself that my hope had not been realized.

This minor suppression, incidental as it is, touches the circle of thought around the Jewish problem like a tangent. In the analysis of Jewish patients in Europe I had sometimes met a phenomenon that was difficult for me to understand emotionally, although it was easy enough to comprehend it intellectually: the fact that there are Jews who are ashamed of being Jews. I had met the same phenomenon in America under different circumstances: patients frequently remembered that they often felt ashamed of their fathers or mothers who had come to this country from eastern Europe as immigrants, had kept their old religious or national customs, and not become "Americanized" like their children, most of whom were born and brought up in the United States. Many memories showed that these children had been ashamed of their parents, for instance, when the father or mother had come to school or when they talked to friends whom the child had brought home. Many of these parents could not speak English well. They had manners and habits that were different from those of American-born parents, and the child often became painfully aware of these differences. All this is natural enough, but I understood it only with my intelligence. I had never felt anything comparable and I could not recall having experienced similar emotions.

This lack of emotional understanding marks the point of departure for the following paragraphs. A line leads from this point on the periphery to the center of the circle, to the unconscious memory that announced itself in the strange comparison mentioned above, and to the clue to this experience. Before discussing my train of thought, let me insert a few sentences about my personal attitude toward the Jewish problem. (It had occupied my thoughts for many years and much of my psychological study was concerned with it. However, this is not the place to discuss this side of the question.)

For a long time I conceived of my people as an extension of my family and believed that my attitude toward them was similar to that which I had toward my family. More than this, I believed that the attitude of any Jew must have its roots in his feelings toward his own family. His individual position regarding the Jewish problem, I felt, is unconsciously determined by these other emotions. The attitude of the individual Jew toward his people reflects his emotional attitude toward his family, especially his father. Other people, friends and lovers, are often and for many years nearer to us than members of our own family; but we have special emotional attitudes toward our parents and our brothers and sisters that we do not have toward other persons who have become dear to us. Childhood impressions, most of which are not preserved in our conscious memories, determine them, give color and blood to the relations that tie us to members of our family. We not only understand them better but in a different manner, and we love and hate them differently. We discover faults in them that are hidden to others and we know them to be in possession of concealed endowments and excellent qualities that are secrets to others outside our intimate circle. Sometimes we are also much more impatient with them than with strangers. Often we are annoyed by features and character traits we gladly tolerate when we find them in others, in strangers.

By this admittedly very personal concept of one's people as an extension of one's family I am attempting to explain to myself emotional facts that, often elusive in character, are hard to comprehend: that the same feelings, positive and negative, can be differently tinged when felt toward a member of my family; that the same experiences can have an emotional intimacy which they lack even with friends and sweethearts. It is as if they had a special personal touch, a distinguishing quality. To speak again in terms of a comparison, the same note sounds slightly different when played on two different strings of the violin. It has a certain timbre on one string that is not felt when it is played on another. The concept of one's attitude toward one's people as being analogous to that toward one's family explained to me, too, how one can feel more attracted to strangers and more hostile or critical toward one's family. A man can prefer to be together with others and even avoid his own people; he can even feel estranged from them—but he can never be a stranger to them. The very intimacy of the experience, which is nothing but common memories that have become unconscious, excludes the possibility of cutting a tie that was formed, not alone by the same blood, but by the same rhythm of living. It is neither congeniality nor consanguinity that speaks here, but the common destiny of our ancestors, of ourselves, and of our children, which forms a bond stronger than relations of another kind. I can admire others more than my family, love them more deeply, and I can feel that they are nearer and dearer to me than members of my family; but I cannot renounce my family. I can choose my friends, my wife, or my mistress, but I cannot choose my father and mother, and I cannot choose to be born an Italian, a Greek, or a Jew. My people—these are the features and the faces of my parents, my brothers and sisters, my grandparents, my uncles and aunts, no longer recognized as such. I look into faces that have a family resemblance although they do not belong to my family, but to my people. They are perhaps not always sympathetic, these faces, but they are always "familiar" to me. I am an infidel Jew; I can scarcely read Hebrew any longer; I have only a smattering of Jewish history, literature, and religion. Yet I know that I am a Jew in every fiber of my personality. It is as silly and as useless to emphasize it as it is to disavow it. The only possible attitude toward it is to acknowledge it as a fact.

This long digression can be justified only if it helps to pave the way to the understanding of the problem, which was difficult for me to grasp emotionally, that Jews could be ashamed of being Jews. My thesis was that being ashamed of one's Jewishness was psychologically identical with being ashamed of one's parents. If this is correct, then I must conclude that this emotion is alien to me, that I have never felt it. But that is impossible. It can only be that I have repressed the memory of occasions when I, like other children, was ashamed of my parents. I cannot remember any situation of such a nature, but that does not mean it did not happen. I had decided to use the very next opportunity for some work at self-analysis in this direction.

Good intentions, such as marrying a certain girl, answering a certain letter, and so forth, become more difficult to carry out the longer their performance is postponed. When the question again occurred to me, it no longer had its original shape. The Jewish theme receded when the question came up again from another angle—from two little experiences with my own children.

My daughter Miriam, not yet eight years old, had invited a boy from her school to lunch. During the meal Miriam, who sat beside me at the table, bent over to me and whispered into my ear, "Daddy, wipe your mouth!" I had drunk some orange juice and it seemed that a few drops were still on my lips. My little daughter was, no doubt, ashamed of me in front of her little boy friend. Was this the first time she had been ashamed of me? It is not likely; it was only the first time I had observed it.

A few weeks later my other daughter, Theodora, who is thirteen years old, had a girl friend as her visitor. When I came into Theodora's room, I greeted them politely and was formally introduced. In the course of the ensuing small talk I ventured the casual question, "Who is the smartest in your grade?" I realized immediately that I had made a blunder because my daughter looked at me reproachfully while her friend giggled and said, "I don't know." It was clear that I had trespassed upon a forbidden area or sinned against the etiquette observed in junior high school circles, but I was not so sure about the nature of my offense. I took my leave shortly afterward with as much dignity as I could muster. My feeling had not deceived me. The next day my wife informed me that Theodora had complained to her that her father had embarrassed her by his "silly questions" in the presence of her friend. Later on I understood that such a question would be embarrassing (1) because the answer is unessential and immaterial in the eyes of junior high school pupils, and (2) because tact forbids a direct answer in either case, whether the girl friend considers herself the smartest or whether in her opinion my daughter is the smartest.

Thus we have two instances in which my own daughters were ashamed of their father and, no doubt, there must have been many others which escaped my observation. I had been taught a lesson not only in tact and table manners but also in child psychology. I tried in vain to recall similar instances from my own childhood. No such memories emerged. My father's image appeared clearly enough; I also realized that he had weaknesses and faults like any mortal man, but I could not remember having been ashamed of him.

Instead, a proverb I must have heard as a child occurred to me, one of those Jewish proverbs that contain so much concealed psychological truth. It says: "He who is ashamed of his family will have no luck" or, more literally, "Upon him who is ashamed of his family there will be no blessing."[1] I had not thought of this line since childhood, and it was strange that it came to mind now. I understood that this saying, heard early in life, had long worked upon me like a warning, yes, even like an unconscious inhibition. It threatens the individual who is ashamed of his family with calamity, with disaster. Only later on did I understand that the proverb has not a magical, but a psychological, meaning.

When no other childhood memory of the described character emerged, I gave up the attempt to recall such memories by any conscious effort. The memory then appeared suddenly, much later, when it was not summoned. It was in connection with the comparison I used,

---

[1] The original is, of course, in German-Yiddish:
> *Wer sich schaemt von sein' mischpoche,*
> *Auf dem is ka broche.*

my analogy of the small boy who tugs at his father's sleeve to tell him something. We know that comparisons are never accidental, that they conceal and often reveal unconscious material. In this case it became suddenly conscious in a flash. I knew that I was the little boy and I remembered the situation with all its details.

I must have been a very young child because my father held my hand as I walked at his side. It was summer and very hot, and my father took me to the Augarten, one of the public parks in Vienna where children used to play. My father was a stout man, as I am now, and he must have suffered from the heat because he puffed and blew out his breath as he walked along with me. I remember that I was very much ashamed of him then and I now realize why. I must have mistaken the noises his loud breathing produced for others caused by flatulence. I had, perhaps, not long before learned that one has to control oneself when tempted to break wind, and I was now under the impression that my father was doing something indecent in public. Perhaps I had once heard similar noises produced by him in his bedroom and was afraid that he would now make these same noises in the presence of people. Maybe the little boy really pulled him by the sleeve to admonish him to behave himself. My memory does not deceive me: I was then really ashamed of my father.

Other memories followed this one, as if a forbidden door had been opened. They all concerned my childhood; they presented other occasions when I was ashamed of my father, like the next fellow. They all had a similar childish character. My parents had been kind and honest people and had their share of human frailties and faults, as we all have.

Only a few remarks about the initial theme should be added to this fragment of self-analysis, which is insignificant considered as such. The result of this self-analysis does not make it necessary for me to change my impression that to be ashamed of one's Jewishness can be traced back to being ashamed of one's parents. In the meantime, many analytic experiences have confirmed this view.

But being ashamed of one's parents is, psychologically, not identical with being ashamed of one's people. I believe every one of us will, if he but digs deeply enough into the realm of unconscious memories, remember having been ashamed of his parents. Being ashamed of our people must have another psychological meaning. It must be the expression of a tendency to disavow the most essential part of ourself. To be ashamed of being Jewish means not only to be a coward and insincere in disavowing the proud inheritance of an old people who have made an eternal contribution to the civilization of mankind. It also means to disavow the best and the most precious part we get from our parents, their parents, and their ancestors, who continue to live in us. It means, furthermore, to renounce oneself. Without self-respect and dignity no man or woman can live. When the Jewish proverb proclaims that he who is ashamed of his family will have no luck in life, it must mean just that: he cannot have that self-confidence which makes life worth living. Strange that the folklore of an oriental people coincides here with the viewpoint of Goethe: any life can be lived if one does not miss oneself, if one but remains oneself.

The thought that my children are sometimes ashamed of the human faults and failings of their father does not sadden me; but, for their own sake, I wish that they will never be ashamed that their father was Jewish. The one feeling concerns only the personal shortcomings of an individual who was striving, sometimes succeeding and often failing. The other shame concerns something superpersonal, something beyond the narrow realm of the individual. It concerns the community of fate, it touches the bond that ties one generation to those preceding it and those following it.

The other, more important part of the train of thought that results from this self-analysis concerns the conditions of psychological understanding of others. If the analyst listens to what others say—and listens even to what they do not say—he will get the messages which, if deciphered, lead to psychological insights that cannot be reached by any other means. If he does not get those messages—if he cannot make out what they mean—he will search for them in vain in books, lectures, and seminars. He must break up the ground, dig deeper and deeper into himself, until he reaches the source of all psychological understanding that is in himself. It cannot be had from others. Not analysis, but the analyst, makes us understand the meanings of those puzzling processes of the unconscious. In contrast with, and in emphasized opposition to, a great number of psychoanalysts, I do not believe in "learning" what the unconscious has to say. I do not believe that the analyst can get his clues from his intelligence and his scholastic wisdom. I believe that the best advice to those who search for hidden psychological truth, was given more than three hundred years before Freud. Here are the lines that a figure of Shakespeare[2] speaks in Vienna, the same Vienna where Freud lived and worked:

> . . . Go to your bosom;
> Knock there, and ask your heart what it doth know—

Much serious learning and years of hard scientific study are necessary to practice psychoanalysis, but study alone will not result in analytic understanding: the real source of our best insights is indicated in Shakespeare's lines. Here is a warning, very up to date, and a lesson more valuable than any given in the psychoanalytic institutes. After all teaching is said and all study is done, do not expect answers from your intelligence, from your "reason." Ask your heart what it doth know.

[2]Isabella in *Measure for Measure,* Act II, scene 2.

CHAPTER VII

The Voice of My Father

ON THE street or in parks you sometimes notice people talking to themselves. These persons, who seem to be carrying on such stimulating one-sided conversations, are not necessarily drunk or insane. I once asked an acquaintance who had this habit about his motives. He answered jokingly that he occasionally liked to hear what an intelligent person had to say, and to feel that he was talking to an intelligent listener. Such a high self-evaluation may be correct in some cases and wrong in others. More important is the fact that in dialogues with oneself one is more sincere than in conversation with others. The speaker is less inhibited and less conventional and will say what he really thinks, while his audience is more tolerant and more willing to listen, not only to reason, but to unreason. Certainly many matters that are never or rarely mentioned in talking to others are freely discussed in conversations with oneself.

Self-analysis is comparable to a conversation with oneself with the difference that its character is not just chattering, but discovering in oneself something which has hitherto been unknown. Self-analysis for its own sake is usually as barren as *l'art pour l'art*. Occasion for self-analysis arises only when we are surprised by our thoughts, when we find in ourselves feelings that seem strange, or when we are amazed over actions and inhibitions we did not suspect in ourselves. Such opportunities occur much more frequently than one might think.

More than a hundred years ago a Viennese satirist wrote: "I believe the worst of everybody, including myself, and I have rarely been mistaken." The remark is certainly justified but necessarily one sided. Self-analysis reveals that there are not only unsuspected vices and horrid impulses hidden within ourselves but also friendly and even generous feelings never dreamed of or only dreamed of. This kind of deep-sea diving brings to the surface not only strange monsters but also unlooked-for treasures. Many surprises beyond good and evil await the diver there on the bottom, if he glides down at the right moment.

The following paragraphs present no more than a fragmentary analysis of a mood, a frame of mind of my own, which I did not understand until some months after it had passed.

Like many of my colleagues I had left the decaying Vienna of the post-war years to live in Berlin, where the new Psychoanalytic Institute was showing a promising development. I had built up a satisfactory psychoanalytic practice in Berlin when, one day, I received from Vienna a request for an appointment. The man who wrote was unknown to me but said that he had a special recommendation from Freud. At the appointed hour the man appeared for a consultation. He was a middle-aged and very wealthy American with a well-known name. He described his nervous symptoms, giving me a good picture of his psychological situation. For many years he had been suffering from a severe obsessional neurosis that necessitated his protecting himself against innumerable imaginary and magical dangers by means of many complicated safety measures. Both because of his nervous troubles and for family reasons, it was not possible for him to come to Berlin for psychoanalytic treatment. Freud had suggested his coming to me because I had treated many similar cases in the past. The patient made me the following proposition. If I would return to Vienna to treat him and be at his disposal for just one hour daily, he would not only be responsible for my living expenses but pay me a fee much larger than the total earnings from my Berlin psychoanalytic practice. After a brief consideration I accepted his offer. Having brought some of my analytic treatments to an end and transferred other cases to colleagues, I returned to Vienna in November, 1932. In spite of the many social and cultural advantages Berlin possessed at that time, I had not been overfond of the capital of the German Reich. When I arrived at the Vienna station, I felt like a son coming home to his mother. All during the journey I had been happily anticipating the prospect of the life ahead of me. I would be free from all financial considerations and would be able to devote most of my time to scientific research. I would be able to see my family and friends as often as I wished. This wonderful opportunity would permit me to see Freud and to attend the weekly meetings of the Vienna Psychoanalytic Association, whose secretary I had been in past years. Altogether it seemed like a fairy tale come true.

The ensuing months brought the realization of these daydreams. Released from the necessity of spending ten hours a day in psychoanalytic practice, I worked on the two books I had planned, saw much of my family and friends, visited with Freud and regularly attended the meetings of the Vienna Psychoanalytic Association. I enjoyed the first days of my return to the utmost. It made me happy just to walk in the morning through the familiar streets of my native city on my way to the university library.

The apartment my patient had taken for me was, like his own, in the Hotel Bristol, which, in splendor and dignity, is comparable to New York's Waldorf-Astoria. I still remember how I could scarcely believe my good luck when I awoke the first morning and looked about me at the magnificently appointed rooms which were now my new home. Humming a Strauss waltz I went down to breakfast at my usual hour. Of course there was no one in the dining room to serve me—it was not yet seven. As I passed the night clerk at his desk, he looked up at me with a startled expression as if I were some ghostly apparition in the middle of the night. It dawned on me that guests in such a place as this would scarcely be expected to appear for breakfast much before eleven o'clock. I took breakfast and lunch in more modest establishments. At the door of the Bristol dining room that evening, I was met by a head-waiter who looked like a duke at the very least and who accompanied me ceremoniously to my table. The waiters at once appeared to hear my wishes. I looked about me and realized with some embarrassment that I was the only person in the great shining room not dressed in evening clothes.

For some days I continued to dine at the Bristol. I was now appropriately attired but I disliked having to shave again every evening and changing into my dinner jacket. Besides, the lordly headwaiter, his three attentive assistants, and the elaborate ritual of the meal made me uncomfortable. The luxury of the place somehow oppressed my spirits. Every morning I left the hotel early to get breakfast at a little coffee-house in a near-by side street. I slunk past the night clerk and was annoyed with myself for being embarrassed when he noticed me. It was really absurd. Why did I feel almost guilty about going to breakfast at seven o'clock in the morning? I must confess that I even began positively to dislike the headwaiter and his three helpers when I thought of how they walked to my table with a stateliness that suggested a procession of high dignitaries. I gave up the Bristol dining room and enjoyed my dinners in less sumptuous surroundings, ruefully admitting to myself that I simply could not feel at home in my magnificent domicile. Gradually it became clear to me that I actually preferred less grand and formal living arrangements. A feeling of not belonging walked with me through the gleaming corridors of the Bristol.

Another factor worked unfavorably upon my spirits. My patient, for whom I had reserved a fixed hour daily, did not show up. True, he had prepared me for this during our talk in Berlin when he had said that perhaps he might sometimes be unable to come at the appointed hour. As it turned out, I saw him in the next three months only a few times. Then he came just once for one hour. After that I did not see him or hear from him again. When we had made our arrangements in Berlin, he had asked me not to write and not to call him on the telephone because that would arouse his fears relating to certain magic ideas. He expected me to stay put until he needed me. Since I had agreed to this, I was bound by my promise now. As the weeks went on I learned that it was disturbing to me to be paid so much money without working for it, without really earning it.

I urged myself to be patient and told myself that I was by no means lazy. Did I not work hard every day? Had I not written one book and done preliminary work on another? Did I not study all the new literature in psychology and psychiatry? Evidently I considered these activities pleasure rather than work. Often I caught myself ashamed at the thought that I, in the prime of life, was not earning my living. This was paradoxical enough since I was "earning" more than I ever had before. This too easy life without duties and obligations was uncomfortable. I even began to feel a resentment against my patient whom, in all reason, I should have considered my benefactor. How often in the past, tired from my ten daily hours of analytic work, had I daydreamed of an easeful life, free from financial burdens, which would permit me to devote myself to the realization of my research plans? And now when kind destiny had made me a gift of just this situation, I could not enjoy it.

I tried in vain to shake off the strangely unhappy mood that had taken possession of me and grew worse as time went on. Again and again I asked myself what kind of odd discontent it might be that, precisely when I had every reason to be satisfied with my lot, prevented me from enjoying it. Measured by my own modest standards, I was now almost wealthy. I was getting a great deal of money without working for it.[1] My life had every possible amenity and I was home in Vienna where I wanted to be—what the hell was the matter with me? The explanations I found were such obvious pretexts and pretensions that I could not consider them valid. A cloud darkened the most beautiful holiday. It was mysterious that I was so often restless or sad without reasonable reasons. To be sure my dark mood left me for hours at a time, but only to return at an unforeseen moment. I recall that it overtook me once after I had walked home from a delightful conversation with Freud, and again while I crossed the street coming home to the Bristol from the opera house, where I had enjoyed *Der Rosenkavalier.* It was with me again as I returned from hearing Mahler's Fourth Symphony. I was still under the spell of the last movement, which is full of gaiety and childlike happiness. Walking in the winter night I sang it over and over under my breath, when suddenly I felt depressed. I had known moods of this sort before, but none so persistent as this. My unrest and dissatisfaction increased, although I put up a good fight against them.

Finally I could bear it no longer. I wrote a letter to my patient expressing my thanks and my regret that it had not been possible for me to be of greater use to him. Without giving reasons—for I had none—I asked him to excuse me and then packed my trunks. The next morning as the taxi took me through the streets of Vienna on my way to the station, I felt wonderfully lighthearted, as if I had thrown off a heavy burden. The air of the radiant spring morning was delicious, and I looked with friendliness into the faces of the people in the streets. My farewell to Vienna was not sad but full of tenderness. It was like taking leave of a sweetheart whom one will never forget.

Many weeks later I began to understand what had happened to me between arrival and departure. I became aware that I had been discontented, not in spite of my good fortune, but because of it. Much later still I recalled just when the first shadow had fallen across my days in Vienna. One afternoon I had by accident—but was it accident?—passed the house in which I was born and had spent my childhood years. My father, who was in the Civil Service, had often been worried about

[1] A few years later, of course, Hitler took all my savings.

money and had had difficulties in making ends meet on the meager salary of an Austrian official. As I walked along, childhood memories crept up from shadowy corners and I saw again the worried faces of my parents. A sudden sadness had come over me by the time I reached the Bristol. From then on the mood only left me for brief hours at a time. Its full psychological significance only became clear to me much later.

It was as if I could not permit myself to enjoy my rich surroundings, my too comfortable life, or the money come by so easily but not felt as deserved for work done. The childhood memories had brought back to me the poverty in which my parents had spent their lives, the sacrifices they had made to give us children educational advantages. Here in the same city, only a half-hour's walk from my childhood home, I had lived in luxury. A slight discontent had already appeared at the Hotel Bristol prior to this incident, but I had explained it to myself as being due to the fact that I was unaccustomed to so much elegance. My mood had continued and had become worse, the longer my carefree life continued.

It was not possible, finally, to avoid the psychological conclusion that my depression had originated in an unconscious guilt-feeling arising from the fact that I was living in abundance and that my parents had lived in so much poorer circumstances. They had deprived themselves of all the pleasant things and had lived in sadly pinched circumstances in order to give their children advantages. It seemed that I might allow myself a certain modest comfort, but that a mysterious factor within, called conscience, forbade my enjoying extraordinary luxury or much money, unless it had been earned by hard work, and opulence that was undeserved. It was as if I had not the right to live sumptuously where my parents had suffered so many hardships. My attempt to adjust to a comfortable, luxurious life had failed.

Later on I admitted to myself that I had been a damned fool but also that I could not then have acted otherwise. When I told Freud the story some months later, he laughed at me cordially (I loved it although the joke was on me), and, if memory does not fail me, it was on this occasion that he expressed the wish that I might "acquire a sclerotic conscience." I hope that since then I have secured this "hardening of the conscience." Alas, I was never given the opportunity to find out whether, after this one experience, I might behave differently in a similar situation. I am afraid that destiny does not have another chance in store for me—it will have to hurry to reach me—but I rather think that

I would take to some comfort and luxury much more kindly today.[2]

Recently a playwright, a former patient of mine, wrote me a letter in which he told me how much he was enjoying a fabulously luxurious life in Hollywood. Engaged to write scripts for one of the big movie companies, he has been drawing an enormous salary for many months, without as yet having written one line for his employers. The young man relishes the high life and his leisure in Hollywood without unnecessary scruples and superfluous moral considerations. He already has the "sclerotic conscience" I lacked.

Later during a brief visit to Vienna, I saw the Hotel Bristol again. Something prompted me to enter the lobby of the hotel, the scene of my triumph and my defeat. I just looked about for a moment, glanced at the guests lounging in their deep chairs, and left. Out again on the Ringstrasse, I heard myself thinking (the expression will be explained immediately), "Those people have just too much money."[3] The sentence was banal; obviously only very rich people could stay at the Bristol. Why had I thought that? It had been thought, or rather almost said, with a certain intonation and in a Viennese dialect that, though familiar to me, I myself seldom use. It had been thought or said as if not I had been the speaker, but some other person, a long way back. It was like the delayed echo of something heard long ago. I do not recall having heard my father say this sentence, but the pronunciation and the in-

---

[2] It seems that the severity of our unconscious conscience lessens as we grow older or after we have paid for our thought-crimes by suffering. The above presentation would be incomplete without tracing the genesis of my strange mood back in still another direction. It would perhaps be more flattering to one's ego if one could assume that an unconscious reaction of conscience emerged, but it would be neither honest nor correct.

Intellectual integrity demands the confession that such a strong moral reaction could not have taken place without having been preceded by a feeling that was unconsciously considered as guilt. What happened may be easily reconstructed. I must have been too proud of my good luck at first. There must have been some feelings of haughty presumption in me, as if it were because of my superior achievements that I could now live in the finest hotel in town. Painful though it may be, it must be acknowledged that there must have been at first some mood of triumph or conceit, that I prided myself on having become so much more successful than my poor father and brothers. The depression which followed was, of course, of a moral kind, as if such pride and presumption were a crime in thought. All the characteristic traits of my ensuing sadness show the opposite of the unconscious tendencies.

[3] The sentence in its original form: *"Die Leut' hab'n helt zuviel Geld."*

tonation were his, not mine. The note of disapproval in the words that came to mind so surprisingly must have been the determining factor in the genesis and development of my discontent while I stayed at the splendid hotel. It was as if I myself had been one of those people who "have just too much money," one of those people of whom my father had spoken so disapprovingly.

Curiously enough, a few moments after leaving the hotel another memory occurred to me, a children's poem that I am almost sure I had not thought of since I was a boy. The verses came back to me as suddenly as if they had popped up from a trap door on a stage. This folk poem that the public school children of Vienna used to recite is called "The Little Tree That Wished to Have Different Leaves." It tells the story of a small fir tree that stands among trees of other kinds in the forest and is ashamed because it has only prickly needles. It wishes to have leaves like the other trees. It receives such leaves, but a goat comes along and eats them up. The little tree then wishes for leaves of glass, but a storm destroys them. The tree now wishes for itself leaves of gold; a peddler sees them, picks them and carries them off in his bag. The disillusioned little tree now only wants its old needles back. It was immediately clear why the forgotten poem had emerged from its long oblivion. I was making fun of myself and my insatiable wishes. Certainly it is significant that the two isolated memories, the sentence heard from my father, and the poem learned in grammar school, both occurred to me within a few minutes. I must have originally heard both when I was about seven or eight years old. They belong, so to speak, to the same geological stratum of my past. They not only served as an indirect confirmation of the psychological analysis here sketched but also convinced me that the moral teachings and codes of my childhood were deeply rooted and continued to live a subterranean life within my personality in the years of late manhood.

Self-analysis of this kind originated in the need to obtain insight into my own moods, thoughts, and impulses as they appeared in everyday life. It brought some surprising revelations concerning my personal peculiarities and information about my character and emotional development. I learned to understand why an enemy or a group of enemies are among my emotional needs, why I cannot imagine myself as a member of a political party, why my ambition goes in one direction and not in another. I learned, too, why I always wish I had written a book or a paper when I admire it, which proves that my admiration is usually accompanied by envy. (Strangely enough, I can read whole volumes of the *Psychoanalytic Quarterly* without the slightest trace of such envious feelings.) Self-analysis has given me these insights and a hundred more, many of them painful and unflattering, a few that are pleasant, all uninteresting to others but of considerable interest to me as a psychologist and as a person.

CHAPTER VIII

Love and the Dark Despot

THIS book denies that the psychoanalyst who treats his neurotic patients has a complete knowledge of himself and it asserts that he is merely better equipped to discover the secrets of his own personality and of others than his patients are. The process of self-discovery is never finished, can never be brought to an end. It is certainly not true that being analyzed brings the task of self-knowledge to a happy conclusion. It merely marks a station on the road. New experiences will add to the knowledge of the psychoanalyst. They sometimes happen when you least expect them. You may be looking for something else and accidentally find a fragment of an unknown you.

One such experience is worth telling because it took place thirty years after I was analyzed. While writing my book, *A Psychologist Looks at Love,* I searched for predecessors of the psychological theory I presented in it.[1] While I did not consider myself indebted to any psychologist in building the theory, I gladly acknowledged the great debt I owe to poets for its genesis. Their words leave indelible traces in us. Forgotten and half-forgotten verses came back to mind as it dawned on me how love is born and bred and what its psychological characteristics are. These verses, long asleep, opened their eyes slowly, like the awakening beauty in the fairy tale after many years of magic slumber. Strangely enough, the verses that rose suddenly from the deep well of forgetfulness were not by Shakespeare, Goethe, Dante, Byron or Heine, but lines and fragments from unknown poets I had heard or read in my teens. I had not thought of them for forty years and more.

[1] New York: Farrar and Rinehart, 1944.

Such surprising revivals remind one of the German folk story told by Baron von Münchhausen. He reports that the postilion, who drove the mail-coach, once tried in vain to give a signal with his horn. He could not make his horn sound while he traveled in severe midwinter. When he arrived at an inn, he hung the horn up on a peg near the kitchen fire. The baron narrates how he and his fellow-travelers suddenly heard strange noises. The postilion's horn began to sound and brought out a variety of familiar tunes. Finally they realized that the sweet melodies had been frozen up in the horn and now came out by thawing. In a similar manner forgotten verses emerged from some hiding place within me. For instance, two German lines suddenly sprang up in me. They expressed the very idea I had just tried to put into shape and they expressed them more clearly and more beautifully than I could ever hope to do. I wondered about them. I could not identify them. They came back at other times while I was writing and they seemed to bring me a message. They wanted to say something beyond their immediate meaning, to communicate a secret and personal thing. What was it? The two lines were:

Denn wo die Liebe erwacht,
Stirbt das Ich, der dunkle Despot.

In English:

For when true love awakens,
Dies the self, the dark tyrant.

I knew, of course, that the two lines were from the middle of a poem, but what was it? I knew, too, that I had read it once, when a boy, and never since. The two lines haunted me while I continued to write. I tried hard to bring the missing part of the poem back to memory. I failed miserably. You know the feeling when you want to recite a poem to yourself whose first verses you have forgotten. You say, "Mm, mm, mm," or make similar funny noises and then start reciting the remembered lines. I did that many times in my futile efforts to bring the missing verses back. Some words emerged, but were they correct? The forgotten verses kept fluttering to and fro and around me like the wings of butterflies, but I could not catch them. I could not get the poem, but I could not get rid of it either. Finally, I gave up the search. What did it matter what the other verses were, whose they were, and from which poem? I decided that I would not quote the two lines in the book. I pretended to be more indifferent than I actually felt. There was that vague sensation that it was not a literary question any more, hunting for the identification of a poet's name, but something personal that had to do with some secret part of myself.

Not that I gave up easily. I looked through many German poems, turned over the leaves of quite a few anthologies of lyrics; but it was in vain. I asked literary acquaintances and men better read in literature than I. I asked several refugee poets from Germany and Austria. None of them knew who the author of the two lines was or where they came from. One of my friends asked me teasingly whether I could not have made the verses myself in my boyhood and then forgotten it. Of course I knew that I was never capable of making such verses. Besides I knew I had read them. There was even an image of the old-fashioned printed type of the page in my memory, which failed me otherwise.[2]

I never made an attempt to find the poet's name and the other forgotten verses by means of systematic self-analysis, and I am ready to accept the justified reproach for this omission from my psychoanalytic colleagues. Many of them, I am sure, will contend that to find such forgotten things in oneself and others is very easy. It is mere child's play for them. They solve such little problems, they will say, in a few minutes—in themselves and others. I admire them, but I do not believe them.

Anyhow, I found the name of the poet and his poem on a strange detour, which I shall report. The way I found them is as interesting psychologically as the motives for which they had been forgotten. I do not know why the two lines I remembered had an oriental touch for me. On one of the many occasions when they haunted me in my writing, the visual image of the small bookcase in my mother's room

---

[2]Most writers have, I am sure, similar experiences and are in similar situations of frustrated mental effort. It gives me a little satisfaction that I succeeded several times in finding a forgotten passage, its author, or its source for Freud, who overestimated my literary education. That I failed sometimes is shown by the following passage from a letter by Freud dated November 11, 1929: "Please do not trouble any more with (the search for the words) 'inch of Nature' and pardon me that I bothered you with it. I renounced the quotation. Nobody could find it. Where I took it from remains a mystery because it could not be my own achievement. As I used to read Milton and Byron among English poets in addition to Shakespeare, there could still be the possibility of finding it in Byron, but I ask you not to search any more and to accept my best thanks for your trouble." Freud quoted the three words in *Civilization and Its Discontents* without naming the author.

came to me and together with it a small gilt-edged volume with yellow-ish pages. I remembered I had read the poem in this book when I was a boy. What books were in the bookcase? I tried to recollect them, es-pecially the volumes of poetry. (The titles given in the following para-graphs were jotted down immediately, because by now I had become interested in the psychological problem. I deny emphatically that such an inquiry deserves the name of systematic self-analysis. At all events it was not successful.) The search had at this moment the character of an intellectual adventure, and I followed its development with the inter-est of a chemist in the result of an important experiment.

The first title that occurred to me was Goethe's *West-Eastern Divan,* but I knew immediately that this was impossible. I knew the poems too well and in my college days I even knew many of them by heart. Then other names appeared: Hammer-Purgstall? (He published a transla-tion of many oriental poems and his name was well-known to me as a boy. I remember having seen his tombstone in Klosterneuburg, near Vienna.) No, certainly not. There was also in the bookcase *The Songs of Mirza Shaffy,* by Friedrich Bodenstedt. (Translations of poems of the Persian poet, Shaffy. Strange that the title of these songs, which had died away a long time ago, was remembered.)

Were the *Ghazals* by Platen there? No. What other books were there? Heine? Yes, the poems of Heine. The title "The Poet Firdusi" suddenly flashed upon my mind. This poem is to be found in the *Romancero* by Heine, but it certainly does not include the two remem-bered lines. *The Hebrew Melodies* by the same poet occurred to me next. No, not there. Then followed the name *Divan,* the chief work of Jehuda-ha-Levi, an association certainly determined by the fact that Heine celebrated this Spanish-Hebrew poet as his brother in Apollo. Was there an edition of the *Rubaiyat* of Omar Khayyam? No, I am sure there was not. Moreover, I had read these famous verses years later and not in German, but in an English translation.

I was positive that the poem I hunted for was either the translation of verses of an oriental poet or an original poem of a German writer who copied most cleverly the manner of oriental poetry; but I was rather inclined to believe the first.

How could I be certain of that? A new name occurred to me then: the title of an anthology of poems that are not from the Middle, but from the Far East—*The Chinese Flute,* by Hans Bethge. But I did not know these poems until I had heard them in the *Song of the Earth,* by Gustav Mahler. The composer died in 1910 and the *Song of the Earth* was performed, I think, for the first time by Bruno Walter in 1911.[3] At that time I was already twenty-three years old, and I know beyond a doubt that I read the verses as a boy—I guess before puberty. To make absolutely sure I sang the *Song of the Earth,* which I know by heart, under my breath. Of course, the lines were not there.

I broke off the attempt at this point. I had again the odd feeling of someone haunted by a thought he cannot escape from, which eludes him whenever he tries to grasp it.

Here are the words of the poem, which I found some weeks later.[4]

> Death ends life's misery and pain,
> Yet life afraid would Death retain.
> We only see Death's threatening hand,
> Not that bright cup it offered plain.
> So shrinks from love the tender heart
> As if from threat of being slain,
> For when true love awakens, dies
> The self, that despot, dark and vain.
> Then let him die in night's black hour
> And freely breathe in dawn again!

[3] The data here mentioned are correct. My good knowledge of Mahler's life and works is not as remarkable as it might appear. I was very much interested as a student in the personality and the creative work of this fascinating composer.

[4] There is some difficulty in finding a good translation of the Persian text, I am told. I am quoting here—with a few slight modifications of my own—the translation which William Hastie published. (*The Festival of Spring from the Divan of Delaleddin, Glasgow,* 1903, p. 2.) W. Hastie admits on the title-page of the book that the poems were "rendered into English Ghazels after Rueckert's version." For this reason and to help readers who understand German, I put Rueckert's version—the same through which I made acquaintance with the Persian poem as a boy—here:

> *Wohl endet Tod des Lebens Not,*
> *Doch schauert Leben vor dem Tod.*
> *Das Leben sieht die dunkle Hand*
> *Den Dunkeln Kelch nicht, den sie bot.*
> *So schauert vor der Lieb ein Herz*
> *Als wie vom Untergang bedroht,*
> *Denn wo die Liebe erwacht,*
> *Stirbt das Ich, der dunkle Despot.*
> *So lass ihn sterben in der Nacht*
> *Und athme frei im Morgenroth.*

It is one of the ghazals of Dalāl al-Din Rūmī, the greatest of the Persian mystical poets. Rūmī lived about seven hundred years before our time. He presented the Sufi philosophy in beautiful poems whose profoundness of thought often comes near to Plato's. He founded the famous order of the dancing dervishes, the Mevlevi. He is not only a great poet but one of the great thinkers and searchers after truth.

Here is the way the forgotten verses of the poem and the name of the poet were found. Or as it would be more accurate to say: "how they let themselves be found." Some weeks after my futile attempt to identify them, so to speak, by a method of elimination, the familiar name of the translator of the poem presented itself to me in a strange connection. I was feeling tired that evening after ten hours of psychoanalytic practice, and in a rather depressed mood I decided to listen to some records. I first played Mahler's Ninth Symphony. I like the first movement especially. Its controlled and virile expression of leave-taking moves me more than Tschaikovsky's boundless and pathetic *Symphonie Pathétique.*

While I listened to the oft-heard themes, I suddenly thought of the tragic words Mahler uttered some days before he died: "I lived falsely." I remembered how he regretted having spent his life in a terrific zeal for work, burned up by his ambition; that in a moment of hope he had promised his wife they would go on trips together to see Egypt and the East. He knew it was too late. A wave of overpowering tenderness for his wife, child, and friends mixed with these regrets in his last days.

Was it this thought of death and regret or was it a musical passage that made me wish to hear the records of the *Kindertotenlieder* of the same composer next? As I listened to them, something beside the music impressed me: the wording of the songs, which are simple expressions of everyday life. The poems were written by Friedrich Rueckert, a forgotten German poet who lived about a hundred years ago.

In that moment I knew at once and with surprising certainty that the poem I had hunted for so long was by Rueckert. I saw his name printed in golden letters on one of my mother's books. At the same time I knew it was not an original poem of Rueckert's but one of his many translations of Persian poetry. I went to the public library and found the verses immediately. As I read them, I had the strange feeling that I had never forgotten them, although I was certain that I had not thought of them once in over forty years.

When I first read them at the beginning of puberty, their mysterious meaning must have attracted and puzzled me. Perhaps I repeated them aloud several times to find out what they wanted to say. I could not understand them, and at the same time there must have been a subterranean kind of comprehension. It seems to me now that the boy, troubled by many unasked questions, must have conceived their meaning as identifying love with sex. Vague but intense fears made him interpret the lines, "For when true love awakens, Dies the self, the dark despot," in the sense that love is something very dangerous, threatening destruction. Puberty, with its anxieties and perplexities, alarmed me as it does so many boys. The contrast of love and death expressed in the two enigmatical lines, and met so often later in life, made a lasting impression upon me. But beyond this misinterpretation there was something in them and in the other verses that then eluded me, but must have been understood in a dim way: the giving up of one's own self in surrendering to love, the losing of the ego in deep affection.

It needed more than forty years to understand what was stirred up when I first read these verses. But is it not strange that the two lines were preserved intact through all these years, like a mummy in an undiscovered Egyptian tomb? I think the seed of my theory of love was sowed when I read Rūmī's poem as a boy of thirteen. How long it takes to recognize something you always knew unconsciously! The main idea of my book had been anticipated by a poet in faraway Persia seven hundred years ago. I never thought I owed it to some mysterious verses I had read as a boy.

What I want to explain now is why the names Rueckert and Rūmī of the poem, were "forgotten," and what it means psychologically that the two lines kept recurring to me during the writing of my book. In all these months I was worried about my son Arthur, my daughter-in-law, and my grandson, then three years old, whom I had not yet seen. They were living in Jerusalem and it seemed—it was 1943—that the German army would attack Palestine and Syria. I hoped that they could get immigration visas for the United States and that they would find a way to make the trip. At the time only the route through Persia was possible; but a revolt, stimulated by German agitators, was brewing in this country and the journey through Persia and China appeared dangerous, too. For many months I lived in fear for the life and safety of my dear ones and in longing for them.

Other thoughts preoccupied me; and other fears, survivals of earlier days, kept the names away from my memory, which nevertheless again and again brought up the two lines, "For when true love awakens, Dies the self, the dark despot." I had a hidden fear, that the war would last a long time and I would die early—before seeing my son again. There might be no time left for me to show them how much I cared for them. I would die, I feared, without having seen my grandson grow up. I would be unable to observe his development and to enjoy his childish laughter.[5] Here is the real unconscious fear expressed in those lines. There must also have been some unconscious regret and repentance about my possessiveness and bossiness toward my son in the old days that came to the foreground, because I am, of course, myself the self, the despot dark and vain, who will die just in the moment when love awakens in him. The lines that came up time and again are full of gloomy presentiment. They want to remind me of what I missed and what threatens me as a punishment for my omissions. At the same time they reach beyond the personal realm as they express the fundamental idea that the victory of love is linked with the defeat of possessive and selfish tendencies in us.

It is remarkable that the name Rueckert occurred to me only after I heard Mahler's compositions again. Concealed here are psychical threads that lead back to the past and connect it with the present and with my fears for the future. The figure of Mahler had a great influence upon me in my twenties, and I identified myself unconsciously with him. He composed his Ninth Symphony when he knew he must die very soon, and the work anticipates his death, giving expression to the various moods awakened in him by its nearness. It was not accidental that I wanted to listen to this symphony. The score corresponded to my own feelings on this evening when I was tired and depressed. Strange how the way led from hearing the symphony to the name I had been searching for! It was certainly unconsciously prepared by thoughts of the last days of the composer. Did he not express his regrets that he had not enjoyed life enough, did he not now feel as never before an upsurge of tenderness for wife and child?

The *Kindertotenlieder* led back to the panic my wife and I had felt when my son Arthur once became dangerously ill as a child. We were afraid at that time that he would die. Those were terrible days. (Rueckert, who wrote the *Kindertotenlieder* after his own two children died . . . Mahler, who put some of them to music before his own small

[5] Fortunately my fears were unjustified. My son and his family arrived in the United States in 1945.

daughter died. He always thought he must have foreseen the death of the beloved little girl . . . Mahler is the favorite composer of my son, who wrote me in a letter that my grandson at the age of three already likes the music of this composer.) The atmosphere around these thoughts of mine is filled with anxieties and death-fears. It is as in *Carmen: "Toujours la mort!"* All thoughts seem to lead to this one goal. They all start from the same point, from the fear that it would become too late for me. The two lines said it: When love comes, I shall have to die.

I must break off this piece of self-analysis at this point because it would lead too far. I would have to recognize that my fears are survivals of obsessive thoughts that worried me in my younger years. I was then afraid I would die just before certain wishes were fulfilled, or rather in the moment of their realization. (Post-analytic remnants of an early neurosis are not the exception, but the rule. The "curing" of a neurosis by no means resembles the picture many psychoanalysts paint. The neurotic symptoms do not evaporate into thin air without a trace, but they pale into insignificance. Scars remain after psychoanalysis just as after a successful operation, and they ache when stormy weather approaches.)

I should mention here that there are other threads between Mahler and my fear of an early death. My first wife, Arthur's mother, had died a short time after we heard a concert together in which Mahler's *Song of the Earth* was performed. The name Rueckert was avoided because it reminded me of the days of fear we passed through when my son was ill. Then we had to face the possibility that he would die like the children of the poet, who wrote the touching songs after they were gone.

How did the forgotten name come back and make it possible to solve the entire little problem? You remember that the words of the *Kindertotenlieder* brought the name back. It was as if an inner suspense became loosened, as if an unconscious question got its answer. It is clear to me how that happened. The *Kindertotenlieder* awakened the memory of the illness of my son consciously where my unconscious fears had blocked the thought-road before. At the same time, hearing these words seemed to say: Your fears are as unjustified now as then when you were so panic-stricken. Arthur became well again then and everything will turn out right now. Your family will be safe and you will see them. You need not die just at the time you begin to feel a new tenderness.

Do not be afraid that the change in you is the signal of approaching death; it means only changing your old self, which should die for a new and better one. The lines, "For when true love awakens, Dies the self, the dark tyrant," formed a somber omen; but the last lines of Rūmī's poem say, "Let it die and change; take the risk and dare to love." As I thus regained courage, the old shadows evaporated and I was able to remember the name Rueckert and to find the poem and its author. The hearing of the *Kindertotenlieder* thus marks the psychological turning-point.

It will interest the student of human emotions to learn that the trends of my thoughts in the futile attempt to recall the name of the poet were all influenced by the repressed knowledge, which did not come through to the conscious mind because it was kept away by my secret fears.

The names that occurred to me as substitutes are all taken from a realm connected with the forgotten poet and his creation. The first are all names of Persian poets. (Persia is the country where danger threatened the journey of my son.) There is Hafis as the speaker in Goethe's *West-Eastern Divan*. *Divan* is also the name of the collection of poems by Rūmī. More than this, Goethe himself translated a ghazal of this poet and praised the profound thought of the Persian mystic in his notes to the *West-Eastern Divan* which I had read several times. The next name is Hammer-Purgstall. He translated many Persian poets into German, among them, of course, Rūmī. Mirza Shaffy is a Persian poet and Platen's ghazals are copies of this national poetry. Heine's "Firdusi" occurs at this point, also a great Persian poet. Omar Khayyam, another Persian name, strikes me then and is rejected.[6]

So many names come up, but not the sought-after one of Rūmī, and not the familiar name of Rueckert, his translator. And I remember many a German poet whom my mother read: Goethe, Platen, Heine, and such forgotten poets as Bodenstedt and Hammer-Purgstall— but not Rueckert. Observe that the train of thought then leaves the realm of Persian poetry with Firdusi, whom Heine praised in verse, and shifts to Jehuda-ha-Levi by way of Heine's *Hebrew Melodies*. The "free" thought-associations seemingly abandon the neighborhood of

[6] Yet compare his ghazals with Rūmī's thought. For instance,

> While the rose blows along the river brink
> With old Khayyam the Ruby Vintage drink
> And when the angel with his darker draught
> Draws up to Thee—take that, and do not shrink.

the forgotten Persian name, although Jehuda-ha-Levi also wrote a *Divan* like his Persian colleagues. My thoughts wander now to Palestine and approach the country where my son and his family live. The associations grope nearer to the source of the forgetting—the fears barring the entrance to the names—Rueckert and Rūmī. The *Divan* of Jehuda-ha-Levi is the thought-bridge to the Persians, but the *Hebrew Melodies* lead to the worries about my son. Jehuda-ha-Levi always wished to see Jerusalem with his own eyes before he died. He saw the Holy City and died there. My son lived with his family in Jerusalem.[7]

Here, my thoughts seem to come nearest to my unconscious fears, but they do not have force enough to make them enter the realm of conscious thinking. It seems that even in thought I am shrinking back from the danger. During the entire search for the forgotten name I never thought consciously of my son, although just at this point my thought came so near. It seems like an unconscious thought-avoidance.

From the *Hebrew Melodies* my associations run to Chinese poets, translated and collected in Bethge's *Chinese Flute.* The journey of my son would go from Persia to China. The name of Mahler occurs, the *Song of the Earth*—next should come the *Kindertotenlieder* and the name of Rueckert. But at this point, so dangerously near the theme of my own death and the memory of the childhood illness of my son, I break off the attempt as futile. It was as if the hands of my thoughts, groping for the remote name, became tired and gave up their search in the dark.

They took hold of the forgotten name the very moment I dared face consciously the possibility of approaching death. It was that evening a few weeks after the futile attempt—the vain search after the forgotten! I have described how the way led from Mahler's Ninth Symphony with its death-theme to the *Kindertotenlieder;* from the songs to their poet, Rueckert; and finally to Rūmī, whom he translated. My feeling at finding the names was similar to that of once again finding an object in a drawer where it has been mislaid. It was right there near you, all the time, and you had not known it. And sometimes, as here, it is a part of yourself that you mislaid many years ago. The motive for avoidance in my thoughts is clear: it is the superstitious fear that my son or I would die before we could meet again. There was not the slightest trace of such

[7] Like Jehuda-ha-Levi I thought I would not see Jerusalem until the unforgettable day in 1937 when I looked down from Mt. Scopus on the Holy City.

a fear in my conscious thoughts.[8] It was discovered only through a self-analysis stimulated by searching for the forgotten name of a poet.

Experiences like this and many others which I could report (and which I shall perhaps report elsewhere) have a power of conviction which no lecture or seminar can convey.

Only such experiences reflect a psychical process comparable to transferring a picture from the negative on to the positive. They are not merely persuasive; they are convincing.

Here we see the great difference between a knowledge that we acquire by learning, hearing, or reading, and what we learn by experience. Only this second kind of knowing cannot be taken from us because it is blended with our experience. The two kinds of knowing are psychologically different even when they have the same content.

As I have spoken so often about my son Arthur in these pages, it is perhaps not inappropriate to quote him at this point. Once when he was the age his own son is now, I teased him by asking how he knew for certain that two and two make four. I refused to accept his argument that he knew it from his teacher and from his arithmetic book. I pointed out to him that it was possible that even these authorities, otherwise not to be contested, could be mistaken. Cornered by the question about the positive source of his knowledge, the little boy finally pointed to himself and shouted impatiently, "But I know it within myself!" Here is the difference between knowledge from outside and conviction by experience, clearly expressed in a child's clumsy manner. It is to be wished that psychoanalysts learn primarily through their own experience and that these experiences enable them "to know it within themselves."

[8] I realized immediately that the lines "For when true love awakens, Dies the self, the dark tyrant," anticipate the main theme of my book on love. I had, however, not the faintest notion that the "dark tyrant" was I and that these lines gave the clear text of an unconscious fear founded on an old superstition I thought I had overcome many years ago.

CHAPTER IX

The Call of Life

No AUTHOR knows fully what his book means to himself, from what dark background it emerged, why he wrote it, nor what place it has in his personal development. But sometimes it does happen that he gets a faint notion of these things, when favorable circumstances bring some usually hidden motives to the surface. The June evening three years ago when I first thought of another book is still a vivid recollection that has come back to me while writing the last chapter.

Before leaving town for my vacation I had collected all the notes for a book that I was planning. Its theme was to be the relationship between the living and the dead, a subject which had interested me for many years. When I once visited the Central Cemetery in Vienna, I saw many small stones strewn around the tombstones on most of the Jewish graves. I wondered what they meant, but no one could give me any real information. The scholars I asked said it was just an old custom. I saw the same thing years later on Arabic graves in Palestine: many small stones covered the barrows. Was this a survival of a primitive stone-worship? I became interested in the subject and I had studied the burial customs of prehistoric men and compared them with later developments and with our modern unconscious attitude toward the dead. Prehistoric men believed that the dead, in an envious or revengeful mood, could return and harm or even kill the living. Because of this fear, our early ancestors bound the dead before they deposited them in caves and then rolled great boulders in front of the graves to further prevent their escape. The burial place was rather the prison than the home of the dead. During many hundred thousand years of human evolution the terror aroused by the dead gradually diminished or became unconscious, while feelings of respect, affection and veneration emerged. The more the deep-rooted fear of the evil proclivities and wrath of the dead decreased, the stronger became the wish to honor their memory. This later development of primitive man's need to placate the restless dead and to protect himself against their revenge took the form of worship, especially in cases in which the dead had been powerful figures, chiefs, priests and sorcerers. In the magnificent pyramids of Egypt as well as in the modest stones we place on our graves today, the contradictory attitudes, fear and devotion, find simultaneous expression. It is reasonable to suppose that the steeples of our churches, and their altars too, are late developments of the big rock which prehistoric man, out of fear, placed before the grave. The tombstone and the altar are the two main results of this ambivalent attitude. Our tombstones are inscribed with words of praise, grief and mourning and certainly these feelings are strong within us, but so also is our unconscious fear of the dead. The small stones that Semetic tribes put on their graves are the last remnants of the prehistoric custom of rolling a rock before the cave in which men buried their dead. My projected book was to compare our unconscious attitude toward the dead with the historical development of the customs.

On the afternoon of our arrival at a small mountain hotel some hundred miles from New York I was resting on the verandah. It was hot and I did not feel like writing. Near by on the meadow men and women were sun-bathing. Most of the women had covered their noses with leaves for protection against freckles. A glamour girl about forty-eight years old, had placed upon her head a peaked soldier's hat made of a copy of the *New York Times* that her little grandson might have envied. All the women wore shorts. The scene was not entirely delightful and I wondered vaguely about the relationship between health culture and beauty. (Later I was not at all astonished to hear that a young male guest of the hotel had fallen in love with one of the kitchen maids. A skirt, a kingdom for a skirt!)

My daughter Miriam, not yet seven, was playing ball near by with another little girl and a small boy. My vague thoughts were interrupted by a tussle that developed among them. A woman got up from her siesta on the meadow and went over to them, and I heard my daughter say to her, "Norman tried to kiss me and I slapped his face!" "Girls don't fight," the woman answered her reproachfully. The remark had a strong effect upon Miriam, although she pretended to be unimpressed.

A half hour later my other daughter, Theodora, who was then twelve, returned to the hotel from a walk with two other girls. Seeing me on the verandah she came to me and asked, "Daddy, what does 'ostentatious' mean?" I explained as well as I could and, of course, asked in what connection she had heard this new word. The three girls told me that they had been joking with a boy of their own age who had said they were "ostentatious, egotistical, adolescent, spoiled brats." Left alone again I found myself wondering about these two daughters of mine. Relations with boys were, it seemed, not always peaceful even when girls are six and twelve. Well, they would be less belligerent later on. Even now the playful tussles and arguments were not wholly aggressive. I felt a vague discomfort at this thought.

After dinner I took a long walk up the road that led into the hills. The outlines of the landscape appeared loosened, the colors softer. Evening seemed reluctant to descend upon the earth. I walked alone but I did not feel lonely. I heard myself thinking, and not only thoughts but images accompanied me. The atmosphere was full of memories. Half-forgotten verses came back to me and strange emotions emerged. ("Now twilight lets her curtain down and pins it with a star." Where had I read that?) I felt a suspense, as if some decision were expected of me but just what decision I did not know. A quieting melody came to me again and again. Later I recognized it as a motif from Mahler's *Song of the Earth:* "Dark is life and dark is death. . . ." The composer too, had had two daughters and he had died early, at fifty-one . . . I caught myself with a strange idea: no man really knows women well who has not seen a daughter growing up beside him. On this detour my thoughts returned to my daughters, no longer vaguely but pursuing a certain direction. In a few more years they would be young women. They would awaken the desires of men and feel the ache of this passion in themselves. The prospect of their facing the dangers of adolescence and young womanhood and of my no longer being there to help and protect them, frightened me.

Schools now teach boys and girls anatomy and biology, but no one teaches them that the psychology of the sexes is different, that men and women go differently about the business of living and loving. Someone, I thought, should write a book about it, that would explain that love does not mean the same thing to men and women, that sexuality has a different meaning for the sexes, that it has a different emotional place in their lives. More than thirty-seven years of psychoanalytic practice have shown me how much unhappiness between men and women is due to lack of understanding, to the misunderstanding of the relationships of the sexes. We use words like "love" and "sexuality" as if they had the same connotations for men and women, but that is true only in the most superficial sense. The images and thoughts which the adolescent boy and girl connect with the words are not the same. From there my train of thought went in the direction of the emotional differences of the sexes, of the two patterns of behavior, of the double standard and finally came to the unsolved problem of the origin of sexuality.

Walking slowly uphill the image of Richard Beer-Hofmann appeared to me as if out of nowhere. I saw him just as he had looked on my last visit in New York where like myself he had come as a refugee from Vienna. I remembered him too, as he had been on my many visits to his beautiful home in the Hasenauerstrasse in Vienna. The last time I had seen him he had spoken of his heart disease. I must write to him, I thought, and ask him how he is . . . A few moments later I understood why his image had suddenly emerged. We had named our younger daughter after his "Lullaby for Miriam," one of the most beautiful poems in the German language. But then verses from his *Graf von Charolais* came back to me. Although much of this play is now outdated there are some scenes in it which can be compared only to the works of the greatest writers. The verses I remembered are from the second act. Do the literary critics not assert that it is almost impossible to find new themes for poets? Yet I know nothing comparable in ancient or in modern literature that expresses the anxiety of a father who suddenly realizes that his daughter must inevitably glide into the whirlpool of sexuality. There is a dialogue between the High Judge, President of the Court of Appeals, and his secretary. On the birthday of his daughter, Desirée, the old man suddenly becomes aware that she is now a grown woman. The old nurse, Barbara, sees on the table the gifts prepared for the girl and she is full of indignation.[1]

> ". . . Low cut shirts
> And stockings above the knee! Garters too!

[1] The translation attempted here gives only an inadequate idea of the power, music and beauty of the original. Beer-Hofmann gave me permission to quote this passage of his play.

The maiden must have been ashamed to death
When the gentlemen saw that. You should
At least have covered the things with a cloth!
Outrageous thoughts must have occurred
To the men! What a scandal!"

She takes the gifts to Desirée's room. The old father is startled by what the nurse has said. He asks his secretary who is working on a brief:

"What did she say there . . . ?"
SECRETARY: (writing)
"She meant only that the imagination of men
Can easily by such things . . ."
PRESIDENT:
"But you do not think with a child . . ."
SECRETARY:
"A child of eighteen years!"
PRESIDENT: (frowning)
"You do not seriously mean that Phillip or
The Senator could have unrespectful
Or impudent thoughts . . . ?"
SECRETARY: (shrugging his shoulders)
"Thoughts know neither respect nor shame."
PRESIDENT: (excited)
"You think then that a man at her sight . . ."
SECRETARY:
"Thinks maybe that which you once
When you were young thought, when a girl
Attracted you very much."
PRESIDENT: (ill-humoured)
"That was something else—But
With my child . . ."
SECRETARY: (smiling)
" 'With my child.' Thus spoke
Maybe, the fathers of those daughters, too."
PRESIDENT: (with suppressed anger)
"Really you suppose that a man
When he sees her, thinks . . ."
SECRETARY: (cautiously)
"May think that she is a woman . . ."

PRESIDENT: (irritated)
"Woman! Why do you call her a woman?"
   SECRETARY: "Well a maiden then."
   PRESIDENT: " 'Woman'! 'Maiden'! As you say it
Every syllable seems spewed out lasciviously.
(in an outburst)
How can you tell me such things?"
   SECRETARY: (quietly)
"You did ask me."
   PRESIDENT: (after a pause)
"That I should never have thought of it! Never 'til now!
Why, we have not been parted for a day since she
Was born. That way you never realize
How something develops and grows tall beside you.
No, not 'beside,' upon me, as a bough upon a trunk—
Nourished by one sap, one blood. 'My child,' I said,
As I would say 'My hand.' Not mine merely, no,
A part of me. I, myself. And that is now a woman!
Something a man may desire and worse still,
What itself desires a man!"

No, the secretary whose wife brought up their children, cannot comprehend what Desirée means to the old man whose wife died in childbirth.

"And now some stranger will come,
He will tell her that he cares for her,
Will kiss her with lips still hot from the kisses of whores!
When I kiss her forehead it is a silent prayer to God
That he may protect the child for me—
But he will kiss her mouth on mouth,
Will press her to himself, body to body
So that she can scarcely breathe. With words
And glances he will rouse her senses
Until they are in storm; eagerly he'll watch
Until he sees the moist ardor in her eyes
That makes her defenceless against him.
And then with fingers disgustingly experienced
He will approach her pure untouchable body—
Ugh! It sickens me! Ugh!"

SECRETARY: (shrugging his shoulders)
"Very few things, sir, can stand up
When old age and wisdom soberly
Examine them. And Love? Love
Can be looked at only by love itself."
    PRESIDENT: "Yes, if it were love, if only a little akin to mine!
Will she be more to the young man
Than something which makes his bed and table comfortable?
She is a 'woman,' and 'women' he knows well, by God!
You pay one kind and you make fun of the other.
Does he consider that she is a creature
Put into the world by God,
Only so much more burdened than himself?
That she is not less than he, only different?
Only the man was weaned; woman is still allowed to dream
On earth's breasts, nearer to creation. Not yet freed
From those primal and mysterious contracts,
Subject still to the same nocturnal planet
Which commands the sea, she is with every full moon
Reminded by blood and pain, like a tardy priestess,
Of her task here below.
What in her appears contradictory, as an enigma
Or as charm, perhaps—to man,
Is that she is still close to the elements,
Is, herself, perhaps, the youngest of them all.
She is for him the only tie
That binds his destiny to the eternal fate of all the worlds.
He need not know, should not;
It must remain unconscious,
Must secretly sleep at the bottom of his love,
Should make him kind to her."
    SECRETARY: "Who knows? Maybe you'll find someone . . ."
    PRESIDENT: (pacing the floor)
"No, I shall not find him, and if I did
He would be an old man. For what is youth but cruel,
And cruel he will be! He will torture her when he loves,
And torture her when he is tired of her. . . .
How many nights did I get up
To see whether she had placed her hand upon her heart

In sleep, because I was afraid a nightmare might disturb her.
Dreamt-of suffering I tried to shield her from,
Dreamt-of pain I would have spared her! Now she will really suffer,
And for one who never suffered for her.
She will like to suffer when she loves him. . . ."

Thus speaks the old man in Beer-Hofmann's play and his words express what every father of a daughter has felt, though he may have been reluctant to admit it to himself.

I had been too absorbed to notice that it had grown dark during my long walk. I turned and retraced my steps down the hill to the hotel. I knew now that I wanted to write a book about the psychical differences between men and women. The desire to write that other book on the funeral customs of ancient and primitive peoples had faded. Had I not always thought that going to a funeral was a waste of time? "To Hell with it!" I heard myself mutter, "Let the dead bury their dead!" Walking along I thought of quoting those verses in a preface of the projected book. This preface could have the title, "The Call of Life." But this is the title of a play by Arthur Schnitzler (who had been a friend of Beer-Hofmann!). In the first scene of this play an old father who is a malicious, sick man accuses his daughter of wanting to leave him alone and helpless and to go dancing with young officers. Am I afraid of becoming such an old, selfish and possessive man? Here is the unconscious reverse-side of the picture of the affectionate and worried father. I cannot disavow any more that the image of sexual relations of my daughters with young men fills me with uneasiness and discomfort. . . . I cannot deny any longer that there is some unconscious jealousy in me. . . .

The decision that I had made or that had been made within me clearly meant that I turned my interest again to the problems of living. The call of life had been victorious.

Reaching the hotel, I went up to my room and wrote a letter to Beer-Hofmann.[2] The voices of the young people, talking, singing and laughing, came up to me from the verandah below. I jotted down my first notes for the new book.

That was three years ago. Theodora is already in senior high school,

[2] His answer came a few weeks later. He said he was recovering from a heart attack but hoped to see me in September. He died on September 26, 1945 at the age of eighty.

goes to dances, discusses dresses and boys with her mother and her girl friends, and is as tall as I. Shortly after our return to New York that fall Miriam asked me to go with her to the Public Library. She wanted to take books home and she explained to me that you can do that only when you are a "member." She became a member and was proud of it. Although three years have passed I have not forgotten that evening because also the books we write and those which remain unwritten, are parts of our destiny.

CHAPTER X

Switching to Another Station

WHEN almost fifty years ago Freud's *Interpretation of Dreams* and *Psychopathology of Everyday Life* were published, nobody asked a question that is near to us today. Where are previous instances of such penetrating and dissecting scrutiny to be found in literature? The answer is echoed in the last words of the question: in literature. But this does not mean in the books and articles of psychiatrists or in medical textbooks and lectures. It means in the writings of Nietzsche, of Dostoyevsky, Tolstoy, and of Kierkegaard. Not what the psychiatrists published, but what their potential patients wrote. There is no doubt that the four men mentioned and many who could and should be listed along with them were neurotic. By that I do not mean simply neurotic personalities; I mean persons whom any psychoanalyst in New York City would consider unhappy neurotic patients, were they to walk into his consultation room today.

And to think that not even the fantasy of a Shakespeare could conceive how superior every one of these men was to every living psychoanalyst in the world—not just as a writer, but as a psychologist! To think how psychoanalysts have to study, to work, to dig by the sweat of their brow to rediscover what these writers found before the first analyst was born! To think that there were passages in their novels and confessions whose profound insights psychoanalysts have not rediscovered, have not even grasped yet!

I am of the opinion that it is more useful for the student of psychology to read the great writers than the *Psychoanalytic Quarterly*. Our students could learn more and better from such sources, which bring treasures of the depths to the surface, than from psychiatric textbooks that muddy the waters with scientific terminology in an effort to make them appear deep.[1]

These writers speak of themselves when they speak of self-created figures who reflect splits of their own personalities. They speak of and for other people when they report their own experiences and psychological insights. How could they have arrived at their subtle and penetrating discoveries of what went on in the souls of others if they had not found it in themselves? And how could they have found it in themselves if they had had no opportunity to compare their own emotional processes with those of other people? In them self-observation and observation of their fellow-men and -women did not compete with each other. They completed each other. Of course, sincere self-observation of incomparable profoundness is not always declared as such. It appears as psychological insight of a general character, disguised as characterizations of other persons. It appears in the form of aphorisms, by-products, asides, in many a work that has no avowed psychological objective.

In every man's memory there are things which he does not reveal to everyone, but only to his friends. There are also things which he does not reveal to his friends, but at best to himself and only under a pledge of secrecy. And finally there are things which man hesitates to reveal even to himself, and every decent person accumulates a considerable quantity of such things. In fact, you might say the more decent a person is, the greater the number of such things that he carries around with him. I, myself, at any rate, have only recently decided to recall a few of my earlier experiences; until now I have always avoided them even with a certain uneasiness. . . .

Where were these sentences taken from? Perhaps from a psychoanalytic article on suppression of unpleasant memories, from an introduction to a fragment of self-analysis dated around 1900 or 1905? Were they perhaps found among Freud's yet unpublished early papers? No, they were written in 1864, forty years before Freud wrote the *Psychopathology of Everyday Life,* where they might fittingly appear. The man who wrote them was Dostoyevsky *(Notes from Underground).*

[1] "Or they sit all day at swamps with anglerods and, on that account, think themselves *profound,* but whoever fishes where there are no fish, I do not even call him superficial."—Nietzsche, *Thus Spake Zarathustra.*

Similar paragraphs taken from Flaubert, Maupassant, Stendhal, Tolstoy, Kierkegaard, Nietzsche, and many others, could be added to prove who were the true predecessors of Freud, psychologist and psychoanalyst.

What, then, differentiates the attitude of these writers from Freud? Three factors: the aim of the psychological scrutiny, its method, and its form of presentation.

The aim of these writers is to give a picture of the inner world, the underground of the soul. The aim of Freud is to investigate this netherworld. They say: There is a labyrinth; how strange! Freud wants to act as the guide in this labyrinth. In the one case the method is that of the artist, of the creative writer. In Freud's case it is not only the method of the scientist; it is the special method of research that he discovered. It cannot be compared with the methods of other psychologists. The presentation in the one case has the form of a novel or a diary. In the other it is a scientific book or paper. Are there other basic differences? No. Here we have the shaping of emotional processes of an unconscious kind as seen by an artist; there, the same or similar processes seen by a scientific investigator. In scope and profundity of psychological insight, in his fundamental approach to the theme, Freud is nearer to Dostoyevsky and Nietzsche than to his pupils. (The same may be said of the creative structure of his personality.)

The first works of most great writers are autobiographical. They seek to present what psychological insights they have obtained when they looked into themselves. The inward look was also what made Freud recognize and understand the processes that are created by the interplay of our drives. With these writers the autobiographical interest is soon put into the background, to be replaced by observation of others and interest in their problems. The same process can be seen in the case of Freud. His interest turns to others, follows the sign of unconscious operations, records the subterranean motives and effects of human behavior. In the phase in which he wrote *The Psychopathology of Everyday Life* and the *Interpretation of Dreams,* psychological self-dissection and psychoanalysis of others already appear side by side. They are treated as one process and it is no longer important which is the object, oneself or another.

It was because of his interest in the psychology of neurotic disturbances that he turned his attention more and more to the analysis of others. We know that much self-analysis was concealed in his research into the emotions and thoughts of nervous patients. He emphasized often enough that there is no sharp, clean-cut boundary between the healthy man and the neurotic and that we are all beset with the very conflicts to which neurotic patients are subjected.

Freud's interest in the psychology of neurosis was, as some passages in his writings show, restricted and sometimes even accompanied by a kind of reluctance. He confessed that his "patience with pathological natures is completely exhausted in my daily work. In art and life I am intolerant of them." In the same letter to me, dated April 14, 1929, he expressed his admiration for the psychologist, Dostoyevsky, but charged against him that "his insight was so entirely restricted to the workings of the abnormal psyche."[2]

Seen from a certain point of view, the psychoanalysis of others, both normal and pathological persons, gave Freud the opportunity to re-examine and verify theories that he had found in self-analysis. In this sense—and only in this sense—Freud belongs to the group of the great confessors of mankind, the men who discover and reveal what happens in the psychical netherworld. He is a powerful link in the chain that extends from Saint Augustine to Rousseau, from Goethe to Tolstoy and Dostoyevsky, and from Ibsen and Strindberg to the writers of our time. That this characteristic of all creative writing became conscious to the poets themselves can be shown by their own words. Compare, for instance, Goethe's saying that his poems are "fragments of a great confession" or Ibsen's statement: "Writing means sitting in judgment upon oneself." One of these confessors, Balzac, said, "We die all unknown." Freud has made the greatest contribution in discovering this unknown self in himself and in us. Posterity will, I am sure, appreciate him more as a psychologist than as a physician. He thought of himself as a psychologist.

From this point of view, the distinction most psychiatrists make, that Freud was a scientist and the writers artists, is not an important one. What is important is that they, like him, conducted a search into the unknown layers of the human mind. That here the spirit is that of an investigator, and there that of a writer; that here what is sought after are laws of mental processes, while there only a picture of them is presented; that here is a sober scrutiny and there an emotional appeal—these are not basic differences. It is not even important that

[2] Quoted from my book, *From Thirty Years With Freud* (New York: Farrar & Rinehart, 1940).

here is a careful aiming and there a shot in the dark. What matters is that the shot in the dark hits the same target. What matters is the fortitude before one's own thought, the fearlessness in the face of darkness in oneself and others. Courage and sincerity are considered the only values. What makes Freud akin to these great writers has deeper roots and is more important than what links him with psychiatrists and physicians.

This is valid even in the realm of psychiatry itself. Let us assume that a well-known psychiatrist is called into consultation to give his opinion and help in the case of a woman who is suffering from obsessional ideas, insomnia, and other nervous complaints. The patient is compelled to wash her hands most of the day and often at night. She is restless and walks in her sleep. We are not concerned with the helplessness of the psychiatrist faced with such a case, but his absolute lack of psychological understanding. Suppose the sick lady was observed about 1907, in England, let us say. Nobody who knows the psychiatric literature of the time will doubt that our physician had no inkling of what the unconscious origin, the motives, and mechanisms of the patient's nervous disturbances might be.

Hers was a simple and rather common case, very well understood today—thanks to Freud—but misunderstood or not understood by the psychiatrists of his time. Who understood it? A poet by the name of William Shakespeare, who presented the identical case on the stage four hundred years ago. At least the Doctor of Physic who observes Lady Macbeth confessed: "This disease is beyond my practice," whereas the psychiatrists of 1907 would have treated it. This doctor of four hundred years ago thought that his patient needed more "the divine than the physician." Freud considered the psychoanalyst as a man who takes care of the soul rather "than as a physician." Freud wrote "The formula 'worldly care of souls' could in general describe the function that the psychoanalyst, whether he is a physician or not, has to fulfill toward the public." [3] Here is the difference. What the physicians until Freud did not understand, a playwright who had not studied medicine did understand. He recognized the hidden motives and mechanisms of obsession neurosis more clearly and deeply than did the psychiatrists four hundred years later. (The doctor in Shakespeare's play at least remarks: "I think, but dare not speak." The doctors facing such a case before Freud's arrival spoke, but did not dare to think.)

[3] *Gesammelte Schriften*, XI, 391.

We would like to remark that such a comparison sheds an amusing side light on a certain situation. Some time ago I remarked in a conversation with a younger psychoanalyst that in Shakespeare's plays there are some psychological insights that even today have not been reached by contemporary psychiatry. The sneering answer was: "You think, then, we should speak of an Ophelia syndrome?" A mentality so remote from the spirit of Freud is astonishing.

What connects the best, the most valuable, practitioners of our psychoanalytic profession with the writers is a certain ability to grasp the products and signs of the unconscious. Both are endowed with a fine apparatus that can apprehend the emotional and thought processes of others. Both are able to receive and decode the messages that go from the unconscious of one person to that of another. In their accurate recording of thousands of little signs of which we were not aware before, in being alive to every little quiver and slightest movement in the lines of unconscious communication. Their antennae are sensitive to little waves and can receive messages from their own subterranean stations as well as from others.

We now turn the dial and we hear the noises and voices of another station. We want to show how the psychoanalyst begins to recognize what takes place in the unconscious layers of other persons, patients and students, during the process of psychoanalysis. It is essentially the same faculty for fine hearing that enables him to find the secret meaning here as there.

We must not forget that it is one apparatus with its hidden mechanical devices that gives you your local station or those of the wide world outside. Our most valuable knowledge about ways to get in contact with the unconscious of other persons is due to the co-operation of the people we have analyzed. It will be useful to be reminded of this fact again and again. This book should be dedicated to the Unknown Patient because it is he or she that has given us, consciously or unconsciously, the best information and helped us reach new psychological insights. If we may borrow a leaf from the musical sphere, the presentation that follows could be introduced the same way Arnold Schoenberg, the composer of the *Gurre-Lieder,* introduced his textbook on harmony. The first sentence of this textbook reads: "I have learned this book from my pupils." [4]

[4] *Harmonielehre* (Leipzig: 1911).

PART TWO

THE WORKSHOP

CHAPTER XI

The Atmosphere

THE waiting and consultation rooms of an analyst look like those of any physician or lawyer. There are desks, tables, a couch and chairs, books, pictures, and ash trays. Yet the furniture and objects in the room of the analyst acquire a significance quite different from that of the furnishings in the office of a specialist in kidney diseases or a corporation lawyer. What is it in the analytic situation that makes the things in the analyst's room mean more than those in other offices?

To the matter-of-fact observer nothing, or almost nothing, in the psychoanalytic situation is unusual. The patient or student who has decided to be psychoanalyzed lies down on a couch, relaxes, and takes the position in which he feels most comfortable. The analyst sits behind him in a comfortable chair. The patient does most of the talking and the analyst, most of the time, is a silent listener. It would seem that there is nothing in this that could appeal to the imagination. Nevertheless this situation that looks so commonplace to the observer becomes so extraordinary that it cannot be compared with any other in our culture pattern.

It seems to me that any attempt to understand the psychological processes in analysis must start here if it is to find the reasons why this situation is different from all others. The little that has been published in contemporary literature about the initial problem misses the point, I think, because it does not differentiate between the situation and the atmosphere of psychoanalysis. There is nothing fantastic about the external situation: what changes it into something extraordinary is the psychological atmosphere that pervades the room and that sets this hour apart from all the other hours of the day and makes it a unique experience. It is the atmosphere between patient and analyst, which transforms a sober situation into a magical one.

But is there really nothing unusual in the external situation itself that favors this metamorphosis? Yes, just one small, seemingly insignificant feature. The patient talks but does not see the analyst who sits behind him. Does the patient or student, then, speak as if he were alone in the room? No, he is aware of the presence of the analyst. Then he speaks to the analyst, to a certain Dr. A. or Dr. B.? No, he speaks not *to* him but *before* him and he has also an audience that is not present. All this sounds mysterious and not very sensible and can only be understood and psychologically appreciated if we realize what it means to the patient as he talks, that the analyst is present but that he does not see him.

Freud gave good reasons for recommending this particular arrangement for the analytic session. He said that he could not endure being stared at for nine or ten hours daily. Also, he said, it demanded too much self-control not to betray his immediate reactions through his facial expressions and their changes as he listened to the patient's communications. These were personal reasons, to be sure, but most analysts will feel as Freud did. There is, however, good precedent for this arrangement. Freud, in following his personal "hunches," found the solution for a general psychological problem. He arrived at his goal without searching for it, with the certainty of a sleepwalker. Historically the psychoanalytic situation can be traced back to the situation during a hypnotic trance. It has moved very far from its origin but it still retains some traces of it.

Psychologically seen, the analytic situation lies somewhere between fantasy and reality. One might say that the external situation is one of matter-of-fact psychotherapeutic treatment while the atmosphere partakes of the magical. The patient comes in from the street with its noises and voices and slowly glides into an atmosphere in which external reality is of no avail, where he hears only what his inner voices say, recollections and experiences, impulses and thoughts. He is himself but he becomes more than the self he shows the world outside; that means he is entirely himself. The analyst is a certain Dr. A. or Dr. B. but at the same time he is also someone beyond this definite personality. He encompasses other figures beyond his own. He is a frame into which the patient puts a familiar picture, for the most part, a portrait of his family.

This quality between the sober and the fantastic, between everyday life and magic, between material and psychical reality, is the essential characteristic of the atmosphere of the analytic situation. Its creation is greatly furthered by the minor circumstance that the patient speaks to the analyst but does not see him. This means that for the unconscious of the patient the analyst is not only a psychotherapist but a figure between reality and fantasy. Here in broad daylight magic penetrates a scene that is utterly matter-of-fact and prosaic. A room like any other, with a couch, a chair, and ash trays, becomes the place for passionate emotions, for deeply felt reminiscences, for good and evil deeds in thought.

We analysts observe many times daily one aspect of the analytic situation changing into the other. We can even observe the transitional stages. Many signs, not only what our patients say but how they say it, show us how they glide into the analytic situation and out of it again. A patient begins his session with "How do you do?" He says a few words about the happenings of today or yesterday, but within a few minutes they are forgotten and the past becomes as vivid as if it were the present. Parents, long dead, come alive again in his memory, childhood scenes are re-experienced as if they were here and now and early sorrows are felt as if today had brought them forth. Rage and love, hate and tenderness, are freely expressed and thoughts that shy away from the light of the day creep out of their hiding-places. And then comes the moment when the self-induced spell is broken. The patient gets up from the couch and sees only the actual consultation room. He must make a sudden emotional readjustment upon finding himself again in the world of reality. There is even a slight physical symptom which shows that the change is not easy for some patients. The dizziness they feel for perhaps half a minute indicates the realization that they must suddenly live again in the actual world, which has different laws from those valid for the world of fantasy in which they have been living for the past fifty minutes. The sensation passes quickly, they breathe deeply and are once more ready to meet the demands of the day.

The analytic situation offers evidence to convince even the hard-bitten skeptic that magic works even in this age of modern technical achievements. It takes only a few moments to make the transition from the realm of the telephone, telegraph, tractor, and radar to the domain where psychical reality alone is valid. Here time and space are unimportant, contradictions may coexist, the rigidity of logical thinking disappears. We are in the land of fantasy, in Prospero's kingdom. Facts lose their force, truth and fancy merge.

The other day a young woman began her analytic hour with the statement: "I cooked the whole night." I understood of course that she spoke of a dream in' which she prepared for a dinner party to which she had invited her family. The same young lady began another hour with the report that the medical examination of her husband's spermatozoa seemed to prove that they were not capable of living. She would have to give up her long-felt yearning and hope for children. She finished her account with the words: "And that's the end of the house plants." This concluding sentence at first sounds perfectly senseless. There is no logical connection between this announcement and what went before. Yet I understood immediately what she meant. Her husband had several house plants which she had taken care of during the past year. It was immediately clear to me that she not only meant that she would no longer take care of the plants because she wanted to punish her husband but also that she herself had unconsciously considered the plants as substitute-children during the time of waiting and that she was now unwilling to look upon them as such any longer.[1]

In the eyes of the patient the analyst is a part of this realm between fantasy and reality. It is psychologically comprehensible that most patients do not know what their analysts look like; to express it more exactly, they know it and they do not know it. He is of course known to them, say, as Theodor Reik; that is, an elderly man who is bald, too corpulent, with a big nose, a high forehead, and who wears glasses through which he looks sometimes observingly, sometimes thoughtfully. At the same time, or rather at different times in the analytic session, he has the features of father, older brother, grandfather, or a good old uncle. Sometimes he looks like a friend whom they love or an enemy whom they dislike or hate. Before the session and after it he is again Theodor Reik. The patient getting up from the couch, faces an old man who says in a friendly voice: "Goodby. I hope to see you

[1]When poor Guy de Maupassant saw visitors in the insane asylum in Passy where he spent his last years, he planted little boughs in the ground of the garden and declared to his guests: "Look, these will all become little Maupassants in the spring."

again tomorrow." Yet during the past hour the patient may have been considering this same man as near to God or close to Satan; he may have seen in him his grandfather or father or a representative of any one of the figures that played an important role in his life. Now he is again nothing but an analyst whose professional services one has sought. Almost in a moment he is reduced to a real figure, a man whom one knows only in his professional capacity.

It is not difficult to find other situations in which a person is regarded in a similar way. I observed, for instance, two little boys in a playground. One of them pretended to be a bear and walked threateningly toward his playmate, who became frightened and ran to his mother for protection. After a few minutes, still clinging to his mother's skirt, he asked timidly, "Jimmy, are you still a bear?" Friedrich Heiler reports[2] that the Catholic peasants in Bavaria were very well aware of the human frailties and even vices of some of their priests. Nevertheless, they retained their respect and awe of them in their priestly functions. This attitude was neatly expressed in the remark, "Our parson is a bum, saving his holy ordination." What appears as the unity of two opposite views that coexist without coming into conflict with each other, can also be found in the contrast of the patient's rational and magical conceptions of his analyst. The difference here is only that the latter view in analysis is unconscious and generally remains unconscious.

I have been thanked during analytic hours for successful business transactions, for winning a law suit, for conquering a beloved woman, for making a technical discovery, for good luck at poker—all achievements of which I was wholly innocent. But I have also been accused of causing the outbreak of World Wars I and II, losses on the New York Stock Exchange, an attack of measles in a child a thousand miles away, defeat in a tennis game, the loss of a husband or wife—all happenings of which I was equally innocent. I have been blessed and cursed a thousand times, killed and kissed in thought, annihilated and royally rewarded in fantasy, and all because I sit unseen in a chair behind a woman or a man and listen to what he thinks or feels— simply because I am an analyst. So powerful is fantasy working in broad daylight.

During the analytic session the analyst shares with the patient this realm between fantasy and reality. He vicariously lives his patient's

[2]In his interesting study, *Das Gebet* (Muenchen: 1923).

experiences and at the same time looks upon them with the factual regard of the investigator. He dives with the patient into the life of old and new experiences, but at every moment he is ready to regain the safe shore of psychological observation. It is his task to keep intact this character between reality and fantasy that is the essence of the analytic situation. This does not mean that he need do anything to promote the illusion; it only means that he must do nothing to disturb it.

It is the task of the analyst to transform the unconscious magical views of the patient into conscious psychological insight. In order to do this, the analyst cannot from the start deny or disavow the magical atmosphere in which the patient unconsciously lives. He must accept its psychical reality. To approach the unconscious processes in the spirit of cold, rational disavowal would be as stupid as it would be to protest, "There are no ghosts!" when the ghost of the king appears in *Hamlet*. One must first accept and acknowledge the psychical reality of the apparition, otherwise it is not possible to understand what goes on in Hamlet's mind. In this recognition the audience follows the advice of the prince himself. When the ghost speaks, Horatio cries, "O day and night, but this is wondrous strange!" And Hamlet answers, "And therefore as a stranger give it welcome." It is in this spirit of preliminary acceptance that analysts listen to the voice of unconscious processes.

The twofold aspect of the analytic situation, its rational and magical sides, is determined to a great extent by one factor: the patient knows the analyst is present, but he does not see him. He speaks as if he were alone in the room, and at the same time remains aware that he has an invisible listener. Instead of discussing the psychological conditions which favor and disturb this atmosphere, I shall show that such situations can exist under quite different circumstances. A young girl who was in her last year at college consulted me because she had various nervous symptoms, insomnia, fears, inadequacy-feelings and so forth. Among the other complaints, she told me that she had suddenly become unable to speak in public, although she had previously been a well-poised speaker. She was ashamed of this inhibition, and it interfered seriously with her work in her class. She remembered the precise moment when this symptom had first appeared. It was on the occasion of an experiment conducted in the speech class. Each student was to speak before a microphone in an empty room. In contrast to many other occasions upon which she had addressed her fellow students, and addressed them well, she now suddenly became inarticulate. She was very frightened, her heart beat rapidly, and she could not get the words out. From then on, she was also unable to speak when she faced teacher and class and when no microphone stood before her. It was as if her symptom had been displaced from that special situation and become generalized. Later on she had great difficulty participating in discussions even in the intimate circle of her friends.

At first blush, this looks like a case of microphone fright that many persons are subject to. Such general classification is never psychologically satisfactory. It does not take the special features of the case into consideration and it leaves unexplained what is the psychological nature of microphone fright. There is also an important difference to be noted. A person who speaks before the microphone during a radio broadcast is aware that thousands of people whom he does not know are listening to him. In our case, the girl was speaking to her teacher and to her classmates, persons who were familiar to her and whom she had frequently addressed in the past. The new elements in the situation are thus the invisibility of the audience and the presence of a microphone.

I cannot present here the psychological evidence for the assertion that this new situation had for the girl an unconscious magical character and that her sudden fear was due to special reasons rooted in her relationship with her mother. Following her complaints about her inability to speak in class, she told me that she did not behave considerately or even politely toward her mother. She admitted contempt for her, and described her as entirely uneducated, though kindhearted. The girl said she never helped her mother at home, that she let her clean her room and pick up her clothes, although she knew that her mother had a serious heart disease.

It was easy to guess—not only by the succession of the two themes in her thoughts—that there was an emotional link between her guilt-feeling in connection with her mother and the inhibition which made it impossible for her to speak in public. The invisibility of the audience and the presence of the microphone must have intensified her social anxieties. The new elements contributed the magical touch to the situation. It was as if speaking in an empty room and to invisible listeners unconsciously meant to her saying something she was afraid to say, giving voice to something which had not been expressed. Her fear anticipated judgment and condemnation by the unseen audience. On the conscious level this audience consisted of her teacher and her classmates. Unconsciously, it meant more: it was public opinion which would judge. Judge what? Consciously, her rhetorical effort; unconsciously, her failures, her "sins." There are only a few steps more to the end of her unconscious train of thought: that the invisible judge before whom she would speak was God, in whom she did not believe, but of whom she was afraid. Not only the fact that she was alone in the room and was to speak into the microphone, but the act of speaking itself acquired in this situation a new, magical significance.

The conscious knowledge of the nature of a mechanical device can here coexist with a nonrational magical conception of the instrument.[3] The two views are on different psychical levels and could contradict each other only if both were conscious. The empty room with the microphone on the desk before her and the awareness of the unseen listeners created for her an atmosphere similar to that of prayer and confessional for pious persons. It filled her with terror as if, guilty and frightened, she were face to face with a higher power. What condemned her to silence was the fearful anticipation of disapproval and punishment.[4]

The case is mentioned here because it shows that a situation which has little in common with analysis can unconsciously take on a magical character for the speaker. Many psychiatrists will, of course, insist that they will stand no nonsense of this kind, but they must first acknowledge the existence and psychical significance of such unconscious beliefs.

Whoever observes people from the analytic vantage point will hesitate to admit that human beings are psychologically in unity. The work of the analyst resembles that of the archeologist who excavates different layers of an unknown or forgotten past. Like Heinrich Schliemann, who found seven cities in different layers when he searched for the

[3] Where such a contrast is consciously felt as a contradiction, neurotic patients often regress to an animistic belief that inorganic objects too have a will and a soul. To one patient who had an obsession neurosis, the telephone appeared uncanny, and she was almost afraid of the instrument, although she was quite familiar with its physical and mechanical character.

[4] Compare the attitude of this patient with the behavior of Rodion Raskolnikov in *Crime and Punishment*. When his mother and sister visit him, he feels suddenly that he cannot speak to them, that he can never speak to anyone any more because every word that he would utter would speak of his crime.

site of ancient Troy, the analyst will discover the remnants of the various phases of an individual life.

What a piece of work is a man! The analyst recognizes that everybody, including himself, lives psychologically at different levels of civilization in different situations. When you discuss the scientific premises of radio or television with an engineer, you speak with a man of the twentieth century, with a modern mind. An hour later, when you listen to the same man attacking Zulu-Kafirs, Ashanti Negroes, Jews, and other primitive tribes, you are under the impression that he lives in the dark medieval ages. When he argues and maintains two opposite views about the same subject at the same time, you can easily imagine that you are listening to a scholastic priest of the thirteenth century. There is the same casuistry, the same futile and quibbling manner of debate, yes, essentially the same kind of obsessional thinking that appeared in the medieval discussion of theological questions, such as, how many angels can dance on the point of a needle, or whether an egg laid on the Sabbath should be eaten. When you then observe this same man in other moods and situations, you will recognize that he is as haunted by the vain fears prevalent in the Stone Age and that he is as primitive and helpless a victim of violent passions as a Neanderthal man. Thus we are not astonished to find that the same girl who knew the exact nature of a microphone became frightened before this neutral little mechanical device. Only when one thinks in one-dimensional psychological terms will it appear strange that the analytic situation may have a rational and a magical character at the same time.

I hasten to add that the magical aspect of analysis, unlike that of this case, is generally of a friendly and encouraging character. There are enough instances of speaking through a microphone which prove that this situation also is, of itself, not frightening. A certain radio announcer is so unself-conscious and natural when on the air that someone remarked of him that "in his presence even the microphone relaxes." (Note that also here the microphone appears as an animated, living object.) The supernatural appears as a friendly and familiar power in the world of children who are not yet estranged from the view that objects too have a life and a soul of their own. They are, indeed, on "speaking" terms with the magical. The other day I heard a charming story about the little daughter of the well-known producer, Cecil de Mille. Her father had taught her to say her prayers before going to bed. One night, listening outside her room, her father heard her say her prayers and finish with the words: "This is Cecilia de Mille, speaking from Hollywood and saying good night."

Magazine cartoons often depict the analytic situation with the analyst conscientiously writing down in a notebook what the patient on the couch is telling him. Such a representation is really funny to anyone who knows what analysis is like, or perhaps I should say it would be funny if there were not so-called "analysts" who really do write down during the session what their patients tell them. Not only do technical reasons forbid note-taking[5] but the whole character of analysis is opposed to such a procedure. Taking notes would change a magical situation into a sober, literal one; the nature of the session would cease to be part of the realm of fantasy and would approximate instead a medical examination, with its adjuncts of record files, anamnesis, and case histories. The psychologist who writes down what the patient says may become a conscientious historian of the case and as such deserve recognition for his industry in the eyes of the patient, who may well regard him as a sort of schoolmaster but never as a sorcerer. Men who practice magic cannot afford bad memories.

There are other psychological reasons why taking notes during the analytic session is impossible. The attitude of the analyst is the counterpart of that which the patient is supposed to take at the analyst's suggestion. The patient of course cannot write down what he or the analyst says. Writing during the session would divide the analyst's attention and disturb the free flow of his thoughts and impressions. It would also distract the patient's attention and disturb him in the unhampered expression of his ideas and feelings.

The analyst, too, must acknowledge the mixed character of the analytic session, he must breathe the same atmosphere as the patient. Only when he is ready to drop all speculation while he analyzes will he be able to catch the emotional undertones in what his patient says. He should not "argue" the case like a lawyer, but face it spontaneously and without preconceived ideas. Only then will the emotional undertones become clearly audible and distinct as if amplified by a microphone of unconscious processes.

The analyst must oscillate in the same rhythm with his patient within the realm between fantasy and reality, sometimes approaching one, sometimes the other. During the analytic session he should remain

[5] In his papers on technique Freud has fully discussed the impossibility of taking notes during the analytic hour.

aware that for the unconscious thinking of the patient he is a figure of the patient's fantasy world. If he is ready to share this attitude to a certain extent, he will also understand the psychological meaning of the arrangement that puts him in a chair behind the patient where the latter cannot see him. It is an essential part of the scene, which is sober and magical at the same time.

From the outset of the analytic treatment some patients show a certain reluctance to abide by this ceremonial of the analytic situation. Freud himself emphasized that this reluctance is especially strong in persons in whose neuroses the tendency to observe sexual objects or processes plays a great role.[6] Newer research proves that many different factors may be responsible for such resistance against the physical arrangement of the analytic scene.

In some instances it is accepted at the beginning, but resistance against it appears in a later phase of analysis. One of my patients, who was already well advanced in his analysis, often got up from the couch to look at me because of a sudden fear that I might have died while he lay talking. Another patient expressed his dislike of the position, saying that he often had the fear that I might kick him on the head with my foot. This fear appeared without apparent motivation even when he had not consciously observed movements on my part. We soon discovered, of course, that these fears occurred after he had repressed some hostile or aggressive thoughts against me. His anxiety was the unconscious expression of his expectancy of retaliation from me. A young woman refused to lie down on the couch after she had been analyzed in this position for several weeks. She said that she was suddenly afraid that I might make a sexual attack upon her. She then told me what she had previously withheld, that a young gynecologist had once used the occasion of an examination to approach her sexually. The suppressed memory had returned with great vividness and made her afraid that the situation would repeat itself.

In these cases as in others in my experience, it is not a realistic factor that determines the patient's reluctance but a fantasy (in the last instance, a memory) that threatens to become real. There are, however, exceptions; and one is remarkable enough to tell here, especially since it shows how the analyst arrives at certain psychological conclusions. A young girl who sought analytic treatment because of severe emotional disturbances had given me a good and graphic report of the experiences

[6] *Gesammelte Schriften,* VI, 97.

of her childhood and early girlhood as well as of her present conflicts. During the first few months of analysis she had not shown many signs of resistance. Suddenly her attitude changed. She had already told me about a young man with whom she had gone "steady" for some years. There had been many petting parties, but she had not allowed him any intimacies beyond kisses. The relationship, which made a lasting impression upon the patient, had been broken off many months before. While speaking of the petting parties, the patient suddenly turned over on the couch and lay on her stomach; at the same time she looked at me in a sharply observant way. She took this position in the sessions that followed, although I tried to persuade her to return to the position usual in analysis. Several times she tried to follow my advice but after a few minutes she felt compelled to turn over and look at me, staying in this position throughout the sessions.

This change in behavior, so sudden and conspicuous, differed considerably from what I had encountered in other cases. It could not be likened to the behavior of men who are mistrustful or who are Peeping Toms, nor to that of women who become afraid that the analyst may make sexual advances. The nature of my patient's gaze, the way she glanced at me, clearly contradicted such an interpretation.

In order to give the reader an impression of just how the patient looked at me I shall have to give my own reactions to her steady observation. She did not look at my face but at my legs or jacket. The glance was searching or penetrating. I had the strange feeling that it had a sexual note. Under this sort of scrutiny of particular parts of my body or clothing I began to feel something close to embarrassment. "It must be something like this," I thought once during such a long, fixed stare, "that women feel when they say a man undresses them with his eyes." But that was impossible! I must have been mistaken. While I mistrusted my own impressions the girl continued her strange behavior. During one of the sessions that followed my doubts vanished. For many minutes the patient, without interrupting her flow of talk, had been looking with fascination at my socks; suddenly she said, "I am seeing a bit of your flesh." I did not react to that. She shifted her eyes to another part of me, talked along for a few minutes and remarked abruptly, "There is a button open on your shirt. Your breast is showing." Then she looked attentively at my face as if searching there for signs of embarrassment. I saw a look of triumph in her eyes when I buttoned the resisting button. It was as if she would have been gratified if I had shown signs of modesty.

The following reconstruction is the result of the analytic work of the days that followed this session. The young man to whom the patient had denied any sexual intimacies had found great satisfaction in embarrassing her by glancing at her bust or legs and making frivolous remarks. What she had just now done in the analytic sessions was to reverse this situation. She had, so to speak, incorporated the personality of her boy friend to whom she remained attached in spite of the separation. Like many other women she had tried to master the loss of the object by identifying herself with the man who had deserted her. She acted out what had happened to her in the past as if she wanted to get even with the man or any man. She tried to embarrass me by spying or staring and saying things to make me as bashful as she had been. It was thus an action or a series of actions that turned an emotional experience to which she had been subjected, into activity. She did unto others what had been done to her. Later there appeared a marked attitude of protest against the "superiority" of men as well as rebellion against the privileges that males in our culture pattern demand for themselves. She said she could not accept the fact that girls have to sit at home and wait for dates and declared that women have as much right as men to woo the other sex openly. Girls, she said, should become sexually self-sufficient and not stay dependent on the initiative of men for sexual gratification.

My early impression or interpretation of this patient's change in behavior was not mistaken. When she arrived at the point in her analysis at which she should have given me a report of her petting parties with the young man, she acted out his part instead. She told me how the young man embarrassed her by acting his behavior and thus belatedly turning the tables on him. Not only was my early impression right, but also the comparison I had used in my thoughts in trying to understand her attitude. Had I not likened my uneasiness to the feeling a woman describes when she says a man undresses her with his eyes? The comparison was not only justified; it already contained unconsciously the origin and motives of her behavior, which I was only able to understand consciously after straightening out the distortion of the original happening.

If the analytic situation produces an atmosphere of fantasy in broad daylight, if psychoanalysis partakes of magic, it is certainly white magic and has nothing to do with black magic and its evil intentions.

I remember a day long, long ago when Freud, after discussing some psychological problems with me, took an American newspaper from his desk and asked me to read an article in it. He observed me while I read and listened attentively to my comments afterward. The article was a violent attack upon President Woodrow Wilson. Wilson's speeches and books were made the object of so-called analytic study. The writer tried to prove by "analyzing" the style and diction of the President that he was selfish, a megalomaniac, a villain, and so on. I expressed my indignation at the shameful superficiality of the psychological views presented in the article. Freud said, "You missed the point. The superficiality in American newspapers is, of course, taken for granted, but what do you say to the fact that psychoanalysis is here put in the service of polemics? People will never understand that our method cannot be used for aggression. It can only be applied to excuse human actions. Here is an infamous way of using psychoanalysis."

Just the other day, more than twenty-five years later, I saw another newspaper article of the same sort. No one who deserves to be called a psychoanalyst could have produced it. Analysts may not confuse conscious wishes and thoughts with the repressed tendencies and impulses that appear in the phenomena we study. No analyst will hold a person responsible for thoughts and wishes that can be considered criminal only if they belong to the world of conscious actions. The unconscious is not concerned with the Ten Commandments.

CHAPTER XII

In the Beginning Is Silence

AFTER the preliminary consultation, the psychoanalyst explains to the patient or student the only rule they will follow during the psychoanalytic sessions. He asks the patient to relax and to say everything that occurs to him as it occurs to him, observing what thoughts, feelings, and impulses come up in his mind. The psychoanalyst is silent.

Once in a session that showed heightened resistance, a patient of mine called psychoanalysis "an impossible situation." Sincerity compels me to admit that in terms of social convention he was right. It is difficult to tell a stranger the most intimate facts of one's life and even more difficult to tell him thoughts and emotions one does not dare admit even to oneself. There are moments when the situation really threatens to become "impossible." Suppose some offensive, abusive thoughts concerning the analyst occur to the patient. What if he feels affectionate or even sexual impulses toward the analyst. Both happen fairly often. The patient knows, of course, that he has to treat such material like any other thoughts or emotions that cross his mind. He is told that he is as much and as little responsible for such thoughts as for the color of his eyes or the quality of his hair.

He has to learn to take this hurdle. It would not help much if we were to appeal to his intellectual conscience or tell him that to make the seemingly impossible possible is one of the essential tasks of his analysis. Even the attempt to convince him by appealing to his moral courage has not much chance of success. We could say to him: "My expectancy that you will be up to this difficult task shows that I have confidence in your energy and good will. If Hercules were to come into my room to give me a proof of his strength, I would not ask him to raise a chair to the height of his head. I would set him a harder task." All this would be of no avail; we can only wait until the patient himself finds the courage to make the almost impossible possible. The rest is silence.

Almost all the difficulties of psychoanalysis are connected with speaking, with the "word." We have often heard—too often, it would seem—the argument that 'it is impossible to imagine that a serious hysterical disease, a grave obsessional idea, a tormenting phobia can be dispelled by "words" alone. This argument is raised by the same people who as children never doubted that a mountain opens at a magic word or that a man can be transformed into an animal by a sorcerer's formula or that a few sounds can bring angels or devils to a given place. The same people later feel enthusiastic about the speech of a statesman, are convinced by the discussion of an idea, moved by the tragedy of a poet, forgiven through confession to a priest—words, words, words. They are the same people who do not doubt—the history of the nations as well as their own lives speak clearly enough—how much happiness and how much misery have been brought about by words and how often great decisions in the lives of people depend upon words alone. It would be incorrect, however, to credit the results of psychoanalysis only to words. It would be more correct to say that psychoanalysis shows the power of words and the power of silence.

Speaking, in psychoanalysis, has been discussed so much that many people overlook almost entirely the emotional effects of silence. When it is mentioned at all, only the occasional pauses of the patient are referred to. Here we choose a lonely path scarcely trod upon, for we shall talk about the silence of the psychoanalyst, its significance in the situation, its emotional importance, and its hidden meaning. No doubt about it, the silence of the psychoanalyst, too, becomes one of the so-called "impossibilities" of the situation.

In a conversation people speak alternately. When a person has said or reported something, the listener makes a remark, asks a question, gives a vocal expression of interest, or tells a story himself. There may be an exchange of views, ideas, or experiences. In company silence is avoided. If the one has nothing to say, the other will speak.

The analyst is not afraid of silence. As Saussure remarked, the unconnected monologue of the patient on the one side and the almost absolute silence of the psychiatrist on the other was never made a methodological principle before Freud.[1] We can guess its concealed meaning best when we note its effect upon the patient. We must correct ourselves here. We should say "its effects" because they are different not only in different people, but they will vary in the same person during psychoanalysis. That means that the silence of the psychoanalyst can have different meanings.

It is noteworthy that the patient attributes a certain emotional significance to this silence from the first session on. Why should he not assume that it is the natural and necessary attitude of the analyst, who has to be silent in order to listen attentively? In the majority of cases this silence has a calming, beneficent effect. The patient interprets it preconsciously as a sign of quiet attention, one that in itself gives him proof of sympathy. This silence seems to ask him to speak freely and to suspend conventional inhibitions in his talk during the analytic session. It has not yet been emphasized that there is another related emotional effect: that the world outside the room is put into the background. The quiet acts like a lampshade modifying a too bright light. The pressing nearness of material reality becomes remote. It is as if the silence of the analyst already marks the beginning of a quieter, less immediate way of looking at others and at oneself.

The patient himself comes into the psychoanalytic situation, which is unique in our civilization, out of silence. He has been silent about certain experiences, emotions, and thoughts—even when he has been most talkative, yes, the most garrulous person in the world. Perhaps he has talked a lot about himself and his experiences, but he has not spoken about the part of himself that emerges in the psychoanalytic situation. In the Pacific, near the Vancouver Island, there is a strange place called the "Zone of Silence." Here many ships have been wrecked on the rocks and lie on the bottom of the sea. No siren is powerful enough to warn the captains. No sound from outside can penetrate this zone of silence extending for many miles. A ship in this area is excluded from the noises of the outside world. What we call the repressed material in psychical life can be compared to this "zone of silence." Psychoanalysis marks the first break-through to this area. When the patient talks about

---

[1] I did not succeed in my search for a discussion of this theme in psychoanalytic literature. A single exception to the general avoidance or neglect of the subject should be mentioned: a few but important sentences to be found in "Remarques sur la technique de la psychoanalyse Freudienne," by R. de Saussure, in *L'Evolution psychiatric* (Paris: 1925), p. 40.

himself, the first, distant, hardly perceptible sounds reach his zone of silence.

When during that first phase of psychoanalysis longer pauses occur, they are (there are exceptions) signs of superficial resistances determined by the fact that the patient has to readjust himself to the unusual and strange situation. Initial resistances are, however, comparable to a distant thunder that indicates a storm is brewing somewhere.

Slowly the silence of the psychoanalyst changes its significance for the patient. Something has occurred to him that he does not like to say or that is difficult to say. He speaks about other things, feels he is avoiding that which wants to be expressed. Then he is silent like the psychoanalyst. The situation has not shown its seeming impossibility yet, but, for the first time, its uneasiness. The patient who feels this starts to speak again, about marginal things and trifles, but the thought that was pushed aside occurs again. It is as if it wants to be expressed or it will enforce silence by intruding into and interfering with every other train of thought. The patient may perhaps now turn to the analyst to ask for his help, but the latter is silent as if that were the only natural attitude and as if the social world which avoids such embarrassing silence in conversation does not matter. A patient who had interrupted her report with a long pause, which she tried in vain to break by talking about indifferent things, fell back into a long silence. It was obvious that she did not want to talk about a certain experience the memory of which was accompanied by feelings of grief. Finally she said, "Let's be silent about something else."

At a certain point in analysis the silence of the psychoanalyst itself becomes a factor in the interplay of emotional forces. It seems to forbid passing over things, and makes one conscious of what remarks about the weather and the bookcase in the room want to conceal. The active power of silence makes small talk transparent and has a force that pulls the patient forward, driving him into deeper layers than he intended.

It is an astonishing and hardly noticed psychological fact that one's own words once spoken are differently evaluated than those which we only think in our representations of words. The spoken word has a reactive effect upon the speaker. The silence of the analyst intensifies this reaction; it functions as a sounding board. An analyst who attentively follows for a period of years this wrestling with the self, increasingly gets the impression that a fight is on between powers that drive for self-expression and self-assertion and others that would hush them into silence. He can sometimes even observe a kind of anxiety after the act. The patient is often slightly frightened by what he has just said and nevertheless relieved because he has said it. There the silence of the analyst works upon the patient encouragingly, and works even more strongly than words could. The emotional situation of the patient, seen by the analyst, resembles the attempt of a prisoner to free himself. In his effort to give voice to the repressed, he reminds me of the pianist who once said, pointing to his instrument, "It is sometimes as if I were shut up there and had to play myself out of it."

This is not the place to follow the psychological significance of the analyst's silence at the beginning of a treatment. It is not just silence. It vibrates with unspoken words. We know that it is the indispensable condition for the reception and absorption of the communications given to the analyst—and more.[2]

The analyst hears not only what is in the words; he hears also what the words do not say. He listens with the "third ear," hearing not only

[2] It is tempting to use the insight into the psychology of silence as a ladder that can be put aside as soon as we have descended to the depths. There are, of course, different kinds of silence; yes, there are even degrees of silence. We speak of a cold, oppressive, defiant, disapproving or condemning, as well as of a calming, approving, humble, excusing, silence. The concept seems to unite opposite meanings, presenting itself with plus and minus signs. Compare, for instance, "silence gives consent" with the rejecting silence of a lady to a man who is forward or objectionable.

Silence can be conceived of as an expression of quiet sympathy or intense hate. To be silent with a person may mean that we feel quite in agreement with him or that every possibility of agreement is excluded. Talkativeness as well as reticence appear as character traits of the women whom men love. Lear disavows Cordelia, who loves and is silent, but Coriolanus returning to his wife tenderly calls her, "My gracious silence." The contrast between speaking and being silent was originally not as sharp as we might think. We are reminded of the characteristic of ancient languages (for instance, of the Egyptian) of forming words with antithetical meanings so that only a small change later indicated a differentiation of the opposites (compare, for instance, Latin *clamare* = to shout, *clam* = secretly; German *Stimme* = voice, *stumm* = mute). We have to assume that silence is primal and that speaking emerged from silence as life from the inorganic, from death. If we live here on "borrowed time," all our speaking is but a fleeting interruption of the eternal silence. We have to believe with the Gospel of John that in the beginning was the word, but before that was the great silence. Carlyle, in *On Heroes and Hero-Worship*, says that speech is of time; silence is of eternity.

what the patient speaks but also his own inner voices, what emerges from his own unconscious depths. Mahler once remarked: "The most important thing in music is not in the score." In psychoanalysis, too, what is spoken is not the most important thing. It appears to us more important to recognize what speech conceals and what silence reveals.

CHAPTER XIII

The Approach

Oh, WHAT a tangled web we weave when first we practice . . . ! I have been teaching and training young analysts for many years and I know that nothing is more difficult for them than to control their impatience. The temptation to help quickly and—what must necessarily precede every therapeutic effort—to understand quickly, is a strong one for the inexperienced. Looking back upon my own early analytic work, I realize how impatient I was myself, how ready to form judgments and to make premature interpretations, how hasty sometimes in my conclusion.

Freud once complained that much in American civilization showed "thoughtless optimism and empty activity." I am of the opinion that these are traits of a young nation, and that recent years have brought our juvenile point of view—the features of our boy-and-girl civilization —nearer to maturity. But even now we are far too ready to believe that we can understand all and forgive all.

The other day I listened to several young analysts talking about their work. What astonished me most was the spirit in which they approached their difficult task. All of them, it appeared, were not only eager to help their patients immediately but also to give them as much sympathy and good will at the start as any human being could give to another. But is this not the natural and right attitude? Is this not desirable in the name of human love and the brotherhood of man?

The brotherhood of man has always seemed to me a utopian idea voiced by American senators. But even if it were something more, what has this philosophical or moralistic concept to do with the specific and restricted task that is the business of the analyst? His problem is simply

a psychological one that it is up to him to solve. It is a question of ex-
pediency and efficiency, not ethics.

The analyst's first task is to understand his patient, to find out the determinants of his illness, to discover the unconscious motives that make
him act and feel and think as he does. But is not the enthusiastic approach, the giving of moral support and sympathetic understanding the
best way to reach this goal? I do not think so. Such an approach is idealistic rather than realistic and I prefer to face the situation squarely. The
analyst's task is not to be a fountain of love and sympathy, but to be a
helper. It is not possible to help until you have understood.

Freud once pointed out that a biographer who is enthusiastic about
his subject is in danger of giving a distorted and unreal picture of him,
of his true character and life story. The hero appears as an angel, not as
a human being with shortcomings and weaknesses, foibles and failings,
however earnest his desire to overcome them. After reading such a
glorifying biography, you may be willing to concede that its subject now
sits at the right hand of the Lord but you will doubt that he ever walked
this earth. Freud asserted that the untrue picture presented by many a
biographer is due to the fact that the writer was in love with his subject. But love is blind. Its presence is most inappropriate when you un-
dertake to understand the psychology of a person.

I remember Freud's telling me two little experiences that illustrate
this point. As his friends knew, the great man had an intense interest in
Egyptology and had given much study to the findings of scientific research in ancient Egyptian history and civilization. At one time a well-
known Egyptologist who had taken an important part in the exca-
vations in the Nile Valley came to Freud as a patient. The analysis
progressed satisfactorily until Freud, as he later told me, had to recognize the fact that he was much too fascinated by this patient, who could
tell him so much about archeological work. Freud felt that his personal
interest was so strong that it disturbed his analytic work. His professional integrity demanded that he send the patient to another analyst
less keenly interested in Egyptology.

The other experience Freud told me proved that he had once unconsciously revealed a critical impulse toward a patient. The man was a
Britisher, and the day before the analytic session in question had been
his marriage anniversary. Freud started the session with the question,
"Well, how was your adversary?" Freud smiled as he told me about this
slip of the tongue because he thought it interesting that he had made a

slip in the English language. He said that it proved that he now spoke English very well indeed because you make such slips only when you speak a language fluently. He admitted, however, that the mistake revealed an impatient or critical tendency on his part. It was as if he had said, "How was the anniversary of your marriage that is so full of adversity?"

I grant, of course, that the analyst must be ready to listen with human sympathy to his patient's story of his difficulties and that he must give them his complete attention and apply all his knowledge. The "sympathetic understanding" is not, as you might expect from listening to the conversation of many American analysts, present from the start of the work. It is one of its optimal results. It comes toward the end of the treatment or emerges when the analysis has already progressed considerably. One may compare its development with the reading of a really great novel. You do not love its figures immediately or it would not be a work of art. It takes time and some psychological work on your part to penetrate to the essence of the personalities you are reading about, to learn what makes them tick and what the motives are that determine their actions and feelings. And should not what is true of reading a great novel, mere "literature" after all that gives only a dim reflection of real life, also be valid when we are facing the variety and complexity of people of flesh and blood, whose deepest secrets we are trying to bring to light? Are the unconscious processes so simple, so patent, that we dare to say we approach these persons with "sympathetic understanding"?

My experience tells me that after the initial phase of analysis, during which we become acquainted with the personality of the patient, learn his experiences, and recognize the nature of his conflicts, his symptoms, inhibitions, and anxieties, there follows usually a period of confusion and uncertainty, a kind of chaotic or erratic vagueness. We grope in the dark and cannot see where we are going. We are not only puzzled and intrigued but also slightly impatient and even a bit annoyed, however well we succeed in concealing these slight feelings. We are impatient with the man or woman under analysis because we are impatient with ourselves. Why does he or she act so unreasonably? Why does he escape into his neurotic symptoms instead of facing reality and overcoming his difficulties like a mature person? Why these quirks and queernesses, these superfluous anxieties, these obsessional thoughts, phobias, and compulsions? What a waste of emotional and intellectual energy that could be put to better use! We do not understand and therefore we are impatient. We are in suspense and very far from knowing all the answers. Our initial sympathy with the patient seems to be endangered because we have become so intensely eager to "understand" him that it is hard to wait. But we must learn to be patient, to gather impressions until they are strong and solid enough to be trusted. These impressions must be re-examined, revised, and verified. They must be compared again and again with additional material as it comes up in analysis until they mature into views and concepts. Given time, the psychological phenomena themselves begin to speak. Certain traits begin to form a pattern; contrasting and even contradictory figures begin to fit into it and contribute to the picture as a whole. After many frustrations and failures the analyst at last wins mastery over his medium. Gradually, as he recognizes hidden connections, sees order in what at first looked like chaos, he experiences his share of creative satisfaction.

And, strangely, the more he discovers of those emotional undercurrents, the deeper he goes into the domain of unconscious processes, the more his patient becomes "sympathetic" to him, the more "reconciled" he becomes to him. At the end he cannot help but see in him a human being like himself, struggling with the same conflicts that are common to us all, proud and humble, almost ready to give up but somehow going on—down but not out. At the end the analyst realizes that there no longer exists a gulf between him and his patient.

Lytton Strachey once told how he approached his magnificent biography of Queen Victoria. Studying the early life of the young Queen, he did not like her very much. He saw her as a spoiled, overly self-assured, and level-headed girl. He treated her at first with a certain ironical remoteness and with little sympathy. The more he studied her life and the more he began to understand her personality and the environment that helped form it the more sympathetic he became. At the end, when he speaks of the Queen in her last years, you feel genuine human warmth, appreciation, and admiration for an impressive personality. He started with little affection for his subject, and ended practically in love with the old lady.

Listening to those young analysts the other day as they spoke of their first patients, I wondered and said under my breath, "Greater love hath no man." But I have trust in them. They will live and learn. They will learn, among other things, that sympathetic understanding does not mark the beginning of analysis, but its end.

CHAPTER XIV

Conscious and Unconscious Observation

IT WAS not difficult to show how a psychologist arrives at insights from careful self-observation. But how can I give my readers a concrete idea of the processes that enable us to conjecture and comprehend the inner processes in others? They are by no means so simple as they appear to the layman, and it is the more difficult to describe them because they are, in part, incapable of expression in words. I propose to begin by dividing the process of conjecture and comprehension into three sections, although I know how artificial this division is, and how misplaced it must appear in face of the living current of the psychical act.

The first section of the way, thus artificially divided, leads from the conscious or potentially conscious perception of the subject matter to the point where it dives down into the unconscious mind of the psychologist. The second would then represent the unconscious assimilation of the observed material. The third stretches from the re-emergence into consciousness of the data so assimilated to the point of their description or formulation. Of the middle of these sections we can say nothing except that we have no direct access to it and that it interests us most of all. The other two sections are more accessible. True, we cannot fix the moment in which a perception dives down below our consciousness. No more can we state precisely the time of its re-emergence. For the rest, it is not only in respect of time that we are liable to error in this matter.

The actual process is only partially accessible to introspective observation. The act of slipping down into the unconscious region, the assimilation there, and the re-emergence into consciousness, may best be compared with the passage through a tunnel. For each of the two sections there is a different degree of light. Whether we can depict them depends upon the brightness of that light.

The first section begins in the clear daylight of consciousness. Let us call to mind the analytic situation that presents itself to us daily. The subject speaks or is silent, and accompanies his speech or silence with "speaking" gestures. We see the play of his features, the variety of his movements. All this communicates to us the vital expression of what he is feeling and thinking. It supplies the psychical data, which the analyst then assimilates unconsciously during the period that we have called the second section.

But is this really the whole of the psychical data that he has at his disposal and uses? If we recall the course of an analytic session, do we not feel that something is missing in this account, something important, nay, decisive? Our feeling is right. *In truth, we are incapable of dissecting into all its component parts the process by which we recognize psychological fact.* The data presented to the analyst must be more extensive and differentiated than appears to him during or after the treatment. His field of observation must be wider. It appears that I have committed errors even in my description of the data at his disposal. What the analyst is able to perceive and comprehend consciously is probably only a selection that he makes retrospectively, after the event. What his conscious memory supplies him with is only a small portion of what he actually uses. In other words, the analyst knows only a part of the data on which his judgment is based, that such and such processes are going on in the unconscious mind of the person he is observing. Our apprehension of the other personality is not restricted to our conscious perceptions.

The individual inner life of a person cannot be read in the features that psychology has hitherto grasped and been able to grasp. Of course I know that there is little that is new in what I am now saying. It is the unconscious mind of the subject that is of decisive importance, and the analyst meets that with his own unconscious mind as the instrument of perception. That is easy to say, but difficult to realize. Psychologists can hardly conceive the notion of unconscious perception. For psychoanalysis the notion presents no difficulty, but to understand the peculiar nature of unconscious perception and observation is not so easy.

For the moment we will turn from the theoretical consideration of the problem, and proceed with the help of any casual example from daily practice. One is as good as another. A patient told me how on the previous day he had had a violent quarrel with his girl (he had been having a sexual affair with her for a considerable time). At first the conversation turned upon the girl's health; she had been feeling weak and poorly of late. She had remarked that she was afraid of tuberculosis; she weighed too little and must put on flesh. The young man, my patient, did not think that necessary. He opposed it on aesthetic grounds. How did the analyst suddenly perceive that the quarrel centered unconsciously upon the question of a child? Nothing in the young man's account pointed that way. Looking back, I discern that my sudden idea must have carried me back at one bound to something my patient had told me about a year and a half earlier. About two years previously the girl had become pregnant and, at his urgent entreaty, had procured an abortion. She had offered no great resistance to the suggestion of abortion, and had undergone the operation, which proved difficult owing to special circumstances, with real heroism. Subsequently she had seldom mentioned the incident, and that only in passing. And my patient had seldom thought of the subject for a year and a half.

Now was it the words "putting on flesh" in his story that roused the memory? How else could the latent meaning of the lovers' quarrel have revealed itself to me? I could not tell, even though I were to repeat the story with the accuracy of a gramophone. It must have declared itself somehow or other, in spite of the fact that the girl's fears, according to the patient's account, sounded entirely reasonable and justifiable. In spite of her perfectly well-founded plea, he must have detected some note of secret reproach in her words—a tone must have conveyed to him that the girl had never got over her loss. What psychoanalysis tells on the subject is that my own unconscious mind had acted as an instrument of perception and seized upon the secret meaning of the quarrel, a meaning hidden, moreover, from both principals. It is good to know that, but is it enough? My unconscious mind is able to conjecture a hidden meaning only through given signs. It requires tokens in order to detect something. Now, I have deliberately chosen a primitive example. This is a case of cryptomnesia, people will say. A memory no longer present in my consciousness was responsible for my recognition of the latent meaning. The unconscious remembrance of that long-past incident, emerging suddenly during the story, set me on the track.

Let us take an example that is only a little more complex and has to do with a like conflict, but in which no such memory of heuristic value can be traced. A young girl under psychoanalysis evinced an extraordinary fear of marriage. She repulsed any man who made approaches to her, and shrank from any chance of marriage or sexual intercourse. The reason she always gave for her attitude was her exceptional terror of the dangers of childbirth. She was convinced that she would not survive the pain, and would die. At the mere thought of childbirth, she was overcome by violent terror. She brought up the fact that many millions of women survive childbirth without injury and mentioned the possibility of preventive measures, but she nullified both factors by stressing the uncertainty precisely in her own case.

Now, she had spoken of this fear of hers several times without my understanding more of the nature or mental origin of her emotion than any other observant auditor. How was it that on a new occasion I suddenly recognized that, apart from all other mental determinants, a profound fear must be at work, overshadowing all other feelings, that she was incapable of bearing a child and that any man must be unhappy with her? Of course I did not give expression to this idea about the suppressed nature of her fear, but waited till the astonishing surmise had been confirmed again and again. I cannot detect in myself any memory of a previous communication, emerging suddenly from the unconscious and helping me to find the connection. Nothing in the girl's statements, so far as I could remember then or have been able to recall since, pointed to her being dominated by an unconscious fear lest she be unable to bear a child. This fear I was subsequently able to trace to apprehensions based upon long-continued masturbation. I had listened attentively to her lamentations and her story without dreaming of any such thing, when suddenly this idea entered my mind, giving me my first and most important means of approach to an understanding of the case. Here, then, there was no memory, or—to put it more cautiously —none traceable. Nevertheless, there must have been something in the patient's words, or something to be read between the lines, that pointed in that direction, something in her utterances, verbal or mimetic or otherwise, that suggested the connection.

Here we are faced with a whole series of questions. The idea must have arisen from something. Why did it arise just at this juncture, since we had talked of her fear previously, since, indeed, she had often told me about it? What went on within my mind, on what mental processes was the idea based, and what preceded it? But is it not erroneous and unjust to lay special stress on this side of the problem? Is it not better to assume that my idea must have been based upon some factor not hitherto grasped, that is to say that it must ultimately be traced back to some sense-perception? In that case, unnamed impressions become the means of communicating psychological knowledge. That brings us back to our starting-point, to the nature of the data at our disposal. It appears to me that it is here that we must begin, if we want to discover the foundation of the psychical comprehension of unconscious processes. If Kant begins with the statement that cognition arises from experience, that true dictum must be supplemented by the statement that experience has its origin in our sense-perceptions, that nothing can be in our intellect which was not there before in our senses. (*Nihil est in intellectu quod non prius fuerit in sensibus.*) This statement is also true for a psychologist who seeks to grasp the unconscious processes in others.

Psychical data are not uniform. We have, of course, in the first place the considerable portion that we seize upon through conscious hearing, sight, touch, and smell. A further portion is what we observe unconsciously. It is permissible to declare that this second portion is more extensive than the first, and that far greater importance must be ascribed to it in the matter of psychological comprehension than to what we consciously hear, see, etc. Of course, we seize upon this, also, by means of the senses that we know but, to speak descriptively, it is preconscious or unconscious. We perceive peculiarities in the features and bearing and movements of others that help to make the impression we receive without our observing or attending to them. We remember details of another person's dress and peculiarities in his gestures, without recalling them; a number of minor points, an olfactory nuance; a sense of touch while shaking hands, too slight to be observed; warmth, clamminess, roughness or smoothness in the skin; the manner in which he glances up or looks—of all this we are not consciously aware, and yet it influences our opinion. The minutest movements accompany every process of thought; muscular twitchings in face or hands and movements of the eyes speak to us as well as words. No small power of communication is contained in a glance, a person's bearing, a bodily movement, a special way of breathing. Signals of subterranean motions and impulses are being sent silently to the region of everyday speech, gesture, and movement.

A series of neurodynamic stimuli come to us from other people and play a part in producing our impressions, though we are not conscious of noticing them. There are certain expressive movements that we understand, without our conscious perception really being at work in that understanding. We need only think of the wide field of language. Everybody has, in addition to the characteristics we know, certain vocal modulations that do not strike us; the particular pitch and timbre of his voice, his particular speech rhythm, which we do not consciously observe. There are variations of tone, pauses, and shifted accentuation, so slight that they never reach the limits of conscious observation, individual nuances of pronunciation that we do not notice, but note. These little traits, which have no place in the field of conscious observation, nevertheless betray a great deal to us about a person. A voice that we hear, though we do not see the speaker, may sometimes tell us more about him than if we were observing him. It is not the words spoken by the voice that are of importance, but what it tells us of the speaker. Its tone comes to be more important than what it says. "Speak, in order that I may see you," said Socrates.

Language—and here I do not mean only the language of words but also the inarticulated sounds, the language of the eyes and gestures—was originally an instinctive utterance. It was not until a later stage that language developed from an undifferentiated whole to a means of communication. But throughout this and other changes it has remained true to its original function, which finds expression in the inflection of the voice, in the intonation, and in other characteristics. It is probable that the language of words was a late formation, taking the place of gesture language, and it is not irrational to suppose, as that somewhat self-willed linguist, Sir Richard Paget, maintains, that the movements of the tongue originally imitated our various actions. Even where language only serves the purpose of practical communication, we hear the accompanying sounds expressive of emotion, though we may not be aware of them.

There are, besides, nuances of smell and peculiarities of touch that escape our conscious observation and yet enter into the sum total of our impressions. They accompany the coarser or stronger conscious sense-perceptions as overtones accompany a melody. In a state of hyperesthesia we may even consciously observe these variations of tone, glance, or gesture, the minutest facial movements, and muscular twitchings; but that is exceptional. In a general way it is only the grossest of these accompanying movements, tones, and smells that reach our consciousness and are consciously used as psychological data. The others appear as part of the total impression. They do not emerge separately in our perception. There can be nothing wrong in likening these unconscious perceptions with the minute sense stimuli that psychology teaches us need only be added together or multiplied in order to become accessible to conscious perception. Each of these minute stimuli, then, must have contributed something to the sensation. We know that technical science has devised apparatus to bring within our grasp these natural processes, which we should otherwise be unable to perceive. And here I call attention to the important fact of repression, which greatly restricts our capacity for perceiving tiny signals of this kind.

Perhaps we shall do well to draw a distinction between this part of our psychical data and another, even though the distinction may prove at a later stage to be purely descriptive. It is true that the facts with which we have just been dealing are unconscious, but they do undoubtedly fall within the group of sense-perceptions of which we have knowledge. I should like to draw a distinction between these data and certain other data, also unconscious, helping like the former to shape our impressions, but such that their precise nature can only be surmised. That is to say, we receive impressions through senses that are in themselves beyond the reach of our consciousness. The assumption that these sense-perceptions have no place in human consciousness, or have lost their place in it, is supported by certain facts and rendered exceedingly probable by others. I mean especially the fact of sense-communications, having their origin in the animal past of the human race and now lost to our consciousness. The sense of direction in bees, the capacity of birds of passage to find their way, the sense of light in insects' skin, the instinctive realization of approaching danger in various animals, all bear witness to sense functions with which we have almost no human conceptions to compare. Of other sense functions that resemble those of the animals, it may be said that our perceptions are much vaguer, weaker, and less certain. It is easy to detect in them the rudiments of originally keen and well-developed senses. We need only compare the large part played by the sense of smell among dogs with its small significance in our own lives.

Freud has established the probability that the importance of the sense of smell has been greatly diminished in man through the development of his upright gait. The fact that the sense of smell tells dogs of things no longer accessible to us may serve as an example of the diminished importance of a number of sense functions in the life of the human race.

Certain senses are reduced to rudimentary remnants because they have been less and less used. Do we not say, "I smell a rat" when we are suspicious of evil and concealed motives behind X's behavior? Is it accidental that we can use such a figure of speech as if we were still olfactory creatures? I am of the opinion that there are more of these rudimentary senses, tracing their origin to the evolution of prehistoric man, which, though not, indeed, totally lost, have lost their significance.

In addition there are other senses of which we have completely lost consciousness and which yet retain their efficacy, that is to say, are able to communicate unconscious impressions to us. A comparison with the sense-perceptions of animals—for instance, the way certain insects can receive and communicate perceptions—points to the supposition that like senses may survive unconsciously in ourselves. I have in mind such a thing as the means of communication among ants, described by K. Frisch, and the signals ants give with their antennae, which the research of Forel, Wismann, and others has explained. Assuredly, there is a significant language in the animal kingdom and means of communication not ours, or no longer ours. The biologist Degener, in his study of simple animal societies, has assumed a kind of telepathic communication. A minute stimulus given by a particular species of caterpillar to a single individual within a large group caused a simultaneous palpitation throughout the whole group. Degener speaks of a hyperindividual group soul in these animal societies. Freud, too, has pointed to the possibility of such direct psychical communication. With reference to the common will in the large insect communities, he thinks that this original, archaic means of communication has been replaced in the course of racial evolution by the superior method of communication by signs. But the older method may survive, he thinks, in the background and human beings revert to it under certain conditions.

It will be observed that, in assuming a direct psychical communication through these archaic, rudimentary surviving senses, we approach the complex of problems known as telepathy. I believe that in the special case of communication between two unconscious minds called by that name, these neglected senses, favored by the weakened action of the others, do really come into action. Such telepathic communication is not supersensory. It makes actual those senses that have become alien to our consciousness. By using as signals the expression of stimuli that do not cross the threshold of our consciousness, and calling them in to supplement or correct our normal sense perceptions, it gives rise to special psychical apprehensions. The conversation between the unconscious of the one and the other mind does not proceed in a vacuum. It is served by certain means of communication comparable with those which we have assumed in the lower animal societies. They are not so much super-sensory as subsensuous phenomena, that is, information conveyed by means of ancient, ordinarily discarded senses. The return to these unknown senses, which must formerly have played a far greater part in the activities of living organisms, may sometimes give rise to the impression that telepathy involves no sense-perception at all.

We have here, not mysterious powers of divination, but rather an interruption of the customary working of our psychical machinery to make way for older methods, not otherwise applied. Thus the unconscious perception passes the bounds of communications received through our known sense organs. We have ears, and hear not with them alone; we have eyes, and see not with them alone. Possibly these unknown senses work faster than those we know, can communicate their perceptions to the unconscious faster than the senses developed later, and so seem to act through the air. And it is further worth observing that this action upon secret feelers of which we are unconscious belongs mainly to the realm of instinct, so that we may speak rather of instinct-reading than of thought-reading. The suspension of customary functions thus renders our less keen senses hyperesthetic—by way of comparison we may recall the greater intensity and subtlety of the sense of touch in people who have lost their sight—and long-forgotten senses recover the power of functioning. The enhanced effectiveness is, therefore, caused by the neglect of the mind's ordinary methods of working.

We have long been aware that the acknowledgment of telepathy as a psychical phenomenon does not imply that higher powers are substituted for the dynamics of mental action. It is not necessary to assume supernatural happenings because some small fragments of what goes on in the world are still unexplained. We need not give ourselves up to magic because the cause and effect of some process is unknown to us. We must confess that our knowledge is not adequate to explain the phenomenon. It does not become more explicable if we refer it back to some greater unknown factor. When we want to drink a glass of milk, we have no need to buy a cow. The psychological valuation of the efficacy of unknown or little known senses has brought us here to the limits of our subject.

While we have thus been reminded of the prehistoric past of sense-perceptions, we may now cast a hasty glance in the opposite direction. The advance of civilization has caused certain senses to perish, and others to become more specialized and differentiated. In general we may say that the development of civilization has reduced the importance of sense-perceptions, has challenged the exclusive dominion they originally held over the life of the individual. The aim is to manage with a minimum of sense-perception and to leave the subsequent process of cognition to the intellect. With the advance of civilization sense-perceptions are more and more markedly degraded to despised acts preparatory to the intellectual mastery of phenomena. We may cite as a sign of this weakening our mistrust of the data with which they supply us. The development of civilization brings a weakening and stunting of sense-impressions that may be compared with the loss of keenness in our sense-impressions in old age, deafness and far-sightedness, which, however, are due to biological causes.

There are reasons to support the hypothesis that refers this diminished significance of the senses to the advance of the age-long process of repression. The concepts "sense" and "sensuality" are not merely loosely associated in speech, but there is an inner connection that gives us an insight into certain psychical processes. The pleasure of the senses really is a pleasure arising from the tension and relaxation of the sense organs. Sense-perception, the significance of which is more and more restricted with advancing civilization by the intellectual processes, particularly memory, is closely associated with the satisfaction of organic and elementary instincts. As memory develops, it comes to represent a substitute for the fading strength of sense-perceptions. It might be argued that the loss of intensity and significance in the senses is a mark of diminishing vitality in the human race since it is associated with a weakening of sexual instinct.

Perhaps the retort might be made that it is precisely civilization that has greatly increased the keenness of our sense-perceptions through the instruments it has created. It enables us to see things through the microscope and telescope that were not formerly visible; enables us, by means of appropriate instruments, to hear sounds formerly inaudible; and communicates sensations of touch and vibration otherwise beyond the reach of our consciousness. That is true, but it is not in contradiction with the previous statement. In part, these instruments serve to correct the very evil caused by civilization—for instance, eyeglasses—for the rest, their efficacy has certainly nothing to do with processes that are of vital interest to the human organism. Undoubtedly, they are of great importance, but it cannot be denied that they are artificial expedients, offering a poor substitute for the direct data communicated by organic sense-perception. Perhaps we may venture to regard memory itself, which, with advancing civilization, challenges the importance of sense-perception as a disposition to feel the strength and immediacy of sense-perceptions over again.

Let us return from this digression to our main argument. We have sought the special significance of sense-perception in psychology in a different direction from that pointed out by modern sense physiology and psychology. We have grasped how varied and differentiated psychical data are when we set about to investigate them from the point of view of sense-perception, but also how hard to differentiate. Besides the main path, they can use a number of side paths, subterranean passages, secret ways. In addition to our conscious sense-perceptions, we receive communications through other organs of perception which we cannot consciously call our own, although they are within us. We can treat these signals like any others. We can attend to them or neglect them, listen to them or miss them, see them or overlook them. There is a very natural temptation not to attend to them or observe them. (A frequent part of our capacity for unconscious and preconscious perception is the observation that something is lacking, the subterranean awareness that something is not there.) It is certainly right and useful to sharpen our powers of conscious observation of things perceived, but we should not overlook the value of unconscious perception. We must not reject what makes itself felt by other means, even if it fails to make itself felt in consciousness at once.

A psychoanalyst must aim at bringing into the field of consciousness those impressions which would otherwise remain unconscious. Undoubtedly individual differences will exercise an influence upon his efforts. The practice and sensitiveness of the individual will vary; the readiness to trust to tiny stimuli and the capacity to register these tiny impressions are not possessed by everybody to an equal extent. And so we should pay attention to the first, hardly noticeable impressions that we receive of a person, however much they may soon be drowned by other, more insistent impressions. Without doubt, first impressions are of importance. First impressions may not be right, but they often contain true apprehensions in a distorted form.

These signals do not convey clear information. They are nowise comparable with modern signposts, upon which destination and distance are precisely indicated, but rather with old milestones whose lettering is weather-beaten and half illegible. Many of the gaps and errors in our psychological comprehension must be attributed to our inattention to these unconscious signals. They may be blurred and their import difficult to determine, they nevertheless supplement conscious perception. In certain cases they alone enable us to discern its significance or correct the significance we mistakenly ascribe to it. It is true that psychological investigation meets here with much that is imponderable and difficult to grasp. Research must not ignore these factors. The best that we owe to the psychology of the unconscious is the result of prolonged observation, without premises. But it would be a mistake to assume that this observation is purely conscious. Not until we have learned to appreciate the significance of unconscious observation, reacting to the faintest impressions with the sensitiveness of a sheet of tin foil, shall we recognize the difficulty of the task of transforming imponderabilia into ponderabilia.

In fact, our psychological impressions are the result of the joint assimilation of conscious and unconscious perceptions. And here the conscious perceptions act, in a sense, like the last fragments of day, to which something different is attached, behind which something different lies concealed, something deeper than daytime thoughts. If we thrust aside the doubtful communications from the unconscious, as being unreliable, indefinite, and contrary to our conscious judgments and prejudices, we shall, it is true, seldom be deceived, but then we shall seldom attain surprising knowledge. Indeed a special kind of keen scent is no less essential than acumen for a psychologist who wants to grasp the unconscious processes.

If we survey our psychological data once more in all their variety and over the whole field, from the strongest expression of emotion to the imponderabilia, we become aware that we are treating them as if they served no other purpose but to tell us something about the inner life of another person. That is certainly not exclusively the case, and yet it is the case. I mean to say that they aim, among other things, at communicating to us something about the hidden processes in the other mind. We understand this primary endeavor; it does serve the purpose of communication, of psychical disburdenment. It has, therefore, a sound function in the economy of the inner life. We are reminded of Freud's view that mortals are not so made as to retain a secret. "Self-betrayal oozes from all our pores." I believe, moreover, that these words indicate the organ that was the sole medium of self-betrayal in the early stages of evolution. Originally most likely it really was first and foremost man's bodily surface, the skin, that showed what was going on within. It was the earliest organ to reflect mental processes. Blushing and turning pale still betray our feelings, and perspiration still breaks out when we are afraid. All self-betrayal makes its way through the pores of the skin. That statement clamors for a sequel. What sequel, may easily be guessed when we reflect that we react to the unconscious with all our organs, with our various instruments of reception and comprehension. *The self-betrayal of another is sucked in through all our pores.*

CHAPTER XV

The Third Ear

THE last chapter spoke of communications for which conscious perceptions have only the function that relays have in telegraphy. It would, of course, be nonsense to assert that this language of the unconscious is understood only by psychoanalysts. (Sometimes it would seem that it is least understood by analysts.) As a matter of fact, this interchange of impulses goes on between all human beings, and analysis only evaluates them as psychological indications. Psychoanalysis is in this sense not so much a heart-to-heart talk as a drive-to-drive talk, an inaudible but highly expressive dialogue. The psychoanalyst has to learn how one mind speaks to another beyond words and in silence. He must learn to listen "with the third ear."[1] It is not true that you have to shout to make yourself understood. When you wish to be heard, you whisper.

What can an analyst teach his younger colleagues in this direction? Very little. He can speak of his own experiences. He can report instances, which have the value of illustrations only. And he can—above all else—encourage the younger generation of analysts to unlearn all routine. We speak of routine only in the gathering of unconscious material through observation, not of the use which the analytic technique makes of it. We have to insist that in the area of observation he keep fancy-free and follow his instincts. The "instincts," which indicate, point out, hint at and allude, warn and convey, are sometimes more intelligent

[1] This phrase is borrowed from Nietzsche, *Beyond Good and Evil*, Part VIII, p. 246.

than our conscious "intelligence." We know so many things that "aren't so" but, we must admit, we guess many things that seem to be impossible but "are so." Young analysts should be encouraged to rely on a series of most delicate communications when they collect their impressions; to extend their feelers, to seize the secret messages that go from one unconscious to another.

To trust these messages, to be ready to participate in all flights and flings of one's imagination, not to be afraid of one's own sensitivities, is necessary not only in the beginnings of analysis; it remains necessary and important throughout. The task of the analyst is to observe and to record in his memory thousands of little signs and to remain aware of their delicate effects upon him. At the present stage of our science it is not so necessary, it seems to me, to caution the student against overvaluation of the little signs or to warn him not to take them as evidence. These unconscious feelers are not there to master a problem, but to search for it. They are not there to grasp, but to touch. We need not fear that this approach will lead to hasty judgments. The greater danger (and the one favored by our present way of training students) is that these seemingly insignificant signs will be missed, neglected, brushed aside. The student is often taught to observe sharply and accurately what is presented to his conscious perception, but conscious perception is much too restricted and narrow. The student often analyzes the material without considering that it is so much richer, subtler, finer than what can be caught in the net of conscious observation. The small fish that escapes through the mesh is often the most precious.

Receiving, recording, and decoding these "asides," which are whispered between sentences and without sentences, is, in reality, not teachable. It is, however, to a certain degree demonstrable. It can be demonstrated that the analyst, like his patient, knows things without knowing that he knows them. The voice that speaks in him, speaks low, but he who listens with a third ear hears also what is expressed almost noiselessly, what is said *pianissimo*. There are instances in which things a person has said in psychoanalysis are consciously not even heard by the analyst, but none the less understood or interpreted. There are others about which one can say: in one ear, out the other, and in the third. The psychoanalyst who must look at all things immediately, scrutinize them, and subject them to logical examination has often lost the psychological moment for seizing the fleeting, elusive material. Here—and only here—you must leap before you look; otherwise you will be looking at a void where a second before a valuable impression flew past.

In psychoanalysis we learn to collect this material, which is not conscious but which has to become conscious if we want to use it in our search and research. That the psychoanalyst immediately recognizes the importance and significance of the data brought to his attention is a stale superstition. He can be content with himself when he is able to receive and record them immediately. He can be content if he becomes aware of them. I know from conversations with many psychoanalysts that they approach this unconscious material with the tools of reason, clinical observation, meditation, and reflection. They approach it, but that does not mean that they even come close to it. The attempt to confine unconscious processes to a formula like chemical or mathematical processes remains a waste of intellectual energy. One doubts if there is any use in discussing the difference between the two types of processes with such superior minds. The Austrian poet, Grillparzer, and the German playwright, Hebbel, lived at the same time (about one hundred years ago) in Vienna, without meeting each other. Grillparzer was reluctant to speak with Hebbel, who was inclined to reflection and brooded over many metaphysical problems. Grillparzer admitted he was too shy to converse with the prominent, meditative playwright. "You know," he said, "Mr. Hebbel knows exactly what God thinks and what He looks like, and I just don't know."

It seems to me that the best way to guess something about the significance of "insignificant" data, the way to catch the fleeting impression, is not to meditate, but to be intensely aware of them. They reveal their secrets like doors that open themselves, but cannot be forced. One can with conviction say: You will understand them after you have ceased to reflect about them.

No doubt, the third ear of which we often speak will appear to many not only as an anatomical, but also as a psychological, abnormality— even to psychologists. But do we not speak of hearing with the "inner ear." What Nietzsche meant is not identical with this figure of speech, but it is akin to it. The third ear to which the great psychologists referred is the same that Freud meant when he said the capacity of the unconscious for fine hearing was one of the requisites for the psychoanalyst.

One of the peculiarities of this third ear is that it works two ways. It can catch what other people do not say, but only feel and think; and it can also be turned inward. It can hear voices from within the self that are otherwise not audible because they are drowned out by the noise of our conscious thought-processes. The student of psychoanalysis is advised to listen to those inner voices with more attention than to what "reason" tells about the unconscious; to be very aware of what is said inside himself, *écouter aux voix intérieures,* and to shut his ear to the noises of adult wisdom, well-considered opinion, conscious judgment. The night reveals to the wanderer things that are hidden by day.

In other words, the psychoanalyst who hopes to recognize the secret meaning of this almost imperceptible, imponderable language has to sharpen his sensitiveness to it, to increase his readiness to receive it. When he wants to decode it, he can do so only by listening sharply inside himself, by becoming aware of the subtle impressions it makes upon him and the fleeting thoughts and emotions it arouses in him. It is most important that he observe with great attention what this language means to him, what its psychological effects upon him are. From these he can arrive at its unconscious motives and meanings, and this conclusion again will not be a conscious thought-process or a logical operation, but an unconscious—I might almost say, instinctive—reaction that takes place within him. The meaning is conveyed to him by a message that might surprise him much like a physical sensation for which he is unprepared and which presents itself suddenly from within his organism. Again, the only way of penetrating into the secret of this language is by looking into oneself, understanding one's own reactions to it.

The reader is asked to think this over. A little known and concealed organ in the analyst receives and transmits the secret messages of others before he consciously understands them himself. And yet the literature of psychoanalysis neglects it. There is one word that may make claim to being a rarity in psychoanalytic literature (with the exception of Freud): the word "I." With what fear and avoidance does the analyst write about his own method of coming to conclusions, about his own thoughts and impressions! The devil himself could not frighten many analysts more than the use of the word "I" does in reporting cases. It is this fear of the little pronoun of the first person singular, nominative case, that accounts for the fact that reports of self-analysis are such a rarity in our literature. The worship of the bitch-goddess objectivity, of pseudo precision, of facts and figures, explains why this is the only book that deals with this subject matter, or which insists that the subject matters. In our science only the psychical reality has validity. It is remarkable that the unconscious station which does almost all the work is left out of analytic discussions. Imagine discussing the science of sound, acoustics, without mentioning the ear, or optics without speaking of the eye.

Nothing can, of course, be said about the nature of those unconscious impressions we receive as long as they remain unconscious. Here are a few representative instances of some that became conscious. They concern the manner, not the manners, of persons who were in the process of psychoanalysis, little peculiarities, scarcely noticed movements, intonations, and glances that might otherwise have escaped conscious observation because they were inconspicuous parts of the person's behavior. People generally tend to brush aside observations of this sort as immaterial and inconsequential, little things not worthy of our attention.

In the hall that leads from my office to the apartment door, is a big mirror beside a clothes tree. Why did I not observe that a young, pretty woman patient of mine never looked into the mirror when she put on her coat? I must have seen it before, but it came to my attention only after the fifth psychoanalytic session. I was aware that she spoke without any emotions about her marriage or her family, and I became suspicious that her remoteness and coolness were expressions of a schizophrenic disease. Walking behind her to the door I observed that she did not even glance at herself in the mirror, but I did not recall perceiving this trait before. I must have perceived it before without noticing it and, when I paid attention to it now, I did so because I saw it as an additional symptom. I had seen the patient walk to the door in front of me five times, and I knew now that, unlike other women, she never looked into the mirror. Now I also became aware of how carelessly she treated her hat, that she threw it on rather than put it on. It gained significance now—why not before? Why did I recall only then what I had often said before, namely, that men who treat their hats with great care are usually not very masculine and women who do not pay any attention to their hats are, in general, not very feminine?

I am choosing this instance as representative of many others in which we become aware of a slight divergence because we miss a certain detail of behavior. Experience in psychoanalysis teaches us that we are inclined to overlook the absence of a usual bit of behavior, although it is often a valuable clue and can become a part of the psychological circumstantial evidence we need. That something is not present where we expect it, or that something is not in its usual place or order, is less conspicuous than the presence of something unusual. Only when the trait appears important or when it is missed immediately will it become conspicuous by its absence. Otherwise, we generally ignore what is not there. Sometimes, just the observation of the absence of such little features leads to understanding. The other day I read a mystery story in which a murder is committed during a theater performance. The audience is searched and the fact that one man has no tie yields a precious clue.

In contrast to the case mentioned above, I observed very soon after the beginning of an analysis that a patient, a middle-aged man, spent a long time before the mirror in the hall, smoothing his hair before he put on his hat, and so forth. This trait came to mind when the patient reported that almost every night through the window of his darkened bathroom he spied on women undressing and that the sight often made him masturbate. My peeping patient was also potentially an exhibitionist. Later on it became obvious that he identified himself in his unconscious fantasies with the women he watched.

Perceptions of such a vague character, impressions that almost elude us, support us in reaching certain stations on our road to insight. We appreciate their value when we have learned to control our impatience and when we do not expect immediate, but rather intermediary, results from these trifles of observations. The smell of a perfume, a gesture of a hand, a peculiarity of breathing, as well as articulate confessions and long reports, give away secrets. Sometimes an observation of this kind scarcely deserves the name of observation but proves important none the less. Sometimes a transient impression remains unnoted until it occurs often. Only its repetition makes us realize its presence. Peculiarities of voice, of glancing, often reveal something that was hidden behind the words and the sentences we hear. They convey a meaning we would never have guessed, if we had not absorbed the little asides on the fringes of the stage that accompany the main action. Men speak to us and we speak to them not only with words but also with the little signs and expressions we unconsciously send and receive. Observation of these signs begins with our isolating them from the total pattern of the behavior. When we succeed in doing this, we can make the impression clearer and stronger by repetition. Their psychological evaluation and interpretation occur sometimes to the psychoanalyst immediately, sometimes later on as we follow the trail. In the process of "catching" these elusive signs we must trust to our senses and not follow the voice of "reason" which will try to brush them aside. The psychologist who approaches this valuable field as sober as a judge will not capture many data because he will also be as unimaginative as a judge. Only he who is fancy-free and opens all his senses to these impressions will be sensitive to the wealth he will encounter.

The trail uncovered by first impressions sometimes leads to insights that could otherwise be obtained only after a long time and by dint of hard psychological digging. A young graduate student at Harvard started his analysis in a very low voice. His manner of speech appeared deliberate and considered. I asked him to speak louder. He made an effort to do so, but after two minutes dropped back to a low tone that became almost inaudible. At first I had the impression that he was shy or timid and that it was difficult for him to speak of the serious conflicts that had disturbed his childhood. This impression could not explain his manner of speaking because his voice was not only low but also exceptionally deep, and it was as if he chose his words very deliberately. Whatever his reasons, whether shyness, disturbance, or emotions that had to be controlled, you cannot analyze someone without hearing what he has to say.

After trying my best to catch what he mumbled, I decided to interrupt what seemed to be a monologue that excluded an audience. My first impression had given way to another. His manner of speaking was much more significant for his personality than what he had to say to me in this first session. Neglecting everything else, I entered into a discussion of his low-voiced and controlled way of speaking and insisted that he tell me all that he knew about it, at the same time asking him again to make himself heard. We soon arrived at the insight that his low voice and dignified manner were a late acquisition that had developed as an expression of his opposition to the shrieking, high, excited voices of his parents, especially of his mother. There was a story in that, a story we meet frequently in American-born children of East-European immigrants. In this case it was further complicated by the neurotic conflicts of the young man. His parents had retained the behavior and manners of the old country when they came to the United States. They spoke loudly and with vivid gestures. They were highly temperamental and made no effort to control the expression of their emotions. Entirely Americanized, the boy began to feel ashamed of his parents and developed this characteristic manner of low speaking and overcontrolled dignity as a counteraction to the temptation to speak and act like the members of his family. He acquired, so to speak, a second personality superimposed on his originally passionate and excitable nature. Early conflicts, especially with his mother, intensified and deepened this reaction-formation whose external signs were his way of speaking and similar traits. Analyzing these features, we soon arrived at the core of his neurotic conflicts.

In this case a practical necessity of the analytic situation forced the analyst to turn his attention to a special trait of personal behavior, which, if it had been less clearly developed, might have remained unobserved. The first analytic session thus started with the discussion of this special characteristic, an exception that proved justified as well as useful.

The analyst can achieve some psychological insight into a patient even before the beginning of treatment if he will only trust his impressions as soon as he becomes aware of them. A young woman made an appointment to consult about the possibility of continuing her psychoanalysis with me. She told me she had broken off her analysis with Dr. A. some months ago. I listened to the story of the conflict that was making it impossible for her to return to her first psychoanalyst. She rapidly sketched the difficulties in her marriage, her social relations, and her professional life. There was nothing, it seemed to me, unusual in what she told me; nothing an analyst does not meet with in many patients. She seemed to be intelligent enough, sincere, and friendly. Why did I feel a slight annoyance with the patient after she left? There was nothing in our conversation that could explain such a feeling. As my attention turned to other patients, I brushed aside the vague impression.

When the patient telephoned two days later, I did not recognize her name and did not remember that she had promised to call me. Now I was forced to follow the rule: Analyst, analyze yourself!

I remembered feeling slightly annoyed, but I had not become aware of any reason for this feeling. It was certain that I had not disliked the patient, and certainly she had not done or said anything during the consultation that could have annoyed me. Well, there was the conflict with Dr. A. I had the impression that the analyst had lost patience with his patient at the end—perhaps after she had provoked him many times—and that she could not take what he had told her about herself. She had definitely rejected my suggestion that she return to Dr. A. and try to continue the analysis with him. But that could not possibly have annoyed me. She was entitled to decide that herself, and I scarcely knew Dr. A.

What was it then that made me displeased with her? Now it slowly came back to me. There were two things she had said the unconscious significance of which I had not realized but had nevertheless sensed. At the end of our conversation she had asked me if I would continue her analysis. Before I had time to answer she had wondered whether I would advise her to go to Dr. N., another psychoanalyst, whom she did not know. The question was asked rather casually, but it had left some trace in me of which I now became aware. It seemed strange. The young lady had consulted me about her neurotic troubles, had asked me whether I would bring her analysis to its end, and then whether she had not better go to Dr. N. instead. I had advised her, of course, to go to Dr. N. Now over the telephone she said that Dr. N. had no time for her and that she wanted to continue her analysis with me. Her question concerning Dr. N. during the consultation appeared at first quite natural and not in the least conspicuous, a question just like any other. Looking back at it, however, it took on another character. I remembered that she had looked at me with a leer, and I understood now, much later, what her sidelong glance and her question meant. It was a provocation of a teasing or malicious kind.

I want to make this element clear. Compare this situation with similar ones. What would we think of a patient who asks to be treated by one physician and then during the consultation asks whether he ought not to go to another physician? It did not make sense and yet I had to assume that there was some concealed sense in it. When you go to a shoemaker to have your shoes repaired, you do not ask him whether you should take the same shoes to another shoemaker. You do not ask a girl to dance and then wonder aloud whether you should not rather dance with another girl.

When I suggested that she go to Dr. N., I must have been reacting unconsciously to the unconscious meaning of her question. I was not surprised or annoyed, as might be expected. On the contrary, I reacted as if her question were the most normal thing. Only later did I realize that it was extraordinary. I reacted not only to the question but also to the look with which she asked it, as if to say: "If you doubt whether to come to me or to Dr. N., please go to Dr. N. I do not want you as a patient." I reacted as if I had understood the meaning of the glance while I did not even notice it consciously. I had been aware of a slight annoyance after her visit, but not of what had annoyed me. My unconscious reaction then (in my answer) and later (not remembering her name and our agreement) showed that I had somewhere, hidden even from myself, understood well enough that her question was really a provocation.

After that I remembered that the sidelong glance had appeared again at the end of the consultation. The patient had casually mentioned reading a rather unfavorable review of one of my books in the *Psychoanalytic Quarterly*. As far as my conscious thoughts went the review did not affect me. But that is not the point here. Why did she mention it? Where was the need to say it? It seems that I felt annoyed, not at being reminded of the criticism, but by her intention in reminding me of it, which I sensed. Well-bred and well-educated, she would certainly not say to a stranger she had just met at a dinner or cocktail party, "Oh, I read an unfavorable review of your last book just two days ago." Why did she do it just before leaving my room and why this sidelong, expectant glance? Considering her otherwise excellent manners, there must have been an unconscious hostile or aggressive tendency in her remark.

What was gained by my insight, what was the advantage in catching these imponderable expressions that had appeared incognito? There was more than one advantage—besides the satisfaction of the psychological interest. That side glance was revealing. It not only observed; it was observed; and for a fleeting moment I caught the real face behind the mask. The situation was like that of a masquerade at which a person has the advantage of seeing a lady who believes herself unobserved, without her mask. Later, when he meets her again in disguise, he will know her identity. This early insight proved very useful later on. It was a promising beginning and it helped me in the difficult situations that merged in the later phases of analysis. It was much easier to understand the masochistic provocation to which the patient resorted again and again. And it was easier to convince her finally that some unconscious tendency in her forced her to make herself disliked. I had, of course, overcome my initial annoyance quickly after I understood its reasons and, forewarned and forearmed by my early insight, I could tolerate the provocations much better than my colleague, who had yielded to the temptation to become angry with her.

The discussion of this case and the many others that follow seems to present a good opportunity to inject a few remarks about the psycho-analyst himself. What kind of psychoanalyst, some readers will ask, can feel annoyed or impatient? Is this the much-praised calm and the correct scientific attitude of the therapist? Is this the pure mirror that reflects the image of the patient who comes to psychoanalysis with his troubles, symptoms, and complaints? Is this the proper couch-side manner? The question is easily answered. The psychoanalyst is a human being like any other and not a god. There is nothing superhuman about him. In fact, he has to be human. How else could he understand other human beings? If he were like a block of wood or a marble statue, he could never hope to grasp the strange passions and thoughts he will meet with in his patients. If he were cold and unfeeling, a "stuffed shirt," as some plays portray him, he would be an analytic robot or a pompous, dignified ass who could not gain entry to the secrets of the human soul. It seems to me that the demand that the analyst should be sensitive and human does not contradict the expectation that he should maintain an objective view of his cases and perform his difficult task with as much therapeutic and scientific skill as is given him. Objectivity and inhumanness are two things that are frequently confused, even by many psychoanalysts. The sensitiveness and the subjectivity of the analyst concern his impressionability to the slightest stimuli, to the minute, almost imperceptible indices of unconscious processes. It is desirable that he be as susceptible, as responsive and alive, to those signs as a mimosa is to the touch. He should, of course, possess the same sensitiveness to, and the same faculty for fine hearing of, the voices within himself. His objectivity, his cool and calm judgment, his power of logical and psychological penetration as well as his emotional control, should be reserved for the analytic treatment. He will not feel the temptation to express his own emotions when his psychological interest outweighs his temperament. He will be able to check and control impulses that he has in common with his patients when he remembers that his task is to understand and to help them. It is ridiculous to demand that an analyst, to whom nothing human should be alien, should not be human himself. Goethe has expressed it beautifully: If the eye were not something sunlike itself, it could never see the sun.

The instances reported above contrast with others—alas, so many others—in which I remained unaware of those trifles, of those little revealing signs, or in which I observed them much later, sometimes even too late. It does not matter how much or how little too late. It makes no difference whether you missed your plane by only a few minutes or by a few hours. In every one of those cases my lack of sensitiveness was punished by additional work, an increased intellectual and emotional effort that would have been unnecessary if I had been more impressionable or observant. In almost all of them there was also a hindrance in myself that blocked me or dulled the sharpness of my observation. Here is such a case, one of many:

A young man had come for psychoanalysis because he wanted to rid himself of many nervous symptoms and some serious difficulties he was encountering in his private and professional life. I succeeded in a relatively short time in freeing him of his most oppressive symptoms, but the other difficulties remained. They seemed to be stationary and did not improve. I often told myself that something in me hindered my deeper penetration into that secret. But I could not find the road that led to it. The young man had obliging, open manners and showed brilliant intelligence, wit, and humor. What a pity that all these gifts remained sterile and displayed themselves only when he talked! His intellectual endowment and his emotional alertness made everything he said interesting whether he talked about his own symptoms, about his complicated relations with relatives and friends, his past emotions and experiences, or of the present, of a sexual adventure, or money matters. He knew how to tell a tale about himself or others. He was stimulating as well as stimulated. Nothing changed, however, in his inner situation after he had lost his most serious symptoms.

One day he told me that his sweetheart, who had listened to his stories for a long time, had smilingly asked, "But, John, why do you make such an effort? I am not a girl whom you met yesterday." My eyes were suddenly opened wide by this remark of a third person. I had really overlooked the fact that the young man had not talked to me, but had entertained me in the last weeks. The girl was right, so absolutely right. He dazzled people. He bribed them with his reports, which were always very alive and vivid, vibrant and interesting. In speaking of himself, however, he did not give of himself. He spent himself, but he did not surrender. He figured in his reports like the story-teller in a modern novel narrated in the first person—a story by Somerset Maugham. In talking about himself, ostensibly quite freely, he was hiding himself. Listening to him with sharper ears, I now received a new impression of his inadequacy-feelings, which made it necessary for him to conquer all people anew whenever he met them, to use his endowments to win them over and thus overcome his deep sense of insecurity. I had let myself be bribed like so many others by these great, ever recurrent efforts. Then along came a young girl whose psychological knowledge did not surpass that of other students of Vassar or Smith and gave me a lesson I would not forget. She hit the target easily and casually, reminding the young man that he need not exert himself. She had said, "I am not a girl whom you met yesterday," and with these nine words she had shown the path for which I had searched in vain. I took my hat off to this unknown Vassar girl and felt thoroughly ashamed of myself. Who had taught her the fine art of psychological observation and discernment? You do not learn such things in the psychology department at Smith or Vassar. I was ready to believe that the girl was smart enough, but it was not her intelligence that had spoken like that. It was her heart that had told her.

Experiences of this kind (I could tell many more) make us psycho-analysts modest about our psychological endowment—or should make us more modest. There was I, who thought myself a trained observer, and I did not recognize what was so obvious. "What is a trained observer?" I asked myself. He is a man who is trained to pay attention to certain things and to neglect others. He is a man who overpays attention to features he expects to see and remains in debt to others that escape his notice.

CHAPTER XVI

Free-Floating Attention

Do YOU picture the psychoanalyst as a man leaning forward in his chair, watching with all five senses for minute psychological signs, anxious lest one should escape him? I've talked about tiny signals, the faint stimuli that flit and waver, slip past, and attain such suggestive significance for the conjecture of unconscious processes. In the face of such differentiated data, so hard to take hold of, you would think that the keenest attention is called for. Do you imagine the analyst not just attentive but tense?

The picture is false, and the analyst's attention is of a different kind. Freud defined this particular kind of attention as *"gleichschwebend."* The word is difficult to translate; simultaneously with its connotation of equal distribution, it also has the meaning of revolving or circling.[1] The closest I can come to the German word is "freely floating." Another possibility, which emphasizes the psychological balance rather than the motion, would be "poised attention." Two factors induced Freud to recommend such free-floating attention.

It saves tension, which, after all, it is not possible to maintain for hours, and it avoids the dangers that threaten in the case of deliberate

[1] A. A. Brill translates it "mobile attention." This is correct only in the sense that a lamp, which can be carried from one room to another, may be called mobile. It cannot be denied that the dancer Pavlova, can be described as mobile, but it does not give one a good picture of her activity on the stage. As so often, Dr. Brill's translations of Freud's writings, which are read by most American students, are worse than bad; they are mediocre.

attention directed toward a particular aim. If we strain our attention to a certain point, if we begin to select from among the data offered and seize upon one fragment especially, then, Freud warns us, we follow our own expectations or inclinations. The danger naturally arises that we may never find anything but what we are prepared to find. If we follow our inclinations, we are sure to falsify the possible perception. The rule that we must note everything equally is the necessary counterpart to the demand we make upon the patient to tell everything that occurs to him without criticism or selection.

When we hear free-floating attention recommended, we get the impression that it is a course easy to pursue. But in practice it is hardly less difficult than the course required of the patient, of which it is the counterpart.

Only ignorance of how the basic principle of analysis is carried out has prevented psychologists from beginning to criticize this point of psychoanalytic theory and practice. By way of experiment, I shall anticipate their criticism and begin with the last sentence of Freud's recommendations, in which he advises the particular kind of attention in which everything is noted equally. It is plain that two notions are here confused that, strictly speaking, have nothing to do with one another: poised attention and taking note. The first notion has to do with a particular attitude of mind or reaction to data presented, the other to a feat of memory. It is true that the word "note" can be used for both. But in fact it seems that Freud passed from the subject of attention to the far-removed theme of capacity for taking note, without being fully aware of it. Is attention inseparably associated with taking note, with memory? Assuredly not. When I stand at a crossing and direct my attention to the traffic, is there anything of which I need take note, that I need impress upon my memory?

And now, how can free-floating attention and taking note be brought into consonance? If from the wealth of a mass of passing data we want to take note of something, we must direct a keen gaze upon special points, turn our attention to them in particular, must we not? How can I take note of anything, if I do not direct my whole attention to it, if I treat insignificant detail in exactly the same way as that which is important? Perhaps it will be said that the notion of "poised" attention aims precisely at taking note of everything and remembering everything. But is not that notion self-contradictory? Attention is always directed only to particular objects. Attention, we have always been taught, implies selection. How can we avoid the danger of selection, if we want to be attentive?

Anyone who has studied the psychological literature on this question will immediately cite passages from a number of books by distinguished psychologists, in which particular stress is laid upon the statement that the notion of attention does imply selection, nay, that without that essential feature it is meaningless. Let me quote a representative passage from Hermann Ebbinghaus' *Outline of Psychology* (*Abriss der Psychologie*):

"Attention is a phenomenon of selection and limitation. The mind escapes from the excessive mass of demands that are perpetually being made upon it in favor of a few that bear a special relation to its own aims."

Indeed attention has been defined as "the preference consciously shown to certain mental contents." We might also point to the "narrowness of consciousness," fully investigated by science. It is a well-known fact that only a certain number of ideas can find a place in our field of consciousness, and that a kind of rivalry or struggle goes on at its threshold among the ideas pressing for admittance. A large number of experiments, prepared and carried out with remarkable precision and acumen, have led to the establishment of the exact number of perceptions and ideas for which our consciousness has room. All this argues against the possibility of "poised" attention. Let us consider, further, what academic psychology tells us of the origin of attention. I will take as a representative example the hypothesis of Karl Groos, a distinguished investigator who claimed, with the support of very intriguing arguments, the "instinct of spying" as the original form of attention. Out of this primary form, which, indeed, represents the "expectation of future events," out of what we may call motor attention, theoretical attention has evolved. Allowing for the distance traveled from this basic form, we should be compelled to recognize in every type of attention its derivation from an instinctive motor reaction. But surely the idea of a poised spying appears absurd.

I would beg my readers to note that my improvised criticism does not aim at investigating an analytic theory of attention, for no such theory exists, certainly none set up by Freud. We will, therefore, only treat the subject insofar as is necessary in connection with our problem, attention in analysis. And here we must first admit that in one direction the criticism is justified. It would have been more to the point, more advantageous, to treat the question of attention separately, and not to confuse it with that of memory. Still, the association of the two sets of problems may be accounted for by the peculiar nature of the technique of analysis. Freud himself points out that the analyst is usually told things whose significance he cannot recognize until afterward, sometimes long afterward. Perhaps Freud's frequent use of the term "taking note" (*sich merken*) is a peculiarity of Austrian speech. At the same time, it is not mere chance that we speak of attention and the capacity for paying attention. An important psychological association is here revealed. It generally remains at the back of our minds because we are accustomed to connect attention with a mental achievement corresponding to an instantaneous or immediate reaction. For instance, we test the attention of a subject in the laboratory by causing auditory stimuli to act upon him at definite intervals, and telling him to make some movement, give some signal, as soon as he hears them. A teacher tests his pupil's attention by calling upon him suddenly to continue a sentence that another has just begun to translate. It will be objected that these are very primitive examples. No doubt, but it is just such examples that I chiefly want to bring forward. Attention generally enables us to react immediately to an event or impression. This cannot be the kind of attention used in analysis because we often do not recognize the psychological significance of the things that we are told until afterward. Even when we recognize a certain meaning immediately, our reaction is restricted to the acknowledgment of the recognition; we have to wait until new insight leads to its full understanding.

I have already said that attention directed—for instance in a laboratory experiment—to an impression, serves to grasp it clearly, to appraise its significance at once, to master it, so to speak, by understanding as soon as possible. That, of course, presupposes that, simultaneously with the impression or soon afterward, its significance can be recognized. If I go for a walk in a field and something leaps up out of the grass and runs across the path, I recognize it at once: Oh-ho! a hare. If I have good eyesight and there is sufficient light, there can be no doubt. I need not wait until later, perhaps several hours afterward, for the conviction to come over me: That was a hare. My attention was, so to speak, rewarded at once by recognizing the object, and perhaps, if I had had a gun, there might have been a further reward.

There are, of course, other impressions whose recognition requires time and severe effort. Think, for instance, of the psychical process which we call observation. Such observation may be prolonged, our recognition of the significance of a process may not occur for a considerable time. And here we are really approaching the essential character of analytic attention. It is akin to that of an observer, but important differences remain to be considered. An observer generally selects a definite section of a process, and his attention helps him to recognize the meaning of one or the other feature. Undoubtedly the analyst does something of the same kind. He, too, selects a section, for instance, the utterances and expressive gestures of a person, and he wants to know what they mean. But we must reflect that he grasps this section in two different ways. We may say that he reaches two apprehensions: one in which he clearly recognizes what the words and movements of the person observed mean, just what they say; and a second that sets small value upon the conscious meaning in contrast with another, which he does not know and which is still to be discovered.

That is not very clear. Perhaps, then, I may have to resort to an analogy.

Let us suppose we are in a foreign country and that we hear a certain sentence in the native language, of which we already know many words. We come upon an unknown expression, retain the word, and resolve to look it up later in the dictionary. There we find it, and we immediately understand the sentence. Here, too, then, our attention is directed to preparation for subsequent understanding.

Let's vary the example a little. We do find the word in question in the dictionary. When we insert it in the sentence, it gives a definite meaning, but not one that could possibly have been intended by the speaker. The whole situation refutes it; the word must have another meaning not in the dictionary. Perhaps we have a case of an ordinary, everyday expression that is used in a special meaning in those circles, e.g., among students, or perhaps it is an allusion only understood in that particular social sphere. The dictionary has been of no use to us, and we decide to await future illumination, when, for instance, the same expression appears in a new connection. We save up the expression, so to speak, and on some future occasion we mean to guess the hidden secondary meaning. Now many impressions that we receive during analytic observation are of a like nature.

We shall occupy ourselves a little with the most important distinctions drawn by psychology in respect to attention. It is one of the most disputed subjects of research. In fact everything about it is the subject of dispute; whether it is an activity or a state is as hotly debated as its premises and motives, its psychogenesis and its psychopathology. Nay, its very existence is open to question. Not long ago a Copenhagen professor seriously maintained at a psychological congress that it was only a pseudo conception, and spoke of the nonexistence of attention.

We shall not be surprised at the importance attributed to the problem of attention in psychology, if we bear in mind how inseparably it is connected with the phenomena of consciousness and the system of memory, how it accompanies the psychical process from sense-perceptions to ideas. It applies equally to our sensations and emotions, is placed in the service of our will, and runs like a thread through our whole inner life.

Psychology distinguishes voluntary and involuntary attention. The former is derived from selective interest, conscious of an aim, while the latter is sometimes described as a partially mechanized instinctive function. The former is mainly active in character, the latter mainly reactive. We may say that, in general, voluntary attention is directed toward a selected content; involuntary attention, toward an obtruding one. Since the days of Lotze and Wundt it has been a favorite illustration of psychological writers to compare the phenomenon of attention with a searchlight. Rightly so, when we realize that attention marks out a zone of light in the field of experience.

And now let us turn to another distinction, determined by the content. External and internal attention are distinguished by their object, that is, by the question whether we direct our interest to the external or the inner world. Let us revert to the comparison and imagine a searchlight turned upon the walls of a fort. It can be turned either upon the foreground of the fortification or upon the interior, the separate objects belonging to the fort, the courtyards, and storehouses.

It is, of course, possible to unite these two kinds of attention. The justification of associating active or passive attention with the external world is self-evident. The second connection, with the inner world, is much more difficult to grasp. As an example of voluntary attention directed inward, I need only cite self-observation as a psychological action. The second possibility, too, will be made clear to us if we think, for instance, of surprising ourselves in a sudden feeling of sadness under cheerful circumstances, or cheerfulness in a tragic situation.

But after all, what we want is to learn more of the nature of attention in analysis. We are coming to that. We distinguish the result of attention directed inward toward our own psychical processes by the very name that we give it. When, perhaps in trying to solve a problem, we turn our attention inward and try to realize causal and other connections and to understand the phenomena genetically, the outcome is thought. But if we approach the problem differently, if we tackle it indirectly or allow it to act upon us, so to speak, without directly attacking it, if we only pay attention to what arises in our mind on the occasion, then the outcome is that ideas occur to us, or at least that they may occur. We now realize that the analyst's heuristic activities are especially dominated by inward, involuntary attention. There remains room enough for the other kind of attention as well, which is automatically called in when needed.

The quality of the attention in psychoanalysis may be well illustrated by the comparison with a searchlight. Voluntary attention, which is restricted to a narrow sector of our field of experience, may be compared in its effect to the turning of the searchlight upon a particular piece of ground. If we know beforehand that the enemy is coming from that direction, or that something is going to happen upon that field, then we have anticipated the event, as it were. It is advantageous to illuminate that particular sector brightly. Let us assume a different case, that something, for instance a noise, has turned our attention to a particular zone. Only then do we turn the searchlight upon it. Our attention did not rush on in advance of the perception, but followed it. This is the case of involuntary attention. If we drive at night along a road near New York, we may notice that a searchlight in the middle of the road is scouring the surrounding country uninterruptedly. It illuminates the road, is then directed to the fields, turns toward the town, and swings in a wide curve back to the road, and so repeats its circuit. This kind of activity, which is not confined to one point but is constantly scouring a wide radius, provides the best comparison with the function of free-floating attention.

From out of the wealth of psychological problems arising at this point, I will pick out one special question as being of interest to the technique of analysis: that of the relation between the various kinds of attention and surprise. It will be seen at once that the time factor plays a great part in this matter. If I know that the enemy is coming from one particular direction and turn the searchlight in that direction from the outset, I shall be able to determine the precise moment of his appearance and thus be in a position to recognize the nature of the danger and the steps to be taken for defense. He will not succeed in surprising me. The great advantage of voluntary attention, which knows its object from the outset and maintains a particular direction, is especially that it enables us to be mentally prepared. "Readiness is everything," might be its motto. Involuntary attention offers a much feebler protection against the danger of being taken by surprise. If it is an external stimulus, a sudden perception, that first calls my attention to the appearance of the enemy, he has the advantage over me in the matter of time. I have less time to prepare myself. "Poised" attention maintains the mean between the two extremes. I cannot escape the danger of surprise, but only attenuate it.

But voluntary attention, which offers such excellent protection against the dangers of surprise, also deprives us from its advantages. It involves an excellent protection against irritant stimuli; but it may, in a certain sense, almost amount to an exclusion of stimuli. And that brings us to its negative aspect, one which many psychoanalysts have failed to appraise at all adequately. Now attention consists of the fact that certain images present themselves vividly and become effective at the expense of others. The concentration of attention involves a setting up of inhibitions, so that keen observation of particular things corresponds to the ignoring of others. Withdrawal of certain contents from consciousness is no less a part of attention than the appearance of others at the center. It is open to question which part is the more significant to the essence and action of attention, the illumination of particular objects, the bestowal of intensive interest upon them, or its diversion away from others. Some investigators, for instance S. Ferenczi, regard the inhibition of all actions except the one contemplated as the prime feature of the act of attention. If all the paths leading to consciousness are blocked, with the one exception, then psychic energy flows in the one direction that is still free, spontaneously and without the need of any exertion on its part.

Ferenczi explains the process thus: If I want to look attentively at something, I block all my senses except that of sight. Enhanced attentiveness to optical stimuli follows of itself. I would not adopt this view without reservations. But there is much to support it and it leads to original and alluring results. Think, for instance, how in the light of it we must alter our conception of the lack of capacity for concentration in children to the incapacity to exclude certain stimuli. Educationally, too, it is of importance, for training in attention assumes a new aspect. The well-known feelings of tension, which vary in degree and are associated with acts of attention, may instead be due to the effort necessary to achieve and maintain this isolation, to provide the inhibition. The narrowing of consciousness may not be a result of attention, as psychology has hitherto assumed, but its cause. Indeed, the whole controversial question of the nature of attention is placed in a new light, if it is not a matter of an active principle, but of arresting and switching off other contents; if the clarifying and strengthening of one perception is simply due to the obscuring and weakening of others. I will only indicate in passing that training in attention may succeed "too well," so that the child is shut off from a whole flood of freely emerging associations and ideas.

And now what about the contents which fall into the background due to the act of attention? Let us inquire what kind they are, why they are neglected or excluded, or, in other words, what is the determining factor in the process that we understand as attention? We now realize that he who approaches the answer to one, raises new questions. We cannot deal with them here, nor do I think that our knowledge is sufficient to answer them, and I prefer to emphasize what we have undoubtedly gained from our discussion of attention. That is the fact, biologically and psychologically significant, that the function of attention was originally negative and consisted of the exclusion or inhibition of all psychical contents except the one sharply outlined. Voluntary attention, which brings so much into a clear light, causes so much more to sink or lose its clarity. While raising the significance of some things vigorously and definitely, it degrades others to insignificance. To return to our former analogy, the searchlight, which casts a brilliant light upon a small area, plunges the greater part of the field into profound darkness. The proverb, "Where there is much light, there is also much shade," is true of the phenomena of attention, too.

What I like to call the reconnoitering character of "poised" attention does not enable us to discern objects and their connection as sharply and clearly as does voluntary attention. Its aim cannot, therefore, be instantaneous understanding, immediate placing among things known. But that disadvantage is accompanied by a number of advantages that fully counterbalance the renunciation of sharply and narrowly outlined immediate clarity. Perhaps I ought to establish the nature of poised attention theoretically, but I choose to illustrate it by means of an example, the solution of a picture-riddle. We should certainly not despise an illustration of this kind when we remember that Freud compared dreams to such a riddle, and the interpretation of dreams to the intellectual labor of solving them.

The first picture is of a piece of cloth with a rent in it, and a needle and thread mending it. *Rent? Hole? Darn?* Then two *LL*'s. *Rentells? Holells?* Both nonsense. *Darnells? Mendells?* Or should it be: *Mendels,* because the two *LL*'s signify just *l*'s? Let us go on. We next have an arrangement of letters: S, and beneath it GS. GS under S? No, that does not make sense. S. over GS? That is no better. Or S above GS? Also nonsense. S on GS? *Songs*—that is it, of course. Then the first part must surely be *Mendelssohn.* But where is the last syllable of the name? *Mendelssohn? Mendels-sohn?* Why, it is *Mend-els-on-Songs.*

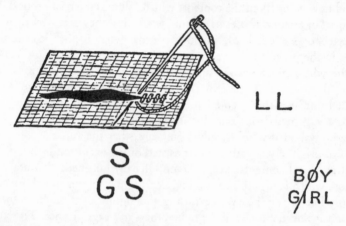

We must not let ourselves be put off by orthography, nor by the exact pronunciation. We must be satisfied with the sound represented under the conditions obtaining in a rebus. To proceed, the crossing out of a letter or syllable often means something negative in these puzzles. *Songs not? Songs deduct? Songs take away?* None of them promising beginnings, followed by *boy girl.* What can these mean? *Songs without?* Then of course it must be: *Songs without Words.* We have it in a flash. On reflection we realize that it is the sense of the riddle. *Boy girl* means nothing. They are simply words, two words crossed out, which means: without words. The solution: *Mendelssohn Songs without Words.*

After all, the solution of a riddle like this can teach us something of the nature of poised attention. Let us recall the minor difficulties that we had with the initial word, and overcame. We were checked by picturing the exact spelling of the word to ourselves. Our attention was not exactly imprisoned, and yet it was a little hedged in, by an ortho-graphically determined image of a word. Every dream-interpretation displays the same phenomenon, and every psychoanalyst can report cases of this kind in which his understanding of the hidden meaning of the dream was delayed by precisely this difficulty. I am in the fortu-nate situation where I can cite three instances that represent three lan-guages.

A patient dreamed of a dress she had seen. In the dream she was in doubt as to whether she should buy the dress. What is more appropriate than that she should consider the waistline in a subsequent part of the dream? The meaning of the dream escaped us, however, until we paid no attention to the spelling and then it occurred to us that the *waistline* really meant *the line of waste,* namely, whether it would not be a waste to take a certain line of action in the situation of the patient.

A man had a long and complicated dream in which he went to the Sorbonne and walked about its rooms. His thought-associations led back to the time when he really visited the University of Paris. Who would think of a connection between *Sorbonne* and *Soeur bonne?*

I can give another example directly, not taken from the dream world but from daylight, waking life, in which orthography played a certain part that I failed to recognize. It struck me that, during the early months of his analysis, a certain Viennese patient stopped short at cer-tain points in his account of his experiences, as if there were an un-known obstacle just at these places. I could not account for it and thought he was concealing some part of his experience. It was the more striking because his statement was altogether honest and serious. Nor did I find any sign in the subject matter of his stories that could lead me to surmise the nature of the block. For instance, he told me of a little quarrel that he had had with his sweetheart the day before, and ended with the passionate words, "I hate her." I did not surmise that the thought that checked him, and which he himself afterwards ex-plained, was that the sentence could be applied to me, the analyst, by a change in the way of writing a single initial letter. The German for both "her" and "you" is *"sie,"* but in the latter case it is written with a capital *S.* (The German *"Ich hasse sie"* and *"Ich hasse Sie"* thus differ only in the writing of the pronoun.) Even at a later stage the double meaning of the word, caused by similarity of sound, acted as a check on the patient's talk, and he often had to wage his "war on the capital *S,*" as he prettily called it.

But let us return to our rebus. We have speedily cast off the slight burden of orthographical and phonetic differences, and read "Mendelssohn" as if the strict rules of spelling and pronunciation did not concern us at all. No less lightly, or light-heartedly, we have dealt with "songs." We have jumped the small hurdles with assurance and speed, and, cheered by our freedom from rules and obligations, we have got as far as "Mendelssohn, Songs . . ." We observe that we do not really owe this easy advance—we came, we saw, we conquered—so much to our ordinary attention as to its relaxation. If we had obeyed the usual laws of attention, if we had not ignored the customary ideas of purpose, we should still be at "Mend," and might have gone on to "stockings" or other fancies. In short, we should have been caught in a tangle of mending wool. But let us suppose that we had disentangled ourselves and turned our voluntary attention to the next step, we should never have found the last syllable of the name "Mendelssohn." If we employ the purposive, active kind of attention that is so necessary, so indispensable in life, the situation would soon have become hopeless. We owe our advance precisely to our escape from the strict demands of attention, which holds all other associations at bay and follows the one train of thought unswervingly.

Our psychical action when we guessed the last element of the riddle —"words"—was of a different nature. When we remember how we beat our brains over that mysterious sign, and how we came to solve it, and then compare the process with that which preceded it, we shall be driven to note a marked difference between the two. At first we wanted to proceed according to the familiar method of solving picture-riddles, and simply guess the word concealed behind the sign. Did it mean boy and girl, boy over girl, girl under boy, or what? It all produced no sense and yet the correct, logical solution was close at hand. Concentrated attention was no help. We have here one of the cases in which strained attention, conscious, purposive effort, can at best lead us to the conclusion that we are on the wrong track.

Attention, which is intended to facilitate intellectual achievement, or, indeed, to make it in any way possible, has misled us. In those cases in which, in spite of our utmost and most strenuous endeavors and the bracing of our attention, we do not succeed in recalling something, in reproducing a forgotten content, we know that there is a tried remedy: we drop the idea of purpose and stop turning our attention in that particular direction or on that particular set of circumstances.

And what happens? The withdrawal of attention does not give rise to inattention, but to a shifting of attention, to a readiness to receive a variety of stimuli emerging from the unconscious or the unknown. As in the case cited above, a rigid, one-sided attention has detracted from our mental achievement and injured our success because it prevented us from moving in any other direction. We gazed as if spellbound upon the words "boy girl," which we read as if they absolutely had to be a part of what we were seeking. Not until we freed ourselves from this fixation of attention, not until we allowed our attention to turn in other directions, did the solution occur to us.

We often hear patients complain that they fail to concentrate their attention. In analytic investigation we find that this complaint conceals a totally different situation. The attention of these patients is concentrated, though, upon an unconscious content, for instance, certain fantasies. They fail to detach attention from particular psychical contents and direct it to others, which is what life demands of them. We often hear that a patient cannot concentrate his attention, without thinking that it is already concentrated upon a subject, unknown or unconscious to him.

When we beat our brains so long over the last part of the picture-puzzle, we were behaving like people who find it difficult to escape from concentrating on one point and to keep their attention free-floating and unattached. In a sense we were unable to throw off the chain of our concentration and circled, like dancing mice, round the words "boy girl." Analytic practice brings daily proof of what a hindrance any rigid concentration on a particular idea can be to the heuristic task. It is only when we replace it with poised attention that it becomes possible to capture unconscious processes.

In the early days of my work as an analyst, when I was faced with surprising symptoms, puzzling dreams, and incomprehensible trains of thought, just the same thing happened as when we were seeking the last part of the solution of the picture-riddle. Not until I cast off the customary restraint of voluntary attention was I able to get hold of the hidden psychical data. Not until I had left the firm and broad high road did I reach the goal along side paths. The secret meaning escaped my conscious, active attention, and was not found until I had become "inattentive" in the popular meaning of the word, that is, until I gave myself up to unconscious ideas of the goal.

Now of course it would be nonsense to declare that analysts work with poised attention only. The statement would be false if only because at certain points poised attention must be changed to voluntary or active, when the significance of a symptom or a latent relation has been recognized and it has now to be placed and evaluated. Let us return to our comparison with the searchlight. The searchlight that scours the whole foreground equally will, of course, stop at one point if the enemy is sighted there. It must be noted that what we have here is the replacement of one form of attention by another. On such occasions, the original, free-floating attention gives way to the voluntary, direct form.

Another form of substitution is more important. On special occasions attention is definitely withdrawn from the object before it and turns with a jerk, so to speak, to other, seemingly more remote, relations. A special significance attaches to this withdrawal of attention from the immediate aspects of the data. Our thought goes off and reaches a goal by an unusual path that it could have attained by no other. Thus the psychical process of conjecturing the secret meaning of an obsession or part of a dream or mental reaction is often like that of solving the last part of our picture-riddle, "boy girl." The essential thing about it is the withdrawal of attention from what is immediately before it, or at least its slackening, and the fact that in this way the emergence of sudden ideas is facilitated. It is possible to attain an understanding of many unconscious processes only after this temporary switching off of direct attention has prepared the way psychologically. The contents that previously had occupied a central position and were then thrust into the background by the shifting of attention will acquire a new and often undreamed-of significance later.

While we adopted an attitude of poised attention most of the time in solving the picture-riddle, when it came to the solution of the last word our interest was withdrawn from the object for the fraction of a second, and poised attention was interrupted for a moment by "inattention." It is as if a swimmer were suddenly to break off his regular motion through the water in order to plunge into the depths. We can observe two types of distribution of mental energy in analysis, too, and introspection may easily distinguish them. Moreover, the momentary plunge into unconscious depths, hitherto undreamed-of, is akin to the mental phenomenon of the birth of wit. Indeed, the result is sometimes similar: in our rebus the solution had something of the quality of wit. The psychical effect of discovering this last word of the riddle is different from that of solving the others. It partakes of the character of surprise.

Earlier in this chapter, I made a paradoxical statement and I owe it to my conscience to revert to it. I said that attention of that special voluntary kind prevented surprise. People who practice it always find confirmation of what they already know. Attention as a hindrance to the progress of scientific knowledge—assuredly that is a bold assertion. Still, it is not its boldness but its falsity that I dislike. But I have spoken in this derogatory manner, not of attention as such, but of its special active and voluntary form if applied to unconscious data. This latter often leads to a fixation of our minds, which may be called autohypnotic, on the immediate object or on the one relation that happens to be in the forefront of our thoughts. Under certain circumstances this kind of attention may prepare our minds for the reception of knowledge. Its main effect is that of clearing a particular path, disposing of particular possibilities, which must then make way for the consideration of others.

Furthermore, I should disagree if anyone were to say that Isaac Newton's straining of attention when he was struggling with the problem of gravitation was useless or superfluous, because the law did not come to him until he withdrew his attention and saw the apple fall from the tree in the garden. His laborious and consciously directed thought constituted, we may say, an important psychological prerequisite for the idea that occurred to him unforced. In a sense it gave sanction to it inwardly, and had economic and dynamic value. Every serious research-worker knows that voluntary attention in the form of intellectual labor often stimulates ideas, just as unforced ideas sometimes give birth to thoughts. It is true that we cannot produce valuable unforced ideas by an effort of thought, but thought is often their preliminary condition. Tschaikovsky once called inspiration a guest who does not care to visit lazy people. That is equally true of scientific and artistic labor and of attention in association with productive work. If, in the searching labors of analysis, psychical energy must be differently distributed, that is due to special qualities of the region to be investigated and the data to be examined, the most important parts of which seldom reveal themselves to reflection, but usually in an unforced idea. It is the condition that helps the oppressed minorities in the kingdom of the mind to win their rights.

I have said that active attention generally precludes surprise, while poised attention attenuates it as a rule. But this process of momentary slackening of attention and diversion of interest in another direction, with subsequent return to the object, is a preparation for surprise. We shall recur to the question of how this preparation is connected with the effect of surprise; for the present this allusion to the fact may suffice. We had wanted to solve the last part of the picture-riddle separately and in isolation, like the others, without troubling about what had gone before.

We failed. The solution did not emerge in our mind until we had abandoned the effort and remembered the previous part of the riddle, which we had already solved. The way to the solution was paved by the words "Mendelssohn Songs." We then saw two words, but they were crossed out. Of course, the solution was *Songs without Words*. Really it ought to have occurred to us at once, we see now, wondering at ourselves.

In not quite the same way, and yet similarly, the surprise is prepared in analysis, and as it dies away we ask ourselves incidentally how it came about. Tracing our mental process backward, it seems to us that we had really no justification for surprise if we had consciously noticed small signs, which we now remember, or if a symptom that now occurs to us had been noted consciously when it first appeared or was repeated in some obscure place. Then a psychical implication, which we now remember, strikes us as a clear indication of what we took so long to recognize. A symptom, the fragment of a dream, a long-forgotten fact suddenly appear in a new light; widely scattered data arrange themselves in a new relation. Retrospective reflection shows that unconsciously we had understood the meaning of the separate facts very well, and that this unconscious comprehension was, so to speak, a necessary preparation for the present surprise. Things that were not in the center of our attention, things that were at the fringe, a passing impression, a fleeting presentiment, now take on importance.

We now discern the great importance of the time factor in appraising the different kinds of attention. Poised attention generally involves the renunciation of the immediate recognition of links of association. It apprehends the several details of the psychical data equally and prepares the way for us to work our way among them later. Free-floating attention provides, so to speak, a storeroom of impressions, from which later knowledge will suddenly emerge. It also creates the prerequisite conditions for those surprising results that appear in analysis as the product of a prolonged unconscious condensation and dissociation of impressions.

We rarely realize that there is a pre-knowledge within us while we wait for illumination. A case gets more impenetrable and everything looks dark and overcast; yet everything is preparing for the coming flash of insight. There are no bolts from the blue in psychoanalysis. Sudden clarity is preceded by increasing darkness. To speak with Nietzsche: "That which will kindle the lightning must for a long time be a cloud."

CHAPTER XVII

Who Am I?

AT PRESENT New York has a favorite parlor game called "Who am I?" A name, let us say Cleopatra or Einstein or Mary of Scotland, is written on a scrap of paper and pinned on the back of a person who is not told what this name is. He must find out who he is by asking questions of the rest of the party. In most cases twenty questions are allowed and they must be answered truthfully. He asks, "Am I dead or alive?" (concerning, of course, the person who is represented) or "Am I real or fictitious?" (that is, whether the unknown person appeared in real life or belongs to the realm of novels, plays, poems, and so forth). The game is, of course, to put two and two together and guess the identity of the unknown personality.

Every psychoanalysis that is not superficial leads to the question, "Who am I?" in terms of psychological reality. The frontiers of the personality reach farther than we think. Moreover, what we hate and what we love, what propels us and what hinders us, all constitute a part of us. "The soul is a wide country," says Schnitzler. It has room for so much; opposite tendencies can coexist in us, feelings contradicting each other live together, and what is true and what false can be confused. A man said to his mistress who had been trying to convince him that she had spent the last few days with her girl friend, "Please stop lying; I already believe you." Did he believe or disbelieve? So much lives in us— wishes and their denials, faith and mistrust, appetites and distastes. They change places so frequently that what is fair becomes foul and what is foul, fair. Psychoanalysis has demonstrated that the ego has built up an ego-ideal, a picture of oneself, an image of oneself as one wishes to be.

Analysts have neglected taking the opportunity to find the counter-picture: the ego-horror, a picture of oneself at which we shudder, the picture of an ego-possibility that frightens us and that we reject. Ego-ideal and ego-horror are sharply contrasted with each other. They present, so to speak, the opposite ends of our psychical potentialities. But our patients, like ourselves, occasionally love what they detest and detest what they love. Not only are the realities of the personality contrasted with its potentialities, but they are also sometimes fused with each other—a possibility that is only imaginable if one accepts the fact that the unconscious does not know the word or the concept "no." The frontiers of the personality reach farther in both directions: into what is commonly called good and into what is commonly called evil. A man's unconscious self also contains possibilities of his life that were lived only in imagination, potentialities of his destiny that never became real. Sometimes it seems as if a shadow has fallen on the ego and changed it. There are mysterious repetitions in the choice of similar objects of love, puzzling resemblances in failure and success, friendships broken up under the same circumstances, affairs that take the same development along with seemingly quite unexpected interludes that show the reverse side. There are self-deceptions about one's own personality and role, interrupted by sudden insights. There are necessary "life-lies" that go hand in hand with a clear understanding of the truth; tendernesses that are only the cover for cruel actions; and cruel actions that hide affectionate feelings. Dr. Jekyll is shocked because he is really Mr. Hyde, but Mr. Hyde is also astonished when he discovers that he is Dr. Jekyll. We are still living with the preconceived idea of the unity of the human soul, and man appears to us to be made of a single material, like a statue. We say a person is good or evil. In reality he is good and evil, better and worse than he thinks.

Here are problems that until the present were not even considered as such, but only as turns and plays and byplays of individual character and destiny. Such problems are not to be handled by men who know almost everything about psychiatry and almost nothing about people. These problems are not to be touched with iron fists but with the tips of the fingers. It is true that it is convenient to differentiate "complexes" and to have differential diagnoses and to attribute this psychological phenomenon to hysteria, another to an impulse neurosis, and a third to a compulsion neurosis; to call one attitude masochistic and another sadistic. But all these terms are rough-and-ready characterizations that have only a very general meaning and value. They do not convey the special note of a particular case and fail to do justice to the nuances and shades of the phenomenon. As you listen to analysts and psychiatrists discussing their cases in these terms, you often get the impression of an observer who sees little boys proudly showing each other marbles of different colors. It is a harmless pleasure.

None of these ready-made classifications gives a real insight into the individuality of a case. They do not solve its riddle; they only put it into a pigeonhole. They get rid of its finer psychological and personal traits by slipping it into the wide-open mouth of analytic terminology. The mouth can swallow it, but the case remains undigested. The description and discussion of psychical processes that we read and hear often give a rubber stamp instead of a characterization. This may remove the chaos that is the natural atmosphere of unconscious processes, but it does not put clarity in its place, merely categories, terms, and labels. It does not give us an insight into the complexities of a man or woman. It lets us look only into his or her "complexes." That may be very attractive to the formalizing minds of psychiatrists, but our interest, that of true psychologists, begins just where theirs ends—beyond complexes and diagnoses, with the individual traits of a person, with the characteristic psychological features of this Mr. Smith or that Mrs. Brown. The general classification is convenient and informative. It is no more than that. What we desire is a deep understanding of the person, of his conflicts and inner contradictions and destiny, not the pattern into which they can be fitted.

What is needed at present is not an enlargement of our knowledge of classifications and complexes, but a sharpening and refining of our psychological capabilities, a better understanding of the individual case, a more acute observation of one's own responses to the data given us in psychoanalysis.

Let me give a few instances of what I mean. A patient received a gold cigarette case as a birthday gift from his father. He reported the gift to me and described it. He said that the gift was much too expensive to carry and added: "It contradicts my trend to simplicity."

If we follow the prescriptions of most psychoanalysts we would at this moment turn our attention to the relationship of this young man to his father. We would note his reluctance to accept anything from his father, and we would arrive, of course, at the Oedipus complex. It seems to me that this way leads into a blind alley. What occurred to me as I listened to him say "It contradicts my trend to simplicity." It resounded but it sounded false to me; it was as if a pianist had touched a wrong key. Would you, in casual, everyday conversation, say, "It contradicts my trend to simplicity"? It sounds stilted. Such a manner of self-expression is always revealing. In this case it revealed a hypocritical attitude of the patient, who liked to think of himself as very unpretentious and undemanding, full of pity for the underprivileged.

Another instance: A patient told me that she had eaten too much the previous day at a dinner to which she had been invited and had thus sinned against her vow to lose weight. Later on, so she told me, she had blamed herself severely for her misdeed, had called herself a "spoiled brat" and "without self-control and self-discipline." She expressed the view that she often committed these offenses in order to blame and punish herself, and she considered them as masochistic devices. It cannot be denied that there was much truth in what she said about herself, but why did she say it? Listening to her, I had the distinct impression that there was something false in her self-abasement, that it was, to use the slang expression, "phony." She wanted to cover the psychological fact that she got a great deal of morbid satisfaction of vanity from her self-reproaches. At this point analytic insight achieves a result which Nietzsche anticipated in his assertion that he who looks at himself with contempt also appreciates himself as a self-contemptor.

What I want to point out here is that in such situations the analyst is faced with the question, "Who are you?" rather than with the problem of what is the special meaning of a symptom. He will try to find the depths of the personality, which are as hidden as the roots of a tree. The nature and the extent of these roots will determine the growth of the tree and what its trunk, its branches, and its flowers will be like. The roots cover more space than the branches and spread themselves wider than the crown. When we have recognized what these roots are, we shall not have many difficulties in following the growth of the tree.

When analysis has penetrated deep enough, many problems that present themselves later on will be solved more easily by the knowledge now obtained. The analytic understanding of many symptoms and behavior patterns of the patient has resulted in a sufficiently clear picture of his personality, and this picture now unconsciously before my mind will help me later on to understand new symptoms and expressions true to his character.

Let us take a fragment from the psychoanalysis of the young man who did not like the cigarette case he received from his father. What follows here took place a few weeks after the beginning of his analysis. The young man had given me his autobiography and had told me about his complaints, among which his social shyness and loneliness troubled him most. Besides various neurotic symptoms, an unhappy love affair, which had ended a few months ago, made him restless and miserable. He had fallen in love with a young married woman whose husband was overseas at the time. (This was during the war and the husband came home on short leaves from time to time.) Mary, the married woman, had given herself without much hesitation to the patient, whose happiness was restrained only by fear of the husband. The young woman broke off the affair after she discovered that she was pregnant. She remained friendly toward her previous lover, who implored her, in vain, to continue their relationship. He finally left the city where they both lived. In New York he was not only tortured by longing for his previous sweetheart, but also by the thought that the child she expected was perhaps his. He could not say why he had this doubt, nor could he deny that husband and wife had had sexual relations at just the critical moment. Mary herself had certainly never suggested that the patient might be the father of her child. Her withdrawal and her decision to end the relationship and remain faithful to her husband in the future seem to me a rather good sign that not the patient but the husband was the father. After the break with Mary and before leaving Chicago, the patient had a short affair with another married woman, Margot, whose husband was also away in the war.[1] He knew that he was not the only man who helped to console Margot. The episode was, however, short and casual and in no way did it diminish his grief over Mary.

A few days after the patient had reported this part of his life story, he started his analytic session in an unusual manner. Instead of lying down as usual, he sat on a chair and began: "I need to talk to you as man to man." He then told me that he had to interrupt his analysis for some time because he had to fly to Chicago. Friends of his in that city had written to him that Margot was pregnant and in despair. It was his duty to look after her because it was most likely, yes, almost certain that the child was his. When he told me about this emergency he was very anxious, emphasized his moral obligations toward Margot and the child and gave a vivid picture of Margot's terrible situation with all possible

[1] All names of persons and cities are, of course, changed in this report for purposes of discretion.

consequences for the young woman. He then lay down on the couch and gave himself to free association.

This instance is perhaps as appropriate as any other to demonstrate the special analytic way of looking at emotional phenomena, of seeing traits in them that cannot be found in textbooks, of hearing in the words things they do not say to others, which are audible only to the third ear. I do not doubt that most analysts in this situation would have wondered about the resemblance of the two situations that emerged for the young man within such a short time. They would think that here is one of those cases in which a mysterious "compulsion of repetition" seems to operate. Such a term comes readily to the analyst but it is not very helpful as long as one remains content with it. May I use a comparison? It is as if you wanted to open a trunk to find what is in it and someone gives you a label on which the destination is marked instead of a key. The resemblance between the situations occurred to me, too, of course, even the term "compulsion of repetition" emerged. But that was much later and it was not a clue.

As has often been said here before, the attention of the analyst oscillates between the patient and himself, between observation of the expressions of the object and of the voices within himself. In this process of switching from the one to the other station, all voices are not equally audible, but I am trying to present as precisely as possible what I caught of the inner perception as I looked at, and listened to, the excited patient. While I observed that his voice sounded higher than usual, I became aware that he was looking sharply at me. I heard what he said: He had to fly to Chicago this very evening. Something deflected my attention, something in his behavior. There was a kind of fogginess in my thoughts, a muddle and a medley of contradictory impressions out of which the following thought-words (or word-pictures) emerged: "Confessions . . . the cover of a book . . . Rousseau . . . Jean Jacques Rousseau. . . ."

I did not yet know what these thoughts meant when the patient lay down on the couch and began to speak again. I listened and I heard him say, "When I looked at you just now, I saw an expression of mock sympathy on your face." I had felt neither sympathy nor mockery when I listened to his tale. My attention was turned to the observation of his way of speaking and, of course, to the report itself. But now I suddenly understood (as if reminded by the remark about my face) what I had thought half a minute ago and why the words "confessions" and "Jean Jacques Rousseau" had occurred to me. As I observed the patient I must have thought that there was something false or theatrical in his story, in what he had said about his worry, about the destiny of Margot and her child as well as about his responsibility. It did not sound genuine. It was as if he were acting a part. Was it something in his choice of words that sounded so false or was it the whole tale? Of course, it was both. His diction made me suspect the sincerity of the feelings he expressed.

The words "confessions" and "Jean Jacques Rousseau" concerned, of course, the story itself. Rousseau tells in his *Confessions* that he had five illegitimate children by his mistress and confesses that he placed these children in a foundling home. The biographers of the great writer doubted the truth of this self-accusing tale, suspecting that its purpose was to conceal the fact that Rousseau could not beget children, that his spermatozoa were incapable of living.[2] It seemed, then, that I did not believe that my patient was the father of Margot's child as I did not believe that he had produced Mary's child before. I was reacting to the repetition of the same situation with mistrust and disbelief. I must have shown these unexpressed feelings even in my silence and the patient must have interpreted their nature in looking at me; otherwise it would be unexplainable that he saw an "expression of mock sympathy" on my face. I doubt that my face had such an expression, but, of course, I cannot be certain of it. There is the other possibility, namely, that he himself in telling his story became conscious that it did not sound genuine, that he projected this feeling onto me, and thus unconsciously anticipated my reaction to it. What he then imagined he read in my face would be the expression of mocking sympathy that he had expected.

Be that as it may, it seems I was suspicious that my patient was really not worried about his being the father of an illegitimate child, nor about the child's mother who is married to another man, but about something else, something that reminded me unconsciously of Jean Jacques Rousseau. With Mary as well as with Margot it was a false alarm, but the apprehension that was felt, this intense worry and fear, could cover the doubt that he could ever produce a child. Now, only now, after I had

[2]It is not essential here that more recent biographers, for instance Matthew Josephson, *Jean-Jacques Rousseau* (1931), are inclined to give credence to Rousseau's confession. My thoughts were determined at this point by books I had read many years ago.

thought of Rousseau and his tale of his five imaginary children,[3] I remembered what the patient had told me at the beginning of his analysis: his testicles had remained undescended until shortly before puberty. He had frequently been taken to a physician, and the fact that his scrotum was underdeveloped must have made him doubt that he was "a real man," as he expressed himself later on. His present worries about being the father of an illegitimate child were pushed into the foreground in order to hide from himself and others his doubts about his potency.

What interest us here are two things: the psychical situation in the patient and what went on in the psychoanalyst, who guessed what was taking place behind the stage of conscious feeling and thinking. It became clear that the young man played hide-and-seek, so to speak, not only with me but also with himself. The little scene that he enacted in the analytic session was not the only presentation of his private theater. Before his visit to me, he had confided in a casual acquaintance that he had become the father of an illegitimate child—a bit of conduct that contrasted conspicuously with his usual reticence. After the analytic session, he went to a young couple, friends of his, to whom he gave a vivid description of his situation and whom he asked for advice and help. He asked them to find out about an abortionist for Margot, who expected a child by him.[4]

The response of the analyst to the story was certainly not in the nature of conscious mistrust in its verity. I was, of course, astonished by the resemblance between the present situation and the one about which he had told me before; but there was no suspicion of an act played before my eyes. There was, however, a reluctance as if I had felt something false or theatrical in his sentences. Then the word "confessions," the memory of the book with its cover, and the name of its author came to conscious mind. Let me emphasize here that the thought about the unconscious sexual inferiority-feelings of the patient emerged much later, only after I had understood what my own associations had meant, what they wanted to say. My emotional response reacted here as

[3] As mentioned before, it is immaterial for this psychological reconstruction whether Rousseau told the truth in his story or not; what matters is that I had the impression that his tale was untrue.

[4] Let me add that the patient really flew to Chicago the next morning to make certain what the real situation was. The father of Margot's child was neither himself nor her husband, but another lover, as she had told a girl friend.

in most cases much more precisely than my conscious thought-process, and it was cleverer than my intelligence. (It is necessary to repeat here the recommendation to pay attention to one's own inner voices, which are now so readily drowned out by "reason" and "knowledge." Such repetition becomes necessary when one realizes that it is much easier to make a new idea enter the head of the Statue of Liberty than the minds of many psychoanalysts.)

I am of the opinion that the impression of the "phony" nature of my patient's worries would not have emerged if it had not been prepared by previous impressions, which were received and perceived during the preceding weeks of analysis and which had to a great extent become unconscious. As one representative instance of such impressions I refer to the sentence previously quoted, in which he asserted that carrying the gold cigarette case "contradicts my trend to simplicity." The way he told me about Margot's expected child, yes, even his introduction, "I need to talk to you as man to man" sounded equally stilted. I realize only now that there was another link that tied my patient to Jean Jacques Rousseau; some of the opinions my patient expressed—especially those about the state of society—his emphasis on simplicity, his sentimentality as well as a certain juvenile attitude toward the world, had reminded me unconsciously of Rousseau, just as his theatrical self-accusation had.[5]

At this point I yield to the next association. It is connected with the word "theatrical" only superficially. The next thought that occurs to me is the dream of another patient, which concerns the theater. It is certainly not this surface association alone that determines the succession of this instance to the previous one. There are, perhaps, other connecting links to be seen later on, but here is the dream:

I am walking on the street and I meet Joe and Lillian. They tell me that Lillian got that part in the play and will be understudy in another play. My first reaction is anger. Why didn't Alice get the part? I cordially congratulate Lillian, but I feel like a hypocrite. I am curious about how Alice will take the news that her sister got the part. Alice comes into the room and I tell her the news. To my great astonishment she is greatly pleased.

I am not concerned here with the details of the interpretation of this

[5] It cannot and should not be denied that I have no great sympathy for the Genevese writer in spite of my admiration for his style. It occurs to me now that my patient had an attitude toward Mary similar to Rousseau's toward his mistress, Madame de Warens, whom he treated like a mother and even called "mama."

dream, but with the way I arrived at an essential part of the dream-interpretation and at its impression, which became important for the character image of this patient. It will be sufficient to give a little information about the dreamer and his relationships to the persons here mentioned.

Lillian and Alice are sisters, both actresses. Lillian is married to Joe, and Alice, who is single, lives with the young couple. The dreamer is Alice's lover. He is very interested in her theatrical career, praises her talent, and helps her, whenever he can, to get parts. There are some data that must be mentioned as day-remnants: Alice tried to get a certain part in a new comedy and had an audition for it the day before the dream. The patient had met the stage manager, who told him: "Alice gave a good reading, but she is perhaps not the right person for the part."

The dream starts, it seems, from this situation: not Alice, but her sister, got the part. The dreamer is angry because Alice did not get the part. He is curious about how she will take the news and relieved when he finds she is pleased. The hidden wish-fulfillment in this dream cannot be guessed from its manifest content, but from insight into the secret emotions of the dreamer. Although he is consciously very eager to see Alice succeed as an actress and although he would be sincerely grieved if she really did not get the part, such a frustration would satisfy another part of his personality. He is very jealous and he foresees that his charming sweetheart would be the subject of much admiration and wooing from many men were she to get the part. Yes, he even foresees that some stage manager or actor might make a pass at her, a possibility which he does not like a bit.

The dream starts, then, with the feared and unconsciously hoped-for situation, that the decision would be negative for Alice. Not she, but her sister, would get the role. The last part of the dream brings the removal of another worry, namely, that Alice would be depressed by her failure. She even appears highly pleased because her sister succeeded. One is entitled to call such a dream hypocritical because the dreamer expresses emotions that he does not feel, but only pretends to feel. The factor of hypocrisy even appears openly in the manifest dream-content. (*I cordially congratulate Lillian, but I feel like a hypocrite.*) However, it is displaced to another element of the dream. The distortion, never missing in the dreams of adult persons, concerns the nature of the feelings that are displayed. In reality the dreamer would be very pleased if Lillian, and not Alice got the part because his sweetheart would then not be exposed to the passes of other men. Although he does not admit it to himself, he does not like to see Alice so ambitious and so keen about her profession as an actress. He would prefer that she give up this dangerous career, although he pretends even to himself to be very enthusiastic about her successes and sad when she is disappointed.

The decisive impression I had as I listened to the report of the dream and of the events that contributed to its production could be put as follows: He would be very glad if Alice did not get the part—clearly in contrast to the manifest content of the dream, in which he is angry that not Alice but Lillian got the part in the play. This impression was strong and remained while the patient was saying that he would be very disappointed if the stage manager did not choose Alice for the part. How did I get this impression? I cannot account for it now; there was nothing in his voice or gestures to suggest such a suspicion, nor was there anything in the preceding hours that pointed in this direction. I can assert that until then, at least in so far as my conscious thinking went, I had assumed that he wished Alice would become a great actress —in conformity with her own wishes, of course. In the manifest content of the dream and in the associations he made, there was nothing that could be interpreted otherwise. Where did this new impression come from? I do not know, but I guess it was the echo of a short sentence which introduced the report of the dream. He had said, "I had a dream last night . . . that was funny."

The remark concerned, of course, the remembered content of the dream in which Lillian, not Alice, gets the desired part. Something in the remark worked upon me as a kind of warning signal. When I now attempt to translate this feeling into the language of conscious thinking, it amounts to the thought: he, the dreamer, makes fun of something or someone in the dream. Many hours after the dream-interpretation I remembered, of course, what we had learned from Freud more than thirty years ago. It is the fact that remarks that are made about a dream or its content apart from the report of the dream itself are in reality parts of the dream, belong to it as one of its elements.

Here is another instance from my practice:

A man dreamed that he took a girl on an excursion; in the evening they lay down together in a meadow and he attempted to make love to the girl who was resisting. He tried to undress her. At this point in his account of the dream, he added: *"There is something missing here.*

There is a hole in the dream." The remark concerns, of course, not the dream-content; it is itself a part of it. It describes the impression that the sight of the female genitalia makes upon the young man who is in a transition phase from homosexuality to heterosexuality. In the same manner the remark, *"I had a dream . . . that was funny,"* means that some fun is made in the dream, not that the dream makes a funny impression.

Where is the fun? Where is the mockery? For the outsider no such fun is to be discovered, but a psychological observer who knows the patient will sense it immediately and understand it soon after. To recognize its nature one has to know two facts: Lillian, the younger sister, is (in the opinion of the dreamer and of competent people) not a good actress (in contrast to Alice). Alice is very jealous of Lillian; there is a concealed rivalry between the sisters. The dreamer has the character of the obsession neurotic and is inclined to make sarcastic observations and remarks and amuses himself sometimes with strange possibilities in an ironical or mocking way. Before falling asleep he had thought of Alice with affectionate feeling. Also the remark of the stage manager that Alice is perhaps not the right person for the part must have occurred to him. If the dream now shows that Lillian, whom the dreamer considers a bad actress, gets the part, it says: That is ridiculous, fantastic, impossible. But it is also ridiculous, fantastic, or impossible that Alice would be very pleased if Lillian and not she got the part. The dream thus starts from the thought: I wish that Alice would not get the part because I am jealous and would be very much annoyed by the attentions men would pay her. Someone else should get the part, any other person, even Lillian. This possibility is now presented in the dream as realized: Lillian got the part and he, the dreamer, congratulates her. During the dream comes the expression of the sarcastic, the opposite, tendency; that it is quite unimaginable that Lillian, who is such a bad actress, should play the role. This thought is not expressed directly but by connecting one impossibility or absurdity with another, namely, that Alice would be delighted by the news of her sister as a star. In other words, if it is possible that Lillian can get the part, then it can even be imagined that Alice would be very much pleased by Lillian's success. Both cases are beyond human imagination. It cannot be denied that intense negative or hostile feelings against Alice break through here in the form of biting sarcasm. In the dream the patient makes fun of both sisters who consciously live together very harmoniously. His dream says: Lillian is a miserable actress and Alice is a jealous person who would allow no success even to her sister. Beside these features the wish that Alice should not get the part is still recognizable as the original cause of the dream. The mockery belongs, so to speak, to a different geological stratum, another psychical layer. The original thought or wish appears here, too, but distorted by hidden sarcasm.

It is not the dream itself in its interpreted, deciphered meaning, but the thoughts out of which the dream is born, the emotional raw materials and the way the dreamer used them, the special twist and turn he gives them, that are significant and present precious clues to the analyst about the character of the dreamer.

In the few instances I could describe here, only a very small fragment of the contrast between potentialities and realities appears clear. It is strange how far our self-deception goes. When I think of my patients at the moment, I realize that they all fool themselves about themselves. (I do not doubt that I am nursing some illusions about myself too.) There is, for instance, a man who is convinced that his boss hates him and looks down upon him. The shoe is on the other foot. Unconsciously the patient hates his boss although he believes that he has pure benevolence and good will toward his superior. There is a girl who asserts that most men are inferior human beings—"Are men people?" she asks— but unconsciously she is afraid that she is unattractive and men will not pay attention to her. There is a middle-aged man who thinks analysis will enable him to carry through the plans of his early youth, ambitions and erotic daydreams whose realization he himself has unconsciously sabotaged for too many years. But analysis does not work miracles. He went out once to build a palace for himself and dreamed his life away. We shall be very pleased if enough energy can be recovered and enough material is left to build a modest cottage in place of the proud palace of his dreams.

I could go on reviewing my cases and show that it is not easy to follow the advice, "To thine own self be true," when this self has itself become uncertain. Many neurotic patients could ask, "Which self?" The analyst who sees the realities and potentialities of a personality can help to find the answer to this question. He functions here as a representative of the social world around his patient, only with better psychological insight and in the spirit of kindliness. Sometimes the people around us, our family and our friends and even our enemies, guess things about our personality of which we are entirely unaware. If we listen to the opinions of those about us, we shall not hear the whole truth, but we shall hear some of it. If memory does not fail me, a Hungarian proverb advises: "When a man says you are a horse, laugh at him; when two men assert it, give it a thought; and when three men say you are a horse, you had better go and buy a saddle for yourself."

CHAPTER XVIII

Insight

P SYCHOANALYSIS, like imagination, cannot be learned by rote. The most important things in the whole technique must be lived. Can we, for instance, "teach" an eager student the insights that come to an analyst? No doubt they form only a part of the train of thought that leads to recognition of an unconscious process and its hidden meaning, but nevertheless they mark the most pregnant moment during analysis. This is the moment when an idea emerges from the unconscious or, in the language of analysis, passes from the primary to the secondary psychical process.

I propose to call this moment the "point of departure." I am tempted to yield to the slightly comical love of the academic mind for Latin words and call it *status nascendi*. I will refrain from doing so, not because it sounds somewhat pretentious, but because it would not be quite correct. The moment I have in mind, in which an idea emerges from unconscious assimilation and is consciously grasped, is not the moment of its origin. That is always earlier, often much earlier. For instance, we may have "comprehended" the secret meaning of a psychical process very soon, but not yet be aware of it. I "knew" Dr. A.'s ex-patient hated men before I "thought" it. That means we have not yet consciously taken cognizance of it. But our own reactions and certain previous trains of thought bear witness all the same that the hidden meaning of one or another trait has already been fully understood unconsciously.

How do we recognize this point of departure? To answer that question is more difficult than to experience the process.

In Holland back in 1935, I was analyzing a young doctor. He said that he was expecting a private caller that afternoon, a young, attractive lady who was coming to visit him for the second time. The first time he had not tidied his flat, and had told the lady so. He had added that he always disliked it when a hospital was specially cleaned and carefully tidied upon the announcement of a visit from the Queen. He was particularly disgusted with the feverish activity shown at such times. It struck him as false and spurious. Today he himself had thoroughly cleaned his washstand. We will ignore the sequence of these opposite attitudes of mind, and turn our attention to the gallant comparison, and to his expression of disgust at the special cleaning the hospital got when a visit of the Queen was announced. From what regions of the unconscious did the idea occur to me that the patient had, as a boy, often befouled the seat of the toilet with his urine, and had been scolded for it by his mother? I communicated the idea. The patient reacted with memories from his twelfth and thirteenth years that might indirectly support the supposition, but he had no conscious knowledge of the behavior indicated by me. Then he mentioned incidentally that, in case of more or less urgency, he was in the habit of urinating into the washbasin, which was quickly cleaned by the hot running water.

Some time ago I had to interpret the dream of a patient: *He says to his sister: "Ha-ha, a nickel is more than a dime."* Nothing occurred to the dreamer that would throw any light on this dream except one thing: he had the feeling in it that he had cracked a magnificent joke. He remembered the dream immediately upon waking up and wondered about it. Why did he roar with laughter in his dream? Where is the joke? He added that he sometimes had dreams in which he coined very witty sentences and when he awakened and remembered them, they were either quite banal words or nonsense. Let us consider this one. That a nickel is more than a dime is, of course, incorrect, but what is there to laugh about? What is witty in such a sentence? He knew beyond doubt that in the dream he felt proud to have made such a splendid remark. I could not help the patient understand the dream because I did not understand it myself. I was helpless when he couldn't contribute any thought-associations to its interpretation. The situation is comparable to that of an Egyptologist suddenly faced with an ancient inscription of hieroglyphics, a key to which had not yet been discovered. I was entirely in the dark except for some vague impressions I got from knowing the patient's circumstances. I know, for instance, that he had given money to his older sister (the one who appeared in the dream) and has had to hide from his wife the fact that he was supporting this sister. Some weeks ago he had complained that Betty, the sister, came to him again to ask for money for the dentist. Another time he was worried because he had to contribute to a trip his niece, this sister's daughter, had to make. The demands Betty made upon him became greater and greater. Yet he could not refuse her because he knew how poor she was. On one of these occasions he quoted a Jewish curse: "You shall be the richest in your family." That means: When you are the richest in your family, you will never have peace of mind because your conscience demands that you give money to all your relatives, that you share your fortune with them, that you permanently worry about supporting them so that you are not able to enjoy life. Suddenly, as I remembered these data, it seemed obvious to me that the dream must have the character of mockery. I repeated the sentence in my thoughts: "Ha-ha, a nickel is more than a dime." That was really not funny; it was rather odd. And then in quick succession followed these thoughts or thought-fragments: Odd, ha-ha . . . odd. . . . eccentric, strange. . . . Hamlet. . . . Suffering also makes laughter. Then I told the patient that he had given his sister a piece of his mind in the dream and had told her in a sarcastic manner that he would no longer stand for her increasing demands for money.

The sarcasm concerned his sister's tendency to present the situation in such a way as to leave the impression that the amounts he was giving her were really not much. He had mocked the absurdity of her statements by saying something absurd himself. She used to minimize the amounts she asked him for. When in the dream he asserted that a nickel was more than a dime, he was saying something absurd to prove that what she said was ridiculous.

Here are the links of my thoughts: I first thought of "odd," which has the two connotations of "funny" and also "strange, eccentric" . . . then the scene from Hamlet occurred to me in which the prince makes fun of the two courtiers, Guildenstern and Rosencrantz (Act II, scene 2) . . . he says absurd things to reveal their hypocrisy . . . the names Guildenstern and Rosencrantz in German mean "golden star" and "wreath of roses" . . . the names are of the kind that the German officials often forced upon the Jews to make them appear ridiculous . . . the Jews . . . the patient is a Jew . . . his recalcitrant devotion to all the members of his family is a characteristic feature of certain Jewish circles . . . a Jewish proverb occurs to me (Yiddish: *"Leid macht auch lachen"*) "Suffering also makes you laugh."

I have followed here my trains of thought leading to a certain concept of his dream. Let me hasten to make two remarks before proceeding. I do not consider the dream fully analyzed, but I believe that I grasped its emotional character, so to speak, its psychical atmosphere. It says: If you assert that the money I regularly give you is just a bagatelle, then you can also say a dime is less than a nickel; or, what you say is nonsense, ridiculous. This view was expressed in a very sarcastic, sharply ironical manner.

The other trait that became obvious is that this saying appeared to the dreamer so witty that he laughed in his dream. His laughter was not gay or cheerful; it was full of bitterness, of grim humor. It was not merry but reckless and sardonic. He made a joke that took the place of a tongue-lashing. After I had told the patient the meaning of his dream, he confirmed it indirectly. He told me something he had not mentioned before, that he had heard from his mother the day before the dream that his sister again planned to ask him for money because she had to cover some expense. Before falling asleep he had thought of the future conversation with her and had enjoyed in anticipation telling her at last how intolerable her demands had become.

It is very unusual for an analyst to give an account of the personal thoughts that lead him to a given interpretation of the material presented to him during analysis. However, in certain cases the unusual becomes a necessity. I am not ashamed that my thoughts at first sound very bizarre or that the connections between them lack logic and reason. When you observe them more closely certain logical ties appear. Take, for instance, the strange bridge that leads from Hamlet to the Jewish proverb. The thought-connection, of course, is the irony hidden in both, the sayings of the Danish prince and the sentence of my Jewish patient. But what is the bridge between the two spheres, which are so remote from each other? I pointed it out: the names Guildenstern and Rosencrantz. They are German-Jewish names that the German clerks of the seventeenth century gave to the Jews who originally had only Hebrew names and were then forced to adopt ridiculous German names. The ridicule is thus one point of the arc in the circle: Shakespeare to Jews. The other is, of course, the very fact that there are two German names in the middle of a Shakespearean tragedy, names that remind me more of the Jews than of the Germans. How did these two names come into the play of the British playwright?[1] A third point is secured by a memory which is as odd as the two facts just mentioned. It comes to mind only now when I try to analyze how I glided in my thoughts from Shakespeare to the idea of the Jewish proverb.

Many years ago I liked to visit a certain delicatessen in Vienna because the sausages and other dishes there tasted so good. The name of the owner, well known in Vienna Jewish circles, was Biel. Over the counter of this delicatessen store was a wooden board with a printed text. The inscription read: "Already Hamlet asked himself, as the play says, 'To Biel or not to Biel, that is the question.' " This caption made me smile, as it did many others. Did not the pun say: if only Hamlet, instead of occupying his mind with metaphysical problems, had asked himself the more immediate question, whether to go "to Biel or not to Biel"? Thus we have another funny connection between Hamlet and the Jews. The Jewish proverb (heard in my childhood) that asserts that our own suffering, too, sometimes makes us laugh, marked, so to speak, the last step to the other side of the bridge. With it I reached the conscious understanding of the character of the dream. It was precisely of this nature: out of his suffering a bitter and sarcastic laughter is born.[2] His dream was sheer mockery.

In general the analyst will, of course, make no effort to observe his own psychical processes in an analytic or rather self-analytic spirit. It was done here for the sake of scientific research. Such a process during the practice of analysis is unnecessary because it is not the details of the analyst's thought-processes that are important, but rather their results. When the analyst listens with a third ear to his own ideas while following those of his patients, he will do so only to get at the hidden meaning behind the sentences of the analysand. It is necessary for him to

[1] As far as I remember, I did not find any information on this point in the commentaries on *Hamlet* that I have read.

[2] The instance mentioned above leads to the solution of a little analytic problem that is not contained in the literature on dream-interpretation. Dream-contents that arouse the laughter of the dreamer or of his audience in the dream are often the expression of irony or mockery. Occasionally the irony can be turned against oneself, for instance, in the dream of a patient who called herself two names that did not match, like a prostitute and a saint. The phenomenon that something in the dream seems very witty but upon awakening appears trite and banal, is not infrequent. Continued research into these phenomena promises not only a deeper understanding of wit but also of a certain type of dreams.

grasp this concealed sense, and his own thoughts are only one of the media that help him reach this secret. A scientist occupied with optics will use his eyes in the observation of the phenomena of light without thinking of his eyes. His attention is directed to his object. But no scientist will understand light, shadow, shape, and color, the whole process of seeing, unless he knows the apparatus of the eye. In the same way the analyst must become familiar with his own unconscious, which is the very instrument that communicates to him the concealed meaning of what he observes.

I have deliberately confined myself to primitive examples, which may perhaps show where the point of departure is to be found, and how the idea emerges from the unconscious fashioning of the material.

I do not know whether many analysts have the same experience, but with me the emergence from the deeper or obscurer planes of thought is preceded for the fraction of a second by a sense of alienation, a rapidly passing feeling of absent-mindedness, even a kind of foggy sensation. It is as though an act of analytic cognition of this kind and origin were announced by a moment of eclipse preceding it. (It is darkest before the dawn.) Perhaps this moment of eclipse, of "absence" in the French meaning, before conjecture is only an expression of the unconscious resistance to the cognition that is pushing itself into consciousness, and at the same time the signal of its imminent emergence. The psychical situation may well be compared with the effect of Rembrandt's treatment of light; the French call him a *luministe,* and one observer writes that he carries "dark lanterns under his cloak, which he suddenly whips out and holds in our faces, so that at first we can see nothing for brightness." This passing chaotic situation, of which I am not so much ashamed as may be supposed, is ended by the immediate lucidity with which the idea crosses the threshold of consciousness. We must assume that certain factors of a dynamic and mentally economic nature are responsible for the process, and that at the particular moment an enhanced psychical tension is suddenly relaxed.

There are phases during analysis in which we arrive at psychological conclusions by means of reasoning. There are certain problems that can be solved by common sense and logic, it is true, but they are not the most important problems that face the psychoanalyst. He arrives at his deepest insights neither by searching for a conclusion nor by jumping to one. The best way is for him to wait until a conclusion jumps to him. It is at this moment when a longer or shorter suspense is lifted, when he has this special and psychologically significant, "Oh, that's it!"-experience. I shall attempt to give the reader a concrete idea of the process by reporting two examples of this kind of experience.

Shortly after World War I, in a large provincial town in Austria, a young architect whom I knew socially, asked me for help because he had fallen prey to a serious depression.[3] He was about thirty-five and lived a comfortable bachelor life in an apartment with his old mother. Ambitious and successful, he had enjoyed his profession, his pleasant circle of friends, and the pursuit of his artistic interests. He had just finished a building, a kind of modest skyscraper, the first of its kind in the town. Its many apartments had just become ready for occupancy. Since there was a housing shortage in Austria at the time, he might well have been pleased with his accomplishment, to which he had given his best energies over a period of many months. He was intelligent and had always appeared to be mentally stable. Serious but usually cheerful, he was generally liked and respected.

When I called on him at his home I found a changed man. He was lying on a couch in deep despair. He gave me a graphic report, which was interrupted by sobbing. He knew exactly what was causing his depression, he said, but he also knew that nobody and nothing could help him. Nothing could avert the terrible calamity that threatened his whole existence. All was lost. His depression was caused by a doubt that emerged after he had finished the main structure of the new apartment building and now haunted all his hours. He could not remember whether this doubt first appeared spontaneously or whether it had come after some remark by a member of the official commission that had inspected the building. It concerned the safety of the building and centered upon the possibility that, in the not too distant future, underground water might endanger the foundations. He remembered that the first wave of doubt had overcome him just after the cellars, roof, walls, and ceilings had been examined. He explained to me in technical terms but with deep emotion, just how he had taken every conceivable precaution and protested that he had very carefully examined the ground and the site before beginning work. At first the fatal doubt seemed to him like any other casual thought, but it kept recurring and became intensified until at last it became a terrible conviction: the underground water would find its way and undermine the foundations of

[3] This case has also been discussed in my book, *The Unknown Murderer* (New York: Prentice-Hall, 1945).

the building so that one day it would collapse. A catastrophe, hideous beyond imagination, would destroy a thousand lives. With the knowledge of the expert he sketched for me a good picture of the slow but increasingly effective work of the underground water and its dangers for the tenants.

Harassed by his doubts he had requested a re-examination of the building by a special commission of the best experts in the field. He showed me a report of its findings. Of course I could not understand the technical language, but to my layman's mind the report seemed to exclude the existence of any danger in the forseeable future. To be sure, certain passages might be interpreted to mean that the underground water constituted a remote potential hazard. The patient, intelligent and much better trained in dialectics than I, tried to persuade me that the commission had admitted the danger in veiled terms in order to spare his feelings and save his reputation. I reread the report but, lacking understanding of its technical terms, I could not decide whether or how far my patient's fears were justified.

Was it not natural that he was desperate, refused to go to his office, avoided his friends, and broke down weeping in despair? A young, ambitious architect realized that the work of many months was not only a failure but a menace to the lives of hundreds of people. Was it exaggerated that, facing such a calamity, he was panic-stricken?

Everything he said seemed logical and sound, clear and consistent. Nevertheless the presence in me of vague but decisive feelings suggested that factors other than those of the reality-situation were responsible for his state of mind. There were also a few inconsistencies or slight inaccuracies in his tale. Imponderable impressions indicated that his grief, genuine and sincere as it was, came from some other source. When he tried to prove to me that the report of the building commission came to certain conclusions in guarded terms, his argumentation, though persuasive, was not convincing. His own statements at this point seemed somewhat "reached," as the script writers would say.

His yarn was good but there were little imperfections in it, slight unevennesses not apparent to the eye but perceptible to testing hands that glide slowly and carefully over the fabric. Small imperfections caused by a twisting of the threads are known as "slubs" to textile experts. There were a few slubs in his otherwise perfect argument. Other inconspicuous features that elude description suggested that unconscious factors had a share in his depression.

At one point in our conversation the patient remarked casually, with a touch of self-mockery, that it was ironical that he, a builder of houses for others, had no house of his own but lived in an apartment with his mother. I had a very fleeting feeling that there was more in that remark than met the ear. At another time he told me that for the past few years he had been carrying on an affair with a married woman. I sensed some inner complications when he admitted that there were a few external difficulties. He said that it was not prudent for him to meet his mistress anywhere here in town where gossip flourished. She could not visit him in his home because his mother would have strongly disapproved of the relationship. He had thought of renting a small apartment in the building he had just completed but had decided that this would be impossible without arousing suspicion. In order to keep their secret he and his mistress found it necessary to meet in a neighboring town.

Was there a clue here? I had the impression that my patient's happiness in his love affair was not unalloyed, that it had its unpleasant aspects. It seemed to me that there might be a connection in thought between the married woman and the building about which my patient had such terrifying doubts. Was it possible that a thread ran from unconscious death wishes against his mistress to his fears concerning the new house? Were murderous tendencies hiding behind his doubts?

I recalled then the case of another patient whom I had treated long before in Vienna. A married man, involved in a sexual affair with a young girl whom he frequently visited in her apartment, was haunted by the fear that his wife might find out about it through some unfortunate mishap. He was afraid of her jealousy and rage if she knew of his infidelity and took all possible precautions. He had a recurring fantasy that filled him with panic. He imagined that late some evening, after he had left his mistress, a prowler who had observed them together, would break into her apartment and rob and kill her. The investigations of the police would discover that he was the last person who had been with the girl and he would be arrested and accused of murder.

It had been clear to me of course that unconscious murderous wishes against his sweetheart had found expression in this fantasy, in which the crime was displaced upon another, unknown person. Did my present case present a similar situation? The architect certainly also had hostile feelings toward his married mistress. He freely admitted that he was sometimes jealous of her husband and that he resented the inconvenience of their clandestine meetings. Was this the Ariadne thread that led out of his emotional labyrinth? But this clue failed to throw light upon the special nature of his doubts. Where was the connection between the furtive love affair and the danger from underground water, between his hostility to his mistress and the unsafe condition of the new building? One could construe several such links, to be sure, but they seemed artificial. I decided I had been barking up the wrong tree.

I began now to feel increasingly that suspense which so often precedes the solution of an intellectual problem. The atmosphere was foggy, I was in the dark, groping my way, not sure where I was going. Just at this time the patient mentioned, it seemed quite incidentally, that another worry had preoccupied him just before the building was completed. His aged mother had developed symptoms that made it advisable for her to consult a gynecologist. The physician told my patient that it was possible his mother had cancer of the uterus and advised a more thorough examination in a hospital. This, of course, had disturbed him badly. The second examination brought no conclusive diagnosis. He told me all this without connecting his mother's suspected disease with his own depression. I knew immediately that here was the clue for which I had searched so long in vain. "Now," I said to myself, "I have the key that will unlock the forbidden room, but where is the room?"

The image in which this thought occurred itself indicated the direction I must take, which was a detour to the goal. Had the architect not spoken of an apartment and had not the thought of an apartment come up in connection with his mother and his mistress? I wondered as I wandered and I waited for further material. It appeared in another context and I was soon able to reconstruct what had taken place in my patient's unconscious thoughts and so discover the real concealed cause for his depression. My reconstruction was a psychological patchwork but it went only a few steps beyond the facts known to my patient and me and merely bridged two separate realms of thought.

Here is the psychological result. One evening when the young architect was worried about his mother's illness, he felt a sudden sexual and affectionate urge to see his mistress. Or course it was not possible to meet her, but he had a great desire to hold her in his arms. She would have consoled and comforted him. If only he had an apartment of his own! For one moment the two sets of thoughts, the desire to see his mistress and the need to have his own apartment had met. The effect of this encounter was the sudden emergence of another thought, which he rejected with all possible mental energy. This terrible thought was as follows: "If my mother dies of cancer this apartment will be entirely mine. My mistress can always come to me and there will be no more obstacles to our happiness together." Later on he admitted that this thought had indeed presented itself as a remote possibility but he denied the inescapable conclusion that originally the idea had had the character of a wish that his mother should die and make it possible for him to have the apartment to himself so that he could receive his mistress at his convenience. It is clear why he reacted with such horror to this thought and why his anxiety over his mother increased, why he felt increased affection for her and had no desire to see his mistress.

There in his reaction against the wish for his mother's death, which had emerged from unconscious depths, was the real cause of his depression. Its intensity corresponds to the energy with which he rejected the forbidden tendency. It is not surprising that in the rearrangement of the material the subterranean force of water stands for the hidden work of the destructive disease. The powers of irresistible natural forces facilitate such an unconscious substitution.

Those minute unevennesses, those small inadequacies I had noted at the beginning, paved the way for the reconstruction of the emotional processes, but it was actually made possible by psychological clues that seemed very remote from the scene, by casual remarks the patient made and treated as if they were irrelevant. It seems to me that the analyst must differentiate between psychological facts and psychological clues. Facts are data that are known and fully acknowledged as to their significance for the origin and motivation of the emotional process under observation. Clues are material of a special kind, whose importance has not yet been examined and whose significance is not immediately clear. Such clues can contribute much to the solution of a problem. Facts help us to figure things out; clues help us to discover things that were always there but that we did not see. Facts are to be used consciously; clues come to us when they emerge from the storehouse of our memory. Facts are before the analyst in broad daylight; clues have to be found. Facts appeal to our powers of reason and reflection; clues evoke response from our imagination. Facts are connected with solid knowledge; clues are related to hunches. Facts give us intellectual security; clues arouse suspense in the realm of thought and ideas.

In reading the usual clinical descriptions of neurotic cases the process of understanding sometimes appears to be a cut-and-dried affair. The iron curtain of psychoanalytic terms shuts out the reader from the living experience of the birth of an idea. It does not allow him to be present at the silent daily battle in which the analyst wrestles with a problem like Jacob with the Angel of the Lord, saying, "I will not let thee go except thou bless me." In such accounts the twilight atmosphere of incipient understanding has evaporated. There is no longer any uncertainty, no fumbling and groping, all has been classified and formulated. The reality of the happenings in the analyst's consultation room is very different from the impression created by such articles, many of which are masterpieces of psychiatric clichés. Lucky breaks and unfortunate mistakes, the combination of trial and error, suspense and surprise—everything that makes psychoanalysis an intellectual adventure has been removed. It is a case history, and its scene is at the periphery of experience.

Another analytic experience will show that the suspense of which I have spoken does not necessarily concern the solution of the central problem of a neurosis. The following case is presented because the puzzle that intrigued me here was not the concealed content of emotional processes but the motives of a patient's behavior. A young man told me, shortly after beginning his analysis, of certain fantasies that excited him sexually either in intercourse with a woman or in masturbation. The fantasies were strange enough, but stranger still was his behavior in his love life. In my thoughts I called him "the Reluctant Don Juan."

He reported that he felt impelled to seduce women who were tied to another man. Whenever he met such women and the circumstances were favorable, he was compelled to use all the considerable means at his disposal to go to bed with them. After the sexual act he felt no desire to see them again. So far his tale sounded like that of the classic Don Juan, a common variety of male animal. Closer observation, however, revealed special traits that do not appear in the usual behavior pattern of the Don Juan type. One would search for them in vain in that category of literary figures. The combination of these traits gives a picture that differs from the Don Juans portrayed by many writers from Tirso de Molina to Molière and Byron, from the Don Giovanni of Mozart's opera to Shaw's *Man and Superman*. The abundance of my patient's individual traits makes their characterization in a few paragraphs difficult, but a selection will be sufficient to prove the difference.

The women who became the objects of his quickly aroused and

quickly passing desire had to be decent women who were in love with another man; adventuresses and trollops were not considered worth the effort. He liked to think of the women he desired as being at first reluctant but as yielding finally to their own sexual urge even though they loved another man. Here is a special feature that is alien to the common or garden variety of Don Juan, a trait that will appear even more strongly when we inquire into the nature of the fantasies that were so exciting to him. Here are a few of them: A woman is involved in an affair with a man whom she at first rejects. Later she enjoys his lovemaking in the presence of her husband. . . . Sometimes a woman is raped while her husband whom she loves, looks on and sees her in raptures in the arms of the criminal.

My patient had read a short story by John Erskine in which a young couple makes a pilgrimage to a distant shrine to pray for a child, which until then has been denied them. On the road they are attacked by a band of robbers. The husband is knocked unconscious and while he is in this condition the chief of the band, a red-haired brute, rapes the wife. What excited my patient especially in reading the description of the scene that followed was a single word. The writer says that the wife approached her husband, who had meanwhile regained his senses, and that she was "ashamed." The patient sees in this word an indication that the wife, although devoted to her husband, enjoyed the sexual intercourse with the brigand. The accent in these fantasies is concentrated on the abandoned sensual pleasure that the woman experiences with one man while she loves another.

He was, for example, greatly excited by the description of a case he read in a newspaper. A prowler had broken into a house, tied the husband to the bed, and had had intercourse while the husband was forced to watch his wife's pleasure. Situations in which husbands and wives were exchanged were extremely exciting to his fantasies. He liked to think of the wives as enjoying, against their will, the embraces of an unloved partner. There was another fantasy of a related kind. A woman is madly in love with a certain young man but marries another either because of pressure from her parents or for money. On her wedding night she experiences ecstasies in the arms of her unloved husband and says, "You made me come across."

I called my patient a reluctant Don Juan because he fought in vain against his compulsion to seduce women in the described circumstances. He resented the sacrifices of time and money in the preliminary courtship and entertainment and would have been happy to be free of the compelling urge. Actually he felt relieved and happy when external circumstances prevented him from making a pass at a woman or when she did not keep a date or when he himself was prevented by his duties from keeping an appointment. It was as if the situation of a young and pretty woman in love with another man presented a challenge he could not resist. The fantasies that have been described provided, as it were, the spark that inflamed his sexual desire.

It was not surprising to learn that he used these fantasies in masturbation, but it was amazing to learn that he actually verbalized them with his wife from whom he had been separated but whom he nevertheless visited frequently. He had virtually forced her into the arms of a lover and he made her tell him all the details of the sexual situations with the other man who was unknown to him. He made her describe to him precisely what she and her lover had done sexually and her recital stimulated him in his intercourse with her. In these curious conversations with his wife before and during intercourse, he not only asked about the sexual details of her relationship with her lover but tried to excite himself and her by picturing aloud in voluptuous language the ecstasy she would experience with her lover in the near future. Truly, here was a Don Juan of a special kind.

I discussed this case with some of my psychoanalytic colleagues, giving them the data here mentioned. It was interesting that they saw its essential character in a way different from my own. One of them said: "The man is, of course, a homosexual." Certainly it cannot be denied that the patient's symptoms strongly suggest such a characterization. Is it not a necessary condition for the stimulation of the patient's desire that the women he wants as sexual partners be tied to another man? Is it not as if he wished to meet another man in the common object of sex? In this connection his attitude toward his wife speaks an unequivocal language. There is not doubt that another man has an important place in his fantasies; but is latent homosexuality really the chief unconscious motive for his attitude? Why does he choose only "nice, decent" women and why the strange emphasis on their loving another man while they enjoy sexual pleasure with a man they do not like?

Another colleague characterized the case as belonging among those involving a certain type of love-choice once described by Freud. Men of this type are impotent with decent women in the mother or sister category but regain their full potency with women whom they despise.

This very common type seeks out women who are tied to another man and enjoys the triumph over him. Although this psychological explanation is well founded, many of my patient's traits could not be accounted for by it. My patient is not interested in the prostitute type, on the contrary, it is just the mother or sister type that intrigues him. His accounts make it perfectly clear that he does not enjoy triumph over a rival, it almost seems as if the reverse were so, that he enjoys the rival's triumph over himself. It is indeed true that a triangle is a necessary element in his fantasies, but in his imagination his attention is directed, not to the other man, but to what the woman is experiencing. In most of his fantasies he is either an onlooker of the scene or himself plays the part of the deceived husband, as he does in his frequent verbalized fantasies with his wife.

The fantasies themselves have all the characteristic traits of lechery and lasciviousness. They are orgies or manifestations of debauchery. Superficially it might seem that the patient is simply an extremely sensual person who uses every woman as his sexual object.

But this leaves unexplained the particular nature of his fantasies. The high moral standards and great delicacy of feeling that marked the patient's personality as a whole, made it impossible to explain him as a crude, primitive sadist. The whole emotional atmosphere of his peculiar orientation toward women, puzzling and contradictory in so many of its features, left no doubt that he was more the victim than the aggressor, that he was cruel to himself rather than to others.

Since the patient is still in treatment at this writing, I am bound by discretion to omit certain data that would contribute to a more complete description of the case.[4] Instead, I shall give my own conception of it and sketch the process by which I arrived at my conclusions. The first impression was simply that of a classic Don Juan whose ambition was directed to the conquest of many women. I recall that as I listened to my patient's recital of his experiences, tunes from Mozart's *Don Giovanni* came to my mind.

But gradually it became clear that the patient really did not want to be subjected to his compulsion to seduce women and that his urge to do so was by no means a simple sexual drive. On the contrary, a secret

[4]Freud, in a certain passage in his writings, emphasized that it is much more innocuous to describe a patient's most intimate fantasies than to give even a few details concerning his external life. People keep their sexual fantasies more secret than other things that play a minor part in their lives.

dissatisfaction seemed to compel him to his seductions, which he himself disliked. The analysis of his fantasies gave a deeper insight into his concealed motives. What was the meaning of the recurring theme of the ecstasies of a decent, well-bred woman in the arms of a tramp, a robber, or generally a man she did not like? Why was the woman always thought of as in love with another man? And why did the patient never think of himself as this beloved man? Why was it exciting to him when his wife, who said she loved him, told him all the details of her sexual relations with another? All these features seemed to tend toward a certain goal and partook of a common quality, but the essence of this quality was difficult to define.

Two impressions that I received during one analytic session helped me to arrive at a preliminary formulation. The first was given by the patient's report of a proposition he had made his wife. He would restore their marriage if she would promise always to have a lover. He explained to me that this condition seemed necessary to him because it would increase his sexual appetite in his relations with her. His way of putting things was so paradoxical that it seemed like an unconscious travesty born of hidden sarcasm.

The second impression was given in the same session but in another context, of which a more complete description must be omitted for reasons of discretion. He quoted a jingle that he had heard sung by other children when he was a boy:

> I should worry, I should care,
> I should marry a millionaire.
> He should die, I should cry,
> I should marry another guy.

He explained to me that it was sung in the spirit of "I don't care what you do to me. I'll be all right. You can't hurt me." That is to say it was the girl's statement of defiance. He recited the lines in a half-mocking, half-pathetic manner as if they were the expression of the *Weltanschauung* of all women. A few minutes later, with the knowledge of an expert, he discussed, as if in contrast to what he had just said, the Hindu word *"sati,"* which signifies a woman who is considered virtuous because she has sought her own death upon her husband's funeral pyre.

I was certain then that my patient's behavior as well as the essential features of his fantasies could mean only one thing: he wanted unconsciously to prove that love is a stupid illusion, a pretense of all women, however seemingly decent, for all of them are willing to sleep with everybody. Later on he actually said with sardonic bitterness that all the talk of love was "a lot of crap," a cheap fake, and that sex was the only thing that counted with women. Any woman would sleep with any man provided he is persistent enough.

His fantasies demonstrated just this point of view. His heroines or victims were always "nice" women, who in spite of their love for one man fully enjoyed sexual intercourse with another. His compulsion to seduce women was, so to speak, the practical demonstration of his conviction about them. It was as if he had to prove to himself that there is no such thing as a faithful woman. He often quoted verses by Donne that bore out his belief.

> All strange wonders that befell thee,
> And sweare
> No where
> Lives a woman true, and faire.

Here to my mind lies the essential character of his behavior. It seems to say in many different ways that there is no love, that all that women say of their love is hypocrisy. Like men, and even more than men, they are led only by their selfish interests and especially by their desire for sexual lust. Such a pessimistic view of women's nature as is implicit in his bitter and cutting sarcasm is unusual in a young man of his cultural background. There is nothing cheerful about his enjoyment of sex, there is even something grim and desperate about it. His hostility toward women, which we sensed in his fantasies and which all his gallantry and surface amiability toward them in social life could not hide, came from a deep source. Considering too that the patient was under compulsion to prove his unformulated thesis by his attempts at seduction and that just this proof excited him sexually, one gets the impression that there is grief and disappointed idealism behind his unconscious mockery. It became quite clear to me that his fantasies were cruel travesties of his ideals, mocking demonstrations of them in terms of their opposite. By a defiant twist he turned what he deeply resented into the only desirable goal.

Another factor that must be considered is his lack of jealousy. Had he not driven his wife into the arms of a lover? And is not the imagined presence of a lover a prerequisite for his sexual excitement? No doubt the factor of latent homosexuality is operating here but in his fantasies, he, himself, is often the deceived lover. In the face of all these clues are we not justified in calling him a masochistic character? Here is the reversal so characteristic of thought-masochism. For the ordinary man the idea that his wife or sweetheart should have intercourse with another man is intolerable; worse still, the thought that she should greatly enjoy it. Yet with the patient it is just this situation that has become the premise for his own sexual excitement.

Is it not likely that originally he was extremely jealous and that he changed an idea that was so painful that he could not bear it into the condition for his lust? What was at first an excruciating horror to him has been transformed into a source of delight. Here is almost precisely the psychological formula for masochistic characters. The degrading and deeply humiliating is turned into the requisite for lust. The patient is not only without jealousy but the very situation that would arouse the most violent jealousy in the average man is the essential condition for his sexual pleasure. This humiliation of the self, this heaping of shame on oneself as the forerunner of extreme pleasure, shows the very stamp of masochism. If this degradation in thought has been demonstrated, one must suppose that a very great pride is one of the unconscious motives of such a peculiar attitude. A person must be very proud indeed, not only to admit his shame but to draw attention to it, to boast of it.

If I have sketched here the portrait of a man who is a masochist in his thinking, where is the complementary sadistic, aggressive trend? Self-degradation such as we have uncovered here must be related to its opposite, the desire to bring about the shameful exposure of others. Masochism and sadism are only two aspects of the same thing, like the inside and the outside of a glove. It is obvious that the patient's wish to expose and degrade others expresses itself in his thoughts against women. Does not the patient's attitude seem to proclaim: "All women are hypocrites. They are all to be had, even and especially when they are in love with another man. They are all trollops and sluts. All talk of faithfulness is a fraud; they are only out for sexual pleasure."

In this case too, in which it proved necessary to understand certain aspects of a complicated personality, I promised to show that suspense and surprise are felt by the analyst. In cases like this, as in others, the impressions the patient's history makes upon the analyst are of psychological importance. The analyst must be aware of what this material does to him before he does something with the material. As I have said, the session in which the patient told me about his proposition to his wife and in which he recited the children's jingle was a turning-point in my concept of his personality. Until then I had seen him as the Don Juan type. The tunes of Mozart's *Don Giovanni,* especially Leporello's "Madamina" aria in which he lists the many women to whom Don Giovanni has made love—"But in Spain, a thousand and three"—had occurred to me as I listened to him. Whenever the same tunes came to mind later in the analysis, the hidden melancholy of Mozart's music seemed to drown out its gay façade.

At a certain moment in the session of which I have been speaking, I suddenly recalled the Viennese actor, Max Pallenberg. I saw him on the stage, was aware of his facial expression in a certain scene, of his gestures as well as his telling way of speaking, especially his tones of torturing mockery and bitter sarcasm whose effectiveness was increased by a seemingly polite, amiable, and humane manner. The mental picture was vivid but fleeting. I saw the actor put two rulers on his head and fix them there. And then I saw, if I may use this expression for a sharply clear image in my thoughts, the interior of an architect's office with its drawing boards and desks, drawings, pens and pencils. Immediately I recognized this mental picture. It was the memory of a scene in a French play in which I had seen Pallenberg act the leading part. I do not recall its title and author, but the names Duval and Duvernois occurred to me at the time. I remembered the theme of the play. A young man discovers that his wife has been unfaithful to him but instead of hiding his humiliation he founds a Society for Cuckolds in the provincial town in which he lives. He sets up committees and gives his society of deceived husbands the widest publicity. If I am not mistaken an open meeting was even held at which the mayor of the town, who shares the lot of the other husbands, makes a speech. In an amusing reversal of the usual attitude the hero of the play, the architect, turns into pride and glory what is usually a source of shame and humiliation. Like my patient he degrades his wife by his emphasis upon his own humiliation. He too, shows no jealousy and on the contrary prides himself upon having let his wife dupe him. The image of Pallenberg which had so suddenly flashed up in my mind, was from a scene in this play in which the architect, while talking to his unfaithful wife, picks up two rulers from the desk and places them conspicuously on his head. He wears horns. The horns symbolize his honor, they are the emblem of the Society of Cuckolds he has founded. If I remember rightly the architect experiences a moment of ultimate triumph. By giving the most glaring publicity to his domestic shame he makes his wife the object of public contempt. In making himself a tragic clown, he exposes her. At the end he has forced her literally and morally to her knees and she asks his forgiveness.

It was this memory of a masochistic demonstration so like that of my patient that broke the suspense and heralded my understanding of the case. The image of the actor, which so surprisingly emerged from my memory, initiated my first conception of my patient's personality structure.

This case is still in analytic treatment and I am grateful to my patient for allowing me to publish this psychological outline. Discretion forbids my going beyond this point in presenting his analysis. Suffice it to say that his fantasies have gradually lost their hold on him, that is, their sexually stimulating quality has diminished. They still occur, but he no longer really enjoys them. He told me the other day that he feels twitches of the old desires when they appear but they are no longer the real thing. He even spoke of a certain nostalgia for his old fantasies; he misses the enjoyment in thought they used to give him. Theoretically at least, he still holds the view that all women can be had and that they are hypocrites, but the compulsion to prove his point in practice is greatly lessened. If my impression is correct, his reluctance has gotten the better of his compulsion to play the role of Don Juan.

This analytic sketch of an interesting personality was necessarily limited to one side of the patient's life, his sexual relations. However the same sardonic and carefully concealed sarcasm came out in other ways. Symptomatic of the many contradictory and contrasting traits of this complex character is the fact that he has now developed an affectionate relationship with a charming young girl. In the realm of sex with her he never employs those fantasies which were so exciting to him with other women, especially with his wife. While he quickly tires of the company of those "other dames," he likes to spend as much time as possible with this girl. He enjoys sexual union with her but beyond that he also feels affectionate concern for her and wants to see her happy. He is also jealous of her, yes, he is even jealous of the slightest attention shown her by another man. He becomes not only annoyed but very angry.

Perhaps I should say here that it became clear as his treatment progressed that during the first years of his marriage he had also been very jealous of his wife. In the beginning he had been furious if she even looked at another man or indulged in a little mild flirtation with one of his friends in his presence. His conspicuous lack of jealousy when he began his analysis was the result of a late masochistic development, in which pride played an important part. It is as if at the height of his jealousy he had said to his wife, "If you like this man better than you do me, go to him! I don't want to stand in your way. More than that, I *want* you to go to him, to go sleep with him. I am asking you to go to bed with him." We have seen that this development led to those fantasies which were masochistic orgies in thought.

Tracing these character traits back to an earlier phase permits us to see the patient's real features behind the cynical mask that had become second nature to him. He must have been a shy boy who worshipped women from afar and who originally had a very idealistic conception of women's place in life. We came then to the reconstruction of an earlier phase in his boyhood when he thought that women were above sexual drives and only yielded reluctantly and without pleasure to the sexual demands of men. His present evaluation of women is the exact reversal of this with an extra self-mocking twist. Women want only sexual gratification and love is nonsense.

Schopenhauer says somewhere in his writings that the most infamous way of trying to invalidate the theory of a philosopher is for the critic to prove that the writer contradicts himself. How much more infamous would it have been if I had tried to show my patient how he contradicted his theory that there is no love, that only sex is valid and valuable in the life of men and women. Man is not a psychologically homogeneous creature. He is supposed to have contradictory tendencies in his character. Indeed what we call character is nothing more than the predominance of certain emotional trends, their preponderance over others that are nevertheless operating and effective within him.

Just the other day I asked my patient after he had once again proclaimed his theory of the non existence of love and the dictatorship of sex, what in his view was the nature of his feeling for the girl whom he wants to see happy. He hesitated a moment but answered then as if in amazement at himself, "Well—it's almost love."

Not infrequently it happens that the idea that leads to the solution of a puzzling trait slips from our grasp as soon as it occurs, and we try in vain to recapture it. It has withdrawn into the unconscious; or should we perhaps say it was pulled back into the unconscious? What has happened is a mental blunder, following the same psychical tendencies as similar occurrences in everyday life. In principle it is nowise different from losing a key and being unable to find it. We think repeatedly that we have got the lost idea, and we only snatch at empty air, or rather at air filled with rational reflections. Our difficulty in capturing these ideas is similar to that of the patient, and their mental conquest requires a special training, as with the patient. What I have already said indicates how important are inner susceptibility to, and retentiveness of, slight irritants and barely noticeable features, in order for the idea to take shape beneath the surface.

Experience shows that it is advisable to formulate in words every idea occurring to the analyst that has reference to the analytic data. I do not, of course, mean that we should tell the patient every idea, that we should immediately communicate to him the conjectured meaning of a network of symptoms, the hidden bearing of his inner attitude, the unconscious connection between what he experiences and his repressed motives. To have an idea and to utter it are two separate things —or should be, at least. I only mean that we should give the idea expression in words in our own minds, as if we wanted to tell it to the patient, or, better, as if we wanted to tell it to ourselves.

It is a true statement that thoughts are speeches not made, or condemned to silence. When I advise analysts to formulate in words in their own minds the ideas that occur to them, psychologists will immediately perceive the advantages of such a course. Thanks to the inner connection between our consciousness and language, an idea formulated in words will be better able to resist the suppressing and repressing forces than one not so formulated. It will be more capable of opposing the tendency to withdraw into the region of the unconscious again. The best ideas and thoughts, those that often lead, like Ariadne's thread, out of the labyrinth of the creations of the unconscious, are indeed the result of processes that lift the analyst's repressions. These are the thoughts which sometimes enable the analyst to leap, so to speak, right into the center of the secret of a case with the help of a single formulated statement.

Ideas of this kind need not, therefore, be uttered when they first emerge, but they ought to be spoken inwardly on the first occasion. Nor should we shrink from this effort when the idea emerging from the unconscious is confused and self-contradictory, when the impression lacks unequivocal clarity and is difficult to express in words. Resistance to senseless or absurd ideas will, of course, make itself felt with particular force. The humorist, Wilhelm Busch, has said, "Everybody has silly thoughts; only a wise man does not utter them." To this we may retort that he is still wiser who seeks meaning and hidden substance even in his "silly" thoughts. And in this instance we need not pause over the objection: That is all very well, but there must be some notion attached to the word. That is only necessary with a finished, thought-out idea, not in this early form. In truth, in the truth that logicians and psychologists do not like to hear, the conscious notion often follows upon the inwardly spoken word. Words will arise of themselves; we need not be concerned about that. *It is not at all difficult to find words for what we think. It is much more difficult to find out what we think.*

It sometimes happens that when we meet for a second time an analytic idea that has slipped from us—sometimes it even comes from the lips of the patient—we recognize it in a particular way. In Vienna it is said in jest that one knows so-and-so "by looking the other way." We may know our own ideas "by looking the other way," too. The limits set to this book hardly allow me to give my reasons for another recommendation, namely, to drop the idea once it has been formulated, to forget it—we know that can only be a metaphorical expression. Then when we unexpectedly come upon the idea again, it will often have developed, will show new aspects that we had not seen formerly. I heard a famous pianist say he played a Mozart concerto much better now that he had not played it in a long time. "It is," he said, "as if my hands got new ideas during the time I did not practice." It is necessary to forget it in order to remember it.

The point of departure marks our entry upon the significant initial stage of comprehending unconscious processes. Let me illustrate the psychical situation by a comparison. Experienced sportsmen tell us that the best moment to shoot partridges is when they rise out of the corn. It is more difficult to hit them in free flight. In like manner the point of departure seems to be the best moment to seize an analytic impression or idea. Once we miss it, it is not much use to pursue it with the devices of conscious reflection. It has already moved too far from the ground of the unconscious, like the partridges a few minutes after their upward flight. And any sportsman will be able to teach us that by this delay we lose much more than the single partridge. In the same way, if we allow the point of departure to slip by unused, whole chains of ideas and thoughts may be lost. In the shooting illustration, we have to make up our minds to wait until we have flushed a new covey of partridges—sometimes it will be the same covey, settled elsewhere in the meantime. In analysis we have to await the return of the ideas we have let slip. ("Shall I try to hold you this time?" says Goethe in his Dedication to *Faust,* speaking of the memories of his youth.)

The point of departure is a psychological moment *par excellence* in the act of tracing the hidden meaning and purpose of unconscious processes. A practical analyst will attach value to other moments in addition to this. Perhaps the mysterious flash with which an analytic idea arises makes it impressive. But its unconscious preparation, the silent mental labor from which it emerges, is yet more important. For it is the outcome of innumerable impressions, conscious and imponderable and incommensurable, the final product of mental labor accomplished for the most part unconsciously. When the unconscious preparation is far enough advanced, it only needs a slight external impression, the tone of a voice, a pause, or a movement, to thrust the idea across the threshold of consciousness. We might call this maturing phase the *latency period of psychological comprehension.* But when we realize that, in the typical process, certain hardly tangible, preconscious impressions are assimilated unconsciously (and then come to light as psychological perceptions, or at least presentiments) the designation *unconscious interval* seems best. It will often happen that during this interval one or more impressions will be repeated and so strengthened. When our ear catches a very faint note, it can hardly distinguish what it is. But if it is repeated several times, it begins to be more easily recognizable, distinguishable. The repetition of an impression has the effect of making it clearer and more capable of interpretation.

The psychological comprehension of unconscious processes requires, like all comprehension, a definite time, which varies in each case. The analyst, too, must have a care to allow his perceptions to mature—or to mature himself for the perceptions that await him. He must learn not to pluck them too soon, like unripe fruit. For the analyst, too, who seeks to penetrate to the depths of the soul, the charming Tyrolese greeting among the peasants when they go mountain climbing is valid. "Take your time!" It is not good to try to force the comprehension of repressed contents, to coerce it mechanically. It is an organic process, like any other. The birth of an analytic idea can be as little hastened as the birth of a child. If we try to accelerate the progress of the pregnancy, the result will be miscarriage.

We have no call to feel ashamed of ourselves as analysts if we take a long time to comprehend the details of unconscious processes. At least any such shame must appear exaggerated in contrast with the self-assurance of others who never attain to comprehension at all. The cautious disentangling accomplished during analysis often takes a very long time. I confess myself an opponent of the breathless chase after interpretations, which rushes helter-skelter after every symptom, every association of thought, in order to snatch from it its unconscious secret. It is possible to miss things because we have been too greedy in seeking them. Even our own ideas must be allowed time to reach consciousness. Some analysts are like a Paris authoress, famous at the turn of the century. This brilliant lady venerated the pope profoundly, but said that unfortunately she was unable to believe in God. She told her friends that for decades she had been assailing God in vain with her entreaties to give some sign of his existence and activity. Really he might have revealed himself to her in so long a time. One of her interlocutors said: "Perhaps you never let Him get a word in, madame."

For the rest, during the interval, during this phase of passivity, which is nevertheless full of hidden activity and movement, the patient's unconscious will continue to express itself, to communicate its secret instinctive life. We have no need to set the comprehension of unconscious constellations artificially in motion. It moves of itself. What is repressed shows traces of itself in concealing itself. It thrusts itself forward in the offshoots that it sends out with growing boldness, all the while demonstratively withdrawing itself. It rises to a crescendo of clarification. What is repressed shows traces of itself until it has found a solution—and even a little longer, so that we may not think it is the solution. There is no analytic timetable for the unconscious.

It is not necessary—I say this in conscious opposition to well-known recent tendencies—that every single treatment should show results. It need only have consequences. We know that what is psychologically most important in analysis often occurs, not during the treatments, but in the intervals between them. Why should we deny it? The long duration of the analytic process is undoubtedly due in part to the analyst, who will not pretend to be able to take in the secrets of the inner life at a glance. These pages, which tell the inside story of psychoanalysis, show how much unconscious and conscious labor is done by the psychoanalyst while he sits smoking, apparently passive, in his easy chair.

The unconscious interval between the preconscious impressions and their conscious psychological capture is a break in our efforts to attain comprehension of psychical phenomena by direct means. In making the break we cherish the expectation that the impressions will develop during the period of latency, will become clearer and take fruitful effect. How often has it happened that we have been able to reach only very imperfect comprehension of some particular network of symptoms, have been able only very partially to explain a complicated case of neurosis or character-distortion? We have been obliged to interrupt the treatment on account of some organic disease of the patient's or some unavoidable journey of our own. After an interval we return to the analytic treatment of the patient. Nothing essential is changed in his symptoms in the meantime, the neurosis or the character-difficulties remain the same. And yet their hidden meaning has suddenly become clear to us; we recognize some relation hitherto unconscious, veiled from our sight; we conjecture the purpose of the repression. Something has happened within ourselves, in the relation between the preconscious and the unconscious, that has clarified our dimmed sight. We hear again what we have heard so often, but we hear something different in it. Now, at last, we feel psychologically at home after a long absence.

The essence of the unconscious interval then, this fruitful pause, consists in our not striving consciously to comprehend the inner processes and trusting to the psychological efforts of our own unconscious the while. Nameless psychical forces within us have accomplished the work in the pause, like the brownies of the fairy tale in the darkness of night. And then it is as if a wall, which we thought to be firm and immovable and against which we had beaten in vain, suddenly vanishes spontaneously, leaving a free view of hidden things. We really ought not to be surprised at psychological comprehension taking shape, unobserved by us, in this interval, for we know that man is aware only of a small part of what he experiences. Once again, as so often in our investigation of mental processes, the significance of the time factor in the analyst's work appears in a special light. Here it stands in close relation to the factor of psychical readiness to comprehend the unconscious; we must on occasion be able to wait in order to reach our goal.

Often in the moment when our ideas and thoughts about unconscious processes emerge, we know no more of their significance and trend, whither they are leading us and how far they are preparing and determining further perceptions, than we do of what precedes them. We do not always know at once, when we have discovered something, *what* we have discovered. It is therefore of importance not only to seize upon the point of departure of an idea or thought but also to return to the idea or thought later and to pursue it in all its possible implications. Only when it is so resumed will it show what it was worth and how far it can lead the investigating intellect. In psychoanalysis, as in all sciences, there are sterile truths and fruitful errors.

It is often particularly difficult to detect the conjectured unconscious significance in the more remote offshoots and derivatives of a repressed thought, to pursue it into all its retreats and hiding-places. For these unconscious, instinctive traits, once they have been discovered and interpreted, will make themselves harder and harder to detect in the further course of the analysis, will conceal themselves better and more carefully; they will assume, with the help of conscious powers, distortions more and more difficult to penetrate. Let me again resort to a comparison; let us suppose that we are playing hide-and-seek with a child of two. It is enough for us to hide behind the nearest tree. If we play with the same child ten years later, we shall assuredly not choose so easy a hiding-place.

If a thought or idea proves valuable when we take it up again and subject it to examination, the requirements of analysis demand that we should, so to speak, let it sound till it fades away spontaneously. To get hold of an unconscious thought or emotion is only one part of the analytic process. To follow it, to observe its consequences, reverberations, and repercussions in the unconscious life of the person is the other part. It is important not to lose the thread one has seized. We shall then, certainly, allow conscious intellectual effort to play a great part in following, slowly and carefully, the further intellectual possibilities thus emerging. At the same time, it will not be possible to dispense entirely with the co-operation of the analyst's unconscious. We might compare this pursuit of our own idea to the end, with the manner of bowing on the violin called *molto sostenuto.*

CHAPTER XIX

Conjecture

IF I AM asked why I do not demonstrate the difference between conjecture and comprehension by describing a complete case of neurosis, I must admit that it would have been more interesting, and probably more illuminating, to show, by describing a case of hysteria or phobia, how we make our approach to analytic comprehension. That would make plain how a first, preconscious presentiment of the hidden purposes and the psychogenesis of the disease emerges from a number of impressions, how it grows clearer and clearer, and how new perceptions help us to understand the conditions and development of the psychical processes and to grasp the case in all its local, dynamic, and instinctive-economic conditions. In such a description, moreover, we could show what manifold corrections and modifications this first conjecture undergoes, how it sometimes proves false, and more often inadequate and incomplete; and that no less often it is partially or wholly confirmed by the further progress of the analysis. But such a description would require many hundreds of pages. It would be a book in itself, and there are a few things I want to say that are not contained in one case history.

As a poor substitute, I shall cite a few examples from the symptomatology of neuroses:

Shortly after the first World War, Freud referred a British patient to me. The man had been a physician in the British army and had spent a few years in India in an advanced post near the jungle with three other white officers and a few hundred native soldiers. He now suffered with disturbances in his work, psychic impotence, and social shyness.

214

Shortly after beginning his analysis I became aware of two of his personal peculiarities: he was unable to say "no" and could not contradict anyone. While he appeared soft-spoken and overpolite, other features showed that he was difficult to deal with, and in contrast to his meek manner, he was stubborn and defiant. The amiable grin he very frequently showed puzzled me: it was like a mask he could not take off. It seemed to be the expression of a "keep smiling" attitude but it appeared at the most inappropriate times when other people would have been sad or furious.

It was on his face when he told me the story of these years when he lived near the jungle cut off from civilization. Although there were many reasons for friction, he never had the slightest disagreement with any of the three officers, the only white people he saw. I assumed that he was afraid of them, that he yielded to everything they wanted and never expressed his own views in conversation. Once when he smilingly related a scene in which his superior, a drunken major, had abused him before the others, I caught myself feeling the same mysterious grin on my face and I knew immediately what it meant. The man was not afraid of his superiors, but of himself. He was afraid of the intensity of his own rage. He felt he would lose all self-control if he once gave in to his emotions. He would, he thought, get into a frenzy of violence and run amuck, if he contradicted others to assert himself. He must have thought he would kill the brutish major and the other two officers who made fun of him if he let himself get angry. His grin was thus compulsive and covered his murderous impulses. He had built a wall of protection around his real self which prevented the break-through of his violent and aggressive tendencies.

Compare this case with the following: A young man now under analytic treatment had been in love with a girl who had promised to marry him. She suddenly declared to him that she would marry another suitor who was a wealthy and socially prominent acquaintance of the young man and who had showered her with gifts and flowers. The other day, a few years after this event, my patient thought that he saw his victorious rival on the other side of the street. He felt an intensive fear that threatened to develop into panic, so he walked quickly away. It became clear to me that this was his reaction to a suddenly emerging impulse to walk over and hit the other man over the head. He really ran away from his own senseless fury.

The character of their own emotions was unconscious to both patients. The initial insight into the nature of their reactions does not deserve the name of understanding them. The difference between guessing and comprehending corresponds to a flash of light which illuminates for a few seconds the concealed entrance into a shaft and a thorough investigation of this shaft in a permanent light. To understand means in analysis to trace back a symptom, a nervous disturbance, to its origin to find whether it belongs to the repressed, the disavowed, or the conscious. And to grasp what place the suppressed impulse or thought has in the psychic household of the patient, what significance it has for his personality and what are its connections with other symptoms.

Yesterday a young girl from a southern state consulted me and told me in a nice drawl her nervous complaints. Among them was a fear that haunted her. Some years ago she had a date in her home city with a married man to whom she had felt attracted. There was a petting party and others followed. Their intimacies did not go beyond kissing and fondling. She broke up the relationship after a few weeks. In spite of all the reasons she herself brought forward, she could not overcome her fears that the fact she had had these dates could become known not only in her home town but also in New York, a few thousand miles away, though she knew nobody here before. And she imagined this gossip would prevent her getting married. There was not the slightest reason to assume that anyone knew of her previous flirtation, or cared if the fact were known. What reasonable man would expect that a girl of twenty-nine had never been kissed before? All this she said to herself, but reasoning did not help. She sobbed when she told me the story. I shall not pretend to understand the determinants of her fears.

After listening to her for fifty minutes, there was only a single suspicion which had occurred to me while I followed the story. The date with that man was the first in which she was really courted and kissed. When she was much younger and in high school, she had been rather fat and unusually tall. On account of these handicaps she had not been very popular with the boys and had acquired an inferiority-feeling which remained though she later came to have a normal figure. The thought occurred to me that there must have been something in her fears that was unconsciously wished. Would she, who was considered unattractive, not have unconsciously wished it to become known among her girl friends and other people that a man wooed and desired her? Was it not so that what she was most afraid of was at the same time of some comfort for another part of herself, more than that, even a source of pride? Her complaints sounded so exaggerated, so unreal, that one could well suspect she unconsciously wished that everybody back home might know that this man had loved just her to whom nobody had paid much attention. Like other girls, she also wanted the man who now wishes to marry her to know that other men had found her desirable. Hidden from herself, there was satisfaction in the very thing of which she was afraid. My impression did not amount to more than a hunch, but even if it could be confirmed and verified later, it certainly did not mean I understood the case. It only meant I got a glimpse of some contours in the darkness, a faint notion that is not very useful in its isolation from the other factors in the case that are perhaps more psychologically important. It would take a long time and much analytic study to understand the nature of the girl's fear.

I once had a patient, suffering from a serious compulsion neurosis, who forced the chambermaid in the hotel where he lived into the service of his complicated compulsion to wash. Among other things he set up an elaborate washing ceremonial, the central feature of which was the manipulation of towels coming back from the laundry. The chambermaid had to bring the towels made up in packets of thirty, bearing them on arms outstretched in a particular way. She had to knock at the door and wait till the patient had spread a linen cloth on the floor, upon which the towels were laid. Thereupon the chambermaid had to advance a certain number of steps, then walk leftward at a word of command, with her arms still outstretched in such a way that she touched neither the washstand nor the door leading to the bathroom, and so forth. The slightest deviation from the prescribed movements, the smallest nonobservance of the steps or pauses enjoined excited the patient to fury. No questions were allowed about the special object of the actions. Particular little movements had to be performed just so, even if they seemed quite senseless.

I will not describe the structure and origin of his compulsion, nor show how the compulsion to wash had grown up as a psychical reaction to an exaggerated method of training him to cleanliness at an early age, nor just how it bore evidence of a bitter struggle against masturbation in childhood. Each of the actions and omissions of the ritual with the maid had its adequate unconscious meaning within the system of the compulsion neurosis. I will not enter here into the meaning discovered by analysis, but only into a secondary feature of the patient's conduct during the ceremonial, his tyrannical stubbornness. I will merely demonstrate the difference between psychological conjecture and comprehension through this one feature. It often seemed as if he only wanted to assert his will against every demur, and to suppress maliciously the smallest notion of independence in the fulfillment of his commands.

What was the unconscious meaning of the senseless doings with the chambermaid? We could conjecture it, if we trusted to the unconscious images in our own minds, that accompanied the repeated descriptions of the ceremonial given during analysis.

The analytic idea that emerged at this point led to the conclusion that the scene might be understood as the caricature and reversal of a situation in the patient's childhood. A certain nursemaid had played a great part in the little boy's life. This woman had trained the refractory boy very strictly to a degree of cleanliness that he intensely disliked. Every one of her orders had to be obeyed unquestioningly by the exceptionally intelligent child. It looked like belated revenge when the adult demanded the same behavior as the nursemaid had formerly done, grotesquely exaggerated, with the position reversed and with a displacement-surrogate. It looked like a representation in caricature. Each single movement was exactly laid down. The utmost care was taken to prevent the clean linen from touching the furniture of the room. The patient fell into a rage the moment there was the slightest deviation from the ceremonial; he could not tolerate the smallest criticism and had to assert his will. In this reversed situation he let a representative of the hated, but also admired, nursemaid feel what he had had to suffer as a child; and he played the part of his former tormentor. The element of unconscious defiance and scorn in his behavior was clear.

In such a case, I knew, the step from conjecture to comprehension would be attained chiefly by acquiring a knowledge of the patient's life story. Of course, the interpretation that occurred to me to explain the nature of the patient's ceremonial had only a provisional character and had later on to be replaced by a detailed and penetrating analysis of each single feature of his behavior. For the time being it was, however, the only way in which I could approach an understanding of his actions.

Where, for instance, did I get the idea that the real text or content of his behavior could only be recognized by a reversal? Certainly not from remembering the reading of analytic books or attending lectures or seminars, because I did not think of my student days. It must be that I traced this mechanism as operating while I listened to his description. It was an idea that accompanied me. Then, when I tried to find whence it came, I could only answer: from experience, that is, from memory-traces of phenomena I had observed before. But which? I could not say because none of the cases presented themselves to my memory at the moment.

Wait a moment. Here was one, at least. I remembered the dream in which I first met such a mechanism of reversal. Was it not the present patient himself who was educated to cleanliness with such severe discipline? Another patient once told me that he had dreamed a very nonsensical dream that made him laugh. *He is himself in the dream, just as he is now, a man nearly forty years old. He is in the bathroom and near him on a chair stands his mother (who died many years ago). He puts a sponge into the water, covers it with soap, and washes his mother's face most energetically. The old woman cries bitterly.* It was, of course, obvious that the latent content of the dream would be revealed by turning the persons around. In the dream he got even with his disciplinarian mother at this late date. (It seems that I guessed the meaning of my present patient's obsession with the help of previous cases wherein I had recognized the distorting effects of reversal.)

It goes without saying that the way leading to conjecture of the unconscious meaning of a symptom, a fantasy, or given behavior, varies with the nature and extent of the available psychological evidence. At an advanced stage of the analysis, when we have already discovered much about the patient's psychical conditions and motives and are familiar with his individual manner of reacting, we conjecture with greater assurance. The results of our own mental activity, unconscious and conscious, come nearer to the psychical facts under investigation than at the initial stage.

For instance, the patient just cited could hardly touch anything with his bare hands. In order to touch door handles, money, or letters, he had to use gloves or paper napkins, which he afterward laid down in a particular place. At a later stage of the analysis, in which the symptoms became for the time being worse and more intense, he avoided contact by using ordinary brown toilet paper instead of gloves, because it was cheaper. Each time he threw down the crumpled piece of paper with which he had touched an object in one particular place in the room, where a heap of brown paper soon collected.

It was no great analytic feat to detect in this behavior one of the original motives of his fear of contact. Here, as so often in this later stage of a compulsion neurosis, the repressed content emerged from what was repressing it. Whereas one of the essential aims of his neurotic precautions was to protect himself from pollution, especially by faeces, a belated protest against his exaggerated training in cleanliness here broke through the very heart of his neurotic efforts at avoidance. The earthly remains, which he consciously found it so unpleasant to carry, were demonstratively piled up in the room. Behind the adult, who, with his compulsion neurosis, takes such pains to preserve cleanliness, we discern the defiant child who flings the soiled toilet paper into the middle of the room, to the displeasure of those about him.

Experienced analysts sometimes succeed soon after the beginning of the analysis in conjecturing the, or rather one, hidden meaning of a neurosis, or the clue to one of its chief symptoms. Let us take the following case. A young woman suffered from the obsession that on every possible (or not so possible) occasion she might have been used sexually by a strange man. She protected herself against the situation she feared by extensive neurotic precautions. She must never be left alone for a moment; her husband must always be close at hand. If he went into an adjoining room to fetch something, or retired to the toilet, she suffered from the fear that in the interval the waiter in the hotel where she lived might come in and seduce her. She loaded her husband with bitter reproaches on his return because he had left her alone again and abandoned her to her tormenting doubts. For instance, she drove through town in a taxi with her husband and he stopped at a tobacconist's to buy cigarettes. He found her despairing and in tears when he got into the taxi again a few minutes later. She feared that the driver might have violated her in the interval.

Undoubtedly it is correct to deduce, in such a case, a neurotic defense against unconscious seduction fantasies, but the special character of the lady's fears and the emotional effect produced enabled us to conjecture other, additional unconscious aims. The result of her obsessive fear was that her husband had always to be close at hand, and that she tormented him in a special way by her grotesque anxiety about preserving her chastity. One early conjectures how much scorn and bitterness lie concealed in the behavior due to her compulsion neurosis; presumably, also, it represents a cruel revenge for a long-past aberration on the part of her husband, secretly discovered by her. Needless to say, this effective form of vengeance had the secondary purpose and secondary effect of keeping the untrustworthy husband at her side and under her eye.

To conjecture these hidden tendencies is certainly not the same as comprehending them in the analytic sense. That is proved by the mere fact that further analytic study of the origin of the neurosis enabled me to establish the historical conditions, the strata of the case.

With morbid and unjustifiable suspicion, the parents had hardly ever allowed the girl to go out for an hour alone, had supervised her friendships strictly and had constantly and urgently warned her against the seductive arts of the young men of the town. Her memory revived an experience, dating from a much earlier period, that she had had as a little girl at home. A workman employed in the house had approached her with signs of sexual excitement, which she reported to her mother at once. A less clear memory recalled a time when she had been ill as a child and had lain in her father's bed and had by chance felt his penis touch her body.

It is interesting to note, moreover, that the intense jealousy, which was so important a factor in the origin of this patient's compulsion neurosis symptoms, likewise appeared in a characteristic form in her younger sister, who underwent analysis for certain hysterical troubles. This girl, who had recently become engaged, passed many hours of the day in reveries made up of scenes of seduction with various types of men. In these daydreams she "tested" the men, as she said, that is, she imagined how such and such a one would behave in sexual situations, and what sensual pleasure she would feel with each. She especially enjoyed imagining that she was going to deceive her consciously beloved fiancé just before the wedding, so that another man would rob her of her virginity. Here, too, certain features pointed to these fantasies being revengeful in character, and betrayed her resentment that in her country the young men were allowed full sexual freedom, while the girls were strictly guarded. She accounted for her fantasies by saying that she suffered so much from the fear that her future husband would assuredly often deceive her later, that she wanted to take her revenge in advance. It is easy to conjecture the psychological significance of the identification with a man and the repressed homosexuality in the psychogenesis of both sisters' illnesses. I must stop, or I shall really yield to the temptation of describing a complete case of neurosis.

Let us now go back to the two intellectual activities in the analytic process, to the differences between conjecture and comprehension. Let's suppose a crime has been committed somewhere. The unknown culprit has left certain clues at the scene of the crime, has lost a handkerchief or left a cigarette butt in the ash tray. The detectives follow up the clues and pick up someone as the suspect. And now the interrogation of the culprit begins, the close investigation of the circumstances of the crime, the examination of the prisoner's statement, and all the processes designed to throw light on the crime and the evidence. We may compare actions of the first kind—criminologists distinguish between the preservation, the examination, and the employment of the clues—with psychological conjecture. Then the reconstruction of the crime and the conviction of the culprit correspond to the intellectual processes that I call comprehension.

Let us pause a little over this comparison with the investigation of crime. In spite of the fact that both procedures have the same goal, namely to throw light on the deed, there are important differences between them. In spite of the various points of agreement, the methods of a judge differ essentially from those of a detective or police officer. The means employed to accomplish their common purpose are as different as the analyst's in the processes of conjecture and comprehension. The first endeavors to ascertain the facts about the crime are of a provisional nature. Inevitably, they allow much more room for uncertainty and doubt than the procedure of proof, which requires the strictest and most careful examination, criminological and logical, of each separate item and of the whole process, and must aim at a perfectly consistent reconstruction of the course of the crime. The common features of the two methods are due to the fact that the work of the examining magistrate is linked up with the preceding investigations by the police, that he tests, corrects, and supplements their conclusions and accepts the results of the preliminary investigation as useful, or rejects them as misleading.

In spite of the practical connection, difficulties will seldom arise over the question of competence. A detective will not presume to perform duties proper to the magistrate, nor will the latter occupy himself in tracking the culprit. Corresponding common features and differences show up between the procedures of conjecturing and comprehending unconscious processes in analysis. The two activities are mainly carried on in different mental planes.

Conjecturing may be described as the initial process. In this preliminary stage the analyst behaves like the detective, who ensures the preservation of every clue, follows it up, and makes use of it. He certainly does not concern himself *first and foremost* with the logical proof of his idea, and often pursues contradictory trains of thought. He has an open mind and does not shrink from yielding himself, by way of experiment, to a train of thought that seems senseless and absurd. At this stage it would be a mistake to demand logical justification for his own ideas, or to admit only such thoughts as could establish themselves as "reasonable" and in harmony with the laws of logic. In this period of preparation one must, so to speak, lower one's demands to the social level of one's own thoughts, and give a hearing to disreputable, radical, even wild ideas, the rabble.

And here the withdrawal of the intellectual censor is as important for the analyst who wants to conjecture the purpose of unconscious processes, as for the patient. An analyst must pay regard to all psychological indications, even to those that seem least important. The principle of poised attention holds good in the first attempt to establish the circumstances both of a psychological situation and a crime.

It is amazing to observe how few people really know how to use their eyes and ears, and how much we all shut our minds unconsciously against the reception of more than one or two definite impressions. The same unconscious resistance recurs later in the realm of ideas. There, too, we refuse to recognize certain ideas, have no eyes for images that rise before us for a moment, and no ears for thoughts that "walk on dove's feet," to use a beautiful simile of Nietzsche's.

At the beginning of her analysis, a young woman doctor described her feelings during sexual intercourse in a quiet, objective manner. In doing so she spoke of sensations at the *"orificium uteri,"* the *"mons Veneris,"* and so forth. As I listened I felt a slight touch of astonishment. It was quickly suppressed. Why should not a doctor use these Latin terms? They are familiar to her. The subsequent course of the analysis proved my reasonable reflection to have been misplaced, and my fleeting sense of astonishment to have been psychologically justified. Her markedly objective manner of speaking about sexual matters proved to be mental camouflage. At a later stage it was easy to ascertain that the young doctor's apparent lack of embarrassment in speaking on the subject of sex, concealed a strong hysterical inhibition.

Again and again in analysis we see the difference between the noisy things that strike us and the effective things that hint gently at their presence.

A young Englishman came into my consulting-room with his pipe in his mouth and talked without removing it. I felt inclined to point out his bad manners to him, but of course repressed all comment and said to myself that perhaps this nonchalant manner was the fashion, unknown to me, in certain circles in the aristocratic colleges from which the patient came. The impression was soon blotted out, and only re-emerged much later in the analysis, when it turned out that the patient was an embittered masochist who wanted to provoke the desired punishment by a demonstratively easy, and sometimes impudent, manner. I might have saved myself many a devious path in the analysis if I had held fast to my fleeting impression.

Just as in criminology people long failed to realize the importance of guarding the clues on the scene of the crime from unskilful or careless hands, of preserving small indications of apparently minor significance for subsequent examination and use, so the art of analysis will pay increasing attention to the fleeting, barely noticeable impressions that we generally overlook or fail to capture. In the psychology of the unconscious, too, it is very important to "preserve the clues." It is much more difficult, yes, it is sometimes impossible to follow them when they are "cold."

Experience of analysis shows that the psychological demonstrative force of these small, unsuspicious-looking impressions, which we hardly notice, is enhanced when we remember them as they re-emerge. They gain in intensity through repetition.

It is easy to demonstrate how mistaken and foolish it is to interpolate prolonged conscious reflections and logical processes during the stage of gathering evidence that precedes analytic conjecture, and how it must disturb the free play of the analyst's associations if he reverts to his theoretical knowledge during this time. It would be as inappropriate and mistaken as if a detective who wants to discover an unknown criminal were to employ the juridical and logical methods of the judge. The unearthing of the culprit is not the marshaling of evidence. The detective's work in bringing a crime to light or to identify the criminal is different from the reconstruction of the crime during the trial.

But what I condemn as out of place during the phase of preparation for the conjecture of unconscious processes, is justified fully in the final phase that precedes comprehension. Here the foremost place falls by right to logical classification and reflection, to deduction, to the strict examination and criticism of single facts, to the application of conscious knowledge; in short, to all the processes of rational thought. I have already said why I have not treated these intellectual processes as fully as the psychical processes in the phase of analysis preceding conjecture. It is only in their material, the unconscious mind, that they differ from analogous processes in the other sciences, not in their nature. They are not peculiar to the analytic method, and, in spite of their great importance, they do not require exhaustive discussion in an inquiry directed primarily toward the peculiar characteristics of our method.

CHAPTER XX

Comprehension

Y OU are familiar with a column entitled "Believe It or Not." Mr. Ripley takes strange facts from natural science, history, and the lives of people and communities, and groups cartoons of three or four of them in a daily newspaper feature. What links these brief picture-statements together is that each of them tells an objectively demonstrable fact that the average reader can hardly believe. Reading the captions we are often inclined to cry: "That is impossible. It sounds incredible." And yet they are undoubted facts, taken mostly from our directly accessible surroundings. "Believe It or Not" by no means confines itself to rarities. It also gives a large number of facts from everyday life, of which we knew nothing or which we had not observed.

Analysts could present the reader with a yet larger collection of facts from the inner world, each of which would sound even more incredible. Indeed, the reader of a psychological column headed "Believe It or Not" would quickly decide in favor of the second alternative. And yet he would be wrong, for these statements about strange processes in the unconscious also tell facts, and many of them are more interesting and important than those in Ripley's collection. It is true that in our case it would be much more difficult to prove them objectively, for only a man who has himself learned to apply analytic methods in investigating unconscious processes can convince himself of their correctness.

I have said that in analysis the psychological results obtained are tested and criticized in the phase in which comprehension enters our minds, and that the testing must be performed with all the strictness of conscious and logical thought. What is at first often grasped and conjectured only unconsciously must pass through the filter of the intellect before its truth can be confirmed. The guarantee for the truth of the analytic result depends upon the sense of intellectual responsibility and the mental honesty of the scientific worker in question. Here the analytic procedure differs nowise in principle from other scientific methods. If we proceed in this way, error is not, indeed, excluded, but its possible occurrence is confined within certain limits. To be sure we cannot produce indubitable logical proof of the action of certain repressed impulses, for then they would have to be laid bare, and they do not reveal themselves sensibly to the observer. There is often no objective certainty of the correctness of a situation reconstructed by analysis. But anyone who accepts certain fundamental assumptions of analysis and who thinks psychologically will find his doubts vanishing, if he himself conducts the investigation conscientiously. The appearance of arbitrariness in an analytic deduction or reconstruction vanishes when we have convinced ourselves how many, and what weighty, factors support it.

An analytic example's psychological power to convince can best be realized by one who knows that it generally only seems to rest upon the psychological factors adduced, but is in reality the last link in a long chain of widely scattered perceptions. It would take too long to give examples of such interpretation, with all the determining psychological factors. But any example will show how interpretation is reached.

In her treatment today an American patient told me of an argument that she had recently had with an Englishman. The conversation started with questions of musical taste. The gentleman said that a year ago he had been very fond of Wagner, but this year he preferred Beethoven; nevertheless, his friends were wrong when they called him inconsistent. The patient thought the expression undoubtedly wrong; it would be better to call him inconstant. And now a difference of opinion arose as to the meaning of the two words, which almost turned into a quarrel, thanks to the patient's aggressive attitude. The Englishman asserted that the word "inconstant" was generally used with the meaning of "unreliable or changeable in love." The patient denied it vehemently. People used, for instance, the phrase "a constant sufferer" and spoke of "constant anxiety," she said. The gentleman retorted by pointing to the title of a well-known novel, *The Constant Nymph*, by Margaret Kennedy, in which the meaning he maintained appeared plainly. They referred the question to the *Oxford Dictionary*, but its dictum was only the starting-point for fresh arguments, in which the living speech habits in America and England were called in as evidence.

The superficial impression received is that of a chance dispute in which an emotional mood found expression, arising from the well-known tension between the Americans and the British. And no doubt there were other, more personal, causes of tension on both sides, as is indicated by the reproof concealed in the term "inconstant."

Any auditor who was at all accustomed to regard things psychologically could not help seeing that the dispute turned upon something quite other than the verbal meaning. But are we right in assuming that, in addition to these easily recognized factors, a particular repressed motive was responsible for the patient's emotional attitude? Can we prove that her excitement in this argument about the word "constant" was partly due to an unconscious recollection of the name "Constance"? The patient had had an affair at home with a man who till then had been attached to her younger sister, Constance. If my surmise is right, a dispute about a chance word was carried on so angrily on this occasion because a concealed reference to herself became involved in the discussion of a linguistic question. That only occurred when the gentleman declared that "inconstant" was applied exclusively to fickleness in love. It was only then that the lady contradicted him vehemently. The word must have stirred an unconscious memory distressing to her, of the affair with her sister Constance's lover, and must have touched upon certain inner emotions relating to the sister she loved and envied. Does it not appear as an indication of certain morbid states in her sister when, in refuting her opponent's arguments, she referred to the customary phrase "a constant sufferer"? This interpretation is not, indeed, evident to an outsider. And it would hardly become so, if I were to add that the patient, to whom I had not communicated it, later came to speak of her sister and the man in the course of loosely connected associations. Strictly speaking, only an observer who had witnessed the whole of the foregoing analysis, and had thus received the same strong impressions of the emotional life and the unconscious processes of this particular person, could judge of the probability of such an interpretation or analytic explanation.

Perhaps it is even more difficult to justify the analytic conception of an unconscious phenomenon belonging to the twilight region between reality and fancy that we call transference. Once again, I will give only a simple example. Analytic treatment had successfully freed the young woman suffering from compulsion neurosis, of whom I have already told, from the particularly tormenting doubt whether somebody—a waiter, worker, or taxi-driver—had not seduced her during a few moments in which she was alone with him. During the last stage of her analytic treatment her energy and interest in life were so far restored that she determined to give lessons in dancing, in which she had earlier received training, in order to lighten her husband's responsibility for her maintenance. Although the lessons turned out a success, new doubts arose, this time, indeed, of a different kind. She was now obsessed by the doubt whether she had taught her pupils right, whether she might not have reached her goal as a teacher by some quicker method, whether she was not unnecessarily prolonging the course in order to earn more money, whether she had the requisite knowledge and skill to teach her pupils as much as they wished to learn, whether she was justified in charging high fees. She spent many hours of the day brooding over these and similar questions.

How shall I prove that these questions reflected certain doubts, transferred to herself, which the patient felt about me and the analytic treatment, and that they reproduced the repressed suspicions that made her doubt my intentions and my abilities? She was conscious of none of this, and she stoutly denied any such doubt or mistrust of me at the present time. None the less, countless little things pointed to unconscious thoughts of the kind. Perhaps I could not give a stronger impression of the correctness of my interpretation, even if I were in a position to recount all the insignificant-looking indications, and to show how her doubts owed their form to the action of the same mechanism that revealed itself in her anxiety about the maintenance of conjugal fidelity, and in other obsessive symptoms not here described. Consciously her doubts referred to another person closely connected with her, to whom her intense ambivalence found expression in the veiled form of accusations.

Once again at this point there arises the still unanswered question of the evidence in support of analytic interpretation. Like every scientific method, analysis aims at securing objective evidence to support its statements. That is more difficult than with other methods because, in order to achieve it, the critic must be willing to accept particular assumptions, since certain psychological assumptions are indispensable—for instance, a conviction of the existence and action of repressed impulses, and of the universal determinism of psychical phenomena.

Even then it is more difficult to prove the objective correctness of an interpretation than in other sciences, not because the analytic method ignores experience, but because *here experience is of a different kind.*

To state the case more trenchantly: the difference lies, not in the more or less empirical character of the investigation, but in the *nature of the subject of investigation.* In many cases we can do no more than rest content with the subjective evidence. As is well known, it often happens in analysis that the analyst adheres to a certain interpretation or explanation of a mental phenomenon, even against the contrary opinion of the patient. Full psychological confirmation is inherent in the interpretation itself, before such confirmation is received from the patient or from outsiders. If the analyst has done his work honestly, if he has tested his ideas strictly and convinced himself conscientiously, by their application to the psychological data, that they are true, he will have the right to hold to his opinion, even when those around him try to shake his conviction by every method of opposition, accusing him of rigid dogmatism and heaping scorn upon him. To quote Freud's unforgettable words, "Nothing remains (for the analyst) but to maintain his conviction, based upon his experience, with all his might, after listening to the voice of his own self-criticism very carefully and to that of his opponents with fair attention."

Of course, every analyst will readily admit that his interpretations have not always hit the mark, that his psychological explanations have erred in one case or another, that an assumption has later proved a delusion. We know—indeed, we know better than our opponents—that limits are set to our psychological knowledge, and we know what they are. So obvious an admission, which every worker is ready to make in his science, must not be interpreted as a special apology for analysis.

For the rest, I may take this opportunity to point out that errors in our psychological assumptions need not by any means always prove useless, if we have worked conscientiously to the best of our knowledge. Sometimes a partial justification of the error emerges later, occasionally it proves fruitful, in that the assumption, though it did not hit the bull's eye, came very near to it. Sometimes an error, corrected later, calls our attention to the truth, which we should not have detected without it.

I trust that in my description I have distinguished clearly enough between the two phases in the analytic illumination of what goes on in the unconscious mind—perhaps, indeed, too clearly, a mistake which can only be justified by the descriptive purpose of the account. In real life there is no such sharp dividing line as is here indicated between the processes of conjecture and comprehension. Nevertheless, we can see even in real life that the productive element in our psychological labors, in which I include the reproductive element, can be separated from a critical element. There, too, we detect the Janus face of analytic work, turned toward the free play of fancy and toward conscious intellectual effort. Though the two faces may show a certain family likeness, they are nevertheless different. No analyst will deny that the process of cognition in our science generally passes through the two phases here depicted, that its beginning is dominated by one of the faces, its end by the other.

We have traveled far, from a description of groping presentiment almost to that of a clear, scientific, definite cognition of the hidden impulses of the soul. We may compare our journey to the change from early dawn, which only shows things in vague outline, to the morning, when they appear sharply delineated. The fact stated with such excessive emphasis, that the aim of psychoanalysis is to bring the investigation of unconscious processes "within the range of reason" assuredly does not mean that this aim can be attained solely *by the methods* of conscious reason.

It would seem advisable to come to a psychological understanding about the nature of comprehension, since that is our goal. Comprehension appears to me to be a purely intellectual process, indeed the model of such a process. If, meanwhile, we submit the question of the origin of the act of comprehension to a closer psychological examination, we shall realize that originally it was a kind of taking possession, in a much more material sense. The root sense of the word points to that, and may be compared with "understand" (to put oneself in the place of something). The German word *"begreifen"* (used almost synonymously with *"verstehen"*), the French *comprendre,* and the Italian *"capire"* approach more nearly to the earliest meaning of the process. They show that originally it amounted to "taking possession of things, seizing them." The physical quality of the object, the material nature and proximity of what was to be comprehended, must at first have been very important, indeed a necessary condition of comprehension.

In the early days of the human race there can have been no comprehension of abstract things in our sense. It would have been self-contradictory. To comprehend something, people had to catch hold of it, to "grasp" it. It is no mere chance that we use this word, too, in the sense of comprehend. If we compare the word "conceive" in its root meaning, which is undoubtedly material, with the word "conception" in the sense of a purely logical structure, we shall realize how far the process of comprehension or conception has traveled from its original nature. Intellectual, non-concrete comprehension in logical inferences and conclusions represents the latest stage in this development. Man undoubtedly lived many hundreds of thousands of years upon the earth without feeling any need to comprehend his surroundings in our sense. Every day teaches us that even in our time that need is by no means one of the strongest in the human race.

Comprehension is a special way of reacting to the impressions that life brings us, a special case of mental mastery of them, certainly the latest and most spiritual type. In psychology we should express it by saying that to comprehend another, to grasp the mental processes in the world around us, is a particular way of mastering inwardly the stimuli that we receive from the existence and behavior of others, a way of assimilating our impressions mentally, in a sense. The objection will be raised that our comprehension of another person is often just the way to prepare a particular reaction or action. It is not as a rule an end in itself, but is made to serve other ends. Quite true. But that does not exclude the possibility of its representing in itself a definite type of reaction; a preparatory action, if you like, a provisional attitude. We can all confirm from our own experience that comprehension often postpones or modifies our primitive or elementary motor reaction. That, perhaps, is the glimmer of truth in the false and sentimental saying: to understand everything is to forgive everything. The latent sense concealed in the proverb, which we fully understand, refers to the obvious fact that our original reaction was the reverse of pardon, and that it was afterward replaced by understanding.

I have said that in a general way comprehension is the result of the effort to seize or grasp something physically, and that psychological comprehension denotes a special form of mastery of mental excitement. The most primitive and crudest form of this mastery is doubtless incorporation. To incorporate something, to devour it to the last morsel, is the elementary way in which primitive man made things "comprehensible," made them his own. He then knew all that was worth knowing about the object, that is, what it tasted like. Working backward, he could infer—in so far as he was at all concerned with logical processes—what the object was, or rather, what it had been. We cannot deny the historical connection between the most sublimated passion for knowledge and the primitive desire to devour. Psychoanalysis has arrived by clinical methods at the derivation of our desire to know from our urge to seize.

We find a surviving trace of this origin when we see how children open their mouths when they are surprised. One need not be an unquestioning adherent of Darwin's theory of expressive actions in order to assume the likelihood that this movement gives expression to the reflexive residuum of an original impulse to devour something. Everybody knows that the little ones do not always make a halt at the "preparatory action." Surprise then finds expression not only through the hands but also through the mouth. It shows that we must look here for the most infantile, the archaic form of comprehension.

What has the derivation of comprehension to do with our purpose of studying certain psychological problems? Something at any rate, for this peculiar origin of the process of comprehension will never quite lose its force. It will make itself felt, in a distorted and utterly emasculated form, even in the complicated and, so it seems, intellectually determined processes of conceiving and forming conceptions. The fact that the origin of comprehension was the act of incorporating an object, that at the beginning of human evolution it amounted to feeling the object within oneself, will never quite lose its significance. Originally, one may suppose, it did not matter whether a man swallowed the object dead or alive. What mattered was the swallowing. The object comprehended must be changed from "it" to a part of the ego, from something without to something within. To this very day we use the expression "thirst for knowledge." It is not accidental that we can speak of a subject's being incorporated, and that we speak jestingly of lapping up a story, etc. Later this physical meaning was quite lost sight of; comprehension had become assimilation in the well-known intellectual sense.

Psychological comprehension of another person is a special case of this sublimated seizure and incorporation. It is, in a sense, psychological cannibalism. The other person is taken into your ego and becomes, for the time being, a part of your ego. Thus in the process of psychological comprehension man's craving for power is satisfied, not only in its most refined and sublimated form, but unconsciously in its crudest. It is true that the process of taking in the object, of introducing it into ourselves, is much more complicated from a psychological point of view than might appear at the first glance.

The division between the ego and the external world is a relatively late product of individual development. Anyone observing a very young baby can see that he knows nothing of the difference. In the beginning, from the psychological point of view, there is only the ego. The external world, subsequently separated from him, belongs to him as much as his own body, external objects as much as his own organs. Only after a long time is the external world divided from the ego, and then with hesitation. But in a certain sense it always remains a detached part of the ego. In the process of taking in an object, of introducing it into ourselves, we only take into the ego once more what originally belonged to it, we only reconquer what we were formerly compelled to yield up under the stern compulsion of reality, and what has been temporarily separated from the ego.

Originally there was only one way of taking possession of an object: one devoured it. Now we know various ways of taking possession, including the possibility, so rich in cultural significance, of taking it into ourselves by comprehension. The introduction of an object into oneself results in a change of the ego. For the moment the ego becomes the object. It is changed into the object. We know the archaic prototype of this attitude; ethnologists and scientific travelers who have lived for a long time among the most primitive Australian tribes assure us that a savage who has eaten a man hopes for certain bodily and mental changes through the act of incorporation. For instance, a man who has made his dinner off a white missionary is convinced that he has made his own the secret powers and excellences, the *mana,* of the man whom he admires and envies. He has "incorporated" him, and not merely in a bodily sense. This belief rests upon an ancient magical principle: a man is what he eats. The Indian who has killed an old grizzly bear and wraps himself in its skin is filled with the bear's spirit; he assumes its movements, and is called "Bear" by his relatives and friends. When a man incorporates an object, he not only sets up certain psychical processes in his organism but also takes the qualities of the object into his ego.

The assumption of a change in the ego is not confined to people in the lowest stages of culture, nor to the effect of the crudest manner of incorporating an object. We detect a late and highly sublimated trace of this savage belief in the proverb: "Knowledge is power."

CHAPTER XXI

From the Truly Startling to the Startlingly True

ANALYSIS stirs us up; it is an emotional process. Its essential character is marked by the recurrent perturbation accompanying the cognizance of repressed processes. I say cognizance deliberately and not cognition, because the former word describes something different and more deep-seated than mere intellectual knowledge. It's like the difference between confiding something to a person and saying something to him. People speak lightly of somebody's having undergone analysis, and yet it makes a great difference whether he has simply been through it, so to speak, or experienced it. Perhaps the reader may ask with annoyance or merely with astonishment—according to his familiarity with the process of analysis and the way of the world—whether such a passing-through deserves the name of analysis. But life demands compromises and half-solutions.

And now, if I probe the peculiar nature of the mental perturbation that is the specific mark of analysis, if I seek to determine its peculiar character as generally and yet as accurately as possible, it appears to be *surprise*. I have already referred to this factor in connection with the nature of attention in the analytic process. In pointing up this factor I ignore the special conditions and peculiarities of numerous cases, and take only what is common to all. Do I hear a storm of protest, with special reference to many cases of analysis in which something other than surprise was most to the fore, and to those in which nothing surprising was ever detected? I beg the reader to desist for the time being from raising these objections and to allow me, in order to make my meaning clear, to refer to a proposition that I tried to set forth in 1926.[1] A fact is there designated as "surprising," when expectation of it has vanished from consciousness and it comes upon us at an unexpected time or under unexpected circumstances.

This is equally true of external and inner perceptions of material and psychical facts. In both realms surprise is a defensive reaction against the suggestion that we turn away from what is familiar and recover in what is new something ancient that we no longer know. In other words, surprise is an expression of our opposition to the demand that we recognize something long known to us of which we have become unconscious. Where the object is to reveal unconscious processes, it means recognizing once more a part of the ego formerly known or glimpsed but lost to knowledge. We have discovered resistance in analysis as the emotional expression of this opposition.

It may be advantageous to suggest here that there is an ultimate connection between surprise and curiosity. I am inclined to assume that an investigator is curious; yes, it is difficult for me to imagine research without curiosity. There are, however, research workers who do not seem to be afflicted with this human weakness. Anatole France asserted that scholars are not curious. Where this factor is absent, no surprise will be felt. Those who are in possession of secure knowledge will no longer be curious and cannot be surprised. People who know all the answers will ask no questions.

In analytic practice those acts of recognition will prove most efficacious that possess this quality of surprise. Their efficacy will progress as recognition penetrates to deeper and deeper planes in the mind. It will prove most lasting where the ancient expectation to which the analysis has penetrated has been repressed. The effect is easy to explain psychologically. It is brought about by a fragment of psychical reality of an unconscious, repressed character coming into contact with material reality in the act of analytic cognition.

Let us take quite a primitive example, such as may be studied daily in practice: In one of my patients violent aggressive impulses against a close relative appeared, and led to an unconscious desire to commit murder. I guessed that this was going on because the patient, in order to repel the murderous impulses, produces certain compulsions whose secret meaning I recognized as a ceremonial of punishment or penitence.

Let me now try to characterize the psychical process that I set in

[1] In a book *Der Schrecken* (Vienna: Psychoanalytischer Verlag.)

motion if I tell the patient the latent meaning of his symptoms and their hidden connection with the unconscious wish to commit murder. By speaking of the secret meaning, I brought a fragment of psychical reality in touch with the external world, and set up a most fertile contact. Utterance released the unconscious process from the dumbness and the oppressive heaviness that weighed upon it. Actually I have only done a piece of translation; my explanation meant exchanging the means of expression used by the unconscious for others, more familiar to us. It may be said that I have translated something from the language of symptoms into that of words. But the making vocal of this translation or transformation distinguishes the coincidence, the meeting of psychical and material reality.

The most significant case of the surprise that recurs so frequently and in such various forms is the phenomenon of the belief in omnipotence. This belief, which originates in our childhood, amounts to a secret view that what we think, can become a reality; in other words, that we have the power to make our wishes come true. Our experiences and our reason contradict such foolish fancies; but reason is often too weak to discredit this belief, especially when it remains unconscious. Let me cite a commonplace example of this belief in the omnipotence of thought. The patient just mentioned told me how often it happens to him that he is just thinking very vividly of an acquaintance, and at that very moment the acquaintance meets him quite unexpectedly. The coincidence of the thought and the external fact caused a slight mental shock, in some instances even a shock that was no longer slight.

I used to see a young girl, a college graduate, who suffered seriously from such thoughts and fought in vain against the belief that she met "coincidences" everywhere. Against her better judgment she had to believe that people in a bus were talking about a man or woman of whom she had just thought the minute before; that certain events took place that she had foreseen, and so forth. What frightened her was, of course, that she could think of the possibility that her mother would die.

The situation described in the analytic treatment is similar to such coincidences. A patient's unconscious thoughts are occupied with the murder of the relative. Nobody knows, of course, that such thoughts have occurred to him. He scarcely knows it himself and does not dare admit it to himself. And then he hears the same meditated possibility spoken by the mouth of another person; it confronts him, incarnated in words. It is as if he has experienced a miracle in the full daylight of consciousness that seems to confirm his belief in the omnipotence of thought. Yes, it works the more strongly upon him because thoughts that belong to the area of the night are expressed in full daylight. The weird impression that some events make upon us will be more strongly felt when they occur in the middle of a street or in a modernly furnished room. What strikes us then as uncanny is intensified by the fact that it emerges from everyday life, from the atmosphere of radio and radar, telephone and television. To the ancient Romans, not midnight, but noon was the ghost hour.

Another surprise feature in analytic treatment connects that phenomenon with the verbal capture of mental processes. We have frequently found that evil or grossly selfish wishes were at work at the root of the belief in omnipotence. The apparent confirmation of the belief pointed to the possible fulfillment of these wishes, nay, actually involved their fulfillment in thought. The strange behavior of a compulsion neurotic may often be explained by the conflict of wishes and opposing tendencies. It is meant to protect from the remotest approach to wish-realization. He resists the possibility so vehemently that what he secretly wishes becomes reality.

But, strange as it may sound, the analyst's utterance of these wishes implies a partial fulfillment of the repudiated wishes. It is thought-play that has attained verbal reality and it gives shape, in a way most nearly approaching material actuality, to what is wished and yet repudiated. In this way, too, the analyst's explanation approaches the nature of those phenomena that seem to confirm the belief in omnipotence. It offers in a verbal formula some satisfaction of forbidden impulses. But the fulfillment involves also something of mastery of impulse by the mind. And so through this function analysis bears witness to the magic power of words.

The simplest and most natural form of the surprise caused by the coincidence of intellectual and material reality occurs when the patient says things that surprise himself. He did not know that he had such thoughts, cherished such feelings, and harbored within him such impulses. What we ourselves think, spoken by others, often enough sounds alien to us; so alien that it occasionally requires a mental effort to recognize it as part of our ego. It often suffices to hear a sentence, which we ourselves have spoken, repeated by another in order to read something different into it. A patient of mine once remarked, "Some-

times I say things here and I realize only later how true they are."
Traditional psychology endeavors in vain to convince us that mental
processes are immediately self-evident data.

On the threshold of psychological research we find, not familiarity
with ourselves, but astonishment at the phenomena of our own minds.
That is to say, the subject of analysis is suddenly confronted with his
own thinking as something alien. At first he will reject it as alien, and
only much later will he acknowledge it as something of his own that
had become alienated from himself. Paradoxical as it may sound, we
cannot learn to know ourselves before first becoming strangers to ourselves. When a person in analysis is surprised by what he has said and
when he realizes the meaning of his actions through analytic interpretation, he is, so to speak, introduced to an unknown self. His surprise
shows, however, that this part of himself was only covered up and
hidden to him. Somewhere he knew about it and his surprise is only
a reaction to his reluctance to admit a secret expectation and foreknowledge.

The case of a mistaken interpretation or erroneous deduction offers
a kind of counter-test. There, too, a psychical emotion is produced, but
not surprise in my sense, no confirmation of unconscious expectation.

Now let us consider the experience of surprise from another aspect,
that of economy of emotion. What happens in the mind of the patient
if we tell him what we have guessed about the unconscious motives
and meanings of his symptoms, his actions, and his thoughts?

A certain physician came to me to be psychoanalyzed because many
compulsions and obsessions had disturbed him considerably in his
practice as well as in his private life. The most important of his measures of protection, with the help of which he tried to fight his obsessions, was an oft-repeated examination of everything written. He had
to convince himself that everything he and others wrote was correct.
He had to scrutinize every letter and every number many times. Making up prescriptions took hours instead of minutes, and so forth. What
looked like a grotesquely exaggerated conscientiousness was in reality
his effort to fend off his obsessive doubts. They interfered with almost
all his activities and threatened finally to make work and enjoyment
of life impossible.

I cannot present here the course of his psychoanalysis and must
restrict myself to the origin of his main doubts. The symptoms had
started at a certain phase of his life when his mother, a widow of some

wealth, had asked him to act as trustee of her property, to check her accounts, to take charge of her stocks and bonds, and so forth. It seemed that the new activity and responsibility, to which he was not accustomed, marked the beginning of his many doubts. He had then started to count again and again, to re-examine the accounts, and so on. He wanted to fulfill his mother's expectations, which had been previously disappointed by her older son, the physician's brother.

There were other important motives, but I shall emphasize here only the one unconscious impulse against whose power most of his measures of protection were directed. The analysis of his symptoms led to a reconstruction of his unconscious situation. One day while he was very carefully checking his mother's accounts, the idea occurred to him that it would be very easy to deceive her and put a certain amount aside for himself. It was just an idea, but it was obvious that behind it there was a strong temptation, especially as he was then having serious financial difficulties. He rejected the idea, of course, but his compulsive symptoms showed their power and continued effect because they were directed against the temptation to use the many opportunities to cheat given him by the trusteeship. The doubts and re-examinations were later on transferred to everything he wrote by a process of displacement and generalization that distorted the connection with the original thought and made its true nature unrecognizable. After careful analytic preparation I presented to the patient the solution at which I had arrived. I introduced him to this other self, which stood in such sharp contrast to his integrity.

A patient's first reaction to such an encounter with his repressed impulses is usually not surprise pure and simple, but a particular case of the emotion of surprise, *shock*. The patient often becomes aware of the repressed impulses with shock. Shock may sometimes be definitely taken as an indirect proof of his becoming aware. The reaction of shock or violent repulsion is due to the fact that our interpretation represents an inroad into the realm of emotional and intellectual taboos, into a carefully guarded secret region of the soul.

As a psychical process, shock reminds us of what happens in the mind when we hear a joke. The first reaction at hearing a joke is a kind of unconscious fear or shock. It is as if a latent anxiety, which lives in all of us, has suddenly become intensified. The joke has touched upon certain taboos, forbidden ideas that exist in our unconscious and awaken the temptation to break through the inhibition that our cultural pattern considers valid. This temptation is at first rejected in the form of fear at the thought expressed in the joke. Then we realize that the fear is superfluous and we enjoy the joke. Children laugh like that when they have been frightened and then suddenly realize that there is no reason to be afraid. Humor lives thus in an emotional realm between fear and laughter.[2]

We enjoy the form of the joke, but unconsciously we enjoy even more the aggressive or sexual tendencies that are concealed and revealed in it. We can take any example of a malicious or cynical joke to put our theory to test. I have just been reading a biographical sketch of the famous painter, Max Liebermann, who was—before Hitler— president of the German Academy of Arts. The old master once expressed his opinion of female artists rather boldly: "There are two kinds of female painters; one kind want to marry and the other kind also have no talent." We realize, of course, that we meet here an aggression against women. We are at first inclined to protect them as cavaliers should, but our laughter proves that somewhere we agree with the aggressor. When the latent meaning of the joke has been unconsciously recognized, the first reaction, lasting only for the fragment of a second, is in the nature of a shock. This unconscious shock is justified because the expression of repressed tendencies secretly contained in wit appears like a suddenly emerging danger. Both here and in the case of an analytic explanation that lays bare the most secret impulses of the ego, we have a momentary intensification of inner inhibition, comparable to the too hasty mobilization of a defensive force. In analysis, too, this shock of thought is realized to be superfluous, but not quickly and easily, as with a joke. It requires the gradual conquest of inner resistance. Demobilization is effected with such hesitation because only in that way can the special circumstances of the mind's economy bear a profound reorganization. We know the psychical factors that help the patient overcome his surprise and recognize the alien content as only alienated but still a part of his repudiated ego.

From the standpoint of economy of thought, analytic explanations are themselves surprising. Since the analyst's idea emerges from the

[2] The psychological significance of fear in the hearer of a joke and of the factors of suddenness and surprise were overlooked by Freud when he made his inquiry into the psychology of wit. They were discovered and discussed in two books by this writer, *Lust und Leid im Witz* (Vienna: 1929), and *Nachdenkliche Heiterkeit* (Vienna: 1933).

unconscious—a part of the part that was once the whole—it seems to arise from the void. This origin allows the condensation and displacement that belong to the primary process and appear intellectually inacceptable to our conscious thought. In this way special abbreviations become possible, since various links in the chain of thought are dropped out, or, in other words, skipped over, and many conditions necessary to the conclusion remain unspoken. Thus surprise is effected by a saving of conscious intellectual operations, because the intervention of the unconscious allows a short circuit in place of logical inferences.

I shall try to make my point clear by putting a witty remark and an obsession-thought side by side. In both the factor of surprise is obvious; in both some connecting link is omitted and what is left out must be replaced with the help of an allusion. The painter, Max Liebermann, whom I mentioned before, was once visited by a beautiful young lady to whom he showed his pictures and with whom the seventy-five-year-old master had an animated conversation on the subject of art. Thanking him and saying good by, the young woman assured him: "This has been the most beautiful hour of my life." The old master answered with a friendly glance: "Well, let's hope that is not true." What has been omitted and the meaning of the allusion are clear: looking at pictures and talking with an old man cannot be as happy a time as an hour in bed with a young one, and you are quite right feeling like that.

Compare now the mechanisms of this joke with those of an obsession-thought that occurred to a patient. Her husband had expressed the wish that she have herself photographed in a certain position and that she send him the picture. She told me that at first she wanted to show me the picture, but she could not do it because a "terrible" thought had occurred to her. The idea was so terrible that she could not communicate it—even in psychoanalysis. After much persuasion, she told me the mysterious thought, which was certainly surprising at first. She had thought that if she showed me the photograph she would have to slap my face. The insertion of the missing links in her train of thought and its analytic interpretation are not difficult: if I were to look at the picture which shows her in a seductive position, I may perhaps become sexually attracted to her; I would make a pass at her, whereupon she would have to slap my face. Here, as in Liebermann's joke, the omission deals with a sexual theme. The suppressed thought that returns from its hiding-place produces in the one case a smile, in the other a symptom of anxiety. It is, of course, not always the subject of sex that is suppressed and then expressed by an omission, but it is one of the outstanding subjects for which we have to search in neurotic symptoms and in wit. In both types, in which the unconscious plays a decisive role, sex can often be found behind the omission and allusion. The Viennese actor, Alexander Girardi, answered a newspaper inquiry as to what his favorite pastime was with these words: "Secondly, to row."

It is easy to give an outsider an impression of the surprising character of an analytic idea, but difficult to make him realize the power of conviction inherent in one. We need only recall the general disbelief with which the establishment of a system of unconscious sexual symbolism was formerly regarded, though it was not the discovery of psychoanalysts and must clearly be charged to the lustful mental attitude of mythologists, folklorists, and ethnologists. Symbols are products of the creative power of imagination that lives in all people. Their appearance in dreams and other products of the unconscious where our mental activity returns to more primitive forms of thinking is only natural. The sexual symbols that Freud discovered for modern psychology are parts of a primal concept of thought. We all understand their meaning when they re-emerge in wit and comparison. Psychoanalysis asserts, for instance, that vehicles in dreams usually symbolize women. But how did a cartoonist arrive at this symbol? He shows a man in a hurry and a friend warning him: "Never run after a bus or a woman. In one or two minutes another will come along." A man in a comedy remarks: "Women are like cars. It is unpleasant not to have a car. To have a car is expensive and dangerous. It is best to have a friend who has a car." The writer has, I am sure, no knowledge of the psychoanalytic idea of sexual symbolism.

Many American analysts make the mistake of assuming that symbols are fixed and permanent figures of collective fantasy. I remember that I received the same wrong impression when as a student I learned for the first time about the sexual symbolism in dreams. A few days afterward I took a walk in the Vienna Prater. It was early summer and there was a crowd at a certain spot. The people formed a circle around a wife and husband, elderly people who were selling frankfurters at a miserable hot-dog stand on the street corner. They were having a furious quarrel in which both lost their tempers. I heard the wife say angrily to her husband: "You will never again put your frankfurter into my boiler." I walked on a sadder, but with respect to sexual symbolism, a wiser, young man. The psychoanalyst who identifies himself with the analyzed person can decipher these symbols through the unconscious knowledge he shares with everybody.

Here is an instance that shows how the understanding of symbols emerges surprisingly in the psychoanalyst. It is the story of how I "discovered" a new dream-symbol, that is, how I suddenly understood the secret significance of a symbolic expression that, as far as I know, had never before been explained in psychoanalytic literature. Shortly after my arrival in this country (1938) I had the following dream of a woman patient to analyze: *I see a lady falling off the roof*. No helpful associations could be given and the meaning of the dream seemed to escape us entirely. I do not know how and why, but somewhere the thought occurred to me that this dream had something to do with menstruation. I communicated my guess to my patient with all due caution, but she laughed and said, "Of course, that is it." When she awoke in the morning, she found that she had become unwell. I learned then that the expression, "I fell off the roof," and similar ones are used in American slang to indicate the onset of menstruation. I had never heard the expression before—I can take a solemn oath on that—how, then, did I guess this hidden meaning? Nothing the patient had said pointed in this direction. Since then I have had many opportunities to verify that falling off the roof has the same significance in the dreams of women.

How, then, shall we convince stubborn skeptics, who think, indeed, that they know everything about analysis, but will hear nothing of it, of the firmness of the hidden foundations upon which an analytic interpretation is built? Let us take another chance example—not one from the interpretation of dreams, not a complex effort at reconstruction, nothing that calls for long and complicated description, but a primitive example from an analysis of a neurosis, say a screen-memory. A case occurs to me: A patient who had been under analysis for about six months told me of a childhood memory. As a boy of five or six he had seen on the floor of the passage leading from the dining room to the bathroom a black tail of hair belonging to his much older sister. His sisters often lost their tails of hair, he said. Is it possible to make an outsider understand that this scene, emerging in isolation, represents a screen-memory behind which another, unconscious memory lies concealed, according to which the little boy once saw his sister's genitals, presumably in the bathroom? Of course we can trace the logical operations that led us to the view; we can explain to our hearer the psychological conditions that determined the occurrence of the idea to us. Perhaps—perhaps—we shall be able to recount all the factors that contribute to making the idea probable—the associations surrounding this screen-memory, the many single elements that went to make up our interpretation like a mosaic picture.

Doubtless the hearer will understand my explanation, nay, he may even admit that it has a certain justification. Nevertheless, he will not be convinced that the idea is intellectually inescapable, for he is un-acquainted with the imponderabilia of the situation, and I cannot communicate an impression of them to him. I cannot tell him what unconscious ideas, what memories of vague impressions, arising from earlier statements by the patient, arose in my mind. I cannot convince him that everything drove me on toward that particular assumption while I followed the chain of associations: from the sister's black tail of hair on the way to the bathroom . . . it has come off . . . something that girls have . . . something that girls lose . . . something that girls have not, and so on. I did not communicate my interpretation to the patient. I remained silent, and he proceeded—in another direction, if we judge only by the manifest content of his former statement—to tell me that as a little boy he usually played with a little girl of his own age in the neighboring garden. On these occasions he examined the girl's genitals once, or several times. He described the impression made by the pubic region and the vagina, which struck him as resembling an ugly dark wound after an operation. It seemed as if the patient's further chain of associations had confirmed my idea. It seemed as if—surprisingly enough—he would now be able to formulate the unconscious links, or as if he were nearly able to, after the analyst had recognized them consciously.

A patient is always surprised when he is told something that un-consciously he already knows. This follows from our designation of surprise as the reaction to the fulfillment of an unconscious expectation. He will take in what was formerly known to him and has only been alienated, as if it were something new, and will repel it. We may now understand the effect, which often does not appear until later, of such a surprising communication, if we recognize it as a kind of psychical shock that it takes time to master.

We shall not be put off by the fact that the patient experiences these *surprises within his ego*, although he thinks that he is well acquainted with his own inner life. It will seem strange to us that the analyst, too, who has such wide experience, is largely dependent upon receiving such knowledge from unknown powers of the ego, and upon listening for the stirrings within him in tracking the hidden meaning of psychical phenomena. Where the analyst's idea penetrates to the profoundest depths of the other's inner life, it may be recognized as the offspring of what is repressed in the analyst and appears to him as something alien. In short, to sum up the matter: *The most vital knowledge obtained by the analyst of the unconscious-repressed is, for him too, a surprise.* It is true that this surprise reaction will lose intensity as the analyst gains insight and deeper psychological knowledge. There may come a time when it does not appear at all. But at least in the early years of an analyst's work it remains as a sure signal that his own unconscious is involved in the recognition of unconscious relations. It is not logical reflection and theoretical learning that constitute the core of the preconscious and unconscious knowledge, so helpful to the psychologist in later years in recognizing repressed processes, but the memory-traces of the surprise he has experienced. If, in our analyses of mental effects, we can so often infer hidden, unconscious motives, the inference is of value, not so much as a logical operation but rather as the outcome of repeated insight into the mind that surprised the analyst at first.

We mistrust psychologists who declare that they experience no such surprises, that the unconscious of those whom they study is immediately transparent to them and easy to penetrate. There may be psychoanalysts of such a nature. They are, so to speak, professional experts in the depths of the human soul. The netherworld is their oyster. The psychologist "who is surprised" then stands consciously opposed to those for whom there are no surprises left in the inner life. If these gentlemen boast that they find it easy "to read the other person," that the unconscious lies before them like an open book, then they do not know how to read it. The wonders of the inner reality are hidden from their sight. I know that there are many psychoanalysts who shrink from what is astonishing and set up a defense against what is surprising in the psychological field, and try to protect themselves against it. They put up a barrier of theoretical learning, to parry and intercept it. But the best of our profession, the most valuable of our art and craft, have learned to appreciate the heuristic value of surprising ideas emerging from the unconscious, and gladly welcome them. (You shall be welcome whenever you come.)

The surprise that is felt when the unconscious meaning of individual phenomena is recognized, when the latent significance of individual symptoms, dreams, strange reactions, is understood, may increase at a later stage, toward the end of the process of analysis. When we survey the development of a neurosis or a special character, our surprise does not diminish when we recognize how the co-operation or conflict of particular impulses has produced just this emotional result, how inevitably and yet how naturally just this type of character arose in the play of psychical forces. And so, when his task is accomplished, the psychologist is struck with amazement as he surveys what he has seen of the dynamic and economic conditions of the inner processes. His incipient understanding of the methods by which our mental machinery works will not lessen his amazement, but rather increase it.

No analyst will be able to give an adequate account of his own inner experience involved in the conjecture and comprehension of unconscious phenomena. I have denoted the nature of the impression made by the knowledge gained in the process of analysis, in the title of this chapter: *it develops from the truly startling to the startlingly true*. Not one of us will be able to reproduce the impression of that sudden or gradually increasing clarity of vision, when data that seemed heterogeneous and unrelated come to life through the development of an idea. The scattered and isolated fragments fit together like the loose, dry bones that, suddenly covering themselves with flesh and skin, became a crowd of men in the vision granted by God to the prophet Ezekiel.

What we experience is a twofold surprise: amazement at the significance entering into the psychical data, which at first seemed puzzling, bizarre, or absurd; and amazement at what went on in our own mind, enabling us to penetrate their hidden meaning. I confess that for me this is one of the fascinating rewards, one of the silent triumphs of my psychoanalytic labors. To all of us, as we follow the trail of unconscious relations in analysis, there comes a feeling like that of Max Liebermann at the first night of Hauptmann's *Rose Bernd*. Those who sat next to the old artist, attentively following the presentation of human destinies on the stage, heard him murmuring admiringly: "How it works!" Something of this amazement remains with an analyst who has followed unconscious psychical processes for many years. Like every scientific investigator, he has learned to discern the variety and wealth of organic processes and recognizes how, in spite of great freedom, they obey unchangeable laws.

CHAPTER XXII

Psychoanalysis and Wit

PSYCHOANALYSIS is not a cheerful science, no *gaya scienza* in the meaning of Nietzsche. New questions arise, difficulties pile up, tragedy looms. Yet, as we saw in the last chapter, analytic conjecture parallels the mental process involved in hearing a joke.

Dreams—a major source of data in analytic work—often sound like bad jokes.

An American patient of mine had a dream about a variety of incidents in a Viennese hotel. *In the center of them was the figure of Metternich.* The manifest content of the dream gives the impression of order and sense. The patient has few associations with it. The only striking feature in the forefront of the dream was the appearance of Metternich.

What is the Austrian statesman doing in the dream of an American businessman? He strikes us as curious in the surroundings. Strange to say, the despot of Austria's past does not show up here as the representative of a political viewpoint or course of action. He has only his name to thank for his appearance in the dream.

During the analysis-hour that followed, the patient and I dissected the name and got "met her *nicht*"—an Anglo-German sentence meaning "I did not meet her." Doesn't it sound like a bad joke? And do not suppose that this instance of analytic interpretive technique stands alone; it is built up like many thousand more.

This dream reminds us how, as children, we played with words in the same way. We seem to feel pleasure that the dream has succeeded in saying what it wanted to say, not only in such a hidden form, but also in so condensed and concentrated a manner. Let me recall what I have already said about the significance of the factor of economy in surprise. It appears here in the form of condensed expression. In analysis, too, the effect of surprise is secured by suspending the forces of suppression and inhibition. Only a superficial mind could expect that the analogy between analytic interpretation and wit would be confined to their formal aspect.

A comparison of the mental dynamics in both cases shows that there is an inner likeness between analytic explanations and jokes. I recall, for instance, that in anyone listening to a joke, there is enhanced preparedness for inhibition that is recognized to be superfluous and released in laughter. I have already shown how originally it was a case of shock, of an encounter with a former fear, that is suddenly made actual and overcome in the mind. A man who hears a witty remark laughs like someone who gets a sudden shock and realizes at once that he need not be alarmed. Not, indeed, in the same, but in a similar manner, the analyst's communications produce a kind of shock in the patient. For a moment his preparedness for inhibition is enhanced and then slowly overcome. Here, then, is a psychocathartic effect common to the analytic process and wit. The fact that the patient often has to laugh when his analyst tells him about the repressed impulses lying at the root of his neurotic symptoms and troubles bears witness to this effect.

There are three parties to a joke. The party of the first part is the man who tells it. The party of the second part is the subject—the butt— of the joke. And the third party is the hearer, the man to whom the joke is told—the man who laughs.

The patient in analysis experiences the laugh—that is, he is the third party in a joke, in spite of the fact that the subject of the psychological surprise is himself. But notice, it is an alienated part of his ego, the second party, who is the butt of the "joke." Let us consider, moreover, what laughter at one part of the ego means. It indicates that the patient is capable of looking at something he has hidden away for a lifetime and is acknowledging it as something familiar.

Let me carry the comparison a little further still keeping the surprise element in mind. The comparison is in itself surprising enough, so surprising that some colleagues have admonished me that it ought to be excluded from the field of serious scientific labors. Others, on the contrary, have told me that I was reading into the joke-process too much that was not there at all, and others again that it was a question of minor common features resulting from the fact of a common origin, but that they did not apply beyond a very narrow sphere.

I am a stubborn man and I would still oppose all the arguments of my fellow-analysts even if I should fail to demonstrate the essential likeness in the psychological field between analytic interpretation and wit. For the strength of a conviction is not dependent upon personal ability to prove its truth. First and foremost I should want to trace what lies back of their contempt for wit: an emotional residue applicable to the whole type. If it were not so, analysts would attribute greater significance to wit as the subject of psychological study. We might almost claim that wit deserves greater attention on the part of psychologists, if only because of its Cinderella role.

The surprise felt at the solution of the dream-element "Metternich" is the same kind that occurs with a pun. Indeed, it could quite well be used for one, although it would hardly satisfy the fastidious. I will not make the effort of thinking up a similar joke: I can cite one which will immediately convince the reader of the position. Some months ago a New York newspaper columnist wrote about the President: "To err is Truman." The joke combines the allusion to the many undeniable blunders the President has made with an expression of condescending pity for him. Technically it is only a pun dependent upon sound, a play upon a proper name, and really not a very good one.

Comparing an element in another dream of the above-mentioned patient with the peculiar characteristics of this pun, we at once confirm our impression of the similarity of the methods in the dream and in the pun. He dreamed of Voltaire. Ideas occur that lead to the breaking up of the name. It then refers to the fear of the patient suffering from compulsion that in crossing a street in process of repair he might have got his shoes full of tar (*voll Teer*). We recognize that the mind is working here—in the dream as it does in the pun—attending to the sound rather than the sense of words. In both cases the machinery of the mind reverts to an earlier kind of operation. In the dream as in the pun, we escape from one range of ideas to another, often far removed, by means of the identity or similarity of sound.

Freud argues that we get a bad joke when we take a verbal short cut from one range of ideas to another, if there is not also some connection of sense between the two. In a bad joke of this kind the verbal bridge is the only link between the two disparate ideas. Now the compression of "met her *nicht*" in the dream makes just the same impression. It is a bad joke. Perhaps we might assume that these verbal links between the elements of puns and dreams are common to these two processes alone. It does not seem unnatural that a dream, in which conscious thinking is eliminated, should allow of a use of words rejected by the waking reason, just like the pun.

I will proceed at once to cite an example that leads farther; here there can be no question of sleep favoring the appearance of such verbal links, or of wit reviving our old delight in sporting with assonance in words. Yet this example, too, displays the same psychical peculiarities. In this case, which, of course, is only put forward as representative of many others, and which in its general structure may claim to be typical, the transition from one set of ideas to another is brought about through verbal assonance under the control of the waking senses.

A German-born patient of mine, a woman no longer young, suffered from an obsessive fear that her husband would soon die of cancer, although at the time he was in excellent health. In order to repel her obsessive fear, which pursued her almost without interruption, she had to utter certain charms, make certain magical movements, and observe a large number of protective measures. Like all compulsion neurotics, she avoided certain things to protect herself from an attack of fear. We expect the things avoided to have some connection with the object of her fear, the terrible disease. In the symptomatology of the compulsion neurosis, the connection would be neither simple nor direct.

Her avoidance will surprise only those who are not closely acquainted with the nature of compulsion neuroses. One day the lady came very late to her treatment. She was obliged to make a long detour, she explained. On the way from her hotel to my house she found herself in a street in which there was a food store. To her horror she saw live crabs in the window of this shop. In German the same word, *"Krebs,"* stands for "cancer" and "crab." Here, too, we see it is a question of using the same word, and passing from one set of ideas to another remote one only connected with it by verbal identity. This avoidance is certainly more serious, and has deeper and more vital effects, than a bad joke. Crabs are avoided, as if they were identical with the disease she fears, although they have nothing in common with it but the name. The two sets of ideas—cancer and crab—meet only in the common name. It cannot but be clear to us that the treatment and evaluation of words in this experience, culled from the symptomatology of neuroses, is psychologically the same as in puns.

There is a third area in which words are treated in the same way as in the compulsion avoidance: the sphere of primitive religion and superstitious customs. In many tribes of Australia and Africa it is forbidden to pronounce the names of certain members of one's family. A Zulu woman will, for instance, never utter the name of her brother-in-law, but will use a paraphrase. If, for instance, the man has a name that is the same as "sheep," she will avoid speaking of a sheep, but will use the circumlocution "that of the tail." The avoidance goes so far in those tribes that even syllables that make part of the forbidden name may not be used. A woman whose brother-in-law has, for instance, a name in which the syllable "ja" appears, will never pronounce the word *"mkenja"* ("bachelor"), because it contains the sound "ja," but will use another expression.[1] Here we find not only the same psychological evaluation of words as in the case of "crab," but also beneath the verbal avoidance there is a similar avoidance of thoughts. Moreover, a similar emotion is present: the patient who avoids the store with crabs in the window is afraid of the magical consequences of being near them (the husband could die). The utterance of the brother-in-law's name by a Zulu woman would not only be counted a breach of etiquette by an African Emily Post; the offender would be afraid of being accused of witchcraft, an accusation that would have serious consequences for her.

Taking these examples for a starting-point, we may compare the analyst, who recognizes the hidden meanings and intentions of unconscious processes, with a man listening to a joke. Freud has told us that the psychical process in the listener imitates that in the maker of the joke, tracing, so to speak, the same path the wit has already trod. An essential element in analytic comprehension is understanding hints, filling gaps, smoothing out distortions; in short, in tracing the way back to the repressed core of communications. I may mention here in passing that such reproduction of the inner processes of another mind is not possible without certain prerequisite conditions in the listener. In the process of reproduction the analyst must use the same technique as the patient, must apply the same mechanism of condensation, displacement, and omission, because by no other means has he any prospect of under-

---

[1] Compare the interesting paper, "Die Frauensprache bei primitiven Völkern," by Flora Kraus. *Imago* (1924), X, No. 2/3.

standing the secret meaning of unconscious processes. The analyst must therefore be capable of using the methods adopted in the joke to attain pleasure, in order to grasp the unconscious intention of, say, some element in a dream or a special symptom.

It is easy to lay stress upon the inanity and folly of an interpretation like that of the dream-element "Metternich," and then, arguing plausibly, to ascribe the character of a joke to the process of interpretation itself. This attitude, which sometimes even claims to be scientific, overlooks with a grandiose gesture the fact that the interpretation is not left to the free choice of the analyst, but only reflects what may be conjectured from hints and allusions. The interpretation, in its intellectual and verbal expression, must adapt itself to the peculiarities of unconscious processes, that is to say, to their infantile character.

At this point we are reminded that Freud was led to investigate the phenomena of wit because he was reproached with interpreting dreams in a way which suggested a joke. The analyst can be made responsible for the supposedly absurd or inane content of his interpretation exactly as much and as justly as an Egyptologist for the content of a hieroglyphic text that he deciphers. None of the keen critics who reproach analysis for its fantastic interpretations supposes that, say, Naville or Maspero believes a prayer to the god Khnum with the ram's head will cure him of rheumatism.

I have indeed likened an analyst conjecturing the repressed meaning of a psychical phenomenon to a man listening to a joke. But the simile shifts around as soon as I picture the analyst telling the patient what he has detected. We might then sometimes compare him with the wit himself. In the former case the secret meaning of the repressed content is made clear to the analyst; in the latter he makes it clear to another. I have already said that the recognition of repressed tendencies often finds expression in the patient's laughter. It is as if he were releasing in his laughter the tension that was necessary to suppress the forbidden impulse.

In the analyst, too, who wants to conjecture something repressed, a great number of preconscious thoughts and ideas dive down into the unconscious, are subjected there to a certain recasting, and are then seized by consciousness. We see, too, the differences between the two processes. Primarily, of course, the difference in mental attitude is of importance; we will return to that. In the process itself, our attention is called to the importance of the time factor.

In joking the unconscious recasting only lasts for a moment. There is no such time limit to be observed in the act of recognition in psycho-analysis. Nor is it incompatible to say that the analyst's idea, which we have seen to be a consciously grasped outcome of something repressed in his mind, is the product of a moment. For he can point to a long course of conscious observation, and often still more prolonged unconscious labors.

We find a further difference when we turn our attention to the final phase. The analyst, like the wit, has counteracted a mental effort of repression and overcome a certain resistance in himself before the idea occurs to him consciously. But the analyst's power of discharging the energy he sets free is subject to much greater checks than that of the first party in the joking process, for this energy is straightway turned to another use—namely, that of explaining the suddenly acquired knowledge psychologically and formulating it in words. His conscious interest is its psychological application, in fitting it into the network of relations that he is beginning to discern; in short, his intellectual effort, will, of course, render a psychical effect such as we find in wit impossible. Nay, the different attitude toward the object, as well as the difference of aim, calls for a different result.

The hidden links between the genesis of an analytic idea that puts an end to a repression and the genesis of wit may be illuminated from two angles. It is easy to show that a large number of jokes contain an unconscious pith that is essentially akin to the explanation of an unconsciously repressed impulse or idea. When it is reduced to this pith, we see that the idea became a joke only through the form in which it was clothed. We all know examples of jokes of this kind. A single one will suffice here to represent the type. When Gustav Mahler was conductor of the Viennese Opera a young violinist was recommended to him for an engagement in the orchestra. The intercessor reported that the young musician had not, it was true, great powers, but he was very modest. Mahler fired up in his impulsive manner: "What is he modest about, then?" Our laughter proves that this remark, of the humor of which, by the way, Mahler was not aware, hits off the sham nature of the modesty, and exposes the unconscious, exaggerated self-assurance of the violinist. In psychoanalysis we often realize that conceit hides behind a display of modesty.

The problem can also be approached from another angle. I have already shown that one of the decisive differences between the process of acquiring knowledge of the unconscious and the invention of puns lies in the direction and application of the psychical energy set free. This turned our attention immediately to the different mental attitude in the two cases. A wit conceives of his subject with hostility or contempt, his tendency is aggressive or sexual in character, while an analyst's attitude toward his subject is definitely otherwise.

It happens—though rarely—under special circumstances that, searching into the most secret recesses of the patient's mind in order to transmute what is detected into the form of psychological knowledge, we produce a witty thought instead of an analytic idea. A momentary mood of the analyst, aggressive or merely exuberant, may find expression for the idea in some such witty formulation of a thought. The analyst has no difficulty in overcoming the temptation to utter the joke. For our argument it is not the utterance but the emergence of such a mental product that has importance.

The discretion that is due even to oneself accounts for the fact that thoughts of this stamp are not brought forward for scientific discussion. There might be a slight personal sacrifice in communicating such a thing. But this book is supposed to give the reader insight into the workshop of the psychoanalyst, that is, into his mind. In order to be true to this task, the book can't skip the shadows, the dark nooks and corners of the picture. The following example is only intended to characterize the type of these thoughts. The idea, which lenient judges may allow to be witty, occurred during the analysis of a young woman patient who had found her powers of work considerably weakened after a bitter disappointment in love. At the same time she evinced a marked inclination for alcohol, which had just been forbidden by the Prohibition Act. The best opportunities to indulge her taste presented themselves at small parties, to which she invited for the most part much younger people. On one of these occasions, she reported, an acquaintance once said to her that she would never achieve anything in life because she was "too full of the milk of human kindness." (The reader will remember that these words are used by Lady Macbeth who is urging her husband to commit a murder: ". . . yet do I fear thy nature; It is too full o' the milk of human kindness To catch the nearest way. . . .")

It was during the treatment, in the course of this report, that the idea emerged: What a pity that she has no milk of the other kind! Regarded as a joke, the idea is certainly poor. Perhaps it merely contains the elements of a joke. But it must be noted that the "witty" idea really was destined to anticipate a psychological relation that later grew increasingly clear. In addition to many other psychical determinants that we need not enter into here, it came to light much later that the patient's taste for alcohol and her offering it to her young guests was a displaced substitute, a surrogate, for the fulfillment of the unconscious wish to suckle a child. Ideas like this, which nevertheless bring a fragment of the repressed content to consciousness, would certainly create the impression of cynicism if they were spoken. It is easy to trace their origin to those impulses which we find as unconscious tendencies at the root of cynicism. There is no need to emphasize how radically an analytic interpretation differs from a joke that unveils the unconscious, even if the content is essentially the same. *C'est le ton qui fait la musique.* In the case of an analytic explanation it goes without saying that the tone would be different, more suited to serious work, even if the analyst said essentially the same as the wit.

The important point, which I believe that I myself have discerned, is to be found in the similarity of the psychical process by which the hidden meaning of unconscious processes is discovered both in an analytic idea and in wit. In certain important points the mental process by which the pith of the matter is grasped is the same, whether the case stirs our deep sympathy or raises a laugh. It makes a difference, of course, in which spirit one approaches this pith. Goethe said of the now forgotten brilliant satirist, Georg Christoph Lichtenberg (1742-1799), that wherever this writer makes a joke a problem is hidden. It is just the reverse with many an intellectual; wherever a problem is hidden, he makes only a joke.

CHAPTER XXIII

The Surprised Psychoanalyst

I F WISHES were horses and beggars could ride, we psychologists would always be able to recognize the what, the how, and the why of what goes on in other people's minds. However, we learned long ago to renounce this wish and to be content with what we can discover by trial and error and hard work. The funny thing is that there are times when it seems as if our wishes were indeed horses and we poor beggars could ride. It is when we realize in a flash the secret thoughts of others and understand their hidden motives.

There are enviable people who boast that they have telepathic gifts and there are thought-readers who give performances of their mysterious ability. There are, however, situations in which every one of us seems to have these gifts of thought-reading. Strange that we do not make a fuss about this and that nobody discusses the matter at greater length.

We do not report to the world that on our last walk with a friend he expressed exactly what we had thought ourselves just a minute before, or that we were able to say precisely what on this or that occasion our wife was thinking. If we feel any satisfaction about it at all, we do not boast about it, and it occurs to us rarely to connect it with extrasensory perception. It seems that we are content to register such occasions, and, were we asked about them, we would perhaps answer that such thought-reading is a natural result of our intimate knowledge and understanding of the other's personality. Yes, we would even deny that the phenomenon deserves the name of thought-reading. But why? Whether we know a person or not is not the essential question, it seems to me. If it were, our astonishment at the gifts of a professional thought-reader would really concern the fact that he can read the thoughts of unknown men and women while we common mortals can do the same magical thing only with a few, very well-known persons. It would be only a difference in degree.

The existence of the phenomenon itself cannot be doubted. Why do we not make any attempt to find a psychological explanation for it and why do we take it for granted? We need not observe the shadow of an obelisk in order to recognize how high the sun stands in the sky. A post on the road tells us the same story. For practical purposes it might be even more important to read the thoughts of persons who are near to us rather than those of strangers upon whom we chance and whom we shall never see again. It might be more interesting to know the thoughts of your sweetheart, your friend, your sister, than those of an unknown lady or gentleman you have met at a cocktail party. If we could always read these thoughts, if we could predict them—it would have consequences that no fantasy, not even that of a thought-reader, would be able to foresee.

These and similar reflections could preface an inquiry into the unconscious communication between the analyst and the analyzed person. Not only are thoughts read here, but unconscious thoughts at that; and not only thoughts, but emotions, impulses, and drives as well. The streamlined run of psychoanalysts make their observations and put their trust in God and Freud. They are confident that they will understand what takes place in the patient when they only apply what they have learned in books, in courses, and in seminars. As if you could learn experiences! There are courses in music appreciation and much can be learned about composers and compositions, but what is best in music cannot be "learned." Some analysts teach their students that they have to "identify" themselves with the patients, as if that were a process dependent upon one's will, like raising one's arm. Identification is an anemic and theoretical name for what really takes place. To that no name can be given.

An old American novel is prefaced by the sentence, "Whatever is incredible in this story is true."[1] Similarly an analyst reporting his experiences with puzzling communications could tell incredible cases that are true. They would, however, lose their incredibility were we to trace them back to what happens in the minds of the analyst and the patient. This is the difficult task we have never attempted. If we could

[1] *The Circuit Rider,* by Edward Eggleston.

approach the problem from both sides, if we could grasp the psychological material and the mechanisms in a pincer movement, we would understand so much better what happens, whereas now we only know that it happens.

Every analyst has had the experience of having the patient speak words that the analyst has thought a few brief seconds ago. Sometimes the patient introduces his remarks in this way: "You will perhaps think now that . . ." But he only projects what he himself thought. It has happened to every analyst that the patient who may have energetically rejected an analytic interpretation unconsciously, confirms it in the next sentence that he speaks. These are very simple cases that are not surprising and their psychological explanation is not difficult to reach.

It is also easy to understand that the analyst sometimes grasps something the patient did not know because he did not want to remember it. In these cases the analyst's memory is not handicapped by the repression that handicaps the patient. But even here the process is not purely intellectual, is not mechanical understanding like that of a mathematical problem. This, however, would be inconceivable were not the unconscious of the psychoanalyst co-operating with his intelligence.

A man remembered that after the death of his mother he lived with an aunt and his cousins. Among the many memories he could reproduce from those years was one that appeared puzzling to him. He was not, as far as he could remember, especially squeamish as a boy of ten. He remembered clearly, however, that he had refused to eat from a plate on which the food of other members of the family had been served or to touch a fork his cousins had used. He even remembered that more than once he had quarreled with his benevolent aunt, who reproached him for his behavior. He could not understand such fastidiousness now.

What happened in me, the analyst, that made me say: "I think that must be traced back to the precautions your mother took during the years of her disease"?

Here is nothing mysterious. In the beginning of his analysis the patient had given me a sketch of his life. His mother had died of tuberculosis after many years of suffering. Only a few memories of his mother, none of them significant, were preserved. It seemed as if all that mattered in his life happened after her death. The only thing that appeared important to him was that his mother never kissed him or his sister. When now, many weeks later, he told me about his fastidious behavior in the home of his aunt, the idea occurred to me spontaneously that the boy was simply following a caution he had acquired earlier in his life. The presentation of his earlier boyhood years and the memory he had told me before, that his mother never kissed him, were suddenly there. I suddenly understood why the boy had refused to eat from used plates and why his mother never kissed him. It was not that he was fastidious, but he had been warned by his mother herself, who knew that she had tuberculosis. He remembered, after my interpretation, that his mother had plates and knives and forks of her own that no other member of the family used. Most memories of the disease of his mother as well as of his own boyhood years had been repressed and had made some traits of his behavior incomprehensible to him.

One afternoon another patient complained of a heavy feeling on his chest. "It is," he said, "as if a stone were laid on me." Unconscious memory and emotional understanding of the patient enabled me to remind him that his family planned to erect a tombstone on his father's grave the next day. I realized this suddenly—but why? The patient was talking about other remote subjects in this session—but he unconsciously thought of his father whose death did not consciously grieve him.

I am in the fortunate position of being able to report two cases that will illuminate the psychology of such unconscious communication, with Freud himself as the psychoanalyst. The first concerns me. I had an emotional conflict that caused me considerable disturbance in my middle forties and I asked Freud for help. Almost twenty-five years after my own psychoanalysis, and after many years of practicing analysis, I found myself for a few weeks as a patient on the couch of the best analyst. Those were unforgettable weeks. The penetrating sagacity, the human understanding, the wisdom, and the kindness of the great man were never clearer to me than in those short weeks. The old man seemed to know all that was in me, my weaknesses and shortcomings as well as my strengths—all that was hidden to others and to myself. From a height of observation, with a psychological discernment never met in any other human being he showed me a picture of myself whose traits, strange and familiar at the same time, I would never have recognized as my own. And how true were these traits! I knew it then and learned to know it even better later on.

Toward the end of these too short weeks I found myself reconciled with myself and ready to accept myself. Strangely encouraged, I had occasion once again to admire his fine unconscious understanding. In the last session I clinked the coins in my pocket while giving myself up to free associations. I casually remarked that playing with money showed my anal-erotic tendencies. Freud answered seriously: "That is, of course, nonsense. You think of your brothers and you are glad that you are now able to send them money." I tried to trace my thoughts back. I had not thought of my brothers consciously just then, but the thought had crossed my mind a few minutes before, a fleeting thought that I could now, because I was earning more than my two older brothers, give them a certain amount monthly. I had let the association pass by unexpressed but had instead listened to the metallic sound of the coin with which I had played at the beginning of the analytic session. I had often before spoken of my two brothers, who used to slip bills into my pocket when I was a student. Instead of the by-passed thought I had half-jokingly mentioned a psychoanalytic theory—but this theory had a connection with the unspoken association. Another psychoanalyst, a representative of an older-brother figure, had published a paper the other day concerning anal eroticism. In clinking the coins I had unconsciously demonstrated: I am now rich; I am richer than my brothers. Freud swept aside my theoretical remark contemptuously, as it deserved, and penetrated to the essential thought, which concerned my feelings of superiority to my older brothers.

My other report antedates this revealing incident by twenty years. It, too, concerns Freud. At that time I was twenty-six years old, an inexperienced analyst and much worried about the numerous problems my first patients presented to me. I had a British patient who had come to a standstill in his associations. He asserted that nothing occurred to him, that he had no thoughts. When he spoke it was obvious that it was only to pass the time of the session. In this emergency I asked Freud what I should do. He told me smilingly: "Ask him to think of something that is remotest from his thoughts, something he would never think of." I followed his advice. At first the patient was silent. It was obvious that he was making an attempt to think of something very remote. He then said: "The swamps of Wutipe." That was certainly geographically remote. It nevertheless gave me the clue Freud had expected. Some months ago the father of the patient had died. It was in these swamps that, as a missionary in China, he had contracted the disease that led to his death. I was able to remind the patient of what he had told me about that long ago, and he broke into sobs. At the end of the session he said, "I don't know what the hell I cried about."

I have thought of Freud's advice often enough since, the last time a few weeks ago. During his psychoanalytic session, a patient said that nothing occurred to him. Silence. After ten minutes: "It is a blank, a complete blank . . . like a curtain in a theater." Then without asking him, I could tell the patient what he had thought. He had read in the newspaper that day that the play of a young writer who, as he knew, had been a patient of mine, would be produced in a short time. He himself had written a play some years ago, which had been performed on Broadway and had not been a success. The concealed thought concerned the play of this other patient and his own intense jealousy of the young writer who had won success and fame before him.

All this is less convincing than instances in which the analyst walks to the hidden spot with the directness and the certainty of a somnambulist, apparently led by nothing but blind instinct. It seems there is no clue to the train of thought, nothing in the preceding life story of the patient that could serve as a hint or be used as an allusion to the thing that emerges suddenly from the analyst's memory. A case sometimes contains material consciously and willfully kept back by the patient. In some of them there is no way for the facts to come to the knowledge of the analyst. I have notes on two such cases.

The first concerned an experience in Holland in 1935. I was treating a young German woman who had been a member of the Socialist party. Despite the fact that she came of an old gentile family, she had had to flee Hitler's Third Reich. In Holland she had come to psychoanalysis because serious disturbances interfered with her work. Among them was the memory of a love affair that had lasted for several years and had ended before she left Germany. The man had been a prominent physician. He was married and he had promised to divorce his wife and marry my patient. When Hitler came, he did not have the moral courage to sacrifice his career. He had broken off the relationship with her and returned to his wife. It was obvious that my patient had suffered more from this disappointment than from the other blows of destiny and that she still loved the man to whom she had been devoted for so long and who was lost to her.

We had been discussing the problem for a few months and she still had not overcome her grief. At a certain point the analysis reached a deadlock. One session at this time took the following course. After a few sentences about the uneventful day, the patient fell into a long silence. She assured me that nothing was in her thoughts. Silence from me. After many minutes she complained about a toothache. She told me that she had been to the dentist yesterday. He had given her an injection and then had pulled a wisdom tooth. The spot was hurting again. New and longer silence. She pointed to my bookcase in the corner and said, "There's a book standing on its head."

Without the slightest hesitation and in a reproachful voice I said, "But why did you not tell me that you had had an abortion?" I had said it without an inkling of what I would say and why I would say it. It felt as if, not I, but something in me had said that. The patient jumped up and looked at me as if I were a ghost. Nobody knew or could know that her lover, the physician, had performed an abortion on her. The operation, especially dangerous because of the advanced state of her pregnancy, was, of course, kept very secret because abortion in the case of gentiles was punishable by death in Germany. To protect the man she still loved, she had decided to tell me all except this secret.

When I look back on the psychological situation, I can, of course, realize what brought me to my surprising statement. I must have felt for some time that the patient was keeping something secret when she spoke of the physician. Then came the session with the long pauses. I can follow the subterranean thread between her few associations now. Toothache, the injection by the dentist, the pulling of the wisdom tooth, the book that stands on its head. If I had followed this train of associations logically, I might perhaps—perhaps—have come to the same conclusion. Here was a displacement from below to above, from the genital region to the mouth . . . an operation . . . pain . . . the position of the book and the embryo on its head. I did not, however, use my logical powers and I can only warn my students against using them in such situations. Logical operation subjects the analyst to errors and mistakes he would not make if he trusted his psychological rather than his logical gifts. An understanding of the process and the insertion of the logical links in the chain can and sometimes should be attempted afterward but not during the process.

When I look back on the session, what was it that happened in me? At first there was silence in me as in the patient; then suspense, a waiting for something to come; her words echoed in me; a new suspense; a new resounding of her words, and then all blank and dark for a second, out of which came the knowledge, nay, the certainty, that she had had an abortion, that she thought with grief of the baby for which she had longed and which she had to give up. I did not give a damn about logic and what I had learned in the books. I did not think of any psychoanalytic theory. I just said what had spoken in me despite and against all logic, and I was correct.

The second instance, though less impressive, proves that the analytic technique, if only applied with inner sincerity, operates with the precision of a scalpel used in surgery. An Englishman, who had become a professor of mathematics at an unusually early age, was sent to me by Freud for psychoanalysis. He complained about different nervous symptoms but mostly because his work was never as complete as he had foreseen. The problems he told me about were, of course, far beyond my poor understanding of mathematics. What became obvious, however, was that he often approached the most difficult problems with a courage and boldness that won him the admiration of other professors of mathematics. He had published a series of articles on certain problems that, until then completely unsolved, he brought close to solution. But he could not go beyond this point to a complete solution. He failed and felt frustrated whenever this point was reached in his thinking. It was as if all his intellectual powers left him suddenly, as if all that had been so ingeniously prepared and built up faded and evaporated. It came to nothing, as if a bad demon had suddenly wiped it away.

He had described the process several times with all its specific mathematical traits. I had gained no insight. His life story showed nothing conspicuous. He was, it seemed, happily married and had a child. What then impelled me after a few months to tell him that I was convinced that he had a premature emission in sexual intercourse? I suddenly felt the impulse to tell him—it was certainly at the "psychological moment." The patient, shy in this respect as so many British young men were twenty years ago, had not spoken of his sexual life and nothing in his report led me to surmise such a sexual peculiarity. Nothing but his vivid and repeated description of what happened when he dealt with a mathematical problem. I could tell him what I unconsciously guessed. He approached his wife with strong desire and he was bold and energetic in the first phases of the sexual act but suddenly he had to let go without pleasure, without reaching the climax of sensations and the release had rather the character of weakening than of resolving the tension. He had never discussed his present sex life with anybody.

He looked at me with amazement. The sudden revelation was rewarded. It opened the door to the center of his problem. Back at the university he could write to me that he had overcome his difficulties in both fields and that he was happy and grateful to psychoanalysis upon which he looked as upon magic. There was, however, nothing magical in my conclusion. I had unconsciously transferred what he had told me about his mathematical difficulties to the sexual sphere. But note: while I verbalized it, I was not conscious of any logical operations of the kind.

Let me add one little instance. It is representative of hundreds of others attesting to the secret communication that takes place between the psychoanalyst and his patient. A man told me a dream in which the following part appeared. *I am with my father on board ship. My father shows me a cabin near that of the captain. I ask my father: "Does mother know that you are leaving?" He begins to cry and says, "I have forgotten to tell her," and we decide to telephone before the ship leaves the harbor. We move and we come to Lands End.*

There were no associations to the dream. He did not know where the name Lands End came from nor any ship on which he had gone with his father. Nothing occurred to him about the dream. Why did I ask him then and there whether he knew the play, *Outward Bound?* "Do I know it?" he answered astonished. "I saw it in the theater and then as a movie and I just thought of it. That is strange." The play, which I had seen many years ago in Vienna, shows a ship on which the passengers are all dead without knowing it. The captain is God.

What did I know of the patient that would have led to this idea? Nothing beyond the fact that his father died two years ago and that now, stirred up by going over his life in psychoanalysis, his old relations with his father have won increasing significance for him. In the preceding session I had quoted a sentence Freud once wrote—most of his students overlook it—that the death of his father is the most important event in a man's life. The dream regressed to another experience that had subterranean connections with the subject, the play, *Outward Bound,* which shows the transition from death to life in the form of a ship voyage. The patient was, as I realized without saying it, under the ban of a superstitious fear that he would soon die, as his father had. A great part of the dream, whose interpretation here would lead us too far, is only to be understood when one turns certain sentences around. They have to be read like Chinese and Hebrew writing. Thus it is not his father but himself who would cry if he had to leave without saying farewell to his mother, and so on. It is remarkable that the play occurred to him as well as to me. It had never been mentioned between us before. Something in the atmosphere of the dream, the ship, Lands

THE SURPRISED PSYCHOANALYST 267

End, the mood of leave-taking which pervades it, the strange mixture of everyday language and something extraordinary—all that and perhaps more must have made me think of a half-forgotten play seen many years ago on another continent.

I know that many analysts add theoretical considerations to their interpretations. They explain minutely and conscientiously how they arrived at their results. I do not consider such a technique false, but wasteful and unsatisfactory. Wasteful because it means an unnecessary intellectual effort on the part of the psychoanalyst. He has to expend energy and time needed for other things. Suppose I consult a physician and he makes a diagnosis of my disease after careful examination. Perhaps he tells me that I have bronchitis. He does not go into a long discussion of the reasons and considerations that led him to this conclusion. I consider the technique unsatisfactory also because the psychoanalyst will be able to name only a few of the reasons that led him to a certain interpretation. Many others, such as previous impressions, little signs, intonations, gestures, and so on, remain unconscious, but they were operating and contributed to the interpretation.

And of what use would such theoretical discussions and explanations be? To convince the patient? But he will not be convinced by logical and theoretical arguments if he is reluctant to accept them. And if he is ready to trust the analyst, he does not need them. Yes, we sometimes realize that a patient *does not believe* that an analytic interpretation is true. *He knows it.* That may sound paradoxical but experience proves that it is possible. My recommendation to the student is thus to present his impression or interpretation in the form of a statement without adding his reasons or adding them only in exceptional cases. (Training another analyst, for instance, is such a case.) I need not emphasize at this point that precautions have to be taken before interpretations of this kind are uttered; we shall discuss them fully later on.

Here are a few cases that at a given moment were beyond the comprehension of the analyst. The conscious understanding of the psychological foundations of an interpretation here did not precede the grasping of their concealed meaning. It followed the penetration. Of course, these are exceptions, comparable to sudden advances of a military force that makes use of a favorable situation on the spur of the moment. Such improvised movements take place side by side with the long-prepared, tactical procedures. It will be obvious from the reports of these cases that the conjecture of concealed meanings and motives takes its point of departure from an actual symptom or a combination of traits. After grasping the hidden meaning the psychoanalyst is often able to use this insight for the psychological evaluation of the patient's personality. What he guesses sometimes affords the possibility of looking into a shaft of the unconscious that was not perceived before. Understanding the single symptom helps bring to light aspects of the patient's character.

In some cases where the psychoanalysis has progressed a good deal, the process is reversed. The analyst has won a good insight into the personality of the patient. Many sessions have given him opportunity to study his character, to observe his peculiar traits, to understand the forces that govern his neurosis. When a new symptom is discovered, a fear has come out of hiding, a compulsive activity or an obsession idea has emerged, the analyst can use his psychological understanding of the whole person to guess more quickly and adequately the unconscious meaning of the symptom or to find the motives and mechanisms behind its production.

I had been analyzing a young American artist for a few months in Vienna when he told me of a phobia he had not mentioned before. Our sessions up to this point had been occupied with his life story and the compulsion against which he desperately fought. He had grown up in a very puritanical milieu. His parents had been very religious people and the child was strictly educated. On Sundays every activity except praying was forbidden. A spirit of gloominess and sinfulness had cast a shadow over his boyhood. In his late teens he had freed himself from the religious beliefs and practices of his parents, whose house he had left. He had come to Vienna because he wanted to get rid of a terrible compulsion that tempted him to play sexually with six- or seven-year-old girls. He had in fact yielded to this temptation several times and was later on crushed by guilt-feelings and fears.[2] After several months we arrived at a reconstruction of the events and motives that had led the patient to his perversion. When he was six or seven years old, he shared his room with a governess who had often taken the little boy into her bed and used him sexually. What he now tried to do to little girls had at first been done to him when he was a small boy. It was a case of turning a passive experience, which the child could not master psychically, into an active one. This reconstruction of the seduction story was, of course, the result of hard and patient analytic work comparable to

[2] As is known from the biographies of Dostoyevsky, it was this same temptation that beset this writer. It is likely he gave in to it at least once.

the solution of a jigsaw puzzle and obtained with the help of all the means that the analytic technique has at its disposal.

In a pause in the work centering around his obsession, he told me about a phobia that had frightened him for many years and which he was again experiencing on his walks in the streets of Vienna. He became panicky when he saw smoke, from chimneys for instance, or sparks. It was not difficult to guess that forgotten impressions from his childhood played the main role in the genesis of this phobia. Ideas of hell-fire and the punishments of the damned emerged suddenly in my thoughts—I understood immediately the origin of his fears.

In the recognition of the motives of his compulsion (and other symptoms not discussed here) before he brought up the phobia, I had followed the usual path of analytic penetration, putting together into the picture all elements that had emerged. The insight into his other symptoms, into his doubts and fears, had made me familiar with his particular personality. When he gave me all the details of the fire-and-smoke phobia, I could already use this knowledge. I recalled the description of his religious background. I was aware of the contrast between his official freethinking and the old convictions that lingered in his unconscious. The solution of his compulsion took many weeks; the guessing of the meaning of the smoke-phobia, only a few minutes. The contrast of the two procedures can best be compared to the following situation.

Some boys study with their botany teacher the leaves, flowers, and fruits of an apple tree. When they recognize such a tree in a garden later on, they assume that it will bear apples, not nuts or plums, because they remember the special leaves and flowers of an apple tree.

At this point I want to introduce a new term for the reaction of the analyst to the communications, words, gestures, pauses, and so forth, of the analyzed person. I call the sum of this reaction, which includes all kinds of impressions, *response*. The analytic response is thus the emotional and intellectual reply to the speech, behavior, and appearance of the patient, and includes awareness of the inner voices of the analyst. Every interpretation, all that the analyst says, the form of his explanation and exposition, are all preceded, and to a great extent determined, by this response. The response is, so to speak, the inside experience of that which the analyst perceives, feels, senses, regarding the patient. It is clear from the preceding chapters that the main part of that response is in its nature unconscious or, to put it otherwise, that only a small part of it becomes conscious. The response is thus the dark soil in which our understanding of psychical processes is rooted. Out of these roots, which are hidden deep in the earth, emerges our intellectual, logical grasp of the problems. Out of these concealed roots grows the tree of psychoanalytic knowledge.

The student is warned not to trust to the false teachers who instruct him that he should approach the material offered by the patient from the start with the instrument of conscious knowledge and theoretical learning. *This form of approach is false, leads the analyst astray, and gets the analysis nowhere fast.* Rather than trust to what he theoretically knows the analyst should trust to what he feels, to what his senses tell him, the known senses and the unknown ones. Mistrust conscious and theoretical knowledge as a receiving station for the language of the unconscious. It will be difficult, I know, to make the analysts unlearn what they have so long applied and to undo the damage that instruction in their training has done. *It is better not to understand than to misunderstand.* To follow one's misconstructions and misapprehensions with great logic is much more dangerous than to admit to oneself that one has not yet understood and is ready to wait until one begins to comprehend. It is better to wait for the dawn than to strike out in the wrong direction in the dark.

The response of the analyst is the emotional answer to the communications of the patient. It is that which takes place in the analyst's mind from the first vague impressions until he sees the unconscious processes of the other person with full clarity. ("The other person" is, of course, oneself in the case of self-observation and self-analysis.) *Response at the moment in which we reach the deepest insights into the unconscious has the nature of surprise.* Such suprise-response will, of course, never emerge when the analyst approaches unconscious material theoretically. He will then see only what he expects to see and neglect, distort, or overlook what does not fit his scheme. The new things he meets will not become objects for new study because they will be labeled quickly and put on theoretical file. For these analysts psychoanalysis will always be a "science," a drawer full of formulas and terms, and never an experience.

In that case, how can it become an experience for the patient? Only he who has once been caught by surprise and has experienced and mastered that sudden emotion can catch another by surprise. I have already warned the student not to follow those false teachers who recommend the use of "intelligence" in the approach to the unconscious. What emerges from the depths can only be caught with something originating in the depths. I am teaching my students to do the sensible thing, but the sensible thing is not always that which our intelligence demands. The analyst who absorbs the noises and voices of the day too keenly will never hear the secret fountains that speak loud only in the night.

The analyst, as he is often trained in psychoanalytic institutes, is an interpreting automaton, a robot of understanding, an independent analytic intellect who has become a person without ever becoming a personality. He confuses the calmness and control of the observer with lack of sensitivity, objectivity in judgment with absence of sensation and feeling. When he sits behind the patient, he tries to be everything else but himself. But only he who is entirely himself, only he who has the sharpest ear for what his own thoughts whisper to him, will be a good psychoanalyst.

I am of the opinion, not shared by many New York analysts, that the personality of the psychoanalyst is the most important tool he has to work with. My stand here is in sharp contrast to that of those teachers who train their students to forget themselves when they try to understand unconscious phenomena. I admonish my pupils to be acutely alert to their own responses. The most important advice on the technique of psychoanalysis is nowhere to be found in the textbooks. The teacher who has discussed technique and technicalities should at the end remind his student: *"This above all: to thine own self be true."*

CHAPTER XXIV

The Young Girl and the Old Lady

A YOUNG psychologist who studies psychoanalysis with me asked me the other day what were my reasons for assuming that he had certain character-traits. The question, put modestly enough, had a subtly teasing or challenging character. I admitted that I was entirely unprepared to answer it adequately. My assumption was founded on many impressions that I had gathered during the past weeks of his psychoanalysis. I frankly admitted that I was unable at the moment to enumerate and describe these impressions. I told him then that I found myself in a situation similar to that of Honoré de Balzac, whose biography I had read a few weeks ago. The writer, once again penniless, awakened in the middle of the night and saw a man in his room who was frantically searching in the drawers for money. The burglar became frightened when Balzac suddenly roared with laughter. The comparison of the analyst's situation with Balzac's in the story, is however, only partially justified. Challenged by the student, I was rather like a man who has not a cent at home at the time, but knows there is money available somewhere. The reasons for my assumptions about the young psychologist were not within my reach at the moment, but they could be recalled in time. Many of them can be remembered and some come to us with clarity and precision, not when our thoughts are concentrated on finding them, but when we are most absent-minded.

Analysis is a good school for modesty. We rarely know where our first and decisive insights come from. We observe certain traits but are not aware of them. Recollections surge up within us, and we have no idea why they arise. We know things about a person and have no inkling of how we know them. We lack definite and cogent reasons for our knowledge.

In the search for unconscious secrets, our intelligence and conscious knowledge are of little help. It is as hopeless to try to use these instruments in the initial phase of conjecture as it would be to attempt to photograph someone who is not present. There remains, to lead us in our search, only what we call intuition, that is, experience which has become unconscious. Intuition serves us like a blind man's dog.

Psychoanalysts rightly point out that all the defenses, built up during many years of living, all reaction-formations and unconscious counter-tendencies will show themselves as resistances in analysis and will block the road to the unconscious territory. The deeper we penetrate the more powerful will these resistances become. Yet we have a secret ally within the personality of the man or woman under analysis. Not all the inner forces are working toward concealment and in defense of the entrance, toward keeping the secret. Under the seemingly impenetrable surface something is moving in the dark until it can be felt and understood. Something is going on down there that has its own purposes and its own development. It is elusive and yet draws attention to itself, it hides itself, yet wants to be discovered and tries in spite of all the twists and turns to come out into the open. There are always small signals, little incidents that have escaped the person's notice but become meaningful to the analyst when they catch his attention. We are in danger of neglecting them and passing them by if something within us does not warn us to look at them. We do not immediately understand their significance but we anticipate that they will reveal their meaning because

> . . . in such indexes, although small pricks
> To their subsequent volumes, there is seen
> The baby figure of the giant mass
> Of things to come at large. . . .[1]

A strange transformation takes place after the first weeks of psychoanalysis: the facts our patients tell us in their autobiographies and reports of their daily lives lose the great significance they seemed to have at first; and events, thoughts, and impulses on the fringes of their attention acquire an unexpected importance. Hard facts become shadows and elusive shadows become facts.

Take the case of a young man who came to analysis because he realized that there was something wrong in his relationship with his wife. On the surface everything seemed fine; the young couple lived com-

[1] Shakespeare, *Troilus and Cressida,* Act I, scene 3.

fortably and there were children. The young man had an excellent position in his father-in-law's firm. He was, apparently, in love with his wife. She, however, complained that he showed indifference and, sometimes, even mental cruelty toward her and that their sexual relations were unsatisfactory. We had come to the fourth week of psychoanalysis, and my patient had told me the story of his life. He came of a poor family and fell in love with the girl who was now his wife while he was a poorly paid clerk in another firm. The girl's parents were wealthy and took her on a trip to Europe. Under pressure from her parents she married another man, and he tried to forget her. It soon became evident that this marriage was a failure; the young woman divorced her husband, looked up my patient, and soon afterward they were married. His wife's family now welcomed him and he became a partner in his father-in-law's department store. Up to this point his tale sounded like a *True Romance* story. My patient had no complaints to make. He was satisfied with his wife and did not understand why she thought that he was difficult and harsh. His psychoanalysis led us back into his childhood and we were busy digging up early memories of his boyhood days in a little town where he lived with his mother after his parents had been separated. In the fourth week he told me a dream he had had the previous night.

He and his wife drive to a roadhouse outside the city. During the drive there is lively talk, joking, and a lot of laughter. Arriving at the restaurant, they walk up to the entrance and he lets his wife walk in first. At this moment a man who must have been hidden behind the door hits his wife over the head with a blunt instrument and she falls senseless. Horrified, he does not know what to do, whether to notify the police or to run.

This was the first dream he had remembered since the beginning of his analysis and it is a technical rule that you do not interpret the first dream recounted by a patient. Then what do you do with it? You deal with it as you do with the modesty that women sometimes show in intimate situations. You ignore it. That does not mean you do not notice it, but only that you treat it as if it were not there. So I made no comment on the dream. The patient spontaneously recalled that he and his wife really had driven to a restaurant the day before and that they had talked on the way. Their conversation had been about friends and happenings related to the time before their marriage.

It was easy to guess that in this conversation something had been mentioned that brought close to the conscious surface the emotions he had felt when his present wife had jilted him for another man. Wounded pride, jealousy, rage, hate, and despair were, so to speak, unconsciously revived, reawakened for a moment, although no hint of these emotions was consciously experienced. They emerge, however, in the dream. We guess the identity of the killer behind the door. The dream revealed the hidden entrance to the shaft that we shall descend later on.

I have already said that we reach disavowed and repressed emotions in the early phases of psychoanalysis with the help of our own unconscious experiences. That means that we recognize them by the echo they find within ourselves. This echo is by no means always consciously perceived and recognized by the analyst. Someone has said that the origin of poetry is emotion recollected in tranquillity. In some such way the initial insights in psychoanalysis are won with the help of our emotions recollected in tranquillity, or our unconscious memories of those emotions. I have said before that the discovery of those secret thoughts and feelings is not achieved by logical process but by unconscious introjection. This means that for a moment we have changed into our patient, as it were; we live his life and feel what he feels or felt. This process has none of the characteristics of conscious activity. It takes place wholly in areas that are not accessible to our thought-efforts and it is almost unthinking. Then when we emerge from the dark stream we dived into, we have often found what we could never have obtained by conscious thinking, what knowledge and scientific training alone could never have discovered. Down South they tell a story about a farmer's horse that broke out of its pasture and seemed lost. All searches were fruitless; the horse could not be found. At last an old Negro who lived on the farm found the horse and brought it home. Asked how he did it, he answered, "Waal, I set and figgured where Ah'd put foh if Ah wuz a hoss, and Ah did, and 'e wuz." The hiding-place of the horse could not be found by common sense, but by "horse sense," by a kind of momentary transformation of the searcher himself into a horse.

But how is such a fleeting unconscious transformation possible? Do we imagine that we can change into so many and different characters? Can we, even for a few seconds, feel like men, women, and children we generally have nothing in common with, who have problems unlike our own, different griefs and joys, and a way of experiencing life alien to our own? Is such a swift metamorphosis not fantastical? Indeed it is. It belongs entirely to the domain of the imagination. But the classification does not mean that it is impossible. It only means that analysts need to be imaginative as well as trained in psychiatry and psychoanalysis. If so modest an achievement were impossible, if we were incapable of reaching what is hidden in the emotional life of a few people, how then, has it happened that the great writers have brought to the surface the deepest feelings, the hidden thoughts, of hundreds of different characters? Shakespeare, Tolstoy, and Dostoyevsky could feel and think what king and beggar, genius and simpleton, whore and virtuous woman, murderer and savior, neurotic and demented, thought and felt. And that was only the beginning of their achievements. They created this multitude of people and made them talk and walk, act and suffer, in their own right and under the power of the forces within themselves. Did not Dostoyevsky, Balzac, Goethe, and all the other great writers swim in that same stream into which we dive for only a brief moment? When Flaubert wrote the scene in which Madame Bovary died, he felt the bitter taste of the poison in his own mouth. The great Austrian poet, Richard Beer-Hofmann, once told me that when he got up from the desk at which he had written the scene in *Jacob's Dream* where his hero fought with the angel of God, he felt that he was limping. No comparable achievement of imagination is needed in analysis, but there are lucky, unguarded moments in which the analyst can reach the unconscious processes of another person merely by means of his own unconscious imagination. Such moments occur without direction from the conscious will of the analyst. In him too, the psychical process follows its own laws and cannot be consciously directed. The material that emerges in him, the subject he gives his thoughts to, only *seems* to be his free choice. In reality it is determined in all its details by unconscious processes within himself. Some understanding, deeper than any product of reason, causes him to select one aspect of the patient's experience and neglect another.

The other day I got a friendly letter from a young woman who had been a patient a few years ago. The photograph of a healthy and handsome baby boy was included. When I looked at the smiling face of the infant, I remembered the brave fight the young mother had fought with herself and won during her analysis.

A number of nervous symptoms, anxieties, and inhibitions had brought her to analysis. Her marriage was precariously near a breakup. She could not stand her husband, whose neurotic peculiarities embittered her. She yielded to sexual intercourse only with great reluctance and she was frigid. Her husband was an American who had spent most of the war years in England, where she was born. She had fallen in love with him there and had had an affair with him that she had kept secret from her parents and friends. She had become pregnant and felt that she had no alternative but to get an abortion. Later her lover, who had meanwhile been sent to another country returned and asked her to marry him. In the meantime she had an affair with another man. She no longer wished to be his wife and gave her consent only in the last moment before his departure to America. Their married life was full of arguments and bitter battles, in which she showed extreme cruelty toward the man whom she had once dearly loved. She gave me a long and detailed account of all the difficulties and dissonances.

God knows, we make many mistakes, but in some cases the needle of an inner compass points unerringly in the right direction. Why was it that listening to this patient, my mind returned again and again to the memory of the abortion? She had mentioned it in the most casual manner, saying merely that it was, of course, necessary to have the operation performed; it was impossible to be an unmarried mother. Nothing in her report or in her complaints seemed to indicate that the abortion had an emotional meaning for her neurosis that was different from the usual one for other young women who have been through similar experiences. True, she had afterward become sexually frigid but she herself explained this change by pointing out that at that time she had discovered that her lover had been unfaithful to her. Her present unwillingness to have a child was justified, she felt, because she did not love her husband and was not sure whether she would stay with him. She explained too that there were good reasons for her mental cruelty to him; he had been cruel to her. It became obvious that she wanted to get even.

I cannot say what made me concentrate my attention on the abortion experience. Was it the matter-of-fact way in which she mentioned and dismissed the subject? Did it have some subtle and concealed connection with her strange fears and neurotic symptoms that I sensed? The character of these symptoms certainly contrasted sharply with her attitude and behavior otherwise. Like so many young British girls of her class and generation, she was very intellectual, emotionally cool, and even cynical in her outlook on life, or at least she pretended to be so. Her most prominent neurotic symptoms were an intense fear of an impending calamity of a vague and mysterious nature and a guilt-feeling of unknown origin.

I no longer recall just when I first received the impression that below her unemotional and detached surface there existed superstitious survivals of her religious upbringing. These survivals were in sharp contrast to the Communistic and materialistic convictions she held. Sometimes it seemed to me as if she was unconsciously punishing herself for some thought-crime, indeed it seemed as if she was unconsciously determined to wreck her marriage and make a mess of her young life. The course of her analysis proved the accuracy of my at first vague impression that the abortion experience she mentioned so casually had been of paramount importance for the development of her neurosis. We learned that she was preoccupied by the unconscious idea that the abortion had been an act of murder for which she would be punished by God or some higher power. Apart from and in contradiction to her avowed freethinking and atheism, there coexisted a stream of unconscious convictions that now actually governed her life.

Our analytic sessions returned to her memory of the abortion. Her recollections were hazy at first and she was reluctant to call to mind a situation she considered unimportant, "peripheral," as she said. In overcoming her strong resistances against recalling these scenes she succeeded in reliving the experience and in releasing the long pent-up emotions connected with them. She lived over again her anxiety, her despair, and her deep guilt-feeling. Vividly she recalled her search for an abortionist, the preparations for the abortion, her fear and revulsion, the furtive behavior of the physician and the nurse, the excruciating pain, and her grim determination not to show her feelings and never to let her lover know what she had been through. These recollections marked a turning-point in her analysis; they acquired the significance of confession and atonement together with the character of therapeutic emotional release. Some months after this, her analysis came to a satisfactory end; her chief symptoms had virtually disappeared. A few months later she wrote that she was pregnant and proud and happy at the prospect of motherhood.

When I freely admitted a little way back that I do not know just when I first felt that my patient thought of her abortion as a murder— a concept in accordance with the teachings of the Catholic church—I neglected to state that I at least do know what impressions made me think of a literary work in which this theme occurs. These were two scenes, concerning situations before the abortion, that the patient described in an analytic session.

A few days before the abortion was performed her mother had come to visit her in London. In the conversation between mother and daughter the subject of the relations between the sexes was touched on; the girl, who must have been on the point of a break-down, did not confess her affair with the young man although she was aware that her mother knew or guessed the truth. It seems that her mother was astonishingly tolerant and understanding toward the attitudes of the younger generation, whose standards of sexual conduct differed so much from her own. The girl was deeply touched but suppressed her wish to tell her mother that she was in trouble. But then her mother went on talking as if she were trying to warn her daughter. Her tolerance stopped short before the problem of an illegitimate child and she spoke condemningly of the casual way in which modern girls sometimes deal with this situation. The patient became silent and later, when she took her mother to the railroad station, could scarcely speak to her.

There was about my patient's report of this scene a peculiar and oppressing atmosphere. Its essence was that the first nearness and sympathy between mother and daughter was followed by a mutual withdrawal, in which both women suddenly felt as if a wall had risen between them. The sense of separation lay in the things they said and in their silences full of things unsaid. The scene seemed to remind me of something. Where had I felt a similar emotional atmosphere?

The girl, whose lover had left the country as a soldier, did not know where to turn in her misery. She could not confide in her women friends and she had no idea how to go about getting an abortion. In her distress she thought of a young man who had been her good friend in their student days. She knew that the young man, who was very shy, had loved her for many years without telling her his feelings. She phoned him, met him, told him her story and asked him to help her. He proved to be a real friend. He found an abortionist and accompanied her to his office. He told the doctor that he was the father of the child and made the arrangements for the operation. My patient's description of this helpful and reticent young man, who had been her unhappy suitor so long and behaved so selflessly in her need, also reminded me of another figure. It was shadowy, but I had certainly encountered it somewhere.

And then suddenly visual images occurred to me, images not from life but from its reflection on the stage. I remembered two scenes from the play *Rose Bernd* by Gerhart Hauptmann. I had seen it maybe twenty-five years ago in Vienna and recalled the outlines of the plot

rather vaguely, but two scenes arose before me in full vividness.[2] The
action takes place at the beginning of the present century in a village in
German Silesia. One of the leading characters is a bailiff and commissioner of forests, a temperamental man about forty years old, whose
wife has been hopelessly paralyzed for many years. The heroine of the
play is a young, full-blooded, attractive peasant girl, Rose Bernd, whom
all men pursue. Rose is in love with the commissioner of forests, and
has a secret affair with him. A serious-minded and deeply religious
bookbinder loves Rose and wants to marry her. The play follows the
affair of Rose and the married man. She has become pregnant and is
helpless. Another man has found out about her relations with the
forester and she succumbs to his brutal courtship. In her terrifying need
she goes to the forester's wife. I see the scene in this house. The paralyzed wife is understanding and kind to the girl who begs her help and
advice. She does not condemn the love affair, but she withdraws her
sympathy when Rose confesses that she is pregnant. I see the scene:
the graying woman in her wheel chair and the way she looks at the
tortured girl, who is so strangely inarticulate and cannot say what she
feels. The girl sits there with her head bowed and is silent.

Rose gives birth to her child in a field. In her shame and despair,
deserted by her lover and pursued by other men, she kills her child.
Here again a picture emerges, that of the last scene of the play. It takes
place in the house of Rose's father. There at the table sits the bookbinder,
August, the girl's fiancé, a thin, gloomy figure who has one eye and has
forgiven the brute who hit him. He had sensed what was happening
to Rose, but yet was not able to help her. A State-Trooper comes into
the house. I see the bayonet fixed on his gun. And there is Rose who
suddenly breaks down and says, "I have strangled my child with these
hands. . . ." There is the final scene before the curtain slowly descends.
The State-Trooper walks to the door to take Rose away. The one-eyed
man, August, gets up from the table and says in a strange, halting voice,
"Inspector, this girl . . . this girl . . . must have been through a
lot. . . ."

It is in this sentence, spoken by a minor figure, that we find the leit-
motif of the play most clearly put into words. It is this melody that I
must have heard again as I listened to the unemotional and strangely
impersonal report my patient gave me first of her abortion. Listening

[2] For the following discussion it is not essential that my recollections of the play
be accurate in detail. Only the psychological reality of my recollections matters
here.

to her tale so scant in words, so bare of feeling, and so remote, my ear must have caught the undertone of a destiny common to a peasant girl on a Silesian farm and an intellectual young woman of London—sisters under the skin. At a certain moment during the analysis I became so acutely aware of that common destiny that the memory of the play emerged in my conscious thoughts. It was odd that this melody was heard in a Silesian dialect and that it was spoken in a halting voice, "Inspector, this girl . . . this girl . . . must have been through a lot." When you penetrate to what is deepest in the soul of women and men, cultural and local differences do not matter any more. Before psychology as before law, all men are equal.

An old folder I came across the other day contained, among other things, a cartoon that reminded me of a case I treated many years ago in Vienna. There was only the cartoon with no notes, but I knew immediately why I had kept it. My patient had been a young and very beautiful woman who for a short time had been tortured by the thought that she would very soon become ugly, ill, and old. This tormenting thought pursued her and made her depressed, yes, even made her think of suicide. She spent many hours before the mirror examining her face and her body, scrutinizing every feature for signs of old age. She used more cosmetics than any Hollywood film star, and all in vain. She could not free herself from the mysterious fear of old age. She once described to me how her image in the mirror appeared to her like that of an old, wrinkled woman she had never seen before. How absurd this obsession idea was will be obvious when one considers that her age was twenty-two and that she had won a beauty prize in one of the contests in Vienna, a city of beautiful women. She was celebrated as beautiful and charming and many admirers surrounded her whenever she appeared at parties or in her box at the opera. She also had other obsessive symptoms, but this fear haunted her especially and made her life miserable. Her husband adored her while she had scarcely more than sympathy for him. Her symptoms were so time- and energy-consuming that she could just about fulfill her social obligations. She loved her little daughter, but did not spend much time with her, leaving her in the care of a trained nurse.

After some weeks of psychoanalysis, in which she relived her life in vivid reports of past experiences, I did not understand much more about the genesis of her obsessive thoughts than I had before. About this time I happened to be sitting one day in a dentist's waiting room and looking at some old copies of *Punch* that were on a table beside some Viennese comic journals. I saw the cartoon that is now in my folder, looked at it for some seconds, and turned to other cartoons. When I was called in, I put the magazine aside and did not again think of it.

The next day as I listened once again to the complaints of my patient about her dread of old age, I suddenly remembered the *Punch* cartoon. I immediately understood at least one of the unconscious roots of her fear. I asked my dentist for the copy of *Punch*. Looking at the cartoon in the waiting room must have aroused certain unconscious thoughts in me that recurred during the analytic session and presented the clue to the puzzling symptom of my patient. Until then not understood, its core was touched and unconsciously comprehended when I looked at the cartoon. The words of my patient functioned only like the up-beat in a musical composition. They reminded me of a tune, often heard, that had penetrated to my conscious mind only the day before.

We see in the cartoon a news photographer who is going to take a picture. No doubt he wants to photograph the young, beautiful girl who is looking dreamily at the sea. The old lady who is sitting near by on a beach chair covered with blankets will certainly not disturb him. She pays attention neither to him nor to the girl, and is deeply engaged in reading a book. We see in the second picture that the glamor girl is not willing to be photographed unprepared. She has not the slightest objection to the publication of her picture but she must pretty herself first. The artist shows us how she uses powder and lipstick, how she puts on the wide-brimmed hat that flatters her face, and how she chooses a pose that shows her figure to best advantage. The old lady is unaware of what is going on beside her; she reads. The last picture shows the young girl the next day. She grasps the latest copy of the local *Bright-beach Observer* ready to admire her photograph. Horrified, she sees the picture of the old lady, and reads the caption: "Distinguished Visitor To Our Town."

The comical effect of the cartoon is determined by the contrast between an effort and an expectation and the disappointment that follows. We smile somewhat maliciously because we observed all the expressions of feminine vanity and we recognized finally its futility. The sequence of the drawings allowed for an increase in this effect because all efforts were wasted. We smile at the mistake of the girl who expected to see her own charming picture and looks instead at the photograph of the old, sick-looking matron. It is as if we had unconsciously expected that so much enjoyment of one's appearance would be frustrated or even

THE PRESS PHOTOGRAPHER.

Reproduced by permission of the Proprietors of *Punch*

punished; otherwise we could not smile at the misunderstanding, of which the girl was the victim.

The comical effect is thus founded on a surprise, but this reaction soon yields to a foreknowledge that the presentation of the comical misunderstanding has a concealed meaning. We suddenly feel that the hidden content of the cartoon—hidden perhaps even from the artist who drew it—is only understood when we recognize that there is some sense behind it, that some special relation exists between the young girl and the old lady.

Here is the point at which the tragic appears from behind the comical. Out of the bottom of the comical cartoon emerges an idea, at first vague, but soon acquiring distinct shape. The connection between the two women, the young, healthy girl, and the old lady of poor health, is a latent identity in which present and future of the self flow together. There are now not two persons there, but one present at two stages of life. The picture at which the girl stares presents herself, perhaps forty years from now. It is a vision of the future, of her own future. The view of the loftily dressed nymph in the wide-brimmed straw hat with the quick and vivid gestures side by side with the old lady peacefully reading in her old-fashioned small hat—the juxtaposition and the contrast of the two figures must have stirred up an unclear and transient idea in us that became confirmed. Our surprise at the end bears witness to the fact that a previous subterranean expectation was justified, that the fancy that occurred to us was not entirely nonsensical. We look at the sequence now with new eyes. We are still amused, but no longer are we merely amused. The matron appears as an episodic figure in the first drawing and then reappears in the one before the last, just as the girl strikes a victorious and glamorous pose, at the moment when the picture is snapped. Is it accidental that the old one is there again at the moment of greatest enjoyment of the girl's beauty, like a concealed reminder of what will inevitably come?

The tragic that now comes to light is only slightly beneath the surface of the comic aspect of the cartoon. When we realize that there is a secret identity between the two women, our smile disappears and we become serious. The latter impression goes beyond the first. Here in a comical cartoon is a glimpse of the futility of all attempts to escape the common fate. We look here at the impossibility of arriving anywhere but at renunciation, to which all ways lead, even that of flight. Our better understanding of the psychical processes in the young girl, to whom at the peak of self-love and vanity there appeared a visible messenger of illness and old age, wakens in us sympathy toward her. There is truth in the sentence of the honorable Horace Walpole, fourth Earl of Oxford, who wrote that the world is a comedy for those who think, and a tragedy for those who feel.[3]

But we did not want to discuss the concealed meaning of the cartoon. The pictures recurred to me when I listened to my patient as if they presented the clue to her symptom. Of course, it must have been the right psychological moment during this session, which made me give her my attempt at a reconstruction of how the symptom had first appeared. She had mentioned previously that she had once seen her little daughter look at her with great curiosity when she undressed before taking a bath. Something in the glance of the little girl must have reminded her of a similar situation with her own mother who had died some years ago. There was perhaps a moment when she, the patient herself as a child, had looked at her mother and realized with hidden satisfaction that mother was beginning to get old. This feeling of satisfaction had come in conflict with her love for her mother and with her moral demands on herself. They forbade the small girl to get gratification from the fact that she was so much younger and prettier than her aging mother about whose beauty she had often been told. It was only a fleeting moment and the emotions were repressed and forgotten. This reaction must have reoccurred with great intensity in the years when her mother was ill and sought help in many health resorts and sea-side resorts, accompanied by the growing girl.

When later she caught the glance of her own little daughter, something in the scene must have reawakened the unconscious memory of her childhood, the moment of looking at her mother and seeing that she was old and ugly. Shortly afterward there appeared the mysterious fear that made her feel that she herself was becoming suddenly old, with a wrinkled face and graying hair. It was her mother's face that looked at her when she saw herself in the mirror. It was as if an unconscious fear of retaliation pursued her and made her tremble at the thought that she would soon look like her mother. Her concealed guilt-feeling about a minute of triumph reappeared just when the world

[3] The old lady is perhaps reading the famous letters of Walpole whose thoughtful sentence we just quoted. What this gentleman writes to his friend, Sir Horace Mann, in Florence, gives a brilliant description of the England of 1790. Between sketches of London at the time, stories of court, remarks about the Lords and the Commons, there are occasionally some personal lines about the writer. The health of the old gentleman is not good. The other day two servants had to lift him from his bed and he suffers agonies from gout. There are people who sing the praises of old age: "O, my dear Sir, what self-deluding fools we are through every age."

around her celebrated her beauty. Her daughter's glance, which reminded her of her own childhood, warned her like a signal: now it is your turn, you will appear to the child (and to all) old and wrinkled. Let me add that my reconstruction was confirmed by memories that appeared later on. The symptom persisted, however, until we worked through the psychological material that concerned the complicated relationship of my patient and her mother in the years of her childhood and maturity. Then the symptom decreased slowly in importance and finally paled into insignificance. My patient now saw in the mirror her own image, which she liked, and her fear of becoming old was in scope and character no different from that of other women of her age.

After I had—with the help of the cartoon—arrived at the understanding of her obsession-thought, I was reminded of other cases of a similar nature. In these cases the self appeared suddenly as a stranger or as another self that was hideous; one's own figure seemed deformed, one's expression villainous or nasty. A middle-aged man could not look into a mirror because he had seen the face of an old, beastly, lust-murderer, a kind of Landru or Jack the Ripper, looking back at him. In other cases, too, the self had gotten a glimpse of its other part, of its counter-picture, and reacted with terror. In the second self not only one's repressed ideas and impulses come to light, but also one's latent possibilities, which the ego knows about but does not want to acknowledge. The young girl in the cartoon looks at her photograph, which is not hers, as my patient saw in the mirror her self, which was not she. Oscar Wilde's Dorian Gray, who wishes to remain young and handsome, sees himself thus changed and distorted. He is only a representative of many figures in literature who are haunted by the fear of becoming old and ugly and who run through life as if chased by their second self, their *Doppelgaenger*. In the destiny of these figures the concealed psychical potentialities become, or threaten to become, realities before which the ego shudders. We recall the cartoon and can scarcely say what made us first smile at it. Oh, yes, there is the comical disappointment of the young, vain girl who made herself up for the photograph and then looked with horror at the picture of an old, strange woman. My patient saw herself thus when she looked at her mirror. The effect of the cartoon was comical, and the description of my patient's symptom made at first a grotesque and absurd impression. When we begin to understand their hidden meanings, we no longer wonder that such comical misconceptions and bizarre thoughts touch sore and painful spots within onself.

CHAPTER XXV

Neurotic Camouflage

I SHALL describe in the following paragraphs a typical bit of behavior at a certain phase of obsessional neurosis and how I became aware of the common character of a feature which was quite unknown before and scarcely noticed in analytic literature. This time we shall not deal with the origin, development, and unconscious meaning of the neurotic symptoms, but with the social behavior of obsessional patients and its psychological conditioning.

Someone has said that a speech is made three times: once when it is planned and anticipated, the second time when it is made in reality, the third time when the speaker thinks of what and how he ought to have said. An obsessional character would make a speech a hundred and more times in imagination or anticipation, but perhaps never in reality. Recurring doubts make every move doubtful and scruples and reflections renew themselves until the slightest move becomes impossible and everything is thought rather than done. Everything loses "the name of action." An intelligent patient of mine once said, "Bad conscience takes the place of work with me." Instead of working, he really felt permanently guilty because he did not work. Such obsessional patients stop at that pre-phase of action that I call "thought-rehearsal."

In contrast, these neurotics have to repeat in their compulsions the little ceremonials that appear so insignificant or senseless to a superficial observer.[1] Doubt whether and how correctly the ceremonial or the

[1]Compulsions are small and often meaningless acts which the individual has to perform and repeat against his conscious wish and will. Obsessions are ideas that are persistent and govern the thought-processes despite the patient's insight that they are of a morbid character. Usually compulsions and obsessions are both present in a certain type of neurosis; the patient is unable to control their reoccurence.

magical measures of protection were performed forçes the person to repeat them until he can be certain that he has done his duty or what amounts to the same in neurotic thinking. It is well-known now that such ceremonials have the purpose of protecting the patient from some danger he expects, should he neglect to fulfill them. He could become ill or die, some calamity could befall him or his nearest. All his ceremonials are calculated to turn those magical dangers away exactly as prayers or sacrifices in religion.

But why should I describe general characteristics, when I can give a beautiful and representative instance? A middle-aged man had the compulsion to stamp on the ground with his right foot whenever he entered a room, crossed a line, and on other similar occasions. On account of his mounting doubts he had to repeat this stamping several times. If he did not carry out this ceremonial he was subject to an intense anxiety. For our purpose it suffices to say that the magical ceremony had the meaning of warding off a definite expectation of harm that might overcome him.

What interests us here is the behavior of the patient who was compelled to carry out his ceremonial conscientiously, yet wished to do so secretly when other people were around. Naturally there arose countless occasions when he found this necessary. The patient (he was an American) had promised to take a young lady in whom he was interested in his car to a resort outside Vienna. She had expressed a desire to visit the place. He foresaw, of course, that on leaving the precincts of Vienna and on entering those of the neighboring city he would have to make that gesture with his right foot. He knew also that he must convince himself through repetitions of the ceremonial that at the moment of crossing the city line it was with the right foot or an evil mischance would be brought about in the new district by an entrance on the left foot.

With the obsessional neurotic's peculiar forethought and precaution, which takes account even of minute details that could endanger the carrying out of a ceremonial, he foresaw that during the excursion a whole series of difficulties would arise. What follows here is the result of analytic work of many hours with the conclusions and aspects we reached. At this point he had to tell me of a couple of instances and sketch the way he mastered the difficulties. How should he, a stranger, recognize the place exactly and the time at which he was compelled to make the gesture? And how should he, sitting in the car beside the charming woman, strike out now and then with his foot without offending her, or indeed without appearing ridiculous, or what was almost as bad, without acting conspicuously?

The first difficulty, that of locality and time, was more easily overcome than the second, which was of a more psychological sort. He contrived what could be called a trial performance of the excursion the day before. Some hours earlier that day he had been talking with his Viennese chauffeur. This conversation provided the occasion for proposing the tryout. He mentioned as if by chance the well-known resorts in the neighborhood of Vienna and expressed the wish to learn something about them. When the chauffeur referred among others to the resort in question, the patient inquired whether it was far, whether it belonged to the district of Vienna, or to that of a neighboring town and so on. After discussing the state of the weather he decided to take advantage of the sunshine and make an excursion into the district that very day. During the trip he frequently asked if they were yet in sight of the place, and when the chauffeur suddenly remarked that they were quite close, he got out of the car. He remarked that it was much farther than he had thought and laughingly said that his foot had gone to sleep from sitting so long in the car. With this as an excuse it appeared quite natural that he should stamp with his foot on alighting. He now asked interestedly just where the boundary line of Vienna was, and whether there was a tablet marking the place, as there would be in the United States. When the driver pointed out the marker to him, he spoke of taking a short walk to get rid of the cramp in his foot. With this he really went a bit farther to be sure of the exact position of the boundary line and of the particulars of the spot. It was no trifling matter considering the constantly occurring doubts and uncertainties. Indeed, at the same time he carried on a harmless conversation with the driver who accompanied him, which, while it showed only the interest of the foreigner, also made him acquainted with the exact boundary line of the city district. As he crossed the line, he could, with a comment about the foot that had gone to sleep—"that's a damned uncomfortable feeling"—stamp several times. After having made himself thoroughly familiar with the lay of the land with respect to several landmarks, he returned to the car, mounted with the right foot, and, somewhat reassured, returned to Vienna.

The actual carrying out of the excursion was now somewhat facilitated as the result of this trial. Nevertheless it remained difficult enough. When on the next day he went with the young lady on the same trip there would be opportunity to look frequently out of the window to discover where he was. He could, of course, after his conversation with the chauffeur, make comments to the woman, who, like himself, was a stranger in Vienna, pointing out places and scenes of interest in the city. Carrying on an animated conversation he so contrived it that at the approach to the border of the city he could carry out in an inconspicuous way his magic foot-ceremonial. Primarily it was a matter of "timing." In an easy conversational tone he asked whether she had already made another excursion, extolling the tour of the environs of the city. He remarked that he was especially drawn to the musical and theatrical life of Vienna and asked about the last operetta she had seen. Leaning back in the car he nonchalantly put his left leg over the right. He did that in order to prevent accidentally passing over the boundary of the city with his left foot on the ground, which could have disastrous magical effects in the sense of his obsession-thoughts.

Meanwhile he led the conversation as follows: "Do you remember the *Waltz Dream*? I have seen it twice." To a remark by the girl he said, "Yes, there are a lot of good melodies in it, but my favorite is still the great waltz in the second act." A rapid glance through the window. The boundary was near. "Do you recall it? How does it go? Oh, yes!" The man laughed a little as if enraptured by the recollection of the melody and began to sing:

> Softly, so softly, float through the hall
> Melodies fairest, waltz, music hall
> In gladsome chorus
> Love's tender pain
> Swells from the heart
> That is joyous again. . . .

While he softly sang the verses, which are not more stupid than other such operatic ones, his right foot beat the three-four rhythm, lightly striking each beat on the floor of the car. It was the most natural thing in the world. At the same time it assured the most rigorous carrying out of the obsessional ceremonial during the passage over the border of the one town and the entrance into the next. It was, as he said, above all a problem of "timing," but certainly not only that.

I would draw the reader's attention first to that trial performance described above. Trial performances of this sort are a peculiar kind of protective measure and have scarcely been mentioned in analytic literature. They are first carefully thought out and later just as carefully acted out. Their aim is to eliminate danger and to take reassuring precautions against the disturbances anticipated from the difficulties that may arise in the carrying out of the obsessional acts and ceremonials. These trials are surely to be compared to dress rehearsals before the premiere of a performance and like them are designed to make sure of the best form of presentation. In such circumstances it often happens that the resolutions sicklied o'er with the pale cast of thought do not lose the name of action but gain it. The neurotic gains courage to venture otherwise "dangerous" undertakings from anticipatory thinking out of the best way to eliminate difficulties from his path. The deliberations and resolutions that result from this trying over in thought may be compared to the reading of a new play, to the "run through," as stage language calls it. The selection of the material in the test-activity—in our case the preliminary visit to the spot—would then be comparable to a dress rehearsal. There also, as in the obsessional testing, certain features will be eliminated; the possibilities of the coming situation are examined and the best of them selected.

Thought-rehearsals are governed by the easily recognizable wish to insure the compulsion or the ceremonial against any mishap and to secure inconspicuous execution. The reiteration, the loving deliberation over anticipated details and other particulars, make it clear that new features afford a secondary gain of pleasure. Not uncommonly the patient spends many hours in this sort of anticipatory deliberation. ". . . sweet rehearsal of my morning's dream," says Shakespeare. The tryout in fantasy or in thought produces ideas incited by the new situation and the particular difficulties created by it. Originally quite indefinite they soon take on a sharper form and a more definite contour. Under certain conditions they can, so to speak, become free from the imagined actual situation and autonomous, free creations of imagination, determined by obsessional thinking as well as by concern for public opinion.

We have given no instances of the intellectual work that preceded and prepared the performance because our interest is here directed to the two lines of activity, the trial performance or dress rehearsal and the real performance of the obsessional ceremonial. We neglected the thought-rehearsals, those anticipations of the situation in imagining and considering all circumstances and possible incidents.

Leaving the customary path of analytic observation, we are here interested in the strange behavior of the man during the test and during the excursion. We note that this patient wants to protect himself against the observation of the outer world and represent his neurotic symptoms not only as insignificant but also as though their very existence is harmless and incidental. These features are easily recognizable in both lines of action in the given example. The patient behaves toward the chauffeur, from whom he wishes to conceal the purpose of his test, as if the excursion were to be treated like any other little jaunt. His interest in the boundaries of the city is represented as merely the passing interest of a stranger. The wish to take a little walk at this spot follows as a matter of course. The orientation appears to be merely the expression of a tourist's curiosity; the stamping with the right foot a natural movement on account of the stiffness of the leg.

The same characterization holds for his conduct on the next day during the trip. It was not only "adapted," it just fitted. There was nothing unusual or forced. The observer would have noticed nothing odd in his conduct. No single feature could have seemed unnatural: not his occasional glance out of the window, nothing in the course of his conversation leading up to the operetta, and certainly not the crossing of his legs and the beating of time with his foot while he hummed the beautiful melody. The compulsion was completely hidden behind his natural and nonchalant behavior. This behavior, however, is determined by the combination of the two tendencies, which in themselves appear to be irreconcilable: he must carry out a striking ceremonial in conformity with an inner compulsion, and he wishes to conceal and mask from the outer world the conspicuous gesture.

Is the patient incapable of checking the stamping of the right foot? Not at all, he had often enough done so when necessary. If he does not do it here it is for the reason that he does not want to bear the discomfort and anxiety that will certainly follow the omission of the act. He foresees that the suppression of the ceremonial will result in severe expectations of misfortune and he would avoid this discomfort. Certainly his behavior is directed at hiding his symptoms and his illness, but even more it is directed at letting his illness have the right of way. His chief motive is to be able to carry out his magic ceremonial without hindrance. Besides this, of course, other motives work effectively: he does not want others to recognize the real nature of his illness. He is ashamed of his symptoms and of the peculiar actions to which his illness forces him.

I propose to call the typical bit of behavior which we observed in this case *neurotic camouflage*. It represents an attempt to reconcile two psychic processes that tend to go in opposite directions. The patient has to be obedient to the compulsion imposed by the neurosis, but at the same time he feels impelled to heed the psychic necessity of making his behavior conform to the requirements of his social milieu. The illness itself wants to meet simultaneously the requirements of the inner world and those of the outer. The social camouflage is thus a compromise formation resulting from the conflict of these two opposing urges.

I venture to assert that social camouflage constitutes a typical feature in the behavior of all psychoneurotics at a certain stage in the development of their neurosis. It can be best observed at the time when the neurosis takes on definite form and it is again clearly evident during the phase preceding recovery, although it is frequently recognizable during intermediate phases also. This is easy to account for. In the first stage after the establishment of the neurosis, consideration for the good opinion of the world is still strong enough to justify a certain amount of care to conceal the symptoms. In the healing process, although a definite force is still exerted on the ego by the neurosis, yet the consideration for society is again sufficiently strengthened to become noticeable.

Social camouflage shows up especially clearly in the compulsion neurosis, because in its symptomatology the distance to be bridged is especially great. Ordinarily the neurotic is as much aware of the contrast between the magical and the rationalistic ways of thinking as the normal individual and this explains his need to hide the ceremonial from the outer world if possible or, if not, to belittle it and represent it as an act conforming to the social code.

As I stated before, the presentation of a case of social camouflage is the result of putting together and interpreting isolated pieces of analytic observation. I can no longer remember when and by what means I arrived at the theory of social camouflage here presented, but I still remember that I received the first and decisive impression of what its meaning and general character is when I listened to the report of my patient about his excursion. As I followed his description with poised attention, picking up the details with relaxed wrist, so to speak, for observation, suddenly a Bruckner anecdote, one of the many the Viennese tell, came to mind. It is well known that the great composer, who had been a choir boy and cathedral organist of St. Florian, wanted to become a priest. During his whole life he piously clung to the Catholic creed, to the spiritual power of which his *Mass* and *Te Deum* as well as his nine symphonies bear witness. When Bruckner's name as a composer was already well known, he was visited one day by the director of the Vienna Conservatory, Franz Herbeck, who attempted to persuade the peculiar and shy organist, who could never give up his peasant ways, to come to Vienna. Bruckner and Herbeck went for an afternoon stroll in the neighborhood of Linz. They were deep in conversation about music, when from a church near by the bells of the Angelus sounded. As a pious man Bruckner wished, of course, to doff his hat. But he feared the scorn of the great man from Vienna, whom he suspected of being an agnostic. Torn between his religious conscience and his fear of appearing ridiculous, Bruckner found a way out that must be considered an expression of the most clumsy ineptitude. It was December and bitterly cold, but in his psychic emergency the composer took off his hat and sighed, "Gosh, but it's hot!"

This anecdote presents a case of unsuccessful camouflage and proves that the phenomenon is not restricted to the field of neurosis. A direct line goes from it to numerous kinds of behavior among normal people who find themselves in special difficulties or situations of embarrassment. They arise frequently when people attempt to reconcile strong urges with definite social usages and attitudes of the environment, since they try to mask their expression as harmless and moderate. Attempts at social camouflage that do not belong to the domain of pathology usually arouse in the observer who recognizes their aim a pleasure in the comic. In the case of miscalculation this pleasure can take on the nature of *Schadenfreude*. The spectator spares himself the expenditure of sympathy because he recognizes that the person in question wished to outwit his audience and was unmasked in the attempt. Thus it is to be compared to the swindler who has unintentionally betrayed himself.

The Bruckner anecdote did more than help me to understand the general character of neurotic camouflage because here was a conflict, not between obsession and social conduct, but between religiosity and environment.

Let me give a few more representative examples from clinical practice to show the general character of neurotic camouflage. A woman suffering from a fear of blushing was aware of a number of unavoidable situations that produced the dreaded symptom. Leaving or entering her apartment house she frequently encountered the janitress, who was accustomed to loitering with some of the other women on the stairs or near by. From past experience she knew the curious glances of these influential people and she had the quite justifiable expectation that the janitress would pass some remark about her to the other women that would cause her to blush. What the patient did in this contingency was designed to make the redness of her cheeks appear natural. As she passed she opened her purse and pretended with bowed head to be looking for something, a mirror, perhaps, or lipstick or comb.

Another obsessional neurotic was obliged to pick up and inspect every piece of paper that lay around anywhere in the room. He suffered from the fear that he might "unintentionally" have mislaid or lost some important business notes he had made. This obsession, naturally enough, got him into many unusual situations, which assumed even more curious forms when his doubts forced him to satisfy himself many times over with regard to the contents of papers lying around. For example, as he sat in a restaurant he noticed a piece of paper on the ground at a great distance from his table. Obviously he must pick it up to convince himself that it contained nothing indiscreet written by himself. Before he passed the spot where the paper lay he opened his appointment book and flipped the pages in passing. Turning around as if to see whether he had lost anything, he picked up the piece of paper and inspected it, then threw it away again. When he had left the vicinity the doubt came over him as to whether there might not still be some notes of his on the paper. He had to return. He asked the waiter where the telephone was, then went slowly through the room until he again discovered the paper on the floor. He stooped as if to tie a loosened shoelace, incidentally picking up the bit of paper, which he looked at in the telephone booth. Obliged for a third time to return he was able to say to the waiter, moreover quite in conformity with his mounting anxiety, that he feared he had left an important notice in the telephone booth.

This same patient was tortured with anxiety lest he might inadvertently and unwittingly have caused an injury to his small son. This anxiety had begun with the doubt whether he had not once, in entering a room impetuously, banged the boy on the head with the door knob as he stood near by. This doubt, which soon shifted to other children, could only be stilled by taking precautions that assured him he could not possibly have injured a child. But the precaution would surely appear to the outer world to be senseless or silly. What would his friends and acquaintances think if they saw him in the middle of a sentence stick out his arm as if to measure his distance from the door? He must surely look a perfect fool since no one would understand that by such an improvised measurement he wanted to free himself from a torturing doubt. The patient wished, of course, to preserve his social standing. When such doubts mounted, he very cleverly gave to his remarks a turn that permitted him to make this gesture without arousing suspicion, indeed even to include it as a gesture appropriate to the context. He could, for example, make an animated gesture when he spoke of something over there, or when he pointed out how big an object was, or on meeting a friend by spreading his arm and burlesquing an extravagance of feeling.

One may point to the great amount of intellectual work done in the clever preparation and carrying out of the obsessional camouflage. I believe that this spiritual expenditure, which in the strictest sense is squandered, has hitherto found a most inadequate evaluation by analysts. The presence of mind and cleverness with which every opportunity is utilized to carry out these mysterious ceremonial and obsessional acts in spite of all social difficulties and yet inconspicuously in manner, are often surprising and one only wonders at not seeing them put to the service of some more worthy cause. Besides these qualities another feature in the neurotic camouflage becomes obvious to the analyst: derision at both the demands of social convention and the strictness of their own ceremonials. This characteristic corresponds throughout to the ambivalent attitude that marks every feature of the obsessional neurosis.

The derisive note gives way occasionally—in favorable circumstances —to a humoristic strain. The neurotic then shows a sort of amusement at himself. A cheerful feeling of superiority to his neurosis and the difficulties into which it precipitates him. Many times there appears an enjoyment of his own dexterity and cleverness at overcoming certain embarrassing situations. The patient has brought it about that not only is his neurotic symptom hidden from the world but it is also put into effect and this so adroitly that his ceremonial or obsessional activity passes as a natural and unsuspected bit of general social behavior. In such plausible and artful mimicry there is visible no neurotic symptom. Where would a clever man hide a particular leaf? In the forest.

Perhaps at this point I may make some remarks on the impression the report of such successful camouflage can make on the analyst. Aside from the obvious and dominant psychological interest and the high opinion of the patient's cleverness and presence of mind the analyst sometimes discovers in himself on hearing such a report a surprising feeling: that of pleasure in the comic. The occasion for such cheerful feeling is sometimes provided by the telling of a particular difficulty and perplexity that the patient has overcome by social camouflage. The pleasure in the comic then results from the happy combination of ways and means found to get out of the dilemma into which the patient has been precipitated by the compulsion of the neurosis on the one hand and the obligations of the outer world on the other: his particular tactics, his pretexts and elusions, his compromises and "evasiveness," to which he is compelled to resort to master unusual difficulties. One is often tempted to think of the genial art of Charlie Chaplin and to imagine the tragicomic clown struggling not with the needs and difficulties of the world of reality but dealing instead with a severe obsessional neurosis—its compulsions and inhibitions in collision with social obligations. Mysterious injunctions and vetoes of the neurosis, against which his reason rebels but obeys under the whip of anxiety—scorning the opposition of society, yet respectful of it—force the obsessional neurotic to attain to these intellectual acrobatics and tricks of neurotic camouflage. The reports of many cases of especially successful camouflage that secures by a crafty manner of execution the carrying out of the compulsion and at the same time masking it from the outer world, indeed making use of the milieu to facilitate the carrying out of the compulsion, awakens in the analyst very frequently a sort of intellectual pleasure, like his pleasure in the comic, if not identical with it. It is similar to that awakened in the hearer of a tale in which someone finds by some most cunning way egress from a difficult situation and at the same time has outwitted the others who got him into the fix. No doubt, on such an occasion we share to some degree the pleasure the patient himself has derived from the success of the camouflage. We share this pleasure after we have unconsciously participated in the act. We do not laugh at the patient but with him. Sometimes we laugh together at the neurotic nonsense in which so much sense is concealed, unrecognizable to outsiders.

We mentioned previously the patient who became so embarrassed and blushed so furiously when she encountered either the janitress or one of her representatives in the hallway. What could be the reason for this embarrassment or rather one of the reasons? Nothing was to be learned about this aside from the painful fear that the janitress would gossip about her with other women. We know how she protected herself against the blush becoming too visible: she looked quickly, in passing, into her purse as if seeking something. Analysis was able to make it clear that the rummaging in the purse was a symbolic substitute for her masturbation in childhood. As a little girl she had been very much ashamed of her masturbation and at one time was afraid her mother had been informed of her secret activity. Mostly she feared that her mother would discuss her and her wicked habit with other women—with relatives or friends, for instance. The protective action, which in this instance had the character of social camouflage, brought back in symbolic disguise just what she wanted to hide.

Another situation that made the patient blush was being alone in the apartment and having to answer the door bell. There were some dodges of camouflage by which she could hide her embarrassment. Experience has shown her that she appeared less embarrassed if she rapidly stuck her hands into warm water in the washbowl and, while drying her hands with the towel, opened the door. While reporting this in the analysis she recalled an occasion in childhood when she had feared being surprised in the midst of her masturbation by the return home of her mother. One also sees here that what spared or weakened the embarrassment for her was precisely the restitution of the action that had made her embarrassed. Another camouflage technique for the same occasion of hearing the bell consisted of quickly popping a piece of bread or a bonbon into her mouth and chewing on it as she opened the door. In the same analytic hour in which she reported this she recalled in another connection that she was once surprised by her mother as she was eating a cookie set aside for her little sister and once again when she took something out of the cookie jar.

In these examples, and many similar ones that could be added here, a new tendency becomes visible within the camouflage, the revelation of the very thing one seeks so carefully to hide. Sometimes the suppressed tendency suddenly breaks through. These fiascoes and abortive efforts are of particular interest because in them can be observed especially well the conflict of the two tendencies and because they prove that the anxiety dictating obedience to the compulsion is more powerful than the desire to conform to social obligations.

It is odd that the new insight into this other, opposite tendency of neurotic camouflage, namely to reveal the secret meaning of the symptoms, also occurred to me with the help of a Bruckner anecdote. The biographers of the composer tell us many stories about how strangely he sometimes behaved. They did not realize that the composer clearly showed in his behavior symptoms of an obsession neurosis. He was, for instance, compelled to convince himself many times that he had turned off the light. He had to count the windows of houses as he passed them, and so on. Once 'this compulsion took possession of him when he was in company of a charming young woman who wore a pearl necklace. To conceal his compulsion to know how many pearls were in the necklace he pretended to admire it very much. At the end he doubted whether he had counted correctly and yielded to the urge to touch the single pearls on the throat of the shocked young lady. The memory of this anecdote about the old composer helped me to understand how a suppressed tendency frequently gives itself away just in the attempt at concealment.

It may be easy to make a compulsive gesture of defensive or magical character so inconspicuously that it appears indifferent or harmless. An obsessional neurotic whom I had under observation, who was obliged to follow a ritual of stopping in front of a mirror and sticking out his right hand when he entered a room, could get away with it if he continued the movement into one of straightening his tie. At most people might note only his vanity. It was certainly more difficult to find a plausible pretext for other obsessional actions. Out strolling with a friend once, he was obliged to turn back suddenly because he was about to meet a woman in mourning. Furthermore, he could not take a single step forward. His obsessional anxiety demanded that he should return to his hotel whenever he met a person in mourning because otherwise he suffered the anxiety that some member of his own family would die. The pretext he found for breaking off abruptly and returning home this time was characteristic. He stood still and said to his companion that he suddenly remembered that he had forgotten to send a telegram of condolence in answer to a notice of bereavement he had received from his family just before starting out for the stroll. So even in his excuse he could make use of the meeting with the strange woman in mourning, for it was the very sight of her that had reminded him of the bereavement. When his companion pointed out to him a telegraph station across the way he replied with something that already sounded less plausible, that he did not know the new address of the family and must look it up in the letter in his room. Every one of these excuses retained a bit of psychological truth: the woman in mourning had really reminded him of his fear that a member of his family could die. He did not, of course, know which member.

With the progress of the neurosis the compromise formations between concealment and display move finally toward revealing the hidden. The intention of the camouflage becomes increasingly less successful, the neurosis braver or more defiant. We well understand that the neurotic person becomes impatient after so many pretexts and pretenses, having sacrificed so much to pride and prejudice. It is a relief to throw off the burden of secrecy and social hypocrisy. Arthur Schnitzler was referring to such a relief when he once spoke of the "truthfulness of tired liars."

CHAPTER XXVI

Out of the Mouths of Babes

NOT everything the analyst labors to uncover is repressed material. The area of the unconscious reaches far beyond the sphere attributed to it by many psychoanalytic lecturers. It includes material which is displaced, distorted and disavowed. There are further events and emotions that were never conscious because they happened when the person was too young to grasp their meaning. They belong to the prehistoric period of the individual personality.

We grown-ups are so far removed from the peculiar ways and forms of our childhood that they have become strange to us. Everybody has experiences of this sort. Our parents or old friends of the family have told us that as a small boy we said or did this or that odd thing. In most cases we do not remember the statement or action. And even when we do, we can no longer discover why we acted or spoke like that. We cannot doubt the truth of the story but we do not recognize ourselves in the picture it shows to us. We have to admit that we were this little boy or that little girl, but we cannot acknowledge any psychological identity with our past self. It has vanished like the snows of yesteryear.

Memories of this order come up many times in psychoanalysis. They are conscious in that their content can be ascertained, but their meaning has been lost. This meaning was not repressed. It grew strange because a man cannot recover the thought-processes peculiar to childhood. Loss of an old way of feeling or thinking can be observed already in children themselves. A little girl of eight cannot believe that, once when she was three, she had wanted to catch a snail and had been worried that the snail would run away. If, after some years, children cannot recognize themselves, how can we expect men and women to accept their psychological identity with an infant? The activities, joys, and griefs, the little games children sometimes remember represent their true selves, but the self from the past seems foreign. They are astonished at themselves and cannot imagine what made them behave so oddly or say such funny things. The psychoanalyst frequently has a difficult time with memories of this kind since no conscious effort on his part, either, can help him regain infantile ways of looking at the world. He would have to study children for a long time and with particular psychological skill in order to understand what his patients tell him about some episodes of their childhood days. Not longing for paradise lost, but his wish for psychological comprehension reminds him of the song by Brahms that goes: "Oh, if I but knew the way back, the dear way back to childhood days. . . ." ("*O wusst ich doch den Weg zurueck, den lieben Weg zur Kinderzeit. . . .*")

Sometimes we realize how remote we are from the child's way of feeling and thinking when we hear the funny things children say. I do not mean the "bright sayings," but remarks and comments that we call naïve, which make us laugh because we are so charmed. I heard that a little girl on the beach complained about her playmate: "Mother, Bobby should not take so much water out of the sea. The sea will become quite empty." The other day I saw a cartoon showing a painter seated before his canvas in a field. He is immersed in his work and pays no attention to the little farm girl who is an attentive observer. The child interrupts the silence suddenly: "I have had the measles. . . ." The two instances, that of the little girl who is worried lest her playmate exhaust the sea, and that of the other child who wants to appear important and opens the conversation with the interesting news that she once had the measles, represent a whole group of sayings that show how differently the world reflects itself in little heads.

Sometimes, in the middle of a psychoanalysis, memories occur that puzzle us because we cannot immediately understand what they mean, nor what they meant to the child who twenty or thirty years later is now a patient in our consultation room. Sometimes it is easy enough to grasp their meaning; we have no difficulty in putting ourselves in the emotional world of the child because we find in ourselves echoes of the same feeling when we dig down deep enough in our own memories. I believe everybody will hear an echo when I tell what a patient remembered from her childhood.

When she was a very little girl she sneaked from her bedroom into the dining room in the dark because she wanted to know how the furniture, the table, the chairs, and the lamps behaved when they were alone, without people around. She was convinced that the room and the furniture would behave differently when they thought they were not being observed. Children's animistic conceptions of the world are further illustrated by another patient who remembered that he once asked his older brother whether the telegraph poles speak with the lampposts. We understand immediately that the hum of the wires suggested the question.

Every psychoanalyst has met difficulties dealing with the childhood memories of patients who do not themselves understand the meaning of their recollections. A woman remembers, for example, that as a little girl she once began to cry when her father led her into the elevator of a hotel in which the family, interrupting a journey, was to spend the night. Her recollection tells her that the elevator was much more spacious than any other she has seen since and that there were plush benches along three sides. She is also sure that this was the first time she had ever been in an elevator. She clearly remembers that she was desperate when she entered it and that her father tried in vain to console her and stop her tears. Although the recollection recurred several times during her analysis, we could not figure out why she had behaved so strangely at that moment. She denied being scared when the elevator began to move because she was already sobbing before that happened. We—the patient and I—were both puzzled until all at once it occurred to her that she must have thought that the spacious elevator was a room and that she, on this, her first visit to a hotel, would have to sleep in this room with her father. She had thought of the upholstered benches as couches. The memory was of course, significant for the analytic understanding of the patient's relationship with her father.

In other cases the special meaning of a child's behavior or talk is not so easily grasped. There are times when no learning, no expenditure of conscious intellectual energy, and no hard thinking can penetrate to these lost ways of a child's emotional processes. There is no other path to this hidden area but unconscious identification with the patient as a child.

A man remembered that as a boy he once behaved very strangely riding on a bus with his mother. A woman who had stepped down from the bus while it was in motion, fell on the pavement without being seriously hurt. The little boy began to cry and protested desperately that he had not pushed the woman down. Actually he had been standing at some distance from her so that it would have been impossible for him to attempt anything of the sort. There was no doubt that his memory of the incident was correct. The analytic interpretation of this childhood memory started from the assumption that in some way his emotions must have been appropriate. We learned later that at this time he had felt very hostile and aggressive toward his mother, who stood beside him in the bus. In a serious marital conflict between his parents, he had sided with his father. It seemed likely that his hostility against his mother had led to aggressive wishes, which reappeared when the accident on the bus occurred. His feelings toward his mother were displaced upon a stranger. The woman who was hurt was unconsciously thought of as a mother-substitute. When she was hurt he must have felt guilty, as if he were really responsible because he had entertained evil wishes against his mother. It was as if his wishes had become reality in the accident to the other woman. There are many instances that show grown-up people behaving similarly when a crime they have wished for is actually committed by others.[1]

I am choosing a relatively simple instance from my psychoanalytic practice in order to demonstrate that only a return to the thought-world of the child can solve the puzzle of a memory that has become unintelligible to the person himself.

A British patient remembered that as a small boy he had said something to his sister (two years older than he) that does not make sense to him now. He recalled the situation precisely. They stood at the window of their country house and it was early evening. They looked at the cows coming home along the village street. The little boy turned to his sister and asked her, "Can you imagine Uncle Harry being a cow?" Well, that sounds silly enough, and the patient was inclined to dismiss the remembered sentence as one of the funny thoughts children frequently have. He remembered that his sister had roared with laughter and quoted his saying teasingly to him later on.

I tried to convince him that the sentence must have made sense then.

[1] See this writer's book, *The Unknown Murderer* (New York: Prentice-Hall, 1945).

His associations seemed to lead him far away, to later memories of Uncle Harry and Aunt Mabel, his wife, to other relatives, and to the contrast between life in the country and in London. The only fact that seemed to be worthy of consideration in these associations was that shortly afterward Aunt Mabel had a baby. I guessed that something in the child's remark alluded to this event, perhaps to the pregnancy, which the little boy had noticed. But I still could not figure out what the sentence, "Can you imagine Uncle Harry being a cow?" meant. Nothing indicated that the boy had suspicions about Uncle Harry's lack of masculinity. On the contrary, this particular uncle came to be known as quite a philanderer. We did not arrive at a satisfactory solution of the puzzling memory that day. There was only the vague idea that the sentence might have something to do with Aunt Mabel's pregnancy.

The recognition of its meaning occurred to me much later, when the patient on another occasion and in another context mentioned that cows sometimes behave strangely in the spring. They jump at each other's backs as if imitating the bull. Everything suddenly became clear. The children, the boy and his sister, must have spoken before about what the grown-ups do in sexual intercourse and compared it with the playful sexual behavior of the cows. The question, "Can you imagine Uncle Harry being a cow?" had thus the meaning, "Can you imagine Uncle Harry behaving like a cow jumping at another cow's back?" It therefore meant: "Can you imagine Uncle Harry in sexual intercourse?" The children might at this time have noticed Aunt Mabel's pregnancy and their thoughts turned to the sexual experiences of their relatives. The boy's question is of a sexual nature. It makes sense now after we have translated it from the child's language into expressions familiar to us. The laughter of his sister, we understand now, was not only determined by the way the question was put. The girl laughed as an adult would at a sexual allusion that is comical.

It turned out that this interpretation of an unintelligible childhood memory became crucial in the analysis of this patient. He had denied that he had any knowledge of sexual processes before a certain age. No longer understood by the adult, here was perfect proof that he knew what the sexual secret was before that age. His parents postponed sexual information; they seemed to wait with it indefinitely, "until the cows came home." But the children knew the secret long before, and the return of the cows only gave them an opportunity to review what they had learned. Often enough just such uncomprehended childhood memories, when psychoanalytically interpreted, give important clues to the life history and the character-formation of our patients.

The child is the father of the man. In reality, there are three persons in the consultation room of the psychoanalyst: the analyst, the patient as he is now, and the child who continues his existence within the patient. We recognize how old childhood convictions live subterraneously side by side with the opinions and views of the adult. Old values consciously discarded long ago operate in the dark and influence the lives of our patients. It would be a serious mistake on the part of the analyst to underestimate the power of the ideas and ideals of the child who continues his existence in the adult. They rise sometimes quite suddenly from their submergence into the bright daylight of conscious living. An adult feels suddenly afraid of the dark and imagines that a picture has come alive. He has revived the animistic belief of childhood days, when every inanimate object had a life and a soul of its own. To our astonishment we often realize that childhood beliefs remain intact in us, are not dead and buried, only submerged.

It would be erroneous to neglect this phenomenon. The psychoanalyst must search for the child in the man, in himself, and in others. He will not understand the depth of emotions if he is not aware of these vestiges of childhood in maturity. Those childhood ideas need not be childish because they are childlike. Some of them are built around a nucleus of early-understood truths and reveal an astonishingly clear vision of the social environment within the narrow circle that makes up the child's world.

About a hundred years ago there lived in Vienna a brilliant satirist and actor, Johan N. Nestroy, whose witty plays the Viennese loved. In one of them a figure speaks about cobblers' apprentices, who were known as very clever and impudent youngsters, prematurely wise, like the urchins of New York's lower East Side. "I would like to know," says this figure, "what became of all those clever, witty cobblers' boys?" Freud, who frequently quoted this line, replied, "They became stupid shoemakers." Freud said that at a certain point in childhood sexual repression begins to operate and puts an end to the natural and brilliant intelligence of the child. I think this answer is one-sided. The child learns also to accept authority and to suppress its natural aggressions, rebelliousness, and independence of thinking. Nevertheless it is true that frequently very bright children suddenly show at a certain age a kind of weakening of their natural powers of observation and judgment, as if the adjustment to society forces them to sacrifice these early personal qualities.

These ideas of children, we said, often contain a grain of truth presented in a childlike manner that sometimes appears funny. A patient was enlightened about the sexual processes by his parents at an early age. Nevertheless, the boy puzzled about the sexuality of men because he tried to imagine it in terms of the animals and the flowers about which his parents had spoken. He imagined that a husband knocks at the bedroom door of his wife on certain evenings and says, "Mary, seed is here." There is no blinking the fact that there is a certain biological truth in the boy's conception. When you remove the trimmings and arrive at the core, you will realize that as little Johnny sees the world, so it is.

We are often reminded in our analytic work that the child lives on in the man and the woman. Life itself bears witness to such survival. When my daughter Miriam was a little girl and we took her to the dentist for the second time, she crawled under a desk and no amount of persuasion could overcome her anxiety. Her mother appealed to her in vain, "Do you think that a lady would crawl on all fours under a desk in a dentist's office?" My little girl answered, "They would like to, but they are too big."

CHAPTER XXVII

In Search of Lost Thoughts and Emotions

T HE layman is inclined to assume that it must be very difficult for the analyst to find the concealed meaning of dream-fragments, symptoms, symptomatic actions, fears and inhibitions that have an especially strange or fantastic character. Experience shows that it is much easier to discover their meaning than the secret of inconspicuous symptoms and little deviations in behavior and thought that do not attract notice. Extraordinary and eccentric symptoms and trends of thought are much more approachable than those which appear to be average and everyday. We do not tend to pay attention to what is familiar. The other day a well-known artist who teaches drawing at an Eastern college told me that he had made an experiment that confirmed this impression. He asked his pupils to draw an elephant from memory. The class did very well. Then he asked them to draw the chairs they sit on daily at dinner, and the drawings were decidedly poor. The elephant had been an object of much better observation than an object seen and used daily. Likewise, in the realm of psychical phenomena the conspicuous is more easily recognized than the common order of events.

The great advantage, however, in dealing with the average or the usual is that we can unconsciously compare it with what we normally feel and think, realize the differences, and "sense" rather than understand in which direction we have to search for its origin or nature. We discover, for instance, that the other person has done something we should not do, but which we have thought of and considered as a possibility for ourselves. At this point I can give an instance that appears strange at first sight but will be understood immediately by every woman.

A patient who was having an affair with a married man was subject to many compulsive commandments and prohibitions to which she had to submit. She tried to pull her lover into this web of mysterious orders. One day she asked him to promise her that he would not come from home when he visited her and that he would not return home when he left her. She formulated what she expected from him more clearly the next day. "You must not come from her or go to her when you see me." It is obvious that the wife of her lover was meant. The patient wanted her relationship with the man in no way, either in time or place, to be "mixed up" with his married life. By this prohibition, by putting an insulating layer between herself and the wife, she kept the two relationships apart. As time went on she extended the time of isolation the man had to go for long walks or sit for an hour in a cafeteria before coming to her and again before returning home.

We know the mechanism of defense that operates under the name of isolation. By isolation two realms of thought that threaten to touch each other are kept separate. Space and time intervals are put between the two in such a way that a strict isolation is attained. We observe avoidances in compulsion neurotics who keep certain thoughts strictly separated from each other, as we see them in the social order (compare the Indian "untouchables" or religious ceremonials (clean and unclean). I doubt whether the student feels enlightened when he reads or hears that isolation "consists in the isolation of ideational content from its emotional cathexis";[1] but I do not doubt that he will be able to understand the compulsive thought: "You must not come from her or go to her when you see me." The idea that led to this isolation is clear enough and it cannot be difficult to discover "the emotional cathexis" that isolates its "ideational content": the patient is jealous and possessive. She finds it intolerable to think that her lover comes from his wife to her or leaves her to go to his wife. It is obvious that the isolation has the purpose of keeping her relationship and that of the man with his wife separate. One needs no great psychological discernment to understand the underlying motives of the ritual to which the man is required to submit himself.

[1] Otto Fenichel, *The Psychoanalytical Theory of Neurosis* (New York: 1945), p. 267.

When the patient told me that she suggested this new command to her lover, she spoke of it as if it were an indifferent thought that had occurred to her, a convenient arrangement, yes, even a kind of amusing idea. She did not think of it as an expression of emotions. It was just one of her numerous compulsions—a newcomer to the old company of her thoughts. Consciously she did not connect it with any feeling and she could not easily be convinced that deep emotions had led to the decision that occurred to her, which she tried to support by reasons.

The process in the analyst who first hears such a compulsive ritual is just the opposite of what took place in its creator. He realizes that it is not dictated by logical reasons, but by strong emotions, by emotions that the patient disavows. I take this opportunity to warn again against approaching the problem of such compulsions, which have a logical or "reasonable" façade, in the spirit of conscious and formalized thinking. When you want to rescue a person from drowning, you have to jump into the water, into *his* water. The first approach to the conjecture of the concealed meaning should be from the emotional side.

What takes place psychologically when we guess the motives of this patient? The analyst knows the story of the relationship of the girl and the man. It started as a casual affair. The man would have liked to keep it that way. The girl, however, slowly but surely became more and more emotionally involved. She scarcely mentioned the wife of her lover to me. She seemed to have accepted the fact that he was married and that he never had thought of leaving his wife. Suddenly the isolation-idea occurred to her and she suggested it to the man who smilingly promised that he would try not to come direct from home or to go home immediately when he visited her. (Little did he think what consequences this small concession would lead to.) The analyst who listened to the report had unconsciously, for a few seconds, put himself into the place of his patient. He dived, so to speak, into the realm of her unconscious emotions. He was the girl for the length of a few heartbeats. He underwent the feelings out of which the decision was reached and rose again quickly to the surface. In these few seconds he captured what he reached for in the depths. He held it in his hand and he looked at it. He could now realize what must have gone on in the mind of his patient. Because he found himself in it and shared it in this tentative way, he got an inkling of what her emotional state was. It was, of course, not to be compared to hers in intensity or time. It was more like a faint echo of the emotions of his patient: her jealousy, her suffering from the thought that her lover left her to go home to his wife; the image becoming more and more intolerable to her until finally she came to the compromise-solution, which took the reality of his marriage into consideration but insisted on her own rights too. Only by becoming a psychological deep-sea diver can the analyst hope to find the secret motives and the strength or intensity of the emotions beneath them. He who remains safe and dry on the shore will never experience the fascinating adventure of analytic understanding of deep-running waters. He will only perceive the play of the waves, not what goes on beneath them. Emile Zola once defined his novels as a fragment of the world "seen through a temperament." Psychoanalysis is a fragment of the netherworld *"vu par un tempérament"* and not, as some want us to believe, through the pages of a textbook. It is with the antennae of our own unconscious that we feel what is the essence of the thoughts and emotions of our patients, not with the tools of reasoning and logic.

The compulsive regulation, "You must not come from her or go to her . . ." was easy enough to guess. Other instances need more psychological preparation, require a longer study of the life history and character of the person; but the instrument of conjecture remains the same. In all cases the same unconscious organs communicate to us the secret motives of the phenomena, the same means convey their meaning, and the same interplay of two unconsciouses results in the conjecture of hidden impulses. Let us choose an instance of an obsession idea, or rather a doubt, of an obsession character. Here also the patient's "complexes," to use an ugly term, do not interest us. We are, however, interested in the psychological process in the analyst who wants to understand the concealed springs of the thought.

A patient spoke with enthusiasm of the books of a philosopher with whose system he had lately become familiar. He admired the profound and penetrating thoughts of the philosopher and had bought his collected works so that he could always have them on hand. Some days later a friend with whom he discussed the teachings of the thinker asked to borrow one of the volumes for a few weeks. The patient lent the book to the friend reluctantly because he wanted to have the volume at hand whenever he wanted to look up something in the admired work. After the friend had left with the book, doubts, increasing in scope and intensity, attacked the patient. Will his friend treat the book with enough care? Will he be painstaking in putting the book in a safe place after he reads a chapter? Suppose his friend is disturbed by some visitor while he is reading. Will he take care of the precious volume so that it will not get dirty while he puts it aside?

Listening to these doubts, the analyst might get the impression at first that they were not very far removed from scruples other people have with regard to highly valued books in their libraries. He might consider the doubts exaggerated but, knowing that his patient is especially orderly and conscientious, he might imagine that here was the expression of a high degree of these qualities. Perhaps it would occur to him that these scruples were expressions of the same feelings that determined the reluctance of the patient to lend the book.

Was that all? Did they reveal nothing else? I listened to the continuation and realized clearly that I no longer had before me mere exaggerated considerations, but real obsession-thoughts. For here are the doubts that followed: What will happen when the friend, fascinated by the original ideas of the philosopher, holds the book and reads it while he eats his supper? Suppose he enjoys his bread and butter during the reading: Will he not leave spots on the page he is studying? And now, submerged in a philosophical idea and unable to interrupt the highly stimulating reading even for a short time, what if he takes the admired book with him to the toilet so that he can study it while he fulfills this other vital function. Then when he wipes himself, the book in his hands can —The patient did not dare to think of the consequences. At this point he broke off this train of thought.

Let us again shift to the psychical process within the analyst. I had followed (with free-floating attention) my patient's train of thought to the point where the worry about the book reached a climax around the imagined situation at supper. Reflections about the possible behavior of the reader of the volume that now set in, seemed at first to be a continuation of the preceding worries, brought to an extreme. But, I wondered, was there not something new now? Did not the doubt about the book's safety take another rapid turn in the following thoughts? There was the idea that the friend might take the book to the "secret place" (the expression is Goethe's) and that he would touch the pages with hands soiled by the necessary cleaning operation. No doubt any more. At the final point of this train of thought these pages were reduced to the rank of toilet paper. The exaggeration of the imagined interest in the book, which could not be put aside during supper and not even during evacuation, had reached a degree that was grotesque and absurd. No analyst could at this point avoid the impression that the worries about the book by the consciously admired thinker were interrupted at this point by another emotion: violent and bitter mockery against the philosopher had succeeded in breaking through at this climax, to which the worries were leading all along. On this thought-detour unconscious scorn against the philosopher revealed itself. It had been covered up before by conscious admiration, even by enthusiasm.

The patient was astonished and of course indignant when I told him at the end of the session that his obsessive thoughts were full of concealed mockery and that in his unconscious view the books of the highly appreciated philosopher were only good for a purpose for which their author certainly had not destined them. I tried—I do not know whether with success—to sketch the inner process that took place while I listened to the complaints of the patient about what could happen to his valuable volume.

My report would be incomplete and therefore insincere if I do not add that twice during his account I had anticipated the continuation to which his speculations would lead. The first point was after he told me about the imagined scene at supper. It was as if I foresaw that he would now lead his thoughts from digestion to evacuation. The next sentence brought the expected sequel. The second time was at the point where his thoughts accompanied the enthusiastic reader to the toilet and let him continue his study during the natural function. At this point, an anecdote came to me out of nowhere.

The famous composer, Max Reger (1873-1916), once wrote a letter to a critic who had published a very negative review of Reger's new work. The letter began, "Dear Sir: I am sitting in the smallest room of my apartment and I am reading your review. I still have it before me . . ." Remembering this anecdote, I had, of course, anticipated the course and had arrived at an understanding of the unconscious meaning of the obsession-thought of my patient. Perhaps the fact that the anecdote had occurred to me was an indication that I had already found this meaning. Perhaps it was an indication that what had been anticipation had now become conviction. I do not assert, of course, that the anecdote is the only way to arrive at this unconscious meaning. There are thousands of ways by which other analysts could arrive at the same result. My way just led through this musician's anecdote, if it were not—what I consider more likely—already following the unconscious understanding that dawned upon me when the patient's thoughts led the philosophical reader to the threshold of the secret place.

It is not the value of this particular association as the instrument in finding the concealed meaning of the obsession idea that we want to discuss. What is to be emphasized is that such associations, such vague but none the less indicative sensations as those which accompanied the hearing of the patient's report, are instrumental in reaching the most important analytic insights. Their symptomatic value cannot be over-appreciated. The psychological implications to which they lead cannot be overrated. The analyst who misses them deprives himself of a great advantage. He has renounced his ability to listen "with a third ear" and he has retarded the progress of understanding. Is this all he loses? However great such a loss, he has perhaps let slip something even more valu-able. He has missed the precise psychological moment to grasp the meaning of this symptom *and* the concealed character of the neurotic disturbance, the hidden springs that determine the actions and thoughts of the patient. Such a single obsession-thought appears, it is true, as only one of many expressions of the deeper neurotic conflict. It is, com-paratively speaking, only one of the threads out of which the whole cloth of the neurosis is woven. But to get hold of the threads means to seize the cloth. A little neglect may breed mischief, and, to vary the say-ing of Benjamin Franklin, for want of understanding one symptom the comprehension of an emotion is lost. For want of the understanding of the emotion, the nature of the leading conflict is lost. And for want of understanding this conflict, the analyst as a psychoanalyst is lost, at least for this particular case. It is not only that the loss of the case will dimin-ish the self-respect of the analyst whose ambition is not restricted to the therapy of neurosis. It is more important that he did not achieve psy-chological understanding and has therefore added one more case to his list of intellectual casualties that hurt his self-esteem.

It is not true that the attention given to the emotional undertones is rewarded only by the understanding of one or several cases of neurosis. It goes far beyond this restricted area into the realm of psychological insights into human nature. Here is an instance of such extension or enlargement of analytic results. More than twenty-two years ago I got the impression from the study of certain cases that an action or deed that is felt as sinful or wicked, demands repetition if the unconscious guilt-feeling is not satisfied by punishment. In certain cases I recognized that an intense hostility or hate is directed against the very persons whom one has wronged. The sight of them fills the offender with un-conscious self-reproach. Such an oppressive feeling will then be relieved by repetition of the deed or by fantasies of such a character. Thus we have the psychological paradox that the offender feels revengeful against the very person whom he has hurt. This analytic view[2] and the theory founded upon it was at that time, 1925, still the object of many doubts and arguments. The thesis that an unconscious guilt-feeling can lead to crime and criminal fantasies against the persons one has offended had not yet been heard of. I was able to locate one single instance presented by another observer, who had anticipated what I had found in living people.[3] But what an observer, and from what deep resources of observation was this instance taken! Dostoyevsky gives the following characteristic traits of Fyodor Pavlovitch Karamazov, the father of Ivan, Dmitri, and Alyosha:

He wished to take revenge on all for his own ignominies. Then it occurred to him that he was once asked: "Why do you hate this man so much?" and that he had answered in a fit of foolish shamelessness: "Why? Look: he did not do anything to me, it is true; but I have once inflicted a mean and base thing on him and almost at the moment of this I already hated him just on account of it."

Confirmed in my opinion by a psychologist whose knowledge of human nature surpassed that of all the members of the International Psychoanalytic Association, I stood my ground.[4] Today this piece of psychological insight which the genius of Dostoyevsky anticipated is generally accepted and constitutes an oft-verified part of analytic knowledge. Eugene O'Neill much later (I doubt whether independently of psychoanalysis) formulated this same insight in *The Iceman Cometh* in 1946.

Freud gave his immediate students more than special insights into the specific symptomatology of neurosis and psychosis; more even than the understanding of the different psychological mechanisms and the structure of our psychical apparatus. He trained our inner ear to hear almost imperceptible undertones, to value the impact of elusive psychical nuances and shades. Those who, like this writer, were fortunate enough to follow Freud for thirty years, will never forget instances in which he gave the outlines of a case or described a psychological type or let a human destiny unfold itself before them. In addition to the incompa-

[2] Published in my book, *Gestaendniszwang und Strafbeduerfnis* (Vienna: 1925).
[3] *Gestaendniszwang und Strafbeduerfnis*, p. 128.
[4] Even Freud doubted at first the great importance of an unknown compulsion to confess, but admitted later that my view was correct in a letter that I possess.

rable insights we gained on those Wednesday evenings, first in the Vienna Psychoanalytic Association and later in Freud's home, we got from him a taste for the psychological values of the almost unfathomable, the elusive, although allusive, undertones and a little of his sensitiveness and fine response to minute emotional indications. It is unforgotten and unforgettable how, out of small and seemingly insignificant details, slowly the picture of a human destiny used to arise with all of its many griefs and joys, how the slightest signs led to the reconstruction of a personality, the faintest echoes of unconscious processes to the discovery of a life-melody. He never gave us a blueprint of how to think along certain lines of theory. We received an idea of how these theories came into being from living experiences. We did not get an outline of the mechanisms of unconscious processes, but an idea of how to arrive at them ourselves. We were not taught what to think, but how to be courageous enough to think for ourselves, how to register small indications in others and in ourselves, how to react to impressions with the sensitiveness of tin foil without asking ourselves what the analytic theory was. We forgot the theory entirely and were therefore able to arrive at it finally as if we had discovered it ourselves. And some of it we did discover ourselves.

CHAPTER XXVIII

The Psychological Moment

THE question arises, when is the best time to communicate one of these surprising interpretations or ideas to the patient. Freud discusses this question in a particular passage in his writings. Here the analyst explains the special characteristics of his technique of interpretation to an imaginary auditor. He says that we must await the right moment to communicate the interpretation to the patient. The auditor, anxious to learn, very properly asks, "How can one always know the right moment?" "That is a question of tact, which may become much subtler through experience," Freud answers. The German word "*Takt*" that Freud uses here has a double meaning. It not only signifies "social feeling," but it is also synonymous with "musical beat, time, measure," also "bar."

Is it not surprising to find the notion of tact mentioned here as being so important in analysis? What has tact to do with grasping an objective psychical content? This is not a reference to the effect of tact in the general treatment of the patient; but that it is tact, we are told, that determines the right moment to communicate an interpretation.

Let us by the way of comparison imagine that a psychologist, say of the school of Wilhelm Wundt, requires tact to determine the moment in which to tell the subject of an experiment that his reaction to light is of a certain speed. We see at once, of course, that the analyst has to give information of a different kind. They are things that we do not like to talk about, that we do not like to say, nay, things that tact itself forbids us to mention. Tact forbids it, but necessity requires it. And so tact is called in to perform the necessary task. Well, the situation is not unique. There are a number of occasions in social life in which we are actually compelled to say what, under other circumstances, tact forbids. No doubt; but then tact tells us to avoid direct or immediate expressions and to use allusive, roundabout phrases. Consider, for instance, matters in spheres that, according to Freud, civilized mankind is particularly hypocritical about: sex and money. What a number of circumscribing and indirect expressions we use, instead of admitting our physical needs straight out! How many allusive words we have for sexual processes! To pick one example from among thousands, I read not long ago the expression *"il n'est pas orthodoxe,"* meaning that a man was homosexual. And it is not only on these two subjects that people use such indirect means of designation. How often do we allude to death by indirect means when we write letters or pay visits of condolence? Not only does analysis speak of things that we tactfully avoid on other occasions, but it gives direct expression to them, speaks of them in a quiet and objective manner that would never be possible in any social situation. Was not an American lady patient in Vienna right when she complained at the beginning of her treatment: "Analysis is so intrusive"? If we do not wish to subscribe to this lady's opinion, who felt analysis to be a little indiscreet, we must take refuge in the realization that tact in an analytic situation is different from what we ordinarily understand by the word.

We can point out that an analyst will certainly not tell his patient the delicate things that must be communicated to him, without preparation. It would be tactless to fling at a patient's head the statement that he had been sexually in love with his mother and had wanted to kill his father. A certain mental introduction and preparation is needed, some understanding of the contrast between conscious and repressed ideas, and so forth. But I do not wish to pursue this subject here; rather it is my intention to use it as a steppingstone to a more general problem: the relation of tact to time. It is only at the first glance that this temporal factor appears strange; upon further examination it proves natural enough. How? people may well ask. Is "tact"—a word that we apply to a scarcely tangible quality in social bearing, an imponderable, incommensurable capacity, a name that may be regarded as the very type of the class of imponderabilia—is this word to be associated with what is certainly measurable, with time, a thing that we can determine so accurately by clock and chronometer, a magnitude that can be gauged by the coarsest mechanical means?

I admit that this impression has its justification, but all I have asserted is that tact stands in relation to time, I have not said what the particular relation is. Nor have I, in stressing this relation at this point, denied the existence of other factors. We have to distinguish between objective and psychological time. Only the former is measurable and divisible, whereas the latter is altogether subjective.

Those who still object to this association of tact and time or find it unconvincing, need only think of music, the other sphere in which the German word *"Takt"* is used. It can hardly be denied that there is the closest connection between music and time, indeed, that the very essence of music can be derived from a function of time. And is not music, of all the arts, the most difficult to grasp intellectually? Are we less deeply moved on hearing the adagio of Beethoven's Fifth Symphony, less delighted by Mozart's "Divertimentos," when we reflect that waves of sound are striking our ears at definite intervals of time, which determine the acoustic impression? We remembered at the right moment that the notion of tact belongs to two fields, the musical and the social, and that in all probability it has retained something of its temporal character even in the secondary, derivative meaning.

I really need not have taken so roundabout a way to establish the connection, for we started from the passage in Freud in which he discusses *when* we should communicate an interpretation or the hidden meaning of a symptom to the patient. In a popular sense tact may be regarded as the ability to do the right thing in social intercourse, but then the right thing is dependent upon the proper moment. Something that is right just now might be wrong five minutes earlier or later. Something that must be said just at this moment is, perhaps, quite unallowable a few minutes later. I heard of a teacher who said to a girl in her class, "You are too impatient to be tactful." Everyday life offers us examples in plenty of the relation between tact and time. If a young man is wooing a girl and tries to kiss her too soon, he is lacking in tact as a lover. It may be that at a later stage the sexual approach is expected, indeed its absence may be felt as tactless. I willingly admit that tact includes other factors, but I insist that the time factor plays its part.

Perhaps I shall do best to start with a psychological description of tactlessness, or lack of tact, in order to define tact. It would be quite wrong to regard lack of tact, or the proper feeling for the requirements of social intercourse, as an ultimate and inexplicable psychological phenomenon, a constitutional defect, so to speak. Whenever we elucidate these cases of tactlessness analytically, they will appear to us in the form of blunders serving secret, unconscious purposes. We must, therefore, regard these blunders in social intercourse exactly like others, such as forgetfulness, or mistakes in reading and writing. To leave a door open that ought to be shut, to drop an observation that is felt by everybody to be embarrassing and out of place, must be judged almost exactly like stumbling, a slip of the tongue, or dropping some object. One makes a slip in manners, a faux pas, and the very words tell us how near the two kinds of blunders are to each other.

If we look at the subtler instances of tactlessness analytically—social cases, so difficult to nail down, of deficiencies in good breeding, good taste, and good manners—we shall find again and again that such errors are expressions of unconscious impulses that have broken loose from their repression. In support of this view, which associates tactlessness psychogenetically with blunders, we might point to the nature of our own reactions. When we have made a faux pas we feel ashamed, we are angry with ourselves, and afterward it is often difficult to understand and how we could have said such a thing or made such a movement. This psychical reaction is so well known that a great lady once declared that the best way to repulse a tactless remark was a courteous "I beg your pardon?"—as if we had not caught what was said or had misunderstood it. It embarrassed the speaker, she said, and made him aware of his tactlessness.

This quality of social blunders is shown in the fact that even people who in general fill their place particularly well in society, and are definitely tactful, may fall into gross errors of tact. One will, for instance, always become suspicious when a well-bred woman makes a tactless remark by "mistake." Often enough the mistake has an unconscious purpose. A lady pushed an object from the piano during a cocktail party. "Oh, is that a hat?" she asked, astonished. It was the hat (a bit unusual in shape, it is true) of another woman whom she suspected of "chasing" her husband. Some of the nice, nasty things women sometimes say to each other are by-products of errors of tact and unconscious symptomatic slips. Analysis has convinced us that with children, too, "tactlessness" need not be a simple expression of naïveté or uninhibited sincerity. One is often justified in assuming that there are unconscious purposes and motives behind the untimely or improper sayings of the little angels, and in being suspicious of their demonstrative innocence. Many family feuds have originated in guileful remarks that pose as innocent sentences and sometimes reveal hidden motives of the children. A patient remembers with some pleasure that as a girl of four years she looked down from the window of her bedroom on her mother who sat on the porch in confidential conversation with an admirer and that she suddenly shouted "Daddy" as if she had mistaken the man for her absent father. The idyl was unpleasantly interrupted.

We have now learned a number of unconventional things about tact, things that are not to be found in compendiums of good manners. Among them are the close relation between tact and time, and the nature of tactlessness as a particular kind of blunder. We shall not be surprised at this designation, if we reflect that we are not concerned with aesthetic and social valuation, but with psychological explanation. We will venture a few steps farther. I do not know whether I may count upon general agreement when I say that an adult is tactless who treats children with whom he is talking or playing condescendingly or markedly as inferior beings. Let us say, he uses unnatural, pretty-pretty, childish language. Can we reconcile this with the supposition that tactlessness is a case of unconscious social blunder? For this is a perfectly conscious, deliberate change in a person's usual behavior. And yet the foregoing designation retains its validity in a certain enlarged sense. It is the intention of the adult to get into social contact with the children, to bring himself to their level, so to speak. And now let us consider, does he achieve the purpose for which he takes so much trouble? Hardly, for precisely the affected, pretty-pretty manner of speech, the marked condescension in his bearing, will prevent the children from regarding him as one of themselves, or even as a friend. We can only explain this by saying that they sense in his unnatural manner the intention of degrading them—the arrogance of the "big person"— through the transparent veil of his condescension.

But let us suppose that the adult deliberately treated the children exactly like adults; that is to say, expected from them the same self-control and the same "good" manners, or, if he wanted to explain something to them, did so in the same form and the same terms as, let us say, a professor to his students, then he would be acting not only foolishly, but also tactlessly. In both cases he humiliates the children, either by condescending without justification, or else by exalting himself. He would show tact if he neither ignored nor stressed the difference of age and maturity, but took it as a matter of course. And here we touch in passing upon a quality of tact that it is surprising not to find mentioned more often. Tact is self-evident; much more so, in my opinion, than morality. I may remark, by the way, that children often show marvellous tact, often more than adults. Watch children playing with adults. They are capable of chasing them and romping with them without restraint, of treating them as perfectly equal playfellows and yet at the same time as superior adults.

Let us take another example, this time from a country where the concept of class differences differs from ours. A lord dealing with a laborer would be tactless if he imitated the worker's manner of speech and thought to a marked degree. It would sound to the worker like mockery. But it would be equally tactless to adopt an aristocratic manner in speaking to the worker, and so to stress the social distance between them. He need only be natural, need only be himself. And this brings us to a special aspect of tact that, I believe, has hitherto been ignored. We are in the habit of associating tact closely with consideration for others, for their feelings, their particular interests, and so forth. Now, it is my belief that this aspect is not nearly so important as people try to persuade us, and, especially, that it is not the most important. In my view tact requires much more attention to what our own endopsychical perception demands as right and proper, to what we hear "with a third ear." Anyone who has learned to pay attention to the minutest expressions of his own impulses, and especially to his reactions, will be tactful without consciously troubling overmuch about other people. And here I must stress that the perception of warning, checking voices within ourselves is of special value in developing tact. No consideration for others will help anyone who does not pay attention to the guiding voice within himself; indeed the direct expression of "consideration" may be felt by the others as embarrassing, nay, as tactless.

The same psychology applies to social intercourse (which is partly governed in secret by these underground affective currents) as to one special sphere of social life, that of sex. Here, within certain limits defined by the obvious respect for the freedom of the other party, the man or woman who pursues his or her own pleasure—in the popular sense, the egoist—gives the other party the greatest possibility of pleasure. We all know cases of husbands and lovers who show great and deliberate and apparently tender consideration for the woman in matters of sex. Either they are men of feeble potency or else they pursue unconsciously abnormal sexual aims. Such great consideration is unconsciously felt by the woman as a repulse or brutality, even when consciously she is greatly pleased by it.[1] Our nature is such that we make our neighbor pay—and often not him alone—for any excess of conscious consideration toward him to which we are driven by hypermorality. Let us, then, not forget that tact is the outcome, not only of consideration for others, but also of attention to our own impulses, and especially our own reactions.

In music it is a matter of course that questions of "tact" (measure) are treated from the standpoint of time. For *Takt* means time as counted and consolidated in units. The transference of this metrical term from music to social life shows that here, too, temporal factors come into play. And here, moreover, sexual life may claim to have typical significance, the society of two may be taken to represent society in general. The temporal factor, as seen in the seasonable beginning and ending of the sexual prelude and in the final ecstasy, is decisive in character. A poet has spoken of the ideal of love as "two hearts and one beat." Even those who are accustomed to regard sexual attraction as a matter of instinct, in accordance with its dominant element, cannot escape the conviction that successful sexual union is largely dependent upon the temporal concordance of the individual rhythm of two human beings. Man and woman are timed to each other in sexual intercourse: their excitement and orgasm is unconsciously "timed."

Human intercourse is governed by a certain measure of yielding to impulse and denying impulse, differing according to the social and cultural level of the parties, their race, the epoch in which they live, etc. We may regard tact as the unconsciously active force determining that measure, as a state of being in harmony with the varying attitudes that prescribe the limits of what is permitted and what is pleasing within any society. To be tactful is to grasp and obey this socially determined rule of conduct. It seems to me that in tracing tact back to its instinctive basis, we have stumbled upon a hidden element of the notion of tact. We have discovered it as an authority that decides on each occasion the measure in which instinct is to be satisfied or denied in social intercourse.

Conventional tact gives rules of conduct for the individual, according as this measure is determined by the society of the time. It is, so to speak, adapted to a medium time, a certain modicum of satisfaction and denial. Anything more or less than this medium time, anything that falls above or below, is held by society to be tactless. Analysts generally

[1] See the analytic discussion on this subject in my book, *Psychology of Sex Relations* (New York: Farrar & Rinehart, 1945).

consider the conventional measure to be too small to satisfy our sexual and aggressive instincts. And so we find in it an agent that tries to cover social inadequacy by means of conventional lies. If we were less "tactful" in the conventional sense, we would be much more decent and sincere people.

Returning to our theme after this long digression, we ask ourselves whether analysis has nothing more positive to tell us about the nature of tact than the rather slender information so far offered. I must confess that I really have no positive and tested results to present. Instead, I may perhaps draw attention to certain experiences, culled in the course of analytic practice that do at least show important, if partial, results. Here, again, it is better to start with the negative results, that is to say, with the experience gathered from the numerous errors and mistakes made in practice. What happens when we do not communicate the interpretation to the patient at the right moment; that is to say, when we are not guided by tact but by other considerations, when we allow ourselves to be ruled by strong feelings or rational arguments? The results are not uniform; they vary, from the absence of success to the rousing of violent resistance.

Let us for a moment turn our attention from these results to the analyst himself. Generally if we watch the reactions of the patient to whom we have communicated an interpretation or the hidden meaning of a symptom at the wrong moment, our endopsychical perception soon tells us that we have not proceeded in the right way. And then a feeling that will not be denied teaches us that the occasion was not right. It was altogether the wrong moment for the interpretation. We should rather have held our peace, or this particular interpretation came too soon, or—much more rarely—too late.

There are moments in almost every psychoanalysis when we feel that we ought to say certain things but remain silent and there are moments at which we say what should not be said just then. The first mistake appears to me to be much more dangerous than the second. If we become shy or afraid of the impression our communication may make on the patient, if we become "gun-shy," we behave just as our patients do when they suppress what occurred to them out of shame or for reasons of tact and consideration or conventionality. I once heard a man say that one should be tactful in small matters but as tactless as possible in vital, decisive ones. If we demand full sincerity of our patients we are obliged to give them full sincerity in return.

What we have to say should be said as it occurs to us in plain words. We should speak not like psychoanalysts, but like human beings. We should not refer to an implement for digging or to an agricultural instrument but should call a spade a spade. Caution and consideration have their place in psychoanalysis as well as courage and daring. There are moments in psychoanalysis when the analyst, not the patient, makes the serious mistake of keeping back things that ought to be said. He too must take hurdles; he too must overcome conventional considerations. When the right moment comes he cannot afford to be silent but must speak up. Inner necessity will tell him when this moment has arrived. The other day a young man told me what his girl answered him: "I cannot say I love you until it says itself." This is also right for the decisive things the psychoanalyst has to tell his patients; they should not be said until they say themselves.

There is no use considering carefully what should and what should not be said when the psychological moment for speaking has come. Some intuitive knowledge decides the what and the how of the analyst's communications. Every argumentation, every reasonable consideration, every well-founded theory or logical thought is disturbing at such a moment. Many experiences in situations of this kind have convinced me that I am clever only when I do not think.

Experience of analysis gives a kind of rule of interpretation, a safeguard against acting unseasonably. I got it from Freud and have made it my own. Do not interpret until the patient himself is near to discovering the interpretation for himself, till, so to speak, he need only take one step more in order to find it himself. This final step the patient does not take alone, or, at least, very rarely. The analyst must help him to cross the threshold. Counsel is good, but it is not enough.

There are important exceptions to the rule, two of which I will emphasize. It cannot apply when it is a question of symbols and their interpretation. The meaning of symbols, which originate in archaic ways of thought, is generally lost to the individual consciousness. And the rule equally fails to apply in the wide and important realm of the transference-processes, that is, of certain feelings and thoughts that the patient has transferred to his analyst from persons important in his childhood. Here numbers of psychical processes are beyond the reach of the patient's consciousness, and there is no sign of his being anywhere near grasping them.

We must also remember that the rule is of a general character, embodying negative guidance only. It amounts to a "don't." And how do we know that the patient has reached that point, that he need take only one step farther in order to find the interpretation himself? It can sometimes be inferred from the speed of his associations, from his bearing and mimicry, and from a number of small signs. The interpretation seems to hang suspended in the air, or can be read between his words. If we assume that that is so—but the assumption is by no means always correct—we must yet admit that it is not an objective and reliable criterion. And so we find ourselves driven back to that mysterious tact of which Freud speaks. And now let us recall the connection between time and tact, our idea that tactlessness is a kind of unconscious social blunder, and our sense of malaise after an unseasonable interpretation that readily assumes the character of shame or dissatisfaction with ourselves. There must be a psychological connection. But what can it be?

In order to find a means of approach from the positive side, I propose a provisional definition of tact. I hold that tact is a fine adaptation of our own vital rhythm to that of our social environment for the time being. I am well aware how vague and hard to grasp, indeed, how unscientific, such an expression sounds, and I hasten to put forward two excuses. First and foremost I would stress the provisional character of the definition. And secondly I must point out that we are entering an undiscovered region of psychology, a region yet untouched by scientific research, so that for the time being we must content ourselves with the most indefinite statements. It is not the problem of rhythm in itself that is so difficult to grasp, but its psychological significance, or its significance for the understanding of psychology.

Rhythm is a universal vital function, belonging to every living creature. This function, which runs throughout organic nature, regulates the flow of vital processes, governs waking and sleeping, hunger and satiety, work and fatigue, ebb and flow, warmth and cold, and the changes of day and night and the seasons. It governs our pulse and breath and extends from the vegetative system to the forms of expression of the more complex mental processes. Kretzschmer, who rightly stresses the importance of rhythm in mental life in his *Medizinische Psychologie,* points to the clocklike circular movements of beasts of prey in cages, the rhythmic movements of idiots, the tendency of little children to turn over every quarter of an hour, as well as to the extraordinary monotony of the refrains and verbal repetitions in the dancing songs of primitive peoples. He shows how the primary requirement that the rhythm should give satisfaction is afterward concealed by practical motives and more complicated considerations, but that nevertheless the basis of our psychokinetic system remains. We know that as civilization develops rhythmic movements give place to more complex, non-rhythmical ones. But the others never quite disappear. And here our attention is called to the instincts that spontaneously follow a rhythm governing the living substance. It would seem that the instinctive rhythm of all men was originally identical, or at least approximately the same, and that the prehistoric and historical development of the race has brought about differences. The advancing differentiation of mankind caused significant differences in the strength of instincts and far-reaching changes in the periodicity, the ebb and flow, of our instinctive impulses.

Man's affective expressions are partly governed by the rhythm of his instinctive processes, and originally no doubt they were much more clearly subject—as they are in animals—to the periodicity of the instincts. However much other factors have subsequently restricted the field of action of rhythm, it yet remains a power beneath the surface. It is my view that the utterances of our patients, in which we recognize the unconscious, instinctive element, also obey the secret power of rhythm in all their variety. Anyone who has conducted analyses for a series of years will have noticed that what is unconscious and instinctive in his patients' communications follows a definite rhythm. We cannot define it, but we are able to divine when the hidden aggressive and sexual tendencies will appear in these communications, and when they will reach their height, die away, and repeat themselves. The psychoanalyst often perceives this rhythmical rise and fall of the hidden instinctive process behind the patient's communications, without being able to tell by what signs he can detect the rules governing the movements of these nameless forces.

And here a point arises, very vague, that comes nearer to answering our original question than any arrived at previously. That is to say: the most favorable moment to give an interpretation—to communicate the repressed meaning of a series of symptoms or the hidden sense of some attitude of mind—is conditioned by the unconsciously felt rhythm of the patient's instinctive processes. If I may venture to define it more accurately: before his unconscious instinctive impulse has reached the greatest capacity of expression, or, to use the comparison of a process in nature, just before it has reached the crest of the wave.

No doubt this explanation merely shifts the problem. The notion of tact, which determines the moment for interpretation and communication, is thus merely referred back to an all-embracing phenomenon. That is true. For all scientific progress consists in such reference back to a new, wider problem. Moreover, we must reflect that this reference back is fairly far-reaching. It very nearly touches the limits of psychology, that is to say, it is close upon that region where psychology is obliged to give place to another science, biology, for the investigation of rhythmically determined instinctive processes falls within its sphere. The prospect that we have reached is this: without intending or knowing it, the analyst becomes aware of the rhythm of his patient's instinctive impulses, and this unconscious knowledge will tell him when to make his communications. Unconsciously he follows this rhythm of instinct, vibrates with it. Perhaps it is better to say that he is a fraction ahead of the patient, reading ahead a bar, let us say, so that he divines in what direction the unconscious will move. Thanks to this start— of the length of a psychological phase, to use an expression of Freud's— he can conjecture and anticipate what is to come or what is unconsciously purposed.

And here let us recall the single step which, in Freud's opinion, the patient would require in order to discover the interpretation himself, the step that the analyst must take for him. That step, then, corresponds to the length by which the analyst is ahead of him. The analyst owes the psychological advantages that he enjoys over the patient very largely to the broadening of his consciousness, and to his knowledge of the nature of instinct, which he has gained through his own analysis and his analytic experience with others.

Even after this explanation, the importance of the subjective factor in the problem does, indeed, remain, but at least we can detect in addition an objective factor in its hidden character. It is still the analyst's response, our own mental reaction to the communications of the patient, that illuminates our path. The tact that determines the time of our "telling" (what I call the psycholanalytic moment) is nothing but an unconscious knowledge of the direction, strength, and sequence of the instinctive impulses. The connection with the time or "beat" factor, which I stress in this matter, is established by our subterranean knowledge of the ebb and flow of the other person's impulses. If we offer an interpretation at precisely this moment, and no other, it is because we know unconsciously in what direction the wave of instinct that we have apprehended, will move. This knowledge arises from our commonly unconscious vibration in time with the instinctive rhythm of the other. To make a comparison: we act like the members of many Indian tribes, who put their ear to the ground in order to detect whether horsemen are approaching from a distance, and so hear the beat of the horses' hoofs long before the riders can be discerned.

I must stress the fact that I have been dealing in this chapter only with a specialized question: when ought we to communicate an interpretation to the patient or open his eyes to the secret meaning of his unconscious means of expression? It is only the question *when* that I wished to answer. In seeking the answer we have touched the limits of psychology; we have been led into the discussion of a universal phenomenon of all living beings. The same thing happens to the student of the theory and practice of music when he tries to grasp the action of the pulsing basic force in music. When he has reduced the capacity to understand melody and harmony to its elements, he is driven to adopt a view that likewise points to the fundamental biological processes: in the beginning was rhythm.

CHAPTER XXIX

Hide-and-Seek

LET'S compare the analytic setup with the game of hide-and-seek our children play. The patient would correspond to the person who hides himself—or a part of himself—and the analyst is "it." There is, of course, something wrong with this picture. The patient hides not only from the analyst but also from himself. Furthermore, the patient wants to hide but he also wants to be found. He not only conceals, but also reveals, himself. Something else is wrong. The seeker, unlike the person in the game, does not walk around looking here and there. He waits until the other comes out from hiding.

Seek not and ye shall find.

Seeking in this case would mean examining the puzzling phenomenon with what one has learned in one's studies, with what one has recognized as valid in courses, lectures, seminars, and books. The approach I recommend here is different. I suggest that the seeker forget what he has learned, neglect what he has heard and read, and listen to his own response. Let's take a few examples contrasting the intellectual or theoretical approach with the one I characterized as that of inner experience or observation of one's own response.

A patient told me he had felt a very intense impulse of a most puzzling kind. During a performance of *Parsifal* in the Vienna Staatsopera, in the middle of the most solemn scene he had the most irresistible impulse to shout at the top of his voice: *"Mazzesknoedel!"* (Matzoth-balls). The impulse became so intense that he almost succumbed, and only quick flight saved him from the unpleasant scene that would have resulted.

Does it help me penetrate the mystery of this impulse when I remember that I learned (from Fenichel) that impulses are "ego symptomic and not ego alien"?[1] Does it explain their irresistibility to know that it "is different from that of a normal, instinctual drive" and "is caused by the condensation of instinctual urge and defensive striving," and that irresistibility means the patients are "intolerant of tension"? I know that such patients "are characterized by oral and skin-erotic fixation." But what am I to do with this knowledge? Where do we go from here? It does not enlighten me when I remember: "In general, the impulse neuroses show, as does no other neurotic phenomenon, the dialectic connection between the concepts of gratification of an instinct and defense against an instinct." While I am still brooding over the term "dialectic connection," I realize that the hidden meaning of the intended shout, "Matzoth-balls!" eludes me. I admit, of course, that the impulse had something to do with the "oral fixation" because Matzoth-balls are food. But only God—in this case the God our forefathers called Jahweh —knows what the connection is. Should I look for a traumatic experience in the childhood of the patient, something to do with those delicious dumplings? No doubt, the impulse also has a sexual character because the oral phase, according to analytic theory, is the first in the development of the libido. That the impulse has aggressive character cannot be denied either, because acting it out would mean disturbance, indignation from the audience, punishment for the offender. Even when I arrived at the conclusion that the impulse is of an oral-sadistic kind and is to be traced back to a childhood scene, it does not help me understand it. The knowledge is abstract, formalized thought, and nothing else. I want to fill it with content. I remember that the patient had seen his parents, his brother, and his sister-in-law in a box at the beginning of the act. The impulse is perhaps an oral aggression against these members of the family. Well, I say now (or rather I would say now if I express myself in Psychoanalese), here is a regression to the oral-sadistic phase of libido-development directed against the objects of his infantile libido. Should I now lose myself in a consideration of the cannibalistic tendencies of the patient?

Now contrast this theoretically correct picture with the one presented by the inner observation of my response to the patient's tale. While he was describing the scene, his voice had a plaintive or complaining tone.

[1] Otto Fenichel, *The Psychoanalytic Theory of Neurosis* (New York: 1945), p. 367 ff.

Why did I want to laugh? Here was something serious, indeed. Had he yielded to the impulse, my patient would be in jail for disorderly conduct instead of on the analytic couch today. What was there to laugh about? Yet, the temptation to laugh got stronger the longer I followed his story—it became nearly as irresistible as his impulse had been. Apparently he became aware of my fight with laughter, because he began to laugh himself as if relieved of a tension. Whereas just before he had been complaining, he now acted like a man who has told a joke quite seriously and finally joins his audience in laughter. Where was the joke?

As far as I could catch my response to this tale—as far as I can reconstruct it—it is the following: What did I think? I see the Vienna opera . . . the stage . . . the solemn scene in *Parsifal* as I have seen it once myself . . . now the picture of my patient in one of the front rows . . . his parents in the box . . . his impulse to shout "Matzoth-balls!" . . . it is Easter Week: . . . the Vienna opera always does *Parsifal* during Easter Week . . . Passover . . . the Jews . . . a joke about a Jew at *Parsifal* in Bayreuth . . . Nietzsche . . . a passage about *Parsifal*. Is it from *The Case of Wagner?*

I now perceived clearly the secret motive of the impulse as well as its unconscious premises. While the patient followed the devout scenes of *Parsifal* he must have thought of his parents, his brother, and his sister-in-law, whom he had seen in their box before the curtain went up. Just a few weeks before he had been told that his parents wanted to be baptized because they had been promised they would be made baronets.[2] He himself had decided to remain Jewish in fact and in name and he had made an effort to control his indignation about the snobbishness of his family. Christianized Jews and King Arthur's knights were unconsciously contrasted. Then came the contrast of the Holy Grail and Matzoth and with it the memory of the Matzoth-balls that he and his family had enjoyed when he was a boy and his people were poorer and truer to themselves. Thus the impulse to shout "Matzoth-balls!" was really an expression of a sarcastic, sharply aggressive tendency against his parents and with them a group or class of Jews who are social climbers and eager to forget and disavow their Jewish origin. It cannot be denied that "Matzoth-balls," the idea that forced itself upon him, was

[2] In Vienna about twenty-five years ago it was possible for converted Jews to be made members of the Austrian nobility.

a picturesque expression of the contrast, and it is not very essential in this connection that the impulse was of an oral character. It is peripheral that the idea was "ego symptomic" and immaterial that there might have been other childhood experiences with Matzoth-balls.

Let us now return to the response that gave me more information about the meaning of the impulse than these theoretical considerations. It is clear that I must have perceived the reluctance my patient felt during the performance. Perhaps something in him (as in myself) rejected the Wagnerian Weltanschauung as it is presented in this late work. This something that rebels against the mysteries and the mysterious might well be connected with his rationalistic Jewish attitude. While I must have sensed the mockery early in his report in spite of his complaining voice (or because of it?), the mention of his family, who listened attentively to the *Parsifal* festival, intensified the impression.

Why did the Jewish joke occur to me? The connection is given by *Parsifal* itself because the joke (which loses its idiomatic pungency in translation) reports that an East European Jew, accustomed to the comic in his theatrical experiences, visited the Festspielhaus in Bayreuth. During the performance of *Parsifal* he turns to his neighbor and complains: "I cannot laugh at it. Really, I can't laugh." It sounds like nonsense; exactly like the impulse to shout, "Matzoth-balls!" Nobody expects that listening to the tragic play of the Holy Grail will cause laughter. It is clear that the complaint of the Jew is hypocritical. He makes us believe that he thought he was attending a comedy and that he is disappointed that he does not feel like laughing. Behind his make-believe is really the temptation to roar with laughter at the sight of all those knights of the sorrowful countenance, to consider them highly comical.

It is interesting that these fleeting associations in my response contained not only the transitions to the solution but the solution itself. Although it was in an undeveloped form, it is, so to speak, in the negative proof. Here are the links: *Parsifal*—Bayreuth—the Jew in the anecdote—his concept of *Parsifal* as comical. I had already vaguely grasped the sarcastic nature of my patient's impulse—its motive, to ridicule those snobbish Jews, including his parents, who pretend to be deeply touched by the mysteries of the Holy Grail. And Nietzsche? A hazy memory of a passage by Nietzsche, which proves that gentiles too consider *Parsifal* comical.[3] With this association the meaning of the impulse was entirely clear. It passed over the threshold of conscious thinking. It stepped, so to speak, from the twilight into the serenity, brightness, and distinctness of the day.

Which of the two procedures is psychologically more useful and appropriate, the objective one or the subjective one? Which leads to the core of the little problem, the road over a textbook or the path over one's own response?

What kind of instance should we choose now? An inexhaustible wealth of experiences and impressions offers itself at this point so that choosing becomes irksome. Should we make a careful selection and take instances of "human interest"? But whatever instance you touch has human interest. There is no instance without it because everyone is always an expression of men's drives, joy, and suffering. Should I favor instances in which hidden motives had to be found or instances where emotions concealed themselves or instances in which I had to search for unknown thoughts? The best I can do, it seems to me, is not to make a careful selection, but to take what comes along.

Take a pathetic human experience contrasting with the cheerful one mentioned before. In the previous case we tried to understand what a puzzling impulse meant. Here we had to ask ourselves why certain emotions did not appear although we would have expected them.

A girl reported how she received the news of the death of her father. It had happened almost ten years before, but she remembered many details of the day. She and her older sister had been visiting an aunt when they were called to the telephone and told that their father was very ill and that they should return immediately. The sister packed her things and hurried to the station to catch the next train home. My patient took a long time, missed the train, and arrived home much later. Her mood was almost apathetic. She felt no vivid mourning. In the following weeks she was oppressed rather than grieved. Her description of the state she had been in left no doubt that it was not one of the depersonalizations that we meet so often in people after the death of a close relative. It was rather as if she had expected the news at that

---

[3]The passage in Nietzsche's *The Case of Wagner* reads as follows: "Nothing is more to be recommended to a man who takes a walk than to imagine Wagner in a rejuvenated shape: for instance Parsifal as probationer of theology with a college education (which is urgently needed for pure foolishness)."

moment. The father had suffered from cancer, but she did not know the nature of his disease and could not have expected his death right then. Also, the contrast of her behavior with that of her sister was conspicuous.

At the time I could not discover how her apparent aloofness could be explained. The next thought would, of course, concern her relationship with her father. Some analysts would perhaps search in the realm of the Oedipus complex for reasons for this absence of grief. They would perhaps assume that it expressed latent hostility, that jealousy of the sister played a role, and so forth. Nothing of this kind could explain her strange psychological situation. Even if such tendencies were present or could have been assumed, their general nature made them inappropriate as explanations for this particular case. I think it is futile to go hunting for motives of this kind without a clue. It means that one gets entangled in a theoretical web. Lack of understanding is regrettable, but misunderstanding in the form of a misconstruction is deplorable.

I waited. It was the only thing to do. Some weeks later in another connection the patient related an occasion on which she had shown herself inconsolable. That had been a few months *before* the death of her father. A dog belonging to her and her sister had been run over by a car and killed. The patient had sobbed for hours, and for weeks nothing could mitigate her grief. She was quite exhausted from crying. When she told me the story, I had the odd feeling that it must have something to do with her father's death, but that was, of course, impossible. The dog had perished at least two months before the father. The dates were certain. I rejected the idea, which appeared to me now not as a mistake but as merely stupid. Later on the patient told me that she and her sister had had much fun with the dog. They played hide-and-seek with him, and she remembered certain tricks. For instance, they would both hide and then simultaneously call him from their separate places of concealment. They were very amused when the dog ran around undecided whose voice to follow. A few minutes later she remembered that her father and mother had played a similar game with her in the garden of their house when she was a very little girl. Strange, there again is the connection between father and dog. But the data could not be doubted and my feeling must be decidedly wrong. It was just a thought connection in the mind of the patient that was helped by the fact that, to a child, beloved animals and persons do not appear so distant from each other. Also, in phobias animals appear as objects of infantile fears that are transferred to them from mother or father as substitute living beings.

What I had considered a lead seemed to disappear before my eyes, or rather to shrink to the proportions of a psychological equalization in childhood. When the girl spoke of the hide-and-seek game with the dog, she had remembered a similar one with her father, which was very natural. There was nothing more to it. No mistake about the time of the father's death and the accident to the dog was possible. It was just conspicuous and puzzling that she had cried for days about the dog and that the death of the father did not arouse her grief. But why did this feeling that there was a connection between the two events not cease? Why did it reappear like an insistent preconception on later occasions when she spoke of her father? I tried to reason with myself and made an effort to explain to myself that an early conflict with the father as it was now remembered was explanation enough for her attitude after his death. I tried to convince myself. But an analyst and a woman convinced against their will are of the same opinion still, even when that opinion is contradicted by their own reason. Nothing else occurred to her about the subject.

Another memory, however, that apparently had nothing to do with it emerged a short time later. She told it casually. A few days before the fatal accident of the dog, she had been with him in the garden as she often was on summer days. She saw her mother and the doctor who was treating her father at the time leave the house. Her mother accompanied the doctor downstairs and they walked slowly through the garden to the door. They had not seen the girl who was behind the bushes, but she had seen tears streaming down her mother's cheeks while the doctor spoke to her in a low and consoling voice. She had never seen her mother in such a state of despair. She could not remember having heard what the physician and her mother had said and she could not decide whether she had heard some words and later repressed them or not— but was the scene not telling in itself? The girl had, of course, well understood that it meant her father was to die soon. She must have made an unconscious effort to forget the impression, to hide it from herself and from the others. When two or three days later the dog was killed, all the grief, the terrible feeling of loss, shook her to the depths. Consciously it concerned the death of the dog, but unconsciously her mourning anticipated the death of her father. It was for him that she cried day and night until she was exhausted and had no more tears left. She had experienced his death and had sobbed farewell to him without knowing it. By a mechanism of unconscious displacement she had transferred her grief to the dog, whose death could not possibly have affected her so much while the death of the beloved father left her cold.

The nature of the subject with which we deal here compels us to shift from the object to the subject and back again, from the observed person to the observer, from the phenomenon back to the analyst. To return to the analyst again. My initial feeling that the absence of grief at the father's death and the excessive mourning for the dog must have been connected subterraneously was correct. Contradicted by all reason, which made it appear impossible, its recurrence proved that it was in tune with the psychology of the case, although opposed by logic. The feeling became stronger when the report of playing hide-and-seek with the dog was followed by the memory of a similar game with the father.[4] My intuition had to struggle with a most energetic inner refusal to believe in preconceived notions or hunches against all the laws of logic. When the patient a few days later casually mentioned the memory that the physician and the mother descended the stairs together, I felt as if an inner tension were released. I no longer believed; I knew beyond a doubt. I saw the connections with full clarity. I had not spoken of my ideas to the patient and I had waited until her memories began to speak and my waiting was rewarded by sudden insight. Added memories emerged in her analysis later on and confirmed the conviction that the events had indeed taken the course suggested by my reconstruction. In cases like this an analyst gets the lasting conviction that the analytic technique, if only applied conscientiously, works with the precision of chemistry or other natural sciences. When the analyst listens very attentively to his inner response again and again and remains critically aware of his personal prejudices, he will realize that presentiments are confirmed and that his hunches do not deceive him. The feeling of vagueness and confusion that is so often unavoidable gives way to a feeling of certainty. The experience, "Oh, that's it!" marks the end of the inner contest. As in this case, a sudden flash confirms that the first impression, although necessarily modified, was in essence correct.

I spoke previously of sudden flashes that illuminate a complex situation for the analyst, show concealed connections to him and reveal

[4] It is interesting that I gave this chapter the title "Hide-and-Seek" although I had not consciously planned to use this case in which the game is so significant.

motives that had been secret before. When such a surprising insight emerges, it can often be recognized as the result of the return of impressions that have either become unconscious to the analyst or that have never left the realm of preconscious thinking. What appears thus as a flash is really a flash back. I am going to make use of the preceding instance—or rather of associations connected with essential parts of it— to show how the analytic flash-back technique works.

Here is a part of a long dream that was analyzed: *There is a dog and I am afraid of him. He will hurt me.* This dream-fragment obviously had no connection with the rest of the dream, the latent content of which had become transparent in our analytic session. No association, beyond memories that the patient had been afraid of dogs when he was a small boy, helped to elucidate the meaning of this part. The other content of the dream had been recognized as concerning the desires and sexual wishes of the patient, who had made the acquaintance of an attractive married woman. He had fondled her the evening before the dream but had not dared to go any farther. Why should a dog appear in the dream together with the fear of being hurt at this point? No associations occurred to the patient at this point, and I was ready to drop the passage as not penetrable at this time when, as if led by an invisible hand, I asked him to repeat this part. When I heard the sentences spoken by him again, *There is a dog and I am afraid of him. He will hurt me,* I was no longer uncertain as to what they meant. They were a continuation of the dream-text. After the scene that brought a visual image of his wish to approach his married friend sexually, a dog appeared on the dream scene out of nowhere, and he became frightened. As I heard the sentence repeated, the idea suddenly had occurred to me that the word *dog* meant *God*. Only a few moments later (not before) I thought consciously that the word *dog* turned around is the word *God*. Let me now for a moment put aside the question whether the idea is correct. Why did it occur to me? God had not been mentioned in this session. We had discussed the dream and what had occurred to the dreamer about it. Among these associations was also the report that he had met the admired woman the evening before, that they had had a petting party, but that something—perhaps the thought of her husband?—had stopped him from reaching the goal of his wishes, which, it seemed, were vividly shared by the object of his desire.

When I now analyze or scrutinize the reasons that made me think *dog* in this sentence replaces *God,* I find three factors that must have unconsciously led me to this assumption. The patient had, it is true, mentioned neither God nor religion in this session, but he had often discussed religion in his analysis before. He had been brought up in a very religious family. Yes, he had even seriously considered becoming a priest himself, but he had lost his religious belief in the puberty years and had become a musician instead. He not only asserted that he was an atheist, but also he liked to blaspheme. In jokes and in serious discussions he mocked religion and used strong and often vulgar language to tear the idea of God to pieces. I mistrusted the sincerity of such demonstrative atheism, especially since he turned too frequently to the subject without any apparent reason. I sensed that somewhere beneath his official atheism and blasphemies lay concealed the old consciously disavowed religious belief. This impression of mine, which I had never mentioned, must have been one of the main factors that paved the way to the interpretation of dog–God. This impression, which had remained unconscious, conceived of the dream-element as an expression that was true to the character of the patient. It secured, so to speak, the general psychological atmosphere, the emotional background, against which this part stands out. Is the reversal God–dog not in conformity with the many blasphemous remarks I had heard from the patient often enough?

So far the general factor. But there must have been others of a special kind contained in this particular situation that gave me the idea. Two indications had registered on me without being consciously recognized. The first was an impression, obtained this time from the interpretation of the preceding part of the dream. Its understanding had been reached by turning certain elements around. Only by such a reversal of their manifest sense did their secret meaning become recognizable. It was clear that the distortion to which the original dream-content was subjected could only be undone by turning those parts around again. While thinking of the part with the dog, I had paid no attention to the interpretation of the other dream-content. I had forgotten that dreams often turn words around as children do. Only after I had found the interpretation dog–God did I remember that the patient liked to play with words in an infantile way. I had often heard him make puns and word distortions.

The other indication that must have unconsciously determined my interpretation, or the suddenly occurring idea that led to it, was, I am sure now, the wording or the style of the dream-sentences. They must have sounded somewhat differently to my inner ear than the preceding ones. These contained the picture of the advances the patient made (in the manifest dream the young woman made the advances); then came a little hesitancy and then the sentence, "There is a dog and I am afraid of him." Does it not seem as if a new story begins here? The impression is similar to the effect of a contrasting color that appears in the middle of a wall or a velvet trim on a woolen dress. The dream pretended to be a unit, to be homogeneous, as if this sentence only continued the story. But here began a new tale, which interrupted or disturbed the other. When the dream told the progress of his sexual adventure that did not go beyond a certain point and then continued with this sentence, should we not assume that the sentence itself contains the disturbing element? What held the dreamer back in the pursuit was just that. It was a religious fear that originated in his early belief: "There is a God and I am afraid of Him." It was his fear of God, hidden from himself, which lingered on in him (in spite of his declared atheism) and prevented him from having an affair with the woman. He unconsciously considered it sinful to have sexual intercourse with a woman married to another man. Petting with her appeared permissible to him, but when he was tempted to go farther he became afraid of punishment by God.

It is, of course, impossible to imagine how analysts who apply their tools of interpretation consciously would proceed in the attempt to understand this part of a dream for which no associations were available. Perhaps they would actually interpret the dog as a father-substitute the patient is afraid of. Such an interpretation cannot be called entirely false, especially since the image that the child makes of God is itself influenced by the infantile idea of a father who becomes unconsciously God-like, deified. The difference between the two kinds of interpretation is, nevertheless, very great, not only because one is closed to the secrets of the dream but also on account of their psychological depth. If the analyst mechanically translates dog = father, using the bridge of childhood fears, he brings an alien element into the concealed dream-content. It is not an analytic interpretation, but rather a translation from the analytic dictionary and it does not convey the real meaning of the original dream-thought. The fact that a big animal in many dreams, as in children's phobias, appears as a feared father-substitute, is proved. That it can be interpreted in the same way in this dream is not proved. To assume this meaning means only that such a fact mechanically pressed into the dream-interpretation does not belong there, that it is, to use the language of the lawyers, "immaterial, irrelevant, and incompetent" at this point. The sentence, "There is a dog and he will hurt me," did not concern the father of the patient. It was not this distorted thought that made him interrupt his sexual adventures. A direct expression of his religious belief disturbed him: "There is a God and He will hurt me"— a sentence and an opinion that sharply contradicted his conscious thinking.

Another train of thought branching off from the next to the last analyzed instance leads me to a case that showed an even stranger reaction after the death of the father. The girl in my next case was, as she clearly remembered, pleased that her father had died or rather relieved as if a burden had been taken from her. It would seem sound to assume that she had hated her father or that certain memories showed that he had maltreated the girl in her early childhood. Nothing of the kind. The father had been a mild and very kind man, and the child had adored him. Other motives for such a puzzling feeling of fleeting satisfaction after the death of the father are possible, as for instance when his leaving fulfills certain secret wishes whose realization his existence seemed to prevent. I once had a girl patient who felt that her father had become a rival in her love of the mother. She used to daydream that her father would die on one of his trips and she, then eight years old, would grow up to be a school-teacher and live with her mother, whom she would support. Nothing of such secret wishes as appeared in the daydreams of that other little girl could be discovered in the present case. My patient had dearly loved her father, who had been a kind and generally honored man. The reason for the paradoxical feeling of joy at his death was to be found in the past. The little girl had often been left alone in the apartment, and a man who was an old acquaintance of her parents' had sometimes come in. One day this man had started to play sexually with the child, who in a mixture of fear and pleasure allowed him to do what he wanted. The little girl understood that it was wrong and did not need the man's repeated warnings not to tell her father. She carried this secret knowledge together with increasing guilt-feelings through the years of her childhood and suffered from fear that her father would in some mysterious way find out what had happened. When he then suddenly died, she had a vivid feeling of relief as if a burden had been taken from her. This emotion did not correspond to the intensity of hostile feelings, but of her burning shame at the thought that he would discover her terrible secret.

The discussion of the case in which the absence of grief at the news of the father's death was so conspicuous would not be complete without some remarks about related phenomena. I mean depersonalization in the mourning phase. This is a state of apparent emotionlessness accompanied by sharp self-observation in a situation where intense feelings of grief and sorrow are expected. The person himself is often not only surprised, but also painfully aware of the fact that he does not feel anything. Yes, sometimes serious self-reproaches occur when, for instance, no grief is felt, no tear shed at the burial of one's father or mother. I do not want to enter into a discussion of the complicated psychology of mourning-depersonalization. I want only to point out how often we can discover a displacement of emotion such as we found in the hide-and-seek case.

A patient of mine felt like a lifeless automaton in the days after the death of his father and he complained that he had no sensations of grief and mourning. He realized that people expected expressions of grief from him, but he could not feel anything. He explained this absence of sad emotions by the fact that a conflict with his father had lasted many years and made him a stranger. He scarcely thought of the father any more when something happened that puzzled him. On Saturday, some weeks after the funeral, he went as usual to his club where he occasionally played chess. The waiter who was serving him said casually, "Do you know, Mr. A., that your chess partner has died?" The old man who had died was nothing more than a casual acquaintance about whom he knew scarcely anything. They had often played chess together because the patient liked the old man's game. To the astonishment of the waiter and of the players in the room, but even more to the patient's own surprise, he broke into uncontrollable sobbing, as he felt an overpowering wave of grief submerge everything else. Clearly, this strong emotion could not concern the old chess partner and was to be explained by a process of unconscious displacement that brought his delayed grief for his father to the surface. It occurred to me to ask him what the name of the old chess player had been. It was Immergut (German—"always good"). A wave from the depths must have suddenly reached the surface here. His father had really always been good to him.

CHAPTER XXX

Memory and Reminiscence

H AVE I not hitherto, in my account of the conjecture of unconscious processes, too little recognized and admitted the importance of conscious knowledge and reminiscence? I am bound to admit that the misgiving is justified. The conscious knowledge that we acquire from experience, reading, and attendance at lectures and discussions is of great importance in this process, but this admission is so much a matter of course that there is no need to stress it. On the other hand the claims put forward by this conscious knowledge had to be brought back within the bounds of its efficacy. I assert that in conjecturing—note that I say *conjecturing*—psychical processes, unconscious reminiscences or, as I prefer to say, *memory-traces* are of far greater importance than conscious knowledge.

What! people will say. You argue that the experience gathered throughout long years by a psychologist, what an analyst has comprehended and learned from a number of cases, is of slight significance, does not make itself felt in the easier and quicker conjecture of unconscious processes? Oh, yes, but such acquisition is not identical with conscious knowledge. Our comprehension of a case of neurosis, a difficult character-deformation, or the unconscious, submerged causes of a severe conflict, widens our psychological comprehension, but that is not the same as present reminiscence. If, confronted with a new case, a clear straightforward reminiscence of my analytic comprehension of a former case arises in my mind, I have an exceptional phenomenon, conditioned by special circumstances.

In a general way the process of conjecturing the latent meaning and

343

the mechanism of what goes on in the mind is governed by knowledge that has become unconscious. That is equally true of each particular case regarded as a whole in comparison with previous cases, and of single phenomena in which we have to conjecture the repressed instinctive impulses. Of course I do not deny that, in the act of conjecture, conscious reminiscences help, but I am almost tempted to venture the paradox that these conscious reminiscences generally occur *after* conjecture. It is as if they want to offer themselves as confirmation, giving clarity and strength to our later comprehension. After the analyst has conjectured the nature of a given repressed process, reminiscences of similar cases, of which he has already attained comprehension, occur to him.

Indeed it sometimes happens that he tells the patient about the hidden meaning of the earlier case, just recalled, when he gives him a psychological explanation of his unconscious process by way of illustration. So, too, it often happens that after the analyst has conjectured an unconscious relation a number of connecting links occur to him, which show him where former impressions of the same patient belong. Admitting that there are exceptions, we may state that such conscious reminiscence does not occur until shortly before or after we have penetrated to our first comprehension of the unconscious phenomenon. It is an astonishing psychological fact, but there are plenty of analogies in scientific work and in everyday life. We need only think of some sudden realization the preliminaries and causes of which do not reveal themselves to us till afterward. You reach a goal, look back, and realize by what path you reached it, what foundation you have built upon.

Thus, in conjecturing repressed processes, unconscious memories are the ruling factor, some of which may later become capable of conscious realization; but they need by no means always become conscious. I recall, for instance, the case of the girl Judy, who had such intense terror of marriage and childbirth, and my first presentiment of the meaning of her fear.[1] In discussing the case I said that, so far as I know, no reminiscence of anything she had told me before helped me to get at the secret meaning of her fear. At the same time I pointed out that "something" in the story and the lamentations of the patient directed my thoughts to the opposite meaning, fear of sterility, only I cannot say what it was.

Although, when I reflected upon the way by which my mind was

[1] See Chap. XIII.

first led to approach the comprehension of the symptom, no reminiscence of anything previously told me by the patient occurred to me, yet a reminiscence of another case did occur—but note this was after I had made my conjecture. When I had given expression to my surmise of the latent meaning of Judy's fear symptom, there arose in my mind the idea of another young woman whom I had treated many years earlier. This idea, grasped for the fraction of a second, followed upon a reminiscence of several essential features of the old case. My earlier patient, Anne, had told me that during her engagement she suffered from an oppressive fear that when she was married she would be unable to bear children, so that in the end her husband would be alienated from her. She had gone in despair from one doctor to another, and had had difficulty in allowing herself to be convinced that there was no organic reason for her fear. Although from the point of view of the examining gynecologist there was no visible reason for panic—later she gave birth to four healthy children—the analysis had revealed the unconscious motive of her fear, and especially its psychical origin in a struggle against masturbation. The differences between the two cases, as also their common features, were plain; my recurrence to the unconscious memory-trace of Anne must have helped me later to attain psychological comprehension of Judy's case.

Any analyst can tell of numerous examples of such unconscious knowledge, consciously grasped afterward, and every one of us would have many more examples at his command, if we accustomed ourselves to track the origin of our psychological knowledge. Recurrence to earlier memory-traces, combined with the perception of small, barely observed signals from the patient, will always contribute something, more or less, to the psychical result of conjecturing repressed features.

And, now, will the reader accompany me on a short digression? We have learned the psychological significance of the difference between reminiscence and memory-trace. As a rule we contrast reminiscence with forgetfulness: what is forgotten is lost to reminiscence, and a reminiscence has been saved from forgetfulness. Our insight into the structure of the psychological mechanism and into the peculiar characteristics of mental dynamics makes us skeptical from the outset of such an excessively simple assumption. For we know that there is no such thing as real forgetfulness, with the exception of the exhaustion of extreme old age, perhaps. Stressing the contrast between memory and reminiscence makes more sense. Memory, which has been designated as a universal quality of organic matter, is by nature unconscious. The small portion of it that becomes conscious confronts us as reminiscence.

We will turn our attention to the deep-seated changes wrought by the act of reminiscence upon material that has lain under the protection of "forgetfulness" or unconscious memory. Memory, as a covered or hidden reservoir, has primarily the power to maintain and conserve. In our study of an important part of the material so conserved—that which is repressed—we have come to understand why the protection is necessary. It consists of painful, or merely unpleasant, impressions, ideas, or impulses that were incompatible with the existence of other mental forces and so were obliged to quit the field of consciousness.

Freud's later researches made it clear that this view had to be enlarged to include impressions that were too intense or too sudden to be assimilated mentally within a given time. We will pay special attention to this more general case. If we form a true conception of the extraordinary extent and depth of the unconscious memories in our possession, we are led to the supposition that indeed the majority of impressions come to people too intensely or too fast to be assimilated at once. In other words, we live to a large extent unconsciously; or, very little of what we experience, only the upper planes, reaches our consciousness. What each day brings us is generally too forcible; so that our mental machinery would not be equal to mastering such a number of impressions, if we had not the power of setting many of them aside for later assimilation. This state of affairs is most easily demonstrated when we think we have grasped the meaning of one of these experiences properly. Often enough subsequent endopsychical perception shows how little we were aware of what was going on in our minds. For instance, we experience the death of a close relative, the loss of some beloved person, and believe that we feel our grief in all its depth. Not till later do we realize how shallow was that conscious depth, in what hidden abysses our grief persists, how petty was our conscious sense of the real inner meaning of the loss. We think that grief has overcome us, but our grief only reveals its depths long after we think that we have got the better of it.

As a rule we experience an event a long time after its occurrence. In many cases the interval is so long that the causal connection is quite lost to us. In fact we know only a small fraction of what goes on in our minds during a single hour. This ignorance, which is to some extent the will to ignorance, implies a protective measure on the part of the mind for, if we knew, we should not be equal to receiving the knowledge. *To experience means to master an impression inwardly that was so strong that we could not grasp it at once.* The mechanism of repression, which carries on within the ego the process of suppression originating from without, is, from this point of view, a special case of the dynamically and economically significant process that occurs when the ego is unequal to meeting certain demands made upon the mental machinery. The more general process of defense does not cancel the strong impressions. It only lays them aside, to bring them out again later.

It will be in the interest of clarity to state the contrast between memory and reminiscence with deliberate bluntness: the function of memory is to protect our impressions; reminiscence aims at their dissolution. *Essentially memory is conservative, reminiscence destructive.* Thus single reminiscences involve a perforation of our unconscious memory as a whole. An incipient dissolution is already present in the process of becoming conscious. Not long ago I read an observation in a novel by one of our writers (Franz Werfel) that well expressed the functional relation between the two mental faculties. Somebody says in the novel, "I have a very good memory because I am bad at reminiscence."

It might, indeed, be urged against this view that reminiscence revives our unconscious or preconscious experiences, that, for instance, history makes ancient events live for us, enables us to realize and possess what has long lain hidden. *"L'histoire c'est une résurrection,"* is written on Michelet's tombstone. But this resurrection generally amounts to an evaporation of hitherto hidden forces, a slow attenuation of their subterranean psychological potency. Egyptian mummies, buried deep in the earth, are preserved for thousands of years. The moment that they are excavated and exposed to the sun's rays and other atmospheric influences really marks the beginning of their dissolution. When Howard Carter and Lord Carnavon opened the excavated burial chamber of Tutenkhamon in the Nile Valley, they found among its treasures a small statuette, excellently preserved. There was just enough time to look at it, to measure it, and photograph it. Suddenly it collapsed without a sound and became dust. Three thousand years of preservation in the dark and one moment of light and destruction!

Seen in this light, one mental function of reminiscence is revealed to which too little attention has as yet been paid. It represents a particular kind of mental labor, leading to the liquidation of impressions. Not till we have recalled an experience in sufficiently frequent and clear reminiscences, can it escape our memory. What is not brought to reminiscence is psychically immortal. With a certain reservation we may say that *the past cannot fade until it has again become the present.* Only what has become reminiscence is subject to the process of exhaustion common to all organic life. Reminiscence is the best road to "forgetfulness" in the sense of emotional mastery of experiences and events. The absence of reminiscence has a wonderful conservative power. It may sound like a joke, but it is one with a serious note that we say that, a man who is always asking his beloved to recall the happy hours they have enjoyed together ("Do you remember how we . . .") is well on the way to destroying the lasting power of those hours. *Not common reminiscences, but common memory-traces, are a strong bond in human relations.*

It is my belief that this secret common possession of memories, shared sorrows and joys binds the members of a family and of a nation closer than conscious tradition and draws a dividing line between them and the outer world. This unconscious community is more essential to the persistence and further development of cultural forces than the conscious reminiscence of history. Reminiscence drags the past into the full light of day, but it illuminates as the setting sun does a landscape, soon to set in darkness.

I have said that, as regards the depth and significance of our impressions, we live as a rule unconsciously. Our experience, I said, is too strong and direct (or our ego too weak and unstable) to be mastered in the requisite time. If I may compare our consciousness with an official, and the impressions we receive with the papers that come into his office, I should say that the business of that office is always badly in arrears. We have very few resources to enable us to keep pace at all. And so, for example, dreams do something to clear up the arrears of the day. This explains the psycho-economic significance of the day-residues for the structure of our dreams. It is not strange that, to these arrears of the past day, others are linked, dating from the past years; nay, that impressions attach themselves that we failed to master in our childhood. And so the overburdened official, who wants to clear up the papers left over from yesterday, will find in them references to earlier documents, and will discover to his consternation that there are quantities lying locked away in steel files, undealt with for years past. Behind the pile of yesterday's letters, which we have not been able to work through, we shall find a long series of earlier arrears, still waiting to be dealt with.

How, then, we may ask, do we manage to work off our psychical experiences? The answer is not simple. In the first place, it seems to me by no means certain that we always manage it. Possibly none of us ever catches up with, and experiences all, the impressions received in childhood. In many cases the ego must, so to speak, be content with payment in instalments. Of course individual differences will affect the issue; besides the nature of the impressions, we must gauge the constitutional character of the ego, its intellectual and affective capacities, its weakness and independence. But in my opinion human life is and remains a patchwork also in the matter of assimilating impressions. To dispatch all our experiences psychologically is an ideal to which we can only more or less approximate.

Complete emotional and intellectual mastery, in the sense of a full inventory, must not be expected, if only because a definite time, which, however, we cannot define, is required in order to master an experience. Reminiscence only throws what we may call narrow emergency bridges across the gulf of that time interval. The neurotic symptoms are, in this sense, compromises between a tendency to forget and the opposite tendency to remember certain impressions. In one of the plays of the Viennese writer, J. N. Nestroy, a man is asked why he always carries a cane. He answers, "I carry this cane in eternal memory of a girl whom I never want to think of again." That is precisely the nature of the neurotic symptoms.

If I have rightly understood the function of reminiscence (or rather one of its functions) it cannot be difficult to compare it with another phenomenon that we often find described in analytic literature as its precise opposite. Repetition-compulsions take the place of the impulse to reminiscence, as Freud once observed. We may regard it as a successful effect of analysis when conscious reminiscence replaces this tendency to repetition. In cases where repetition occurs in place of reminiscence we have regression, a return to a more primitive way of mastering experience.

The compulsion to repeat is the earlier, archaic attempt to dispatch our experiences. The tendency to reminiscence is a later, more spiritual form of the same attempt. When we persuade the patient to proceed from action to reminiscence, we are trying to lead him from an infantile method to one that came later in evolution and is more rational and comprehensible to us. But we know that the attempt is not always successful, because sometimes reminiscence proves inadequate when confronted with the strength of experiences. That we can understand, because reminiscence is so much more remote from reality than a repetition of experience; it is only a blurred copy of it. Analysts know a number of situations representing a blend of repetition and reminiscence, processes between *souvenir* and *recréation du passé*. A simpler example is that of patients who show great excitement and make it plain that they are occupied with a certain experience without being able to tell what it is. Perhaps they say, "I should like to beat somebody," or, "I feel like screaming." They feel sulky or tearful and inclined to perform senseless or eccentric actions. Often the reminiscence of the experience that stirred these impulses occurs later on.

A child tries to keep abreast of the impressions that flow in upon it by obeying the tendency to reproduce them. Adults try to dispatch them by means of reminiscence. We know that the value of such a general statement is merely relative. It is only true within limits. That is shown by the fact that adults remain grown-up children. Freud's account of a child who played out the disappearance of his mother is a typical example of the way in which, at an early stage, the attempt is made to master experience by means of action. It may be that, as Wälder has shown to be probable, all children's play serves such purposes.

Children evince an unwearying impulse to repeat the same impressions unchanged—for instance, to hear the same fairy tale with the same words again and again—and they do not at first want to have a "reminiscence" of their impressions, but to master them. A system of education rightly influenced by psychology should be able to derive valuable guidance and new ideas from the realization of these facts. At quite an early age mental processes occur that show how the tendency to repetition blends into the other, newly arising way of mastering experience, that of reminiscence. Thus one patient remembered from his early boyhood the special manner in which he confronted surprising, or merely new impressions. For instance, he heard an unaccustomed word at play or saw something new that made an impression upon him. He still remembers how he said the new word to himself or imitated the action, if only sketchily, and resolved to repeat the process before he went to sleep. And before the child fell asleep he lay quietly for some time and repeated the word several times to himself or pictured the action to himself again and again. We may assume that many children at a certain age go through such an imaginary stage.

And this directs our attention to the relation between receptivity and reminiscence, as it changes with advancing years. Children seem most receptive to new impressions. A French psychologist speaks of the *cerveau de cire* (brain of wax) of children and primitive man. This remarkable receptivity may assume the character of the love of sensation. A child is curious, that is, desirous to see and know new things, *novarum rerum cupidus*. A very feeble ego confronts this receptivity, and, incapable of mastering so many new impressions, it is forced to hand over the greater part to the unconscious for later assimilation. It is not, therefore, because childish experiences are specially forceful that they are mastered later, but because it is too hard for the feeble ego to master them. In this sense, then, we must attribute a traumatic character not only to particular events but to the sum total of childish experience. This goes far toward explaining the extreme importance of childish impressions in the subsequent life of the individual.

The impression that children quickly dispatch their experiences is illusive, as any analysis may prove to us. The infantile mind works like a coarse sieve, letting through a number of impressions in order to re-examine and dispatch them later. As the ego grows stronger and more independent, it is better able to stand up to its impressions. It restricts the field of its attention, and, by distinguishing between what is important and what is immaterial, between what harmonizes with the ego and what is alien, it can apply greater mental energy to the mastery of fewer experiences. Thus with a finer sieve a great deal is prevented from slipping through. Old age shuts out new impressions more and more, as if it were satiated or knew that the time left to it would not be enough to assimilate newly received impressions. It is like a sieve with only a few small holes.

We can see how varying must be the significance of conscious reminiscence in these different ages. A child lives for the present; he is, so to speak, without reminiscence but, to make up for it, extremely receptive. An old man lives in his reminiscences, shut off to a large extent from new impressions. Thus receptivity and reminiscence are functionally related to one another, although here we can only throw light on one aspect of their relationship. And so reminiscence, which later takes the place of repetition, of the tendency to reproduce, not only becomes a substitute for experience but also its final phase. Appreciation of the significance of the brain's degeneration in old age does not, of course, exclude the validity of my thesis of the emergence of early reminiscences and the rejection of new impressions then. Nor does it aim at being anything more than a psychoanalytic contribution to the explanation of amnesia and hyperamnesia in old age.

Have I not already stated that an experience is not mentally assimilated until it has been often and clearly enough recalled as a reminiscence? The fact that childish experiences are so vividly and forcibly recalled as reminiscences in old age is presumably a sign that they are losing their effective significance. Perhaps we need a whole long life in order to reach some degree of psychical mastery of what we experience as children. To live in reminiscences means that we are growing old, for it means that we are dispatching earlier experiences instead of entering upon new ones. Goethe felt this in his old age: "What I possess I see as if from afar, and what has vanished becomes real to me."

I believe that the validity of this psychological theory extends beyond the individual life, and that the lasting, unconscious traces of ancestral experience are among the undiscoverable and yet effective factors determining our lives. Young nations, or other types of communities, seek sensation; old nations live in their reminiscences or traditions.

It seems clear to me that the impulse to reminiscence is not opposed to the original tendency to repeat, but is its continuation in another form. We have in it a late differentiation of the archaic repetition-compulsion. Originally reminiscence implied the attempt to assimilate an experience by reliving it in the imagination. It is, therefore, the repeated performance of a play on the stage of thought or idea, while in the earlier form of action it was really acted out again. In the psychopathology of the traumatic neuroses, which so frequently repeat the original situation, the play is performed again, so to speak, because of its overpowering effect.

Let us trace the psychological development a little farther still. Psychology distinguishes sharply between reminiscence and sense-perception. Thus, for instance, B. Wundt, in his *Grundriss der Psychologie,* points out how wrong it would be to describe reminiscences as copies of the direct sense-perceptions, weaker but in the main faithful. The two processes, he says, differ not only in their origin and intensity but also in their composition. "However indistinct we let a sense-perception become, yet so long as it is perceptible at all, it remains essentially different from a reminiscence." That, of course, is true. But the fact remains that a reminiscence is the imaginary repetition of the sense-perception. To use a good phrase of Driesch's, it is a "present experience with a finger pointing to the past."

Is the repetition that I have described as an early archaic form of reminiscence perhaps a connecting link between the sense-perception and the reminiscence? In that case it is not the sense-perception as such that is the last link of the psychological chain we are following, but the tendency to recall it to the present. At the other end of the chain we discern the sense-perception as the model of the reminiscence, for that strives to reconstitute in imagination the full sensuous force of the original perception. When we have a clear reminiscence of a particular person, we are apt to say, "I see him before my eyes," or, "I can hear him saying it." Everybody knows from experience that specially strong reminiscences may easily assume the character of hallucinations.

Reminiscence is thus an externalization. The end of the chain connects up again with its beginning. In my view reminiscence was originally an hallucinatory image of experience, and what we now call reminiscence is in general a mere faded, sketchy development of that original form. But if so it anticipates repetition or action, or rather it denotes a first phase that was, perhaps, a condition of action and rendered it possible. A little child tries to master strong impressions by recalling them in hallucination, causing them to reappear. He then reacts to the hallucination as if it were a real impression. In place of hallucination, which he later fails to produce or finds insufficient and unsatisfactory for the mastery of an experience, the tendency to revive the former experience appears in other forms, such as play and other actions that reproduce the earlier situation. The reminiscence of later days has its primitive prototype in the primary hallucination of an impression or childish experience. This later endeavor to assimilate experience is linked with the earliest, that of the baby.

I will only add one or two remarks, slightly connected with this subject. I should like, for instance, to call attention to the *economic* significance of reminiscence, hitherto inadequately appreciated. It makes room for fresh mental undertakings by clearing away the old ones. We know how important this function is in the analytic process. In this respect analysis acts as a kind of cultural spring cleaning and so hastens the necessary discharge of emotional excitation, hitherto unresolved. The evolution of our culture involves the piling up of more and more undischarged emotions, or, to refer to our former simile, an alarming degree of arrears in our correspondence. (Alarming, too, in a literal sense.) In this nonstop life, analysis works off the undischarged emotions that force their way into our everyday life and hamper us in meeting its demands—processes them so that they can be put away in the files.

There is a further economic aspect of this discussion of the relation between memory and reminiscence. It is often pointed out that the surest way of retaining impressions is to repeat them frequently; hence the importance of constantly repeating lessons we want to learn. While granting what is obviously true in this view, we must not forget that frequent repetition of something that is to be impressed upon the memory has its dangers, for, in accordance with the foregoing considerations, it will lead to emotional discharge of the thing to be learned. We must interpose intervals between learning and repetition, for accumulated repetitions weaken the memory-trace. We must forget what we want to retain, in order to possess it.

I now return to the point from which this digression started, with apologies for its length. We have discussed the genesis of analytic knowledge, and I have urged that the conjecture of repressed ideas springs from the depths of unconscious knowledge, and does not connect with our conscious knowledge, based upon theory and practice, until a later stage. We have been considering the part played by conscious reminiscence. We can now state that the impressions the analyst receives from the data offered in analysis are generally too strong and too immediate to be mastered at once, that is, in this case, comprehended. At this point we realize once more the value of Freud's counsel to give the reins to free-floating attention in analysis.

We need not strive to retain the single impressions. We do retain them, without effort. They will re-emerge from that storehouse of the unconscious, from memory, when we have need of them. Analysis is an experience for the analyst, too, and as such has its place in the general process of mental assimilation that I have described. Assimilation demands a certain distance from our impressions, and it is often not till long afterward that we can recognize their significance. Once we have a conscious reminiscence of these impressions, it is a sign that we are beginning to master them inwardly, a sign of incipient comprehension. But the psychological comprehension of people is only a special form of the mastery of the emotional excitation that they arouse in us. What if we could thoroughly understand "all people around us"? By that I mean all their motives, the whole of their nature, all their actions and thoughts. Then we would be lonely indeed, even more lonely than we now are when we understand so little of them and so little of ourselves.

CHAPTER XXXI

One Unconscious to Another

LET us return for a moment to the starting-point of this inquiry. What happens to the psychological data, of which, as I have said, there is such a wealth and variety? The obvious answer is that they are seized by our consciousness at the stage of observation and used for the psychological comprehension of unconscious processes. At this point criticism will immediately begin: an indeterminable number of these signals are beyond the reach of conscious observation; they never reach the psychologist's consciousness. Our corrected version of the answer, must, therefore, state that the analyst receives impressions of his subject that he uses for the purpose of psychological comprehension, although a large number of them do not enter his consciousness. Others do not reach his consciousness as such. What reaches his conscious mind are the things they point to, allude to, or announce. Others, again, are consciously seized upon by observation. Even this description cannot claim universal validity, for the psychical process in the observer is certainly not from the outset so thoroughly and markedly intellectual. In truth the inner process must be far more complicated. We can ascribe such an unequivocal, purely cognitary tendency only to one special phase.

I note with a certain envy that my difficulty in describing the process of psychological comprehension adequately does not exist for many psychologists. Faced with my problem, the expression "empathy" readily occurs to their minds and flows from their pens. Indeed, this expression sounds so full of meaning that people willingly overlook its ambiguity. To speak of empathy has on occasion been as senseless as to discuss

sitting in a box without distinguishing whether one means a compart-
ment in a theater, the driver's seat, or a big case. The word empathy
sometimes meant one thing, sometimes another, until now it does not
mean anything.

The conception has its origin in aesthetics, the theory of the beautiful,
which does not deal with life directly, but with its reflection in art.
It was not until later that it was transferred to the process of cognition
in psychology and was made, so to speak, the sole principle of psychological comprehension. It is hard to form any idea of the psychological nature of empathy, for in the controversy over the conception
the process appears sometimes as the natural, unconscious condition of
psychological comprehension, sometimes as the result of a special effort
and conscious endeavor.

As a rule the process is described as if empathy were an act dependent on the conscious will and to be performed mechanically. Thus I
read lately in a book on the psychology of criminals written for criminologists how such and such a mental process was to be imagined.
These words were added: "Of course we must be able to feel our way
into the criminal's mind." The energetic, untroubled tone of a demand
like that reminds us of the ease with which the caliph in the familiar
fairy tale changed himself into a stork as soon as he uttered the mysterious word, "Mutabor," and at once understood the conversation of
the storks, incomprehensible to everyone else. In like manner, according
to the ideas of some psychologists and psychiatrists, an observer can
change himself into various persons by a slight effort of the will. Such
a process of empathy can have heuristic significance only for the surface strata of the mind, those nearest to consciousness. But we are
primarily concerned with learning the content and mechanisms of the
unconscious.

So far as the psychical process of such cognition has hitherto been
made clear to us, its character is in general as follows. The united or
conflicting effect of the words, gestures, and unconscious signals that
point to the existence of certain hidden impulses and ideas will certainly not at first stimulate the observing analyst to psychological
comprehension. Their first effect will rather be to rouse in him unconsciously impulses and ideas with a like tendency. The unconscious reception of the signals will *not at first result in their interpretation, but
in the induction of the hidden impulses and emotions that underlie
them.* I do not hesitate to borrow the word "induction" from the sci-

ence of electromotive force, even though I am aware how little adequate it is to the much more complicated character of psychological
processes. We can now discern the instinctive basis of psychological
comprehension. In popular language, the unconscious and repressed
impulses that betray themselves by these signs act like stimuli or en-
ticements that release certain effects of a similar kind in the analyst.

Let us suppose that a patient is telling something of his life story,
and in his account he betrays the part played by unexpressed libidinous
or aggressive impulses by just such unconscious signals as I have often
referred to—his tone of voice, a pause, a movement. The secret impulses are communicated to the analyst by means of unconscious perception. The essence of what we have hitherto learned brings us thus
far. The further step that I will venture upon is this: *these unconscious
impulses communicate themselves to the analyst.* That means that the
patient has revealed emotions and thoughts without being aware of
them. These unconscious feelings are, so to speak, tentatively felt by
the analyst himself when he listens to the patient.

If this be so, the patient's latent impulses would act as a stimulus,
stirring kindred tendencies in the analyst. This account of the matter
cannot be true, or only true in the crudest sense. The thoughts, ideas,
and fantasies thus intimated are so manifold and of so peculiar a nature that they are confined to the one person, and are dependent upon
his experiences and opinions. This is true, indeed, but it is not generally the unconscious thoughts and ideas that are induced—even that
occurs sometimes, and then it strikes us, when it reaches consciousness,
as a telepathic phenomenon—but the unconscious impulses behind
them.

I was told of a little girl who was given the nickname of "Me-too."
The child reacted to everything that happened or was given to her
older brothers and sisters with the words, "Me too." And it made no
fundamental difference whether a sister got the measles, a basket of
flowers, or sweets. We react spontaneously to the unconscious signals
that betray the hidden wishes and inclinations of others to us, just as
the little girl did when she was told that this or that had happened
to her sister. This rousing of the same unconscious inclinations by induction proceeds on a different mental plane from the various conscious
observations and reflections that may occur almost at the same time,
running parallel, so to speak. It is obvious that fears, doubts, griefs can
be tentatively induced, as well as wishes and desires.

In designating the psychical effect produced upon the analyst by signals of the unconscious, I have intentionally avoided the term "identification." It is not a simple process of identification. It is said that in order to comprehend another person we must be able to imitate in our own experience what is going on in the other's mind. To me that assumption seems misleading, not because it suggests a difference in the intensity of the experience, but also because at the same time it denotes an essential difference in the quality.

I will try to indicate, by means of a comparison, the difference between the process of identification and that which I have intended to describe here. All the world's a stage; why not choose a comparison from the theater? Let us suppose that an actor is studying one of the great characters of the classical dramatists; that he imagines how, let us say, Hamlet might have felt in the scene with Ophelia. He "enters into" the mood of the prince and then acts his part in accordance with the idea so acquired. While studying it, he grows more and more into the part, and clothes it with all the passion and intensity of emotion with which nature has endowed him. I do not believe that the greatest and most convincing actors are those who apply themselves to the study of a poetical character in that way. The greatest actors do not enter into the personality of a tragic hero, but they become Hamlet, so to speak. They do not imitate his experience, they actually experience his destiny, with the help of the same psychical possibilities within themselves, and of memory-traces of their own experience.

There is, therefore, no identification, but a change in the ego taking place in the unconscious. And then what their acting expresses is the part of the ego thus transformed. We might say, a memory of what the ego might have become. They do not enter into another's feelings, but unconsciously those feelings become their own. They are not resonance chambers for alien experience; but the resonance comes from the unconscious memory and revival of their own experience. Poetry has touched upon a fragment of buried inner life, has stirred the actor's own hidden possibilities. His acting is not the reproduction of an alien destiny, lived through in mimicry, but a possibility, unconsciously experienced in the past, of his own lot, which has found a point of contact with the other's. Unconsciously sharing the experience of Hamlet, he is enabled to revert to his own experience, and strives to master it inwardly by acting out the part. This comparison certainly fails to make thoroughly clear the differences in the mental origin and in the development of the process. But perhaps it may give an idea of the emotional process, and so may be used to describe the analytic situation. The psychological condition of analytic conjecture of repressed impulses is a similar unconscious change in the ego for the fraction of a minute, together with a subsequent reversion to a former state and the power to discern our own former (transformed) ego objectively in the other person.

Does not this assumption bring us near the theory of empathy, which I have rejected as inadequate? Certainly—but only near to it. The difference will be clearer if we revert once more to a description of what goes on in the actor's mind. We have a presentiment that he has developed in his art what we have all possessed in embryo since our childhood: the capacity to share the experience of others, not *like* our own, but *as* our own. Undoubtedly that capacity was once far more active, and faded more and more in later years. And it applied not only to organic beings but embraced the inanimate world. If we recall our childish games, we must confess that it was not imitation in the usual sense; it was a transformation of the ego that grown-up people might then have observed in us. There is little of this capacity left in us by the time we are grown up. Nevertheless, we involuntarily exchange the manifestations of our own personality for those of another person when we want to depict his character. Indeed, it may be that there are hints of a change in our muscles, an involuntary variation in the tone of our voice and our manner of speech, when we speak with animation of somebody else. If I read a newspaper article to somebody else, its contents influence the rhythm and modulation of my voice, as if these latter were trying to render the events related independently of the meaning of the words. Our gestures are, perhaps, the last expression of this original transformation of the ego, but our voice also bears witness to it, even if we want only to describe objectively how high a mountain is or how terrible a storm was. All these signs still point to the animistic outlook that dominated both our own childhood and the thought of primitive peoples and of early antiquity.

The capacity to transform the ego easily and variously must have played an incomparably larger part in the early days of the human race than it does today. It is not for nothing that myths and fairy tales are full of such metamorphoses. With the disappearance of the animistic outlook and the mounting repression of instinct, civilization has caused this capacity, likewise, to shrink to a feeble residuum. Evolution is tending to suppress to a great extent not only the instinctive life itself but its form of expression as well. The history of civilization shows that this tendency, displaced as it may be, still affects our looks, our bearing, and our gestures, and goes far toward cramping all our expressive movements. A refuge for the ego, in readiness to transform itself under the influence of lust, remained in the unconscious. There, what it has lost of that capacity in the conscious mind, is still preserved. It is part of the growing tendency to suppression that dramatic art, which formerly found much freer utterance in tone and mien and gesture, is more and more restricted to mere suggestion through speech and gesture, and that, indeed, it may be losing its former cultural significance more and more decisively.

We now see clearly the difference between the theory of empathy and the genetic view here put forward; what appears in the former as the environment and atmosphere for the comprehension of other minds, is in the latter only its prelude. What in the former appears as a special function within comprehension, is pronounced in the latter to be a general psychological prerequisite.

If, after this digression, we revert to the consideration of that prerequisite and its significance for the apprehension of the unconscious, the following emotional process emerges: through induction of unconscious impulses, the psychical possibilities in the observer's ego are realized for a moment. In other words, by means of the repressed content in the manifestations of the other person, a latent possibility in the observer's ego becomes actuated for an instant. This image of the ego, turned to psychical reality, is projected into the external world and perceived as an object.

We can best compare the psychical process with the act of vision, in which a stimulus is transmitted to the brain by the optic nerve, and every ray of light is projected again into the external world. The other person's impulse, which has unconsciously roused a corresponding impulse in the observer, is seen externally like the image on the retina. The observation of other people's suppressed and repressed impulses is only possible by the roundabout way of inner perception. In order to comprehend the unconscious of another person, we must, at least for a moment, change ourselves into and become that person. We only comprehend the spirit whom we resemble. Within certain limitations, which we will investigate directly, the principle holds good in the psychology of the unconscious that only he can understand another's experience who experiences the same himself.

Thus comprehension is preceded by a reproduction of what goes on in the other person's mind. It is an unconscious sharing of emotion, seized upon by endopsychic perception. The observation of another is here diverted into observation of the ego, or rather a part of the ego, transformed by taking some object into itself. In language fitted for philosophers, we might formulate it by saying that the essential element in experiencing another is an unconscious experience of the ego. Let us admit that by this long, roundabout route we have reached the perception of a psychological fact to which the German poet, Friedrich Schiller, gave utterance more than a century ago: "If thou wouldst understand others, look into thine own heart!"

The special form in which the ego is transformed by taking another person into itself for a moment can only be called an introjection. We are accustomed to use that term to denote a permanent change of the ego in consequence of the incorporation of some object. But nothing prevents us from speaking of temporary introjection. Psychoanalysis obliges us to assume a large number of these introjections, since every important act of comprehension of repressed processes can be achieved only by means of introjection.

And then the process of introjection is followed by projection, whereby the transformed ego is thrown outward and perceived as a psychological object. This sequence—the incorporation of the psychological *Thou* into the ego and its ejection—are conditions as essential to psychological investigation and the observation of other minds as the inhaling and exhaling of breath are to the organism. They constitute the primary psychological condition for the comprehension of other people's unconscious processes.

A few remarks by way of explanation, supplementation, and correction will prove necessary after this compressed account of the psychical process. Introjection of another person into the ego naturally assumes that on the deep plane on which the object is "received" the ego resembles the object, or at least that its psychical structure is appropriate to the purpose, just as the retina is prepared for the reception of light rays. There are no psychological errors on this plane of the unconscious. The unconscious of the one person can quite well comprehend that of the other, thanks to the hidden resemblance. Psychological errors, if they take place, may be charged to the account of the agents of the *conscious* mind. Misunderstanding or erroneous interpretation of what is in another's mind generally pertains to what has been superimposed. Misunderstandings and errors of judgment about the psychology of others are due to the effects of the same unconscious forces that made us deceive ourselves about our own character and misinterpret our own actions. The same or similar motives are at work in self-analysis as in the analysis of others. Here again we are led back to the conviction of how necessary are inner sincerity and moral courage, because those are the qualities most important for the understanding of ourselves and others.

We all make mistakes of commission and omission in analysis and we are lucky if we discover them and learn from them. We then realize that we failed because we did not succeed in our tentative transformation, in taking the analyzed person into ourselves, in becoming that person. Limitations of space force me to restrict myself to the report of two simple instances which occur to me now because both belong to my analytic experience of recent days and both cases are concerned with people who have been only a short time in analysis.

A young chemist told me that he always felt somewhat relieved when I "criticized" him. Of course I did nothing of the kind; but he was inclined to take every analytic interpretation as a criticism and he knew very well that he was making this mistake on purpose. But why should he feel relieved when I "criticized" him? The only explanation at my disposal at the moment was that he was a masochistic character and the "criticism" satisfied an unconscious need for punishment. I did not communicate my view to him, but this was my interpretation. Now, although his analysis proved it was generally correct, it was wrong because it did not make me understand the special phenomenon. A few days later he told me that he felt somewhat relieved whenever his boss at the chemical laboratory discovered a slight mistake in his work. I was suddenly capable of understanding the nature of his feeling.

It seems that I understood it now not only because it recurred but also because it did not concern me any more. I understood that there was a concealed and deep guilt-feeling in my patient, which made him always expect to be "found out," that is, that his thought-crimes would be discovered. He was afraid others would realize that he was cruel, aggressive, and mean. Therefore, whenever his chief or I found some fault or mistake, he felt relieved because they were harmless and not of a serious nature, compared with the condemning, yes, annihilating criticism he unconsciously expected. He lived, so to speak, in permanent expectancy of approaching calamity, in a kind of floating anxiety. He had to be forearmed against unpleasant surprises. He differed from other young men whose thoughts were fleeting and turned to love, lust, and fame. He could say with Housman:

> Mine were of trouble
> And mine were steady,
> So I was ready
> When trouble came.

My mistake in this case can only be excused by an unconscious unwillingness to realize the special meaning of his paradoxical emotion. Self-analysis would reveal what motives were responsible for my psychological blunder.

In the second case I was ready to be contented with a superficial interpretation of a dream. A patient reported that she awoke that particular morning from a dream, but she remembered only one thing from the dream, the word "clandestine." She could not contribute anything to the dream except a remnant of the day before. Her teacher in an English lesson had spoken of the connotations of the word "clandestine" and mentioned synonyms like secret, furtive, sly, and so forth. He had added that clandestine has, in contrast to some of these words, the character of harmless secrecy. Nothing else occurred to her that might throw any light on this dream-fragment of a single word. I assumed (without saying so) that the dream had something to do with sexual thoughts or facts that she had kept secret from me, and we proceeded with the order of the day, which, in this case, referred to other events she had wanted to tell me about on the day before. She spoke of her father and her brother, but suddenly she interrupted herself and said, "I know now what the dream with the word 'clandestine' means. Of course, that's it! The word is really 'clan-destine.'" She reminded me of the fact that I had told her in the last session that conflicts such as hers have deep roots in the relations of the individual to members of her family. I had added an anecdote that Freud had once told me: he had given the same information to one of the first American patients who had undergone psychoanalysis. The man, a New Yorker, was not in the least astonished. He said, "Oh, Dr. Freud, I always knew that. We are all suffering from familiritis." He had coined a new word analogous to arthritis and similar expressions to convey his meaning.

My patient had not reacted to my statement yesterday, but she had thought of something she did not say: she knew that she, too, suffered from "familiritis" and that many of her nervous troubles had originated in her relations with her family, her "clan." Her mother had been a borderline case, near a psychosis, and her sister had died in an insane asylum. A brother was seriously neurotic. She was often afraid that she would share the destiny of her mother and sister. The dream was thus interpreted by the patient herself. As she listened to my anecdote, she had thought of the destiny of her family, which she had kept secret. Put to shame by the superior sincerity of my patient, I could now continue that the dream must also amount to a self-admonition to speak of the "clan-destiny" during the analytic hour. She had used the day-remnant "clandestine" for a play on words (clan-destine) in a manner similar to Freud's patient, who had coined the word "familiritis." Even the contrast between the connotations of "clandestine" and "secret" and "furtive" that the English teacher had mentioned now gained some psychological meaning. Here is perhaps an echo of thoughts that encouraged her to speak of her mother and sister; "clandestine" means secret of a harmless kind, her teacher had said. She need not be ashamed of those family secrets during her psychoanalysis. The "clan-destine" can be openly discussed with me.

My analytic mistake in this case is obvious enough; I should not have given up so quickly; I should have followed the slight circumstantial evidence of her day-remnants and, above all, I should have thought of the possibility of word-plays so often used in dreams. If I had, for instance, asked my patient to divide the word clandestine into clan and destine, she would have arrived at her interpretation immediately and perhaps I myself would have arrived at it later. Again, there must have been an unwillingness to put myself unconsciously in the place of the patient at the time. I cannot go into this uninteresting piece of self-analysis here. Suffice it to say that it would unearth the unconscious motives that prevented me from understanding the meaning of the dream.

These instances may perhaps give the impression that it is necessary to follow a quite distinct direction as we feel ourselves into the emotional situation of the observed person. That is not so.

In the psychology of the unconscious we have the antinomy that we best comprehend the special direction and aim of an impulse, the individual character of a psychical situation or conflict, if we trace it back to the universal and still undifferentiated instinctive element that lives its unconscious life in us all; this includes you and me.

I was watching a little boy play ball with an adult. After the child had thrown the ball for about five minutes to the man, who had been catching it, he suddenly ran away with the ball and flung it into a bush some distance off. Then he came back to the man and looked at him in astonishment, saying, "You must cry!" He meant that his playfellow ought to feel the same disappointment that he, the little boy, would feel himself, if the ball had been taken from him in so inconsiderate a manner. Psychologists will note that his behavior sprang from a mistaken and primitive inference by analogy. What interests us more than this problem of logical classification, is the question whether the child was *psychologically justified* in expecting from the adult severe disappointment and its expression in tears. Well, of course an adult is not in the least seriously cast down because he may not go on playing with a ball. But we may assume without hesitation an unconscious, or perhaps preconscious touch of displeasure because he could not go on catching the ball, as a residuum of like situations in the long-past games of his childhood. The little boy's psychological error applied only to what went on in the plane of consciousness, where the throwing away of the ball was certainly not registered as a disappointment. Applied to the adult's unconscious, which after all remains a child, the little boy's assumption was perfectly justified.

There is a further observation that must hold good with regard to our readiness for introjection. There must be a psychical readiness to take the object experimentally, so to speak, into the ego, or else no psychological comprehension of the unconscious of another person is possible. If I want to know the taste of an unknown dish that is set before me, I must at least try a mouthful of it; I must not refuse altogether to taste it. Readiness for introjection is nowise identical with tenderness or love toward the object, any more than the fact that I try a dish means that I like it. A hidden lack of readiness for introjection is often the cause of our not comprehending another person, of our inability to discern what is going on in his unconscious mind. It is not so much ignorance of the other person's unconscious as the refusal to know. To change the comparison, if I turn off my radio this evening, when it is set to receive Boston, that does not mean that there is no concert in Boston just now, but that I do not want to listen to it. But I may have turned it off without knowing (that is, without conscious intention), and may then be very much surprised to have missed hearing Boston. One consideration of a special nature is worth mentioning. People ask how it is possible to maintain any continuity of psychological comprehension, so necessary in psychoanalysis. I must reply at once that we have to draw a sharp distinction between conscious and unconscious comprehension. The difficulty obtains, of course, for conscious comprehension. Unconscious comprehension can keep its psychical continuity through all transformations of instinct, changes in the aims of instinct, and variety of instinctive expression. I have described the process as temporary; indeed, it can often be called momentary introjection, from which the ego speedily emerges. The question of the possibility of psychological continuity is easily answered by a reference to the fact that we go back to older, earlier processes of introjection on the part of the ego. In psychological conjecture a connection is established between the patient's present and his earlier experience through the analyst's going back to earlier processes of introjection, thanks to unconscious memory-traces.

What takes effect in the mind is easier to depict by means of an example. A hysterical woman patient had attempted suicide, in a way that could hardly be taken seriously, after a quarrel with her husband. This attempt had occurred before she started her analysis. She had taken a dose of poison. In her analytic session, while she was describing the scene, which dated some years back, the thought of her mother, who had also attempted suicide, occurred to her. There followed a series of associations that pointed to a disappointment in love with another man. The patient herself ascribed her attempt at suicide to her mood of despair after the disappointment, and also to her mother's example. After she had talked of other things, she mentioned casually at the end of the session that in the early days of her marriage she had really copied her husband in everything. When he read the paper, she did the same; when he smoked, she had to smoke, too. At that time she had been so much in love with him that she always wanted to do what he did. Her husband had been annoyed because she had no opinions of her own, but repeated what he said like a gramophone record; and so on. And that did not cease until she made the acquaintance of the other man. And now it must be understood as a reversion to an earlier process of introjection that the idea occurred to me that she wanted to attempt suicide because her husband had once tried to kill himself in the past. It was a fact that her husband had attempted suicide many years before. It was at the time when his first wife lay dying. He had swallowed the sputum of the consumptive woman in order to infect himself. Now a new aspect of the problem emerged. An unconscious motive for her attempted suicide appeared in addition to the reasons adduced by her that were capable of conscious realization. She was still jealous of her husband's love for the dead woman. She still copied him by showing him: See, I, too, can love another as you loved your former wife; so much that, like you, I will die if I can no longer have him. On another psychical plane she identified herself with her mother, but that does not conflict with the identification just described, for her mother, too, had married a widower and continued to be jealous of his first wife. The patient's actual disappointment in love, relating to another man, was genuine. But this love had the secret aim of making her husband jealous and avenging herself for the jealousy that she had had to suffer.

Of course we had discussed her relation to her husband fully during her many treatments, her jealousy, and so forth, but it seemed as if these strong feelings had receded when the other man entered her life. How, then, did it come about that I suddenly comprehended the connection between present events and long-past experiences? How was it that the remote inducement to her attempt at suicide, of which she herself was not conscious, now seemed to me undoubtedly the primary and more important motive? The case was that the chance mention of a past situation led to the revival of a former object-introjection in the analyst. When, a few months previously, she had told me about her behavior in the early days of her marriage, I had not estimated its full psychological significance. At that time, too, there had been an introjection on my part; but not till now, not till the present occasion, did the former memory-trace rise partially into consciousness. We have here a case of subsequent comprehension due to a reversion to a former introjective experience. Thus the question of the psychical continuity of sharing other people's experience presents no special problem of psychological comprehension. It represents a special case of the phenomenon of reminiscence based on unconscious memory-traces. And it is not specifically a question of the comprehension of other people's minds, but a question

of the possibility of reproducing knowledge that has remained or become unconscious.

The process of psychical introjection, which I have assumed, still
seems puzzling enough. If once again we trace the psychological process, this is the course of events that presents itself to our consciousness:
conscious observation of the other person, perception of his utterances
and gestures, conscious recognition of the hidden meaning contained
in them, of the latent motions and impulses at work in them. Here all
our attention is consciously fixed on the other person, and there seems
to be no room for the process of introjection. Where can we thrust it in?
Well, we know that the above account is very incomplete; it only
refers to conscious processes. And we have recognized that even in the
first stage of the process, that of taking in the psychical data, unconscious observation runs side by side with conscious. But there is another
and more significant omission in the account. We can make it good by
reminding ourselves that the stage of observation passes into another,
governed by the unconscious assimilation of the psychical data we have
taken in. The most important part of the process of introjection must
take place at this assimilation stage, even though it began in the initial
phase. But the detachment of the object taken into the ego, and the
projection of that part of the ego, must occur at this stage, for in the
next we already find the conscious assimilation of psychical processes
that seem to have their place in the other person.

If, then, we have thus determined the stage at which the process of
introjection takes place, the question arises how it comes about that it
generally remains unconscious, and that consciously we see only the
other person. The part played by self-observation in the psychological
comprehension of other people's minds is seldom consciously recognized. I am unable to give a satisfactory picture of it myself. Perhaps a
comparison will transform the situation. into one more familiar to us.
For again we are reminded òf the physiological and psychological act
of vision; there, too, only the smallest and least important part of the
processes by which we see the image—and see it as an external object
separated from ourselves—ever reaches consciousness. From another
aspect, too, a comparison with the act of vision is instructive; it is well
known that we must be at a certain distance from an object in order to
be able to see it. We can only see ourselves in a mirror or in the eyes of
another person. This peculiar fact may be cited to explain why we do
not easily grasp the part played by the ego in recognizing unconscious

processes in others. That psychological process we have still to consider in detail. Our concept cannot remain uncontested and we shall have to meet serious arguments later on. We are prepared for the worst, but we are in full swing now and no opponent can prevent us from following our idea to its consequences.

PART THREE

TWO-WAY STREET

CHAPTER XXXII

An Uncomprehended Case

I HAVE a story that makes it clear how the unconscious of the analyst himself may prove a hidden source of his failure to comprehend. I wrote an account of this "case within a case" on the evening of the day that I was occupied with it, while the impression was still fresh.

The Dutch psychiatrist, Dr. X., whom I liked, had undergone a long analysis with a third colleague and had been under training analysis with me for three months. It was 1934, and I was in Holland (The Hague), where I practiced psychoanalysis for a few years after leaving Vienna. One day he came to his session in a bad temper.

"I am getting on badly; I can't understand anything," he began, and went on to report that he had been particularly bad at comprehending what was going on in his patient's mind that day. Only yesterday, he said, he had been present at a discussion at the analytic society, and had noticed once again how far his colleagues were in advance of him and how little able he was to give analytic interpretations and explanations. It had made him mad, and in the morning his ill-humor had returned during the treatment of a lady patient, for he had failed altogether to comprehend what the woman wanted, what she feared, and so forth.

And then he began to talk about the case of this patient, as he had already done twice before during his analysis. Mrs. Anna Z. came of a family of comparatively low social standing and had been brought up very strictly. Her parents' marriage had been unfortunate. The father, a drunkard, had taken a number of pretty housekeepers as his mistresses, so that the mother, who was slowly dying of tuberculosis, was finally obliged to quit the house with the youngest daughter, Dr. X.'s patient. As a girl Mrs. Anna Z. had had no social intercourse whatever with young men. In her early twenties she made the acquaintance of a doctor much older than herself, who took a kindly interest in her and finally married her. The busy doctor, a good-natured but rather brusque man, soon proved a very inattentive husband. He loved his wife in his own way, but that was presumably not of a kind to bind her to him. During her analysis she constantly complained of his inconsiderate conduct. One of the things that Dr. X. emphasized as a mark of an inconsiderate attitude, was that the husband forced her to share his pleasures even if she was not in the mood or felt ill. For instance, one evening her husband wanted to go to the movies, but she had previously complained of feeling unwell, which he called an excuse. When she protested more and more urgently, the doctor at last made up his mind to examine his wife, and found to his horror that she was suffering from acute inflammation of the lungs.

And now, after she had recovered from this illness, a conflict arose in the woman's life that threatened to destroy her marriage and drove her, with her husband's consent, to resort to analysis. After her severe illness she had gone to a German sanatorium to convalesce and had stayed there for a considerable time. Among the doctors there was a young assistant who first attracted her notice by his beautiful eyes. She felt soothed by the friendly and confiding manner of the young doctor, who was many years her junior. And now, in our analysis-hour, Dr. X. told me briefly how Mrs. Anna had gradually fallen in love with the much younger man, and how this affection conflicted with her feeling for her husband. Her affection was the more astonishing because she spoke very little German, while the doctor did not understand Dutch. There had been no sexual approaches, but Mrs. Anna thought she discerned clear signs of love in the young doctor, too. At any rate, the conflict tormented her more and more after her return home, so that she confided in her husband.

It was during this time, too, that the first serious neurotic symptoms appeared, which induced her husband to take her to Dr. X.—the man who was undergoing training-analysis with me. On the morning in question Dr. X. said that he understood very well that the woman, repelled by her husband's lack of consideration and attracted by the young doctor's sympathetic manner, had felt drawn to him. It had the effect of a kind of revenge on her husband; he really was a remarkably unattractive man. But Dr. X. said he could not comprehend why the woman constantly complained that she could not forget the younger doctor, while at the same time she declared that she knew very well that she did not really love him and that she wanted to stay with her husband. Nor could he, Dr. X., understand how the young doctor could be a surrogate for the woman's father. The theory of analysis did not fit Anna's case. Altogether, he said, he did not understand the whole case, neither its unconscious conditions nor its purposes.

That was our starting-point. Dr. X. said that he did not comprehend how the young doctor could be a surrogate for the father of a lady so much older than himself, and I may add that I did not comprehend it either. What I did understand was that Dr. X. had fallen a victim to the danger of applying the analytic theory of the Oedipus complex mechanically and rigidly to the case, of doing violence to reality for the sake of theory. Such a mechanical and wholly unjustifiable application of analytic knowledge was itself a sign of severe latent resistance to analysis. The absurdity of it indicated Dr. X. unconsciously scorned analytic theory. When he complained that he could not comprehend how the young doctor could be a surrogate for the father, we recognized that he was mocking at the theory of the Oedipus complex, which consciously he defended. In this unconscious rejection and denial of analytic theory, we shall, I think, find the first source of his lack of comprehension.

Now instead of giving the result of our conversations—the explanation, that is, of the other emotional barriers that hindered Dr. X. from comprehending the case psychologically—let me tell how I myself made an approach to the comprehension of the patient's unconscious situation, although I did not know her and had learned so little from Dr. X.'s recitals. While Dr. X. was describing the somber aspects of the patient's marriage and giving an account of her relations with the young doctor, a question arose in my mind, and, as it persisted, I finally put it to Dr. X.: "Has Mrs. Anna any children?" He then told me that the lady had three children. I asked the age of the eldest son. He had just reached his tenth birthday. Why did I ask? I did not know when I put the question, but I realized it so promptly afterward that we must assume that unconscious knowledge of the significance of the question had preceded it. And I was able immediately to conjecture part of the secret motive force in Mrs. Anna's history, and not only to communicate it to Dr. X. but also to show him at a later stage what unconscious motives had prevented him from grasping the hidden connection psychologically.

My question was not accidental. After Dr. X. had said he doubted whether the theory of the Oedipus complex fitted this case, I told myself later I must have unconsciously understood very well the subterranean mockery contained in his words. Wherein lay the mockery? Surely in the emphasis laid upon the fact that he could not understand how the young doctor could unconsciously represent her father to a much older lady. Of course he meant the question quite seriously, but the quality of unconscious mockery was unmistakable. Every experienced analyst knows how often unconscious mockery is only a repudiated confirmation of what is mocked, that mockery merely serves the purpose of repudiation. It simply means: "I am struggling against the acceptance of what I am yet forced to admit." For the unconscious knows nothing of rejection, it cannot say "No."

I myself had unconsciously seized upon the latent mockery that found expression in the absurdity of the assumption and the consequent failure to comprehend, and had reacted as if Dr. X. had said, "I do not understand the case if I look at it from the point of view of psychoanalytic theory. There is no such thing as the Oedipus complex. It is all nonsense." I must have reacted, unconsciously, in the sense of meeting the hidden attack by proving objectively how little it was justified.

As I have said, it was not till later that I understood the purpose of my question as to whether the patient had children. I then suggested, as one possible explanation of her mysterious love and the neurosis connected with it, that resistance to incestuous impulses toward her son, who was approaching puberty, might be one of the causes of her condition. I assumed as a not too remote possibility that, when more and more unmistakable approaches on the part of her elder boy left no room for doubt as to their nature, the patient had felt and repressed a sensual impulse. But this violent rejection of an unconscious incestuous impulse was not equivalent to its inner mastery. It had persisted in relation to the young doctor, as a displacement-surrogate, and had there found a new battlefield, so to speak. Perhaps, I continued, the lady had refused to notice consciously the sexual nature of her son's approaches and in her reaction had repulsed them the more brusquely. In that case her subsequent behavior not only showed greater compliance toward the surrogate but also expressed her unconscious contrition for her hardheartedness toward her son.

Dr. X. listened attentively and respectfully to my attempt at a psychological explanation, without expressing his opinion of its credibility. His only remark, that the patient had troubled very little about her children during her stay abroad and afterward, seemed evidence of doubt. But shortly afterward, without any connection with the subject under discussion, he recalled an episode the patient had recounted to him that had occurred during her stay in the sanatorium. The woman's inner conflict did not reach its full intensity until she had offended the friendly young doctor. Once they had been talking about a modern novel, and the conversation, in spite of difficulties of language, had been carried on eagerly on both sides. The young doctor had spoken very feelingly of the description of the lovers in the book. She had answered laconically—and this not only because of the difficulty of expressing herself correctly in the foreign language: "Oh, what does love matter? Work is better." Soon afterward the doctor took leave of her, rather abruptly, she thought. After that he had been more reserved, and had not let himself be seen with her so often. He seemed to be hurt. The patient had felt very penitent for her repulse, indeed her neurosis dated from that moment, for it was only then that her depression and other symptoms began to appear. When she returned home she had said to her husband again and again that she must see and talk to the doctor once more. She did not know, indeed, what she would say to him, but the urge to see him again was strong, for she felt that she had hurt him and owed him some reparation.

It would take too long to recount here all the small signs, all the widely ramified and circumstantial data, that led me to reconstruct from the words of the colleague treating the case the psychological framework—most certainly not more than framework—of the unconscious conflict in which the neurosis had its origin. It was something like this: In the sanatorium, where she felt strange and lonely, the aging woman had unconsciously thought of her son often and with yearning. These thoughts, in which I need not prove the unconscious sexual stress, became associated with the pleasant impression that the young doctor had made upon her. They had jumped across to a second object, so to speak. Why? That we can only surmise. Anyone better acquainted than we are with the woman's inner life will be better able to account for the intertwining of her mental pictures of two persons so very different. It may be, I think, that when the mother's thoughts were occupied with her growing boy at this time, ideas of his future came into play. Perhaps she had indulged in one of those daydreams that are so typical of women: Some day my boy will look like the nice German doctor, who is so courteous and capable. It would be natural for her to think that her son might be a doctor like his father. Sometimes she may have wished in earlier days that he might become a better copy of his father. Thus her liking for the young doctor received support from an unconscious source, making it stronger and deeper. That source was the displacement of tender and repressed sexual impulses originally directed toward her own son.

Psychologically it is easy to understand that her incestuous impulse, unconsciously transferred to an alien and remote object, appeared far less dangerous than in its former direction, nay, that it even became capable of entering the region of consciousness. But it is significant that the previous mental forces of inhibition that had acted in relation to her boy asserted themselves later in her relation to the displacement-surrogate. Her relation to the young doctor was soon clouded. You see it in her reactions in the conversation about the novel, when she said, "Oh, what does love matter? Work is better," in an attempt to resist once more the tender and sensual impulse. Perhaps, indeed, these words are an echo, only slightly modified, of an opinion that her husband had once uttered to her and that she—at least consciously—had adopted. If we look and listen closely, we shall recognize in her behavior toward the young doctor at that time the repetition, modified by the circumstances, of a process that had played a great part in her inner life. A repetition that we may regard as a kind of unconscious memory of certain situations in the life of her family. She must have opposed her son's demand for love in a similar way with a remark about the greater importance of his school work. She had repulsed his tender approach in the same way that she felt preconsciously in the talk with the young doctor.

We had long conjectured that the psychologically essential part of the inner process must have lain in her resistance to her own sensual impulse, alike toward her son and toward the surrogate. We recall the fact that her neurosis dated from the moment in which she felt contrition for her repulse of the doctor and yearning for him, and wished to make up for her lack of tenderness. Is it too bold to assume that here an earlier emotional process was being repeated, and that what, for various inner reasons, could not and must not reveal itself in the original mother-son relation, came out in the displacement onto another object?

I believe that in the loneliness of the sanatorium not only her yearning for her son, which would be psychologically easy to understand, but also contrition for her occasional irritation in repulsing his tenderness had been aroused and, with it, increased fear. It is clear why these natural feelings could not enter the field of consciousness. They were mingled with the memory and revival of sexual impulses, forbidden in relation to her own son. Whereas the road to consciousness was thus barred to them in relation to their original object, no equal psychical barrier confronted them when displaced onto a secondary object. It is in keeping with the psychical process indicated here that at this time the patient troubled very little about her son and was not conscious of any longing for him.

Obviously it was not here that we looked for the ultimate causes of her neurotic disturbance. Nevertheless, by following this path we were led to the inner conflict from which, between the pressure of unconscious impulses and the failure of the compromise solution, the illness arose. It is plain that the neurosis revived old states of conflict, which we will not touch upon here. It is equally plain that secondary, unconscious purposes were fulfilled through the neurosis. I had long surmised that these included revenge upon and torment of her inconsiderate husband, as if the wife wanted to make him jealous by showing him: See, you ought to treat me as this young doctor does, and behave as considerately to me! It is equally certain that, on the other hand, tender memories of her own engagement played a part in the psychical situation, of the time when her husband was still a young doctor.

Dr. X. recounted the case of his patient in his own treatment, just as a patient recounts any part of the material occupying his mind, and at first we treated it just like any other indifferent material. I had the impression that my colleague brought the case forward unconsciously in order to show me that he, who had long been attached to one of the schools diverging from psychoanalysis, had held to his doubts even in the earlier analysis, but without expressing them. Why I had this impression I did not know, but his analysis later on proved that the impression was correct.

I should like to enter here into the technical reasons why, as a general rule, we ought to avoid discussions of this theoretical character, and in what exceptional cases it is possible to defend them. But I will only observe that I did not take up the challenge thrown at me in his words in order to cast it back at him, but to see what lay beneath it, what it was meant to conceal. There really was something beneath it; my colleague could not comprehend the case, because it touched complexes of his own. The still unconscious application to himself thrust itself in as a barrier, shutting off the psychological connection that he sought. My patient was himself father of a little boy, whom he loved dearly, and whom, until recently, he had protected from punishment and from certain unjustifiable educational experiments on the part of his mother. In recent weeks an inner change had taken place in his wife; presumably she was overcome with compunction, for now she had begun to spoil the little boy very much, allowing him to indulge in all kinds of naughtiness and showing him great tenderness. I conjectured one of the inner checks that prevented our analyst from understanding what was going on in his patient's mind. In order to understand her, he would have had to see more clearly that unconscious impulses of jealousy and hostility toward his own little son had recently been stirred in him.

His psychological comprehension was checked from another direction. Not long before, his own mother had died of a prolonged illness. In recent years his relations with his mother had been good. But he could not forget that in his childhood she had not treated him lovingly. She had often been domineering and impatient with him. In her latter years the old lady's character had undergone great changes. She had grown kinder and gentler. Her character had mellowed; it seemed as if some tension had been relaxed in her. She had grown especially tender toward her middle son, our Dr. X. At the same time she had felt a kind of pride in him, socially the most successful of her children.

Perhaps this brought Dr. X. nearer to the unconscious comprehension that there had been an incestuous element in his mother's relation to him, now more clearly discernible than ever. He came near to perceiving that her treatment of him in his boyhood had principally denoted a defensive reaction against unconscious sensual impulses on his part and on hers. And then, in the after-effects of her death and his consequent memories, together with his melancholy and tender feelings, the ancient sexual impulses tried to force their way into the son's consciousness. Their repulse was reinforced by his reaction to the obvious parallel of the relation between mother and son in his own wife and their son. That he failed in psychological comprehension of his patient's relation to the young doctor must be ascribed to the action of these same defensive forces. He betrayed a great deal to me by his unconscious mockery:

by denying one side of the Oedipus complex, he confirmed the other, which forms its natural and necessary psychological complement.

Why have I recounted this case? What purpose had I in view? We have always known that the comprehension of unconscious processes in others is checked by individual repressions, analysts will say. The case here recounted only gives further confirmation. Perhaps it will be allowed at least that it offers an exceptionally good opportunity of confirming what is already known. Undoubtedly the fact of psychological scotoma has been sufficiently recognized and appreciated in analytic theory. The expression "blind spot" has established itself in the psychology of the unconscious. That is true, yet when that convenient expression is used, it does not always imply living experience, but sometimes only what might be called a terminological deposit. I have taken the opportunity to trace once again the path leading from a scientific term to the inner reality of which it formed a convenient deposit.

I had other reasons for taking the liberty, after some hesitation, of describing this individual case. We have seen how the analytic comprehension of the case was checked because it reminded Dr. X. of certain inner conflicts, from the after-effects of which he could not escape. He brought up the case for discussion because he did not comprehend it psychologically. But the explanation of the unconscious forces that would not let him comprehend, had an unforeseen effect upon his own analysis. Some things that I had only surmised hitherto, things that were not clear to me about Dr. X. with his reserved and pent-up character, now assumed fixed and definite psychological outlines as he told me of the case he did not comprehend. May we deduce an unconscious purpose from this psychical effect? While my patient told me of the case, he told me, without knowing or intending it, of his own difficulties and conflicts. What he failed to comprehend in another's case showed, in the light of analysis, why he could not comprehend it. The unconscious self-betrayal rose from his account of the neurosis of another, which he did not comprehend and yet grasped unconsciously. I will not yield here to the temptation of entering into several problems of supervision of analysis, though they are both important and interesting.

But what about myself? Is it not a fact that certain vital inner processes in my patient did not come fully to light until he presented me with data so remote as the analysis of a person unknown to me? My patient's unconscious scorn must have embraced the secret purpose of saying to me, "I can offer you something toward a solution if I choose. You are dependent upon my good or ill will." At this point, therefore, in the surrender of part of his own data, a positive tendency was at work which appeared even in his resistant attitude.

We can trace a number of technical and psychological problems from a case like this. Is it not remarkable, for instance, that I pursued just this tactically risky path with the assurance of a sleepwalker, or, rather, of the unconscious, in defiance of all technical rules? Undisturbed by the perceptible mockery of my patient and with my attention actually roused by it, I picked out this remote case of neurosis, the telling of which appears to a superficial view as an attempt to evade important data of the patient's own case, and treated it in his analysis as if it were a part of himself. Is there not something here that we can only call an unconscious node where many threads are joined?

Psychological comprehension of the unconscious may be no more bound up with the ego than comprehension in other fields of research, but it is more dependent on the ego of the investigator. In other words, the fact that a man has his M.D., that he has successfully studied psychiatry, that he has had his training analysis, yes, even that he is a member of a psychoanalytic society—all that does not prove that he understands the psychology of unconscious processes. Music appreciation, too, can be "taught," but what a symphony says and sings can only be experienced. Whether and to what extent a man is a psychologist depends upon what kind of man he is. Psychoanalysts are born, not made, or, better still: only those who are born as such should be made psychoanalysts.

CHAPTER XXXIII

The Question of Evidence

A PSYCHIATRIST referred to me for analysis a patient he had treated in a sanatorium. In my consultation the patient, an intelligent man in his early thirties, had told me that he had become increasingly nervous and depressed last year and had to interrupt his work for a few months. He then began the first psychoanalytic session with an autobiographical sketch which reached from his childhood to the time when the present crisis came into his life. He emphasized at the beginning that he had been lucky; he had an excellent position, his marriage had been fairly good and he loved his children. His parents had made considerable sacrifices for his education. He had been successful in high school and college; especially in college, where he had made social connections that became very useful in his later life.

The father of a friend had given him a small job in the big manufacturing company in which he had a leading position. A department chief in the company asked him after a short time in the office, whether he would like to work for him. The young man accepted the offer gratefully and his work was so good that he was promoted. His patron died and was replaced by an older man, who also liked the young, efficient and well-mannered clerk. He soon became not only the assistant of his new boss but also his confidential adviser. The old man made many complaints about the management of the company and about some of his superiors, including the man who had first helped the patient to get this job. Also his original benefactor had remained friendly with the ambitious young man and had confided in him, among other things, his growing dissatisfaction with the department chief, the patient's boss.

Thus the patient was in an ambiguous situation; he had to listen for hours to complaints and accusations from both sides. Finally his boss, who was a grumbling and dissatisfied man, was removed from this office to another branch of the company and the young man was asked to take his place.

Now a strange thing happened; slowly, and at first imperceptibly, a change in his attitude took place. He began to doubt his ability to handle the position and became afraid of the great responsibilities connected with it. He felt an increasing apprehension and nervousness. Previously, if anything had gone wrong in the department, he could share the blame with others. Now he alone would be responsible. He was especially apprehensive when facing business conferences that he had to attend in other cities. His new position made it necessary for him to go to Chicago, Detroit, and other cities and to make important decisions that would determine the future sales and profits for the company. He admitted finally that he would be unable to travel. He felt increasingly reluctant to go to the office where he had to take over his new position. He was afraid to face the task that awaited him. He stayed away. At the end he refused to leave the house. The displacement and generalization, so characteristic of inhibitions and doubts of this kind, had made him a prisoner at his home. It was at this point that he had to take a long leave of absence from his office. He decided to consult a psychiatrist and landed in the sanatorium. The treatment helped him to the extent that he was able to return to his office, but his fears, though diminished in intensity, remained.

While I listened to the patient's report, I felt some hidden emotional connections. It was as if out of his tale some cues emerged, some elusive lights appeared here and there. The initial cloudiness of his situation seemed to recede in a few spots. It was obvious that the man became ill when a wish that he had nursed for a long time became a reality. He had been very ambitious and had certainly wished to take the place of the old man and thus obtain a prominent position in the company. Once before he had been promoted when a superior died. When the old man who had favored him and had confided in him left the office, he was offered the desired position. And just then doubts, apprehensions and fears emerged that made it impossible to take his new place in the office. It was as if some inner power wanted him to renounce the very aim of his wishes as soon as they became fulfilled. No doubt, I said to myself, here are powers of conscience operating in the dark.

The patient had wished for a long time that the old man who had been so kind to him would be removed from the position that he wanted for himself. He must have listened to the complaints of the old man and to the expressions of dissatisfaction of his chief with great suspense, and always with the wish that the outcome of the conflict would be that he himself would succeed his boss. And when the old man was finally removed, an unconscious moral reaction set in. It was as if he was responsible himself for the old man's dismissal, as if his own unconscious wish had the power to direct the events that led to the other's downfall and his ascent. After he had reached what he so much desired, he punished himself. He robbed himself of the fruits of his efforts because he unconsciously felt that the wish directed against the old man amounted to a mean deed, a crime in thought. He unconsciously forbade himself to enjoy his successes, he condemned himself to a kind of house arrest, became a voluntary prisoner. It is strange that men become mentally ill not only when they are frustrated in their wishes but also when these wishes are fulfilled.

The patient was well aware of his ardent ambition. He freely admitted it. What was unconscious in this case was not the power of the drives, but the intensity of the moral forces that worked upon him. What the patient did not guess was that his conscience was so delicate that he could not stand having his success paid for by the defeat of another who had been kind to him. I heard him boast in that first analytic session that he had freed himself from the inhibitions that were imposed upon him by his moralistic and religious upbringing at home. He had not the faintest idea that he was like a man dancing in chains. We often meet people in analysis who proclaim how they have thrown old moral concepts overboard and we often discover that behind the official libertine the "last Puritan" emerges.

My impression that my patient broke down under the assault of unconscious guilt-feeling on account of his wishes will have to wait for proof. When I shall tell him much later what I discovered about his own hidden character, he will, I am sure, deny that his unconscious conscience got the better of him. Yet he will at the end admit that he must have thought he did not deserve the position. Doesn't his behavior already amount to an unconscious confession of his guilt in thoughts?

In one of the novels of Anatole France a Catholic priest discovers accidentally that the archbishop whom he had just visited had lied to him. The abbé is very indignant about His Eminence: "That man will never tell the truth except on the stairs of the altar, when he takes the holy wafer into his hands and says: 'Domine, non sum dignus' " (O Lord, I am not worthy.) Similarly, this patient and many like him will play hide-and-seek with themselves. The whole amount of inner sincerity they are capable of will come to expression only when they confess their sense of unworthiness.

But how can I prove that my hunch about the patient is correct? How do we generally know whether an idea occurring to us in analysis is really in keeping with the true unconscious situation of the person we analyze? Can it not be simply ascribed to the fancy of the analyst, to his arbitrary desire, or his preconceived notions? The answer is that, with one exception, there are no direct and objective criteria equivalent to those applied in chemistry or any of the other natural sciences—none, at least, of such a nature that every thinking mind must recognize them without the slightest doubt. If we mix a certain substance with another in the test tube and observe unequivocally a certain reaction, we can say positively that the original substance was such and such. There is no analogous test in the analytic process. A determined skeptic to whom we point out that, say, the explanation and analytic treatment of a vehemently repressed impulse has effected a radical change in the patient's inner life, can always retort that there is no guarantee that the change is due just to the said process. Success cannot decide the question.

Does it give us any objective surety that our unspoken psychological assumption occurs simultaneously or later to the patient—that is to say, independently? Certainly not. His mind may have been prepared for a similar idea by something previously said or read; he may have acquired his knowledge from psychological experience of other people, or, lastly, he may have conjectured our thoughts by telepathy. There is no objective, immediate, and indubitable proof that our interpretation has really hit upon the unconscious reality in the patient's mind, has demonstrated the effect of the particular impulse in the emotional result, and conjectured the repressed nature of interrelated phenomena. The sole exception which a consistent skeptic might perhaps admit would be our inferring an event, a date, a fact that we could not possibly have known otherwise. Let us suppose, by way of example, that our analytic idea represented the essential factor in the reconstruction of events having reference to the patient's childhood and that it assumed an event, of which we had no knowledge from any other source, that was confirmed afterward by a third party.

If, then, we can seldom have objective proof that our idea corresponds to the unconscious facts, would it not be better in the process of analysis to dispense with "ideas" that just come to us and simply to trust to what our assured and conscious knowledge of psychology and psychiatry tells us? What kind of science is it that goes to work with involuntarily occurring ideas and uses the unconscious of the investigator as recipient, instead of his conscious, critical reason? Has this science so little respect for empirical methods? Doesn't it overstep the limits within which reason is acknowledged as the supreme principle?

I expect these reproaches from opponents who are unacquainted with the essential character of analysis. I am more surprised when some analysts, who really ought to be better informed about the peculiar nature of their profession, fiercely attack my view of the function of unconscious cognition. Some objections raised in the discussion must be admitted to be material and objectively justified. The same cannot be granted of others, because they are based, not upon a presentation of my argument, but upon a misrepresentation. They must, therefore, be taken less seriously than their propounders would wish. Perhaps it will be best to give an example of this kind, and so to make an example of it. In a recently published criticism[1] a colleague recognizes two ways in which an analyst may err; he may make too much or too little use of the reflective reason. But my critic expresses his fear that I go too far toward the second extreme and forget Ferenczi's admonition that we should test our data logically and base our interpretive activities solely upon the results of our intellectual labors. Just as psychoanalysis leads from the intuitive grasp of the unconscious, which poets have always had at their command, to a natural science of the human soul, so it must lead to ranging analytic technique within the rational categories. My critical colleague, referring to the process described in this book, censured me severely: a technique that was supposed to be able to function without the application of rational categories did not deserve the name of analysis. He pointed out that I had quoted the saying, "To him without thought, It comes unsought" (that is, cognition). According to him I thereby reduce analysis to the level of simple people's knowledge of human nature, and rob it of its scientific character. He defends a systematic technique and blames me for recommending "the lack of all system, the absence of any definite plan." My formula is in conflict with

---

[1] Dr. O. Fenichel in the *Internationale Zeitschrift für Psychoanalyse*, 1935.

the aim of psychoanalysis, which is precisely to bring our field of research within the range of reason.

I must concede that what my pugnacious colleague has published sounds very well. It captures us by its appeal to reason and the scientific method. I must acknowledge the great skill with which single sentences are resolutely torn from their context in order to show acumen in proving them false. Again, I must acknowledge the large-mindedness with which an "as if" is ignored, as though I had never used it, and the dexterity and quickness of wit with which the technique I recommended is so reinterpreted as to seem to "function without the application of rational categories." My critic courteously refrains from saying straight out that the absence of rational categories is attributable not only to the technique in question but also to its practitioner. That is only hinted by a discreet reference to the level of "simple people's knowledge of human nature." No fault, therefore, can be found with this criticism, if we regard the barefaced distortion of important facts and the clever falsification of the essential points in my statement as harmless and incidental.

It is more material to examine the general psychological assumptions from which a tragicomical misunderstanding like this arises. We all regard reason as the supreme authority in scientific research. In the actual course of research conscious and unconscious processes of thought will co-operate in variable proportions to reach our result. In the field of analytic technique this ratio of conscious intellectual effort to unconscious comprehension of the psychical material will be special and peculiar. An analyst's real instrument is his own unconscious, which has to seize upon the patient's unconscious processes, "intuitively," as is incorrectly said.

What, then, can be the meaning of intuition in research? The word denotes immediate cognition through the inner vision. In science intuition can only mean the ability to grasp complex relations in an instant, to perceive solutions, or at least partial solutions, of difficult problems directly. Now it seems to me that the word "intuition" is incorrectly applied here, unless we explain and establish the nature of intuition psychologically. Such an explanation would characterize intuition as a form of vision, in which a hitherto unconscious recognition of certain relations forces its way right through into consciousness. This "intuitive" cognition may in a certain sense be compared with an act of perception, and it makes no difference whether its object belongs to the outer or the inner world. The essential thing is the immediate, or seemingly immediate, conscious apprehension of hitherto unconscious cognition. The gist of that cognition proves to be a repressed experience, or suppressed knowledge, of unknown origin. The unexpected reappearance of this repressed possession justifies the emotional effect of surprise, which any observer may note in himself in the act of cognition. Here we light upon a psychological factor that we have often discussed. The experience of surprise has reference to two elements in the process of cognition: that the result is apparently immediate and emerges unprepared, and that it is attended by a peculiar clarity. The decisive part played by the unconscious offers an easy explanation of both qualities. The clarity of cognition is produced by contrast with its previous unconscious character; what is essential in it was unconsciously ready and prepared.

The analytic technique of cognition of unconscious processes is marked by oscillation between the conscious and unconscious labors of the intellect and imagination. The proportion of unconscious ideas in the searching process is variable, but they always play a part in determining the result and are undoubtedly of peculiar significance. For several reasons I have here placed the realization of this unconscious element in the forefront of psychological discussion. The employment of the unconscious as a vital organ of apprehension constitutes a *peculiarity of the analytic method, which differs in that particular from other scientific methods.* There is a second reason: to the best of my knowledge, the nature of the special function of the unconscious in the psychological process has not hitherto been treated exhaustively, even in the literature of psychoanalysis. It goes without saying that I have not here paid equal tribute to the important share of conscious and rational thought in analytic investigation, for it is not peculiar to the analytic method, which has it in common with every other method. In all methods it will go far beyond the mere arrangement and comparison of the constituent parts of the material. It will be at work not only in perception and conscious observation but also in testing and verifying the ideas that arise from the unconscious, in linking them with previous knowledge, in drawing certain conclusions, in criticizing them, and, generally, in the strict examination of the psychological data.

In truth, it is no part of my intention to minimize the share of the conscious mind and purposive thought in analytic investigation. Fenichel's touching concern lest I should ignore the need of testing our data logically is misplaced, both in substance and in his manner of expressing it. A recognition of the supremacy of the unconscious as an organ of psychological perception is fully compatible both with the strictest self-examination and with continual logical scrutiny. The scientific character of the analytic method is to me so much a matter of course that there is no need to stress and emphasize and laud it again and again. It seems to me unnecessary and rather absurd to stress the fact in these days that psychoanalysis "leads to" a natural science of the human soul—heaven help us! where else should it lead?—and to seize upon every opportunity of pointing out its scientific character ("I am a natural scientist; do you recognize my colors?"). There is no occasion to be concerned lest reason should be denied its fair share in analytic investigation. There is far more occasion to fear that it may be used in the wrong place; that is to say, it may be granted an unfair share. The real danger is not that analytic technique may "be supposed to function without the application of the rational categories," as my keen-witted colleague thinks, but rather that it may apply them where they are out of place. Reason is needed even to see where it should itself be employed, and where its employment is premature or inappropriate. The analyst should be intelligent enough to realize where mere intelligence is unable to uncover secrets, and when other kinds of mental operation present the possibility of solving a problem. Truth is a woman who cannot always be wooed in the same manner.

Our enhanced theoretical knowledge of unconscious processes, gained from the results of analysis, makes the temptation the stronger. It misleads us in making use of theoretical results where only comprehension springing from the unconscious can help us; and it tempts us to content ourselves with psychological word symbols culled from what we have learned, instead of enticing us to penetrate the data of immediate experience. Other people's experience can direct our attention to certain relations, but only *our own* psychological experience proves permanently useful in analysis. To me the presentiment of a hidden association springing from the unconscious is still more productive than a certainty arising from theoretical knowledge alone. More productive, not merely for further investigation, but in its unconscious action. The patient cannot distinguish a true statement about the unconscious mind from a false one, but he has a subtle, unconscious or preconscious, power of distinguishing its nature; whether it springs from theoretical knowledge or from the analyst's psychological comprehension and sharing of experience, whether it is genuine or faked in our sense.

An anaylst is first and foremost a psychologist, and in his approach to his psychological data he must respect the separate life of the unconscious, which reveals itself, not to critical reason and purposeful thought, but just to the sagacity of the unconscious. It has a life the hidden meaning of which is discovered by these psychical forces within us; here a conscious and purposeful search rather hinders than helps. At this point a conscious knowledge of the forms in which the unconscious expresses itself proves to be of far less importance than a sensitive ear for the unspoken that is yet expressed. A knowledge of the nature and mechanisms of drives is a prerequisite for the practice of analysis, as indispensable and also as universal as a knowledge of anatomy is for the general practitioner. With that alone—let us say, for instance, with a knowledge of the mechanism of hunger—you cannot even entice a more or less intelligent and well-trained dog from the fireplace. Even for that purpose you need some applied psychology.

I have a third reason for stressing the part played by the unconscious in my account of the way we conjecture repressed processes. I want to urge that the attempt, hitherto hardly made at all, promises to produce results that may be fruitful in scientific psychology and its application. If we pursue this path farther, we are bound to reach important conclusions that throw light upon the unconscious motives and emotional drives at work, processes our psychological knowledge and judgment of other persons are based upon. An examination of conscious and logical thought, on the other hand, produces no such important results for psychology. If it is true, as Poincaré once said, that a science grows at its periphery, then we analysts may expect a peculiarly significant extension of our knowledge from the illumination of just those unconscious processes which usher in and determine our psychological perceptions.

I agree with my opponents that conscious and unconscious elements, co-operating with and supplementing one another, work together to bring about the results of analytic investigation. All that is at issue is the size of the share each takes. What is primarily at issue is the *point where the work of the unconscious should begin, and where the work of the critical, classifying, and associative activity of conscious reflection should start.* I maintain that conscious knowledge and reason should have not the *first,* but the *last,* word in the process of analytic discovery. I want to see respected the peculiar character of the unconscious method, which lies in the function of unconscious sagacity. I believe that to call in the rational functions and conscious knowledge in our *approach* to unconscious phenomena is erroneous, both as regards matter and method. Such early and premature employment of consciously logical thought for purposes of investigation blurs the special character of our psychological labors and checks the free play of associations and the emergence of fruitful ideas that draw the hidden meaning of the products of the unconscious into the region of consciousness.

Hidden meanings first reveal themselves, not to the conscious intellectual effort, but to the unconscious struggling to overcome one's own inner inhibitions—which, by the way, is no slight or negligible mental achievement. In this initial stage of analytic investigation of the unconscious mind, the wet blanket of conscious reflections and knowledge is out of place. To apply them here robs analysis of the better part of its efficacy, and *amounts to a misapplication of reason.* It puts the cart before the horse. Anyone who thinks differently about the analytic process may, perhaps, study psychology, but that does not make him a psychologist. His wealth of theoretical knowledge may, perhaps, conceal his poverty of ideas for a time, but it cannot take their place. Let critics hold that I allow too much room in the process of analytic cognition for the "unscientific" unconscious, and too little for logical thought. He who declares for the light of reason need not therefore deny the profundity of darkness.

It was necessary to argue against the view stated above, not because of its real significance, but because of its false claims. The place allotted to the analyst's unconscious labors in this account—differing therein from all previous works—is not, as my simple critics suppose, a result of my undervaluing the powers of reason. *There is less danger that analysts will be too little logical than that they will be too little psychological in their thought.* Let me conclude this discussion of principles with a quotation from Goethe, which gives beautiful expression to the contrasts that have come to light: "There is a great difference between striving to reach light from darkness, and darkness from light; between trying to envelop ourselves in a certain gloom, if we dislike lucidity, and seeking, in the conviction that what is lucid rests upon profound, hardly fathomable depths, to raise what we can from those almost unutterable depths."

I am grateful for these attacks. The necessity of meeting and examining them, and the attempt to hold my own against them, has drawn my attention to something the psychological significance of which was not previously so clear to me: the distinction between conjecture and comprehension in the investigation of unconscious processes. To conjecture is to find one or more tracks along which the mystery of the phenomenon may be cleared up. To comprehend is to examine the track, to convince ourselves where it leads, and to follow it to the point where it joins paths already familiar. Applied to our special subject, we say that to conjecture means to grasp the nature and trend of unconscious processes, to bring the instincts and psychical mechanisms lying at the back of them nearer to consciousness. But comprehension amounts to understanding them as accurately as possible in their definite significance, making ourselves familiar with their psychical conditions and aims, and placing them in the chain of cause and effect so that they are illuminated, both in isolation and in their manifold relations to other mental processes. If we conceive of conjecture as an approach to the intellectual mastery of unconscious phenomena, then we shall designate comprehension as the attainment of the goal.

We shall best reach an understanding of these distinctions if we put two or three examples side by side. A young girl undergoing analysis tells of her habit of standing in front of the mirror when she undresses before going to bed, contemplating herself for a while, and kissing both her upper arms tenderly. Nothing in this strikes me as remarkable; it is not uncommon for young girls to take pleasure in their own beauty. (The other day I read in a book on the Holy Inquisition that a young Spanish woman confessed to her priest that every evening she stood nude before her mirror and admired her beauty. She asked the holy man whether this was a sin. "No," he answered. "It is not a sin, it is only an error.")

Still, it is not quite usual for the pretty scene to be repeated every evening in a stereotyped succession of actions, and for the girl to whisper words to her reflection or herself that she cannot afterward remember. The proceeds of conjecturing the unconscious meaning of this little scene is easy; the vital element in its hidden significance occurs to me at once. It represents a particular man, or one yet undetermined, seeing the girl with her bare shoulders, being charmed by her beauty, whispering words of tenderness or sexual excitement to her, and kissing her on both arms. The conjectured meaning enables me to go on tracing the mystery of the action psychologically. When shall I be able to say that I have comprehended it? When I can recount exactly the single features of the scene and their special meaning; when I have discovered the actual or imaginary events from which it arose, the kind of satisfaction that the repeated intermezzo gives the girl, its significance for her mental state, the psychical mechanism at play; and when, moreover, I have established the inner connection with the patient's other emotional processes.

Another example: A middle-aged woman, unhappily married, showed in her daydreams distinct traits of cruelty in her character-formation. They found expression in long drawn-out fantasies in which an element of lust was markedly present. That is, a slight sexual excitement was evinced at first, rising, in the presence of certain images, to the *moment suprême*. Some of these images originated in the reminiscence of harmless little everyday experiences of her own, which were elaborated to narrative fantasies, some from the books she was reading. For instance, she had read a novel by Benoit in which the life of the farmers on the large islands of the Australian continent was described. There was an account of several Europeans going on an expedition to the interior and being captured by a cannibal tribe and tortured most cruelly. The fantasy started from the description of the various forms of torture to which the Europeans were subjected, and lingered over the torments of a farmer who was hanged by the feet from a post and tortured. There can be no doubt of the sadistic character of such a fantasy, which was accompanied by all the signs of sexual excitement. The patient herself called it a form of masturbation.

My conjecture of the unconscious meaning of this fantasy had its origin in this last image: the European hanged by the feet, head downward. My idea had reference to this particular position, which reminded me of that of the embryo in the womb. The conjectured latent meaning of the image springs from the mental picture of childbirth, which involves such great pain for the woman. Thus the still earlier masochistic pleasure in suffering appears behind the facade of cruelty. The fantasy image represents the displacement onto a man of the instinctively desired but consciously rejected situation of childbirth. Perhaps the unconscious thought will extend to the motives responsible for this displacement, of which the principle motive corresponds more or less to the idea: I wish a man might find himself in such a position and suffer such pain.

Comprehension will test this piece of interpretation, trace its separate elements, and correct or supplement it. For instance, it will establish the connection of this fantasy with the patient's emotional reaction to the birth of her youngest child. It will work back to the ideas, some forgotten, some repressed, that the patient had as a young girl about the nature of sexual intercourse and birth; and it will find how an element of instinctive cruelty is welded in these images with an unconscious feeling of guilt because of the forbidden masturbation. The psychological motive for displacement onto a man appearing in the fantasy, has still to be explained, as well as the characteristic unconscious identification of the mother (in labor) with the child, and other special features.

Another quite similar example: A young girl who was a social worker in a hospital had clearly sadistic images that concerned a young instructor (an interne in the hospital) and her analyst. She wished to see these two men in all kinds of humiliating positions—for instance, laughed at, physically tortured, and mentally incapacitated. These images, vividly painted and expressed during the analytic session, gave her emotional satisfaction. Is not this fantasy almost the same as that of the lady above? No doubt, here too the tendency to take revenge for the anticipated cruelty of men is one of its motives. Nevertheless, it would be a mistake to interpret this fantasy in the same way as the previous one. Even before he "comprehends" it, the analyst will already sense in the phase of conjecture that here is a different note—a different ratio of components, if it is permitted to use a comparison from chemistry. Much more emphasis is laid upon the shameful and the ridiculous. The physical pains occur, it is true, in this fantasy too—even the image of a man about to be hanged emerges—but they are not in the foreground. In her picturesque descriptions of the situations these men should be subjected to I sensed another motive. The two men appeared to the girl as especially intelligent, yes, even as "intellectual giants," as she later said, while she had a very low opinion of her own intelligence and considered herself a nincompoop.

Her fantasy, in which these men were subjected to humiliations and degradations of many kinds, was in reality the transformation of another, original fantasy that concerned herself. In this original version, which we had to reconstruct, she herself was badly humiliated, laughed at, and made ridiculous. As I listened to her descriptions of the subtle, and not so subtle, tortures she had ready for the instructor and myself, I remembered that she had often told me of the great efforts she had had to make in seminars and discussions at the hospital to cover up her own ignorance and her lack of intelligence. She was often so ashamed, she said, that she would have preferred to have died, but she "put up a front" and pretended to be unconcerned. Now I could guess that she inflicted these imaginary tortures of shame and ridicule on just those men who had impressed her by their intellectual achievements. In her fantasy they had to suffer the deadly feelings she had when she imagined how stupid and ignorant she must appear to them. Her cruel fantasy is thus an attempt to devaluate these highly appreciated men in anticipation of their looking down upon her. She had to degrade and humiliate them in fantasy in order to bring them down to her own (imagined) mental level, otherwise she could not have kept her self-respect. The phase of conjecture reaches this point, that is, the guessing of the unconscious meaning of her fantasies. To understand them we would have to go much farther; we would have to follow them in all their details, connect them with the life history of the girl and with her relationship to men in general, and so forth.

The difference between conjecture and comprehension in psychoanalysis can thus be compared to the finding of an object and examining it in a laboratory. The analyst is the man with the divining rod, but he has the geological and chemical equipment also. In the phase of conjecture he is ready for all flights of fancy. In his attempt at comprehension he is the examiner who insists on logic and reason, the man of now and here.

CHAPTER XXXIV

It Works Both Ways

THE analysis of another person may also lead, in a peculiar and indirect way, to the conjecture of secret processes in our own ego. Analysis of a subject outside himself makes a constant demand on the psychologist to understand himself. I have also said that it would not be possible to grasp the unconscious mental processes in the other person if we merely appropriated the other person's experience and it had no point of contact with our own.

The road to the conjecture of the unconscious part in another person's mental processes leads through the inner perception of actualities or possibilities in the ego. And this stretch of the road is itself almost wholly unconscious. Only on exceptional occasions does this part of the process of cognition reveal itself to our consciousness so that we can grasp its psychological meaning for the analysis of the subject and for our own profounder knowledge of self. I will call this process the *reciprocal illumination of unconscious happenings*.

The affective and psychotherapeutic value of the analysis of another person to the analyst himself is recognized and acknowledged even less frequently than its psychological and fact-finding significance for his knowledge of his own ego. Regarded in this light, the analytic investigation of the other person continues one's own analysis, penetrating to profounder depths. We always maintain that nobody is justified in expressing a serious scientific opinion about psychoanalysis who has not felt its effects upon himself. That involves not only his own analysis but also its continuation in the analysis of many other persons. Apart from the scientific point of view, it may claim to be of great inner value. Any analyst of long experience can confirm the statement that his analyses of others help him master old accumulations of emotion whose nature and, still oftener, intensity have remained unknown to him.

As far as I know, this therapeutic reaction of analysis has not been accorded its true significance in our professional literature. Moreover, the significance of reciprocal illumination of unconscious processes extends far beyond the sphere of analytic investigation into that of all psychological apprehension of hidden mental processes.

The literature of analysis has emphasized again and again that repressions in the analytic observer set definite limits to his powers of psychological cognition. It has not yet been pointed out how the removal of a repression in the analyst helps and deepens his psychological comprehension and what psychological surprise it leads to. A biased view has emphasized the subjective and misleading element in his own ideas. Too little has been said of how fruitful they can be, if strictly checked and repeatedly tested, in the investigation of problems that confront us psychologists.

It often happens that these ideas, rising from unknown regions of the mind, open the way to hitherto inaccessible planes of the unconscious. They succeed in penetrating to the spontaneous inner life of another. And at the same time it not infrequently happens that a subsequent realization of the origin of the idea teaches the analyst something of his own hidden processes by roundabout and hardly fathomable ways. If he knows more about himself than other psychologists, he certainly owes it principally to the analysis that he has himself undergone, but also to the analyses that he has conducted.

This deeper knowledge of the ego is undoubtedly due primarily to the analyst himself, but secondarily to the "unknown patient" whose analysis leads him back to his own problems. Here, as far as I know, is a unique case in science. Its character can best be understood when one compares it with analogous situations: the examination of the condition of a patient's heart is itself not a means for getting a better insight into the function of the doctor's own heart.

I shall show by means of a single example, described in detail, how psychological comprehension of another person passes through a point of contact with a fragment of our still unconscious ego, and that analysis of another leads secretly and indirectly to the unconscious consideration of our own inner problems, too. Nobody will expect that the road traveled should always be the same. It is in each case individually differentiated. And my example is designed to show, too, how our approach to the hidden meaning of the other's inner life is partly governed by latent processes in our own ego.

While analyzing a woman patient, an idea occurred to me at a particular juncture, which, though nowise unusual, may illustrate what I have to say if we pursue it psychologically. The patient, whose condition, according to the dominant symptoms, could best be described as hysterical neurosis, suffered among other things from accesses of rage against her children, for which there was no adequate conscious ground. The word "suffered" is the right one here, for in these outbursts of passion the woman beat and abused her children against her own better knowledge. It was striking that she had no feeling of guilt for these excesses, though she was convinced of their ill-effect. It was possible to understand this remarkable absence of any feeling of penitence and guilt only if it was taken in conjunction with another feature. After these castigations, but often too in place of a castigation she refrained from administering, she maltreated herself grossly. For instance, she inflicted considerable injuries upon herself by striking her head with hard objects. She felt no sense of guilt, therefore, because she had imposed painful punishment upon herself through these self-inflicted injuries. In studying this case I understood for the first time what I presented later on in a book as a thesis.[1] I have since confirmed it by numerous cases, although many analysts do not understand it to this day: that self-punishment and conscious guilt-feelings are almost mutually exclusive.

When, by a slow process of analysis, we succeeded in uncovering the hidden sources of her sudden accesses of rage and the reactions to them, a sense of guilt really did appear. There were several striking special features: it was her little son that the patient chastised with such ungovernable passion, a child who had become difficult to manage, certainly not without fault on the mother's part. It soon became clear that the little boy's naughtiness specially roused his mother's anger when her husband had previously irritated her or hurt her feelings. It seemed as if she then worked off her rage upon the child. Sometimes the attacks were preceded by a strong sense of inferiority. There was a similar reason for her outbursts of rage when the children had behaved badly in the presence of adults whose good opinion she valued greatly or whose criticism she feared. A second feature of these accesses of rage was that they increased in intensity as they proceeded. Once the woman had lost

[1] *Masochism in Modern Man* (New York: Farrar & Rinehart, 1942).

patience and struck the boy a blow, that very act drove her to strike him again harder and harder. Sometimes it seemed as if she could hardly stop, once the chastisement had begun. Sometimes during these crescendos of rage the thought occurred to her: "But now I could stop," or, "I can still stop"; and yet she was impelled to go on beating. It was as if the one blow she had given forced her to continue chastising the child.

In accordance with our analytic experience, we shall associate this feature, too, with the absence of a conscious sense of guilt. Indeed, we shall see in it precisely the expression of an unconscious sense of guilt. The accompanying feeling, which analysis had to supply by way of supplement, was: "Now I have done something wicked and mean; I have incurred guilt and already deserve moral condemnation. Now that I am already lost, I had better commit a crime, ruin myself and my whole life by beating the child senseless and making a cripple of him." I need hardly say that other instinctive impulses beside this unconscious sense of guilt drove her to repeat the chastisement. The term "orgasm of rage," which, incidentally, she applied to her attacks, indicates the most important element in these unconscious impulses, which I will not discuss here. The contrast between these excesses and her bearing toward her children on other occasions, which was often particularly patient and tender, was certainly worth noting.

When in the course of her analysis distinct feelings of conscious guilt took the place of her accesses of rage and self-inflicted injuries, the patient often brooded over the anxious question, what consequences her harsh chastisement would have for the inner development of her son. Another question arose, too: What would the boy think later of so cruel a mother? Would he ever forgive her for what she had done? As I listened to her lamentations over the serious injury she had done to her boy's mind, a short sentence came to my head, something like this: "It is possible for someone to beat a person violently, and yet for it not to hurt at all." I was surprised at what I had said, for I had not consciously thought of it before, much less thought it over. Whence came these words? I knew at once that I had heard them somewhere. And a few days later I realized that it had been at a performance of Ferenc Molnar's play, *Liliom*.

I had seen the play eight or nine years previously and had hardly thought of it since.[2] What was it that now made my thoughts revert to it, and why had I spoken those words? It is clear that they applied to the

[2] The report given here was first written in Holland in 1935.

question that was occupying my patient's mind. They sounded like comfort to her in her anxiety. But why did my thoughts recur just to that particular play and that sentence? What subterranean path had my idea followed?

My first glance into the workshop of the idea, if I may use that expression, struck a chord of memory from that evening at the play. I had not wanted to go to the theater, and the first pictures in the legend, *Liliom,* had not impressed me favorably. Certainly there were a few pretty and attractive scenes, which even had something of the charm of a folk song, at the end of the first act. There were a few moments of witty dialogue, and even a few that gave food for thought, but the predominating sense was one of dislike. The methods favored by the dramatist were decidedly coarse, and the effects that he wanted to and did produce were rather cheap, both in comedy and tragedy. I liked the direct characterization of the persons and the almost undisguised contrast between the scenes as little as the obtrusiveness of the feelings displayed, which frequently had an element of falsity and sentimentality. It was a mediocre piece by a capable dramatist, written for a gallery that extended to the boxes. It was—to put it crudely—trash, with a few pleasant features.

But this drama, which is really a bungling and artificial piece of work, takes a remarkable and unforeseen turn toward the end, and there is a scene in which the emotional content is certainly not artificial, but the outcome of deeply felt experience. After I had watched the pictures in this play pass before my eyes, occasionally with amusement, often with annoyance, and more often with indifference, I lived through two minutes before the curtain fell in which I felt an emotion that could not be shaken off—without knowing whence it came but divining that its echoes would long persist. Whenever the memory of *Liliom* occurred to me later—and that was seldom enough—whenever I heard or read the name, the reminiscence always came, not only of the somewhat dull evening at the theater but also of this impression, and with it a hint or sense of constriction in the throat that I had felt on that occasion. At one time, too, I had asked myself why I felt the deep emotion, and had found no answer. Was it not unique, so strong an effect produced by a few sentences in an otherwise mediocre play?

Let me recount the plot briefly: the chief character is Liliom, by trade an especially competent barker and bouncer at a carousel in the Budapest City Park. The owner of the booth, the middle-aged Mrs. Muskat, thinks highly of him not only for his commercial ability but also for very personal services rendered to her. And the servant girls, too, hungry for love, who come to the merry-go-round on their days off, like his rude vigor and his masculine gaiety. One of them, Julie, though she has been put on her guard against him, cannot escape the charm of the rough, pugnacious, defiant child of nature. She remains with him. Liliom is hardly capable of expressing his deeper feelings. Whenever he feels guilty he curses rudely and strikes hard.

As represented by his creator, Liliom is meant to hide a soft heart beneath a rough exterior. The faithful, gentle Julie is dismissed from her place on his account. The jealous Mrs. Muskat finds herself obliged to dispense with Liliom's valuable services. Poverty and care do not make him gentler. Failing in everything, he strikes Julie often and brutally. Only the tidings that she is expecting a child rouse him to exultation, which, however, he carefully conceals as a matter of course. It also makes him an easier prey to the temptation to take part as an accomplice in an assault on a bank messenger. The crime fails. Liliom stabs himself as the police try to seize him. The dying man is brought to Julie. Even now he can betray nothing of the gentler feelings that were his motive; he has hardly time to say, "Hello, my lass!" before the end.

And now comes the surprising turn to which I have referred. We accompany Liliom straight from the bier to heaven, or the suicide department of the heavenly police court. There he is no more communicative, answers questions with, "That's none o' your business," and remains defiantly seated when the heavenly clerk of the court appears, a person of heavenly patience with a long, white beard. He gives information only reluctantly and rudely. He denies being sorry for anything and shows himself defiant and impervious to gentle persuasion. He is condemned to fourteen years' purification in purgatory and led away by the heavenly policeman, from whom he begs a cigarette in a whisper. After the period of purification he is to return to earth again in order to prove his moral progress by doing some good to his wife or child.

The last picture shows Julie, now grown gray-haired, living in a little house with her thirteen-year-old daughter. Liliom appears, and behind him two heavenly detectives. He is a beggar, and talks with his daughter incognito, partly about her father. He would like to show her one or two card tricks. Then he pulls out a large red handkerchief, in which he has wrapped a star. He has stolen it for her in the sphere of supermundane purification. His little daughter will not accept the star, and shows the unknown tramp the door with great energy. He looks at her and strikes her a resounding blow on the hand in an outburst of rage. And now comes the moment when the spectator feels moved by a power that acts as strongly and incomprehensibly as music. The girl is amazed. The blow resounded, but she felt no pain. "It was just as if he'd kissed my hand." As the two heavenly detectives escort the incorrigible Liliom out into the street amid headshakings, she asks her mother, "Is it possible for someone to hit you—hard like that—real loud and hard—and not hurt you at all?" And the mother says, as the curtain slowly falls, as if remembering: "It is possible, dear, that someone can beat you and beat you—and not hurt you at all."

The question arises, why should the memory of these words, of which I had not thought for many years, emerge during this particular treatment hour. The superficial connection is clear: the anxiety of the mother who had so often chastised her boy presents the essential point of contact. But when we draw the parallel between the patient and the dramatic character, we have only designated the most superficial plane, just the crudest and most tangible of the emotional connecting links. Here, therefore, we receive not so much explanations of the psychological process as of the outward circumstances. I am less concerned with demonstrating the associative data in the thought, which are clearly visible, than in the unconscious source whence it springs and whose outcome it is. To use a metaphor, I can indeed discern the shaft leading down into the depths, and the short passage at the entrance that is half dark. But what interests me particularly is the depths where the metal is won from the ore, and the subterranean passages by which it was tapped and raised to the light of day.

Perhaps we shall have the most hope of discovering the unconscious origin of my idea if we throw the light of analysis upon the latent content of this legend among common people, and trace the plot to its unconscious core. Let us, therefore, suppose that a psychoanalyst who is also interested in the problem of artistic creation, has been present at a performance of the drama, and afterward asks himself what applied psychology has to contribute to the comprehension of the hero or of the inner processes of poetic creation.

He will recognize the hero's Oedipus complex clearly: both Mrs. Muskat, who enables Liliom to earn, and Julie, who bears him a child, represent the mother. Regarded from this point of view, the robbery and assault of the bank messenger represent a displacement-surrogate of patricide. Nor shall we overlook the effects of the castration complex. It will be easy to recognize the nature of his suicide as a punishment and atonement for the attempted murder. Furthermore, the police officers and constables, both on earth and in the higher regions, will present themselves to the interpreting analyst as representative figures of the father. Liliom's behavior in heaven is seen to be a continuation of his revolutionary attitude directed against his father. No doubt the analyst will be obliged to note the negative Oedipus complex, the original fantasies, and other effects of infantile development. He will not omit to point out that the poet's imagination is fed from these subterranean sources. I should choose to call such a way of looking at the play, the essence of which is the reference to certain emotional constellations of childhood, an analytic explanation on the plane of the complex. No doubt, such general and schematic interpretation will be considered highly satisfactory to many analysts. It is as valid—and as elementary—as A B C.

Another spectator with the psychoanalytic outlook—or the same one on a different occasion—will perhaps turn his attention rather to the particular fateful instincts that determine Liliom's life and character. It is not out of the question that he might designate Liliom as a man with an instinctively sadistic disposition, since it seems to afford him sexual pleasure to beat the woman he loves and treat her brutally. The other, complementary, and antagonistic instinct appears more clearly in the course of the plot, when the hero fails in everything and refuses or spoils all his chances. So, too, the turning of his sadistic impulse against himself, the destructive tendency that affords him a gloomy pleasure even in his own ruin. We might feel tempted to designate Liliom as a case of moral insanity. His unconscious sense of guilt, enhanced perhaps in reaction, drives him into crime and makes him go from one act of brutality to another. Various drives, alternating in strength, find expression in Liliom and break forth. No one of his aims has gained the upper hand in his inner life. He has not succeeded in effecting that synthesis in the ego which appears to be the prerequisite of character-formation. It is needless to say that instinctive impulses, hidden even from the poet, have found plastic expression, but it usually is said. The manner of regarding the play indicated here must be designated as a psychological attempt made from the standpoint of instinct psychology.

Today it is no longer possible to deny the validity and value of these analytic explanations. But today it is not only possible but also necessary to ask, whether such interpretations have more than a rudimentary character. Their psychological significance is enhanced if we penetrate deeper into the special features of the character and destiny presented, and if we trace carefully the development of the drives, as conjectured from scanty hints. For instance, the fact that Liliom was an illegitimate child and grew up without the authority of a father will not lack significance to the observing analyst today. It may have contributed something to the formation of Liliom's instinct-ridden character, and to the genesis of his attitude toward women.

I will now speak of a different manner of regarding the play, that is, as a psychologist of the unconscious processes. It does not, like those just sketched, start from conscious inferences and definite psychological assumptions, but from the unconscious assimilation of single impressions received by the spectator. Such a way of thinking and looking at psychical processes, in real life or in fiction, is something new in psychoanalysis and has not failed to arouse the indignation of my learned colleagues. It is, however, nearer to the spirit of psychoanalysis than their learnedness. The contrasting of the two ways, given here and continued in a later chapter, will speak for itself. At first sight my way appears to resemble the manner in which some critics look at works of literature. One of them, Anatole France, even called a critic a man "who tells the adventure of his soul while he experiences a work of art." There are, however, two essential features that make clear the difference between the ways of those literary critics and of the psychologist. The first is that the psychologist will observe his own emotional process in the spirit and with the means of his science. They will appear to him only as the subject matter of psychological research. The second difference is that the critic wishes to reach an artistic evaluation of the work and of its content. The psychologist wants to make an inquiry into hidden mental processes in order to arrive at new psychological insights.

I have already said that the last scene in the drama occupied my thoughts for some time after the performance. At that time I could not understand why it had moved me so deeply. Nor did my knowledge of analysis help me beyond pointing to an especially marked psychical reaction to a representation of irascible and violent impulses. And yet the memory-trace of this impression cannot have been inactive in the intervening years. After I had, to my own astonishment, spoken the words, "There are some blows that do not hurt," during the session, single ideas arose in my mind that told me, when I pursued them, what the scene meant unconsciously and what it had meant to me personally.

These ideas, and the thoughts that succeeded them, did not come all at once. They were isolated, divided from one another by intervals of many hours or days, and I was not consciously giving special thought to the play. At first these uninvited guests, my thoughts, seemed to be nothing but a continuation or confirmation of the psychological explanation or interpretation attained through the other ways of regarding the matter, from the standpoint of the complex- or of instinct-theory. But these explanations certainly did not offer any psychological information about the one surprising thing in the drama, the sudden passage to the heavenly scene and then back again to earth. Nor did they throw any light upon the last scene, the remarkable conclusion, or its emotional effect.

Here is a condensation of impressions dating from the performance that had lain passive within me for many years, together with those springing from the psychological re-examination of what I remembered, and the consequent formation of definite trains of thought. Liliom's trade, that of a barker at a carousel, pointed to the sphere of childish interests. His uncontrolled character, his wild unruliness, his rebellious and defiant attitude, his failure to adapt himself to his social surroundings pointed to the psychical conditions of his instinct-ridden childhood. The scenes in heaven, in association with his suicide, suddenly appeared to me as a typical childish fantasy, poetically recast. All at once an image of the fantasy that boys sometimes have in the years preceding puberty, when they feel themselves neglected or unjustly or unlovingly treated, emerged, detaching itself from vague and ambiguous impressions. The boy pictures to himself that he will commit suicide. Then his mother or father would reproach themselves bitterly. Then they would see what a good child they had lost and how unjustly they had condemned his childish naughtiness.

So that would be the unconscious core of the poet's fantasy, the latent possibility evinced as reality in the dramatic form. But would that not also indicate how the passage from earth to heaven came about in the fantasy? Of course the heaven of a child's imagination must appear as a continuation of his earthly surroundings. The Last Judgment is nothing but a slight variant of the police cell, so much feared by the naughty boy. In a typical childish fantasy the lust for vengeance upon the parents is mingled with vain and self-assertive images, bitter feelings of disappointment, and motions of love toward the parents the denial came from.

Regarded from this point of view, the whole drama appears in a new light. Does Liliom still appear to us as an adult with an instinct-ridden character, as a case bordering on moral insanity, as the barker at the carousel in the Budapest City Park? Does he not now rather appear to us as a boy who loves to ride the merry-go-round and dreams how splendidly he would perform the part of the barker? And here we find a surviving echo of childish ideas: the barker is envied partly because he can use the merry-go-round as much as he likes, without paying. His trade combines the agreeable with the useful. (As a feminine counterpart let us take the exclamation of a girl during the period of puberty: "I should like some day to have a dentist for my husband and a confectioner as a friend of the family.")

It is not, then, a criminal who is acting here, but a naughty boy who loves pleasure, yet who may, indeed, become a criminal under certain psychological conditions, for instance, very harsh or too indulgent treatment. Not an adult in insurrection against compulsion and law, but a child who does not see why he should go without pleasure and is indignant at the incomprehensible reproaches and punishments of his parents and their representatives. The boy, who is certainly a social misfit and does not know how to control his impulses, feels himself unjustly condemned and punished. Perhaps he really has boyish fantasies of a robbery to procure money. Perhaps, also, dimly lustful ideas of forbidden meetings with a servant girl, a surrogate for his mother. This fondness for the kitchen employees, also felt by the precocious boy, is accompanied by an unconscious feeling of guilt. So, too, anxiety to procure the precious money that a boy needs in order to visit the merry-go-round and for his other pleasures is sure to appear in his childish fantasies.

The essential point in the assumption here outlined is that the poet, without having the faintest idea of it, unconsciously depicted Liliom not as an adult but as a child, a defiant boy. Regarded from the point of view of this secret, unsuspected assumption, a great deal is psycho-logically illuminated as if by a flash of lightning. A vagabond and a ruthlessly egoistical fellow like Liliom is certainly well adapted to rep-resent a bad boy dressed up as an adult. The dwellers in the slums are nearer to children in their instinctive and mental life than the dwellers in more aristocratic quarters. In the pictures of this play childish im-pressions of the City Park have found a belated and vivid expression. The adult Liliom is, so to speak, the enlarged snapshot of a Budapest street Arab who is bad but not wicked, of a boy who is at once wild and kindly, whose heart is half filled with childish games, half with God. It is this element of real experience that grips the audience and gives the final scene on earth with the incorrigible and defiant ne'er-do-well something heavenly that is lacking in the scenes of the Other World.

The scene of the suicide and those in heaven fit on to the whole as the prolongation of a boy's fantasy, a boy who later became an adult and a poet, and who never knew that in his comedies and tragedies he was repeating the play of childhood, and that in creating dramatic characters he was reverting to the images of his boyhood.

It would be an error to say of the author that he was dreaming him-self back into childhood. He gave actual shape to the vision of an adult, and yet did not know that just in doing so he was dreaming himself back as a child. It is only apparently in contradiction to the above assumption that, as we are reminded, Molnar has written an obviously autobiographical book for boys, *The Lads of Paul Street*. The uncon-scious character of childish impressions, which played a part in its pro-duction, is more actively displayed in the fairy-tale world of his dramas, *The Fairy Story of the Wolf* and *The Devil,* than here. And there is something childlike in the whole fantasy of Liliom's reception in heaven and his return to earth, with its half-grotesque, half-popular ideas. It has its origin in the region where the fairy tales spring up that continue so long to influence the thinking of children and of adults, too.

In these fantasies Liliom satisfies his childish craving for vengeance, shows his grief for the denial of love, asserts his personality in defiance and waywardness, and yet expresses his penitence and the boyish love for his mother that he keeps shyly concealed—the mother who has punished him. So much, and so much that is contradictory, finds a place in the inner life of this boy, and not only this one. The robbery and assault, which strikes us as so outrageous in an adult, becomes in this light merely the realization of a childish fantasy; and the beating of the woman he loves only the wildness and defiance of a naughty and badly brought up boy, who has come to be bad, and will grow worse if he is forced to feel guilty.

When he wants to steal a star from the sky, the idea is not nearly so strange in a boy as in an adult. (But is it so strange in an adult? We are told of poets—when they are in love, it is true; and that is a relapse into childishness—that they would like to fetch the stars from heaven for the beloved. Mephistopheles points out the childishness of such desires, which know nothing of the limitations of reality:

> To please his sweetheart such a lovesick loon
> Blows bubbles in the air
> Of all the stars and sun and moon.
>
> —Goethe, *Faust*)

The result we have reached is not satisfying. The deep emotion stirred by the last scene is still unexplained psychologically. It would be in keeping with the foregoing to imagine the boy continuing his fantasy and picturing himself becoming a father some day and understanding and treating his own child much better, showing him card tricks and giving him something beautiful. That might be a description of the continuation in another direction of the fantasy of suicide and Liliom's journey to heaven and back to earth. Then the return to earth would be associated with a temporal transformation: the little boy has grown to a man and is now the father of a daughter. Such a supposition is not unreasonable if we compare it with other childish fantasies, but it has no great inner probability.

At this point a fresh analytic idea threw light on the problem, an idea again referring to the scene in question. There was something in it like a picture-riddle, which provoked one to discover what was hidden. In this confrontation of the three characters—Liliom returned to earth, the gray-haried Julie, and her thirteen-year-old daughter—there was something that gave my analytic curiosity no rest, and that yet I could not solve. It was certainly not striking that Liliom beat both his beloved and his daughter. Psychologically it is not unlikely that the same reactions appeared in both cases. This instinctive reaction can well be explained in keeping with our interpretation; no doubt the wild boy had sometimes struck a little girl who was not nice to him and would not play with him at once.

Slowly the whole picture is transformed. We need not abandon the assumption that, without knowing it or unconsciously, the author has portrayed a bad and yet kind-hearted boy in Liliom. Nor need we give up the hypothesis that the essence of the scenes in heaven is a late remolding of a typical boyish fantasy. We may assume that in the final scenes another, second plane appears, superimposed upon the first and still allowing a glimpse of that first beneath. The first plane has not vanished; it has only receded in these final pictures, in order to make way for other images.

But we can understand the later plane of the fantasy and its content only when it is taken as the effect of a process of reversal; if we realize that in it the same emotional data are applied in another way. That is to say, our analytic explanation, according to which the character of Liliom is, so to speak, a bad boy grown up, who, unjustly punished and chastised, avenges himself in a suicide fantasy, retains its psychological justification. We may grasp the later, unconscious application of the same fundamental psychological data, if we invert the situation (Liliom and his daughter), so to speak. It is then no longer the father, returned from the beyond, and his thirteen-year-old daughter who confront one another, but the mother, who has died, and her son of about fourteen. We have learned to understand the action of such a mechanism of inversion psychologically in the interpretation of dreams and myths.

On one plane a boyish fantasy was woven: the offended boy means to commit suicide, he will even behave defiantly in heaven, as he did on earth. He will not be impressed with God and he will say, "So what?" to the divine Examiner. Returning, he will bring his mother what is loveliest for a present. But side by side with this, or rather above it, quite a different series of images pass by, a fantasy tending in the opposite direction. This fantasy may even start from a real situation: his mother is dead. And now the little boy dreams that his mother returns to him and brings him a present from heaven.

At this point there is a break in the structure of the fantasy. It is caused by the memory arising of his former unruly and naughty behavior. Perhaps the daydreamer, starting from that memory, imagines himself being just as naughty and defiant again. His mother would strike him hard on the hand again, as she did in her lifetime, punishing him with a blow, she who was yet ready to fetch the stars from the sky for him. But here bitter knowledge dawns upon the little boy, coming late, too late: those blows did not make any difference to his mother's tenderness. They did not mean that she had withdrawn her love; they were blows that did not hurt. Here, too, an experience recalled from childhood finds expression: the child, who has so often felt his chastisement as a sign of the irrevocable loss of love, nevertheless understands unconsciously that it was not hatred that struck him, that the punishment did not break the bond between him and his mother, nay, that it never would be able to loosen it.

Now I think that we are in a position to survey the situation in which the author's fantasy originated, and to reconstruct the fantasy in its original form. It consists of two main elements. The first: a naughty little boy, often punished for his mischief and misbehavior, dreams that he becomes the barker at the carousel and that he is punished for fresh misdeeds that, accordingly, are presented as the crimes and brutalities of a man. Then he will commit suicide; even the heavenly police and the celestial children's court will not impress him. He will be sent in vain to the reformatory generally known as purgatory. And here the Promethean defiance of a Budapest street Arab rises in revolt against the educational powers.

And now the fantasy, carried thus far, takes a decided turn, signalized by definite changes both in time and place. In the last picture we have a different scene again. It is staged upon earth once more, whither Liliom has returned, but little purified in spite of all the effort expended on him. In time the action is thought of as taking place fourteen years later. Apparently the plot is continued in a straight line; in reality it goes in a reverse direction. We must assume that this reversal is itself indicated by the shifting of the place of action. That inversion has already been hinted at in the change of scene from earth to heaven. According to our interpretation of the later plane, there would be here a secret indication that it was not Liliom, but his mother, who died and went to heaven.

As in fairy tales and folk songs, it would then be the mother of whom it is assumed that she can return to earth to watch over her children and render them services in secret. Expressed in the form of a wish or fantasy: "If only Mother would return from heaven! If she came back now and beat me for my naughtiness again, it would not hurt me at all; it would be like a caress. For, after all, she loved me." Indeed, the wish to have his mother back again may perhaps be represented here by the wish: if only she would beat me again! It is at once the expression of comprehension after the event and a plea for forgiveness. Thus the turn in the play corresponds to an affective inversion, an emotion turned about and intensified in reaction. The boy, hitherto so wild and defiant, bows his head in sorrow and yearning as he remembers his mother, with whom he was often angry because she punished him.

That other plane, which I have here raised from its latent condition, undoubtedly permeates the whole plot. The boy suffers from his mother's harsh punishments, and grows up amidst privations as the illegitimate son of a servant girl. In the manifest action, on the contrary, Julie is ill-treated by Liliom.

Here, then, must be the hidden cause of the emotion stirred by this final scene; and, further, in our assurance of the bond between mother and child, which remains indissoluble in spite of the pain they are bound to give one another.

Thus not only the characters but also the plot appear to be the outcome of a far-reaching unconscious effort at condensation and distortion of the original content. It was assisted by the possibility of deep-rooted identification suggested by the relation of mother and son. In this, perhaps the serenest of human relations, there is comprehension that we may almost call telepathic, enabling each to grasp the hidden meaning of the mental processes in the other immediately, in spite of all conscious misunderstandings. Thus the mother can comprehend unconsciously that even in her son's naughtiness there lies concealed a secret courting of her love. She lets the little boy know unconsciously that even in her denial of love, resistance to the mother's own claim to love is at work, that even her angry scolding and punishment do not exclude, but include, undying tenderness toward her child.

CHAPTER XXXV

The Roundabout Way to the Self

T HE deep emotion I felt in the last scene of Molnar's play, now seems almost accounted for. My solution thus far is, indeed general. It only tells us that it was the latent effective content of the scene, the content that we have been able to reconstruct, that roused such strong feelings. Hitherto our inquiry has only produced the explanation of a common emotional event in which the individual participates. It does not answer other questions. Why did the reminiscence of the scene thrust itself upon me at this juncture, and what did it mean to me? But we would not be satisfied with the banal statement that the idea just fitted the question asked by my patient, represented a reaction to her lamentations, and had the analytic meaning of reassurance. Not only the superficial character of the statement prevents us; a merely external conception like that is also refuted by our conviction that every detail of our mental processes is determined throughout.

How did the idea happen to come up? Assume that the patient's words, what she said and what she left unsaid, acted upon me as a stimulus. She stirred ancient emotions that lay hidden in me. What emotions? I was trying to recapture and reconstruct their development by applying the method of free association. Now a few fleeting images presented themselves to my inner perception. All sorts of things emerged from the darkness, until the image of my son Arthur thrust itself into the center of the picture, clearer than the rest. The events of recent weeks that had occupied my thoughts vividly now appeared among my associations. Some little time before the analytic treatment

in question, Arthur had gone to Palestine to try his chances for a profession. (The events of this chapter and the preceding one took place
in 1935.) In recent years he had been obliged to change his school and
his course of study several times because of our repeated moves. After
we left Berlin, he had passed matriculation examinations in Vienna,
and then came at once to our new home in Holland. There he had
begun to study medicine, which, however, soon proved impracticable.

In these latter years I had been very much dissatisfied with him. He
had seemed to me to take life too easily and to neglect his studies for
his pleasures and social engagements. I had been constantly obliged to
remind him of our reduced circumstances and of the serious and uncertain character of the disturbed times. As an only, and certainly a
spoiled, child, he had been displaying a careless and thoughtless attitude, and far too little energy, to my mind. He had been working too
little and too negligently. And it had seemed to me that he did not
take my admonitions, to which he listened in silence, seriously enough.
But on his long journey and in the distant country, to my great and
joyful surprise, he showed an unusual degree of energy and prudence,
acted with wisdom and independence, and evinced a maturity of judgment and action I had not credited him with. And to us, his parents,
he was showing so much consideration and tenderness that in my
thoughts I often begged his forgiveness for having done him an in-
justice. Decidedly I had underestimated his character. I, a psychologist
by profession and, as I believed, by vocation, had judged only the external aspect of his conduct.

In the previous misunderstandings, which seem unavoidable in the
relation between father and son, a fear had arisen in my mind, faint
at first, then more and more distinct. It had clothed itself more or less
in the thought that I should die and my son, who had hitherto shown
himself so lacking in energy and practical ability, would not be equal
to the struggle for existence when left alone. (How mistaken I was,
was shown in the years following the time of the "Liliom case." Arthur
predicted that the Nazis would invade Holland, which I then considered impossible. He often showed more practical sense than his
father.)

Afterward a change took place in this train of thought, in which the
affective foundation is so clearly displayed. Arthur would not work
seriously or make any effort so long as I lived. Not until I was dead
would he begin to take life seriously, and that might be too late for

him. To an analyst who looks beneath the surface it will not be surprising that this train of thought sometimes wound up in a mood of longing for death.

Here it was no far step to recur to my own youth. True, I had never had such carefree days as my son, but I, too, had been fairly negligent at school and—except for one or two subjects that interested me—had shown only just enough zeal to satisfy the requirements of my teachers. My father, too, had often evinced anxiety for my future. After his death, which occurred only a few days before I sat for matriculation, I had plunged into my studies with remarkable zeal. In my early years at the university I worked as if I had not only to make up for lost time but also to achieve something extraordinary for my age. Without my knowing it, this compulsion to work which dominated not only my days but also many of my nights was a severe penitence, which I imposed upon myself, for the anxiety that I had given my father by my carelessness—and doubtless not only by it. It was as if I wanted to prove to my dead father that I was worthy of his love, as if I wanted to honor his name by my achievement now that it was so late, too late. Was it not an unconscious fear of a reprisal that emerged behind the anxiety lest my own son might not take his work seriously until after my death?

Is it here that we must seek the deeper reason for the strong effect produced by the final scene in *Liliom?* Was it not that unconsciously I feared a punishment for the anxiety I had caused my father, and that in the stage picture I was shown that I had been forgiven? Certainly penitence and love appear in the scene and prove victorious against the impulses of enmity and violence. Their reactive nature is demonstrated in the fact that on the stage the blow is felt as a caress and has become the expression of a mixed impulse.

Now that my son had become energetic and competent, he had not only allayed my fears for his success in life, but also undermined the secret apprehensions lest I must die in order to make way for him. I must beg his pardon, too, for my lack of confidence in him and my underestimation of his character. But he, I hope, will not resent my many admonitions and the largely undeserved reproaches; for he knows that I love him in spite of all. As in the figure of Liliom, so, too, in these thoughts we detect a high grade of psychical condensation. Now that I myself feel the anxieties of a father and have a sense of rapidly growing old, I begin to understand my own father better, his anxiety on my behalf, his distress at my laziness, his reproaches, which often seemed to me superfluous or unjust at the time. (I am inclined to think that these sentences mark only the beginning of my understanding of my father's character and that the twelve years since then have made this understanding deeper and more intimate. Also another insight in the meantime became clearer through self-analysis and analysis of others. It is the psychological acknowledgment, not to be found in psychoanalytic literature, that one of the roots of ambition is the wish to obtain the approval and appreciation of the father, or his substitute. Later on this wish will be displaced to teachers, to public opinion, and even to the nation or the world. Upon reaching middle and old age, the character of ambition seems to return again to the circle of the family. Now the wish is to be appreciated and remembered by one's children.)

A few days after these reflections or reminiscences, I was forced to realize that the trains of thought here indicated were still secretly occupying my mind and still stirring strong emotions in me. Inwardly I had by no means done with them. The new impression at first did not seem to have any connection with the earlier ones. It seemed to be an isolated and recent fragment of emotional experience. It was only later that I discerned how many threads there were connecting this new experience with the hidden experience in the past.

In an absent mood I had opened an English anthology and run through it pages. In doing so I came upon a poem entitled "The Toys," by Coventry Patmore, a writer of whom I knew nothing. This is what he describes: the poet's little son had disobeyed his father again and again, and had received a sharp slap by way of punishment. He was sent to bed "with hard words and unkissed." Later the father went to him, fearing lest grief should prevent the little boy from going to sleep. But he was sound asleep, his eyelashes still wet with tears. On the table beside his bed he had carefully arranged a stone with red veins, a piece of glass, six or seven marbles, and two French copper coins, to comfort him in his unhappiness. But the poet prayed penitently in the night: One day, when we fight the last fight, may God reflect that our human joys are like these childish toys. He will know how little we understand his commandments. May God then put aside his anger like a father and say, "I will be sorry for their childishness."

Again in reading this poem I felt a faint shudder of emotion, as if something were under discussion that concerned me more personally than other products of the poetic art. It was much later that the application to myself became clearer to me, this time in the form of a reminiscence dating many years back. Once when Arthur was a little boy and could not yet swim well, he had gone far out on a lake in a rowboat in defiance of my repeated prohibition. When we heard of it we passed many hours in agonized waiting. When he returned home, in my agitation I slapped his face, which must have shamed him all the more because there were acquaintances of ours on the lakeside. Thus the emotion revived by reading the poem was caused by penitence and sorrow for my uncontrolled outbreak on that occasion. This, then, is the psychical plane to which the emotional effect of the scene with the forgiven blow in *Liliom* applies—the mortifying reminiscence of the blow I struck, my sense of guilt for it, and my hope that my little son would not always feel resentment against me for my maltreatment. He must have felt unconsciously how great a part my anxiety on his behalf had in causing the regrettable excess.

The inner identity between my fear that I should die soon and the thought of death expressed by the poet of "The Toys" is plain; likewise its unconscious relation to the previous chastisement of the child. The fear may very well have appealed to the death wishes of the castigated son, anticipated but secret and not consciously recognized. It is clear enough that here, as in the latent content of *Liliom*, the fear of retaliation betrays itself. In *Liliom*, too, there is a hint of punishment —of judgment in the beyond—as in the father's anticipatory fantasy in "The Toys" and, still traceable, in my own fear of death. The special emotional effect may be explained as the consequence of a sudden reassurance or allaying of an ancient fear persisting in the dark. In *Liliom*, too, the agitation stirred by the last scene presents itself as an emotional reaction to some such secret fear relating to an expected punishment for a sadistic and cruel satisfaction of instinct. The reassurance contained in the final words tells us: The subject of your chastisement will renounce all vengeance and forgive. He will sense the impulse of love even in the pain you caused him.

In all three products of fantasy—in the play, the poem, and my train of thought—parents and children appear side by side and confronting one another. Our emotion corresponds to the outbreak of loving impulse and a sense of guilt that, strengthened by reaction, have overcome the tendency to hatred and asserted themselves triumphantly over all the pain that two generations are destined to cause one another.

Both the outcome and success of our inquiry now equally urge a return to the examination of the psychical situation in which my thought of *Liliom* arose. What happened? The patient had expressed her anxiety about the future development of her child, lamented that her boy would one day harbor a grudge against her for her castigation, and told me of her doubts of how he would regard her in the future. Her lamentations and self-accusation revived in me a similar kind of memory and thoughts no longer conscious. In a kind of automatic and fragmentary self-analysis, these thoughts revealed themselves as the expression of emotions of penitence and fear because of my hostile and unjust treatment of my own son, emotions now hidden but continuing active over a long period. We see clearly the strictly determined character of the train of thought, if we accept the very likely assumption that for a definite part of the way it proceeds underground or unconsciously.

Less clear is that part of the mental process that led to my discovery of the psychological significance of my own experience. Nor is there much light in the gallery along whose devious passages the sentence about the blows that do not hurt was brought to the surface of the mind. By the process of induction, the emotion here met with *similar emotions* of my own, occurring as a reaction to certain experiences. They had never been fully mastered and they carried on a subterranean existence, betrayed by the emotional intensification of certain impressions—remember the final scene in *Liliom*. The taking of another person into the ego, which I have explained to be the primary form of comprehension, led to my grasping psychologically the unconscious processes in the other mind. For my reaction shows that I unconsciously understood the nature of my patient's fears very well, and conjectured what she herself knew unconsciously.

At a first glance we cannot but be surprised at the way taken here to reach comprehension of the unconscious processes in another. It is a roundabout way through the ego and its latent experiences, actual and potential. As a rule our own experience, which helps us to conjecture that of the other person, remains hidden. Sometimes it becomes capable of conscious realization at a later period, seemingly without any connection with what the other person has recounted. Ordinarily the most important part of our own experience is, indeed, veiled from our inner perception, and is not discovered till much later, if at all. And here the analysis of another offers an opportunity, hardly ever appreciated, of deepening our psychological comprehension of our own ego. While consciously we only see the psychological subject, unconsciously we see also our own self as a psychological subject within the former. In an earlier passage I equated the comprehension of another with a process in which the most important element is a transformation of the ego, the becoming another. We have devoured our subject—here I must say metaphorically, although there was a time when it was more than a metaphor—and so have wholly become the subject. We ourselves are no longer there; nothing of our ego is there. And it is just through such a mislaying of our ego that we may succeed in penetrating to a deeper comprehension of our own personality. Not infrequently just after careful and attentive observation of our psychological subject, a moment comes in which we no longer seek the solution of the enigma in the other, but find it in our own ego. And thus the analysis of another may lead, in an indirect sense that is difficult to describe, to enlarging and deepening our knowledge of self in a way beyond the power of our own analysis.

I must emphasize the fact that this road to the comprehension of the happenings in the depths of our own being has not yet been appreciated in its importance to psychology, not even in the literature of psychoanalysis, so far as I can see. Whereas otherwise we learn something of these hidden processes in our own ego by being ourselves the subject of psychoanalysis—that is, by being analyzed—here all conscious attention is devoted to the subject. By taking it into ourselves we learn something indirectly too of what is going on or has gone on, in ourselves. In the present case it has been clear how my own latent experience illuminated the other person's; and also how my own became conscious with the help of the other's. In the case here described there was a *psychological point of contact; my own unconscious was touched,* as so often happens at a particular stage in analysis, and this exercised a decisive influence in engendering insight into the unconscious of both of us.

The reminiscence of the performance of *Liliom,* or rather the unconscious memory-trace of it, had presumably already helped me to comprehend the patient's mental processes. She, like Liliom, suffered from paroxysms of fury; her unconscious sense of guilt and her deep dissatisfaction with herself made her more and more enraged with the very people toward whom she herself should have felt guilty.[1] When I quoted those words from the last scene of *Liliom*, I was not consciously thinking of the plot of the play, still less of its unconscious core that was capable of being grasped by psychoanalysis. But it was just that latent meaning of the scene that constituted the consolation the patient expected from me: The blows received by the little boy from his mother had not hurt or injured him so much as she feared, for he understood her very well unconsciously.

Let it be noted that in the manifest plot of the drama, in contrast with our interpretation, it is not a little boy that is beaten by his mother, but a little girl by her father. It appears strange to me now that I said the words, that there are hard blows which do not hurt, before I understood their real meaning, said them, so to speak, automatically. The utterance of those words shows that the goal was attained sooner than it was consciously recognized, nay, sooner even than it was conceived as a goal. It was not an insight occurring like any other, but rather the utterance, the signal, of something taking place in the ego, one of those processes in the ego of which it knows nothing. A train of experience from which I had not yet escaped was proclaiming itself. (Not escaped, did I say? I had not yet reached it. It was the patient's anxieties that first led me by an indirect road back to those concealed queries, doubts, and fears.)

Not till I had spoken the sentence about the blows that did not hurt, did I realize that it might comfort the patient; and it was still later that I comprehended that I had tried to comfort myself with it. But the comfort, the nature of which I did not at first recognize, had itself come to me—and even then I did not consciously understand it as reassurance— from another person who must have experienced the same emotions, arising from like sources, and had mastered them by giving them poetic form. (And the fact that his artistic labors were only partially successful indicates that they were not completely mastered.)

The psychological road I followed may, therefore, be mapped as follows: I understood the patient's experience with the help of my own, which had always remained unconscious or had lapsed into the unconscious. This experience of mine reached my consciousness by a roundabout way through a literary work, of which I was unconsciously re-

[1] A psychical mechanism that was first described in my *Gestaendniszwang und Strafbeduerfnis* ("Compulsion to Confess and Craving for Punishment") (Vienna: 1926).

minded by the patient's emotion. The author had tried to master his experience inwardly by giving it literary form. At this point we will only touch upon the question that arises, of the degree and quality of psychical energy necessary in order to master an unconscious experience, by indicating that the strong effect of the final scene in the performance of *Liliom* is the counterpart of an unsuccessful effort to master it. The fresh attempt, inaugurated by the patient's lamentations and troubles and agitating the former region of experience anew, led to a better result. Why? I guess because in the first instance the outward occasion for the revival of unconscious conflicts had been a human destiny presented in dramatic form, while in the second real life spoke to me.

If we examine the method here described, it will be seen that "the reciprocal illumination of unconscious processes" is not inapt as a designation. While I was trying to fathom the quality of my patient's mental reactions, an experience of my own was illuminated and entered consciousness. The psychological understanding that came so late and so tardily helped me in turn to comprehend much in my patient that had hitherto been only dimly conjectured. If we examine the part played by the effect of the final scene in *Liliom,* we shall see the way by which reciprocal illumination of unconscious processes comes about.

I propose to use an expression of Goethe's for this psychological process, and to call it *"recurrent reflection."* The poet speaks on several occasions of this term, which he borrowed from entoptics. In one essay he tells us that recurrent reflections "not only keep the past alive, but even raise it to a higher existence." He reminds us of the entoptic phenomena "which likewise do not pale as they pass from mirror to mirror, but are actually kindled thereby." In a letter about obscure passages in *Faust* (to Iken, September 23, 1827) he observes: "Since we have many experiences that cannot be plainly expressed or communicated, I have long adopted the method of revealing the secret meaning to attentive readers by images that confront one another and are, so to speak, reflected in one another." I believe that the same procedure that Goethe adopted for literary purposes can, *mutatis mutandis,* with necessary changes, be used on occasion in scientific psychological work, in order to "reveal the secret meaning." It will prove specially advantageous when the "attentive" observer, that is, one who is growing attentive, is himself the psychologist in process of learning. Psychology, like physics, must pay regard to entoptic phenomena.

The ego can never be known except indirectly, for it can only become an object when it is at a certain distance. There are doubtless many ways by which a hidden part of the ego can be understood. We can regard the ego as an object by identifying ourselves with an outside psychological observer, taking his place, so to speak. But we can also regard the external object as a piece of the ego, and by that indirect means reach a partial comprehension of our own inner life. Lastly, we can catch special glimpses of the self when, for instance, some event has made the ego a riddle to itself clamoring for solution. Mental phenomena that were little noticed formerly, like dreams, a symptomatic action, curious behavior in certain situations, or an obsession, may cause the ego to become a riddle to itself. Sometimes an action that formerly we had not believed ourselves capable of, one we surprise ourselves with, may have a like effect. As an example from literature I may cite the Marquise de O., who appears in a novel by Heinrich von Kleist. When the Marquise is cast off by her father and resolves to depart with her children, her own picture of herself is changed: "The glorious effort had made her acquainted with herself, and she suddenly rose from the depths into which destiny had cast her, lifted, it seemed, by her own strength." Anyone who has watched human destinies with the eyes of a psychoanalyst knows how a painful experience sometimes leads to such a penetrating knowledge of our own special characteristics, and how often people are "made acquainted with themselves" by a "glorious effort." Such acquaintance may even, on the exceptional occasion, be a pleasant surprise.

The deeper psychological meaning of what we experience is always beyond our reach; access is always forbidden to the more intimate regions of the ego. What others are and experience may often appear indistinct to us and often incomprehensible, like a map on which there are wide unexplored tracts side by side with accurately marked areas. The ego is the last Dark Continent. Assuredly we psychologists know very little of the inner life of others, but of our own we know much less. All efforts to comprehend others originate in inner perception and start with the desire of the ego to be better understood. Every psychological inquiry might bear the motto, *Tua res agitur:* "It is you who are discussed here." In that sense all psychology is a scientific, roundabout way to a deeper understanding of oneself.

CHAPTER XXXVI

Intermezzo Capricioso

TWO chapters back I suggested two ways in which the average analyst might interpret the meaning of *Liliom* and contrasted them with my analytic concept born of personal experience. I sketched how the average analyst would look at the play and its figures, what hidden drives he would recognize, and what meanings he would guess. It was admittted that interpretations of this kind have their merits and values. I added that the value is very limited compared with the discoveries that become possible when one approaches the play in another spirit—with personal impressions and the unconscious to the fore. I tried to be fair. My presentation of an interpretation on the level of the complexes and instinct-theory was, I believe, objective, and not merely critical. I drew a picture of a possibility. What the reality looks like I found in the august pages of the *Psychoanalytical Review*. Compared with my portrait, it was a caricature. What follows is a digest of a study that a well-known analyst wrote of *Liliom*.[1]

The author introduces his study with the statement: "Everything in the play tends to show that Liliom's inferiority was of a sexual nature and more definitely originating in the gonadal sphere." The reader wonders about this because he rather got the impression that Liliom is presented as quite a ladies' man—even if they were not always ladies. The analyst assures us, however, that "we see his compensatory mechanisms displayed in many ways," also in trying to convince himself of his potency. Liliom appeared to us rather unconcerned, not overburdened

[1] Gregory Stragnel, "A Psychological Study of Ferenc Molnar's *Liliom*" (*Psychoanalytical Review*, 1922, IX, 40).

with intellectual problems, but we learn here that "his fatherlessness caused him to wonder about his sexual origin." As we anticipated, this analyst also considers the barker a sadist, but he adds that he found "a clue to one of the underlying factors in sadism—gonadal inferiority. The gonadal compensation finds an outlet in the muscle erotic which on a physical basis releases tension." Here we get an insight into the deeper motives of Liliom's pinching the girls and beating his wife: it is muscle eroticism, which is an outlet of a "gonadal compensation."

You doubt it, readers? When you follow this scholarly psychoanalyst, your doubts will dissolve. He emphasizes that "gonadal inferiority" is one of the main factors in Liliom's behavior. "We know that deficiencies in the gonadal chain in the male lead to pituitary compensation. This is shown much and in various gonadal inferiorities. Present workers in endocrinology, in studying the physiological functions controlled by the pituitary have definitely proved that this gland is the seat of periodicity for the organism. Appreciation of rhythm and anything pertaining to time are controlled by the pituitary. The innate musician or poet has a well functioning pituitary." And now we see why Liliom is at the carousel: "Here we have a clue to Liliom's choice of occupation as a 'barker' and 'bouncer' on a merry-go-round. The music led him to his choice of occupation, his pituitary craving for rhythm and music being gratified. As a 'barker' his infantile eroticism and oral erotic were satisfied. As a 'bouncer' he incorporated his sadism into his occupation. As a further note of interest, Dr. Swan of Cambridge states that atrophied testicles are frequently found in men who have committed suicide." Is another concept possible? Liliom beats his wife, he becomes a bouncer and a barker, he commits suicide—Liliom suffers from gonadal inferiority which means something was wrong with his testicles. Here, readers, are the deepest roots of Liliom's character; the dark motives of his behavior are here explained and clearly presented.

He hits his daughter and she feels the blow as if it had been a kiss? What is a kiss? It is "a pregenital erotic which is an outgrowth of the suckling erotic of the infant." And that is that. What is the reason that the little girl hides her face after the father gave her a blow? "The reason she hid her face was the unconscious shame." She "associated the blow with sexuality."

While Liliom and his accomplice are waiting for the victim of their assault, a train passes by on the embankment. Liliom is fascinated and must watch the train. Why? What is there to wonder at? "He wonders about his own paternity. Who can the father be who intimidated his mother, spat upon them, and thundered by?" The train represents the father who came and was responsible for Liliom, spat on Liliom and his cast-off mother, and went away. The train in *Liliom* corresponds in this analyst's conception to the ghost of Hamlet's father. It is, so to speak the modern edition of the father's ghost. The father appears not only in the symbolic shape of a train, but a few minutes later as a policeman. "We see the father emerging from the background. He wants a picture of himself symbolically seeking his son." Liliom's attitude toward the father-policeman is, of course, an ambivalent one. This father-policeman represents the abyss "which may step between him and his object—money."

The vicissitudes of Liliom seen in the light of this analyst are interesting enough and full of fascinating features that we would never have guessed. Liliom brings a star with him when he returns to earth from the sphere of purification. The stolen star is wrapped in a red handkerchief. The audience is fascinated by this significant detail, but the audience does not know the half of it. Did you have any notion of what it means that the white star is wrapped in Liliom's red handkerchief? The psychoanalyst explains: "Again we encounter the symbolic red and white. The white for his own impotence and his daughter's purity and masochism, as the Acacia blossoms represented the mother, and the red, sadism (infantile energy) and punishment."

Is that all? By no means. An interesting point is the crimson fire into which Liliom is put for purposes of purification: "The red is a symbol for his hate, for his sadism, for his regret, for his self-punishment. Fire and water have been used from darkest antiquity as a method of purification by lustration. Certain American Indian tribes leap over burning fires at ceremonial rites. . . ." Other anthropological data follow. Liliom plunges his knife into his own heart when he realizes that escape is impossible. You think, reader, he did that as many robbers before him have done when they saw that the police would catch them the next moment? That is very shortsighted. "This final act is," we are told, "the prostration before the potent father imago—the law."

I have given here only samples of the analytic concept and the prose. I accompanied this analyst only a short part of his walk on the stilts of psychoanalytic terminology. I have shown only in extract that what should be touched gently with kid gloves is here grasped with the iron fist of schematic, streamlined interpretation.

Dorothy Parker once said that a certain well-known actress ran the whole gamut of emotions from A to B. This analyst runs the whole gamut of analytic terms from castration to the Oedipus complex. "This music mads me; let it sound no more," says Shakespeare. While I am writing this, other music is in my ear: march-motifs in three-quarter time—fortissimo—and I recognize them: Robert Schumann composed them, Opus 9. This part is inscribed: *"Marche des Davidsbuendler contre les Philistins."* ("March of the Members of the League of David against the Philistines." The symbols of David are the harp and the sling.)

The analyst who wrote this study on *Liliom* does not explain why we should be interested in this barker with his gonadal inferiority and impotence (Julie, Mrs. Muskat, and the maids in the Budapest City Park have perhaps better judgment on this point), with his gonadal compensations, with his pituitary craving for music, his infantile eroticism and oral fixation, and his sadism. What distinguishes this sexually abnormal individual from others? Why did the poet put him on the stage and why should his destiny occupy our interest? Why should he end in heaven instead of in Bellevue Hospital?

And how explain that I felt a lump in my throat when his daughter is astonished because the man hit her hard and it was like a kiss? Why did I not think like this analyst that a kiss is—after all, properly seen, in the light of an analytic textbook and looked at from the point of the libido theory—only "a pregenital erotic which is an outgrowth of the suckling erotic of the infant"? I am ready to take a solemn oath on it that I did not think of that while looking at the scene or of the "gonadal inferiority" of Liliom returning from heaven. I took the red color of the handkerchief into which he had put the stolen star for granted, and not the slightest idea occurred to me that it symbolized his sadism and self-punishment. Not the faintest echo of an idea occurred to me that the train that spat and vanished symbolized Liliom's unknown father who had disappeared after making his mother pregnant. It seems that I am especially insensitive to such fine symbolisms.

The other day a student of mine told me something that had occurred to his daughter, not yet five years old. The little girl had been unusually quiet and thoughtful during dinner. She turned suddenly to her mother and said, "But you must often talk to me, mummy, after you have died." I swear to God that this child of five, a little girl called Karen Hellmuth, was at that moment nearer to the understanding of *Liliom* than the analyst, M.D. and psychiatrist, who published a study on it ever will be.

CHAPTER XXXVII

Psychoanalysis by Rote

I T CANNOT and should not be concealed that many of the revolutionary and new insights presented in this book are the result of an inner crisis and self-examination after many years of psychoanalytic practice. Sentences like "There is no analytic technique; there is only sincerity," re-evaluations concerning the part of surprise in analytic findings, the role of the response in the analyst, the conviction that our own unconscious functions like an organ in conjecture—all this emerged out of the attempt to master a wholesome crisis. At that time I became aware that something was wrong with my way of analyzing and I tried to reorient myself by self-criticism and self-observation. There are similar instances in the professional lives of many men who are creative. Here again is an example from the development of a musician, which lends itself to comparison. When the young Bruno Walter, who had already gained prominence, came to be assistant conductor at the Vienna Opera in 1901, he very soon found himself the object of vicious attacks by the Vienna newspapers. (Mahler was probably right in asserting that they really pointed their attacks at him as the person who had invited Walter to the Opera.) At that time Walter passed through a crisis, which he describes vividly in his memoirs.[1] He came to the conclusion that he did not know how to conduct, that his "excessive watchfulness of details interfered when I had to anticipate a longer phrase or tried to satisfy the demands of synthetic interpretation." He increased this watchfulness and self-criticism at the rehearsals. "On the other hand I vetoed every bit of self-observation during per-

[1] *Themes and Variations* (New York: 1946), p. 159.

formances, forcing myself to concentrate exclusively upon the music as a whole. . . ." He tried successfully to regain his self-respect and his former firmness and strength. This double method bore fruit and led to a reinvigoration of his musical work. During his performances he now felt that he could use his growing technical accomplishments, "that I was able to insert a certain amount of critical listening and observation without jeopardizing the flow and continuity of the music." He knew then that the most important part of his struggle, the fight against his own uncertainty, was won.

My crisis was in its nature and development very similar to that described by this artist. Some aspects were almost identical; for instance, the fact that "a certain amount of critical listening and observation" could be inserted without endangering the continuity of the analysis. Out of such experiences came the most important results here presented.

When I ventured upon the declaration that the most vital knowledge acquired during analysis presents itself both to the patient and to the analyst as a surprise, I promised to take up the objections to my thesis. Even now I can answer them only in part. The most weighty reasons in support of my view could only be the product of a complete description of the inner processes of the analyst's own mind, which cannot be given. Still, I can attempt to discuss a few objections that are to be expected in particular from among psychoanalysts themselves. Psychoanalysts will point out that the knowledge culled by the analyst from the psychical data is by no means always of the nature of surprising interpretations and reconstructions, and that I am ignoring a number of consciously logical processes. That is true; but, as it seems to me, it does not in any way affect the validity of my surprise theory.

That theory states that the most important intelligence of repressed processes is, in every case of analytic investigation, in the nature of a surprise, and that in saying this we designate, not just one quality side by side with others of equal importance, but its very essence. In other words: *that the most significant intelligence received in every analysis represents the confirmation of unconscious expectations.* A house is not made of bricks alone, but also of cement, wood, and iron, etc.; nevertheless, bricks are the chief material used in building houses.

What, it will be objected, of the preparation through which so much has been learned? What of everything that theory has done to widen the analyst's knowledge and consciousness? In my opinion, we cannot warn the student emphatically enough not to approach the investigation of the unconscious mind with definite ideas of what to expect, gathered from his conscious theoretical knowledge. It would not matter if it were merely "ridiculous" to interpret every association with, say, an umbrella as a thought referring to a penis, or to "unmask" a friendly impulse toward a middle-aged lady as a recurrence of an Oedipus wish. A man who has not the courage to make himself "ridiculous" when something of decisive importance is at stake—if he does not feel within himself the intellectual independence to adhere to what he has recognized as true in face of the smiles of the cultured rabble—had better look about him for another profession.

In countless cases the interpretation might be correct in substance and yet technically erroneous, that is to say, the interpretation that is true in itself is without significance in the case under consideration. Instances of this sort illuminate the marked difference between the kind of analytic knowledge that I would call card-index science and the knowledge that springs from our own unconscious. As in the smallest things, so in the greatest: such misunderstanding, such lack of understanding of the essence of analytic knowledge will make itself felt likewise where it is no longer a case of one element in a dream, an idea, or a symptomatic action, but where our conception of the most significant unconscious intention of a neurosis is in question; and there it will lead to yet more unpleasant consequences.

I know of cases in which the analyst's investigating proceedings looked as if he had set out with the object of finding confirmation for the theory of analysis, instead of reverting to it after the case was completed. Concentrating on certain theoretically demanded points does not exclude sagacity and penetration.

The study of analytic theory resembles that of law which, as the American philosopher, Morris Cohen, asserted, sharpens the mind by narrowing it. How often we feel, in looking back upon our own cases or hearing accounts of other people's, that this card-index science pulled up the gangplank to reality too soon, that the ship put out into the ocean of theory too early. In my practice I generally become confused in proportion as I think of the analytic theory that is so familiar to me while treating a case, and I only recover my bearings in the chaos of living psychical processes.

Who today, hearing, for instance, the expression "Oedipus complex," thinks of profound agitations, of passions withdrawn from the ken of the ego, determining the life of the individual and forcing it along ways that he did not wish to tread? The designation has become a descriptive abbreviation for a psychical fact, worn flat like an old coin in everyday use. In these days, if we tell a patient from the educated classes that he cherishes unconscious desires for the death of his father or brother, we may receive the answer: "Oh, yes; why not?" And he is ready to admit at once that he wants to start a massacre among his closest relatives and friends. Such ready admission does not of course preclude the same patient, who immediately accepts an important element of the theory of analysis as fitting his case, from thrilling with pain if he thinks in a quiet hour of the possibility that his father might die, his father, so full of vitality and so beloved. The idea of his father dying, uttered in the course of an analytic treatment, and the same idea thought of at another time, may be two entirely different things. To accept the psychological existence and efficacy of such murderous wishes is not comprehension, not self-comprehension in the analytic sense. The patient has heard and read of incestuous wishes, of hatred of fathers, and of children's sexuality. Perhaps certain memories attached to these ideas have emerged in his consciousness, but such preparation makes the psychologist's work harder rather than easier. From the knowledge of the ego aspired to by analysis, it is separated by a great abyss, across which there is only *one* bridge, that of experience. Nowadays it often happens that analytic nomenclature long precedes experience, and the patient has a long time to wait before it comes—if ever. But designation ought to be something like the signal that an experience has been inwardly mastered, comparable to its epitaph, the inscription on a tomb.

Now it seems to me that a beginner in psychoanalysis is faced with a similar danger. The danger, I mean, that threatens when the appearance of complete accord between the special symptoms of a case and the theory of analysis forces itself upon the analyst at an early stage. Then he runs the danger of taking flight to the refuge of terminology, to a manner of forming our thoughts feebler and more remote from reality than any other. Of all the gains secured to us by analysis its terminology seems to me the least valuable. The designations for the subtlest and most complicated mental processes are often—with the exception of a few names given by Freud—marvelously lacking in vividness; they are like tight garments, with the mental content splitting all their seams. Many of these technical terms are hardly adequate to the idealogical content of the mental processes that they are meant to designate, and most of them are not capable of giving so much as the smallest suggestion of their emotional content.

The depth of a cognition is not independent of the way we reach it. If we do not reach it by our own way, there appears, instead of an original perception, a word from the analytic vocabulary, and we think in the clichés of the psychology of the unconscious. The fact that such knowledge is not experienced, that is to say, its profound unreality, cannot be permanently concealed by giving it a Greek or Latin name. Some analysts behave as if analysis were itself the goal, whereas it is only the way to a psychological goal. What matters is not only that the unconscious should become conscious but also that it should be recognized and felt as objective and belonging to the ego. It is not enough for the patient to know about his repressed impulses. He has to know them.

Anybody can talk for hours about an unconscious process without having more than an external consciousness of it; nay, we can even talk for hours about something that is by its very nature inaccessible to verbal expression. In analysis, too, it is possible to remain in the consciously "comprehended" periphery of experience, instead of penetrating to direct mental processes.

Analytic theory is not the fact-finding instrument for which it is often taken, and so used and abused. It is the final precipitate of intelligence received through psychological work with living objects. It is, of course, very useful to be able to observe and study dead butterflies in a case, tidily pinned and labeled, but a butterfly-case is a very poor instrument for catching the creatures. Does not this comparison tell us something more about the problem here discussed? It certainly does. Comparisons are never accidental, and this one says: You can catch objects only with tools or instruments the material of which resembles what you want to capture. Unconscious processes in others can only be conjectured by some unconscious factor in the observer himself. And, moreover, it is dangerous to apply analytic theory in acquiring knowledge because it prevents the peculiar experience of conjecturing and comprehending. The analyst arrives at a false assuredness, a pseudo comprehension. A person who values analysis only as a theory has discovered only what is good in it, not what is best. A man who feels the call to be an analyst should realize that more and other processes are involved in analysis: an emergence of secret things that were not only unspoken, but that never spoke; an encounter with hidden impulses while the ordinary business of life goes on in the upper planes of consciousness.

I maintain, therefore, that in the process of comprehension the vital difference between knowledge experienced and knowledge learned by rote holds good not only for the patient but also for the analyst—also for the analyst who, after all, has undergone the analysis. The process of analysis is not ended when the analytic treatments are at an end; its fermenting effect is not restricted to the duration of one's own analysis. We are still too apt to overlook the fact that we need time to master our experiences, and the more time the deeper their effect upon the tissues of the mind. It is this which makes the process of analysis of such long duration, but also so durable. Analysis is such an experience of profound effect, and must be surveyed from a considerable distance in time, in order to be understood for what it is. Its effects are of less importance than its after-effects. And now, when we come to the practice of analysis: it is true of analysis, as of other experiences, that we come to comprehend its meaning differently and more fully when we see it reflected in another mind, for the deeper planes of the ego can be reached only by a roundabout way, through an object. It is, therefore, legitimate to speak of the psychotherapeutic value to the analyst of the analysis of another person. *In beginning to comprehend another, we discover a clue to ourselves.*

Training in analysis can mean nothing essential to the student but the rediscovery of contents deep down in his own unconscious ego. For anyone who does not rediscover the knowledge conveyed in analysis, it is a dead science of the inner life, and the work of analysis a sort of mental exercise upon a psychological basis. One's analysis is rather the beginning of the process of rediscovery than its fulfillment. We must first stand at a distance, affectively and in time, from our own analysis; the experience must first penetrate to those depths in the inner life where it can make contact with other experiences, must first be rejected and re-emerge, before it struggles through to clarity. Unlike many of my colleagues, I am by no means delighted when a distinguished nerve specialist or psychologist declares his conviction that the results reached by analysis are right. I want to know first how deeply he can doubt, before I believe in the depth of his conviction. Novalis once said that in order to grasp a truth rightly we must have fought it.

Perhaps I can best illustrate by means of a comparison the difference between knowledge learned by rote and knowledge experienced. Suppose we go to a performance of *Hamlet*. Not only do the actors' speeches sound familiar to us; they sound like quotations. A little later we hear the same words in another performance, spoken by other actors, but they have now assumed a new meaning, touched with personality. They seem to spring from the very fountainhead of speech. And yet it is the same tragedy, the same words.

I will return, as to a dominant theme, to the statement that the essential element of analytic technique—I mean in the sense of the application of the method to a living subject—cannot be learned by rote, but only experienced. To me it seems essential that a young analyst should for once leave all "training" behind him and return to it along his own path—so essential that the roundabout way is preferable to marching straight on along the broad high road.

I shall give an example from practice that demonstrates the difference between knowledge experienced and knowledge learned by rote. It is taken from the analysis of a woman no longer young who was being treated for depression, inability to work, and a variety of other symptoms. Her relations with her husband were seriously troubled, and the marriage was on the verge of collapse. The husband and wife only talked together when it was absolutely necessary. The patient had refused sexual intercourse to her husband, whose potence was but feeble. They had had no sexual intercourse for a year. After the husband entered into a superficial intimacy with another woman, there were almost daily quarrels. The patient spoke of her husband only in words of the deepest loathing and bitter hatred. The quarrels had become more violent lately, since the two children had been sent away for the holidays and the couple remained alone together in the house. The patient, exceedingly embittered by her husband's repeated unfaithfulness and unkind behavior, had terrible attacks of rage in which she threatened to kill her husband. One evening there was a fresh quarrel in which the couple said to one another nearly everything that they had on their minds. The next day, in her treatment, she told how she had not been able to sleep for fury. When, toward morning, she was falling asleep, a mouse ran across her bed, so that she was kept awake. She resolved to leave her husband and return to her parents. During the day she so far altered her resolution that she decided to return to her parents the next morning, if the mouse ran across her bed again in the following night. When she came home from shopping about noon of that day, she found the mouse in a trap that she had set for it. She stayed.

In the interpretation of this example we will study the difference between the conception put forward by conscious knowledge, and an explanation arising from the unconscious. Let us assume that during the patient's story the analyst thinks at once of the fact that the mouse is an animal that frequently symbolizes the male genital organ in dream and reverie, in fairy tale and folklore. His conscious knowledge of this symbolism seems to penetrate to the hidden meaning of the patient's thought. We may insert this symbol in her story like the solution of x in an equation. I do not want to deny the value of such a direct translation. It may really lead to a correct psychological explanation of what the formula of the mouse meant unconsciously to the patient.

The other way, which seems to lead to the same goal, is this: The analyst had already studied the woman's sadistic and masochistic fantasies; he had watched the growing bitterness of the conjugal strife. He had long divined how the woman was suffering under lack of tenderness and pent-up sexual feelings, and how cruelly she was tormented by jealousy of her hated, and yet still beloved, husband, when she heard of his intimacy with another woman of her acquaintance. He recalled that recently the patient had complained that she could no longer love her children, and that during the absence of the children the conjugal scenes had become even angrier and her accesses of rage still more violent. At some point while he listened to the woman's stories and accusations there occurred to him a surmise of the unconscious purpose of the violent accesses of rage, for which the husband's cold behavior and his aberration provided a sufficient conscious motive. And this surmise grew to a certainty, thanks to continually accruing fresh circumstantial evidence. Unconsciously the patient wanted to regain her husband, a wish stimulated in part by what was left of her love, partly by pity for him, and partly by the desire to overcome her rival. She knew nothing of this secret wish. Her conduct seemed to tend instinctively in the very opposite direction. In accordance with her choleric temperament, the repressed wish had made use of violent outbreaks of rage to attain its end. Yet the attacks were not merely means to the end, but also its surrogate. We are reminded of the proverb that war is a continuation of diplomacy by other means. Perhaps it may occur to us that the unconscious thought was at work that reconciliation with her husband might be more easily accomplished during the children's absence, and that her rage became more violent when she failed.

Her emotional and physical craving for her husband must have reached a climax on that evening. We shall not err in explaining the subsequent sleeplessness as an expression of sexual tension. In that night the patient, like other women, was frightened by the appearance of a mouse. Her resolution to return to her parents is explained by the unconscious disappointment because her husband did not come to her that night. When, in the course of the following day, she so far changed her mind as to resolve to return home if the mouse ran across the bed the next night, too, we can well understand what the change means: unconsciously she hoped that the secret wish might be fulfilled in the following night. We may also express this thought, which was alien to the patient's ego, in these words: if the mouse, and not my husband, comes to me in bed tonight as well, then I will return to my parents. The contrast, which stands for rejection by the man, need not prevent the one object acting at the same time as surrogate for the other. And when she then remained, because she found the mouse in a trap during the day, the unconscious sexual connotation of her thoughts stands revealed. I need hardly say that in the following night her unconscious wish was satisfied. There, too, the trap was skillfully set.

The psychical road from 'the first surmise to certainty concerning the unconscious meaning of the patient's thoughts is different from the process previously indicated, where the analyst, out of his conscious knowledge, introduced the mouse as a symbol into the train of thought, in order to comprehend it. In the latter case he did not think of symbols, but allowed his unconscious to lead him. He was guided, not by what he had learned from books and lectures, but by clues and undertones of the patient's behavior and personality. Later, perhaps, *after* he had grasped by what hidden, and yet instinctively assured, means the Eternal Feminine pursued its aim, it may have occurred to him that the mouse is a well-known sexual symbol. It may, indeed, be urged that the knowledge helped him preconsciously to conjecture the latent meaning of the train of thought. That is not the question. I have only said that I comprehended the repressed processes of the patient's mind without calling in the aid of my conscious knowledge of the sexual significance of the mouse. Now it might be argued that both ways led to the same goal, and that the first, that which made use of conscious knowledge, is actually the shorter. Even if we admit as much, it is not a matter of indifference by *what* road we reach our insights. The shorter is not always the better way.

Meanwhile closer consideration will show that the goal is not the same. In the case of the direct and conscious introduction of the symbol we have merely grasped a train of thought psychologically, an isolated fragment. From there we can proceed regressively to comprehend the recent conduct of the patient. But in the second case, in which we have followed her conduct with a comprehension arising from the unconscious, the outcome will be a comprehension of a different and deeper kind. Insight will be revealed to us of the varying impulses, the different sides of her character, nay, the nature and secret purposes of the neurosis. The play of inner forces in the patient will be revealed to us in all its variety and with its hidden springs. Her present behavior will offer us certain points of vantage from which to discern explanations of other, earlier, and not yet comprehended processes; and it will take its proper place in inner relation with all the rest of what we know about the patient. I call this kind of comprehension *knowledge experienced,* and place it in contrast to *knowledge merely learned by rote,* operating with conceptions derived from consciously acquired facts. The possibility involved in the latter is that we may cling to mere dummy words, instead of finding ideas that correspond to inner reality.

Respect for terminology may prove to be a residual belief in verbal magic. Theory, which ought to come as the final precipitate of personal experience, often becomes its actual substitute and results in superficial routine. I hold that not only is the scientific value of the two types of knowledge different, but also their dynamic value. It is not indifferent for the progress of the analysis whether we simply apply conscious knowledge to the psychical data presented to us, or whether conscious knowledge arises from its unconscious assimilation—not even if the substance of the knowledge should be in both cases the same. (But it is never exactly the same.) The effect upon the patient is different, and so is the mental reaction upon the analyst. Experience teaches that we readily spend money that falls into our lap by chance, because we value it lightly, whereas money that we have ourselves earned is better spent because, unconsciously, we value it more. So it must be with knowledge that we work for. It is this knowledge that we have earned ourselves that is of prime effect in analysis.

In conjecture it is the idea that occurs freely that will bring the analyst upon the tracks of repressed processes, not the idea that is trammeled by theoretical prejudices. What is heard with a third ear must be heard again and examined in the control room of reason. Both inspiration and perspiration have to be at work. Here is the parting place, the line of demarkation, the marking which will decide *who is an artist in psychoanalysis and who is merely a technician*. The technician will hear only what announces itself with much noise. The artist will hear best what speaks in a low tone. When God said, "Let there be light," He did not shout.

CHAPTER XXXVIII

No Royal Road Through the Unconscious

WORKERS in other fields are also prepared to meet with surprises in their researches. Nevertheless, there can hardly be another method of investigation so lacking in plan, so unsystematic in approaching its data, so free from prejudices with regard to what is coming as psychoanalysis. Let us consider other methods of psychological investigation. Let us picture to ourselves an experimental psychologist, a representative of the phenomenological school, a Gestalt psychologist, or a behaviorist at the beginning of his researches into a living subject. Different from each other as their methods of research into the mind may be, they all agree in demanding the strictest attention to definite and previously defined points in the investigation just begun. A psychologist who starts a scientific investigation of this kind with a person as the subject of his experiment will concentrate all his intellectual powers upon some narrower or wider problem and all his attention upon one or several points that interest him. An analyst who wants to penetrate the deeper planes of the mind approaches his investigation unprepared and without prejudice, and he gives the impression that he is looking for nothing in particular. He conducts himself quite differently from, let us say, a psychologist who is beginning a series of experiments in the laboratory after exact and careful preparation and according to a previously arranged plan. The analyst seems rather like a pupil of the witch in Goethe's *Faust* when he seeks to penetrate to the hidden knowledge of the repressed:

> To him without thought
> It comes unsought,
> He has it without care.

This impression is not quite correct, for the analyst does come to his investigations with certain psychological assumptions and expectations. Think, for instance, of his conviction that everything in the psychical process is determined. Consider also his assurance that the repressed material has means of expression and will betray itself in its offspring. Nevertheless, we must admit that, in comparison with the methods of other psychologists, the impression from the witch-scene in *Faust* is largely justified. Indeed, I must point out that the character of a method of investigation must adapt itself to the nature of the subject of investigation. Clearly it would be absurd if an expedition to explore the Sahara were to equip itself with a ship.

It is instructive to compare the attitude of, say, a psychiatrist of pre-analytic days interviewing a nervous patient with that of a nerve specialist of today. The former listened gently and patiently for a long time to the story of a neurotic patient. But at a certain point he felt constrained to intervene and turn the patient from his meandering tale to an orderly statement. Perhaps, during the interview, he would point out that the story was disconnected, the train of thought desultory. He, the doctor, could not make head or tail of it. With a little imagination we can picture to ourselves the doctor's voice, admonishing gently or sternly: "Your thoughts are too desultory; they jump about all over the place. Do try to keep to the point." Or: "Please do try to tell straightforwardly and in proper order what you have to say to me." If our pre-Freudian doctor had enough insight or patience to refrain from such an exhortation, he himself nevertheless picked out with conscious selection what seemed to him important in the story, and set aside what he thought insignificant. He separated the chaff from the wheat and tried from the outset to bring order and connection into the conscious treatment. In any case, the doctor endeavored to conduct the treatment in accordance with conscious principles and in a clear and systematic sequence. But that was possible only if the patient could be induced to plod along a beaten path of thought and not flit hither and thither like a will-o'-the-wisp. And now consider how radically different is the analyst's way of setting about his investigations. He leaves the manner and sequence of presenting psychical data almost entirely up to the patient.

We shall not be surprised that even within the analytic school there are groups who demand that psychological investigation go back to its systematic, orderly, consistent character. But anyone who, through many

years of daily analytic practice, has proved to himself the way the unconscious of the patient and of the analyst act as guideposts for the
conjecture of repressed processes, will hardly allow himself to be taught
worse by new ideas of this kind. The old German academic proverb
still holds good: With a system, incoherent drivel begins.

Quite recently Wilhelm Reich has put forward such a view very decisively in his interesting book, *Charakteranalyse* ("Character Analysis"), which is valuable in its clinical section. He calls for a vigorous
approach to the complexes, a rapid and consistent advance to the central
infantile conflict, in a sense of prearranged march into the field of the
unconscious. He repudiates passive expectancy, and requires that the
conjecture of unconscious relations shall no longer depend upon uncontrollable "intuitive" ideas occurring to the analyst. If we proceed in this
manner, he claims, so-called chaotic situations will no longer arise. A
program of this kind holds out to the student analyst the promise of
labors systematic and reliable, nay, after the initial difficulties have been
overcome, even smooth. If this expectation were to be fulfilled, the result would be a considerable abbreviation of the treatment for the patient, and therefore a sensible diminution of difficulty and greater success.

This analytic program represents, so to speak, a one-year plan for the
economy of the mind. The situation Reich pictures and promises is the
wishful thinking of every psychoanalyst: a smooth, easy, and elegant
descent into the netherworld. It reminds me of the way some religious
people promise us final salvation. When the French writer, Paul Bourget, was converted to Catholicism, Anatole France wrote about one of
his novels: "If we can believe Mr. Bourget, we will all land in heaven
and we cannot avoid paradise—unless there is no paradise, which is very
likely."

Reich's program sounds admirable, and has secured many adherents,
especially among the younger generation of analysts. If I here subject
Reich's technique to the light of criticism, that is not on account of its
inherent merits, but on account of extra ones ascribed to it by many
analysts. They do so, I believe, not because it shows anything in a new
light, but because it has created a stir. That is what makes me introduce
the subject here, although strictly speaking it lies outside the limits of
my argument. My second reason is one of principle: I am of the opinion
that this tendency must necessarily lead to an abandonment of the most
valuable characteristic of the analytic method. The road upon which

Reich's book sets forth leads far. To me it seems too far. It leads into a blind alley.

Precisely in the name of science we must reject this methodical semblance of accuracy, the false suggestion that psychoanalysis admits of a fixed system. The theory puts forward a claim that is unfounded, gives rise to the notion that, thanks to analysis, we know everything about the unconscious that there is to know, and makes our method appear complete and final. Such a view is inspired by an unjustifiable optimism about the extent and depth of our knowledge of the unconscious, and ignores the fact that it is still as dark and impenetrable as an Indian jungle.

The founder of psychoanalysis was more modest. Freud never indulged in the belief that he had solved all the riddles of the inner life. A few years ago he likened his work to that of an archeologist who had rescued a few temples from the dark earth and brought them to light; but he had no doubt that great treasures still remained below, awaiting excavation. So much for what has already been disclosed and what still remains to be disclosed. For many of my colleagues psychoanalysis is a closed book, a book written by Freud. He would be the first to protest against such an idea.

There is no royal road through the unconscious. I would also remind my readers that even great generals have sometimes attached no peculiar value to a consistent and prearranged plan. Napoleon, asked about the nature of his strategy, answered, *"Je m'engage et je vois."* Since we are dealing with a region that is largely unknown, we can only give a little advice about the first steps leading from the territory with which we are familiar—advice, so to speak, about the frontier. We can recount our own experience in making incursions into the unknown territory. Reich's endeavor, on the other hand, is precisely, as he says, "to establish a standpoint, both general and particular for each case, by which we may apply the data to the technical handling of the case *according to natural law,* and to know exactly in every interpretation what [is] its basis and what its purpose . . ." In my opinion this application according to law, consistent and fixed from the outset, is ill-suited to the unconscious. The technique of analysis has grown from unconscious assumptions. It will always remain essentially dependent upon them and owe to them its most fruitful perceptions. In contact with the patient's unconscious it will always renew its strength, like Antaeus in his struggle with the Titans when he touched the earth.

NO ROYAL ROAD THROUGH THE UNCONSCIOUS

The requirement that in every interpretation we must know exactly its basis and purpose seems to me altogether utopian. And this not because it is too rationalist—I, too, acknowledge reason as the ultimate principle in the comprehension of the unconscious—but because it introduces this rationalization at a stage of the analytic process that cannot be grasped by the understanding mind until later. There can be no prescribed rules for our procedure with regard to the imponderabilia of each individual case. It is out of the question, if only because we cannot define in advance the inaccessible potentialities of the unconscious. A technique of this kind, expecting everything from conscious considerations and plans, shows, moreover, surprisingly little confidence in the searching and finding powers of our own unconscious. An analyst ought to have learned in the course of his practice that his own unconscious drags all kinds of things from the darkness with a thousand polypus-like arms. It is not necessary for an analyst to be constantly occupied with his plan of campaign during the process. If he is a good psychologist, the blind urge within himself will teach him the right way.

Reich aims at "a clear-sighted, regular, and systematic analysis of resistance" making unwaveringly for its goal—that is, he assumes a detailed plan with definite points of attack. The systematic technique that he recommends to us for the conquest of the desired territory may be excellent in itself; but it is so high-flying that it feels able to ignore the nature of the terrain where the decisive battles are fought. Reich upholds his systematic, consciously arranged procedure by urging that the way hitherto adopted "is very uncertain, dependent upon incalculable chances, and lacks the assured foundation of analytical lucidity. . . ." How true! For we work for the most part in unknown territory. On such journeys we certainly are dependent upon chances; we do lack "the assured foundation of analytical lucidity." But I do not think that an exploring expedition is surer of success, if an exact itinerary is worked out beforehand through a land that is unknown. There is no *géographie de l'inconnu*. Varying the well-known sentence, we can say: A man never descends so deep as when he does not know where he is going.

I cannot believe what Reich's systematic technique of analysis assumes—namely, that we shall find a well-arranged card-index and catalog of the unconscious ready-made. Reich reminds us that many treatments fail because the analyst cannot find his way through the mass of data revealed: "We call that a chaotic situation, and hold that it is due to particular errors in the technique of interpretation." I should not call it so, and I hold that these situations are not only due to particular errors in the technique of interpretation but also to particular and far-reaching deficiencies in our knowledge and our psychophysical constitution. We may wait with unruffled skepticism to see whether the technique recommended to us will cure these deficiencies. I doubt whether a change in technique, in the direction of a consistent and systematic treatment of the patient, can teach us anything new. I rather incline to believe that it is possible to find something new that will then create its own technique.

After all, what are the errors that Reich assumes to be responsible for the "chaotic situation"? They are premature interpretations, or interpretations of the data in the sequence that they are clearly presented themselves, without consideration of the structure of the neurosis and the stratification of the material. The error lies in interpreting simply because the data presented themselves clearly; to use Reich's caustic words, "unsystematic interpretation of the meaning." In these cases the interpretation of the meaning often precedes the interpretation of the resistance, he says, or else the interpretation of the resistance is inconsistent. This unsystematic procedure is to be replaced by orderly interpretation and analysis of the resistance. Slightly exaggerated, the technique here described sounds like the affecting plaint of an orchestra: "It is so dreadfully difficult to keep a conductor coherent."

Especially, he says, we must pay attention to latent resistance. "I make a habit of tackling these latent resistances." Reich gives several interesting examples of this "tackling," which seem to indicate that his method deserves the name of an aggressive rather than an active technique. Sometimes we are reminded of the prescription Jaroslav Hasek referred to: "More severity toward the poor!" Militant psychology may be a matter of taste; we have a right to inquire more into the criteria that decide what is to be "tackled" and what passed over. With a sureness of aim that proves Reich is as gifted a satirist as he is a strategist, he remarks that it is not always easy "to convey the simple information that one should always start from the surface." And then he shows what must be interpreted first if by chance two surface contents emerge side by side, both with an unconscious foundation. We shall certainly agree with Reich when he says that there are special reasons for discussing one part of the psychical surface first, and not the other. Doubtless there are such reasons, but they will be largely of a preconscious or unconscious nature, so that it is not till a later stage that they will present themselves as useful reactions for the purpose of illuminating or guiding the analysis.

Certainly there may arise situations during the analysis in which the analyst will consciously—that is here to say, with a consciousness of purpose—interpret one particular fragment of the material offered and pass over another; but these are exceptional cases. As a general rule his "reasons" are consciously realized at a later stage. But they need not even all be consciously realized. As a general rule logical or rational considerations do not decide how we proceed. These considerations occur later when we reflect on our procedure and test it.

The course of the analysis is not directed by a consistent and conscious system on the part of the analyst. In choosing the sequence of the data to be interpreted he is guided by unconscious reasons, the inner significance of which far exceeds any principle of prearranged order and system. We have here a secret understanding and an unconscious order, exceeding in its heuristic value that of any rigid and prearranged consistency. If at first guidance of this kind through the vistas of the unconscious order seems madness, yet it has a method of its own, revealing relations more profound than the professedly consistent procedure according to a prearranged, rational plan. The longer I conduct analyses, the deeper grows my suspicion of any attempt to mechanize and systematize them and the stronger my impression that *in analysis skillful technique counts less than inner truthfulness, nay, that this inner truthfulness is the very essence of analytic technique*. If we regard the matter in this light, it is of small importance whether our choice of material is from memory or from the sphere of the actual, or whether we are concerned with the interpretation of meaning or of resistances. That is to say, the choice of data to be interpreted must also be left to a great extent to the analyst's inner sagacity and tact.

It still remains most advantageous to start from the psychical surface. It is true that the surface is the uppermost plane, but it can mirror the depths. The analyst's unconscious, without the aid of a rational system, without conscious consistency, without precept or prescription, will thence be able to discover what needs interpretation, and in what sequence it should be interpreted. Reich's new school wants to pick out from the mass of material the one fragment that plays a central part in the resistance. It calls for continuity in the analysis by means of a con-

sistent marshaling of resistances, and wants the technique of interpretation of resistances, likewise, to be orderly and systematic. Its ideal is "a
direct development of the transference neurosis and its analysis, in
keeping with the original neurosis; the patient develops his resistances
systematically, and in the intervals he produces affective memories free
from resistance."

Everything here proceeds smoothly, I admit; the transference neurosis
develops exactly as foreseen. The patient develops his resistances systematically, the analysis proceeds with the accuracy of the planets, and
its appointed march is accomplished in conformity with Reich's sched-
ule. This remolding to a comprehensive, mechanical, and consistent
system seems to stamp analysis with the character of a psychology rather
of business than of instinct.

Reich asserts: "Whereas when the work of interpretation is unsystematic we must confine ourselves to sudden pushes, search, guess-
work rather than inference, if we have previously worked at the resistance in the analysis of character, the analytical process advances
automatically." It advances so smoothly that anyone who is really familiar with psychoanalysis is bound to grow exceedingly suspicious. The
region in which this kind of analysis occurs may be situated in the land
of the lotos-eaters; it is assuredly not of this world. In an analysis of
Reich's type it is not determinism of thought that prevails, but a military discipline of thought, an analytically prescribed intercourse of
thoughts, so to speak. The ideas do not occur in a disorderly tumult.
They stand in line and one is admitted after the other.

We are directed to pay heed to the formal element as the great means
of discovering the new consistent and systematic technique. In addition
to dreams, blunders, etc., the patient's deportment merits attention;
that is the manner in which he tells his dreams, makes his blunders, etc.
"The manner is of equal value with the matter, regarded as interpretive
material. . . . Through this experience," we read in another passage,
"the formal element is introduced into psychoanalysis, hitherto mainly
concerned with the content." This astonishes the professional analyst,
and the layman is puzzled. Where shall we find an analyst who has not
ascribed full importance to the deportment of a patient and his individual manner of telling his story, one who does not pay great attention
to the formal element in his impressions? "You're telling me" could be
the answer in New York slang. He is proclaiming, with great aplomb,
the conquest of a land that has always been ours.

There is so little that is new in emphasizing the formal element, so little that is original, that he does not even venture to take a short step farther and declare that form is nothing but content changed to an outer layer, kernel changed to shell. What Reich says here has always been so obvious that it did not need to be said. In fact, it was not *permissible* to say it, if the intention was thereby to designate an essential element in a new technique. What still remains to be noted on this point is less the substance of the statement than the boldness with which it is made. A truism is proclaimed as a gospel of salvation. Never were doors more open than those against which Reich here runs with greatest violence.

Undoubtedly it is justifiable to warn us of the dangers of a chaotic situation, only I fear that the warning does not involve any protection. However consistently we push forward into the darkness of the unconscious, such situations are unavoidable. It happens not infrequently during analysis that for a time the threads threaten to become tangled and we grope our way in the dark. Then suddenly an intonation of the voice, a pause, a gesture, that we had not observed before leads us toward a solution. It is precisely from this temporary darkness, this chaotic situation, that the clarifying and explanatory idea arises, "the strange son of Chaos."

Systematization involves the loss of what is most valuable and characteristic in the technique of analysis. Was it not an advantage that we were not required to marshal our data immediately or manipulate them with violence, that our technique remained close to the mental processes of the moment and could adapt itself to them? It is one of the essential benefits of this technique that the analyst retains his respect for the peculiar laws of the unconscious, and need not state by the sweat of his brow what he does not know. And now he is to be required to make an exact and conscious selection of the material, arranged according to fixed principles, and to push the analysis consistently in a predetermined direction. The understanding between two unconscious minds will, I fear, be replaced by misunderstanding between two conscious minds.

Undoubtedly there are stages in many analyses in which such consistent analysis of resistances comes about of itself. In these cases the special technique is automatically prescribed. We need not prescribe it ourselves. Such selection of material solely from the point of view of resistance does not mean guidance of the analysis, but an affective act of violence against it. In actual fact this much-praised energetic procedure is better adapted to any other object than the repressed elements of the mind. If we survey the description of the orderly, systematic, and consistent technique of dealing with resistance, we shall come to the conclusion that it is easy to be consistent. The difficulty is to know to what end.

My decided rejection of the conscious ordering, the consistent and systematic discipline, of the analytic process is most certainly not tantamount to a denial of any guiding principle. What I repudiate is the totalitarian claim of the new technique of dealing with resistance, the claim that the planning, rational factor is to be our guide in a psychical phase where it is out of place. I repudiate the totalitarian claim of a conscious and systematic procedure where it is a question of conjecturing repressed tendencies. I will not admit that we can extract from the living psychical processes with levers and screws what they will reveal only in the course of organic development. In such procedure the Logos is degraded to mere intelligence.

There is an order governing the unconscious of the patient and the analyst; the analysis obeys the law by which it unfolds. But its order is determined by the reciprocal action of the unconscious. The analysis pursues its aim by ways that are only revealed at a subsequent stage of the process. In contrast with the systematic and militant type of analysis that is recommended to us, I praise the exclusion on principle of order and compulsion in technique, the absence of a consistent system, the lack of all conscious and rigid arrangement. I confess myself an opponent of every kind of conscious mechanization of analytic technique. This establishment of order and plan that is to be forced upon us corresponds in the inner life to the efforts of so many domestics who do, indeed, tidy our writing tables and ruthlessly make an end of all disorder, but, by their consistent and systematic methods, sweep away or destroy, stupidly and senselessly, the fruits of years of laborious work.

Analysts must not allow themselves to be led astray by the prospect of quicker therapeutic results. What is being attempted is to bring back analytic procedure, by a roundabout way, to the old methods of medical and psychological investigation, which were undoubtedly thoroughly consistent, orderly, and systematic. The people who act the rebel are rather engaged in a bold retreat. The Left Wing of a movement to which we owe a scientific revolution is marching with flying colors into the camp of the reactionaries.

The other danger that analysis as a method of investigation has to resist has certain common features with the one just described. A briefer statement will be enough for this other would-be improvement of technique, which also professes to lighten our labors and ensure a smooth working of the process of cognition; for, though certainly it has not fewer advocates, its defects are much more obvious. It is the technique of interpretation advocated by Steckel and his school. Here everything is left to the ideas that occur to the analyst. He is subjected only to a very slight inner control. The analyst has made himself so far independent of the psychical data that it sometimes seems as if he had no urgent need of them at all. The result is that the analyst rather forces the idea that occurs to him upon the patient than communicates it—and in this method almost everything is in the form of such ideas, good and bad, unchecked, subjected to no filter of self-criticism and examination. The common features are obvious. Reich's technique of interpretation is arbitrary in its order; that of Steckel's disciples, in its content. In one case psychological conjecture based upon our own unconscious knowledge is almost entirely excluded and branded as "intuition." In the other, it becomes omnipotent. In one case the discipline of rational thinking becomes, so to speak, a tyranny. In the other, reason abdicates.

I have already compared the investigation of unconscious processes to a voyage of discovery. But that voyage is not to be mere filibustering, but a scientific expedition undertaken with all the caution and care, all the sense of responsibility, proper to such a journey, ready at any moment to give an account of the strange lands visited. It is indeed a journey to an almost unknown land, but no mere random trip.

It will be pleasant to return from this dispute, which proved necessary in order to avert a danger and clarify the issue, to more positive tasks. But before I do so I will utter the clear warning that arises from these critical considerations: We are justified in regarding any innovation in analytic technique with suspicion if it promises to enable us to penetrate into the unconscious smoothly, easily, and quickly. Again and again an analyst will experience—beside satisfaction at the slow dawning of light in the dark places of the mind, and at illumination sudden only in appearance—disappointment at difficulties, his own errors, and "chaotic situations." Again and again, in spite of every extension of the boundaries of consciousness, he will strike against the limitations that bound our psychological knowledge. Anyone who takes part in our labor of investigating the unconscious mind must realize that after the first phase, in which we recognize with amazement how much that is new and undreamed of we learn in the course of analysis, a second phase follows in which we see how much that is unknown and unknowable remains in the realm of the unconscious.

This recognition of the limits of his possibilities will lead the psychologist to set sober bounds to his aims, to reflect, to re-examine, and to come to grips with himself. It will not lessen his keen interest in unconscious processes, nor will it have power to dampen his enthusiasm. Amidst the inevitable obscurities and difficulties of his psychological labors, his interest will undergo the same changes as mark the development of a wholesome marriage. Though passion may fly, yet love must remain.

PART FOUR

THE LANGUAGE OF THE SOUL

CHAPTER XXXIX

Diction and Contradiction

UNCONSCIOUS forces announce themselves, reveal their existence and effects; but they are mute or their language is not the one we speak. Their nature and their aims have to be guessed and have to be translated into words—thought or spoken—because only that which can be caught in word-pictures or sounds can become conscious. Only that which can be submitted to the magic of words can be brought to the daylight of conscious thinking. What cannot be said or thought in words or word-presentations never happened as far as the conscious mind is concerned. It lies dormant. Only words which are uttered or thought can awaken the Sleeping Beauty of unconscious events, emotions, and ideas. The effects of psychoanalysis are, to a great extent, related to bringing to light what is buried in the depths.

A new insight into the dynamics of unconscious processes is bound to the creation of new expressions or to a new meaning of old words already used in another sense. Progress of depth psychology is unimaginable without finding new expressions because only with their help can that which has eluded description be grasped. It is not accidental that the great psychologists, those who reach the remotest recesses of the human mind, are at the same time great stylists, creators in the realm of wording.

Freud was one of them. This seer was a sayer. He renamed the demons of the netherworld and the gods above the sky. He gave shape and substance to the mysterious shadows he discovered in the depths of the unconscious. He gave voice to the silent powers that we feel but cannot see. The plasticity and the dynamic character of the new expressions he found are appropriate to the conflicts between the unconscious forces and the conscious demands of society. He observed an emotional process by which impulses and tendencies that are not in harmony with one's ethical or aesthetic ideas could be banned, sunk, and submerged; and he called it repression. He conjectured another process by which emotion is moved from one place to another, without our knowledge, and he called it displacement. He recognized in dreams, in the genesis of neurotic symptoms, and in many other unconscious productions devices that keep unpleasant impulses and ideas away from us, and he spoke of censorship and of the distortion to which these tendencies are subjected when they reach the threshold of our conscious thought in one form or another. He found hundreds of such dynamic expressions for the unknown powers that operate in us. The discoveries of this genius cannot be divorced from his creation of new words and the new meanings he gave to others that were used up like old pennies.

To appreciate the difficulties in his way it is necessary to understand the decisive differences between unconscious and conscious processes. What takes place subterraneously has a primitive and archaic character. The unconscious does not know and does not care about our logic and our laws. It can tolerate contradictions; it can avow one thing and yet embrace its opposite. It plays with words as if they were things. It is inconsistent and has not the slightest difficulty gliding from one realm to another. Of course, we cannot hope that the translation of such processes into our language gives an adequate idea of these peculiarities. Such translations always have necessarily an "almost" character; they can only come near the hidden meaning, but cannot reach it. "When the soul speaks it is, alas, not the soul any more that speaks," complains Friedrich Schiller.

The tool with which you seize such elusive and strange figures, really such stuff as dreams are made of, should be proper to them. Freud's prose, the magic of which no translation does justice to (least of all Brill's), is in its riches and precision such an admirable tool. In his description and analysis of unconscious processes, he remains close to the emotional realities of life, which are so hard to define. Whoever has read or heard any of Freud's case histories has been impressed by the fact that the precise and acute wording of the description corresponded to the dramatic happenings in the soul of the person, to his individual expression, and to that which relates him to us all. It was never an entirely abstract survey, never a psychology in the void. It remained close to life, full of personal qualities, with all the intricacies, complexities, conflicts, and uncertainties of human existence and with all its manifest misery and concealed pleasure. Nothing of such closeness to life is felt in the books and papers of most of Freud's followers. There is a dryness and colorlessness, a drab and dull descriptiveness, that make one think: How does this concern me? Here are poor words in a terrible remoteness from real life in vain pursuit of emotional processes. There is no frigate like a book to take you miles away (from human experience).

The other day one of our prominent chemists, winner of a Nobel prize, was asked whether it is possible to explain the nature of his present research to laymen in a language they could understand, without formulas and technical terms. The scholar answered: "Yes, it is possible, but extremely difficult." Is it equally difficult to speak about research in emotional processes? Is it equally necessary to use a great many formulas and technical labels? The answer is decidedly in the negative.

It is a bad omen for the situation of a science when the reader or listener must make a great intellectual effort, not to grasp the substance of its statements, but its form and wording. We all know that scientific terminology is a necessary evil, but it seems to me that too much stress is laid upon its necessity and too little upon its evil character. In the case of psychoanalysis there is the danger that it will have its development arrested by a high-sounding and pompous terminology. I can foresee future research in which man no longer appears as a human being but as a collection of complexes with Greek and Latin terms. Sometimes when I hear or read accounts of a neurotic case I am seized with a kind of dizziness as though I were watching acrobats performing. It is as if a rope dancer were walking across an empty space on the heights of abstract theory, along a rope of labels. There is a genuine *horror vacui,* a shock at the void concealed behind such a wealth of terminology.

When you listen to some young psychoanalysts and psychiatrists you sometimes get the impression that they are much more devoted to these technical terms than to psychoanalytic thinking. What they say does not sound like knowledge acquired by experience, but like a terminological deposit. It is not love of the science of the human soul, not an inclination for the analytic way of seeing and investigating, that appears here, but an inclination for analytic terms and clichés. Not long ago I heard a student say that he had again passed through the oral, the anal-sadistic, and the phallic phases, and had mastered the Oedipus complex, and now he was near the end of his analysis. It is difficult to express in words the disgust one feels at listening to such talk. But more important to me than the unaesthetic impression made by this remark is the fact that the student who made the statement seriously could have felt little of the personal and revolutionary experience of psychoanalysis. Beneath the thin veneer of such terminological smoothness, such glib articulateness, is nothing that is related to our science. Here is the dead-end of psychoanalytic study. Analysis is here devaluated by a smart and superficial verbalization. "With pomp and circumstance" the fruits of a new science are sold down the river.

I am afraid of the ease and facility with which they put labels on very complicated human developments. Such throwing around of technical terms can conceal a void full of pretensions. It can easily be confused with a penetrating comprehension of unconscious processes. It can lead to a false show of knowledge that remains peripheral. It can seduce a man into thinking in psychoanalytic clichés and in terms of a card-index science instead of one of personal experiences. Every time those terms are glibly applied, it is like a criminal abortion practiced against the embryo of a genuine psychological understanding. Terminology can be a fatal menace to a science if it is used, not to give names to relations, but as a substitute for real comprehension. Its use seduces us to intellectual laziness, so that we substitute something learned by rote for something experienced, something easily acquired for something really our own. I tremble for the new generation, which makes such short work not only of its experiences but also of the analytic terms that describe them. To speak Psychoanalese fluently does not mean to understand psychoanalysis, and a man who can use all the technical terms correctly can be a very poor psychoanalyst.

Let me dwell for a while on these terms, their use and abuse, their necessity and their valuelessness. Besides his books and papers that spread a new and surprising light into the deepest shafts of the mind and are often breath-taking in discovering unheard-of areas, Freud had to write technical papers, the first textbooks on psychoanalysis for psychiatrists and psychoanalysts. In them he had to use scientific terminology, old and newly invented. He had, so to speak, to deliver the skeleton without the flesh, without muscles or nerves, theoretical schemes and patterns of neurotic and psychotic symptoms. The superstructure of psychoanalysis, technical considerations, and discussions made a different style necessary. These contributions were written in a technical language for psychiatrists who had at their disposal the same material as Freud. The need to communicate with these practitioners necessitated the use of technical terms for well-known symptoms, clinical cases, certain typical situations, and emotional states.

With the years an abundance of such technical terms accumulated, spoken and understood only by the small circle of experts, a psychoanalytic language that was a mixture of Greek and Latin words loosely connected with each other by some expressions from everyday language, which linked them together like a large number of pearls on an inconspicuous thread. Followers and pupils of Freud's found new Greek and Latin words in the dictionaries and enriched the psychoanalytic vocabulary. Later some of these technical terms not understood or misunderstood found their way into wider circles of educated or interested persons. A new language, *Psychoanalese,* was born. Firmly established by 1920, it has flourished for the past twenty-five years. Today we already see signs of its decadence and decay.

Out of the night of the unconscious Freud brought new words into the world of psychology. Out of the day of psychiatric knowledge an artificial terminology was made and manufactured. The first production will outlive our time. The other will perish with the times that invented it. One signifies the birth of new thoughts; the other, their miscarriage. The new words and expressions that Freud created are achievements of an artist who went out to investigate a new world. The technical terminology of psychoanalysis is a fabrication of craftsmen and will be replaced by other, better tools. Both products are necessary and serve their purposes, but craftsmen should not pretend to be artists. Some of Freud's followers tried to steal his thunder. They were only able to seize firecrackers.

The use of technical terms in psychoanalysis today tends to drive away the creative spirit of psychological understanding. Its abuse endangers the progress of research. I can give you an idea of what the new jargon sounds like. I know it well, because I spoke it for more than thirty years and, if my memory does not fail me, I contributed some new terms to it myself.

CHAPTER XL

Psychoanalese (Scherzo)

IF YOU want to hear Psychoanalese spoken fluently, if not always correctly, listen to young and not so young psychiatric social workers discussing a case of neurosis or psychosis. You will hear glib small talk about the great conflicts of the human soul. Fluent, if not always correct, Psychoanalese is spoken at the meetings and discussions of the psychoanalytic societies. Correct and sometimes elegant Psychoanalese may be read in the books and papers the members of the psychoanalytic groups publish. On all these occasions you will get the notion that here is a new language that tries to investigate unconscious processes by means of Greek and Latin terms. Here you can learn that "psychosexual maturity is reached, according to the libido-theory, when the individual passes through the phases of pregenital development, which is of a polymorph-perverse character, to a new integration and adaptation in the phallic phase." You will be informed that "to each period of the psychosomatic growth corresponds an excitability of a specific erogenous zone." You will learn that "some traumatic event can disturb the balance of integration and regression will occur which amounts almost to the same psychosexual effect as a primary fixation of the libido on an infantile love object" and that "the variety of the symptomatology of obsession-neuroses shows such a regression to the anal-sadistic level and dynamically determines the sexual function of the individual and influences the vicissitudes of Oedipal development." It sweeps you off your feet, and you catch your breath. Between the three parts of the fundamental concept of psychosomatic research—psychogenesis, conversion, and specificity—you will be kicked around like a football.

You open a new analytic book and you read: "The impulse to coprophagia which certainly has an erogenous source (representing an attempt to stimulate the erogenous zone of the mouth with the same pleasurable substance that previously stimulated the erogenous zone of the rectum) simultaneously represents an attempt to re-establish the threatened narcissistic equilibrium; that which has been eliminated must be reintrojected." Such a sentence parades before the reader like an armored division. Believe me, there is less in it than meets the eye. You read page after page of formalizing, verbalizing sentences, but the dry terms refuse to come to life. What emerges is not an insight into human nature, but into the jargon of specialists which, as Justice Holmes once remarked, "implies a kind of snobism." Exhausted by this merry-go-round of labels you turn to the new copy of the psychoanalytic journal that happens to be on your desk, and you read the first sentence you light upon: "In a number of cases of ejaculatio praecox I have noted in particular in addition to their typical urethralanal fixations the presence of a wealth of urethro-regressive fantasies." You turn the page and find a paper on Freud's theory of the death and life instincts. While you try to understand a truly admirable speculation on the conflict between the two primary principles, the one that creates life and the other that destroys it, you get confused, because the author of the paper substitutes for Freud's expressions the terms "libido" and "destrudo." For a moment you are under the impression that it is all *abstrudo*. But you are wrong there. All that makes not only sound, but also sense. Here are some facts of life as the new psychology sees them and they could easily be understood if they were put in plain English. The trouble with you, brother, is that you do not understand Psychoanalese. Nicholas Murray Butler's definition should be enlarged: An expert is one who knows more and more technical terms about less and less.

Let me speak here about another peculiarity of Psychoanalese: the use of mythology. I like Greek mythology as well as I like others, but I do not see any necessity for introducing names of many mythological figures into psychological research. Geologists did not take Hebrew names from the book of Genesis in describing the formation of the earth, the Deluge, and so on. It is all right to call on mythology to

make a particular quality or a certain process especially vivid or lucid
to the reader or listener. It ceases to be useful and becomes a nuisance
when we know psychic processes only by the name of a Greek god,
goddess, or hero. In Shakespeare's *The Merchant of Venice* Lorenzo
and Jessica sit on the steps of Portia's house and Lorenzo speaks:

> . . . in such a night
> Troilus methinks mounted the Trojan walls,
> And sigh'd his soul toward the Grecian tents,
> Where Cressid lay that night.

And now he and his sweetheart run into a variety of classic allusions
and imagery:

> Jessica: In such a night
> Did Thisbe fearfully o'ertrip the dew,
> And saw the lion's shadow ere himself,
> And run dismay'd away.

> Lorenzo: In such a night
> Stood Dido with a willow in her hand
> Upon the wild sea banks, and waft her love
> To come again to Carthage.

> Jessica: In such a night
> Medea gather'd the enchanted herbs
> That did renew old Aeson.

It sounds enchanting but it is poetry, not scientific psychology. Words
are, as Emerson put it, "the dress of thought." But many analytic
mythological labels are not thoughts dressed, but thoughts dressed up.
Reading a lot of the newer psychoanalytic literature, you sometimes
feel as if you were present at one of those fancy-dress balls favored by
the French kings. Ladies and gentlemen appeared there in ancient Greek
costumes and telltale symbols. Hercules was there with his cudgel as
the personification of strength; Orpheus with his lyre representing the
power of music; Diana personifying chastity . . . , all the gods, demigods, and mythological figures. Is it then necessary that a psychoanalyst
speak like an instructor in Greek mythology? Is it desirable?

In the analytic books and discussions you meet the Oedipus complex
and its sister, the Electra complex. You chance upon Narcissus looking
into a pool; you make the casual acquaintance of a Pandora complex,

whatever that may be. An English analyst teaches us to discriminate between "Ouranos-" and "Laios-" jealousy and "Zeus-" jealousy. You observe how Eros governs the scene and uses libido as its messenger boy. In the background waits mute Thanatos; Tyche and Ananke appear as the parents of our culture. Daimonion is just around the corner.

It is easy to predict that the analytic terminology cannot and will not stop here. Analysts will understand that such a smattering of mythology is insufficient and does not throw enough light upon the unconscious processes. I claim that a great number of gods and heroes from Olympus who could be used as name-givers have been sadly neglected in our science. I miss the Hera complex describing a woman's unconscious incest inclination toward her brother and the Orestes complex, which includes all murderous tendencies against one's mother. Why not speak of a Medea complex when a patient has unconscious wishes to kill her children?

Psychoanalysts still use the outdated expression castration complex, when every high-school boy knows that Uranus was unmanned by Cronos. Why not speak of a Hercules complex when a patient is overpotent? Shouldn't an unhealthy ambition in a neurotic person shortly and aptly be called a Herostratus complex? There is a certain repeated situation in compulsion neurosis in which the patient cannot make up his mind whether to choose one thing or another because both appear full of dangers to him. I recommend the designation of one situation as Scylla; of the other, as Charybdis. The phenomenon of Narcissism plays a great role in psychoanalytic theory. Why is unconscious guilt-feeling not named Erynism? Would Sapphoism not be a good term for female homosexuality and Ganymedism an excellent expression for the passive homosexual attitude in men? There are so many gods and demigods in Greek mythology and relatively few are put into the service of psychoanalytic research.

There are some signs, however, that this sad situation may improve. Last year a famous psychoanalyst in Boston differentiated between the active motherly woman, the Demeter type, and the intellectual nonfeminine woman, the Pallas Athene type. The prominent British psychoanalyst, J. C. Fluegel, just published a book in which he prefers to speak of Nemesism when he means that aggression is turned against oneself, and of a Polycrates complex when he describes the unconscious need of self-punishment. There is some hope for the future of psycho-analytic terminology.

Seriously now, here are terms used not as a means of scientific communication but for adornment and decoration. Here are flowers and flourishes of speech that do not show the psychiatrist's results, but show him off. Here is a parade of education and learnedness, terms of an arbitrary inconsequence that serve only to distract the listener or reader from the essentials to the ornamentals. You will ask, what's in a name? That which they call Eros by any other name would smell as sweet? But the pretentiousness of analytic terminology cries to the netherworld. Many apply those terms to save themselves the trouble of thinking independently and others to save themselves the effort of thinking at all.

There are, moreover, two possible results of this overflow of mythological allusions. Either you know nothing about all these myths which were godfathers to the analytic terms—in which case they do not mean anything to you—or you know them very well with all their details and inner meaning. In this event the psychoanalytic term often has connotations that are not in conformity at all with their content.

The sadness of it is that with Freud the preference for such terms was born out of his great love for Greek antiquity, which is certainly not the case with most of his followers. Such mythological phrases and allusions were also in conformity with the manner of expressing certain things at the time when Freud was a young man. In those days an Austrian prosecutor characterized a defendant before the court by saying that the man was given to the worship of Bacchus and Venus. (Literally true.) He meant, of course, that the delinquent was a drunkard and chased women. It is obvious that such a manner of expressing oneself is antiquated. It is out of date when written or spoken by psychoanalysts today.

Nowadays when you listen to a psychoanalytic lecture or read a book, you expect to meet human beings, their conflicts, their misery, and their enjoyment, not Greek gods and demigods. The blending of ancient mythology with the bad style of many psychiatrists makes it difficult to refrain from writing a satire on the subject. You imagine a parody "Oedipus in the Netherworld" with music by Jacques Offenbach. (Freud would have had a good laugh at it. He once told me that he enjoyed this composer's operettas.)

At all events we have been fed so many mythological allusions and images, that we are fed up with them. We suspect that these names aim less at enlightenment than at creating an impression. We could endure the absence of many of these figures comfortably. We can afford to lose quite a few more. Sometimes we wish that most of them would go to He— To Hades, I mean, of course.

CHAPTER XLI

Other People's Experiences and Yours

$\mathbf{L}$OOK at this strange situation: the deepest and most vital region of the self is inaccessible to its own contemplative and inquiring consciousness. In order to comprehend it psychologically, it needs to be reflected in another person. Now we should expect that the thou, the other, would be directly comprehensible psychologically. But even that seems to be valid only with reference to the uppermost and conscious planes of the mind; the unconscious planes are not grasped directly. The medium is the ego, into which the other person is unconsciously introjected. In order to understand another we need not feel our way into his mind but to feel him unconsciously in the ego. We can attain to psychological comprehension of another's unconscious only if it is seized upon by our own, at least for a moment, just as if it were a part of ourselves—it is a part of ourselves.

If the unconscious of another can be grasped only through the medium of the ego, is there not imminent danger that we shall recognize only ourselves in him, see in the other person only what arises in our ego? The extreme case of this danger would be that other people could only be grasped in the image of the ego, that essential aspects of their unconscious processes would not be discerned, or—worse—would be falsely discerned. We admit the danger. Does the recognition of its existence imply at the same time that the method of understanding unconscious processes indicated here is false? I think not. There are sufficient means of guarding against the danger: first and foremost, *the careful observation of the subject, free from presuppositions*. If we do not want to abandon the attempt to comprehend the unconscious processes in others, we must follow this road. There is no other. Scientific psychologist and layman alike, the trained observer and the man in the street who only trusts to his "intuition," are obliged, if they want to discover unknown psychical relations, to pass through the stage of taking the subject into their ego.

The way the ego participates in this process of cognition is usually misunderstood. But the fact of participation has always been recognized. And here it is a matter of no importance whether it is described by scientists as empathy, by poets as an act of comparison ("Wilt thou understand another, Look in thine own heart."—Friedrich Schiller), or by the common man as something vaguer yet. There is general agreement that without such introduction of self-observation there can be no knowledge of other minds. Whence should the knowledge come, indeed, if it had no link with our psychological experience in the ego? A psychologist can make intelligence tests and other tests without being in the least involved emotionally. There is not the slightest necessity to call on the psychologist's personal experiences. As a matter of fact, a reference to his own emotional processes is uncalled for. A psychoanalyst, however, who does not draw from his own unconscious experience is not only unimaginative; he is also unimaginable to me—although I know there are many analysts of this kind. This fact is not contradictory to my statement. There are also certain freaks of nature that I cannot easily understand, although I know they exist.

If, then, the road through one's own experience is the only accessible one, scientific psychologists will need certain precautions and guarantees in following it, in order to avoid the danger of a generalization of knowledge acquired through inner perception, and in order not to distort the truth by an unjustifiable intervention of their own emotions. The science of analysis professes to be able to offer a certain guarantee that the mirror in which the processes in the other mind are reflected is not dimmed. It requires the analyst himself to be analyzed, so that his psychological comprehension may not be hindered or distorted by his own repressions. In addition it calls for a strict examination of his own impressions and his own psychological judgment of the data.

A further doubt may arise concerning the way in which the ego participates. I have said that the psychical process is characterized by the other person's unconscious impulse communicating itself to the analyst. Our first scruple will relate to the intensity and duration of this induced impulse. Plainly it cannot be compared in this respect with the corresponding impulse in the patient; otherwise the result would be a sharing of experience. Of course, we do not share the experiences or emotions of our patients. If we did, we could not analyze them; our energy would be used to master these experiences. What really happens in the conjecture phase is that we get just a taste of the menu, no more, just enough so that our tongue and palate recognize the food.

In describing the psychical process, I said that the same unconscious impulses would be aroused in embryo. That means that they are roused only at the initial stage, and then make way for endeavors of another kind. It is as if some external impression stirred the reminiscence of a well-known melody in us; say, for instance, that the opening bars are played on the piano. For a person with a musical memory it is not necessary for the melody to be played all the way through for him to recognize it. After a few bars the reminiscence of the whole melody, or at least of its essence, will occur spontaneously to the listener. In like manner the unconscious memory-trace of the induced emotion is stirred tentatively, so to speak, in the analyst. To retain our comparison: if somebody else plays a bar or two of a melody familiar to me, there is no need for me to recall consciously when and on what occasion I heard it. Nor is it necessary for me to become conscious of whether I liked it or not on that occasion.

Certainly the comparison does not take us far. But it takes us farther than we have yet gone. Outside I hear a voice singing. One or two bars of the melody remind me of one that I know and I join in and sing on a little. Yes, of course I know it! And now the conscious reminiscence may be stirred: Why, that is the Austrian national anthem, Haydn's beautiful melody. But it is equally possible that I do not remember. What rarely fails to appear is the impression made by the melody, its affective content, what the notes are trying to say, to express—and that quite independent of whether I remember the text, or even if I know it at all. Within certain limitations, therefore, our comparison corresponds to a case in which the analyst seizes unconsciously upon the expression of his patient's emotion before becoming conscious of it himself. The conscious recognition of the melody, of the conditions of its emotional content and its connection with the content of the text, would correspond more or less to the process of psychological comprehension in analysis.

The induction of the unconscious impulse at its initial point recalls to us, moreover, the significance of the time element determining the unconscious part of the process of comprehension. By that I do not mean only the duration of the induced impulse but the fact that it would be quite impossible to seize upon the induced impulse just at its initial point in embryonic form, if it had not led back to impulses of our own, experienced at some earlier time. No doubt, they will not coincide with the experience content as such; but the instinctive experiences of the patient have corresponded unconsciously with potential experiences of the analyst. Otherwise he would be able to detect nothing in the patient's words, see nothing unconscious in his gestures and movements. Here, of course, the difference between actual experience and the revival of the memory-traces of experience acquires psychological significance. What the other person tells us generally stirs only unconscious memory-traces in us. And here let me take resolute measures at once to guard against a misinterpretation or misunderstanding. *Nowhere in this inquiry have I advocated a consciously drawn parallel between another person's experience and our own.* The existence and psychical efficacy of the same unconscious tendencies involves no more than a psychological condition; it is not meant to be observed in us in every case. Self-observation is a derivative and secondary process. It is, so to speak, the observation of the ego through the eyes of the other person. Conscious reference to our own experience in face of unconscious processes in the other person, and self-observation for the purpose of comparison with another's inner life, would not only act as a disturbing factor in the analysis but would also be misleading. It would be bound to lead us astray, causing us to reinterpret another's experience in the light of our own, and thus to falsify it violently.

While I reject *conscious* comparison with our own inner processes and reference to our own experience in the comprehension of another's processes, an unconscious reference to self nevertheless seems to me all the more important for psychological cognition. The indirect promotion of our comprehension of self through knowledge of another's unconscious processes is a subject hitherto barely discussed in the literature of psychoanalysis. Sometimes by this indirect method of penetrating another's experience, our own can be better understood, for it is in fact veiled from our inner perception. *Our own experiences are more alien to us than the other person's.* But it seems to me beyond question that to grasp analytically the unconscious processes of somebody else, not only indirectly enlarges our psychological knowledge of self and its psychical conditions but also helps us to master the material of conflict within ourselves.

The second objection runs something like this: It is quite incredible, in view of the great variety of unconscious impulses, that only the same tendencies will be stirred in the analyst. That objection is justified, but merely because it is raised against a statement unjustly represented as too simple. The little word "only" is misplaced here. What I said was that these unconscious impulses in the one mind induced impulses of the same kind in the other—in this case in the analyst. But that only denotes the beginning, generally an exceedingly transient beginning, of the psychical course of events. This momentary impulse is followed by other psychical processes of a different kind; reactions to the other person's and our own (induced) impulses, taking the opposite, or at any rate, another direction. The original impulse speedily made way for another, or several others—let it be noted that I am still speaking of the realm of the unconscious. In that region, therefore, when an impulse of hatred is perceived in the other person, an embryo motion of hatred is stirred in the analyst, and a libidinous tendency in the patient induces a corresponding unconscious tendency in the analyst. In order to avoid misunderstandings, let me emphasize once more that this induced impulse remains at the initial stage.

We have, I believe, seen that it is not the other person's impulse as such, but *its unconscious echo in the ego,* that is the determining factor in psychological conjecture. Thus our own mental reaction is a signpost pointing to the unconscious motives and secret purposes of the other person. Let me admit, moreover, at this point that the rigid assertion that a psychologist maintains an attitude of aloofness toward the mental processes of his subject, and merely observes them, can be upheld at most only for the conscious part of his mind. The assertion of the unfeeling attitude, of the impassibility of the analyst, is a fairy tale, and not even a pretty fairy tale. What is essential in the psychical process going on in the analyst is—after the stage of observation—that he can vibrate unconsciously in the rhythm of the other person's impulse and yet be capable of grasping it as something outside himself and comprehending it psychologically, sharing the other's experience and yet remaining above the struggle, *au-dessus de la mêlée.* The first step in sharing the unconscious emotion is the condition of psychological comprehension: his own hidden affective impulse comes to be a means of cognition, but until it is mastered there can be no objectively valid knowledge of the inner processes of the other person.

Certainly it is only crudely true to say that unconscious impulses in the psychologist are stimulated in embryo by the words and gestures of the patient. But if we adhere to this description of the "stimulating" effect of psychological observation, we still see before us a long road, stretching from the emergence of an analogous impulse to intellectual comprehension. In particular, it is difficult to understand why that road should be taken at all. For these unconscious impulses do not drive us toward psychological comprehension, but toward expression, action, motor discharge. Thus the riddle lies in the transformation of this "roused" impulse into psychological interest, in the substitution of one form of psychical energy by another. Now we may retort that it is just from the analytic point of view that the transformation of unconscious impulses into curiosity and the urge to investigate is a psychological process that we have long understood; we have here just a special case of that process. But it is precisely the special aspect of the process that stirs our curiosity.

We can best conjecture its nature when we study the psychological conditions in transference analysis. Let us choose an instance from negative transference, and assume that the patient's words betray traces of the unconscious intention to humiliate and hurt the analyst. Special features in the patient's behavior show his unconscious tendency to aggravate and mock at the analyst. Apprised by various slight signals, the analyst has struck against this purpose, of which the patient is unconscious. Unconsciously these expressions rouse the analyst's own aggressive impulses. We should expect that these hostile motions within himself would turn against the aggressor. We should expect the repulse of the attack or the humiliation of the aggressor to be the object of the impulse. And these hostile impulses really are roused in embryo, but they are immediately intercepted when they arise, unconsciously or preconsciously. Their instinctive energy is not used for revenge, but is placed at the service of psychological cognition. The analyst notes the intention, but he is not annoyed or at least scarcely ever annoyed. He feels impelled to study it psychologically. We may certainly class these impulses among the "instinctively inhibited" motions, but they form a special subdivision in that the inhibition begins early, actually at the initial point. Within the process we must place the point of reversal very early, immediately after its emergence to the conscious level.

Here is a simple example: during a patient's first analytic session I became aware of a habit he had of ending many statements with "you follow me?" or "get me?" or "you see?" or sometimes with "do you know what I mean?" or simply "catch?" I began to connect how often he would repeat questions of this kind which remained, of course, unanswered. These recurring questions did not concern difficult or abstract problems. They were interspersed in his report about his family relations or events in his past. Why did I think that his questions were expressions of his unconscious doubt about my intelligence or psychological understanding? Such an attitude would be very much in contrast with his otherwise respectful behavior, but it was clear to me that he thus expressed unconscious contempt. No analyst could afford to overlook those little signs that revealed an unconscious attitude contrasting with the conscious manner of the patient. From where did the roots of my analytic interpretation emerge? Scientific reasons justify here a turning to psychological self-observation. While I followed the tale of the patient who repeated those questions, I observed a slight feeling of annoyance in myself. He spoke about his relations with his wife, which were by no means unusual in their character and asked, "You follow me?" He tried to describe his feelings toward his older brother, oscillating between hostility and friendliness, and he asked, "Do you get me?" What was there difficult to understand? When you want to know something about shoes, you go to a shoemaker. When you wish to understand something about the nature of human relations you ask a psychologist. In contrast to his outward appreciation he had in his questions revealed that he considered me either stupid, or an incompetent psychologist. My reaction to these recurring questions was a slight feeling of annoyance as if he had expressed disrespect or contempt. This "as if" translates really what the patient unconsciously felt.

Compare another example with this: A young woman spent the greater part of an analytic session in complaining about her husband, his lack of consideration and his inattention. Suddenly she interrupted herself: "You always say the same things. You repeat yourself. I am bored with it." The sudden charge was a surprise to me, because I had been silent the whole time. My bewilderment lasted only a second, then I knew that her attack was in reality a defensive maneuver to hide an inferiority feeling. It was as if she had suddenly become aware that she had frequently said the same things before and had expressed the same complaints. She was afraid that she would bore me with her repetitions.

Anticipating such a reaction on my side, she attacked me—a form of projection we know so well with women when they feel defenseless or inadequate. How did I understand the nature of her behavior? I observed my own reaction. There was first a momentary astonishment at the entirely unmotivated attack . . . I had said nothing . . . Then a kind of slight amusement emerged, as if I had rediscovered or recognized a trick, a typical feminine attitude often met before. At the same moment I realized that her attack originated in her fear I would no longer be interested in her tale.

The process by which the sum of energy is turned from aggression into the service of the will to know and to understand is introduced by a halt, a check. But as a rule the emotional release of the charge of energy is interrupted from the first, and that makes it easier to employ it differently in the service of psychological cognition. Afterward the aggressive impulse is observed in the subject, according to the formula already indicated. We need have no hesitation in regarding this realization as simultaneous with the process of projection. It removes a certain emotional hindrance and achieves a certain psychical relief. Projection enables us to become conscious of our own impulses, displaced onto the other person.

We may detect the same mechanism in the perception of unconscious sexual impulses in the transference process. There, too, our own desirous impulse is inhibited at the very outset. The sum of energy that accompanies or precedes the crude sexual desire is used for the purpose of psychological cognition. In depicting these representative cases, we can see plainly how psychological interest is derived from a tendency to gain mastery, hardly differentiated as yet. It makes no difference in principle whether that primitive urge to gain mastery is primarily libidinous or primarily aggressive in quality.

Let us sum up: The road that we have to travel is bounded on the one hand by the conscious, preconscious, or unconscious perception (observation) of psychological evidence, and on the other by the conscious psychological cognition of the processes. The most important stations on the road are determined by the introjection of the subject and by its reprojection. There was a moment in the process in which it might seem doubtful whether the tendency to conquer might not triumph in a motor or verbal expression. At that moment, which we may compare with a watershed, the question whether we should, in a literal sense, seize, or should comprehend, the subject was inevitably settled in favor of the latter. While there was a moment (the point of departure) in which the possibility of a disintegration of drives arose and libidinous or destructive tendencies clamored for expression, the triumph of the will to know marked a blending of drives. Although the endeavor to know psychologically had retained so many elements of the urge to conquer, yet the deviation from the original instinctive aim is clear enough. In the place of the will to seize, the will to comprehend appears.

Must the act of comprehending unconscious processes always follow the complicated course here indicated? Is there none shorter and less troublesome? In considering that question I must first remark that I have said nothing of the time taken up by the mental process. It might last only for a fraction of a second. The paths pursued are such as have long been prepared, such as have been traced for many hundreds of thousands of years. And the description here given only holds good for conscious psychological comprehension, that is to say, for the special case in which the observer makes up his mind to comprehend the unconscious processes of other minds.

Nevertheless, the impression made by my description differs from that ordinarily made by the act of comprehending unconscious phenomena. That process seems to us so much simpler and more direct. We believe that we have often understood at once and immediately what is going on unconsciously in another mind. If we examine this objection, we find no material arguments to support it. Let us, for instance, take a case which seems at the first glance to prove it sound: in the course of a conversation a woman recognizes the unconsciously desirous nature of her companion's feelings toward her. In popular psychology an account of such an event would run something like this: certain tones of the voice, gestures, and glances have suddenly convinced the girl of the man's unconscious intentions toward her. In reality that account gives only a poor and inadequate outline of the mental process. The unconscious libidinous tendency in the man stirred a like impulse in the girl, if it was not there from the first; and that induced or enhanced tendency in her ego helped the girl recognize what was going on unconsciously in the man's mind. A fleeting transformation of her ego made it possible for her to realize consciously the unconscious tendency in the man.

Is there, then, no more immediate way to become conscious of the unconscious processes in other minds than the roundabout way through the ego? Here I must plead guilty to a little act of substitution, for I have suddenly replaced the notion of conscious cognition by that of becoming aware of something. Perhaps I did so because the distinction has validity and significance, consciously and unconsciously, only in relation to a higher stage of psychical organization. It is, for instance, hardly applicable to early childhood.

We will, therefore, set aside experimentally the distinction that later acquires such significance. Perhaps it will be useful to choose an example from a remote field of observation. But for the time being I will attribute no other value to it than that of concrete illustration.

What tells dog A., who has just met dog B. and prepares for a fight or a sexual interlude while B. circles round him, the secret intentions of his mate or adversary? We assume that there are certain signals of the sense of smell that perhaps precede visual perceptions—we know that a dog's sight is not very keen. A nuance of smell unknown to us humans—we assume—announces to dog A. that in the next moment dog B. will proceed to attack. A.'s reaction is instinctive and does not wait till the olfactory sensation reaches the dog's consciousness as an idea and is interpreted by him. The reaction takes place rather with the self-evident immediacy of a reflexive movement.

Let us suppose that the dog—and why should we not call him Riquet, in memory of M. Bergeret's clever four-footed friend in Anatole France's novel?—Riquet, then, who reacted to such practical purpose to the sensory signal, is a kind of super dog. Nature has endowed him not only with the gift of speech but also with the capacity for competent self-observation. Let us suppose that he promptly describes to us the experience of meeting the strange dog; their cautious approach to one another, interrupted by pauses; their attempt to make one another's acquaintance, intended to secure an answer to the question: "What kind of a dog are you?" Riquet will tell us how he observed that dog B., or Nero, was going to make a movement of aggression in the next moment, or rather was even then cherishing aggressive intentions.

It seems to me extremely unlikely that Riquet, when asked, would refer us to the process of empathy, familiar to animal psychology, by which he learned his opponent's intentions. If we endow the dog with human qualities, I fear that he would give us only very inadequate information. Perhaps he would not even be able to give us precise information about the exact nature of the smell-signal. Probably he would remark casually that his instinct warned him in the moment preceding the attack. If we pressed him to describe the mental process more accurately, he might mention his own muscular sensations as the last factor accessible to his self-observation. He would refer to a reminiscence of tense muscles, which told him that he himself was just going to leap or run. Of course, we are at liberty to reduce as far as possible the interval between his reception of the signal and his muscular sensation.

In this fancied, and admittedly fanciful, example there is no room for the processes of introjection and projection assumed in us humans. The process really is immediate. We must, therefore, assume that that mechanism cannot develop until a higher plane of psychical organization has been reached and the mind becomes conscious of the other's intentions. Nevertheless the course of animal behavior here supposed—and I have deliberately exaggerated the human-like, anthropomorphic element that generally characterizes animal psychology—offers us material for further reflection. Although the process depicted leaves no room for introjection and projection, yet in Riquet there is a prevision of the psychical process which we assume in the psychological act of human comprehension. We can recognize it in its preliminary stage. Primitive man is informed of the unconscious intentions of others by signals like Riquet's. His own impulses, which may announce themselves by slight, unnoticed tension of the muscles, guide him in his "psychological" perceptions. Paradoxically enough, the whole difference between the process in man and in animals is made all the clearer the more unmistakably we establish certain similarities.

In my example I have represented a psychological process in a dog, and assumed that in him the recognition of intentions in his fellows takes place much more immediately and without mediation. And I chose the dog because he is our housemate, and we imagine—erroneously, I suspect—that we know a good deal about his inner life. And we must take into account that the dog has been domesticated for a very long time and has been alienated from his original instincts by intercourse with mankind. Undoubtedly, as our observations show, he has lost something of the certainty of immediate "comprehension," or becoming aware, of the intentions of others in the course of the development of his species in the company of man, and has exchanged it for new acquisitions attributable to the society of man. Species that have held aloof from human society will certainly become aware of the intentions of other animals more immediately, more in the manner of reflexive action.

We are forced to say to ourselves that we still know so little of the inner life of our own species that we cannot venture to make assumptions about what happens in the minds of other animals. Nevertheless, we have reason to suppose that wild animals have a much simpler and more elementary way of recognizing what other animals want or desire or seek. Thence it is only a step to the assumption that in the early days of his evolution man grasped more immediately what was going on in another mind. A further step leads to the question how he lost that assurance about things psychological that his very distant forefathers presumably possessed.

The question why psychology is necessary could have stood at the very beginning of this inquiry. We evaded it and turned to the problem of how we may reach comprehension of the inner processes of our fellow-men. The question that was avoided re-emerges in a new form: What has made comprehension so difficult? Even now we are too little prepared to give an answer to that question. Perhaps it is even significant that it is raised at all, for in the psychology of consciousness such problems do not arise. Though we cannot at present answer it, we may be better able to some day, when we know more about the genesis and differentiation of consciousness.

In the present state of our knowledge we must be satisfied with quite a general assumption. It points to an increasing loss of this immediate type of comprehension, thanks to the advancing tendency to supplant instinct. And it must be noted that the suppression of instinct preceded the process of supplanting it, and acted in the same direction. Let us refer once more to the example of the dogs. I have said that there we presumably have immediate psychological comprehension. Well, that was true if our example related to two wild dogs. In other species taming and training will already have made a difference in their control of instinct. It will make itself felt in the weakening of "comprehension," or of its immediacy. Not long ago I was observing two dogs, one behind a garden fence and the other outside it, who ran along it and barked at one another in the usual way. Whereas for the most part they ran the same distance, stopping at the same moment in their course and turning round as if at a word of command, it sometimes happened that one of them, a sheep dog, turned sooner or ran farther than the other, a Pomeranian.

It seems as if the *immediacy of comprehension were closely bound up with the state of the individual's instincts,* as though all psychological comprehension were primarily grasping the nature and direction of the other person's instinctive tendencies. But with evolution and training the surety of the original impulses and instincts vanishes, and other secondary tendencies intervene in the play of psychical forces, weakening or changing them, so that the immediacy of the interaction of instincts is lost.

It is the differentiation going on in the evolution of the species, ultimately the different ways in which instinct is suppressed, supplanted, and employed, that makes psychological comprehension between two human beings so difficult. (We should understand more of the inner life of animals, if our own instinctive life had not moved so far away from theirs.) To these differences also are due the uncertainty of our psychological judgments and prejudices. Since the development of human civilization strives in general to weaken the original instinctive impulses in their ancient intensity and to divert them from their primary purposes, comprehension becomes less and less sure with the differentiation of the individual and of many individuals. Thus our lack of confidence in the reliability and immediacy of our own judgment is really lack of confidence in the reliability of our own instinctive impulses, which have been subjected to such far-reaching changes with the development of human civilization.

The fact that we can no longer trust our own immediate judgment, which so often leads us astray, must be attributed to the individual differences in people's repression and supplanting of their instincts. If everybody were on the same "instinctive plane"—and that would mean the equivalent of the same cultural plane—that is to say, if we had all made a halt at the same particular stage in suppressing and satisfying our instincts, there would, indeed, be no immediate psychological comprehension in the old sense, but psychological comprehension of another person would be much easier. Thus the inequality in our use of instinct, that is, in fact, the difference in the rate of cultural development, comes to be a serious hindrance to psychological comprehension.

Animals have no need of psychology, in the sense of a theory of the inner life of other animals, because they know with instinctive certainty what is going on in their minds. Nor had primitive man any need of psychology of this kind, because he still had presumably a large measure of the same instinctive certainty about the mental life of others. That psychology came to be *necessary* must be bound up with the changes, going on for many hundreds of thousands of years, that determined the evolution of mankind. More and more, instinctive certainty must have been lost; the inner life of our fellow-men grew not only more differentiated but also more difficult to know. We are all, it is true, moved by the same invisible strings and checked by them, but they are not equally strong in each individual case, nor is the pull equally forceful in each.

It is true that the ancient reliability and immediacy with which we became aware of impulses in others have only been lost in our consciousness; in the unconscious they are preserved. When people are so fond of declaring that they are all born psychologists, there is some truth in it, no doubt. Their unconscious is an incorruptible psychological organ of perception, but *only* their unconscious, a part of their personality that is, as a rule, inaccessible to them. They are right, therefore, but not in the sense they think they are.

No long ago I read a passage in the Viennese satirist, Nestroy, that sounds like a witty paraphrase of the view put forward here: "If chance brings two wolves together, we may be sure that neither feels the least uneasy because the other is a wolf; two human beings, however, can never meet in the forest, but one must think: That fellow may be a robber."

CHAPTER XLII

The Mechanism of Anticipation

IN THE preceding chapter, I was trying to solve the problem of unconscious comprehension; I used dogs' play in war and sex as an illustration. I have tried to conjecture what went on in the minds of the clever animals, speculating about how they gained so immediate and precise a knowledge of the intentions that their comrades put into action a moment later. And now, with one bold leap, we will clear the barrier dividing human from animal psychology and ask whether there is anything between human beings analogous to an animal's instinctive understanding. And here we enter upon a very interesting section of our inquiry, that of the function of unconscious understanding in social intercourse. For human interplay is very strongly governed by unconscious impulses.

I have spoken of introjection, which seems to me a more fruitful concept for the foundations of psychology than empathy. We see clearly the feint practiced by the advocates of the theory of empathy, when we realize that they regard the action of the empathetic understanding as an ultimate empirical means of cognition, like seeing and hearing—an elementary instinct not to be analyzed psychologically. From this point of view it is certainly easy to do as Max Scheler does and speak of the "perceptibility of inner experience." According to that philosopher there is no psychical *I* and *Thou* phenomologically; there is only an undifferentiated stream of total psychical happening.

If we adhere to the differentiation of a psychical *I* and *Thou*, we are compelled to presume a certain psychical action and interaction. And when we refer to the psychology of the unconscious we see how Scheler could come to his singular theory; the immediacy of the interaction of two unconscious minds might easily lead, or mislead, him to that conviction. In the literature of analysis this immediacy of the psychical reaction, a reflection of which occasionally penetrates to consciousness, is formulated by saying that one person's unconscious comprehends another's. Hitherto when analysts have striven to gain a clearer view of the nature of this unconscious comprehension, they have come up against an almost insurmountable barrier.

It is not surprising that in the attempt to climb over it, the subject has sometimes been clumsily handled or mishandled. Thus, for example, Fenichel distinguishes between two kinds of unconscious comprehension; one based upon signs and one occurring without the aid of signs. The latter supposition seems to me not only mistaken in method, but erroneous. There must be the subtlest signs, unconsciously given and received, and perception by means of senses of which we are not conscious. Especially the term "comprehension" is wrong in this connection. It is rather a lightning-like or slow process of conjecture of what is going on unconsciously in the other person. We see at once how wrong the term "comprehension" is, when we realize that often the conjecture is diametrically opposed to the conscious construction. The unsuitable nature of the term is even more striking when the psychical process is not understood, or is thoroughly misunderstood, by the conscious mind, although its meaning is unconsciously conjectured. Every observing analyst has countless opportunities to note how frequent and how gross is this antithesis between the conscious apprehension and the unconscious conjecture of other people's mental processes in social life.

It is almost as if, apart from the visible relations between human beings, there were others, far removed from consciousness, whose character and action we nevertheless conjecture successfully. It sometimes happens that these secret motions not only find expression but also penetrate to consciousness after many years or even decades. Secret motions are those that struggle in vain against being brought to the light of day. The behavior of our fellows, what they do and leave undone, what they say and leave unsaid, offer unequivocal evidence, even if we are not always in a position to interpret it. Beyond the region of conscious understanding, there is something in human relations that speaks a subterranean, secret language, softer and yet wiser than that of the conscious understanding. Sometimes it seems as if our conscious actions were only a phantasmagoria, while all that was really significant in our mental life took place behind the scenes. In that region true answers are given to false questions; the truth is detected in the false answer; nay, a significant answer is even given to a question that we have not heard or understood consciously. Hints that were not intended as such are shrewdly understood, although we have not consciously grasped their meaning. Unconsciously we sense the purpose of an action or reaction, or of a blunder. Even in the foggy air of human intercourse there is, unconsciously, great clarity. While we have no idea consciously of the hidden purposes and impulses of another person, unconsciously we may react to them as sensitively as a seismograph to a faint subterranean vibration.

Eddington says that the progress of a science is measured more by the questions it raises than by the ones that it solves. If this is true it would almost seem that psychoanalysis has reached a standstill, that what it can achieve is a closed book written by Freud. In reality psychoanalysis today is called upon to raise new questions. How, for example, does the unconscious of one person react upon the unconscious of another? The psychology of interpersonal relations is virtually unexplored as a realm of analytic research. There are psychical mechanisms we hardly notice that we are certainly very far from understanding.

Let us choose as representative a phenomenon I should like to call the mechanism of *unconscious anticipation*. We have here a special case in which our unconscious knowledge of one another finds symptomatic, and not only symptomatic, expression. This mechanism acts in the unconscious anticipation of another person's emotional reaction to our own behavior. It is, so to speak, an experimental anticipation, inaccessible to the ego, of the effects produced by our own behavior.

I can more effectively demonstrate this psychical mechanism by an example of the way it acts than by a definition or description. I choose my example intentionally, not from the sphere of analytic practice, but from everyday life. Moreover, it is not chosen in such a way that the quality of the unconscious is of decisive importance. We have all of us watched a woman, followed by a man, automatically smoothing her hair. The psychical mechanism at work seems fairly simple. The woman tidies her hair because, consciously or unconsciously, she wants to please the man who is following her. Every woman will say that the mental process need not be so primitive. Especially a woman who makes a movement to tidy or beautify herself need not be at all conscious of her action. The fact that the man's eye is upon her makes her see herself, her hair, and her general appearance as another person—in this case the man behind her—sees them. In thus regarding herself with the eyes of another she anticipates—usually unconsciously or pre-consciously—the impression that she will make upon the other. In other words, her action is a reaction to a hypothetical impression. We need not, of course, confine the formula to this behavior; it holds good for a certain part of our unconscious processes.

Let us now think of the rather more complicated example of the disgust with which their own bodies inspire many women during menstruation. Undoubtedly that reaction may be traced in part to anticipation of their husbands' feeling of disgust, which is, of course, taken into account in the education of the growing girl. The mechanism of the anticipation of a psychical effect upon others, whether unconscious or grown conscious, probably dominates the whole inner origin of disgust; that is to say, the anticipated reaction of the parents and of others in the child's environment determines that psychical phenomenon of repulsion.

Meanwhile I will pass beyond the narrow field of typical behavior into the wider region of more general phenomena, in which the mechanism of anticipation governs a vast number of individual actions and reactions. And here it is important psychologically to distinguish between anticipations that occur consciously, those which begin unconsciously but are later recognized by us, and those which owe their existence to unconscious and repressed impulses and remain unconscious. Let me give a simple example of the second type: Mr. A., an American, wants to tell his acquaintance, Mr. B., that his wife was prevented on the preceding day from going to the theater; she was ill. He starts to say "sick," but chooses another word. Recalling the conversation later on, the reason occurs to him: the man he was talking to is an Englishman, and you can use the expression "She is sick" in England when you mean that a woman vomits. No doubt he wanted to prevent B. from supposing that his wife was pregnant, he tells himself later. Here, then, is a definite unconscious motive for avoiding the use of the word. Every psychological observer knows of many hundreds of such cases.

Certainly the psychological significance to which the mechanism of anticipation may lay claim in social intercourse has not yet been adequately explored. To realize that fact we need only think of its psychical effects in private and public life, where it draws its power from repressions, and where conscious thought and action seem in violent contradiction to the assumption of such effects. We need only think of the more or less fascinating play of mutual flight and mutual attraction between two young people, to which Mephistopheles gives the contemptuous name of *"Brimborium,"* that prelude to the satisfaction of the sexual instinct. He warns Faust and admonishes him:

> . . . why seek
> To hurry to enjoyment straight?
> The pleasure is not half so great
> As when at first, around, above
> With all the fooleries of love
> The puppet you can knead and mold
> As in Italian story oft is told.

How many anticipations of this kind there are then in thoughts and little actions; how speech and answer are tuned to one another in their unconscious meaning, in repulse and surrender! Observation has frequently impressed upon us how a drive works its way through to its goal in its psychical manifestations, independent of the conscious will, how it advances with the speed of seven-league boots or step by step, its progress determined by law. Psychologists know how helpful this unconscious anticipation is in the relations between the sexes, so manifold and yet so monotonous.

We may observe the same unconscious comprehension and the same anticipation of the peculiar reaction of the other person, where love or friendship is slowly dissolving: that unintentional and yet unconsciously intended misunderstanding of what has hitherto made the relation precious. The mechanism evinces its effects in all human relations as an important means of comprehension apart from verbal speech. The unconscious anticipation of the way in which another person will react is one of the most important psychological conditions in the development of our relations, whether they develop toward tenderness or hostility, friendship or envy. In the process of anticipation we seem to divine the action of our own unconscious impulses, as well as the mental reactions of the other person. A shy man often makes other people shy, too. A person who adopts a masochistic attitude in his social relations often stirs an unconscious sadistic instinctive reaction in another. Is it not his unconscious desire to stir it?

All this might almost imply that in everything that we do and think we unconsciously picture to ourselves how the other person, to whom it relates, will react to it. And, going a step farther, how he would react to our thoughts. In that case we should never be alone. When I think of Mr. X. or Mrs. Z., whatever my thoughts and ideas may be, whether I picture myself as subject or object in relation to them, they are present, so to speak, in that I unconsciously anticipate what their attitude would be to my thoughts about them and to the actions that concern them. And in actual fact we do unconsciously anticipate the emotional and intellectual reactions of these persons, and allow them to take their course, in a way, experimentally. What the poet says is true also in this sense of a permanent exchange of unconscious thoughts:

> In us are all—none, none is alone.
> You are their life and their life is your own.
> —BEER-HOFMANN, "Lullaby for Miriam"

Where we anticipate the reaction of our environment to our behavior in our conscious thoughts, we have an exceptional case that, under certain dynamic and economic conditions, confirms the regular occurrence of the unconscious mental process. The mechanism of anticipation is not confined to this direct occupation of our thoughts with persons. It accompanies a large number of psychical phenomena that have nothing directly to do with the objects.

It is easy to see the origin of such an unconscious phenomenon: a child fancies the reaction of his parents and nurses during many of his actions. The imagined or supposed presence of these persons will relate at first more to the negative side of the reactions—that is to say, it will anticipate the repudiation or admonition or disapproval of the parents. (We picture the reaction of many a mother in relation to her unsupervised child as expression to these anticipations: "Go and see what Teddy is doing in the garden, and tell him not to.")

At a later stage the imagined presence of his mother will precede the action. The primitive character of the anticipated reaction will give place to greater variety (several kinds and degrees of disapproval, consent, delight, and so on). Children often show a remarkable delicacy of feeling for those reactions. I was impressed by what I heard from a man who had been born a hunchback. He recalled that in his childhood he had no intense feelings at the mockery of some tough boys when he was alone on the street; but when the same boys ridiculed him as he walked along with his mother, he felt deeply humiliated. In the setting up of a supervising factor within the ego, the superego, the most important instance of anticipation becomes a permanent institution. Much more numerous are the cases of anticipation that produce no such deep and lasting consequences in the unconscious life of the mind, and yet reflect the influence of our environment.

Among the cases in which the anticipation of psychical reactions has reference to repressed impulses, we must count all those in which the ego has called forth reactions that it does not desire through its behavior. To be consistent, we must assume that here, too, the ego unconsciously anticipated the consequence of its behavior and, much as we may resist the assumption, secretly desired this or a similar reaction on the part of its environment.

Take any chance case: A young man in financial straits tried hard to get a job; he constantly found himself before shut doors. Where he was given a hearing he was nevertheless rejected after a short time. In such cases we are of course inclined to suppose at once that there were very few jobs open, and that our young man was just a victim of unfavorable economic conditions. Analysis shows that it was often only partly the case. In every case where the young man succeeded in getting an interview with the head of a firm, he made some *faux pas,* behaved awkwardly or arrogantly, suddenly knew nothing about something with which he was usually familiar. There could be no doubt but that he himself unconsciously spoiled his own chances. The analysis showed that he almost staged it, often and with peculiar subtlety, as if he had waited unconsciously for the very moment when he might count upon getting the job, to pull his boner. It really seemed as if he could foresee and calculate exactly the effect of some little awkwardness or exposure of himself—it all happened so accurately, as if with calculated skill, or as in a play. This anticipation of the psychical effect of his reactions upon the other man sometimes produced the impression that the preceding conversation had unconsciously merely served to enable him to take the self-destructive step with the utmost certainty, and to prevent the thing toward which his whole conscious energy was directed—his appointment.

It seems probable to me that *many cases of the dark constraint of destiny, depicted by Freud, can be explained only by means of this unconscious anticipation of other people's mental reaction.* I received this impression, for instance, in analyzing a girl who always suffered the same disappointment, with the same typical termination, in her relations with young men. It seemed as if unconsciously she not only made her choice with this in view but as if her whole behavior from the beginning of the affair had been so determined, as though she had always secretly foreseen the recurring termination, great as were her conscious hopes that this time it would end differently. In this case as in so many others of a similar nature, an unconscious feeling of one's own inferiority was operating. The girl was unconsciously afraid that the young man would, when he knew her better, find out that she had nothing to offer, that she was stupid, shallow, worthless. When the young man wooed her, her anxiety over such a pending discovery of her faults unconsciously increased to the stage of panic, and she used the next occasion to break up the relationship. The mechanism that unconsciously governed her behavior is thus a "flight forward." She became so afraid that she had to run forward to the imagined danger. It was as if she had no other way to remove her panic than by herself bringing about what she feared. The clerk who is going to be dismissed says, "You can't fire me, because I am resigning."

This mechanism of unconscious anticipation describes, as it were, a great vault arched above all our social relations. It stretches from unconscious prevision of another's response to a chance word, to reactions to our whole psychical behavior; from the single deed with definite and conscious motives to the compulsive repetition of a fated train of events seemingly determined only from without. In success and failure the nature and tendency of other people's mental reaction is unconsciously anticipated to an extent not hitherto appreciated. The secret instinctive forces leading to the result that we unconsciously intend are foreseen by some endopsychic power, though they may appear wholly foreign to the ego. We might say that the self guesses more about itself than it knows.

The concept that we unconsciously foresee the emotional reactions of others to our own behavior or attitudes leads to certain theoretical considerations and is also of great practical importance. A Frenchman once said: "Not only is England an island, but every Englishman." Every person observed as an isolated individual is like an island. Alone, he can hide his character and motives to a great extent, but the nature of human relations is such that in the company of others he tends to reveal himself.

The experiences of the young man who could not get a job and the girl who was always disappointed by men speak a language that is quite clear. The mishaps that appear to these people as blows dealt by fate working through external circumstances are really happenings stage-managed by their own unconscious reactions. These, working behind the scenes of conscious wishes and thoughts, could not be effective if they did not foresee the consequences of the behavior they produce. If such unconscious foreknowledge of the emotional reactions of others does indeed exist, we feel tempted to assume that the response is secretly desired however dark may be the motives for such an attitude. Whenever the analyst observes human relations it will seem to him that such reactions from the environment are unconsciously wished for.

A young man complained that whenever he tried to get information from officials he was rudely answered. He reported many incidents of this sort. The analyst could prove to him that his questions were so silly that they could have been asked only to annoy and irritate the other person. Our young man was unconsciously a rebel who wanted to provoke the representatives of authority. His seeming submissiveness and apparent attitude of wide-eyed admiration were so conspicuous that they revealed rather than hid his unconscious tendencies. The person to whom he put his questions did not react to his conscious attitude but to his unconscious mockery. The young man also has a trying habit of repeating slowly and thoughtfully every answer he was given as if he doubted its correctness. No wonder his informant lost his temper. The young man really "asked for it."

A girl was so worried about her mother's health that she insisted the old lady be warmly dressed even on hot days. She would not permit her to go out when it was raining, did not allow her to see visitors who might give her a cold germ. The daughter's concern and apprehension about her mother's health were so exaggerated that they actually amounted to tyranny and a subtle form of torment. The mother, patient at first, always became angry with her oversolicitous daughter finally. She reacted as if she had been treated with hostility rather than loving concern, and her behavior corresponded to the unconscious truth of her daughter's attitude.

The analyst sees many people who apparently have the best intentions but who somehow anger and provoke others. They succeed in making themselves obnoxious and we must assume that that is what they wish to do. Parents and children, husbands and wives, reveal their unconscious tendencies to each other in a thousand different ways. The aim of such unconscious motivation is well understood by others but the actor is almost never aware of it. Its true character is brought to light only by the response of the environment.

A patient of mine had an argument with her boss during which she gave him a piece of her mind. Later she felt guilty and apologized but she framed her apology in such terms that the man had more reason than ever to feel hurt. I assume that while she consciously wanted to ask his forgiveness, she was compelled to give him another piece of her mind.

A girl wanted very much to get married and wondered why all men turned away from her after a little while. From the reports of her conversations with some of them I was able to show her that she told them rude and sharply critical things while she thought she was amusing them with her frankness. Unconsciously she destroyed her own chances; the behavior of the men shows they were offended. Did she not want to offend them? She was unconsciously hostile to men.

I do not like to flirt with an idea; either I leave it alone or I go through with it. The accumulation of many impressions of the sort I have been describing led to a view that had to be re-examined and verified. I subjected all subsequent observations of human relations in analytic experience and in daily life to careful examination. Most of them seemed to confirm a psychological insight, which in my thoughts took almost the form of a law. So far as I know, this general insight, to which there are few exceptions, has not yet been formulated in psychoanalytic literature. It seems to me so valid that it can be applied in almost all cases. *The nature of an individual's unconscious motives is revealed by the effect of his actions and behavior upon others.* Otherwise put: The psychologist can infer, from the effects of a person's behavior, his unconscious motives which often are in contrast with the conscious motivation. If we apply this rule in daily life we may assert that the reactions of the environment to a certain bit of behavior reveal the unconscious motives of the actor, regardless of his conscious intentions and wishes. Of course there are exceptions to this rule as for instance when the environment is itself criminal or pathological, or when extraordinary situations complicate and distort the issue.

To be sure this insight can lead only to provisional psychological results. We observe that a man harms himself by his behavior. The reactions of his wife, his friends, or his employers show that they become angry with him and punish him for his offensive conduct. The psychoanalyst must now discover the unconscious motives of the behavior that causes such definite reactions from others. The analyst must turn the stone—in this case the stumbling block—to see what is beneath it. He may find any one of many different motives, self-punishment, the desire to harm oneself, aggressiveness, and so on. The general insight that I have formulated cannot be used as a key to the inner rooms but it does unlock the door to the hall through which one can enter the interior of the apartment.

I have already tried to depict the instinctive conditions of the mechanism of anticipation, without denying the rational elements at work in it. In the sphere where the drives have their dwelling, may be the origin of the presentiments conditioning the act of anticipation. There, too, we must seek the psychical factors that seem to extend the phenomena of unconscious anticipation on two sides to the border regions of the mind. On the one hand it seems as though the ego could foresee actual future events to whose occurrence no objective signals point. On the other hand, as though it had remarkable, sometimes positively prophetic, powers of guessing the psychical reactions of other people in advance. On this supposition, the ego would possess in its unconscious, not only hitherto undreamed-of dynamic qualities, but similar prophetic qualities. And this appearance has some foundation in fact, when we reflect that in these phenomena we have unconscious forces whose action is largely unrecognized, or at least not sufficiently recognized.

In the first contingency (where events are "foreseen") we can detect, in many a case open to psychological investigation and examination, a blend consisting of the unconscious conjecture of the drives governing the minds of men and women in the environment, and of conscious or preconscious knowledge and experience. What we have is not so much a prophetic vision of coming events as projections of our own unconscious wishes, rooted in our drives, or kindred expectations of future ills. We cannot always lay bare these subterranean conditions. There really is something like an unconscious presentiment of our own destiny, springing from unrealized insight into the peculiarities of our ego. A hidden, or unconfessed, knowledge of our own inner potentialities— or of the things that we secretly strive for or fear—is at work in it.

An experience of this kind from my own youth made a strong impression upon me. In a conversation with Arthur Schnitzler I expressed my disbelief that a man could find himself in a certain situation that is presented in one of his plays. Some months later I found myself in precisely the situation that I had declared inconceivable to me. It was as if I had anticipated the situation unconsciously, and my statement to Schnitzler had been in the nature of an intense reluctance to admit such a possibility, a disavowal of consciously unknown, but dark emotional, potentialities in myself.

The anticipation of the effect of our behavior and our utterances on other people usually appears as the outcome of a similar unconscious projection. Furthermore, we must not underestimate the part played by preconscious knowledge, based upon our earlier experience. But the phenomenon is determined in particular by the introspective unconscious perception of how *we* should behave in such a case, if we were the *other person,* that is to say, the object. On occasion this origin of anticipation even reaches consciousness.

For instance, a woman patient who had displayed strong unconscious resistance said during a treatment: "How you will hate me!" That means: If I were in your place, I should hate a person bitterly who tried to torment me so much. I had a similar case in the utterance of another woman patient, who was always trying to assure herself of my good will and forgiveness. She was constantly begging my pardon and asking whether I would always remain friendly to her, although she was unaware so far of harboring any malicious intentions toward me. It was only much later that I found out what her request for pardon referred to. It had hastened to anticipate the action of cruel and aggressive tendencies, as yet unrecognized by the ego but unconsciously known to it, and was thus fully justified psychologically.

Psychological projection, acting through the mechanism of anticipation, will explain the psychogenesis of many beliefs and many superstitions. It is easy to recognize the protective measures taken to prevent some evil that is feared as a defense against unconsciously projected and anticipated wishes of our own. We protect ourselves, so to speak, against the consequences of the wicked desires that we ourselves would feel if we were in the position of the other person. Appreciation of this anticipation, in combination with projection, brings us near to a psychological explanation of the belief in the evil eye, for example.

I have already spoken of the way in which the mechanism of anticipation presupposes in itself a secret knowledge of our own ego. It is a case of a psychological possession that can no more be unearthed than a buried treasure whose whereabouts cannot be brought to light. Unconsciously the ego possesses more psychological knowledge of itself and others than is accessible to it. On the other hand, it overestimates, as we know, the extent and value of its conscious psychological knowledge—that is to say, what it has at its command and disposal.

In his conversations with Eckermann, Goethe called anticipation "foreknowledge drawn from our knowledge of our inner selves." We can agree with him, if we supplement his definition by saying that this foreknowledge is derived from unconscious or repressed knowledge of our inner selves. It would not appear justifiable to use the term "foreknowledge" if that were not the case. We would simply have to speak of knowledge based upon a psychological foundation. Moreover, this character of the factor of anticipation shows how far such knowledge is distinct from rational knowledge, and from what depths of the mind it draws its strong faith. In particular cases analysis can prove convincingly that this "foreknowledge" is to be traced back to perceptions of our own hidden impulses, either unconscious or lost to consciousness, perceptions of the inner potentialities of ourselves and others. Latin scholars have a proverb which says that learning is nothing but remembering (*nihil aliud discere quam recordari*). I do not think that the proverb is quite true; we learn a great deal without remembering it. And the foreknowledge of anticipation is perhaps, in its essence, only the reflection of unconscious knowledge, of which the psychical origin and precise nature have slipped our memory. It belongs to the dark self-perception of the wide domain which is the self and which reaches far beyond the narrow boundaries of the conscious ego.

CHAPTER XLIII

The Shock of Thought

A FALSE assumption that has almost developed into a myth is that the course of analysis is largely independent of the personality of the analyst. And here I am not speaking of the therapeutic aspect of the psychological task but of investigation. Surely nobody will contend that individual talents for grasping unconscious relations do not vary.

To me it seems an obvious assumption that the individual's psychological qualifications can be improved by his own analysis and his further analytic training. Still, we know very little how far such training is able to enhance receptivity of psychological data, sensitiveness to the significance and range of interpretation of the products of the unconscious, and the gift of sensing subterranean links. At any rate, I doubt very much whether training can equalize differences in talent. Some experience points to the probability that the measure and depth of psychological comprehension are not greatly altered even when the student has waded through the whole course or all the courses. Even analysts learn only what they are capable of learning. I do believe that analytic training can amend faults of character and correct defects in personality. But I do not believe that it can compensate for shortcomings in personality.

Any achievement in one of the spheres where unconscious effort plays a part will always be dependent upon the quality of the worker. In investigating unconscious processes, differences rooted in the nature and character of the investigator will have significance for the quality and depth of his cognition. *The fact that the analyst's ego does not come to*

the fore in his work, that his person is lost to sight behind his achieve-
ment, does not at all mean that it is not at work in that achievement.
How could it be otherwise, when the subject of the psychology of the
unconscious are the most personal and intimate processes of the mind,
which can only be grasped and comprehended by the most personal
qualities in the analyst? Of him, too, it is true that to achieve something
he must be somebody.

In opposition to the majority of my fellow-analysts, I profess the
opinion that the individual manner of conjecturing and comprehending
unconscious and repressed processes comes to be the expression of definite characterological qualities. Like every other scientific method, analysis strives to observe and describe the processes under investigation as
objectively and accurately as possible. To that end it seems essential
that what is personal in the investigator should be, as far as may be,
excluded in capturing the processes, since the intervention of anything
subjective must have a disturbing effect upon cognition. But that is not
identical with the asumption that one of the organs of perception may
be restricted in its functions. A botanist will place his eyes, as well as
his sense of smell and touch, in the service of his scientific work; so
will a doctor who has to ascertain the changes taking places in the
human organism. There is nothing to prevent us from regarding the
unconscious as a sense organ living a life of its own. We know, of
course, that this can only be a comparison, but the function of the unconscious in the process of cognition seems to justify it.

Now the unconscious functions alike in everybody as an organ for
seizing upon the concealed processes in the inner life of others. It has
the same tendencies and the same methods of work. It is, so to speak,
the most impersonal thing in the personality, and yet we speak of the
personal factor and attribute to it great importance in the development
and peculiar character of psychological cognition. But when we speak
of the personal factor, we do not thereby indicate the unconscious as
such, but the individually varying relation of the conscious and preconscious to that system, the dynamics and economy of the play of forces
so introduced, which govern the intercourse between the psychical
agents. The quality of that relation mirrors the history of the individual
and his relation to his environment and his inner world.

When psychoanalysts declare that the psychological comprehension
of the individual is limited by his repressions, they only pick out *one*
factor—a specially important one, it is true—from the many and various

relations between the conscious and unconscious that are of importance to analysis. It is worth noting that this factor is negative: it sets the limits to the comprehension within each one of us. But it assuredly cannot be said that a person whose repressions have been removed in a deep-reaching analysis henceforth understands the language of the conscious and the unconscious repressed as easily and clearly as Solomon, in the legend, understood the language of all animals. For the removal is only temporary, we might say often momentary. Repression is a process governed and rendered necessary by the development of civilization, and renews its advance along the old channel.

In addition to the factor of repression, there are certain negative character-traits; and, on the other hand, there are certain psychological factors that favor the individual's comprehension of the unconscious. We still know very little of these personal qualities, and the little that we do know must be held back till it has stood the test of repeated and careful examination.

I am at liberty to extract only a very small fragment from this large and still unilluminated mass. I dare to assert that the way a person deals with his own emotional experiences determines to a great extent the depth and extent of his understanding of unconscious processes. There is a well-known French proverb that says: *"Le style c'est l'homme."* Freud corrected it: *"Le style c'est l'histoire de l'homme."* In this case perhaps the history not only means the story of the individual life but also takes in the emotional traces of the lives of the ancestors. It seems to me that the personal style of analyzing is also part of the life story of the man. It seems to me that it is ridiculous to exclude this personal factor from consideration in a matter as personal as the capabilities of an analyst.

If I were asked what quality I regard as most important for an analyst, I should reply: *moral courage*. It would be absurd to assert that an analyst must be superior to his patients in brains or knowledge or acumen. But in this matter, in moral courage or, as we might call it, in inner truthfulness, he must be superior. The training of analysts should be directed less toward the acquisition of practical and theoretical knowledge than the extension of intellectual independence. It is not so much a question of acquiring technical ability as inner truthfulness.

In old Austria the soldiers who had specially distinguished themselves in the war received a decoration with the motto: "For bravery in the face of the enemy." The special kind of civil courage that seems to me necessary for an analyst might be called *courage in the face of his own thoughts.* This courage is seen and proven when an individual meets with a thought or idea in his own ego, the nature of which runs decidedly counter to his moral, aesthetic, and logical demands. There are various means of dealing with these thoughts or ideas to which the ego offers special resistance. Just as with the external enemy, you can meet them and suppress them, you can hide from them or deny their existence, or you can run away from them.

An unexpected encounter with a thought of this kind generally releases a momentary psychical reaction in the ego that I call the shock of thought. I have taken this designation from Freud's *Interpretation of Dreams,* where it occurs only once, though in a significant passage. The term "fear" does not seem right here, if only on account of the time factor. If fear is comparable with a line, then we must liken shock to a point.

It is a question of a reaction that frequently occurs when we unexpectedly encounter a thought or an impulse of which we had not believed ourselves capable. We are not conscious of it, however conscientiously we examine our ego. Here, again, we come upon the factor of surprise, which has occupied a particularly important place in this inquiry. In an experience of this order we cannot escape responsibility for the startling idea or impulse that emerged in us, unless we believe that Satan or some Power of Darkness has induced it in us.

But why do I call the reaction to this kind of unexpected encounter the shock of thought? Do we not know that we would not yield to a murderous impulse so long as we are in our right mind? Thoughts are duty-free; ought they not to be free from shock, too? And are they not thoughts everything in us rebels against?

Analysis shows, indeed, that not everything within us rebels against them. A hidden factor within us welcomes them vigorously. There is, therefore, no other explanation for our shock than the assumption that there is within us the fear and the wish that our thoughts might inadvertently turn to reality. It is certainly a fact that the liability to shock in relation to our own thoughts varies in different individuals. But it is also a fact that most of us are already acquainted with this shock at the first and unexpected encounter with something returning from the region of repression. Where we do not notice it, it has quickly made way for some other kind of reaction, but it was there at first, even if we did not recognize it.

But why shock? Would not fear be a more suitable concept and a more appropriate word? Analysis has shown the pre-eminent significance of the emotion of fear in mental disturbances, and has demonstrated that the problem of fear must be regarded as the most important in relation to the development of neuroses. *But the root problem of neurosis is not fear, but shock.* In my opinion *that problem remains insoluble until fear is brought into connection with the emotion of shock.* The memory-trace of the prime shock of the human creature is at work in fear. It is not fear but shock to which belongs the paralysis of our machinery of motion, tightness of breath, pallor, and the sensation of coldness. As contrasted with fear, shock has a simpler, less definite, and more violent character.

Shock is the prime emotion, the first that the little living creature feels. I do not believe in the theory of fear in the trauma of birth, but that the moment of birth is marked by the first, profound shock, from which the later shocks, so frequent in babyhood, are copied. All the physiological and psychological signs support the assumption that nature's first emotion is shock. I hold that shock is in general characteristic of a traumatic situation; fear, of a situation of danger. *Shock is the emotional reaction to something that bursts in upon us; fear, the reaction to something that comes with a menace.* Fear is itself a signal preceding shock; it anticipates the emotion of shock in miniature and so protects us from it and from its profound and harmful effects. Thus, on the one hand it is the expectation of the experience of shock in the situation of trauma, on the other its mitigated repetition.

Not fear but shock is the primary and universal psychical reaction of the newborn human being and animal. A baby reacts to the faintest visual and acoustic stimuli, which the adult ego would not notice, with all the mimic signs of shock. It is only gradually that the reaction of shock yields to an adaptation to stimuli better suited to the child's environment. The little thing's liability to shock gradually diminishes in intensity and frequency.

It would seem that one of the first, unconscious aims of education would be to reduce a baby's liability to shock. To accustom him to the stimulus by repeating it is not only a phenomenon of biological adaptation, but at the same time an educational measure.

Mankind in its evolution passes through the same stages as the little human child in the inner mastery of those stimuli which originally produce shock. Explorers and ethnologists all agree in saying that the most primitive tribes are all exceedingly liable to shock. Everything unknown and unusual is monstrous to them. The advance of human civilization finds expression not least in the conquest or mitigation of liability to shock. Not only the number of objects that induce shock, but also the violence of the emotion, is diminished. The appearance of fear, placed as a barrier before the emotion of shock, is one sign of that mitigation. The emotion of fear is distinguished from shock not only in intensity; its very nature shows that it saves the ego from the suddenness and the overwhelming effect that characterize shock.

We must regard it as a consequence of the advance of civilization that inner shocks take the place of external ones, that we feel shock at our own drives and impulses, whereas in the world of primitive man all shocks come from without. O'Neill's Emperor Jones sees himself surrounded by threatening visions in the great forest—his past becomes alive. In place of the evil spirits that surrounded primitive man on all sides and gave him shocks, we find in the later periods of civilization all the terrors or shocks of conscience. No doubt there are plenty of external causes of shock even for civilized man. But their number seems small compared with the omnipresence of things that caused shock in the early days of the human race. We may assume that the more the cause of shock came from within, the greater was the change in the violence and the psychical effect of shock. Fear as a substitute for shock and a reaction against it constitutes a guarantee that the emotion is no longer able to overcome the ego.

One of the first tasks of civilization was to free men from shock in relation to external objects, or objects projected outward. Perhaps the first heroes of the human race were those who held their own against a shock that paralyzed others. Hundreds of thousands of years later the activities of Epicurus, for instance, served this aim of civilization when he taught men to cease feeling terror of the gods. The continuation of the cultural effort here denoted is the struggle against fear, which has taken the place of the original shock. That new task in the service of human evolution is very far from being accomplished. It now teaches us to struggle against our fear of our own unconscious impulses and thoughts. I believe that a considerable share in this cultural task has fallen to the lot of psychoanalysis, since it diminishes the individual feeling of guilt, or social fear. People would be more sincere if they had more often the courage of their own thoughts; they would also be wiser and maturer. If we watch our own fear and the fear of other people, which prevents us all from being completely sincere, we recognize how we adults have remained minors. How like we are in our nature to little boys and girls who resort to all manner of excuses and dodges to avoid confessing their childish deeds and desires! Perhaps people would even be more capable of love if they had more the courage of their thoughts. It was only a seeming paradox when somebody not long ago characterized love as the "absence of fear."

It is in accordance with the advancing inward tendency in the course of evolution that we now receive a shock, not only when we catch ourselves with impulses and thoughts incompatible with the moral demands that we make upon ourselves, but also with ideas and impulses of a different sort. I mean, for instance, impulses that seem to menace our aesthetic requirements and the rules of cleanliness and propriety. That sounds more paradoxical than it really is, especially because the emotion of shock is not clearly felt in the case of such violation of our customary behavior. We must remember that the emotion is mitigated in intensity and of extremely short duration. It may often occur only as a very fleeting initial emotion, speedily replaced by fear and then by other reactions.

There certainly are people who receive a shock at the mere thought of a small infringement of their customary behavior; for instance, the woman who gets a shock if a vulgar expression or a grossly sexual term crosses her mind. Indeed, if I may trust to single impressions from my own and others' observations, a kind of shock is received when we feel the impulse to say something tactless. We have in these phenomena genuine shock, though it may express itself in a form different from the corresponding, more violent emotion in a traumatic situation.

In the analysis of pathological phenomena this identity of emotion is seen clearly enough, as, for example, in the case of sudden obsessions. One patient suffering from compulsion suddenly felt the impulse to drink the contents of a certain person's chamber pot. It must not be thought that this impulse reflected a perverse preference for a young lady, and that the patient wanted to follow the example of the German knight, Ulrich von Liechtenstein, who, according to the medieval legend, liked to drink the urine of his lady. The person in question in the present case was the patient's grandmother. When the patient was seized by this incomprehensible impulse or command, he received a violent shock. A sufferer from compulsion sustains a similar shock when malicious desires or thoughts of death directed against those whom he loves suddenly enter his train of thought. The wide range of things that cause shock extends far beyond the field of pathological phenomena. Certain phenomena of civilization cause many people to sacrifice great parts of their personalities to protect themselves against shock. They place great restrictions on their egos in order to avoid shock and the consequent fear. Thus conscience does make cowards of us all.

We often find the same reaction associated with ideas and thoughts that are absurd or fantastic, that unite incompatibles, take the impossible for granted, or violate the elementary laws of logic. It seems then as if a power that we might call the categorical imperative in the testing of reality and common sense, forbade us to think what is nonsensical. It is as if, confronted with these ideas and thoughts, a bad conscience that has adopted an intellectual character made itself felt and protested against our own intellectual sins and delinquencies of imagination. In these cases self-criticism acquires a markedly moral tone. We may understand this as being due to the effect of the psychical mechanism of displacement, for it is those nearest and dearest to the child who train him to be reasonable and to respect reality, as well as to be good and moral. The intervention of the laws of reason, and of thought in harmony with reality, continues to depend upon the authority of persons admired by the child. And so a momentary relapse into the primitive manner of thinking not governed by adult logic is often evaluated by us as an act of disobedience. The emotional reaction to it is often a kind of intellectual shock of very short duration.

With some people the reaction may occur consciously, when they meet with a fantastic or nonsensical idea in themselves in the full daylight of conscious and sober thinking. There are, of course, different types of reaction to these unexpected interlopers in the realm of the imagination. It often happens that we smile at their queerness, but sometimes we only smile after a preliminary shock. And in the realm of our own thoughts and ideas it is only a step from the shock-giving to the ridiculous. The momentary shock at the emergence of absurd and fantastic ideas has a psychological justification; once we have broken through the shell of rationality and adaptation to reality, we never know where irrationality, fancy, or whatever you like to call these forces, will call a halt.

One of the duties of an analyst is to stand up to this shock of thought —that is to say, not to start back in alarm when, in regarding his data, absurd or irrelevant ideas arise. Sometimes it is much easier to admit a cynical thought to consciousness than a fantastic or odd idea that is quite out of place in this rational, or would-be rational, world.

It is, of course, necessary that the analyst should not share the attitude of his patient who shies away from his own thoughts like a horse that suddenly becomes aware of the shadow it casts in the sun. This comparison brings to mind a simple example of such an uncanny idea. Pulled from one side to the other by his many doubts, a patient with a serious compulsion neurosis had a mental image of Ravaillac, the murderer of King Henry IV of France. Ravaillac was condemned to be torn apart by horses driven in different directions. My patient saw himself tied to the horses and his mutilated body. He shuddered at the idea, even as he told it to me the next day. "What nonsense!" he shouted. "I have never heard of Ravaillac since I heard the name in school." The analytic explanation took the suddenly emerging idea seriously. He must have identified himself with the murderer of the king. He remembered then that in those school days when he heard of Ravaillac, he had a great interest in the horses his father kept at the time. Then another characteristic was remembered. Henry IV was murdered while sitting in the toilet seat. The patient was often annoyed as a boy by the fact that his father remained in the toilet so long. Many of the doubts that occupied him at the time the surprising image emerged circle around his attitude toward his father whom he both admired and detested. Every analyst knows similar ideas arising from the psychical assimilation of data that sound far more fantastic and bizarre.

Even analysts are severely tempted to reject such ideas as irrelevant or senseless. It takes moral courage to hold onto them as informative and useful and to treat them as mentally real and important. A person who does not acquire that courage will never experience surprises in himself and others. One who takes headlong flight from the shock of thought to reasonable and rational ideas is in the same position as a patient who, having suddenly had a fantastic or nonsensical idea, is ready to dismiss it as nonsense. The merely intellectual belief in the value of involuntary ideas and associations does not insure an analyst against attack by the shock of thought.

The inner truthfulness that I have called moral courage often goes beyond the obligation to think these thoughts to the end—it calls for their utterance. If we do not say what we ourselves think, how can we expect another to have the courage to do so? It goes without saying that this courage must be coupled with special self-criticism and discretion, but the discretion must not be the better part of intellectual valor.

Courage seems to me to be one of the finest virtues, for it excludes many faults, like lying, hypocrisy, and insincerity. In many cases it is not lack of knowledge and acumen, *but lack of moral courage that prevents us from comprehending the hidden meaning of unconscious processes. It is that same moral courage that enables us to discover things hitherto unknown in the realm of the unconscious mind.* We recall that Freud ascribed it to that kind of courage that he was able to make the vital discovery of the hidden meaning of dreams. We see more and more clearly that the conditions of psychological comprehension are less intellectual than characterological. In order to bring the hidden truth of the unconscious to the light of day, we need not only science but also conscience.

This psychological factor, the conquest of fear and the shock of thought that precedes it, is of the utmost importance to the technique of the psychology of the unconscious. Presumably courage plays the same part in the presence of a thought as physical courage does in other fields. Only investigators who are unterrified—"unshocked"—who have, to use Napoleon's expression, *"courage de nuit"*—can press forward into unexplored regions of the mind. Such advance has its dangers, no less than the primeval forest, the polar ice, and the stratosphere. To dare think that which is forbidden and socially tabooed, to be fearless before one's own thoughts, is perhaps the most important part of the education of an analyst. How often in these last years have I gotten the impression that analysts themselves lack the moral courage to say what they think! In supervising young psychoanalysts, in discussing the cases they treat, we frequently discover that the correct idea that would have solved the problem had flashed through their minds and had gone with the wind, "the ill wind that blows nobody good." A delicacy that is out of place, a timidity or conventionality about one's own idea, forces not only the patient but often the psychoanalyst as well to dodge, to evade, to escape. Also, the analyst is tempted to follow the line of least resistance instead of the path of greatest advantage. He will also often feel inclined to brush aside thoughts which are seemingly "silly," far-fetched, fantastic, or odd. He will be tempted to use the same tricks as his patient: to let himself get away with the pretext that the idea which occurred to him was not important or relevant. He also will hesitate to tell the patient unpleasant truths, to say things that sound offensive, unaesthetic or immoral. He also may try to be evasive when consider-ing the reactions which his unwelcome discoveries can arouse in the patient. These are subterfuges and mental reservations in disguise, shallow pretexts before oneself.

It stands to reason that a patient needs a certain psychical preparation before he can assimilate what the analyst will tell him. But when the psychological or rather the psychoanalytic moment has arrived, the ana-lyst has no choice; he has to say the things he has unearthed.

The advice given to the young analyst is thus: Tell the truth, the whole truth and nothing but the truth. No false modesty and no false dignity, no measures of precaution and self-protection! Caution is the mother of wisdom, but the child has sometimes to become disobedient to his mother to deserve his name, to be "wiser" than she. To tell the truth without consideration and concern about the painful conse-quences is in certain situations comparable to a lifesaving surgical operation. It hurts, but it cures. Some illusions about oneself will, of course, have to be sacrificed. You cannot make an omelette without breaking eggs. It is necessary to say those unpleasant things without circumlocutions and adornments, without making them appear pretty, insignificant or easily acceptable. No qualifications, and no "watering down"! Call a spade a spade and do not speak of an agricultural instru-ment! Be gentle in manner, but brave in matter! run Your patient will be able to stand the truth when he feels you mean well toward him. To tell him the truth amounts to a compliment to his intelligence and his moral courage.

One word more about the psychical effect upon the patient of achiev-ing the conquest of the shock of thought. Not only does the analyst win greater freedom in the potential acquisition of knowledge thereby, but he is also able to strengthen the inner claim to sincerity, a claim that is in all mankind. It is not so important to induce the patient to ex-press what he does not trust himself to say as to help him to bring into the daylight of consciousness what he dare not think and feel. And here we may reflect that it is easier for some patients to confess a scheme for murder than a desire to cheat the streetcar company of a penny. Some are readier to avow some very unconventional sexual impulses than an impulse of tenderness or a prick of conscience.

The significance of the factor of moral courage extends beyond its influence upon individuals. It is not only an element of therapeutic value in individual analysis. Inner truthfulness is infectious like lying. It is not always easy to detect a lie behind its myriad masks. But truth is unmistakable; its note cannot be counterfeited. He who is courageous in the face of the hidden shock of thought, makes others courageous and may contribute in his own narrow circle toward making a whole generation more courageous.

CHAPTER XLIV

The Courage Not to Understand

NOBODY can get a good hold on the essential discoveries of psychoanalysis without a certain measure of suffering. The truth lives among us unspoken, and someone should come out with it, whatever effect it will have on our student analysts. It sounds simple enough, and yet it is calculated to stir up debate—even among analysts. In every society there are some things that are taken as a matter of course. Yet we need only utter them in order to make them the subject of serious differences of opinion.

Well, I chose the word "suffering" intentionally. I might very well have said "pain" instead. But my object was to denote the most vital and significant element of that pain, the very element that is associated with the acquisition of the most important analytic experience, and for that I know of no other name than suffering. It may be prudent not to call things by their frequently alarming names; but it is not equally truthful.

What? Can the knowledge of objectively valid truths, of definite laws demonstrable by everyone and to everyone, of typical conditions, be dependent upon the observer or learner suffering under them? It will be said—and often has been said—that a condition of so subjective a nature is unheard of in scientific investigation. People will say it recalls the way religious doctrines of salvation are learned, that it is calculated to endanger verification of the objective facts, that no such condition has ever been attached to the acquisition of psychological knowledge, and so on. Unable to meet such a shower of arguments and unschooled in dialectics, I shall not attempt to put together what can be said in reply to these objections. I will only remind the reader that the conditions upon which we can acquire certain knowledge do not depend upon the teacher's will, but first and foremost upon the nature of the knowledge to be acquired.

It is the peculiar nature of the knowledge that justifies my statement, and not only of the knowledge but also of the experiences that must be acquired. The most important analytic knowledge cannot be acquired in its full significance without the removal of repressions. And here we strike upon a central conception. The motive and purpose of the repression was nothing but the avoidance of pain. The removal of the repression must cause pain—taken here in its broadest significance. But the removal of the repression, the conquest of the resistance against certain ideas and emotions becoming conscious, is the inescapable condition of acquiring the most important analytic knowledge. Assuredly it is not only the individual's sensibilities, his pride and his vanity, that are touched by analysis, but other things besides. Our dearest illusions are brought into question; dear because their maintenance has been bought with particularly great sacrifices. The views and convictions that we love most fervently analysis undermines; it weans us from our old habits of thought. This new knowledge confronts us with dangers that we seemed to have mastered long ago, raises thoughts that we had not dared to think, stirs feelings from which we had anxiously guarded ourselves. Analysis means an invasion of the realm of intellectual and emotional taboo, and so rouses all the defensive reactions that protect that realm. Every inch of the ground is obstinately defended, the more ardently the more trouble its conquest once cost us. But where analysis penetrates to the deepest and most sensitive plane of our personality, it can only force an entrance with pain.

There is nothing misleading in saying that the man who really wants to understand analysis must experience it and its effects on his own person; but it is a vague assertion that paraphrases the position rather than describes it. It is correct to say that the analyst's most significant knowledge must be *experienced* by himself. But it is even more correct and approaches nearer to what is essential to declare openly that these psychological experiences are of such a nature that they must be *suffered*.

What we have to do is to throw light on the problem in its obscurest corners; perhaps the subjective capacity to suffer or, better, the capacity to accept and assimilate painful knowledge, is one of the most important prognostic marks of analytic study. It seems to me that we have no right to withhold from learners the fact that the deepest knowledge is not to be had if they shrink from purchasing it with personal suffering. And this capacity is assuredly not one that can be learned. Suffering, too, is a gift; it is a grace. Let me make my meaning clear. Among my patients at the moment is a talented playwright. His craftsmanship, his dramatic sense, his stylistic endowment are beyond dispute; he is smart, witty, observes sharply, and knows the world. What makes him fail? Goethe gives the answer: he says the poet is a person to whom God gave the gift to say what he has suffered, what we all have suffered. My young playwright would have the ability to say what he feels. The trouble is that he does not feel suffering. He always chooses the easy way out of conflicts; he will not stand his ground in the face of unavoidable grief, sorrow, despair. We analysts often cannot spare our patients pain. In order to make an omelette, you have to break eggs.

But how can an analyst understand others if he has not suffered himself? We return here again to the statement that characterological qualities are more important than intellectual ones for the making of an analyst.

Now does not a good deal of psychological knowledge get through to the patient painlessly? Certainly, I was speaking here of the most significant part of analysis, the most important both in theory and practice, which starts from the problem of repression and remains dependent upon it. But a deeper comprehension of these questions presupposes a clarification of the analyst's own conflicts, an insight into the weakest and most endangered parts of his own ego, the rousing and stirring of everything that slept deepest in him—if it slept. That knowledge can only be purchased at the price of staking his own person, of conscious suffering. Before sitting down on the chair behind the couch, the analyst should have stood up to life.

In this sense the reading of analytic literature and attendance at lectures on analysis only mean preparation for the acquisition of analytic comprehension. They certainly do not give the penetration that alone deserves the name of comprehension; they remain on the surface of intellectual comprehension, and show little power of resistance. But why do I lay stress upon just the suffering? Doesn't anyone who wants to understand the depths of human experience also have to feel pleasure, joy, happiness? Certainly; but a person who has once experienced deep suffering need not be anxious about his power to comprehend other emotions. That intellectual freedom, that profounder psychological insight, that clear vision that come from the conquest of suffering, can be attained by no other means.

To spare ourselves pain sometimes involves sparing ourselves psychological insight. The unconscious knowledge that I have so often spoken of springs not least from the reservoir of our own suffering, through which we learn to understand that of others. Not unhappiness, not calamity, not *malheur* or unfortunate experiences produce it. It is true that misfortune teaches us prudence. But suffering, consciously experienced and mastered, teaches us wisdom.

Before I conclude this contribution to the discussion, I will return once more to the theme of inner truthfulness, which appears to me as one of the essential psychological conditions for the investigation of the unconscious. It is a quality that will not only prove of value in the conquest of unexplored regions of the mind; it is also needed in order to stand out against a pseudo rationality that declares it superfluous to range the distant realm of the unconscious when the good territory of the conscious lies so near at hand. In our analytic work we soon feel the temptation of yielding to that admonition, for the forces of our own conscious habits of thought will influence us to reject at once an idea about the psychological data that seems absurd or scurrilous. And we must consider that the data, emerging rapidly, often vanish and are lost just when they are received. But if we recall one of these ideas later, it often seems not only senseless and in bad taste, but without tangible connection, far-fetched. Although the idea as such has not then been drawn back into the unconscious, its matrix in the conditions of the psychical situation has.

The voices of those around him, to whom he tells the strange idea or impression, will then sound to the analyst like an echo of what resists the surprising perception within himself, and will sometimes drown other voices. Everyday considerations will mount up, ironical reflections will block the way, sophisms will appear to check the action of reason, and the jugglery of consciousness will prevent penetration into the region of repression. In the external world ancient wisdom will unite with modern cocksureness to lure the analyst away from the blurred trail. And it needs moral courage to hold aloof from obvious "explanations." For if the budding analyst, deaf to the seductions of exalted reason, cleaves obstinately to the track once found, like a hound set on the trail that is not to be turned from it by strangers calling him, he will get no encouragement from society, even if the trail brings him nearer to what he is seeking. He will feel the desolation, chill, and gloom of the man who dedicates himself to intellectual solitude and is soon alone. The comfort remains to him of the knowledge expressed in the proverb: "*Se tu sarai solo, tu sarai tutto tuo.*" And this is the blessing of such loneliness: he who is always listening to the voices of others remains ignorant of his own. He who is always going to others will never come to himself.

Rejection by our neighbors and the absence of outward success, joined to our own doubts, is harder to bear than we like to admit. But if we have the hope of illuminating obscure mental relations, these reactions of society may make us lose our temper, but they cannot make us lose courage. That danger is nearer when the way we are seeking seems to lose itself in the darkness ahead or in the far distance, while other people seem to have reached the same goal long ago along the broad highway.

The line of least resistance in psychological cognition does not simply mark off the general opinion from the analytic point of view. We shall find it in our own camp, nay, in each one of us. We, like other people, are exposed to the temptation to try to comprehend obscure psychological relations rapidly and according to formula. Indeed, there is one factor that occasionally brings the temptation nearer: analytic theories are no less susceptible to hasty and false application than other scientific assumptions. We must warn young people not to make short work of the intellectual processes that precede the spoken word, and train them to postpone judgment and put up with doubt. Knowledge too hastily acquired assuredly does not imply power, but a presumptuous pretense of power.

I take it as a good omen of the scientific quality of an analytic worker who has only been practicing for a few years, if the explanation of unconscious processes does not come easily to him when he finds himself confronted with the confusing wealth of psychological data. Thus a young psychoanalyst lamented to me not long ago that he had failed to comprehend a relation in, or to grasp the peculiar psychological character of, a case he was observing. I advised him to wait and not yield to impatience. If a thing is very easily comprehended, it may be that there is not much to comprehend in it. He said hesitantly that from his school days right on into the years when he discussed problems of his science with academic friends, he had envied people who rapidly and easily discerned intricate relations and could solve a problem with ease. His case may permit of a few remarks on something beyond the special circumstances.

Very many of us know these moods well. At congresses or meetings of analytic societies when somebody has boasted how easily he had found the solution of a psychological problem, how deep he had penetrated into the structure of a case of neurosis, and how soon he had discerned all its psychical conditions, I have felt nothing of calm assurance, but sometimes a strong sense of my own inadequacy. While I had not yet really grasped where the problem lay, the other man had solved it long ago. I looked enviously upon a facility, a rapidity of comprehension that I could not hope to attain. My intellectual inferiority seemed to be confirmed by the harsh—and still more by the mild—verdict that contrasted my own dullness and slowness of grasp, my "long-distance transmission," with the other person's ease and rapidity of comprehension. I thought then that the intellectual rating of an individual was essentially determined by these qualities. Scientific psychology had worked out, in its tests, methods of making these conditions appear the only important and unchangeable ones.

And then as my youth slipped away and I subjected their much-lauded ease of comprehension to closer examination, my respect for it was considerably diminished. Was it, perhaps, experience that taught me to be suspicious? I do not think so; experience as such teaches us hardly anything, unless we want to learn from it. But that requires a coincidence of certain psychological conditions. The truth is that I learned to mistrust all that is intellectually glib and slick, smooth and smart. I often recognized it as a mark of shining and worthless superficiality, a "phony," to use the slang expression. I began also to mistrust the rapid power of "understanding" and I remembered what they used to say in Vienna about an Austrian statesman: his grasp of things and persons was always quick, but always false. I acquired the ability to resist the great defensive power of other people's experience, for the experience of others often enough prevents us from gaining any of our own. On occasion it is the downright protector of tradition and the purveyor of false assumptions handed down to us.

I do not speak here of those cases in which such comprehension amounts to the acceptance of the opinions of predecessors or authorities that have come superficially to our knowledge. Such cases are, indeed, of the utmost importance to the rising academic generation.

I am discussing the comprehension that comes after we have examined the facts and found a reasonable and sufficient explanation. The temptation that is perhaps the most difficult to recognize as such, and to which we therefore so readily yield, is that of accepting an explanation because it is plausible, rational, and comprehensible. This easy comprehension is often the sign of intellectual haste, let us say, the expression of an intellectual avidity that is content with the first intelligence that offers, instead of thinking the best obtainable just good enough.

In analytic psychology we have daily illustrations of how liable we are to this temptation. There is, for instance, a wholly logical connection between two elements in the manifest content of a dream; but it is only a shadow bridge across a hidden gulf. We hear a very reasonable inference, a logically unassailable reason for certain personal peculiarities, and yet it forms only a well-camouflaged superstructure in the system of a serious compulsion neurosis. All that and much more besides is only external, a logical façade, intellectual mimicry, and camouflage, set up in order to lure research away from more important things and keep it away from its real objects. Anyone who interprets a slip of the tongue as the absent-minded substitution of one letter for another or the dropping of a sound, need not go on with research. Anyone who regards the compulsion of a nervous patient to wash simply as an expression of intensified cleanliness has allowed himself to be led astray by the logical tricks of a compulsion neurotic. If we once abandon ourselves to deceptive logic and yield to the obscure urge to comprehend rapidly, then we cannot stop. We are soon convinced; it must be so, and nowise else. With less and less intellectual resistance, we shall then comprehend everything on the basis of false assumptions—strictly logically. Everything proceeds swimmingly; single contradictions and omissions are passed over, rifts unconsciously bridged. Any detail that does not fit is pushed and pulled into place, and conflicting elements are guilelessly forced into a new artificial system. The advice that we must give to young psychological investigators must be: Resist the temptation of understanding too quickly. ("*Principiis intelligendi obsta.*")

We hear the boast made on behalf of psychoanalysis that, behind the mental phenomena that have hitherto been regarded as absurd and senseless, it has discovered a secret meaning, a hidden significance, and brought it to light. Confronted with this mighty achievement, which has opened the road to the comprehension of the unconscious

510 LISTENING WITH THE THIRD EAR

mind, I fear that we have too little appreciated the other achievement that preceded it, without which, indeed, it would not have been possible. Psychoanalysis has resisted the acceptance of mental associations simply because they were reasonable, or, indeed, because they were "the only reasonable explanation." It has refused to recognize a chain of cause and effect in the inner life as the only one solely because it seemed plausible and there was no other in sight. The theory of physical stimuli seemed capable of explaining the phenomena of dreams; puberty was thoroughly accepted as the beginning of sexuality. In these matters nature herself offered the obvious explanation. Several physiological phenomena clearly indicated the etiology of hysteria, the phobias, and compulsion neuroses—everything was plain, there were no further problems to be solved. To hold these reasonable and sufficient explanations inadequate, to renounce easy and convenient comprehension of psychical facts—that could hardly be called eccentricity— it was obviously either want of sense or else scientific conceit, *hybris*.

It must be stated more than once—it must be said three times—that not to understand psychological relations represents an advance over superficial comprehension. Whereas such comprehension amounts to arriving in a blind alley, all sorts of possibilities remain open to one who does not understand. To be puzzled where everything is clear to others, where they merely ask: "What is there to understand?"— to see a riddle there still—need not be a mark of stupidity; it may be the mark of a free mind. Obstinately not to understand where other people find no difficulties and obscurities may be the initial stage of new knowledge. In this sense the much lauded rapid apprehension, including that by means of psychoanalytic theories, may be sterile since it touches only the most superficial levels. Regarded thus, a mediocre intelligence, an intellectual mobility, and capacity to be on the spot, which places, classifies, and establishes every phenomenon as quickly as possible, may have less cultural value than apparent intellectual failure or the temporary miss, which is sometimes the forerunner of deeper comprehension.

In the inner world, too, there are situations in which the cosmos, the ordered, articulated universe, seems, so to speak, to be turned back to chaos, yet from which a new creation emerges. We think, perhaps, that we fully understand such and such a psychical event, and then it suddenly becomes incomprehensible. We had worked our way to the opinion in question and made it our own. And then all of a sudden it is lost, without our knowing how. We had tested and examined everything and decided that it was all right; and then everything became uncertain again: in the midst of light we saw obscurity. Problems solved long ago become problematical again.

Questions answered long ago show that there was something questionable in the answer. Surely everybody has had the experience of a carpet pattern seeming to change under his very eyes. Gradually or suddenly we see it seem to lose the familiar form; the lines, combined so significantly and pleasantly in figures or arabesques, suddenly part, tangled, and try to follow their own strange ways, darker than those of the Lord. As long as we have known the carpet, we have seen that arrangement of lines in it, one figure. Our eye is used to tracing the threads that make the memorable form. We never expected to see anything else. And then one day the accustomed order of the lines is dissolved, the old pattern is blurred and hazy. The lines refuse to combine in the old way. They arrange themselves in new, hitherto concealed figures, in new, hitherto unnoticed groupings. A like surprise, in ceasing to recognize something to be transformed later into the light of new knowledge, may be the lot of many investigators. What has long been classified, arranged, judged, and clearly known may suddenly become incomprehensible to an individual pioneer. That means that the conception hitherto current, according to which everything was clear, no longer seems to him worthy of the name of comprehension. The investigator in question might then say, "I am beginning no longer to comprehend."

It would seem that one of the most important conditions of this non-comprehension is an uncommon measure of intellectual courage. I do not mean here the courage to confess we have not understood something that is as clear as daylight to everybody else. That kind of courage would denote something more external, something of a secondary character. What I mean is rather the courage in the world of thought that is able to draw back from what is universally comprehensible and reasonable, and not to join the march into the region of the plausible. It takes courage to mistrust the temptation to understand everything and not to be content with a perception because it is evident. It takes courage to resist the wave of general comprehension (in the sense of superficiality or common sense). It requires inner truthfulness to stand out against our own intellectual impatience, our desire to master intellectually and to take associations by storm. This, too, is a form of belief in the omnipotence of thought and it requires courage to reject it—not to take the path of least intellectual resistance, of speedy and effortless comprehension.

Assuredly it is not true, as a group of scientific nihilists tell us, that man will have nothing to do with truth. On the contrary, I believe that mankind has a great thirst for truth. The greatest hindrance to the advance of knowledge is rather of a different nature; it is that people think they have long been in possession of the truth, the whole truth. The realms in which the human spirit will make new and surprising discoveries are by no means only those hitherto unexplored, but also those of which we have very accurate and reliable maps. It is the problems already "solved" that present the most numerous and difficult problems to the inquirer. If we want to attain new knowledge, we must look around among the old, familiar questions, just as Diogenes sought men in the crowded market place of Athens. But we need a measure of intellectual courage to raise and solve these problems. It is this courage that will, sooner or later, overcome the resistance of the dull world.

Leave-Taking

THE name of Freud stood at the entrance of this book. It shall lead us to the gate. I flew from Amsterdam to Vienna to say good-by to Freud. We both knew we would not see each other again. After we shook hands, I stood at the door and could not say a word. My lips were pressed together so hard that they were unable to part. He must have sensed what I felt; he put his arm on my shoulder and said, "I've always liked you." (He had never before said anything of this kind.) As I bowed my head wordless, he said in a low but firm voice, as if to comfort me: *"People need not be glued together when they belong together."*

I have said this consoling sentence to myself many times since, when I thought of him in the following years; also when I thought of relatives and friends I had not seen for years and of others never again to be seen. I said it again ("People need not be glued together when they belong together") when some analysts have expressed the view that I had turned disloyal to Freud because I had discovered that some of his theoretical concepts needed modification in the light of more recent research. The view that I had become a renegade is so silly that it deserves no rejection. Perhaps it will dampen the conceit of those gentlemen who call themselves "Freudians" when I tell them that Freud once smilingly said to me: *"Moi, je ne suis pas un Freudiste."* (Why did he say it in French? It is perhaps a variation of a French quotation that is unknown to me.)

I am again thinking of the last sentence I heard him say, when I imagine the kind of readers this book ought to reach and the kind of readers for whom it is not destined. This book should come into the hands of a wide circle of cultured readers who have a genuine love for the science of depth psychology and a passionate curiosity about what goes on in the netherworld of the human soul. Like an after-tremor that follows an intense earthquake, these pages bear testimony, emotional and intellectual, to the experience connected with the name of Freud.

These pages are especially destined for the hands and the ears, the brains and the hearts, of the young generation of psychoanalysts and psychologists. They will hear with a third ear what is said here be-tween the lines—and even what is left unsaid. There are, I know, some in this young generation who have a genuine psychological gift, who are endowed with that fine hearing for unconscious processes, with the talent for observing and discerning nuances in psychological problems, with independence of judgment and moral courage. I would like to warn them and to encourage them. I would like to speak to them, to leave a will in words like those the Marquis Posa left to Don Carlos, Infant of Spain, in Schiller's play. "Tell him," says the older friend when he dies, "tell him that he should retain respect for the dreams of his youth when he will become a man. He should not open his heart . . . to the deadly insect of baser reason of which they boast, and not be led astray when he hears enthusiasm blasphemed by wis-dom of the dust." They, the young men and women now arriving on the stage of psychoanalytic research, will know where this deadly in-sect is and what it is like.

We who are in our sixties and will soon leave the scene salute those who are in their twenties. We represent the past of psychoanalysis, its first heroic struggles, and its first glorious victories. They represent its future. We do not know them, but we feel close to them. People need not be glued together when they belong together.